Mass Communication Research and Theory

EDITED BY

Guido H. Stempel III

Ohio University

David H. Weaver

Indiana University

G. Cleveland Wilhoit

Indiana University

Boston • New York • San Francisco
Mexico City • Montreal • Toronto • London • Madrid • Munich • Paris
Hong Kong • Singapore • Tokyo • Cape Town • Sydney

Series Editor: *Molly Taylor*
Series Editorial Assistant: *Michael Kish*
Marketing Manager: *Mandee Eckersley*
Editorial-Production Administrator: *Beth Houston*
Editorial-Production Service: *Walsh & Associates, Inc.*
Composition Buyer: *Linda Cox*
Manufacturing Buyer: *JoAnne Sweeney*
Cover Administrator: *Kristina Mose-Libon*

Between the time Website information is gathered and then published, it is not unusual for some sites to have closed. Also, the transcription of URLs can result in typographical errors. The publisher would appreciate notification where these errors occur so that they may be corrected in subsequent editions.

Library of Congress Cataloging-in-Publication Data

Mass communication research and theory / edited by Guido H. Stempel III, David H. Weaver, G. Cleveland Wilhoit.
    p. cm.
  Includes bibliographical references and index.
  ISBN 0-205-35923-X
   1. Mass media—Research—Methodology. 2. Mass media—Philosophy. I. Stempel, Guido Hermann, 1928-II. Weaver, David H. (David Hugh), 1946-III. Wilhoit, G. Cleveland.

P91.3 .M36 2003
302.23'07'2—dc21

2002066662

ISBN 0-205-35923-X

Printed in the United States of America

Contents

About the Authors

Lee B. Becker is professor and director of the James W. Cox Center for International Mass Communication Training and Research at the Henry W. Grady College of Journalism and Mass Communication at the University of Georgia.

Tom Bowers is professor and senior associate dean in the School of Journalism and Mass Communication at the University of North Carolina at Chapel Hill.

Clifford G. Christians is a professor in the College of Communications at the University of Illinois.

Claude Cookman is an associate professor in the School of Journalism at Indiana University.

Hugh M. Culbertson is a professor emeritus in the E. W. Scripps School of Journalism at Ohio University.

Lewis Donohew is a professor in the Department of Communication at the University of Kentucky.

Everette E. Dennis is a distinguished professor in the Graduate School of Business at Fordham University.

Matthew S. Eastin is an assistant professor in the School of Journalism and Communication at Ohio State University.

Steve Everett is vice president of Strategic Communications, DSD Laboratories Inc. In that position he directs public affairs research for the U.S. Air Force. He was formerly Director of Audience Measurement and Policy Research for the National Association of Broadcasters.

Gina M. Garramone is a former faculty member in the Department of Advertising at Michigan State University.

Donald M. Gillmor is Silha Professor of Media Law and Ethics emeritus in the School of Journalism and Mass Communication at the University of Minnesota.

Elizabeth Maria Grabe is an associate professor in the School of Journalism at Indiana University.

Bradley Greenberg is a professor in the Department of Telecommunication at Michigan State University.

Kathleen A. Hansen is a professor in the School of Journalism and Mass Communication at the University of Minnesota.

Maxwell E. McCombs is the Jesse Jones Centennial professor of communication at the University of Texas at Austin.

Kristin McGrath is former president of Minnesota Opinion Research Inc.

Douglas M. McLeod is an associate professor in the School of Journalism and Mass Communication at the University of Wisconsin.

David Paul Nord is a professor in the School of Journalism at Indiana University.

Philip Palmgreen is a professor in the Department of Communication at the University of Kentucky.

Daniel Riffe is a professor in the E. W. Scripps School of Journalism at Ohio University.

Pamela J. Shoemaker is the John Ben Snow professor in the S. I. Newhouse School of Public Communications at Syracuse University.

Keith R. Stamm is a professor in the School of Communications at the University of Washington.

Guido H. Stempel III is a distinguished professor emeritus in the E. W. Scripps School of Journalism at Ohio University.

Phillip J. Tichenor is a professor emeritus in the School of Journalism and Mass Communication at the University of Minnesota.

Erik Ugland is an assistant professor of journalism at Marquette University.

David H. Weaver is the Roy W. Howard research professor in the School of Journalism at Indiana University.

G. Cleveland Wilhoit is a professor in the School of Journalism at Indiana University.

Acknowledgments

The three editors of this book want to thank all the authors who took the time and effort to respond so well to our requests for updated and new chapters. David Weaver and Cleve Wilhoit also want to thank Indiana University doctoral students Young Jun Son and Eunseong Kim for all their help with the subject index, secretary Grace Carpenter for her help with typing several chapters, former doctoral student Sung Tae Kim for his help with the chapter files, and the Roy W. Howard chair for support of various expenses. Guido Stempel wants to thank Thomas Hodges of the journalism faculty at Ohio University for his help in deciphering disks in software Stempel's computer didn't understand. This book reflects the continuing and pervasive influence on our field of the late Bruce Westley, co-editor of the two editions of *Research Methods in Mass Communication*, the predecessor of this volume. Many of us are in his debt. We would also like to thank the following reviewers for their time and input: Kurt Kent, Gainesville, FL; Wynn Norman, West Virginia University; and Ken Ksobiech, Marquette University.

The three of us who edited this book have agreed to donate the royalties to the Minority Scholarship Fund of the Communication Theory and Methodology Division of the Association for Education in Journalism and Mass Communication. We hope this support and this book will encourage more minority scholars to join and remain in our field.

1

The Systematic Study of Mass Communication

Guido H. Stempel III

Bruce H. Westley

When *An Introduction to Journalism Research*, edited by Ralph O. Nafziger of the University of Wisconsin and Marcus M. Wilkerson of Louisiana State University, appeared in 1949, it signaled a new era in journalism education. Prophetically, it had chapters by Frank Luther Mott of the University of Missouri, Chilton R. Bush of Stanford University, and Fred S. Siebert of the University of Illinois. They, along with Nafziger, were among the small group of men who were creating doctoral programs at their schools that would produce a new breed of researcher.

That book made it clear where journalism research was headed. Nafziger said in the introduction:

> But perhaps the most significant development in the study of journalism has been recent progress in the use of new methods and research tools. Journalism has profited with other disciplines by one of the great modern advances in the field of learning: the invention and adoption of more precise means of studying human behavior in all its manifestations.[1]

Chapters by Bush on statistics and Earl English of the University of Missouri on interviewing supported that thrust. However, there were also chapters on historical research by Wilkerson and legal research by Siebert. Thus, while Nafziger clearly reflected the behavioral research perspective that had begun to emerge in journalism research in the 1940s, the book was also in a sense a guarantee of the coming diversity in journalism research. That diversity made a multiauthored book the logical approach even then.

But if the Nafziger-Wilkerson book seemed to say that journalism research was on its way, the convention program of the Association for Education in Journalism and the pages of AEJ's official publication, *Journalism Quarterly*, seemed to say it had not arrived.

An indication that behavioral research had not arrived was Percy Tannenbaum's finding in a study of *Journalism Quarterly* footnotes that only 2 percent of the footnotes in the pre-1950 era were to behavioral journals. In the 1950s that figure rose to 18 percent, and references to trade journals and general publications decreased.[2] Furthermore, the twelve to fourteen articles per issue in the *Quarterly* in the late 1940s constituted most of the published research on the field.

The breakthrough in the convention program took a while. In 1955, a group of researchers organized their own program for the day after the last day of the AEJ convention at Boulder. The group became known officially as the Quantitative Research Group and unofficially as the rump group. The next year they had a day of research presentations the day before the convention. The convention itself had two research sessions, both at the same time. That's a far cry from current AEJMC conventions with 400 research papers on the program.

It was not until the reorganization of AEJ in 1965 that the Quantitative Research Group was fully assimilated. It became the Division on Communication Theory and Methodology, and under the new constitution it had full status and full rights with the AEJ. It was from the very beginning one of the three largest divisions, a fact that reflects the growth of mass communication research.

In 1958, the second book appeared. Edited by Nafziger and David Manning White of Boston University, it was entitled *Introduction to Mass Communications Research*.[3] Although it was only nine years after the Nafziger and Wilkerson book, a whole new group of authors was included—Wilbur Schramm of Stanford University, Malcolm S. MacLean, Jr., of Michigan State University, Percy H. Tannenbaum of the University of Illinois, Roy E. Carter, Jr., of the University of Minnesota, Paul J. Deutschmann of Michigan State University, and Bruce H. Westley of the University of Wisconsin. Chapters on such topics as experimental method, measurement, and scientific method reflected the change that had occurred in the relatively few years between the two books. In many ways, *Introduction to Mass Communications Research* reflected the gains of a decade of experience in the field. And while Nafziger and White said it was "not intended to be a comprehensive textbook on communication research or even the special area to which it is confined," still it was noticeably more comprehensive—though less eclectic—than the earlier book. Just as the research output of the field was expanding, so the know-how about research was expanding, especially in the behavioral sciences. There was a deliberate decision to omit chapters on historical and legal methods. This did not reflect any reduced interest in those areas, but probably did reflect the content of courses then burgeoning in graduate programs across the country.

Parenthetically, it should be noted that the second edition of Nafziger and White was not the result of any profound change in the field (the only new chapter was one on content analysis by Wayne Danielson). It was believed that a flood in the basement of the Louisiana State University Press building had wiped out the remaining type.

Two decades later, *Research Methods in Mass Communication*, edited by Guido H. Stempel III and Bruce H. Westley, was published.[4] It reflected something that had been happening in our field. As mass communication research had grown, it grew closer to related disciplines. Mass communication researchers have drawn on the methodological insights of scholars in such fields as sociology, political science, and psychology.

Another linkage has grown up between journalism scholars interested broadly in communication processes and like-minded persons in departments of speech, communications, speech-communication, and the like. At the same time those interested in historical and legal research in mass communication have found appropriate models in the base disciplines. As part of this process, text materials from other fields have become increasingly in evidence in mass communication research courses.

Yet, when we surveyed about 100 mass communication research methods teachers while that book was being planned, we found the majority eager for a new mass communication research methods book. They made it clear, however, that what they sought was an eclectic book. They sought a book broader in scope and yet deeper in detail than the two previous texts. Their dissatisfaction with the half dozen or so books really intended for sociology equaled their dissatisfaction with a book as dated as Nafziger and White. The problem seemed to be that, even though the methods we employ are quite similar, these books were not really about mass communication research.

The second edition of that book, coming eight years later, reflected wider use of computers, including computer-assisted interviewing and computerized databases,[5] which had made profound changes in legal research in the short time between the two editions.

This book follows from those two, but there are two major differences. One is the emphasis put on industry applications of mass communication research. We felt a need to do this in part so that students would be aware of such applications. We also felt it was necessary to assess what media researchers were doing against the context provided by academic researchers.

Systematic Study

When we speak of "the systematic study of mass communications," we mean any research discipline that can shed new light on mass communication processes, effects, institutions, and institutional change, its legal constraints, its constitutional imperatives, its technology, its changing response to new challenges. And we mean to get a start, at least, on an appreciation of how these methods differ and how they are similar, how they are changing and how they remain the same.

In opting for an eclectic approach, we knew that we were complicating things for the student. Yet one of the reasons that there are 400 research papers at the AEJMC convention each year is the eclectic nature of our field. This is in part reflected by the growing number of divisions and interest groups in AEJMC. There are now seventeen divisions and eight interest groups. All have research interests, and no two are alike in this respect. The eclectic nature of our field and our decision to follow an eclectic approach raise the question of how we can organize such a tale so that the student could move from one area to the next with ever-widening knowledge and understanding.

We begin with four chapters on applications of mass communication research. This will give the student an overview of the field and at the same time indicate that research is not merely something university faculty members do. These chapters show that research is an integral part of advertising, public relations, broadcast journalism, and print journalism. The student thus will know that research will affect his or her life, even if he or she is not a researcher. We are fortunate to have as authors for those chapters four people whose work is respected by both academics and professionals—Steven Everett, who writes on broadcasting; Kris McGrath, who writes on print media; Hugh Culbertson, who writes on public relations; and Tom Bowers, who writes on advertising.

From those chapters we move to one that offers the basic conceptual context for research. Written by Douglas McLeod and Phillip Tichenor, it deals with the logic of social and behavioral science. Tichenor is one of the seminal theorists of mass communication institutions and processes whose work is known far beyond the world of mass communication. McLeod was one of his students at Minnesota. The chapter raises questions about the nature of knowledge and especially how social and behavioral scientists contribute to knowledge. It deals with such questions as how we deal with causality, how we deal with induction and deduction, how we choose between macro- and micro-system models, and how we move toward verification. It sets the stage for the part of the book devoted to behavioral and social science methodology, which follows.

We focus first on theory and theory construction. Lewis Donohew and Philip Palmgreen, whose previous collaborations include a well-known revision of Festinger's theory of cognitive dissonance, discuss the role of theory in behavioral science and the process of theory building. We are not talking about "building models" in the manner of graphic representations of the communication processes, but the patient work of developing theories to account for data. We often speak of theory *and* methodology, signifying their separateness. Donohew and Palmgreen stress their interconnectedness, which should answer the expected question: Why talk about theory in a book about method?

Measurement plays a crucial role in theory building, and that is the topic we turn to next. It is often the subject of an entire course, but Keith Stamm has undertaken to cover the essentials of measurement in a single chapter. His own research speaks to his qualifications for this task because in that research he has demonstrated keen insight and creativity in dealing with measurement.

We usually test hypotheses by means of statistical inference, so statistics is logically the next topic we cover. David Weaver has surely this book's most difficult assignment: to cover in a single chapter the basic statistical tools of our craft. His own facility in using statistics creatively in treating many journalistic topics is well known. His chapter ranges from descriptive to inferential statistics, from normative to nonparametric, from small-sample to large-sample, from the t-test to the F test, from R factor analysis to Q. It is a huge task for the author and demands much from the student.

Next comes a chapter that we wanted to put in the first edition of *Research Methods in Mass Communication*. It deals with SPSS applications of statistics. It did not make it then because one reviewer insisted SPSS would not last. It has, of course, and remains the most commonly relied on software for statistics in our field. Daniel Riffe, whose work demonstrates a wide variety of uses of SPSS, has written that chapter.

The next three chapters concern themselves with the two most frequently used modes of inquiry in mass communication research—content analysis and the sample survey. Each poses distinct problems. Those chapters are written by authors with years of experience in that specialty. Guido Stempel, whose content analysis work began in the 1950s, writes on that subject. Kathleen Hansen, whose work on databases has been on the cutting edge for more than a decade, writes on the use of databases in content analysis. Pamela Shoemaker and Max McCombs, long-time survey researchers, deal with that topic.

Next comes a chapter on secondary analysis by Lee Becker, one of the first to make use of that research opportunity and produce outstanding work. Becker tells us how to take advantage of the vast accumulation of social science data now highly accessible to any qualified scholar. Why spend $100,000 to do a nationwide survey when answers sought may already be available?

Then we have the chapter on experimental research. Maria Elizabeth Grabe has done an excellent job of carrying Bruce Westley's chapter further.

Bradley Greenberg's chapter on ethics is next. He was a pioneer in this field, and his chapter on ethics in our first edition was one of the first published in our field. It was not that ethics was not a topic, but rather that it did not attract much attention. Greenberg brings us up to date, reflecting the increased attention and new thought on this topic.

Claude Cookman's chapter on presenting quantitative data comes next. It is needed in part because computers print out so much data and in forms that are not always readily understandable. Cookman explains how you get from the computer printout to tables that combine with text to create effective messages.

We shift at that point to other methods of scholarship in the field: qualitative studies, history, and legal scholarship. They are grouped together because they are different enough from the methods already discussed to require separate treatment. They are not last in any sense of priority. Historically, they predate behavioral science and they remain a significant part of our field.

This block of chapters begins with a chapter of qualitative studies by Robert Fortner and Clifford Christians. Earlier research methods books in communication did not discuss qualitative research, and it was not until the 1980s that we had a Qualitative Studies Division in the Association for Education in Journalism and Mass Communication. The authors make it clear that qualitative is not simply the opposite of quantitative and that rigor is part of the method.

Next is "The Practice of Historical Research," by David Paul Nord. This chapter contains some surprises for social and behavioral scientists—and perhaps some journalism historians as well. In the Nafziger and White book, Westley's chapter explained "scientific method" in terms of how it differed from traditional historiography. The happy surprise here is that historiography is moving closer to the methods of social and behavioral sciences, so a great deal more can be said about how they are similar. While humanistic history still makes important contributions to historical insight, Nord makes it plain the historian now uses concepts much as the social scientist does, that is, organizes them into theoretical postures of a tentative nature while evidence is adduced to find support for the theory—or its disconfirmation. Historians seek quantitative data where feasible and they sometimes use statistical tests.

The methods of legal research have changed remarkably over the last quarter century. No chapter in the Stempel and Westley book changed as much between the first and second editions as the one on legal research. Two veteran scholars, Everette Dennis and Donald Gillmor, and a graduate student who has worked with both of them, Erik Ugland, do a remarkable job of bringing this chapter up to date on the emerging resources and how they can best be utilized. They make the point that legal research is at the same time both a scholarly pursuit and a professional set of tools. They also stress the convergence between what legal scholars do and what behavioral scientists do. And they make it clear that legal research makes more use of computerized resources than any other area in mass communication research.

The final chapter, by Guido Stempel and Bruce Westley, discusses writing research results. It offers the maxim that "good writing is clear thinking made visible" and the suggestion that scholarly writing can be good writing. The chapter outlines the standard format for a research article and discusses the difference between journal articles and theses or dissertations. The authors had long experience as journal editors, and they hope with this chapter to help students avoid the common pitfalls of scholarly writing.

The Overview

It might be assumed from its eclectic nature that this book has as its goal creating a true Renaissance Person of mass communication scholarship, one who moves easily from the law library to the museum to the computer center, exuding confidence all the way. We have a few scholars who are able to range widely across the spectrum of methods, equally at home in all, or nearly so. Our purpose is not to emulate them but instead to give the student a broad introduction to the entire field, to pose alternatives in choice of method—a choice that may be made much later. These choices include methodologies useful to the university-based productive scholar, to be sure, but they also include other career choices available to competent people. They may become archivists of mass media collections or writers of official media histories. They may become survey research specialists in opinion or marketing research firms or copy testers applying their experimental research skills in an advertising agency or their survey research skills to the market characteristics of magazine audiences. They may become investigative reporters using statistical analysis of databases. They may become media critics or ombudsmen using content analysis skills to assess media, including their own. In all these examples—and there are many more—what qualifies the person particularly is competence in and commitment to a method—a systematic means of studying mass media processes and institutions and human communication behavior.

So, although we assume the student must specialize eventually, we believe there should be a wide and sympathetic introduction to all the ways that new knowledge may be uncovered in our field. If students cannot be expected to produce in all these areas, at least they can be expected to read the literature. The danger inherent in specialization is the risk of insularity—that in gaining commitment to a methodology we see our phenomenal world only in terms given by that methodology. The saying is that "If a person's only tool is a hammer, everything looks like a nail." Because other methods may work in different ways toward goals somewhat different from ours, we easily fall into the trap that turns commitment into a sort of methodological chauvinism.

But even if you do not go into a research career, you are likely to meet research somewhere in your professional future. More research is being done by and about media than ever before. More decisions are based on research. More news is gathered through the use of research, and more news stories are about research. The question is not "if" but "when." The aim of this book is to start preparing you for that moment when you find yourself needing knowledge about research methods to carry out your duties.

Scholarship is an "adversarial proceeding," a reality that should be more apparent after this book has been studied than before. The historian begs to differ—finds an interpretation based on new source materials. Legal scholars beg to differ—from old interpretations and flawed interpretations of the law. Communication theorists attack the assumptions of their predecessors and erect new theories that account for everything that earlier theory did not and add some new findings as well. This is adversarity with a high purpose. It is as much a matter of showing that what we thought we knew was wrong as it is a matter of finding out what is right. New knowledge comes hard and it thrives on contest. In fact, the careful student may find points in this book where our authors are in some measure disagreeing. What the student should recognize is that each author is writing from his or her own perspective and from his or her own experience. It is for the student to resolve these matters in his or her own way.

But to be productive, the contest should be between like-minded workers toiling in the same vineyard. Effort devoted to vilifying "those other people" with their quaint and stodgy searches through dusty archives, those young smart alecks who have substituted Fortran for English, or those airy qualitative types who love to display their erudition is largely wasted. The goal of this book is to offer the best information we can muster from people who are committed to the search for new knowledge; we hope that they will impart their commitment and enthusiasm along with some knowledge of the research discipline that they espouse. We ask the student to give them all a hearing and to enter the task with an open mind and some sensitivity to the differing ways that we move from evidence to inference.

Endnotes

1. Ralph O. Nafziger and Marcus M. Wilkerson, eds., *An Introduction to Journalism Research* (Baton Rouge: Louisiana State University Press, 1949), 3.

2. Percy H. Tannenbaum, "JQ References: A Study of Professional Change," *Journalism Quarterly*, 38(1961): 203-207.

3. Ralph O. Nafziger and David Manning White, eds., *Introduction to Mass Communications Research* (Baton Rouge: Louisiana State University Press, 1958), vi.

4. Guido H. Stempel III and Bruce H. Westley, eds., *Research Methods in Mass Communication* (Englewood Cliffs, NJ: Prentice Hall, 1981).

5. Guido H. Stempel III and Bruce H. Westley, eds., *Research Methods in Mass Communication*, 2nd ed. (Englewood Cliffs, NJ, 1989).

2

Broadcast Research

Stephen Everett

Chances are you've been a consumer of broadcasting all your life. Radio is just about everywhere—in clocks, in cars, in stereos, in portables, in stores and restaurants. If you stop to count how many radios you yourself have in your home, you might be surprised by the number. Now—is that above or below average? Answer: The average U.S. household has 2.7 television sets[1] and there are so many radios that the radio industry doesn't bother to track it any more.

Don't forget a relatively new way of receiving radio and television programs: your personal computer and the Internet. More than 3,000 broadcast stations put their programs on the Internet through streaming audio and video.[2] Some broadcast stations don't even have over-the-air signals—they exist only as Internet content providers.

All these broadcasters offer products they hope will be of interest to audiences. However, most broadcasters acknowledge they can't be all things to all people. To create their own productive (and most would hope profitable) market niches, broadcasters often define *target audiences* for which they design their programs. Getting to know target audiences (who they are, where they are, what they do, when they do it, and why) is a huge challenge for all communicators, not just broadcasters.

Perhaps it's especially dear to broadcasters' hearts because listeners or viewers are what broadcasters "sell" to their customers. Advertisers spend more than $60 billion annually in the United States on radio and television ad time,[3] with the goal of getting audience members to at least have the *opportunity* to be exposed to the message, possibly think about it, possibly be persuaded by it, and, most desirable of all, possibly buy the product or adopt the idea being sold by the advertiser.

So broadcasters are matchmakers. They try to get advertisers and potential customers together, at least for the fleeting moments when broadcast ads are on the air and customers might encounter them. It's more complicated than that, though, because specialized advertisers want to reach specialized prospective customers—often using specialized media (such as stations or channels) or vehicles (specific programs). The key questions broadcasters and their advertising clients want answered include (a) who the audience is, (b) what the audience thinks or wants, and (c) how many of them are being reached when a client purchases and airs an ad. To answer these essential questions, the broadcast industry relies very heavily upon an army of research firms and consultants. We can describe broadcast research as falling into two general camps: ratings research (counting ears or eyeballs) and all other research (anything that goes beyond audience size estimation and tries to describe the nature, attitudes, or feelings of prospective customers in the audience).

Both are important, but ratings research is the most basic audience measurement conducted in the U.S. broadcast industry, so let's start there.

Ratings Research

At some point you've probably seen at least one of your favorite television shows canceled by the network. Perhaps the reason offered up in support was "sagging ratings." However, it's important to keep in mind that broadcast ratings are *not* measurements of the audience's liking of a program. They're measurements of the audience's *exposure* to the program. Of course, it's human nature to want continued or repeated exposure to something we like over something we dislike, so ratings usually correlate positively with the audience's evaluation of a program. But the question answered by the ratings companies for broadcasters is straightforward: How many pairs of eyeballs or ears spent at least a minimal amount of time tuned to a given program?

Ratings Terms

Though the jargon may sound like rocket science, the arithmetic behind it isn't. The two most important broadcast audience research terms are rating and share, and they're easily defined.

Rating: The percentage of the universe tuned to Program X.
Share: The percentage of the viewing/listening universe tuned to Program X.

Let's look at a simple example, from a simpler time. Perhaps you've heard older folks talk about the days when television meant choosing from three or four stations coming over the air into the TV's antenna. Think of a small town ("Pleasantville") of 2,000 households, all with one television per house. Three television stations' signals (ABC, CBS, and NBC) come into Pleasantville, and there are no other television viewing alternatives. We're going to look at the viewing data for 8:15 P.M. on a Thursday in November. The numbers:

ABC: 240 HH
CBS: 360 HH
NBC: 300 HH

Some quick arithmetic and this formula will give us the ratings for each:

Rating = HH tuned ÷ total HH (for ABC, 240/2000 = .12 or a 12 rating)

So the ratings for ABC, CBS, and NBC are 12, 18, and 15, respectively (the arithmetic isn't usually this easy, so enjoy it while you can). Add all the ratings up and we get *Homes Using Television (HUT)*. In this case, for 8:15 on Thursday evening, the HUT is 45 (45% of homes were watching *something*). HUT levels vary from hour to hour, from day to day, and from season to season. HUT levels tend to be highest in the evenings (that's why they called it "prime time"). They tend to be lowest in the middle of the night. For some times of day, weekend HUTs are higher than weekday HUTs. Due to weather, daylight, and possible alternatives to television viewing, HUTs are higher in the winter than they are in the summer.

So is a rating of 2 a *good rating*? It depends . . . if that 2 comes from the 3 A.M. hour, then it's an excellent rating. If it's from prime time, that show won't be on the air much longer. Because the answer to the question was "it depends," broadcasters and media planners find it useful to report *share* along with rating. The formula:

Share $=$ HH tuned $\div$ total viewing HH (for ABC, 240/900 $=$ .267 $\sim$ 27 share)

The rounded shares for ABC, CBS, and NBC are 27, 40, and 33, respectively. Note that the shares add to 100. When looking at all possible viewing choices, the shares *always* must add to 100, since each individual number describes the "slice of the viewing" for each individual station.

There's another formula for share:

Share $=$ Rating $\div$ HUT (for ABC, 12/45 $\sim$ 27 share)

Armed with these two viewing measures, you can tell a pretty complete story about how a program is performing. Rating gives an indication of *absolute* performance (How big was the audience, regardless of time, season, etc.?). Share gives an indication of *relative* performance (How did the audience stack up with the other program audiences at the same time?).

For both television and radio measurement, ratings usually report on *average quarter hours (AQH)*. Put simply, audience members must tune in for *at least five minutes of the quarter hour* to be counted in that quarter hour's rating figure. Listen to the radio for only three minutes, and you won't be counted in the station's AQH rating for that time of day.

Now it's time to broaden our understanding of the universe, at least in broadcast terms. The formulas for rating and share can be and are applied to many different groups in the audience. The least defined universe would be "all television households in the country." A highly defined universe would be "Minneapolis women 18–24 years old with technical/engineering skills and a desire to serve their country." Alas, ratings companies don't assess skills nor patriotism among their samples, but the gender, age group, and geographic characteristics are tracked by ratings companies.

In practice, far more use is made of "people ratings" than of household ratings. It's not hard to see why—advertisers wish to identify and deliver messages to *people* who, in turn, may be persuaded and/or make purchases. Households are a unit of convenience when reporting ratings, with limited usefulness for target marketers.

The formulas for rating and share work for any universe, so long as you keep the numerator and denominator of the formula in the same units (men 35–49 above the line, then men 35–49 below the line). HUT has a persons analog, as well: Persons Using Television (PUT). Sometimes it's also called *Persons Viewing Television (PVT)*.

Advertisers rely heavily upon ratings points when planning and evaluating media campaigns. In fact, a common mechanism for describing the amount of television or radio advertising being purchased is *gross rating points (GRPs)*. This is a simple concept—add up the ratings points for all the ads planned in the campaign to get the GRPs. Media planners tally GRPs for nonbroadcast media as well, since one can calculate the percentage of a universe receiving yesterday's edition of the local daily newspaper just as logically as a broadcast rating. A closely related concept—*target rating points* (TRPs)—does exactly the same thing but for a more narrowly defined target audience.

Sometimes advertising "weight" is described in terms of *impressions* or *gross impressions*. While it may sound impressive to tell a client its campaign "generated 10,000,000 impressions," it's not as efficient as reporting TRPs. After all, are 10,000,000 impressions a lot? Doesn't it depend on the size of the target universe? If so, don't you have all the ingredients necessary for calculating and using TRPs?

When you're talking about a single program's or ad's rating, you're describing *unduplicated audience*. However, something happens to rating points when they're added together. They become *duplicated measures* of audience. The rating for a single ad counts everyone who sees that specific ad. Run the ad repeatedly and some people in the audience probably will see it more than once. In the GRP or TRP calculation, repeat viewers are counted multiple times.

Broadcasters and advertisers often want to know how many *different* people heard or saw one or more of the ads run during a week. That *cumulative audience rating*, or *"cume,"* describes the advertiser's one-week **reach**. If a local car dealer buys one radio ad each weekday morning at 7:30 for five days, the dealer's going to want to know how many different potential customers heard at least one ad. The dealer is also going to be interested in knowing how many audience members heard *just one* ad, or two of the five, and so on up to who heard all five ads. That's important knowledge because advertisers know that *frequency* is an important part of an effective ad campaign. Prospects usually must be exposed to an ad and/or campaign several times before it begins to "register" with them.

Broadcasters can use AQH and cume ratings to calculate reach and frequency. If you buy five radio ads, each one generating a rating of 2, you've bought 10 GRPs. If your cume rating for the week is 3, then you know you tended to reach the same people more than once rather than reaching new listeners each time. After all, you reached 2 percent of the audience with your very first ad, then you added only one point to that with your other four ads combined. The formula and arithmetic:

$$\text{Frequency} = \text{GRPs} \div \text{Reach}$$
$$= 10 \div 3 = 3.33$$

Put into words, you reached 3 percent of the audience with your ads, and each person you did reach heard your ads an average of 3.33 times. That may be enough frequency for your ads to be effective! The trade-off: You reached only a small fraction of the total universe (only 3%).

Now let's turn attention to processes by which these ratings, shares, HUTs, and so on, are measured in the real word.

Television Ratings

If television is an integral element of popular culture, so are the **Nielsen Ratings**, research that drives the television advertising and broadcasting businesses. Nielsen Media Research, headquartered in New York, has been measuring broadcast audiences since 1936. Nielsen sells ratings research to broadcasters and advertising agencies at the national and local levels. It also offers ratings research for national cable television channels and the specialized Hispanic television audience.

When measuring national audiences, Nielsen uses a random sample of 5,000 U.S. television households. Each household in the sample has devices, called *peoplemeters*, attached to every television in the house. These meters track when the television is turned on, the channel to which it's tuned, and who's watching. The peoplemeters then download their collected viewing information via telephone line to Nielsen's data production center in Florida. That's how the "overnight ratings" are produced. If it's the day after the Super Bowl and you see something in the news about how 50 million households tuned in to the game, that estimate is coming from Nielsen's peoplemeter sample. Nielsen collects and sells national ratings data 365 days per year.

If your first thought about all those peoplemeters and all that phone downloading was "sounds expensive," you're correct. The Nielsen Television Index, or NTI, is useful to networks and national advertisers, and they pay millions and millions of dollars each year to have those data.

But what about *local* television and *local* advertisers? The Nielsen Station Index (NSI) is for them. Nielsen has carved the United States up into 210 distinct television markets, called **designated market areas** (usually abbreviated as DMAs). Figure 2.1 shows the DMA list for 2001. The biggest, New York City, accounts for more than 7 million television households, or 6.92 percent of the total U.S. television universe. The smallest—Glendive—is so small you may not have heard of it (it's in Montana).

Every county in the United States is assigned to one—and only one—DMA, based upon that county's viewing tendencies. Assume your county lies close enough to Big City X and Big City Y so that you receive TV signals from both. If your county watches 51 percent of its television from X and 49 percent from Y, you'll be assigned to the DMA for City X. Nielsen revises its DMA list each year, though typically few DMAs change position in the list from year to year.

A market's position on the DMA list has important business implications, though. Many advertisers design television campaigns to run in a number of the larger U.S. cities (and their DMAs). If a major advertiser tells its agency to "buy spot advertising time in the top ten DMAs," and you own a television station in DMA number 11, well, you'd like your market to get bigger so you can get a piece of that advertising pie.

The process of measuring local television audiences and DMAs is very different from the national measurement approach. In all 210 markets, viewing is measured through paper-and-pencil diaries, which Nielsen mails to households selected randomly to be in

DMA Rank	Market	TV HH	% of US
1	New York, NY	7,301,060	6.924
2	Los Angeles, CA	5,303,490	5.03
3	Chicago, IL	3,360,770	3.187
4	Philadelphia, PA	2,801,010	2.656
5	San Francisco-Oakland-San Jose, CA	2,426,010	2.301
6	Boston, MA (Manchester, NH)	2,315,700	2.196
7	Dallas-Ft. Worth, TX	2,201,170	2.088
8	Washington, DC (Hagerstown, MD)	2,128,430	2.019
9	Atlanta, GA	1,990,650	1.888
10	Detroit, MI	1,878,670	1.782
11	Houston, TX	1,831,680	1.737
12	Seattle-Tacoma, WA	1,647,230	1.562
13	Minneapolis-St. Paul, MN	1,573,640	1.492
14	Tampa-St. Petersburg (Sarasota), FL	1,568,180	1.487
15	Miami-Ft. Lauderdale, FL	1,549,680	1.47
16	Phoenix, AZ	1,536,950	1.458
17	Cleveland-Akron (Canton), OH	1,513,130	1.435
18	Denver, CO	1,381,620	1.31
19	Sacramento-Stockton-Modesto, CA	1,226,670	1.163
20	Orlando-Daytona Beach-Melbourne, FL	1,182,420	1.121
21	Pittsburgh, PA	1,148,340	1.089
22	St. Louis, MO	1,143,690	1.085
23	Portland, OR	1,069,260	1.014
24	Baltimore, MD	1,023,530	0.971
25	Indianapolis, IN	1,013,290	0.961
26	San Diego, CA	975,690	0.925
27	Charlotte, NC	954,210	0.905
28	Hartford & New Haven, CT	953,130	0.904
29	Raleigh-Durham (Fayetteville), NC	939,000	0.891
30	Nashville, TN	879,030	0.834
31	Kansas City, MO	849,730	0.806
32	Cincinnati, OH	836,190	0.793
33	Milwaukee, WI	832,330	0.789
34	Columbus, OH	809,940	0.768
35	Salt Lake City, UT	782,960	0.743
36	Greenville-Spartanburg, SC-Asheville, NC-Anderson, SC	771,680	0.732
37	San Antonio, TX	710,030	0.673
38	Grand Rapids-Kalamazoo-Battle Creek, MI	702,210	0.666
39	Birmingham (Anniston and Tuscaloosa), AL	683,830	0.649
40	West Palm Beach-Ft. Pierce, FL	681,100	0.646
41	Memphis, TN	655,210	0.621
42	Norfolk-Portsmouth-Newport News, VA	654,150	0.62
43	New Orleans, LA	653,020	0.619
44	Greensboro-High Point-Winston Salem, NC	634,130	0.601
45	Oklahoma City, OK	623,760	0.592
46	Harrisburg-Lancaster-Lebanon-York, PA	617,830	0.586
47	Buffalo, NY	616,610	0.585
48	Albuquerque-Santa Fe, NM	607,170	0.576
49	Providence, RI-New Bedford, MA	600,730	0.57
50	Louisville, KY	598,940	0.568
51-100		19,879,170	18.851
101-150		10,121,940	9.6
151-210		4,704,340	4.461
	Total	**105,444,330**	**100**

FIGURE 2.1. 2001–02 DMA List, Nielsen Media Research. Reprinted by permission.

Nielsen's sample. Figure 2.2 shows the diary page you'd use to report your Saturday evening household viewing. Your mission, should you choose to accept it, is to write in the diary all the television viewing by you and other household members for a seven-day period. You're asked to write in start time and stop time, channel number, call letters, program name, and the household members watching with you. For this week-long effort you have received, at a minimum, a crisp new dollar bill tucked in with your diary when mailed to you by Nielsen. Some households receive higher payments, because Nielsen's experience shows that certain ethnic or younger households are less likely to participate in the diary process. Those "special treatment" households receive $2, $5, or even $10.

Now you may be thinking, "For a buck? No way!" If so, you have company. Nielsen has continually increasing difficulty getting selected households to agree to keep and return diaries. Figure 2.3 shows how the NSI response rate has declined over the past several years. The chart shows response rates for the four times per year, called "sweeps," that NSI viewing data is collected by diary. Each sweep lasts four weeks, though each household participating reports viewing for only one of those four weeks.

This would seem to be a serious data compromise, compared to the continuous measurement employed in the national NTI service. The part-year sweep measurement stems largely from cost issues, since small-market stations probably could not afford to pay Nielsen three times more money for continuous diary measurement. Sweeps also open the ratings up to greater chance of manipulation, since stations may employ unusual and/or temporary tactics to drive up viewing during the sweeps periods.

One approach is to run better programs during the sweeps. If you're a station program director and you've bought a movie package comprising three blockbusters and a dozen "dogs," you're probably going to schedule your blockbusters during sweeps periods—and promote them frequently and vigorously on-air.

"Watch-and-win" contests frequently crop up during sweeps. Compared with scheduling better program inventory during sweeps, contesting seems more manipulative since, ostensibly, more viewers watch the station because of the contest, not because of the regular programming. Nielsen takes this "hyping" seriously enough that it has, for some time, listed stations running contests during the sweeps in a separate disclaimer in the front of each ratings book used by clients. This listing loses some of its punch, however, when most or all stations in a market are listed, as is frequently the case.

Nielsen frowns more seriously on another practice some stations have employed in the past to get viewing entered in diaries: on-air announcements to diary-keepers. It can be a simple thing: "If you're watching us now, be sure to write 'News 7' in your Nielsen diary." Because this sort of announcement, if used by all stations at all times, would result in on-air chaos, Nielsen forbids client stations from making diary announcements during sweeps.

Then there are station actions so egregious as to merit a "Nielsen death penalty." If NSI receives evidence that a station has engaged in fraud (such as paying a diary household secretly to write in extra viewing of the station), that station can be "de-listed." The station can be deleted from the viewing data Nielsen reports to its clients, and that means the station will have no current viewing data upon which to base advertising sales. The station, of course, also must endure the stigma of a "scarlet letter" signifying its unethical conduct. Because the penalty and ramifications are so severe, few stations risk being de-listed . . .

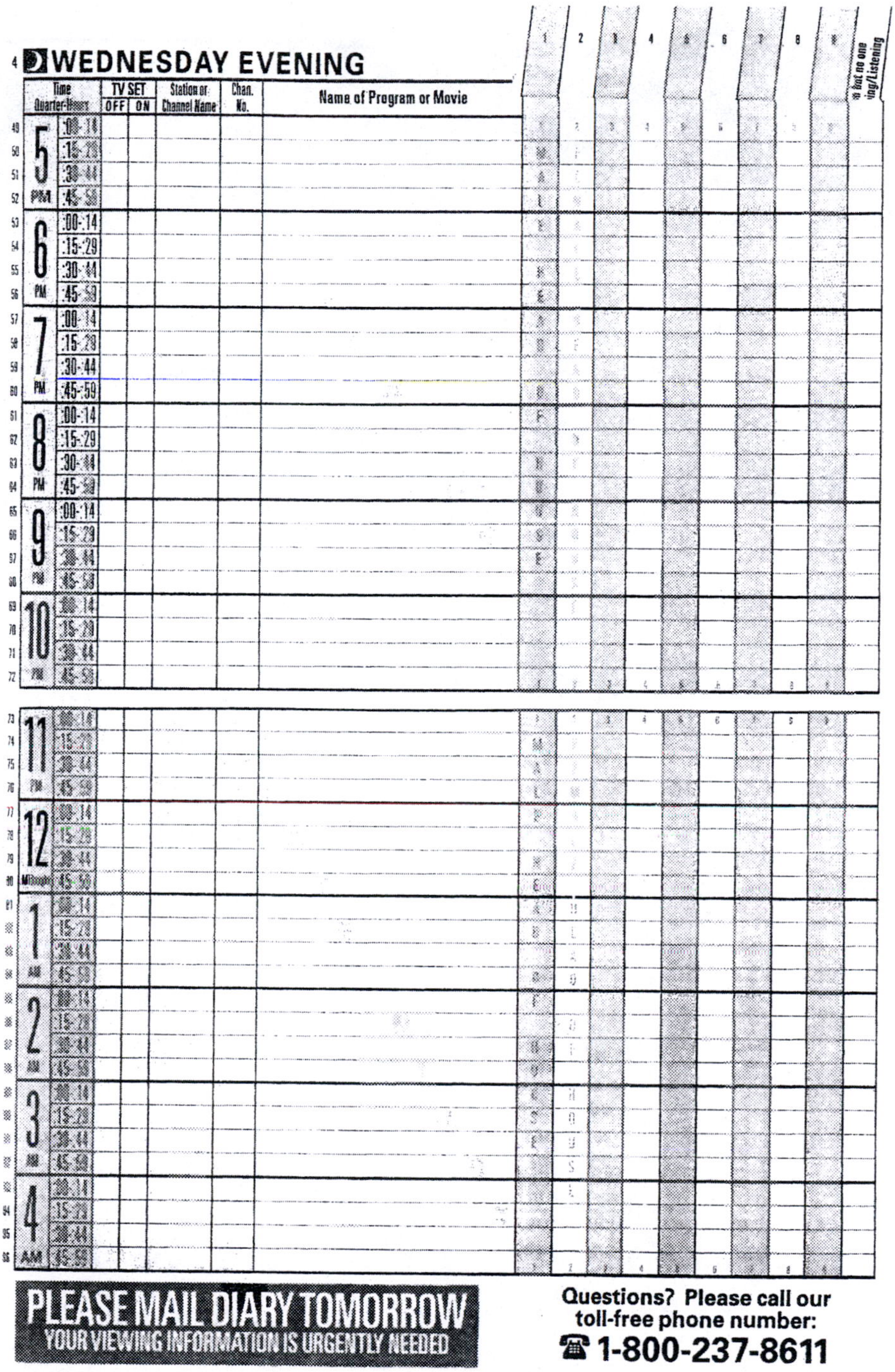

4 WEDNESDAY EVENING

Time Quarter-Hours		TV SET OFF	TV SET ON	Station or Channel Name	Chan. No.	Name of Program or Movie
5 PM	:00-:14					
	:15-:29					
	:30-:44					
	:45-:59					
6 PM	:00-:14					
	:15-:29					
	:30-:44					
	:45-:59					
7 PM	:00-:14					
	:15-:29					
	:30-:44					
	:45-:59					
8 PM	:00-:14					
	:15-:29					
	:30-:44					
	:45-:59					
9 PM	:00-:14					
	:15-:29					
	:30-:44					
	:45-:59					
10 PM	:00-:14					
	:15-:29					
	:30-:44					
	:45-:59					
11 PM	:00-:14					
	:15-:29					
	:30-:44					
	:45-:59					
12 Midnight	:00-:14					
	:15-:29					
	:30-:44					
	:45-:59					
1 AM	:00-:14					
	:15-:29					
	:30-:44					
	:45-:59					
2 AM	:00-:14					
	:15-:29					
	:30-:44					
	:45-:59					
3 AM	:00-:14					
	:15-:29					
	:30-:44					
	:45-:59					
4 AM	:00-:14					
	:15-:29					
	:30-:44					
	:45-:59					

PLEASE MAIL DIARY TOMORROW
YOUR VIEWING INFORMATION IS URGENTLY NEEDED

Questions? Please call our toll-free phone number:
1-800-237-8611

FIGURE 2.2. Sample Diary Page, Nielsen Media Research. Reprinted by permission.

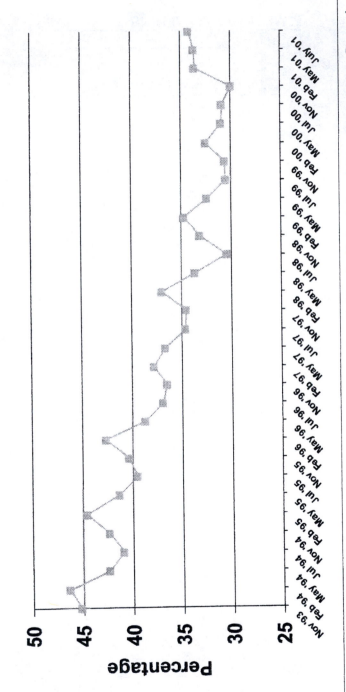

FIGURE 2.3. Nielsen Diary Response Rate (Unweighted Average). Compiled by the National Association of Broadcasters Research and Planning Department.

and few are. However, it's worth remembering that, in addition to its many methodological weaknesses, diary measurement can be influenced (or subverted) deliberately.

Roughly the 160 smallest DMAs in the United States pin their business hopes on Nielsen ratings gathered through diaries. The fifty or so largest DMAs have demanded, and pay for, additional viewing measures to beef up diary-based ratings. These *metered* markets also have electronic devices installed in samples of households within the DMA, gathering tuning information for download by telephone to NSI's Florida operations center. However, there's a big difference in that Nielsen doesn't use peoplemeters in these local markets. Instead, Nielsen uses a less sophisticated device called a *set meter*, which doesn't measure viewing by different members of the household separately. The set meter doesn't know or care if there's one person or four (or zero!) in the room, so long as the set's turned on and tuned to a given channel.

The larger markets' need for continuous measurement outweighs this limitation, and Nielsen continues to market its metered service to other DMAs that haven't yet chosen to pay the higher prices associated with metered viewing data. Some in the industry say Nielsen's desire to sell metered service to more and more DMAs discourages efforts to improve the validity and reliability of diary measurement. Nielsen is a publicly traded for-profit corporation. Since the Arbitron Company's withdrawal from television audience measurement in 1993, Nielsen also has held a monopoly in TV ratings.

Radio Ratings

Radio broadcasters rely upon station ratings to sell advertising time just as television broadcasters do. Radio broadcasters more often sell advertising by "daypart," rather than by program, so they need information describing the audience estimated to be listening at any given moment during, say, "Morning Drive Time" (usually 6 to 10 A.M.). Similarly, they need ratings information for "Afternoon Drive," "Midday," "Evening," and any other dayparts during which their stations may sell ad time.

The **Arbitron** Company conducts local market radio ratings research in the United States, and it has done so since 1965. Reflecting the greater number and spread of radio stations throughout the country compared to television stations, Arbitron defines local markets differently than Nielsen's DMAs. As of fall 2000, Arbitron defined 283 different radio markets, each with its own ratings books issued either twice or four times per year (larger markets tend to want more frequent measurement—and are more willing to pay for it).

Arbitron provides listening information for its client stations on two levels. First, Arbitron reports listening in the **Metro Survey Area (MSA)**. The MSA typically comprises one or more "core counties" in a metropolitan area, city, or town, as defined geographically, demographically, and economically (commuting trends from an outlying county into the metro area figure into that county's metro assignment, for example). Here's an important distinction between MSA and DMA definitions—many counties in the United States are *not* involved in an MSA, while all counties belong to one DMA.

So how is listening reported for the territory outside the MSAs? Arbitron has a second, broader market definition plan to accommodate the far-flung geographic coverage of many radio stations. The *Total Survey Area (TSA)* for a radio market comprises additional counties outside the MSA, based upon listening being reported at a minimal level to stations in the MSA. Some of these TSAs can be quite large geographically. Also, any given county can be (and most often is) in more than one TSA.

As a practical matter, radio broadcasters usually are concerned much more about their MSA ratings than about TSA numbers. Given the tendency of many local advertisers to buy radio ad time in the hope of generating increased local business traffic, listeners who may live 100 or more miles away from the MSA aren't seen as strong prospects.

Radio broadcasters also tend to buy advertising slots (called *avails*) sprinkled at different times within dayparts. An advertiser might purchase an ad schedule that calls for four 30-second ads to run every weekday morning during drive time (6 to 10). Under this *run of schedule (ROS)* buy, the station is free to schedule the ads on a rotating basis anytime between 6 and 10. This approach to purchasing reflects radio's different nature, compared with television. Radio is more of a background medium, with audience members less likely to be tuning in for specific 30-minute programs and, instead, more likely to snap the radio on when arriving at work and snapping it off at the end of the day.

A radio rating point means the same thing conceptually as does a television rating point—one percent of the target audience tuned in for at least five minutes during a quarter hour. However, Arbitron's reports stress *cume audiences* more strongly than Nielsen does with its books, because radio advertisers are more likely to want to know how many *different people* were reached by that week's worth of ROS advertising. Then, using the formula described earlier in the chapter, advertisers can calculate the average frequency their campaigns generated. It's an advertising industry axiom that television is a "reach medium" and radio is a "frequency medium." Figure 2.4 shows a sample page from Arbitron's "Radio Market Reports," the rating book describing local station performance.

All Arbitron ratings data in the United States are collected by diary, and Arbitron faces response rate woes, just as Nielsen does. Figure 2.5 shows Arbitron's response trends over the past several years. It just hasn't been practical to install electronic devices to track radio tuning and listening. Remember that question from the beginning of the chapter regarding how many radios you have in your household? Well, if Arbitron were to take accurate measurements of your listening it would have to meter *all* the radios you use. That would be a very expensive proposition—one that most radio stations wouldn't be able to afford. There also would be enormous technical obstacles to overcome in metering a medium as ubiquitous and as portable as radio.

New Approaches to Ratings Research

Aware that the changing viewing and listening environment may leave them with severely compromised audience research products (relying heavily upon paper-and-pencil records of audience members' tuning behavior), Nielsen and Arbitron are testing new data collection tools—and they've done so for many years. One of the greatest challenges always seems to be economic. The ratings research companies must develop new ways of measuring audiences, without driving up the cost to their clients too dramatically.

Both companies aspire to develop and deploy ratings measurement tools that reduce or eliminate audience responsibility for data collection or reporting. The ideal device

Target Listener Trends
Persons 12-24

	Monday-Sunday 6AM-MID				Monday-Friday 6AM-10AM				Monday-Friday 10AM-3PM				Monday-Friday 3PM-7PM				Monday-Friday 7PM-MID			
	AQH (00)	Cume (00)	AQH Rtg	AQH Shr	AQH (00)	Cume (00)	AQH Rtg	AQH Shr	AQH (00)	Cume (00)	AQH Rtg	AQH Shr	AQH (00)	Cume (00)	AQH Rtg	AQH Shr	AQH (00)	Cume (00)	AQH Rtg	AQH Shr
WAAA-FM																				
SU '01	37	606	3.7	31.4	42	362	4.2	30.7	34	322	3.4	26.2	47	398	4.7	30.5	35	310	3.5	36.1
SP '01	36	542	3.6	30.0	36	319	3.6	29.0	27	263	2.7	21.1	58	408	5.8	32.4	28	257	2.8	29.5
WI '01	39	580	3.9	30.7	44	382	4.4	27.5	28	266	2.8	20.0	54	434	5.4	32.5	41	306	4.1	48.1
FA '00	38	550	3.9	30.4	43	290	4.4	27.4	50	344	5.1	27.6	44	371	4.5	29.3	32	276	3.3	40.5
4-Book	*38*	*570*	*3.5*	*30.6*	*41*	*338*	*4.2*	*28.7*	*35*	*299*	*3.5*	*23.7*	*51*	*403*	*5.1*	*31.2*	*34*	*287*	*3.4*	*38.8*
SU '00	36	581	3.7	30.3	42	335	4.3	30.9	42	303	4.3	28.4	46	433	4.7	29.3	35	340	3.8	35.7
WBBB-FM																				
SU '01	5	96	.5	4.2	6	44	.6	4.4	8	22	.8	6.2	5	34	.5	3.2	8	58	.8	8.2
SP '01	2	85	.2	1.7	1	19	.1	.8	2	22	.2	1.6	3	33	.3	1.7	4	41	.4	4.2
WI '01	6	126	.6	4.3	7	64	.7	4.4	9	43	.9	6.4	9	57	.9	5.4	6	39	.6	6.7
FA '00	4	103	.4	3.2	5	41	.5	3.2	8	45	.8	4.4	6	46	.6	4.0	1	40	.1	1.3
4-Book	*4*	*103*	*.4*	*3.5*	*5*	*42*	*.5*	*3.2*	*7*	*33*	*.7*	*4.7*	*6*	*43*	*.6*	*3.6*	*4*	*45*	*.4*	*4.6*
SU '00	7	127	.7	5.9	4	50	.4	2.9	10	63	1.0	6.6	10	79	1.0	6.4	6	65	.6	6.1
WCCC-FM																				
SU '01		27				7				7				3			1	11	.1	1.0
SP '01	2	29	.2	1.7	1	7	.1	.8	4	10	.4	3.1	2	13	.4	2.2	2	22	.2	2.1
WI '01	2	33	.2	1.6	3	17	.3	1.9	4	10	.4	2.9	2	24	.2	1.2		3		
FA '00	2	43	.2	1.6	3	17	.3	1.9	2	26	.2	1.1	2	20	.2	1.3	2	16	.2	2.5
4-Book	*2*	*33*	*.2*	*1.2*	*2*	*12*	*.2*	*1.2*	*3*	*13*	*.3*	*1.8*	*2*	*15*	*.2*	*1.2*	*1*	*13*	*.1*	*1.4*
SU '00	2	50	.2	1.7	3	13	.3	2.2	3	22	.3	2.0	2	20	.2	1.3	2	9	.2	2.0
WDDD-FM																				
SU '01	3	115	.3	2.5	2	39	.2	1.5	3	44	.3	2.3	6	75	.6	3.9	3	50	.3	3.1
SP '01	5	110	.5	4.2	8	47	.8	6.5	9	56	.9	7.0	7	56	.7	3.9	1	24	.1	1.1
WI '01	2	103	.2	1.6	2	34	.2	1.3	2	41	.2	1.4	2	43	.2	1.2	1	27	.1	1.1
FA '00	3	114	.3	2.4	4	45	.4	2.5	3	49	.3	1.7	3	55	.3	2.0	2	23	.2	2.5
4-Book	*3*	*111*	*.3*	*2.7*	*4*	*41*	*.4*	*3.0*	*4*	*48*	*.4*	*3.1*	*5*	*57*	*.5*	*2.8*	*2*	*31*	*.2*	*2.0*
SU '00	3	138	.3	2.5	3	49	.3	2.2	5	64	.5	3.4	3	65	.3	1.9	2	27	.2	2.0
WEEE-AM																				
SU '01	2	76	.2	1.7	3	35	.3	2.2	1	21	.1	.8	2	33	.2	1.3	1	21	.1	1.0
SP '01	2	100	.2	1.7	3	48	.3	2.4	1	37	.1	.8	4	57	.4	2.2		33		
WI '01	2	90	.2	1.8	6	87	.6	3.8	3	27	.3	2.1	2	32	.2	1.2		13		
FA '00	5	97	.5	4.0	9	40	.9	5.7	13	54	1.3	7.2	5	35	.5	3.3	3	13	.1	1.3
4-Book	*3*	*91*	*.3*	*2.3*	*5*	*43*	*.5*	*3.5*	*5*	*35*	*.5*	*2.7*	*3*	*39*	*.3*	*2.0*	*1*	*15*	*.1*	*.6*
SU '00	3	114	.3	2.5	7	53	.7	5.1	2	46	.2	1.4	3	61	.3	1.9	1	30	.1	1.0
WFFF-FM																				
SU '01		10								3				7						
SP '01		9				3				4										
WI '01																				
FA '00		9								6				8						
4-Book		*7*								*3*				*3*						
SU '00	1	28	.1	.8		13				7				13			1	13	.1	1.0
WGGG-FM																				
SU '01	7	268	.7	5.9	10	120	1.0	7.3	10	138	1.0	7.7	11	136	1.1	7.1	4	82	.4	4.3
SP '01	9	260	.9	7.5	9	103	.9	7.3	15	126	1.5	11.7	13	129	1.3	7.3	5	82	.5	5.3
WI '01	8	246	.8	6.3	13	117	1.3	8.1	13	81	1.3	9.3	11	131	1.1	6.6	3	67	.3	3.4
FA '00	10	275	1.0	6.0	14	105	1.4	8.9	19	162	2.0	10.5	11	152	1.1	7.3	4	63	.4	5.1
4-Book	*9*	*263*	*.9*	*6.9*	*12*	*111*	*1.2*	*7.9*	*14*	*127*	*1.5*	*9.8*	*12*	*137*	*1.2*	*7.1*	*4*	*74*	*.4*	*4.5*
SU '00	12	286	1.2	10.1	12	109	1.2	8.8	17	123	1.7	11.5	17	164	1.7	10.8	9	90	.9	9.2
WHHH-AM																				
SU '01		3				3				3				3						
SP '01										4										
WI '01		6																3		
FA '00										6										
4-Book		*2*				*1*				*3*				*1*				*1*		
SU '00		5				2			1	3	.1	.7		3				3		

FIGURE 2.4. Sample RMR Page, Arbitron, Inc. Reprinted by permission.

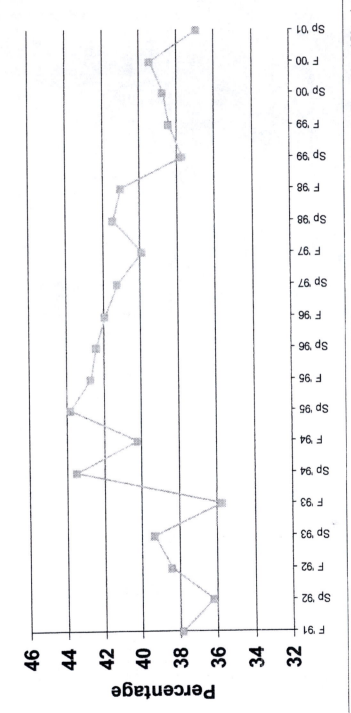

FIGURE 2.5. Arbitron Diary Response Rates (Unweighted Average). Compiled by national Association of Broadcasters, Research and Planning Department.

would be one that tracks what you watch or listen to, without your even knowing it. Or is that so ideal after all? Privacy issues come front and center with that sort of monitoring, and Nielsen and Arbitron don't need to introduce new concerns to audience members already less likely than ever to willingly participate in ratings research.

Nielsen has been working on an improved television meter system for the past several years, and it's continuing to test its "active/passive meter system." At its core, the "A/P meter" relies upon multiple methods of identifying the programs (and, don't forget, the ads) an audience member watches. Most viewing would be measured by encoding the programs with video and audio information identifying the program (or the ad). When the A/P meter senses that encoded information, it matches it with the viewers in the room (who, in theory, have dutifully punched their button on the meter to indicate that they're watching TV). The encoded information is stashed in the broadcast signal in such a way that viewers can't see or hear it—but the meter can.

A potential problem with such a code-based audience measurement system is the requirement that all programs be encoded with that identifying information. Also, of course, television stations would have to pass the encoded information along through their transmission if meters at home are to receive usable information. If you can picture the possibility, some day in the future, a television station might find itself in a dispute with Nielsen and, as a consequence, threaten to "pull the plug" on program encoding, you begin to understand that encoding, by itself, has vulnerabilities. There also will be times when technical difficulties prevent stations from inserting code into local programming (or passing through code on network programs). Some back-up measurement would be desirable.

To provide that insurance, Nielsen intends to take advantage of the new digital broadcast technology being adopted by more and more television stations, using a network of monitoring stations in the larger DMAs that would collect the digital data streams from all digital television broadcasts in the market. Then, if the program encoding failed for one or more stations during a ratings measurement period, the A/P meters in viewers' homes would collect short "samples" of the digital data stream to which the viewer is tuned. At a later time, those samples could be compared to the digital signatures collected by the monitoring stations in order to determine what program was tuned in.

When the A/P system was first announced by Nielsen in 1993, it seemed to be high on Nielsen's priority list. Broadcasters were just beginning to roll out new digital television broadcasts (including "high-definition television," or HDTV), and the Federal Communication Commission had issued regulations requiring stations to broadcast in both digital and analog formats for several years (so as not to render nearly every television in the country obsolete). By 2006, the FCC said, television broadcasters would have to rely solely upon digital spectrum, returning the analog spectrum they've been using for years and years to the government for use in other ways. Nielsen would need a new meter system for that brave new television world, because its current peoplemeters and set meters do not work with digital broadcasts.

There was an additional regulatory stipulation, though: Analog spectrum would be returned to the government only if 85 percent of the viewers in a given DMA had the capability of viewing digital television broadcasts. U.S. TV households have been slow to embrace the new digital television service. HDTV remains the realm of "videophiles" with thousands of dollars to spend on single television sets, and most U.S. TV households continue to use analog television sets. It's likely that very few (if any) television broadcasters in the United States will be abandoning their analog spectrum in 2006. Hence, Nielsen has been given some more time to use its older analog metering technology.

Arbitron has also been developing a meter system for the past few years. Using the same sort of inaudible encoding of identifying information into radio programs and ads, Arbitron's *Portable Personal Meter (PPM)* would relieve listeners of the burden of entering their tuning behavior into a paper diary. Keep in mind, though, the distinction we drew between television viewing (in relatively few locations in a home) and radio listening (nearly anywhere and everywhere). To address this, Arbitron has developed a very small meter device, about the size of a pager. If you were in Arbitron's PPM sample, you'd carry the PPM around with you all day, wherever you happened to go. The meter would be listening constantly, with a built-in microphone, to the sounds from your environment. When you come within earshot of a radio that's playing encoded music, news, ads, and so on, the meter would store that information in its computer memory. Then, just before you go to bed, you would put your PPM in its little recharging stand, which also doubles as a data port for downloading listening data from the PPM to Arbitron's computer center by telephone line.

Of course, this approach has its problems, too. Arbitron's engineers have attempted to cover as many bases as possible. If you leave your PPM on your dresser in the morning, and it sits there all day, listening measurements obviously would be flawed. So the PPM contains a motion-sensing device and, if the PPM isn't moved at least every few minutes, it will let Arbitron know that you didn't take the PPM with you (or that you had a particularly sedentary day, if indeed you *were* wearing your PPM).

The PPM units are much less expensive than Nielsen television meters, so they may not fall prey to that constant economic test of all new audience measurement systems.

The PPM technology seems well suited for radio listening measurement. However, it also could be used to measure use of other media—so long as there's an audible program source to be monitored. That would include television (unless the TV sound is turned down or muted). Nielsen and Arbitron recently announced a partnership, with an eye (and an ear) toward using the PPM to take television and radio audience measurements. There's no reason why you, as a PPM-carrying audience member, couldn't provide radio data to Arbitron *and* television viewing (or, more precisely, TV listening) data to Nielsen. This economy of scale could go far to offset the increased cost of PPMs over paper-and-pencil diaries.

The increasingly complex electronic media environment means it's tougher than ever before to try to capture accurate pictures of audience behavior through paper-and-pencil diaries. According to Bob Patchen, Arbitron's Vice President of Research Standards and Practices, "The current rating standards—personal diaries, household diaries, and set meters—will simply not be able to cope with the coming multimedia explosion. Audience researchers must provide viable new solutions for tracking and understanding consumers' multimedia behaviors, or risk becoming irrelevant."[4]

There's another viewing and listening location that's expected to grow in popularity in coming years . . . your personal computer. As more and more broadcasters place their programming on the Internet through streaming video and audio, Nielsen and Arbitron will want to take advantage of a computer's ability to track the digital data streams coming into it. Nielsen already has worked with Microsoft, in fact, to build television "metering" capability into the Windows operating system. However, the home computer also will present new problems for Nielsen and Arbitron. There's nothing to prevent you, and a few thousand others like you, from listening to a web-based radio station in Los Angeles, New York, your hometown, or anywhere else in the world, for that matter. Arbitron eventually will have to decide how to handle this sort of "out-of-market listening," lest significant numbers of listeners go uncounted, local advertisers be asked to pay higher prices for ads reaching long-distance listeners, or both.

Industry Oversight of Broadcast Research

It should be clear that ratings are the very currency by which the television and radio industries do business. Good ratings make money and further careers. Poor ratings lose money and lead to job change. With so much riding on those numbers, broadcasters (and advertising agencies, the other big customer group for the ratings companies) take a hand in overseeing the way the ratings companies do their business. Both Nielsen and Arbitron have formal customer groups to advise them (the Nielsen Customer Alliance and Arbitron Advisory Council). These groups are intended by the ratings firms to provide sounding boards for potential changes to products, rate structures, and other facets of the business. These groups are *not* collections of research methodologists and statisticians whose interest might lie in the nitty-gritty of the measurement process.

The Media Rating Council (MRC), based in New York, is the industry organization that audits and accredits media research firms and their products. If there are problems with ratings research being done by Nielsen, Arbitron, or any other research firms collecting audience information for electronic or print media, the MRC has the best chance of detecting those problems and working with the research company to resolve them. The MRC also has established standards and guidelines for audience measurement, and research firms are expected to adhere to those standards and guidelines if they wish to receive MRC accreditation of their products. And that's a big deal, for unaccredited research tends to be discounted by advertisers and their agencies.

The MRC is playing another important role as new media hit the market. As George Ivie, Executive Director of the MRC, explains, "Our role has been growing, most recently with quality of the measurements. Particularly in new media areas, the credibility provided by our accreditation process helps gain the buyer's acceptance of the data."[5]

Other trade associations within the broadcasting industry conduct research oversight and provide input to the ratings companies. Most prominent among them, the National Association of Broadcasters (NAB), in Washington, DC, is home to industry committees on local television and local radio audience measurement. While these committees don't have accrediting power (or responsibility) over the research companies, they still have clout. After all, NAB's member stations number in the thousands, and the ratings companies count most of them as customers.

David Gunzerath, vice president of Research & Planning for NAB, works closely with these industry committees (Committee on Local Radio Audience Measurement and Committee on Local Television Audience Measurement) and sees them fulfilling an important oversight function in today's business environment. "In an era in which there is relatively little marketplace competition among the broadcasting industry's primary research suppliers, COLRAM and COLTAM play important roles in maintaining a system of accountability for quality among these companies on behalf of the broadcast community," he says.[6]

Program Research

While the ratings drive the broadcasting business, broadcast stations are constantly looking for ways to improve their ratings and, consequently, generate increased revenue. Better programming is an obvious avenue to higher ratings, and the broadcast industry conducts a great deal of research toward that goal.

Television programs are expensive to produce, so it shouldn't be surprising that producers wish to hedge their bets about story ideas, prospective actors to star in shows, plot lines, and other components of a show *before* they commit millions of dollars to the on-air product. National television advertisements also can be very expensive productions. It's not at all unusual for a 30-second network television ad to cost millions. Special effects, elaborate music and sound, star-quality talent, big-name directors: They're often the ingredients of excellent television advertisements just as they are of Hollywood blockbuster movies.

Producers can answer a great many questions by putting pilot shows, plot variations, story concepts, and just about any other content-related facet of a program in front of a group of viewers, to measure their reaction, opinions, liking, or other factors. At the earliest stages of program or ad development, research participants might be brought together to hear and discuss positioning statements. These would give guidance to the creative team before any script is written or film shot. Then, after writers have had a crack at it, audience members might see *storyboards*, which show artist renditions of snapshots of the different scenes in the program or ad, along with the dialogue.

The next stage in testing probably moves into the realm of actual moving images, called *rough cuts*. These are low-budget executions, though, designed only to convey the way the program or ad will go together and flow, not to gather viewer opinion of the whizbang special effects or million-dollar-a-minute celebrity spokesperson.

If a program or ad production still seems promising at this point, the big dollars are committed and actual filming of the eventual finished product begins. Still, the producers will have the ability to test that final product, or variations of it, with audiences before the "real deal" is distributed to television households across the country. Did audiences dislike the plot twist at the end of the pilot show? Did they want to see more of the new car and less of the driver in the ad? Does something need to be added or clarified before the final production airs? These are the adjustments producers can make in the later stages of program production.

And where is a producer to find these test viewers? They may be residents of a test market who have been recruited to participate in focus group discussions at a central research location. Perhaps they've been pulled off the mall floor to spend 15 minutes or so screening test ads in a "consumer research facility." They may be people at home who receive a videotape of the test program and a questionnaire to answer after watching. Unfortunately, each of these test approaches poses problems for the researchers. Ideally, we'd want the test viewers to be just like the average U.S. television viewers out there. Focus group research is *quali-*

tative research, and it's rarely possible to generalize findings from participants to a larger population in any scientific way. People at the mall tend to be different from those who aren't at the mall (and a myriad of variables are at work here, such as location of the mall, time of day, season of the year, etc.). Even sending videotapes to viewers at their homes will result in evaluation by viewers who have chosen to spend money on a videotape player. Despite these limitations, producers value the guidance from these tests.

Radio broadcasters are just as interested in maximizing the business pay-off from their programming. Many conduct *auditorium tests* (fairly large groups of research participants brought together in a central research location to listen to and evaluate radio program material). The researchers typically play excerpts of music (called *hooks*), snippets of on-air talent, or other elements of their programming for which they'd like listener evaluation. Listener feedback also can also be collected by telephone, through *call-out research.*

Ed Cohen, former research director for Clear Channel Communications—one of the largest radio group owners in the country—and now Arbitron's Vice President for Domestic Radio Research, has conducted many of both types of studies. "Usually they're intended to do two different things," Cohen says. "Auditorium tests are designed to help a station build and maintain its playlists and music library. Subjects in those tests may listen to and rate hundreds of hooks over a two-hour period. Call-out research is better suited for listener surveys focusing on the station's image, talent or other facets not related directly to the music it plays."[7]

There *is* a scientifically rigorous way to test programs, but it can be expensive. Imagine that the U.S. Air Force wishes to test some new recruiting ads for television. The question: Should the ads continue to show fighter jocks "yanking and banking," or should the ads stress the values, commitment, and nobility of service in the USAF? Another important question: What constitutes success in the campaign? Do recruiting numbers have to rise, or would increased public awareness or knowledge of the Air Force be deemed a successful outcome?

It's time to be realistic: Few young people would make a decision of such life importance based upon ad campaign "A" or "B." So let's define "liking of the Air Force" as the dependent measure of interest for this campaign. We would choose several test DMAs in which the Air Force would run the new ads. Several other DMAs, matched as well as possible on important demographic variables with the test DMAs, will serve as control markets and will receive the "yank and bank" ad campaign. The ads will run at the same GRP levels in all the DMAs for the same time period. Then, at the end of the study, we'll conduct a scientific survey of audiences in the different DMAs to measure "liking of the USAF." If the values-based campaign does cause viewers to feel greater liking of the Air Force, this *field experiment* is designed to detect that causal relationship. It does so at a price, however. In this case, the Air Force bought heavy advertising schedules in multiple DMAs and aired two competing sets of expensive advertisements—only to demonstrate that Americans "like" the Air Force more when the values-based campaign airs. While that's important to know, some general is going to want the concrete tally of how many young people walked into recruiting offices *because* they saw the new USAF ad campaign. There are some questions even the best, most rigorous broadcast research just can't answer.

And then there are the mundane questions, still important to those trying to maximize return on investment at the station or network. Would viewers prefer their local news anchorman with a crew cut? Should he be wearing a sweater instead of a jacket? Are audiences getting tired of the theme music for the news show? Would they prefer younger, more attractive newscasters instead of the current grizzled veterans of years of ratings wars? Would they rather see 30 seconds of weather after the first three news stories, instead of waiting for another 15 minutes?

These questions are the business of *program consultants* such as Frank Magid and Associates, Audience Research & Development, and many others. Usually they enter into exclusive agreements with no more than one station per DMA, and they make recommendations for programming alterations—and conduct the audience research to test outcomes. As with the other non-ratings research mentioned earlier, this research is designed to reduce uncertainty for station managers. There's usually too much at stake for management to feel comfortable programming "by the seat of their pants."

Program consultants may get less business in the years to come, because of the dramatic restructuring of station ownership in the United States over the past few years. As a result of relaxed ownership caps by the FCC, more stations belong to a smaller number of group owners than ever before. Some of these large broadcast groups have in-house research capability, and some have chosen to conduct their own program research, in effect putting program consultants on staff full-time. That's more and more the direction taken by the NBC stations group, according to Billy McDowell, Vice President of Research for NBC Stations.

"Most everything can be handled internally between the research and programming assets of the stations division, the NBC network, and the syndication division. There is a good deal of sharing resources across the divisions. This minimizes the need to go outside and reduces the cost of programming to NBC," McDowell says.[8]

An Audience Research Paradox

Most broadcast audiences have more viewing and listening choices than ever before. Cable TV customers typically have dozens of channels they can watch, and direct broadcast satellite (DBS) customers may have hundreds. That means smaller and smaller "pieces of the pie" for individual channels or stations. Targeting of specific audiences, based upon age group, interests, activities, or other demographic and psychographic variables is becoming more important for broadcasters. That sort of detailed knowledge of audiences requires extensive, detailed research. Yet audiences today are increasingly unwilling to participate in research studies.

So broadcasters find themselves wanting to know more and more about smaller groups of people who are less and less willing to "talk." In addition to Nielsen and Arbitron, other syndicated research companies have a difficult time getting audiences to participate in their surveys. Scarborough Research, which collects audience information for print media as well as electronic media and also cross-references media use with product use and purchase, routinely encounters response rates of less than 20 percent for its studies (less than 10% in some markets). Yet customer demand for detailed information remains. What's a research firm to do?

Brace yourself—most firms make up much of the audience behavior they report. Of course, they don't call it "making stuff up." They call it "imputation" or "ascription." It usually involves taking information gathered from some respondents and applying it to "similar" respondents who didn't provide all the information requested. If a household of five is keeping Nielsen diaries for a week, and someone fails to check the box indicating which family member was tuned to Channel 7 at 8:15 P.M. on Wednesday, Nielsen will "impute" the viewing to the most likely individual household member. That means an older member of the house will be credited with viewing CBS, and a younger one will get credit for watching the WB. And if you're a young person who just happens to really like "The Lawrence Welk Show," Nielsen probably will get it wrong if you don't check your box on the diary page.

Nielsen has improved its imputation model recently, though. Until last year Nielsen made its imputations based upon viewing patterns from the 1970s.

Another generally accepted data reporting technique used by ratings companies is *weighting*. If Nielsen finds that its sample includes 4 percent Hispanic households, but the DMA population is 8 percent Hispanic, the results from those relatively few Hispanic participants would be amplified mathematically so that, in the end, the data would look as if the findings came from a sample with 8 percent Hispanic households. In plain terms, each Hispanic household in the sample would be reported as *two* Hispanic households in the final data. The implicit assumption: Hispanic households that agreed to participate have the same viewing behavior as Hispanic households that decided not to bother with the diaries. That's a tough assumption to defend, but the alternative (selling data from samples that are conclusively not representative of the population) is even scarier to the research companies.

There's another source of uncertainty users of ratings (and other sample-based research information) must keep in mind. **Sampling error** prevents us from interpreting statistical findings as precise measures of populations. If a morning-drive radio show receives a 1.4 rating from Arbitron, there's a window of variation around that number in which the "true rating" is expected to fall. Just as with opinion polling, the numbers often are too close to call. However, there unfortunately are too many managers in the business who interpret a rating figure as gospel truth. They're the people who fret a 0.2 rating point decline from the last book to the current book, though that decline is well within the margin of error for the ratings estimates.

False Precision

Broadcast research, especially ratings research, generates numbers upon which billions of dollars of business is based. Those numbers can be reported to multiple decimal places ("The Olympics telecast received a rating of 12.43 among television households in Tulsa last night," for example). A quick review of the potential sources of error should humble us somewhat:

- Sampling error arising because Nielsen measures only a sample of households in Tulsa, not all of them.
- Nonrepresentative samples stemming from differential willingness of different types of viewing households to participate in the diary measurement process.
- Measurement error resulting from people's inability to remember and write in their diaries the programs and times they've actually watched television during the

past week (yes, many people go an entire week without writing anything in their diaries, then do a "data dump" just before returning the diary to Nielsen).

- Measurement error resulting from some people's deliberate disregard of the instructions provided by Nielsen (for example, writing in "Frasier" on the diary because it's your favorite program, though you weren't home to watch it the week you had a diary).
- Imputation errors occurring when Nielsen attempts to replace "missing data" in viewing data.
- The occasional editing and processing errors by Nielsen people once the diaries are returned to Dunedin, Florida, for tabulation.

The lesson for us here is that we should be cautious when interpreting ratings information. Those data shouldn't *determine* management decisions—they should *inform* management decisions. It should be apparent to you that the broadcast ratings process is flawed significantly. However, most industry people would argue that flawed ratings are better than no ratings at all.

There's some logic to this. If the sources of error affect all stations' ratings equally, we can draw conclusions about the *relative* standing of stations' audience numbers (KAAA's 8 rating in prime time means more people are watching that station than are watching KBBB, with a 5 rating at the same time). The *absolute* conclusions are less supportable (KAAA's 8 rating means 8% of the DMA population, or 235,410 people, are watching the program at that time). Unfortunately, evidence suggests that sources of ratings error don't affect all stations in the same way (stations with younger audiences are more prone to undermeasurement by diaries, for example).

One thing is certain. Ratings companies will never please all of their customers all the time. If a change in measurement methodology increases ratings for some stations, other stations probably will lose audience numbers. If Arbitron changes its weighting procedures, some stations will benefit while others will take hits. And if a drastic methodological change results in higher ratings for ALL stations at ALL TIMES, who could be displeased? There's that other major group of ratings clients—advertising agencies—and higher broadcast ratings usually lead to higher advertising costs for marketers. It's quite a balancing act the ratings companies face.

One other environmental factor must be mentioned here. Most broadcast research companies (certainly the ratings companies) are publicly traded for-profit businesses. Sure, they might be able to improve the quality of broadcast research as it's now conducted. But they also must satisfy shareholders and investors. There's a constant tension between research quality and research cost, so we'll continue to hear the refrain from broadcasters, advertisers, and researchers: "The ratings aren't perfect, but they're the best we can afford."

Endnotes _____

1. *Fall 2001 Home Technology Report* (Westfield, NJ: Knowledge Networks/Statistical Research, Inc., 2001).

2. Representatives of major radio research organizations confirmed this.

3. *TV Facts* (New York: Television Bureau of Advertising, 2001).
4. Robert Patchen, E-mail to Steve Everett, Oct. 31, 2001.
5. George Ivie, E-mail to Steve Everett, Oct. 25, 2001.
6. David Gunzerath, E-mail to Steve Everett, Oct. 24, 2001.
7. Ed Cohen, Phone conversation with Steve Everett, Oct. 23, 2001.
8. Billy McDowell, E-mail to Steve Everett, Oct. 25, 2001.

3

Newspaper Research

Kristin McGrath

A 1999 article in the *American Journalism Review* criticized newspaper research as follows:

> Although skepticism is a job requirement in journalism, newspaper people have not been skeptical enough about the claims made for readership research. They have not much questioned the accuracy of the surveys that land on their desks or the pitfalls of the methodologies researchers use. Most have not even questioned research's single most obvious failing—that it has not arrested the decline in readership, as its advocates have claimed it could. Over the past twenty years, at their annual conventions and in their trade magazines and in-house publications, news executives have spoken more and more of the need for journalists to think like marketers. As if it were easy, or possible, to know in advance what people want to read. As if the average citizen, in a brief telephone survey conducted by a part-time, poorly paid, not-very-well-trained surveyor, could articulate that. And as if compelling content somehow originated with readers and not in the individual mind of a journalist with interesting things to say . . . it is apparent that newspaper research yields as much uncertainty and confusion as clarity. Much of it is subjective, unscientific, and amenable to manipulation.[1]

That passage captures the animosity that many newspaper researchers still encounter, particularly from newsroom journalists. This chapter seeks to demonstrate that—contrary to the above quotation—newspaper research, in its relatively short history, has become a credible, relevant, and essential management tool. Five aspects of newspaper research are discussed:

Readership research
Research to develop and monitor news/editorial initiatives
Circulation research

Research to support advertising sales
Research as a tool for newspaper management decision making

Readership Research

The main goal of much readership research is to ascertain how many readers newspapers deliver to their advertisers. Before readership studies of this type became commonplace, advertisers relied on **circulation** numbers to accomplish this. There is still some debate over whether readership numbers or circulation counts provide better information on a newspaper's reach. In particular, circulation directors who started out as newspaper carriers or district managers and came up through the ranks often have more faith in circulation counts than in readership percentages. One of their key arguments is that circulation counts of most daily newspapers are verified by an independent auditor, primarily the Audit Bureau of Circulations. Who, they ask, makes sure that newspaper readership percentages are accurate?

These questions are under continual scrutiny by people who conduct and use newspaper readership research. These consist primarily of researchers employed by newspapers, research firms that conduct proprietary studies for newspapers, and research firms that conduct syndicated studies for newspapers. Syndicated studies measure all newspapers with significant market share in a particular market. These generally consist of telephone interviews conducted among large representative samples of adults in each market with careful attention given to design and data collection. The results are generally sold to anyone who wants to buy them, including newspapers, other media, advertising agencies, and advertisers. There are two main sources of syndicated newspaper research in the United States: Scarborough Research, which conducts studies in the top 100 U.S. newspaper markets, and the Gallup Organization, which conducts studies in several of the largest newspaper markets. Proprietary studies are studies commissioned by individual newspapers. The results belong exclusively to the commissioning newspapers. Other organizations that have been involved in newspaper readership measurement issues include the Newspaper Association of America (NAA) and its predecessor, the Newspaper Advertising Bureau; the Advertising Research Foundation (ARF); and, in recent years, the Audit Bureau of Circulations.

One result of all these efforts has been to develop standardized questions to measure newspaper readership. For example, the industry standard for the past few decades has been to measure daily (Monday through Friday) readership by determining **"yesterday" readership** on an unaided basis. To accomplish this, interviewing takes place Tuesday through Saturday (so that "yesterday" is a weekday) and respondents are asked, "When was the last time, before today, you read or looked into [NAME OF PAPER]?" The standards specify that an equal number of interviews be conducted each day. That's because it would be possible to raise readership percentages artificially by concentrating interviewing in the latter part of the week. Standardized questions and interviewing procedures such as these can help ensure that readership comparisons among different newspapers are indeed "apples to apples" comparisons.

Those who are interested in making sure that newspaper readership figures are solid also pay close attention to other questionnaire design and data collection issues. Order bias in questionnaires is one concern. For example, if the key readership questions are preceded by several other questions about a particular daily newspaper, its readership figures could be artificially inflated. It's also important to draw telephone numbers from good random samples, use well-trained interviewers, and monitor response rates carefully. With these considerations in mind, the Audit Bureau of Circulations has recently developed a readership "product." Bureau personnel oversee readership studies to make sure that the highest possible standards of questionnaire design and data collection are adhered to. Only a few newspapers have participated in "audited" readership studies.

Methodological considerations aside, arguments for relying on readership percentages to measure a newspaper's reach are far stronger than arguments for relying on circulation numbers. Circulation numbers can only document that a newspaper has been purchased, not whether it has been read, by whom, or by how many people. Readership research, by contrast, can answer all of these questions.

The "read by whom" question is particularly—and increasingly—relevant. Initially, the demographic information collected in readership studies was used primarily to support advertising sales. For example, if a retail advertiser's primary target market was women aged 25 to 44, the research could document how many women in that age group read the newspaper.

As readership studies became widespread, discouraging readership trends became apparent. In the mid-1970s, the newspaper industry launched its first major effort to arrest the decline in newspaper readership. Albert E. Gollin, who was a senior researcher at the NAA and, prior to that, at the NAB, described this effort in a speech he gave to a newspaper conference in 1996:

> As an industry, with a few notable exceptions, until fairly recently newspapers were not known for their support of readership research. . . . By the late 1970s, the problem of declining readership—in an environment of intensified media competition— had energized the leadership of newspaper associations to establish a special industry-supported effort called the "Newspaper Readership Project," which lasted for six years (1977–83) . . . . What is relevant about the NRP in this context is that readership research—editorial product research, wide-ranging studies of newspaper attitudes and images, of reading habits and content preference, of strategic reader segments, of news media exposure, and of various circulation marketing issues— received a powerful, unprecedented boost, in the form of large-scale funding and the active involvement of several hundred editors and marketing executives in its planning and implementation. That hands-on experience, and the value derived from more than 70 research reports, conferences, and workshops generated by the NRP, whet industry appetites and accelerated the demand for research at individual newspapers and newspaper groups . . . . The changed attitudes within the industry as to the salience and perceived value of the research function represented a culture shift, one that is still in process.[2]

One of the results of all of these efforts was the development of new ways to segment newspaper audiences. In addition to demographic segmentation, newspaper audiences were analyzed by life cycle stage, lifestyle, and varying levels of attachment to newspapers.

The life cycle analysis eventually challenged a piece of conventional wisdom that had long been a comfort to newspaper executives. According to the conventional wisdom, the young people who don't read newspapers very often now will "join the fold" as they mature, marry, have children, buy a home, and become rooted in their communities. Stuart Tolley, another former senior researcher at the NAA and NAB, traced the newspaper readership patterns of successive generations and found that each generation developed its newspaper reading pattern in its young adult years, and that generation's readership increased only slightly as it aged. He found that each generation's readership level started lower than that of the previous generation, and it never caught up.

When the decline in newspaper circulation began in the early 1970s, the assumption was that the younger people were watching TV news rather than reading newspapers. Robinson's nationwide study in 1975 found otherwise. For every age group, more people read newspapers than watched TV news, and for TV news as for newspapers, use was low for younger people and increased with age. Comparison of Robinson's figures with those of Stempel and Hargove in a 1995 national study suggests that this pattern continues. The age groupings aren't identical, but Robinson found that for persons under 40, daily newspaper reading averaged 58 percent, while Stempel and Hargrove found that twenty years later daily readership for those 35 to 54 averaged 64 percent.[3]

Yet Hazel Reinhardt, a Minneapolis-based consultant on market and demographic analysis, pointed out in a speech to the 2000 convention of the American Society of Newspaper Editors that changing demographics may force newspaper reading below 50 percent in the next decade: "For pre-baby boomers, people born before 1946, on average 70 percent of them read a newspaper on a typical weekday. For baby boomers (born 1946–1964), it's about 58 percent. And for Generation X (born 1965–1976), it's only 46 percent." She pointed out that pre-boomers, who accounted for 31 percent of the adults in 1998, will account for only 17 percent in 2010, and Generation Y (born 1977–1999) will be 29 percent of the adult pool. "Unless Generation Y reads at a much higher level, overall readership will fall below 50 percent by 2010."[4] This cohort analysis offers compelling evidence that newspaper executives need to work toward developing stronger newspaper habits and loyalties among young adults.

In addition to life cycle analysis, lifestyle analysis also provided some insights and strategic directions. For example, the *Boston Globe* conducted research using the Values and Lifestyles (VALS) typology developed by SRI International. The VALS typology found that adults with the most "upscale" demographic characteristics could be divided into two distinctive segments based on their values and lifestyles.[5] These segments were labeled the "societally conscious" and the "achievers." In Boston, a typical member of the "societally conscious" segment would be a city-oriented liberal arts professor at one of its many universities. A typical "achiever" would be a suburban-oriented engineer employed along the Route 128 technology corridor. Research demonstrated that the *Globe* had far stronger readership among the "societally conscious" than among the "achievers." In order to address this issue, *Globe* management pursued two initiatives. Business coverage was strengthened, particularly as it related to technology. And the *Globe* zoned its local coverage for the first time so that people living in different parts of the Boston market would receive local coverage aimed at their part of the market. A comparison of research done before and after the initiatives showed considerable improvement in *Globe* readership among "achievers."

Another way to segment the newspaper audience is to divide people into regular newspaper readers, occasional readers, and nonreaders. Regular newspaper readers tend to be older, while occasional readers and nonreaders tend to be younger. In large, metropolitan markets, regular readers tend to be male and socioeconomically "upscale" (people with higher incomes and educational attainments). In smaller, local markets, regular readers are often disproportionately female, and socioeconomic status is not particularly related to newspaper readership. In all cases, regular readers tend to be strongly rooted in their communities. In fact, community orientation tends to have a stronger relationship to newspaper readership than any demographic characteristic.

Another way to divide people based on their orientation to newspapers was developed by MORI Research and has been used extensively by the newspaper industry, spearheaded by research commissioned by the American Society of Newspaper Editors (ASNE). The results of the research were published in two reports issued during the 1990s, "Keys to Our Survival" and "Beyond Survival."[6] This typology uses discriminant analysis to classify adults as loyal newspaper readers, at-risk readers, potential readers, and poor prospects for regular newspaper readership. The analysis classifies each respondent as a newspaper reader or as a nonreader. Based on whether the classification is correct, the following groups are created:

Loyal readers: Readers correctly classified as readers
At-risk readers: Readers incorrectly classified as nonreaders
Potential readers: Nonreaders incorrectly classified as readers
Poor prospects: Nonreaders correctly classified as nonreaders

Loyal readers tend to fit the profile of regular newspaper readers, discussed above. They read newspapers thoroughly and receive many rewards from them. As might be expected, the newspaper habit of at-risk readers is much more tenuous. They tend not to be interested in "hard news" coverage, but something draws them to newspapers nevertheless. For example, male at-risk readers often are attracted by sports coverage. In the ASNE research, a wake-up call to editors was based on the finding that loyal readers tend to be old, while at-risk and potential readers tend to be young.

As the model was developed, many measurements were evaluated in terms of how well they "predict" newspaper readership. The one that consistently emerged as the best predictor consists of the following question: "How would you feel if you had to live without a newspaper for quite some time? Would you feel lost without a newspaper, would you miss it but could get along without it, or could you easily get along without a newspaper?" This question has been around for many years, and the trend line is startling. In the early 1960s, about half of adults in the United States said they would "feel lost" without a newspaper. In recent studies, that percentage has dropped to about one-sixth. Maintaining newspaper readership strength is obviously an uphill battle.

During the 1970s, when weekday circulation began to decline, Sunday circulation began to rise, going from 49 million in 1970 to 63 million in 1995. However, since 1995, Sunday newspaper readership has been declining as well. In order to explain this trend and offer ways to combat it, the NAA commissioned research by Clark, Martire & Bartolomeo, Inc. The research consisted of telephone interviews with a representative sample of 1,800 adults in six markets: Bremerton, WA; Pensacola, FL; Springfield, MA; Cincinnati, OH; Phoenix, AZ; and Philadelphia, PA. In each market, a minimum of 100 individuals who read the target newspaper less often than previously was included. The final sample was weighted to reflect the actual distribution of readership frequency.[7] Newspaper industry studies often are conducted in specific markets selected to represent a variety of market sizes and geographic locations. A methodological advantage to this type of sample is that the "newspaper" variable remains fairly constant. In this research, a respondent's local daily newspaper was one of six newspapers, not one of more than 1,000 newspapers. A practical advantage of this method for the NAA is that the participating newspapers usually will pick up a large portion of the cost of the research. "**Oversampling**" a key target audience—in this case, people reading the Sunday newspaper less often—also is employed frequently. Oversampling ensures that information is collected from enough respondents in the key target audience to be analyzed separately. As with much readership research, the study found no easy answers. It concludes: "The research makes abundantly clear that marginal Sunday readership is not the result of a single factor; rather, it is a mix of a variety of factors, including content issues, circulation issues, inadequate and ineffective promotion and competitive pressures."[8]

The decline in newspaper readership and loyalty is one of the key reasons why it has become increasingly important to analyze newspaper readership in the context of the media environment as a whole.

Often, this type of research builds on the long tradition of "uses and gratifications" research, which investigates how people use the various media and what kinds of psychological rewards they obtain from their usage. Often, survey respondents will be asked which media they turn to for various types of uses and gratifications. Television and, to a lesser extent, radio generally emerge as the main media used for entertainment and escape. Television and newspapers often share the franchise for obtaining national and international news. Magazines frequently show strength as a way to build one's knowledge and to explore very specific interests. Often, newspapers share the knowledge-building franchise as well. Newspapers generally capture the franchise for local news, although the local news franchise of television sometimes is as strong or even stronger than that of newspapers. Newspapers and magazines generally show comparable strength as ways to obtain useful information. Very often, the strongest franchise for newspapers is as a source of local advertising.

The Internet shows potential to capture virtually all of these franchises. Comparisons of a 1999 study by Stempel, Hargrove, and Bernt with the 1995 study by Stempel and Hargrove showed that Internet use increased fivefold, while use of newspapers and TV news declined. However, the study also showed that Internet users were more likely to read newspapers than nonusers of the Internet were. This may be because readers can go from the newspaper to the Internet for additional information on a story, or they can go from the Internet back to the newspaper. While TV viewers can go to the Internet for additional information, they really cannot go back from the Internet to TV news to find out about a specific story.[9]

The quotation at the beginning of this chapter condemns newspaper research because "it has not arrested the decline in readership." Given that so many of the causes of newspaper readership declines are beyond the control of newspapers, arresting the readership decline probably is not possible.

News Editorial Research

News sells newspapers. Any editor will tell you that, and research bears it out. Very broadly, the three main **"uses and gratifications"** that readers obtain from newspapers are keeping up with the news, obtaining useful information, and enjoying the activity of reading a newspaper. Of these, keeping up with the news has continually emerged as the main motivation. A quarter century ago, when research to obtain reader feedback on newspapers' news/editorial content was in its infancy, editors often expressed concerns that if they paid too much attention to what readers want, the result would be a "dumbed-down" newspaper. Some editors still express these concerns. Most editors, however, have gained a strong respect for the intelligence of their readers and an appreciation for research that can help them do a better job of serving readers.

Of the two other main "uses and gratifications" besides keeping up with the news, obtaining useful information has been increasing in importance, and reading a newspaper for enjoyment has been declining.

The "news sells newspapers" maxim may be a constant, but newspapers nevertheless need to change with changing times and changing media environments. The Internet offers the user the ability to pick out the story he or she would like to see, just as the newspaper does. Broadcast media cannot do this. Indeed, the ways newspapers will need to change to adapt to a new media environment that includes the Internet have only begun to be investigated. Along with the changing media environment, people's information interests—their definition of news—and their preferred formats for obtaining this information change as well. Research can help editors keep abreast of and take advantage of these changes.

This section discusses the following types of research to help develop and monitor news/editorial initiatives:

Analysis of information interests and coverage ratings
Research to help organize the newspaper
Assessment of existing sections
Evaluation of proposed new sections and features
Item readership
Analysis of the role of newspapers on different days of the week
Design and format research
Research associated with "public journalism" initiatives

Information Interests and Coverage Ratings

This type of analysis is done to help editors ascertain whether their news coverage priorities are in line with readers' interests. Survey respondents indicate their interest in a list of news topics and evaluate the newspaper's coverage of those topics. Often, this information is collected in the self-administered portion of a telephone-mail survey. Typically, the telephone portion of the survey will be limited to measurements that require a higher response rate, such as readership and demographic measurements. Then, respondents will be sent a questionnaire to fill out and mail back.

Although this results in a lower overall response rate and, therefore, a less representative sample, this design does have many advantages. Asking respondents in a telephone interview to express their interest in, say, twenty-five news topics and then evaluate the newspaper's coverage of those topics is extremely tedious. The same information can be obtained very efficiently in a self-administered questionnaire.

Once the information is obtained, the following four groups of topics can be identified:

- *Strong interest and strong coverage ratings:* The recommendation to editors is, "Keep up the good work."
- *Strong interest and weak coverage ratings:* The recommendation is to place a higher priority on coverage of these topics.
- *Weak interest and strong coverage ratings:* The general recommendation is to take resources from this type of coverage and move them to the higher priority area. However, topics that fall into this group sometimes have a small but very loyal audience. Editors know, for example, how much the phones will ring if they forget to include the crossword puzzle.
- *Weak interest and weak coverage ratings:* It's not so important to improve coverage of these topics.

Often this type of analysis is done among key target audiences—such as occasional or at-risk readers—as well as among readers as a whole. When this is done, topics that fall into the fourth category often become more important because the target audience is much more interested in those topics than other readers are.

Another type of analysis is to look at the correlation between coverage evaluations of specific topics and a measurement of overall satisfaction with the newspaper. If coverage of a given topic is strongly related to overall satisfaction with the newspaper, that topic can be said to "drive" readership, and strong coverage of that topic assumes additional importance.

Research to Help Organize the Newspaper

Not too many years ago, editors were happy to organize their newspapers such that readers would be forced to page through the entire paper in order to find what they wanted. Advertising directors were happy with this lack of coherent organization as well; if readers paged through the whole paper, they were likely to notice more advertisements. However, as overall newspaper readership declined and as research demonstrated that newspapers' poor organization alienated many readers, making newspapers more efficient for their readers became a higher priority.

Including a battery of information interests in a survey can provide guidelines for editors in organizing the content of their newspapers. Factor analysis can reveal which information interests group together, meaning that people interested in one of the topics in a group tend to be interested in others as well. Some of these topic interest groups are obvious. For example, all spectator sports topics tend to group together. However, others are less obvious. For example, should information on personal finance go in the business section or the feature section?

Assessment of Newspaper Sections

Many newspaper sections are targeted toward specific audiences. Research can reveal whether these sections are hitting or missing their targets. The main news section reaches a general audience, sometimes somewhat skewed toward men. The local news section also reaches a general audience, sometimes skewed toward women. Men overwhelmingly read the sports section. Attempts to attract more women to the sports section by increasing coverage of women's sports have largely been unsuccessful. The audience of the business section is predominantly male and socioeconomically "upscale." Again, attempts to broaden the business section audience by covering more "workplace" issues and more businesses owned or dominated by women have not met with great success. The audience of the feature section tends to be mainly women.

The one section that has the most difficulty reaching its target audience is the entertainment section. When editors are asked about the audience they want for the entertainment section, they always say it's young people. However, more often than not, the demographic segment most likely to read the entertainment section is older women.

Another problematic section is the editorial and opinion pages. The audience for this part of the paper is extremely geriatric. Efforts to attract a younger audience to the editorial and opinion pages have not been successful.

Evaluation of Proposed New Sections and Features. In recent years, the once moribund women's section has taken on new life. During the height of the women's movement in the 1960s and 1970s, women newsroom journalists successfully killed the traditional women's section in most newspapers, a section that often emphasized gossip and celebrity news. More recently, editors have pursued the idea of a section or sections specifically aimed at women. One reason for this is the fact, documented by readership studies, that women—especially young women—have very weak newspaper readership. Another reason is the success of many magazines aimed at women that focus on such topics as home, food, fashion, health and fitness, relationships, parenting, balancing career and family—and, yes, gossip and celebrity news.

Focus group discussions are a very good way to evaluate prototypes for new sections, such as the new women's sections. The women's section investigation is one in which survey research and focus group research likely would reach opposite conclusions—and the focus group research would be more accurate. Surveys are not very good vehicles for prompting people to imagine something new.

Focus groups generally are made up of about ten participants and a moderator. The participants are recruited to fit certain specifications. Women, obviously, would be recruited to evaluate a proposed newspaper section for women. Participants also may be recruited to ensure a variety of ages, educational levels, and newspaper reading patterns (regular and occasional readers, for example). The moderator's job is to lead the discussion but to remain steadfastly neutral.

It's not unusual for participants' opinions to evolve as a focus group discussion progresses. When this happens during a discussion of a proposed new product, it often reflects the evolution that likely will take place in the marketplace once the product is introduced.

In discussions about a proposed new women's section, the typical evolution has been as follows: First, the women are distrustful. They suspect that the section might be patronizing and that it might create a women's "ghetto" in the newspaper, treating women like second-class citizens. Interestingly, women almost always think of newspapers as a male product. Then, after looking over the prototype for the section and thinking about it, the women become much more positive. They agree that women do have distinctive information interests. They also agree that when coverage of topics that interest them are grouped together, it's easier to find what they want to read.

What has happened as a result of this research on "new" women's sections? Initially, several general-interest women's sections were introduced. These tended not to be particularly successful because they were too broad. However, sections dealing with more specific topics of interest to women, such as home and garden sections, health and wellness sections, and fashion sections, have been much more successful.

In addition to doing research to test completely new sections, newspapers also do research to evaluate major changes to existing sections. Editors have learned that making major changes to sections without reader input and preparation can be hazardous. Several years ago, when the *Boston Globe* did a major overhaul of its weekly TV guide without doing any prior research, nearly 50,000 readers called to complain. Focus groups can be helpful in evaluating changes to existing sections. Sometimes, survey research also is appropriate if it's important to obtain a precise measurement of the "upside potential" and "downside risk" of changing a section. The key variable often is a question asking respondents to divide ten points between the existing section and the proposed new section to indicate which one they prefer and the strength of their preference. This method was used to evaluate prototype sections targeted toward at-risk readers and potential readers in research conducted for the American Society of Newspaper Editors.

Item Readership

Occasionally, newspapers measure the readership of every item in the newspaper. This was the method used more than a half century ago in the *Continuing Studies of Newspaper Readership* sponsored by the Advertising Research Foundation.[10] In this type of research, readers are asked to page through the entire newspaper and to recall which items they read. This type of comprehensive item readership research is not done very frequently. One reason is that it's quite expensive.

Recently, however, there has been renewed interest in measuring the readership of specific newspaper advertisements. In the early 1990s, MORI Research conducted this type of study for the Newspaper Marketing Bureau of Canada, and in the late 1990s, the Starch organization measured readership of individual advertisements in a study sponsored by the Newspaper Association of America.[11]

The only way to draw general conclusions from the results of item readership studies is to conduct content analysis of the individual items that have been measured. In content analysis, each item measured in the item readership study is classified according to various characteristics, such as size, placement in the newspaper, and presence or absence of color.

In both the Canadian and U.S. studies, the variables most strongly associated with the readership of an individual ad were the size of the ad and the presence (versus absence) of color. Other variables that often are thought to be related to readership were not, including the ad's placement on the page and whether the ad appeared on the left-hand or right-hand page.

Although newspapers don't often measure readership of every item in the paper, editors often seek feedback on the readership and popularity of key columns and standing features. This type of measurement works well in the self-administered portion of a tele-phone-mail survey because the logo of the item in question can be displayed in order to increase recognition. In addition to measuring the readership of columns and standing features, it can be instructive to measure their image as well, along such dimensions as "entertaining" or "controversial." Demographic analysis, of course, can ascertain whether the columns and standing features are reaching their target audiences.

The Role of Newspapers on Different Days

Much of the decline in newspaper readership is attributable to a decline in readership frequency. The kinds of people—or, in some cases, the same people—who used to read a newspaper every day now may read one two or three times a week. Because of this trend, much recent newspaper research has investigated ways to increase readership frequency.

One way to accomplish this is to give each day's newspaper a distinctive identity. For example, the Friday newspaper often concentrates on weekend entertainment, the Saturday newspaper often features home and garden topics and the Monday newspaper frequently contains a weekend sports wrap-up. Research to develop these day-specific features often asks respondents to select which days they expect to find certain kinds of coverage and which days they would like to see such coverage. When this type of research was conducted for the *Arizona Republic* in Phoenix, it was revealed that although Friday was a very strong day for entertainment coverage, Thursday showed considerable potential for entertainment coverage as well, particularly among young people. For young adults, the weekend entertainment routine often begins on Thursday evening. As a result of the research, the *Arizona Republic* expanded its entertainment coverage. The Friday entertainment section was aimed at a general audience and contained considerable coverage of movies and weekend activities for families. The Thursday entertainment section was specifically targeted toward young adults, both in its graphic look and in its coverage priorities, which emphasized local clubs and concerts by popular entertainers. The Thursday section also was distributed free in locations, such as campuses, with concentrations of young adults. The Thursday section was very successful both as a reader draw and as an advertising vehicle.

Design and Format Research

If you have the impression that the newspaper you read has become narrower in the past few years, you're probably right. Escalating newsprint costs have led many newspapers to "web width" reductions. Research often has been conducted both to assess reader reactions to the narrower pages and to evaluate various layout options for the new page sizes. Much of this research consisted of focus group discussions. The overall reaction to the narrower pages generally has been positive. People have found the narrower pages to be much more manageable.

Another recent trend in design research has been to take a close look at the format and reader appeal of the front page. There's a lot of newspaper tradition associated with

Page One, and traditions can be hard to change. According to the tradition, for example, the most important story of the day belongs at the upper right-hand corner of Page One. That rule often has been followed even when the most important story is likely to have limited reader appeal. Another part of Page One tradition is that if the front page contains a feature story likely to appeal to readers, that story should be below the fold. Single-copy buyers glancing at the top half of the front page in a store or coinbox would, of course, not see that feature story.

Circulation directors, who want to increase single-copy sales, have long argued with these front-page traditions. Until recently, the research they could cite to support their arguments has been fairly limited. A study done several years ago for the *Philadelphia Inquirer*, for example, found that many other things influenced newspaper purchases more than the content and format of the front page did. These included habit, the weather, and the general news environment—including breaking news that people were aware of from other sources. In recent years, this has been changing. Fewer newspaper purchases are habit purchases and more are impulse purchases. When point-of-purchase interviews are conducted with people who have just bought a paper, an increasing proportion are saying that they decided to buy the paper after looking at the front page.

These trends have spurred many newspaper editors to revisit their notions about the front page. In a drastic departure from the traditional front page, the *Pittsburgh Post Gazette*, for example, introduced what it called a "poster" front page on its early Sunday edition aimed at single-copy buyers that many newspapers publish on Saturday. The "poster" front page looked more like a magazine cover than a newspaper front page, since it was generally dominated by one large piece of art.

Another type of nontraditional front page came about largely because many participants in focus group discussions on newspaper front pages said the front page should offer a "menu" of the main stories that could be found in the paper, similar to menus that appear on computer screens.

In order to investigate these alternatives, the *Arizona Republic* commissioned a study in the late 1990s to evaluate the front-page preferences of readers. Respondents compared a "typical" *Arizona Republic* front page with a prototype of a "poster" front page and a prototype of a "menu" front page. As might be expected, long-time, habitual, loyal readers strongly preferred the traditional front page. At the opposite extreme, the "poster" front page was too much of a departure for most respondents. However, occasional and at-risk readers did express considerable enthusiasm for the "menu" front page.

Another type of research on front pages is simply to keep track of which front pages occurred on days with the strongest single-copy sales. Magazines routinely analyze their covers this way. *USA Today* also keeps a running tally of front pages and sales figures. Few other newspapers do this type of ongoing front page tracking, however.

Still another type of design research has to do with how readers would like stories to be presented. Often, this type of research is conducted as focus group discussions. Two main findings of this type of research are that readers don't like long stories, and they don't like "jumps." That does not, however, mean that readers don't want detailed, in-depth coverage when the interest or importance of the story warrants it. The simple device of introducing a story on the front page with a self-contained summary and then referring readers to more coverage inside the paper can do a lot to alleviate readers' frustration about "jumps."

The Poynter Institute in St. Petersburg, Florida, has conducted extensive research on ways to make newspapers more visually appealing. Monica Moses, an associate in visual journalism at the institute, recently summarized some of this research as follows:

> Maximum comprehension and interest came when text was accompanied by both a photo and a graphic. . . . Graphics, photographs and headlines get far more attention from readers than text does. The reader takes in 80 percent of the artwork and 75 percent of the photographs in the paper. She sees 56 percent of the headlines. But she's aware of only 25 percent of the text, and she reads a fraction of that. About 13 percent of the stories in the paper are read in any depth—that is, at least half-read. And that's under the best of circumstances: These test subjects, frequent newspaper readers, were uninterrupted, supervised and given prototypes with well-written, compelling stories.

Moses goes on to criticize editors for paying too little attention to the visual elements of their newspapers:

> Text is literally the last thing people see in the newspaper. That's not to say it isn't important. Text is, in many respects, the meat of the paper. . . . Still, the industry is disproportionately text-driven. It's run by people whose experience and comfort are with text. Yet, the reader's experience is more holistic, more visual. There is a disconnect between how the industry views the paper and how readers do, a disconnect between journalists' values and readers'.[12]

Public Journalism

A major debate among journalists in recent years has to do with how much newspapers should practice "public journalism." Editors generally have embraced the types of research described so far in this section—research aimed at improving coverage balance and presentation. But should newspapers go beyond these uses of research by planning and selecting stories that promote good community citizenship? Those in favor of this approach offer both ideological and practical arguments. They say that, in addition to reporting the news, local newspapers have a responsibility to be good citizens of their communities and to promote good citizenship. They argue that this goal should permeate all of a newspaper's coverage, not just its editorial and opinion pages.[13] As a practical matter, they sometimes point out that community involvement is strongly related to newspaper readership. Those opposed to "public journalism" argue that the good citizenship goal, as laudable as it may be, conflicts with journalists' responsibility to report news objectively.

A recent article in the *American Journalism Review* suggests that sensitivity to community concerns has changed the whole culture of newsrooms. Its author, Carl Sessions Stepp, asserts the following:

> Over the past decade or so, the culture of newsrooms has fundamentally changed . . . these are not your old city editor's newsrooms. In that bygone era, newsrooms and news people were autocratic, aloof and aggressive. They published first and asked

questions later. They brazenly built fences between themselves and their sources and audiences. They guarded an independence bordering on isolation . . .

No more.

A new newsroom culture is settling in. The driving force, more powerful than anything else, seems simple: Newspapers fear for their survival. But the so-called reform efforts matter, too. Day after day in my visits to newsrooms, I saw the footprints of public journalism.

One of several examples of this trend that Stepp cites is the *Journal Star* of Lincoln, Nebraska. He says its editor, David Stoeffler, "turns out to be a big believer in public journalism and in using market data to help improve the newspaper."

The paper has hosted town hall meetings, sent reporters knocking on doors canvassing the public's ideas for issues to cover, sponsored a yearlong literacy project, and teamed with state public television for a series on Hispanics in Nebraska. During last year's city election, Stoeffler presided over meetings in city council districts in which citizens were asked about their priorities, candidates were quizzed on those issues, and the paper focused its ongoing coverage on those areas.

Stoeffler wants "people thinking differently about the newspaper's role in the community." In particular, he is aiming to be "more solution-oriented."

Newspapers often use research as part of "public journalism" efforts. Going beyond the candidate forums describe in the Stepp article, systematic surveys are sometimes done in advance of elections to identify issues that people feel are the most important. Then, coverage of election campaigns focuses on those issues. Stepp points out that "when he commissioned a readership study, Stoeffler turned the results over to reporter Joe Duggan, who wrote a 'story' about it for the staff, headlined, 'Who wants what and why we care.'"[14]

Circulation Research

While debates such as the one over "public journalism" rage in newsrooms, circulation directors stay focused on the goal they've always had: to sell newspapers. Nevertheless, the world of circulation directors is changing as well.

For example, a traditional preoccupation of circulation directors has been to find ways to "convert" single-copy buyers to subscribers. Research has shown, however, that very few single-copy buyers are interested in being converted. As Albert E. Gollin described it in his 1996 speech referred to earlier in this chapter, "Recent studies of single-copy buyers reveal two distinct segments: those who buy one regularly, finding it as convenient as home delivery and with fewer perceived drawbacks, and another segment who buy a newspaper less often, drawn to the newspaper by content appeals that are strong on certain days. Neither seems particularly promising candidates for conversion."[15]

More recent research on single-copy buyers has concentrated on ways to entice them to purchase the paper more often (such as the front page and day-identity research discussed above) and on ways to make buying single copies more convenient. At this writing, the Newspaper Association of America is conducting research on single-copy buyers. Part of this research deals with finding ways to display newspapers more prominently in grocery stores. Respondents also are being asked how much they tend to spend on other merchandise when they go to a grocery store to purchase a newspaper. The purpose of these questions is to demonstrate to grocers that newspapers draw good customers to their stores in hopes of achieving better display for newspapers within the stores.

So-called "stop" studies are another common type of circulation research. In these studies, people who recently have canceled their newspaper subscriptions are sampled. The questions deal with why they stopped their subscriptions and what might be done to entice them to subscribe again. In these studies, the top-of-mind response usually is, "I didn't have time to read the paper." When the subscription cancellation motives are investigated in more depth, the reasons generally can be traced either to delivery service or the content of the newspaper—or both. Occasionally cost is an issue.

Recent research has demonstrated that it's even more important than previously believed for circulation directors to place a high priority on delivery service. The recent findings have demonstrated that subscribers who are unhappy about their delivery service are more likely than those who are satisfied with their delivery service to be critical of the newspaper's editorial content. Unhappiness with delivery service appears to spill over to unhappiness with other aspects of the newspaper.

In recent years, circulation directors have been paying more attention to the highly valuable databases that they control. Most newspapers have up-to-date databases on all of the households in their markets. Circulation departments usually need to have information on nonsubscriber households as well as subscriber households because many newspapers produce and deliver shoppers to nonsubscribers so that they can offer advertisers complete market coverage.

These databases increasingly are being used as secondary research tools. Often, newspapers augment their household databases with census-based geo-demographic databases provided by suppliers such as CACI or Claritas. These databases supply information about the demographic characteristics of people living in different zipcodes and census tracts. One way to use this information is to identify geographic areas where more people should be subscribing than actually are subscribing.

Research to Support Advertising Sales

Newspapers have two markets. They sell the newspaper to readers and potential readers. And, in turn, they sell access to those readers to their advertisers. Most newspapers in the United States receive a far higher proportion of their revenues from advertisers than from subscriptions and single-copy sales. Partly because of this, and partly because of editors' resistance until fairly recently to market research, research to support advertising sales has the longest history of any type of newspaper research, and it tends to receive a bigger budget than news/editorial or circulation research.

Gollin, in his 1996 speech referred to earlier in this chapter, described research to support advertising sales as follows:

This is still the major thrust, justifying the investments made in both syndicated research and custom studies. Research data are used in several ways that highlight the newspaper's value as an advertising medium, alone or compared with local media competitors.

- Circulation penetration or average issue readership in the market, to demonstrate mass market coverage, or high levels of targeted coverage for advertisers with a more segmented customer base. ["We cover your potential customers."]
- Readership reach among specific store shoppers or buyers of advertisers' products. ["Your customers are our readers."]
- Readership and use of newspaper advertising in making shopping or buying decisions, in general or by specific customer categories (e.g., car buyers, food shoppers). ["Newspapers move your merchandise."] . . .
- Sales response to specific ads. This category of "bottom-line" effectiveness research is rare, for understandable reasons. It is costly, prolonged in duration, complex to design and manage, and risky. . . . But the demand for greater "accountability" being insistently raised by advertisers is likely to keep up the pressure on advertising researchers to do more in this vein . . .
- Growing emphasis is being placed on research with newspaper advertisers themselves, in the tradition of "customer satisfaction" studies whose goal— as with circulation studies of this type—is customer retention."[16]

Much of the research done to support newspaper advertising sales is very standardized. Because advertisers with locations in many markets want to be able to compare the results for different markets, newspaper researchers and advertising directors have developed standard questions to use in these studies. For example, when people are asked whether they have shopped at various department and discount stores, the question is generally asked on a "past 30 days" basis. Grocery stores are asked about on a "past 7 days" basis. Since readership and demographic questions also are standardized, advertisers can be assured of "apples to apples" comparisons.

Newspaper Management Research

People in senior management at newspapers have much more challenging jobs than was the case twenty-five or thirty years ago. People used to joke that the main thing that newspapers printed was money. Newspapers continue to be quite profitable, but their profit margins are not as spectacular as they once were. At the same time, competition for both readers and advertising dollars has become much more intense. And it's a dog-eat-dog world. Newspaper acquisitions and consolidations continue at a fever pace. Recently, much of this activity has consisted of newspaper chains buying other newspaper chains, or of chains trading newspapers with one another in order to achieve geographic efficiencies (such as common printing facilities). In the United States, the independent, family-owned newspaper has virtually become a thing of the past.

Research can help newspaper managers address many of these challenges. This section discusses the following types of research often done for senior management at newspapers:

Monitoring the external environment
Developing norms for newspapers within a group
Strengthening a newspaper's competitive position
Acquisitions
Targeting new geographic areas
New products, including Internet products
Research to build the newspaper's brand
Internal management research

Monitoring the External Environment

Newspaper executives need to maintain surveillance over their markets in order to identify both threats and opportunities to their newspapers' market position.[5] Research is one tool they can use. The research used to monitor the external environment is largely the same as that described so far in this chapter. It can address such issues as: What are the newspaper's readership trends and how can declining readership be addressed? How is the newspaper faring compared to its competition? How can we improve the news/editorial content of the newspaper to reach a wider audience and make it more relevant to readers? How can we improve circulation service? What is our advertising market share and how can we increase advertising? How can we improve service to our advertisers?

Some newspapers also use research to monitor their external environment by building on the concepts summarized in a recent book, *Managing Customer Value*.[17] The book is an outgrowth of the "continuous improvement" school of management theory. It says that in order to grow and to compete effectively, businesses need to know which aspects of their products consumers value the most. Then they need to make sure that their products address those values in ways that are superior to the competition. Research can be employed both to identify these core values and to assess the newspaper's performance against those values. Focus group discussions can help identify the values and formulate the way they should be phrased in quantitative research. In subsequent quantitative research, respondents can be asked how important each of the value statements is in their decision to read the newspaper, and they can also be asked to rate the newspaper's performance on each of the value dimensions. Then "gap analysis," similar to that used to compare information interests and coverage ratings, can be employed to ascertain how well the newspaper is performing against the aspects of the newspaper that are the most important to its audience.

Developing Norms for Newspapers within a Group

Groups of newspapers often commission similar studies in all of their markets. These are used as a kind of report card for the various newspapers within the group. The results can show, for example, whether some of the newspapers need to work toward improving their customer service. The research also can be used to highlight examples of "best practices."

Strengthening a Newspaper's Competitive Position

Although head-to-head competition among newspapers continues to exist in only a few U.S markets, competition on the fringe of markets is very common. For example, The *Los Angeles Times* competes with several very strong suburban daily newspapers. Similar conditions exist in many other metropolitan areas.

When this is the case, all of the types of research that have been described so far in this chapter often are applied both to the newspaper commissioning the research and to its main competitor. For example, respondents are asked to give topic coverage ratings and circulation service ratings for both newspapers. When this much information is desired, the research often needs to be designed to minimize respondent fatigue. One way to cut down on respondent fatigue when a lot of information needs to be collected is to divide the sample so that each respondent answers only some of the questions. For example, respondents might be asked to name their "main newspaper." Among respondents who designate a "main newspaper," the subsequent evaluation questions will be asked of that newspaper. Among respondents who don't name a "main newspaper," the questions will either be skipped or the newspapers will be rotated.

Acquisitions

As mentioned above, several newspaper groups continue to pursue aggressive acquisition strategies. Although a newspaper's selling price is based largely on its circulation size, companies that are considering purchasing a particular newspaper often will conduct research in that newspaper's market to identify aspects of the newspaper's strengths and weaknesses that would not be apparent from the circulation statistics.

Targeting New Geographic Areas

The dog-eat-dog environment applies not only to acquisitions. Newspapers often use research to monitor the strength of other nearby newspapers. If a nearby newspaper shows signs of vulnerability, the aggressor newspaper will attempt to take advantage of that vulnerability.

For example, executives at one Southern California newspaper learned from their ongoing market research that the market position of a nearby newspaper was becoming quite weak. The newspaper designated two new geographic zones in the competitive area and stepped up local coverage in those zones. It stepped up promotion efforts in the competitive area, including becoming the marketing partner of a major sports stadium. In addition, circulation solicitation efforts in the competitive area were substantially increased. As a result of all these efforts, the aggressor newspaper's readership in the competitive area increased to the point that some advertisers decided to buy space just in the aggressor newspaper and to drop the other newspaper, thereby increasing the weaker newspaper's vulnerability.

New Products, Including Internet Products

Newspapers continue to attempt to leverage their printing capabilities by developing new publications, such as shoppers and niche publications aimed at segments of their markets.

When potential new publications are evaluated, newspapers often will conduct research to determine the size of the market for the new publication, the likely demand for the new publication, and the strength of the competition.

However, the main new product initiatives of newspapers in recent years have been the development of Internet products. Virtually all newspapers have websites, and many aggressively pursue the goal of being the main Internet portal for their market areas.

Depth interviews often have been used to help develop and fine-tune newspaper websites. Like focus group discussions, depth interviews are a qualitative research tool. They can be a very useful way to gain insights, but they are not statistically projectable. Depth interviews to explore an Internet site often are set up the following way: Respondents are recruited to fit certain specifications, such as young people who are very interested in the news and who are very Internet-savvy. A computer terminal is installed in the interview room, and the same computer screen is duplicated in the viewing room. The interviewer prompts the respondent to search for a certain kind of news or to access and explore the newspaper's website. In addition to hearing the respondent's comments about the website, those viewing the depth interview can see what the respondent actually does. The combination of these two types of feedback can be very instructive.

Beyond developing their own websites, newspapers, like other industries, have begun to explore using the Internet as a research tool. For example, they routinely gauge the popularity of various parts of their websites by counting the number of "hits." It's very tempting, but also hazardous, to conduct surveys over the Internet. The main danger in conducting surveys over the Internet is the same one that has plagued researchers ever since the *Literary Digest* wrongly predicted a presidential election in the 1930s: self-selected samples. Just because a lot of people respond to a survey doesn't mean that they are representative of the population the researcher wants to be surveyed. This drawback can be somewhat overcome by recruiting panels of respondents with known demographic characteristics that approximate the demographic characteristics of the target audience. It's important to "refresh" the panel periodically by dropping long-time respondents and adding new respondents. Respondents who are part of a panel gradually lose their representativeness. They know their opinions count, so they work toward becoming experts, rather than typical users. When careful steps are taken to at least approximate a representative sample, Internet research has many advantages, the main ones being that it's quick and that it's far cheaper than other types of survey research. As methodological problems continue to be addressed, online research is sure to assume a much greater role in newspaper research.

Research to Build the Brand

Particularly compared to consumer products companies, most newspapers have been very slow to embrace brand-building efforts. The *Wall Street Journal*, of course, has a distinctive brand identity, but how many other newspapers do?

To their dismay, many newspapers have discovered that they have a brand identity regardless of whether they have been working to achieve one. Earl J. Wilkinson describes this phenomenon in his introduction to a book of case studies on newspaper brand-building efforts: *Essence and Soul: The Story of Newspaper Brands:*

A brand ultimately is the range of instinctive, emotional attributes assigned to a name or symbol by the marketplace. . . .

In political terms, we newspapers have allowed the market to define us. When I hear of the inherent brand value of newspapers, my mind's eye wanders to the panel of young people at a newspaper conference that assigned words to describe newspapers: old, establishment, boring, uncool. So, it cuts both ways: If newspapers have inherent brand value, the values assigned by the market may be strong—but negative.

Perhaps a better way of describing the newspaper brand is not to say it is "under-valued," but "under-flexed" and "under-utilized." Imagine the centrifugal forces of two objects, one pushing and the other not pushing back. The gap between how the newspaper company wants its brand viewed and how the market views the brand is fairly broad in most markets that have undergone serious examination.[18]

Newspapers generally begin their brand-building efforts by conducting research to find out what constitutes their existing brand identity. The research often is both qualitative and quantitative, and it focuses on the newspaper's perceived image. Cyndi Nash of the *Seattle Times* described some brand-identification focus group discussions conducted by that newspaper as follows:

These were not structured as traditional focus groups. They were smaller, more like six people than ten. And we asked questions in a way we hadn't before. Our moderator . . . used a technique called "brand benefit laddering" to get at some deeper motivations. In essence, this consists of asking consumers what they get out of the newspaper when they read it, how that makes them feel, and then probing to deeper levels about how having that feeling makes them feel. And again, and again. So that by the end of the session, we know whether reading the newspaper is about self-esteem, power, security, pleasure, and others.[19]

The *Kansas City Star*, in a quantitative study, took another unusual approach toward identifying and building its brand. Kim Walden, The *Star*'s director of market research, described this approach:

In the spring of 1999, the *Star* began a month-long inundation study. The study was comprised of women (women tend to be the decision maker to stop and start the newspaper as well as being an attractive demographic for advertisers) ages 25 to 49, who were information-savvy and used many sources to find information—the *Star* was just not their preferred source. The participants were not regular readers of the *Star* but were, in essence, forced to become heavy users for a month. . . . The women also kept journals about their experience. . . . After a month-long study, many of the women's perceived barriers turned out to be real. . . . The *Star* was difficult to scan and identify areas of interest; too lengthy on information they felt was redundant (had heard the news previously through another media channel); too short on issues of relevance to them, too much redundant information; it was irritating and difficult to track articles; and felt guilty for taking so much time to read the *Star* on a daily basis. . . .

However, there was a positive image shift for a majority of these women. The current *Star* is much more aligned with the priorities and values than these women assumed. . . . The Star must teach, model, and demonstrate the most efficient, easiest, and satisfying way to enjoy the newspaper. It is imperative that the *Star* show readers how the newspaper integrates into their daily lives and why it is worth their time to read.[20]

A more typical way to use research to help build a newspaper brand is to start with a battery of image measurements in a quantitative survey. Often these take the form of semantic differential measurements. Respondents are given pairs of opposites and are asked to choose on a scale whether the newspaper is more like one or the other of each pair. Some examples: dull versus interesting; cares about the community versus doesn't care about the community, or written for people like me vs. not written for people like me. Once these measurements are obtained, factor analysis can be used to see which ones group together statistically. The factor "loadings" indicate which individual images contribute the most toward defining each of these image groups. Once the groups are identified, regression analysis can identify which group or groups contribute the most to overall reader satisfaction. The group or groups that are the best predictors of overall satisfaction can be used as the basis for the newspaper's branding strategy.

For example, executives at the *Houston Chronicle* determined that relevance was the core concept of their branding strategy toward readers and that innovation was the essence of the branding strategy toward advertisers. The branding slogan targeted toward readers became "Touch the News That Touches You." Advertisers were told, "We're reinventing the newspaper." According to the *Chronicle*'s Joycelyn Marek, these two slogans can serve as umbrella themes for all of the *Houston Chronicle*'s various products:

At the *Houston Chronicle*, we have our core newspaper product, but we also have a whole array of associated products and services. We have electronic products, a printing division, and a direct marketing department. All of these things I have mentioned are, in their own right, separate products that may be marketed in a variety of ways. . . . But they are one brand. The challenge is to develop a branding theme that works for all the components. . . .[21]

Internal Management Research. Top newspaper executives not only need to deal with an increasingly challenging external environment. The internal challenges are escalating as well. Keeping newspaper employees happy and productive may not be as easy as it once was. Declining newspaper readership and advertising market share obviously can have a negative effect on the morale of newspaper employees. The technological changes that have taken place in all newspaper departments also have made some jobs more tedious and stressful. For example, the job of a copy editor or layout editor once involved considerable face-to-face interaction with other newsroom employees. Now, the interaction is mainly with a computer screen.

David H. Weaver and G. Cleveland Wilhoit have conducted a series of studies assessing job satisfaction among newsroom journalists. Many of the trends have been negative. For example, the proportion of journalists who said they were "very satisfied" with their jobs declined from 49 percent in 1971 to 40 percent in 1982–1983 and then to 27.3 percent in 1992 (p. 100). In 1982–1983, 10.4 percent of journalists said they expected to work outside the news media five years hence; that figure rose to 21.3 percent in 1992 (p. 112).[22] Conducting job satisfaction studies at individual newspapers can help newspaper managers identify the causes of these problems so that they can address them effectively. Often, the same type of "gap analysis" that has been described previously is employed in job satisfaction studies. Employees are asked how important each of several aspects of their job is to them personally. Then they are asked to rate the newspaper's performance on each of these aspects. The job aspects managers need to address the most are those where the largest gap is identified between low performance and high importance.

Conclusions

Newspapers are playing on a ballpark whose lines have been redrawn. Changes in the media environment in which newspapers operate have accelerated. Demographic trends that indicate declines in newspaper readership will accelerate as well. The *American Journalism Review* article cited at the beginning of this chapter said "research's single most important failing" is that "it has not arrested the decline in newspaper readership." On the contrary, research initiatives like the ones described in this chapter have helped keep the decline from being as steep as it might otherwise have been.

Newspapers have continually sharpened their research tools as the pace of change in both their internal and external environments has accelerated. The momentum of both change and of the growth of newspaper research is likely to continue. As newspapers move from being a mass medium to a niche medium—which is likely to happen within the next ten years—research will help newspaper managers adjust to and take advantage of their new situation. As more and more newspapers become parts of large, professionally managed businesses, management demand for research intelligence is bound to increase. And as more of the "autocratic and aloof" newsroom journalists retire, newsrooms likely will increasingly welcome the audience feedback that research can provide.

Endnotes

1. Charles Layton, "What Do Readers Really Want?" *American Journalism Review*, March 1999, 49.

2. Albert E. Gollin, "The State of Local Market Newspaper Research." Speech delivered to a print media research workshop at the Grand Hyatt Hotel, New York, on January 18, 1996. (New York: Advertising Research Foundation,1996), 2–3. Also see Leo Bogart, *Preserving the Press: How Daily Newspapers Mobilized to Keep Their Readers* (New York: Columbia University Press, 1991).

3. John T. Robinson, "Daily News Habits of the American Public," *ANPA News Research Report No. 15*, Sept. 22, 1978; Guido H. Stempel III and Thomas Hargrove, "Mass Media Audiences in a Changing Media Environment," *Journalism & Mass Communication Quarterly* 73(1996): 549–558

4. Beverly Kees, "Shifting Demographics Mandate Change," *The American Editor*, May–June 2000, 16, 19.

5. See Arnold Mitchell, *The Nine American Lifestyles: Who We Are and Where We're Going* (New York: Macmillan, 1983).

6. http://www.asne.org.

7. Newspaper Association of America and Clark, Martire & Bartolomeo, Inc., "Report: NAA Sunday Readership Study" (Vienna, VA: Newspaper Association of America, 1999), 6.

8. Ibid., 17.

9. Guido H. Stempel III, Thomas Hargrove, and Joseph P. Bernt, "Relation of Growth of Use of the Internet to Changes in Media Use from 1995 to 1999," *Journalism & Mass Communication Quarterly* 77 (2000): 71–79.

10. See *138 Study Summary* (New York: Advertising Research Foundation, 1950).

11. http://www.roper.com/starch/; http://www.naa.org.

12. Monica Moses, "Consumer Mentality," *The American Editor*, April 2000, 7.

13. See, for example, Richard C. Harwood, *Tapping Civic Life: How to Report First, and Best, What's Happening in Your Community* (Washington, DC: Pew Center for Civic Journalism, 1996).

14. Carl Sessions Stepp, "Reader Friendly," *American Journalism Review*, July/August, 2000, 23, 24, 30, 31.

15. Gollin, *op. cit.*, 5.

16. Gollin, *op. cit.*, 4–5.

17. Bradley T. Gale with Robert Chapman Wood, *Managing Customer Value: Creating Quality and Service That Customers Can See* (New York: Free Press, 1994).

18. Earl J. Wilkinson, ed., *Essence and Soul: The Story of Newspaper Brands* (Danville, IL: Faulstich, 2000), 7.

19. *Ibid.*, 14.

20. *Ibid.*, 36–37.

21. *Ibid.*, 27–29.

22. David H. Weaver and G. Cleveland Wilhoit, *The American Journalist in the 1990s* (Mahwah, NJ: Erlbaum, 1996), 100, 112.

4

Applied Public Relations Research

Hugh M. Culbertson

Research should be the beginning and end all—the alpha and omega—of public relations. That's implied by one of the field's most widely quoted definitions, the *RACE* formula published by John Marston in 1963.[1] Marston and others of his era suggested that, ideally, public relations involves at least four stages:

> **R**esearch on the client organization—and on audience beliefs, needs, predispositions, and behaviors—to aid planning and implementation of programs.
>
> **A**ction in the form of policies and programs by the client to serve the public interest.
>
> **C**ommunication to enhance audience understanding and use of—as well as support for—these programs.
>
> **E**valuation of messages produced and resulting audience changes, as well as of audience behaviors. Research during a program can suggest needed midcourse corrections. Also, study afterward can show whether efforts have been successful.

Research constitutes the first and last stages in this model. One would expect, therefore, that public relations practitioners would be researchers first and foremost! However, this isn't necessarily so.

We first will discuss some evidence about the nature of applied public relations research. We will then examine methods used and needed in three areas—front-end research on public relations contexts, evaluation during and after a program, and monitoring of media coverage.

Early Days—Little Research

Grunig and Hunt[2] and Robinson,[3] among others, have concluded that, at least until recently, practitioners have focused largely on stage 3 in the RACE formula—communication. Research has often been intuitive, "seat of the pants" in Robinson's[4] terms.

In the 1960s, Robinson searched extensively for instances of systematic applied public relations research. He found only seven studies that clearly indicated problems addressed in research, methodology and use of results.[5] Surprisingly, all seven studies were surveys, just one weapon in the scholarly arsenal. No experiments, quasi-experiments, in-depth interviews of a few informants, focus groups, or systematic content analyses were reported. Also, when Robinson summarized the results in a book, he gave mostly descriptive tables. Even basic cross-tabulations were seldom used to *identify audience segments* or *isolate factors that might affect* people's attitudes, knowledge, opinions, and behavior. These are oft-noted goals of data analysis.

Trends over time were indicated in some instances,[6] as were comparisons between beliefs about a client organization and those about competitors.[7] While no doubt interesting to clients, such data have only limited value in program planning and execution.

Recent Times—Some Positives

In recent years, at least two developments have increased the need for research. One has been growing acceptance of two ideas about effective public relations. First, it requires systematic, careful *listening* to important publics as well as speaking to them. And second, good public relations occurs primarily where a practitioner truly is *part of the management team* that sets organizational direction and policy. A large-scale study sponsored by the International Association of Business Communicators supports the claim that public relations is most effective when these two conditions are met.[8] And it seems obvious that:

- Research is central to the listening process.
- Unless communications people actually participate in designing research—and they actively interpret results in ways that suggest application—they may become marginal on management teams.

Second, the growing importance of research seems apparent in light of two related developments in organizational management:

1. *Environmental scanning:* Systematic study of what's going on in the world and implications thereof via careful media analysis and consultation with experts in such fields as politics, the environment, labor relations, finance, and so on.[9]
2. *Issues management:* Identifying issues relevant to client organizations before they really become issues. Movements and causes go through a complex growth process, spurred by special interest groups, specialized media, and policy makers, before they gain widespread public or media attention.[10] Organizations fare best when they take action early to solve or prevent problems. Once a crisis occurs, open, candid communication can only help damage control. The old saying, "An ounce of prevention is worth a pound of cure," has become gospel in crisis management.[11]

Environmental scanning and issues management have gained much attention. The latter has spawned a monthly journal for corporate executives.[12] These are not exact sciences. Examples will be discussed later.

Growth in these areas leads one to ask whether applied public relations research has gained in sophistication since Robinson's 1963 study. Recent award-winning PR programs suggest there's been some growth, but not a whole lot. Each year, the Public Relations Society of America gives Bronze Anvil Awards to organizations that have been judged as most effective in thirty categories. Emphasis is on tactical solutions. *Public Relations Tactics* reported on 1999 winners in its September issue of that year.[13] Write-ups provided comments on effectiveness. This author looked at types of evidence mentioned. Specifically, of the thirty winning cases:

- Eighteen (60%) described *message circulation and reach*—print circulation, estimated viewership or listenership, number of program participants or people attending an event, and so on. As noted below, such data indicate only opportunities for impact, not actual effects.
- Eight (27%) reported *evaluative comments about programs* by public relations colleagues, executives, news people, and other presumably knowledgeable individuals who did not sponsor or help produce the projects recognized.
- Six (20%) gave counts of *audience responses* to or consumption of a program or articles. Included were number of hits on a website, number of coupons mailed in, number of phone calls received following distribution of a message, and other actions.
- Only four entries (13%) reported readership and responses measured in what appeared to be *formal surveys*.
- Just one research section of a case study (3%) mentioned *focus-group* results.

Such counts say little about the quality and nature of evaluation research. Reports were brief and often incomplete. However, taken as a whole, evidence of impact seemed quite soft. Contestants focused heavily on opportunities for impact and on assessment by outsiders—not on solid evidence of effects.

In a different realm, perusal of entries in the PRSA Silver Anvil Award competition revealed much careful front-end assessment of issues involved and their social, political, and economic contexts. This widely heralded competition focuses on strategic thinking and planning as well as on tactical execution.

In an attempt to gauge research underlying programs viewed in the industry as strong on strategic planning, the author analyzed "research" and "evaluation" sections of all six successful 1999 Silver Anvil entries presented, at least in part, by Ketchum Public Relations.[14] That firm has long been regarded as a leader in applied research. All six cases emphasized literature reviews when describing their *front-end research*. Further, four Ketchum cases reported focus-group results. And two stressed published consumer surveys which did not appear to be paid for by Ketchum or its clients. Turning to evaluation—*rear-end research*—all six cases indicated clip counts and reach (1,000 placements of varied stores in the printed press in one case, 804 million impressions in another, and so on). Also, in their evaluation sections, all six cases reported counts of audience "payoff behaviors," apparently based on little or no formal research beyond routine general observation and record keeping. Included here were attendance at meetings, published letters to newspaper editors, increased stock prices, and loss of few customers during a strike. Two of the cases reported general-population surveys apparently sponsored by Ketchum's clients.

Two others discussed surveys done, at least with Ketchum's advice and help, of conference attendees, client employees, and other specialized publics.

In sum, most research dollars went into evaluative research apparently designed to gauge success or failure. Studies cited in front-end planning were largely borrowed from the literature and from other sources.

Front-End Research on Social, Political, and Economic Contexts

In counseling, practitioners must study the social, political, and economic (SPE) contexts of a client organization. Without understanding of these, one winds up whistling in the dark. Take, for example, problems that the Coca Cola Co. faced in Belgium in the late 1990s. Some children became seriously ill after drinking Cokes. Soon after that, regulators forced the firm to recall products and shut down its plant. To some, this seemed like overreaction. Why did it happen? Veteran consultant John Budd pointed to these contextual factors:

1. Europeans were paranoid about food contamination due partly to hysterics prior to the Coke incident stemming in part from Britain's "Mad Cow" disease.
2. Coca Cola dominated soft-drink sales in nearly 200 countries. As a huge multinational corporation, it was vulnerable to widespread charges of cultural and economic imperialism often leveled at such firms.

Failing to monitor media coverage and survey data carefully, Coca Cola executives underestimated the danger of such problems. The company was taken by surprise.[15]

In another case, the Monsanto Corp. admitted that it had erred in introducing genetically modified crops in the United Kingdom. According to the firm's director of government and public affairs, the company just assumed "good science and regulatory approval equaled public acceptance." Executives failed to see that people might associate genetic modification with such seemingly remote but emotionally loaded factors as Nazi-like efforts to create a "master race" and the destruction of endangered plant and animal species.[16] As a result, the firm was blasted by editorial writers and activists.

Analysis of such issues requires sophistication in social-science theory as well as insightful reading and listening to the media. In a recent book, the present author and three colleagues identified seventeen theoretical notions that they had found useful in analyzing public relations contexts.[17] Here we pause to discuss two especially helpful notions.

Schema and Frame of Reference

Schema.   This is a belief that helps determine how one seeks, processes, interprets, and remembers information. A survey about osteopathic medicine revealed two schemata that created public relations problems for that healthcare school. First, many MDs have been trained as specialists, focusing on particular organs or body systems. In this process, they have tended to ignore ways in which different organs depend on each other and work together. In other words, they have ceased to think about the whole body as a system. Healthcare has suffered as a result. "This is natural," one osteopathic educator commented. "Spend five or ten years studying, say, the pancreas, and you tend to see any patient entering your office as a walking pancreas with a few ancillary appendages."[18] Turning to a second belief, most Americans have great faith in technology and science to solve problems. This schema, embedded in U.S. culture, sometimes contributes to unrealistic expectations that doctors can cure almost anything. When treatment doesn't work, disillusionment and despair about healthcare set in.[19] Also, perceptions that doctors can cure most everything lead some people to avoid taking personal responsibility for their own health. Why bother to exercise, eat well, and avoid excessive drinking? If problems set in, a doctor can solve them![20]

In another area, Americans long viewed the Soviet Union as a dire threat. That belief encouraged them to vote for political candidates largely in light of priority assigned to national defense. That, in turn, contributed to the growth of what Winston Churchill called the "military-industrial complex," which has greatly affected U.S. politics and economics for several decades.[21]

Frame of Reference.   Psychologist Harry Helson noted that whenever we assess a quantity, we do so by comparing it with some standard. For example, water at 80 degrees Fahrenheit feels cool if we touch it just after removing our hand from an environment near the boiling point. But that same water may seem hot if we have just come in from a very cold room.[22] What standard do we use in a particular case? According to Helson, that depends on our past experience and our current environment.[23] In a study of local police work, citizens were asked how many patrol cars they felt should be at work, on average, throughout the day in their small town. The mean response was thirteen—considerably higher than the actual total of four cars on duty at any one time. This finding was used to justify more patrols. After all, citizens felt a need for more than actually existed.[24]

Research on the SPE context takes time and effort, though not necessarily a great deal of money. One normally begins qualitatively—with in-depth interviews and unstructured browsing to identify relevant issues and arguments. Then it's important to collect data on a fairly large scale and count. All of which negates the oft-noted claim by some qualitative and quantitative types that each is superior to the other!

Here are several steps that colleagues and I have found useful, noting examples. It is not essential to include each step in a given study. But the more the better.

Background Reading

We began each project with two to three days of browsing in specialized magazines, overview books, and databases. In studying osteopathic medicine, we found several concerns and developments—health maintenance organizations, AIDS, hospital bankruptcies, constraints of managed care, etc.—that clearly became more salient between our initial study in 1981 and an update ten years later.

In a study of police-community relations, *U.S. News and World Report*, along with *Newsweek*, discussed trends and innovative solutions in enhancing contact between police and citizens.[25] Also, *Essence, Smithsonian*, and *The American Scholar* provided insight on pressures and forces relating to a university's African American studies center.[26]

Recent books of readings in applied disciplines often discuss current issues with clarity, depth, and insight. Such books tend to be quite readable partly because they are designed for undergraduate or introductory graduate-level courses. In our police study, for example, a book edited by Snibbe and Snibbe[27] discussed several important topics. Additional sources were needed to update this eighteen-year-old volume; however, this book and others like it often contain classic, rather timeless conceptual discussions.

Periodicals that synthesize public opinion research also aid SPE-context analysis. Especially useful are *The American Enterprise* (formerly *Public Opinion*), *Public Opinion Quarterly*, and *Gallup Reports* (formerly the *Gallup Poll Monthly*).[28] One must be aware of sponsors' ideological leanings, of course. For example, *The American Enterprise* is published by a conservative organization.

Best-selling books also merit attention, though often they are superficial and one-sided. In analyzing an African American studies center, for example, we could scarcely avoid noting a book by Allan Bloom, *The Closing of the American Mind*, which was critical of such centers.[29]

Publications of the United States Census Bureau are a gold mine of information about income, race, sex, education, and other parameters, at the city, county, and state levels.[30]

Hard-copy indices such as *The Reader's Guide to Periodical Literature* and the *New York Times Index* remain useful, though they have been superseded to a degree by online databases such as Lexis-Nexis. Use of such databases requires careful, knowledge-based choice of key words. In one search, Dialog informed us it had 6,779 items dealing with police! That figure was overwhelming, so we entered a much narrower term, "Police Neighborhood or Town Watch." This yielded a very workable thirty-one items.[31]

In-Depth Interviews of Informed Observers

Having read at some length, one can flesh out important issues and arguments by interviewing, in depth, a few "experts." In the osteopathic-medicine study, the author and his colleagues proceeded in several steps. First, we prepared an interview guide with about thirty open-end questions seeking reaction to or elaboration of issues and arguments identified in our reading. Armed with this, we arranged one-hour interviews with twelve osteopathic educators in 1981 and eight in our update ten years later. Questions asked here were quite general and designed not to put words in respondents' mouths. We recorded interviews, took notes on them, and wrote detailed transcripts followed by an interpretative synthesis. That process generated many quotes presented later in reporting to our client.[32]

Focus Groups

In the initial osteopathic survey, we conducted two **focus groups**, each with about twelve osteopathic physicians. Basically, we asked general questions, tape-recorded answers, probed, and wrote follow-up transcripts. In general, we regarded focus groups as a source of insight in developing and interpreting structured questions used in later large-sample surveys. Krueger[33] and Larissa Grunig,[34] among others, have argued that, when properly chosen and questioned, focus groups can yield valid, reliable results that stand alone.

Clearly this can happen only if one uses techniques of random and/or stratified sampling to select people who are representative of clearly defined populations. Some focus groups are *representative* of large populations. However, *blue-ribbon* groups chosen because of their expertise and experience often do better in articulating questions and issues. Such focus groups, used in our medical surveys, clearly play a unique role. Krueger makes three important points about focus groups:

1. It's wise to structure them so people within a given group have similar levels of knowledge and ability to articulate views. Otherwise, "lesser lights" may say very little. *Variation in focus groups is desirable, but it should occur primarily between, not within, groups.*
2. The moderator who convenes and conducts a focus group needs to be supportive. Important ideas sometimes come to the fore when groups "brainstorm" and say things that initially seem rather outlandish.
3. Focus groups involve several people, usually yielding varied ideas. The job of synthesis—identifying underlying themes and ideas—is quite challenging.[35]

Large-Sample Surveys

After the above three steps, a researcher should have a good handle on what questions to ask in large-sample surveys. In the first osteopathic study of 1981, we did two such surveys:

1. A 30-minute questionnaire administered to 252 doctors of osteopathic medicine—a one-third sample of all DOs in Ohio. This step was important in light of the adage—often noted in modern discussions of public relations as a two-way street—that a client organization's views about its publics is at least as important as the converse. Because they were involved and knowledgeable, DOs "sat still" for longer interviews than would be feasible with a general-population sample. The response rate was a rather amazing 85 percent.
2. A general-population telephone survey of 490 Ohioans in 1981 and 390 in 1991. This permitted estimates of where people stood on a given topic with about a 5 percent margin of error. Respondents were chosen by random digit dialing. Points emphasized by DOs in their survey were highlighted. Interviews lasted about ten minutes.

What does one study in a front-end survey? Obviously the answer depends on the situation and problem investigated. However, certain variables often neglected in mainstream mass-communication studies warrant special attention. We now turn to these.

Knowledge Testing. Traditionally, public relations people have focused heavily on persuasion—on attitude change rather than on enhancing knowledge. However, current emphasis on relationship building and two-way communication argues for a different view. The good practitioner often plays the role of educator.

Teachers often are criticized for stressing *factual recall*—memorization. Some recall is needed, certainly, as a person can't constantly look up information in an almanac or encyclopedia. However, recall does not equal wisdom. In addition, it's important to emphasize:

1. *Concept definition.* For example, in basic economics, demand is inelastic when even a large change in price brings only a small shift in the amount purchased.
2. *Application.* Ideally, respondents should apply terms such as demand elasticity to cases like the following. As a farm boy, this author learned about demand inelasticity the hard way. He and his dad raised peppermint, a crop for which demand was quite inelastic. One summer they had a bumper crop, harvesting about twice as much peppermint oil as they had a year earlier. But, lo and behold, the market could hardly bear this large quantity. To sell twice as much as before, marketers had to reduce the price by about 70 percent. The result: the bumper crop actually brought in fewer dollars than had smaller crops in previous years. The author returned to school the following fall without much money in his pocket—and with the concept of demand inelasticity burned indelibly in his memory!
3. *Relational thinking.* Trends over time and comparisons often are central to understanding. And these analyses involve looking at one fact or quantity in relation to others. For example, is danger of external attack higher or lower now than it was before the collapse of the Soviet Union?

Obviously, it is wise to measure such knowledge with open-ended questions, not multiple-choice items, where possible. For one thing, some respondents answer multiple-choice questions by guessing. And correction for chance responses turns out to be quite tricky. Second, *structured items force the respondent to answer along lines spelled out by the researcher.* Sometimes people come up with open-ended answers that seem correct but had not been anticipated by the researcher. In developing a knowledge test, it's wise to pretest on about thirty to fifty people similar to those covered in the following survey. Then select items for the "main test" to meet two criteria:

- *Items should vary as to level of difficulty*, with some items being hard (answered correctly by very few), some easy (nailed by most respondents), and others arrayed at all points along the scale in between.
- *Those who answer a given item correctly do better on the total test than do those who answer incorrectly.* Since a given item typically is scored as right or wrong, a point-biserial r (r_{pb}) is a commonly used *index of internal consistency or reliability.* If this measure of association is negative, at least two interpretations are possible. First, the item may be tricky in a subtle way, nailing many highly informed people. Second, and more commonly, the item may measure knowledge of a domain different from that tapped by other items. For instance, an item on European history might correlate negatively with other items on U.S. history. Why? Perhaps few students have the time to take courses in both areas, so they wind up studying one area or the other.

Once all data are collected, indices of difficulty and discrimination (r_{pb}) can be calculated again as a check. "Bad" items can then be put aside when summing the number of right answers to obtain a total knowledge score.

Relative Importance or Prestige. One may endorse a proposal as excellent but still take no action relating to it if it seems unimportant. Thus importance warrants attention in public relations research. One can measure this in at least two ways:

1. By having people rank-order several items, including the one of interest to a client. In one study, students at the author's university ranked the school seventh in prestige among ten institutions arrayed evenly throughout a list of 100 covered in a survey of opinion leaders by *Fortune* magazine. Interestingly, *Fortune's* expert panel ranked the university approximately 45th among the 100 schools! Obviously, as the university president had said, students had a near "crisis of confidence" about their own institution.
2. By having people rate importance on a four-point scale with "very important" = 4, "fairly important" = 3, "not very important" = 2, and "not important at all" = 1.

The first approach has the advantage of providing a meaningful frame of reference. Unfortunately, it provides only ordinal data. Ratings, on the other hand, usually are regarded as interval measures.

Expectations. As noted earlier, the author measured people's expectations about desirable levels of police on duty at any one time. He did this with the following wording: "What would you say is the minimum number of police officers necessary to staff an eight-hour shift? You may not know, but give your best estimate." Such an item provides a way of interpreting beliefs about current staffing levels. Of course, many responses may be uninformed wild guesses. Still, they say something about general perceptions.

Linkage Beliefs. A company probably has a positive "image" if people associate it with profitability and serving the public but a negative image if it is linked in people's minds with union-busting and ruining the environment. Many linkages with values seen as important tend to suggest one's attitude toward the company is stable—and is likely to result in "overt payoff behavior."

In one phone survey, the author asked residents of his state:

> Now I am going to read off a few concepts relating to healthcare. Please tell me how closely you believe each concept is linked to osteopathic medicine today. Is the connection with osteopathy very close? Fairly close? Or not close at all?

Concepts rated were manipulative treatment, wellness (diet, exercise, and lifestyle measures), treatment of the whole person, lowering of healthcare costs, and caring physicians. These had been among the notions that, based on early reading and surveying of DOs, a person must consider to really understand this healthcare school.[36]

Information Systems Variables. One of the most oft-noted theories in applied public relations is information systems theory. This formulation attempts to predict *active information seeking* as opposed to *passive information processing*. Active seekers presumably take the initiative in seeking information—and process it carefully once they have it. Passive processors attend to information only when and if it grabs their attention.

James E. Grunig, the theory's primary author, has measured *information seeking* by giving respondents a list of hypothetical brochure titles dealing with a certain topic. Respondents then indicate, on a scale from 0 to 10, how likely they would be to send for such a brochure. *Processing*, in turn, was measured by asking people how likely, on a ten-point scale, they would be to read an article if they came across it in a newspaper.[37] The theory predicts that people's tendency to seek information hinges substantially on three variables that describe their perception of the situation in which they operate vis-à-vis the message topic. These factors, with recommended measures, are:

1. *Problem recognition*, the extent to which folks feel uncertain about any conclusion or decision which they might accept. A recommended measure: Do you stop to think about this problem often, sometimes, rarely, or never?
2. *Involvement*, the extent to which one sees connections between him- or herself and the object under consideration. One operational definition: Do you see a strong, moderate, weak, or no connection between yourself and this problem?
3. *Constraint recognition*, the extent to which a person feels able to act so as to make a difference. One item used by Grunig to measure this: Could you do a great deal, something, very little, or nothing personally to affect the way these issues are handled?[38]

A good deal of evidence indicates that, as the theory predicts, those with high problem recognition, high involvement, and low constraint recognition tend to be active information seekers. Grunig refers to them as *active public* apt to search for information and process it purposefully. Other people are less active.

In practice, communicators dealing with nonactive publics have two choices. First, they can reach passive consumers through loud, catchy messages that, figuratively speaking, hit people over the head and demand attention. Or second, they can make a case that people are more involved and less constrained than they realize—and that certainty is not really high because conclusions aren't "cut and dried."

Data Analysis.   Techniques used in front-end research do not differ greatly from those discussed elsewhere in this volume. However, one point merits attention. Theory often does not provide clear prediction of outcomes, so one needs to "wander" in search of meaningful relationships. Sometimes inexperienced researchers feel swamped in this process. Say one has measured twenty variables. If she correlates each variable against each other variable, she will come up with 190 possible two-way cross-tabulations or other relationship indicators. Few people have the patience and capacity to look at that many tables!

One helpful solution. Take a blank sheet of paper. List in the right-hand column the key *dependent variables* (measures one wishes to describe and understand). Then, in the left-hand column, list what appear to be significant *independent factors* (used to explain variance in dependent variables or segment the audiences with respect to them). Third, scan the lists and draw a line between any one dependent and one independent factors that seem apt to relate interestingly. Usually this reduces the possible cross-tabs to a workable number. And the researcher feels she has found a lifeboat just in time!

Evaluation Research

Until fairly recently, most public relations people evaluated progress during a program—and success or failure at the end of it—mostly by counting newspaper and magazine clippings. Such media monitoring still is a growing business and is discussed later.

However, skeptical clients—along with educators and management gurus—have noted that media coverage is only a means to an end.[39] One can become famous placing articles in *The New York Times* or *Fortune* magazine but still fail to reach a client's key publics.

Good evaluation research measures progress in meeting important, clearly defined goals and objectives *defined in terms of audience beliefs and behavior*. To pave the way, one must think through at least four steps.

First, define *publics* as *clearly* and *narrowly* as possible. A public, as defined here, is a group of people whose behavior is important to a client's success as it strives to fulfill its mission. If a business is to succeed, people must buy its products. If a candidate is to win an election, people must vote for—and contribute money to—her or him. As recently as twenty to thirty years ago, many practitioners wrote mostly for the general media to reach the "general public"—the total population of an area covered. Sociological definition of the mass as the primary audience for mass media doubtless supported this view.[40] Recently, however, public relations has joined the mass media in focusing more and more on relatively small, specialized publics.[41] Often these people are highly involved with—and interested in—a client organization and its projects. High school baseball coaches know and care about baseball, just as bass fishermen know and care about fishing. One can address fairly detailed messages to such "active" audiences and expect meaningful response.[42]

Second, state general *goals* in terms of audience behavior. Such goals are rather abstract. An example might be to improve the credibility or image of the Ford Motor Co.

Third, translate goals into more specific, measurable *objectives*. Pursuing the Ford example, one might specify that "At least 60 percent of Americans name Ford as the top U.S. car company, when presented with a list of such firms, by August 1, 2003." Specifying a target date is essential if one is to prove success or failure. Without such a limit, the practitioner could always plead for more time. And hardheaded clients are likely to balk! Two factors play a part in selecting a time frame:

1. The target date must be appropriate from a *practical* standpoint. It does little good to raise candidate ratings in December where an election is in November!
2. Timing must be *realistic*. Most people have many things to think about. Thus objectives should proceed *step-by-step* without expecting people to climb an entire ladder with one quick, giant leap.

Fourth, specify ways to *measure goal attainment or nonattainment*. Obviously this is necessary in evaluation research. One related point warrants attention. Even if you lack the time and resources to do evaluation research, specifying clearly what to measure aids program planning. For example, executives often speak of raising or protecting worker *morale*. As it stands, this abstract goal does not aid planning of action and communication very much. However, it helps to "translate" morale by linking it to such rather specific objectives as improved *product quality* (e.g., the number of pistons set aside by quality control as defective), reduced *tardiness* in coming to work (e.g., measurable by checking time cards in the personnel office), reduced *turnover* (also computed from personnel records), and so on. A consultant may have trouble influencing morale. But she or he probably can figure out ways to attack such things as tardiness and turnover. Whatever morale is, the listed objectives are imperfect measures of it partly because each one may reflect other factors (e.g., product quality could decline because of flaws in raw material). However, if several such factors go up or down at one point in time with no other clearly defined explanations, there is strong reason to believe morale has changed.

Objectives—Their Definition and Measurement

Marketing and advertising scholars often discuss a "hierarchy of effects" useful in thinking about objectives. This is a sequential list of variables assumed to reflect campaign success or failure. An *overt payoff behavior* such as voting, purchasing, or working as a volunteer is the capstone of the hierarchy. It's widely assumed—but not always proven—that people must score fairly high on any one variable before progressing very much with the next one in the list. Following is a version of the hierarchy adapted for public relations. Marketing and advertising people focus quite heavily on the concepts outside of brackets, while PR emphasizes those within the brackets.

Awareness —— [Information seeking, gain] —— [Comprehension] —— [Client credibility] —— Attitude —— Intention to behave —— Payoff behavior.

Awareness

Awareness often is measured with a direct question, often incorporating a phrase designed to reduce respondent embarrassment that could lead to socially desirable but untruthful answers. Obviously, a *recall* question (in which the respondent provides the answer) is preferable to a *recognition* item (in which one chooses the answer from a list). For example, one might ask: "These days, it is hard to follow personnel in major-league baseball, as players move around a lot with free agency, trades, league expansion, and so on. Do you happen to know who was the starting center fielder for the Cincinnati Reds at the beginning of the 2001 season? If so, who?" That way, a respondent who could not name Ken Griffey, Jr., will not feel like a complete idiot. He probably will admit to being unaware of Griffey's move from Seattle to Cincinnati. And he is likely to go on and answer the next question.

Comprehension

Comprehension really involves factual recall, but comprehension requires concept definition, relational thinking, and application of knowledge. Measurement of these concepts was discussed in the section on front-end research.

Source Credibility

Source credibility is useful in defining image—a frequent concern in public relations. This concept appears to have two fundamental dimensions. The first is *competence*, the extent to which one is presumed to know what he or she is talking about. Second is *trustworthiness*, the presumed goodness of a source's character and her or his fairness so folks feel inclined to trust her or him. Global seven-point semantic-differential rating scales often are used to measure credibility. Reviewing thirty years of factor-analytic research on credibility, McCroskey and Young reported strong evidence for fairly widespread use of the following scales:

- *Competence:* Intelligent-unintelligent, untrained-trained*, expert-inexpert, uninformed-informed*, competent-incompetent, stupid-bright*
- *Character* (trustworthiness): Sinful-virtuous*, dishonest-honest*, unselfish-selfish, sympathetic-unsympathetic, high character-low character, and untrustworthy-trustworthy*
- Another oft-mentioned concept not regarded by McCroskey and Young as part of credibility is *extroversion* (also called dynamism). Recommended scales are timid-bold*, meek-aggressive*, verbal-quiet, talkative-silent, extroverted-introverted, and not dynamic-dynamic*.[43]

In the asterisked adjective pairs, the negative pole is on the left. In other pairs, the order is reversed. Roughly equal numbers of items with positive words on the left and right are recommended to control for mechanical, unthinking checking of one point on a left-to-right continuum while completing a list of scales. Scoring has a value of 7 at the positive pole, 1 at the negative end, in each case. It is recommended, also, that scales from different dimensions be alternated in going down a questionnaire page.

The above scales have shown up in factor analyses involving a variety of sources. However, a separate factor analysis is recommended for any study because each source and audience might yield different scales and dimensions. For example, we expect politicians to be dynamic. Thus extroversion might be salient in rating them. However, that notion might seem irrelevant when assessing psychological counselors or nuns. Semantic differentials can be converted to Likert agree-disagree items for a phone survey.

Attitude

Attitude has long been a focus of communication research. It's generally defined as a predisposition to behave in a certain way toward some object. Basically, it is defined by two dimensions:

1. *Direction:* Does the person studied regard the object as good, bad, or indifferent? Attitudes so defined are labelled as positive, negative, and neutral, respectively.
2. *Degree:* How good or bad does one see the object as being? Clearly, with a neutral attitude, degree has a value of zero.

Operational definition of attitude has long puzzled scholars.[44] Space precludes a detailed discussion of that issue here. However, one question requires attention. Does attitude predict overt payoff behavior? If not, isn't measurement of it rather useless?

More than thirty-five years ago, psychologist Leon Festinger found little evidence that attitude, as usually measured with paper-and-pencil tests, really correlated with overt payoff behavior.[45] Later, sociologist Herbert Blumer[46] and communication scholar James Grunig[47] also criticized attitude research on the grounds that it does not take into account the goal-oriented, situation-specific, socially constructed nature of human behavior.

Recently, however, studies have shown that attitude degree and direction often do predict payoff behaviors fairly well where respondents really have freedom of behavior choice. Kim and Hunter reached that conclusion in a systematic meta-analysis.[48]

Of several attitude-scaling techniques, the Likert Method of Summated Ratings seems particularly useful for applied research.[49] The researcher creates a set of at least three to five declarative sentences with which agreement reflects favorably on a client, project, or some other important attitude object. Also, one should create three to five items that reflect unfavorably. A balance between positive and negative items is needed to control for some people's tendency to agree or disagree in general—almost without regard to item content. *Yeasaying*—positive response set—will tend to raise scores on positively worded items but lower them on negative items. *Naysaying*—negative response set— should have the opposite effect.

In a pretest with about thirty to fifty people, respondents ideally indicate level of agreement or disagreement with each item on a 5-point scale. With positively worded items, values assigned are 4=strongly agree, 3=agree, 2=uncertain, 1=disagree, and 0=strongly disagree. On negative statements, scoring is reversed.

Correlations among items are then calculated, with significant positive r values reflecting a tendency for a given item to measure the underlying concept of attitude. Items that have negative or near-zero correlations with more than one or two others items should be eliminated in the main study.

In some cases, exploratory factor analysis may identify item clusters that reflect separate dimensions of meaning about an attitude object. In such a case, dimensions might be summed and interpreted separately. However, if items are truly evaluative, a simple search for positive zero-order correlations usually suffices. Items that have negative or near-zero correlations with more than one or two other items should be eliminated in later data collection.

Likert scaling has an important advantage over global rating procedures such as the semantic differential. Each Likert item presumably taps a specific belief linking the attitude object to some idea, value, or goal. This, in turn, suggests that attitudes are based on a cognitive structure that gives them meaning. And such *cognitive linkage*, along with fairly high *involvement* and *stability over time as to degree and direction*, appears to increase the likelihood that attitudes predict payoff behavior.[50]

Definition of the neutral point is controversial in attitude scaling. However, applied research usually does not require great precision or clarity in this area. Defining the neutral point at the middle of the range of possible scores or at the median usually suffices.

Intent to Behave

Intent to behave seldom is measured directly in applied communication studies. That seems strange. Intent lies a step closer than attitude to payoff behavior in the hierarchy of effects. Most variables discussed in the section on front-end research also play a part in evaluation, depending on the situation. A thorny problem exists in most cases where respondents report their own preferences, likes and dislikes, intentions, and other subjective states. We simply don't know, in many instances, how we feel or why we feel that way. *Obtrusive* measures that require a self-report often aren't valid. *Unobtrusive* measures, while indirect, are designed so the researcher can infer subjective states.

In one study, for example, respondents indicated how closely they linked osteopathic medicine with three concepts—wellness (diet, exercise, and other general-health activities), whole-person treatment of patients, and having a caring physician. Surely few could report directly how important these concepts were in assessing osteopathy. However, as shown in Table 4.1 below, correlations between linkage to wellness, whole person treatment, and caring physicians and DO credibility were substantial and positive (between r=.28, .43, and .39, respectively) for those very satisfied with their health insurance. Yet the same correlations declined to insignificance (from .10 to .12) among respondents who had no health insurance that they saw as satisfactory. This confirmed a theoretically based, very practical conclusion. When people have insurance—and thus, access—to healthcare, they can afford to worry about luxuries like wellness, caring doctors, and so on. However, where insurance is not seen as adequate, these luxuries appear to fade into the background.[51] The moral of this story: Reform health insurance! Without that, many seem to worry little about such things as a caring doctor. And this may reduce their regular contact with healthcare professionals. Presumably direct reports could not have yielded such subtle findings.

Table 4.2, drawn from a study of how local citizens viewed a set of medical clinics, reports four measures of belief about attitude scores. These are:

1. The point-biserial correlation (r_{pb}) between ratings on a given item and whether a respondent had had direct contact with a clinic in the system.
2. The Pearson product-moment correlation (r) between response to an item and an overall measure of favorability or unfavorability toward the clinics.

TABLE 4.1 *Product-Moment Correlations between Linkage to Osteopathy and DO Credibility among Very Satisfied and Less Satisfied Health-Insurance Customers*

Concept	Very Satisfied with Health Insurance	Not Very Satisfied or Not Satisfied At All	t^a	p
Wellness	.28** (n=70)	.12 (n=96)	1.02	nsd
Whole-Person Treatment	.43** (n=68)	.10 (n=97)	2.09	.02
Caring Physician	.39** (n=64)	.10 (n=88)	1.76	.05

Notes: **$p < .01$, 1-tail.

[a]Probability based on t-test of differences between correlations converted to Fisher Z statistic.

From "Needs and Beliefs in Construct Accessibility: Keys to New Understanding," by Hugh M. Culbertson, Carl J. Denbow, & Guido H. Stempel III, *Public Relations Review* 24 (1998): 125–143. By permission of *Public Relations Review*.

3. The mean rating on each item, scored as indicated above for Likert items. (Here, however, no neutral point was presented, so values ranged from 1 to 4, not 1 to 5.)
4. The percentage of respondents who gave "don't know" responses or did not answer.

Some illustrative interpretations follow.

1. Item 1, "Physicians at the center care about their patients," was a strong point across the board for the clinics. The mean rating of 3.20 was very favorable. The low r_{pb}

TABLE 4.2   Indices Relating to Likert Items Osteopathic Clinic Survey

Likert Item (direction)	r_{pb} with Contact	r with Image	Mean (1–4)	%DK or NA
1. Physicians at center care about their patients. (+)	.04	.35**	3.20	12
2. Use of center for teaching med students means patients get most up-to-date care. (+)	.02	.38**	2.98	6
3. People who answer the phone at the center are usually informed and helpful. (+)	.03	.25**	2.99	23
4. Billing from the center is usually accurate. (+)	−.17*	.32**	2.89	37
5. Physicians at the center charge less than private physicians in the area. (+)	−.17*	.26**	2.70	43
6. Since physicians are available at center on part-time basis, it's difficult to get to know an individual doctor. (−)	.31*	.20*	2.47	12
7. Doctors at center, as DOs, don't offer all treatments that MDs do. (−)	.21*	.19*	2.84	23
8. I'm uncomfortable about being a patient at the center in Athens with students in the exam room. (−)	.13*	.23*	2.83	12
9. Nurses at the center are usually unfriendly. (−)	.23**	.26**	3.16	12
10. Doctors at center only treat those with bone and joint problems. (−)	.25**	.12	3.19	16
11. Parking is a problem at the osteopathic center in Athens. (−)	.05	.21*	2.60	36

*p < .05

**p < .01

From "Linkage Beliefs and Diagnosing an Image," by Carl J. Denbow & Hugh M. Culbertson, *Public Relations Review* 11 (1985): 29–37. By permission of *Public Relations Review*.

of .04 indicates that patients and nonpatients alike had a favorable view. The correlation of r=.35 with "image" suggests this view is linked, in people's minds, with attitude degree and direction. And the small number of don't-know and no-answer responses indicates that most people have definite views here.

2. Item 5, "Physicians at the center charge less than private physicians," suggests problems. This notion matters to people as reflected by the healthy r of .26 with overall clinic image. But the 43 percent no-response figure suggests widespread uncertainty about clinics' fees. Also, the mean rating of 2.70, just above the midpoint of 2.50 on the scale of 1–4, suggests fairly lukewarm approval at best. And the negative r_{pb} of −.17 between contact and this item suggests that current and past patients have stronger concerns than do outside observers. Relatively negative views by those in close contact with clinics surely sounds an alarm![52]

We now look briefly at measurement of people's perceptions and predictions about each other's behavior. Accuracy of such perceptions is crucial given today's oft-noted emphasis on building and maintaining two-way relationships.[53] Adapting the Chaffee-McLeod coorientation model,[54] one can define four basic concepts:

1. The client's own set of priorities or attitudes regarding a program or a set of related objects.
2. The client's prediction of a public's priorities or attitudes.
3. The public's perception of a client's priorities or attitudes.
4. The public's own set of priorities or attitudes.

Assume that each of the four listed sets consists of numerical ratings on an interval scale. Coorientation focuses on similarity or difference among the four sets. The product-moment correlation coefficient, r, usually is an appropriate measure of association in such a case between any two sets of data. Possible measures include:

1. *Agreement* ($r_{1,4}$)—the extent to which client and public actually think or act alike.
2. *Client accuracy* ($r_{2,4}$)—the extent to which a client's prediction approximates what a public actually thinks or does.
3. *Public accuracy* ($r_{3,1}$)—the extent to which a public's prediction approximates what a client actually thinks or does.
4. *Client congruency* ($r_{1,2}$)—The degree to which a client attributes its own view to a public.
5. *Public congruency* ($r_{3,4}$)—The degree to which a public attributes its own view to a client.

Clearly accuracy is important in relationships. Consider, for example, your most recent interaction with your best friends. If things went smoothly, they doubtless did so partly because you and they knew each other quite well. You predicted your friends' responses to your behavior fairly accurately so as to avoid offending them, and vice versa.

Space is not available to consider all of the thorny issues that come up in measuring and defining coorientation variables. We make just four points:

1. *Extremely high congruency often leads, in practice, to inaccuracy.* Two people or groups seldom have identical learning experiences and goals that influence perception. The assumption that they do sometimes amounts to egocentrism or ethnocentrism.

2. *Enhancing accuracy in cases of low agreement is a difficult but important task.*[55] Sen. J. William Fulbright recognized this many years ago when he proposed his famous Fulbright scholarships. He reasoned that, if people from different nations are to get along peacefully, young scholars and leaders-to-be from each nation need to understand others despite large cultural differences. And Fulbright saw no easy fixes. He arranged for scholars to live and work in each other's lands for at least several months.[56]

3. *Often accuracy is a more practical goal than agreement.* In one case, the U.S. Army Corps of Engineers had certain ideas about flood control in the northern United States. Local farmers, a key public, did not share these ideas. But the residents did come to understand the Corps' point of view, apparently contributing to tolerance and patient work toward compromise.[57]

4. *Research is especially difficult when one or both parties—client or public—is a group.* Group characteristics often really are measures of central tendency applied to data about individuals. And a mean or median may actually describe few individuals within a group. To clarify this, consider that the Mississippi River is, on average, three feet deep. In fact, few if any parts of it may have precisely that depth. Some areas may have 20 feet of water, while others are bone dry. The implication: Look for ways to segment publics by dividing them into separate groups with very different views and approaches—and with little within-group variance.

Some coorientation studies measure similarity of views with difference scores between ratings. This procedure may be appropriate in some cases. However, it seems less fruitful than a correlational approach in measuring overall viewpoints and ways of thinking.

Research Design—Evaluation

Obviously, data collected at one time—during or after a public relations program or campaign—does not indicate impact convincingly. Change from before to after the campaign is central. And that suggests collection at several points in time. Unfortunately, even this often is not conclusive. It amounts to an experiment without a control group. One cannot easily separate features of the campaign from outside factors. The Internet allows one to direct a message to one target person but not another. Thus, true experimentation, with random assignment of individuals to treatment groups, has become increasingly feasible. However, the *quasi-experiment* remains an important strategy for studying campaign impact. Here samples are studied repeatedly and are chosen for comparability—albeit without random assignment of individuals to treatment groups. Such assignment may be difficult if not impossible in a mass-media campaign.

Often cited as a model quasi-experiment is a classic study done in 1965–1966 by Douglas, Westley, and Chaffee.[58] The authors studied two small Wisconsin communities, Reedsburg and Richland Center, which were very similar in age, gender, income, population, and other factors, based on data from the U.S. Census. Regular-interval sampling from randomly chosen starting points in the towns' electric-utility lists yielded comparable samples in the two towns. Before measures on knowledge level and attitudes about mental retardation, with attitudes gauged by twenty-one Likert agree-disagree items, were administered in September 1965 to 85 residents of the experimental community, Reedsburg, and 60 in the control town, Richland Center. A six-month information campaign was then carried out only in Reedsburg. Messages included twenty spot-news and five feature stories, and a Mental Retardation Week ad in the local paper, posters around town, broadcast news, and other items. Then, in April 1966, the attitude and information tests were readministered to both panels. Data about information gain were not conclusive. However, as predicted, positive attitude change about mental retardation was significantly greater in the experimental community than in the control. The two communities differed substantially in education level, but the researchers controlled for this factor by making separate comparisons among people with high, medium, and low education levels. Such a study has its limitations. It does not indicate which messages or specific tactics worked best in the campaign. Also, it is difficult to eliminate the possibility that unknown events or messages might have influenced knowledge and attitudes during the six months between measures. However, the study surely represents a step in the right direction with evaluation.

Media Monitoring

Many practitioners wait with anticipation for a bag of clippings every week, two weeks or month. This author was one such person in the late 1950s and early to mid-1960s. He then helped handle press relations for the agricultural college and experiment station at a major land-grant university. The clippings he received were cut out of newspapers and magazines with knives or scissors. Attached to each story was a small sheet indicating the newspaper or magazine in which the story appeared, circulation as certified by the Audit Bureau of Circulation, and publication date. The author quickly carried these clips to the director of the agency for which he worked. Usually the director was impressed. At least, he came to realize we'd gained widespread coverage in dozens of newspapers and magazines—not simply in the local paper. He read that paper regularly, of course. And, unfortunately, it quite often ran stories somewhat embarrassing to the university! One day, however, the director said, with some irritation, "I wish you could show me genuine evidence of impact. Are people really growing better rhubarb, earning more money, etc., because of the work we do?" Usually little such evidence was available. At best, clips indicate only *opportunities* for impact. In fact, frustration about this contributed in some small measure to the author's decision to become a researcher!

Clippings have other limitations as well. They do not indicate readership, listenership, or viewership—or impact. Also, they seldom show clearly the play given within a newspaper, magazine, or newscast. Once in a while, a clip will contain a banner headline or masthead indicating front-page play. But this is rare. Few press releases get such prominence! In addition, readers miss some stories. In fact, one major firm estimates that clipping services usually catch only about 60 percent of all published items containing a key word or phrase such as the client's name.[59]

Recently, computer searching surely has partially solved the missed-story problem. And clipping firms today provide some useful data such as:

1. A story's slant—positive, neutral, or negative—in portraying the client organization and its projects. Unfortunately, information about coding instructions and intercoder agreement, stressed in Chapter 11 of this book, seldom is very precise.[60]
2. Story type. For example, one service distinguished among product announcements, case histories, other fairly long features, and shorter news stories as well as mere brief mentions.[61]
3. Numbers of stories and impressions relating to particular themes presumed to support specific client objectives. For example, one firm studied coverage relating to the objective of establishing an auto manufacturer as a *well-managed global company*. Under that heading, a report to the client counted stories and impressions relating to the themes of leadership, philanthropy, a talented work force, responsiveness, and honesty/integrity.[62]

While helpful, these embellishments do little to eliminate clippings' limitations listed earlier. Further, firms often provide "advertising equivalency" estimates of the dollars required to buy advertising space equivalent to the news coverage obtained. Such estimates are subject to at least two limitations:

1. Many publications do not sell advertising space on certain pages, including front pages. This makes some equivalency estimates quite meaningless.
2. Such estimates sometimes are inflated to reflect an assumption that news coverage has higher credibility than do paid ads. That assumption stems from the fact that news presumably is not paid for or controlled by a client with a vested interest. Unfortunately, the author knows of no clear evidence regarding the size of such a credibility gap—assuming it does exist.

Despite these problems, clips do serve a purpose in press relations.

A final note: Databases—the most sophisticated, thorough clipping services available—play an important part in research about public relations contexts. The author took advantage of this in a study on exploitative use of child labor around the world. A Lexis-Nexis search with the keywords "Charles Kernaghan and the International Labor Organization" yielded 303 articles in magazines and metropolitan newspapers between early 1994 and Thanksgiving 1997. These articles provided much of the background for a write-up about Kernaghan, the ILO director, his crusade against child labor, and related contextual issues.[63]

Conclusion

In conclusion, applied public relations research today cries out for creative thought and innovation. Despite its central role in the public relations process, research has tended to focus on two things:

1. Media coverage and opportunities for exposure to messages generated by communication professionals.
2. Change or stability in audience behavior. Often evidence linking such phenomena to public relations efforts is weak.

Trained social scientists surely see a strong need for data collection *before* and *during*, as well as *after*, communication programs or campaigns. Also, front-end research needs to probe a client's social, political and economic contexts. Too often, studies focus narrowly on audience acceptance or rejection of the client organization and its programs. Two-way symmetrical communication—an "in phrase" in the field—calls for substantial broadening of applied research.

Endnotes

1. John E. Marston, *The Nature of Public Relations* (New York: McGraw-Hill, 1963), 161–169.
2. James E. Grunig and Todd Hunt, *Managing Public Relations* (New York: Holt, Rinehart & Winston, 1984), chapter 2.
3. Edward J. Robinson, *Communication and Public Relations* (Columbus, OH: Charles E. Merrill Books, 1966), 100–104.
4. *Ibid.,* 47–51.
5. Edward J. Robinson, *Public Relations and Survey Research: Achieving Organizational Goals in a Communication Context* (New York: Appleton-Century Crofts, 1969), 105–278.
6. *Ibid.,* 126–134, 146–152, 193–196, 226–236.
7. *Ibid.,* 212–220, 229–235.
8. David M. Dozier with Larissa A. and James E. Grunig, *Manager's Guide to Excellence in Public Relations and Communication Management* (Mahwah, NJ: Lawrence Erlbaum Associates, 1995).
9. Robert L. Health and Richard A. Nelson, *Issues Management: Corporate Policymaking in an Information Society* (Beverly Hills, CA: Sage Publications, 1986), 20.
10. *Ibid.,* 20–30.
11. Otto Lerbinger, *The Crisis Manager: Facing Risk and Responsibility* (Mahwah, NJ: Lawrence Erlbaum Associates, 1997), 19–29.
12. See *Corporate Public Issues and Their Management.* This journal is published 24 times a year by Issue Action Publications, Inc., 207 Loudon St., S.E., Leesburg, VA 20175.
13. Eric Battenberg, Jon Lesser, and Jeff Reese, "1999 Bronze Anvil Winners," *PR Tactics,* September 1999, 13–26.
14. Entries were examined at the following web site: *http://www.prsa.org/award/sawin00.html.*
15. "Budd Recounts Coke's Disastrous Image Loss," *Corporate Public Issues and Their Management* 22 (December 1999): 105–106.
16. "Monsanto Mea Culpa Regains Credibility," *Corporate Public Issues and Their Management* 22 (October 1999): 95–96.
17. Hugh M. Culbertson, Dennis W. Jeffers, Donna Besser Stone, and Martin Terrell, *Social, Political and Economic Contexts in Public Relations: Theory and Cases* (Hillsdale, NJ: Lawrence Erlbaum Associates, 1993), 51–120.
18. *Ibid.,* 232.
19. *Ibid.,* 279.
20. *Ibid.,* 242–244.
21. Oxford Analytica, *America in Perspective* (Boston: Houghton Mifflin Co., 1986), 180–182.
22. Harry Helson, *Adaptation-Level Theory: An Experimental and Systematic Approach to Behavior* (New York: Harper and Row, 1964), 129–151.
23. *Ibid.,* 151–155.

24. Culbertson et al., *op. cit.*, 135.

25. *Ibid.*, 151.

26. *Ibid.*, 209.

27. J. R. Snibbe and H. M. Snibbe, eds., *The Urban Policeman in Transition: A Psychological and Sociological Review* (Springfield, IL: Thomas Publishing Co., 1973).

28. Culbertson et al., *op. cit.*, 35.

29. Allan Bloom, *The Closing of the American Mind* (New York: Simon and Schuster, 1987), 336–382.

30. Culbertson et al., *op. cit.*, 35.

31. *Ibid.*, 36–37.

32. *Ibid.*, 38–40.

33. Richard A. Krueger, *Focus Groups: A Practical Guide for Applied Research* (Newbury Park, CA: Sage Publications, 1988), 29.

34. Larissa A. Grunig, "Using Focus Group Research in Public Relations," *Public Relations Review* 16 (1990): 36–49.

35. Krueger, *op. cit.*, 106–121.

36. Hugh M. Culbertson, Carl J. Denbow, and Guido H. Stempel III, "Needs and Beliefs in Construct Accessibility: Keys to New Understanding," *Public Relations Review* 22 (1998): 125–143.

37. James E. Grunig, "Communication Behaviors and Attitudes of Environmental Publics: Two Studies," *Journalism Monographs* 81 (March 1983), 19–20.

38. *Ibid.*, 19.

39. Robinson, *Communication and Public Relations*, *op. cit.*, 84–86.

40. Herbert Blumer, "The Mass, the Public and Public Opinion," in Bernard Berelson and Morris Janowitz, eds., *Reader in Public Opinion and Communication* (New York: The Free Press, 1966), 43–50.

41. Richard Maisel, "The Decline of Mass Media," *Public Opinion Quarterly* 37 (1973): 159–170.

42. David K. Berlo, *The Process of Communication* (New York: Holt, Rinehart and Winston, 1960), 152–166.

43. James C. McCroskey and T. J. Young, "Ethos and Credibility: The Construct and Its Measurement After Three Decades," *Central States Speech Journal* 32 (1981): 24–34.

44. Hugh M. Culbertson, "What Is an Attitude?" *Journal of Cooperative Extension* 6 (1968): 79–84; Allen L. Edwards, *Techniques of Attitude Scale Construction* (New York: Appleton-Century-Crofts, 1957), 1–14.

45. Leon Festinger, "Behavioral Support for Opinion Change," *Public Opinion Quarterly* 28 (1964): 404–417.

46. Herbert Blumer, *Symbolic Interactionism: Perspective and Method* (Englewood Cliffs, NJ: Prentice-Hall, 1969), 93–100.

47. James E. Grunig, "Communication Behaviors and Attitudes . . . ," *op. cit.*, 4–9.

48. Min-Sun Kim and John E. Hunter, "Attitude-Behavior Relations: A Meta-Analysis of Attitudinal Relevance and Topic," *Journal of Communication* 43 (Winter 1993): 101–142.

49. Allen L. Edwards, *Techniques of Attitude Scale Construction*, *op. cit.*, 149–171.

50. Norman H. Anderson, "Cognitive Algebra: Integration Theory Applied to Social Attribution," in Leonard Berkowitz, ed., *Cognitive Theories in Social Psychology* (New York: Academic Press, 1978), 1–101; Martin Fishbein and Icek Ajzen, "Acceptance, Yielding and Impact: Cognitive Processes in Persuasion," in Richard E. Petty, Thomas M. Ostrom, and Timothy C. Brock, eds., *Cognitive Responses in Persuasion* (Hillsdale, NJ: Lawrence Erlbaum Associates, 1981), 339–359.

51. Hugh M. Culbertson, Carl J. Denbow, and Guido H. Stempel III, "Needs and Beliefs in Construct Accessibility: . . . ," *op. cit.*, p. 139.

52. Carl J. Denbow and Hugh M. Culbertson, "Linkage Beliefs and Diagnosing an Image," *Public Relations Review* 11 (1985): 29–37.

53. David M. Dozier with Larissa A. Grunig and Todd Hunt, *op. cit.*

54. Steven H. Chaffee and Jack McLeod, "Sensitization in Panel Design: A Coorientation Experiment," *Journalism Quarterly* 45 (1968): 661–669.

55. Hugh M. Culbertson, "Role-Taking and Sensitivity: Keys to Playing and Making Public Relations Roles," *Public Relations Research Annual* 3 (1991): 37–65.

56. J. William Fulbright, *The Price of Empire* (New York: Pantheon Books, 1989), 191–219.

57. John E. Bowes and Keith R. Stamm, "Evaluating Communication with Public Agencies," *Public Relations Review* 1 (1975): 23–37.

58. Dorothy F. Douglas, Bruce H. Westley, and Steven H. Chaffee, "An Information Campaign That Changed Community Attitudes," *Journalism Quarterly* 47 (1970): 479–487.

59. "The News Picture," unpublished report from The News Analysis Institute, Pittsburgh, PA, received in May 2000, p. 1.

60. "Analysis of News Generated," unpublished report from The News Analysis Institute, Pittsburgh, PA, received in May 2000, p. 5.

61. "Publicity," unpublished reported from The News Analysis Institute, Pittsburgh, PA, received in May 2000, pp. 1–2.

62. "Analysis of News Generated," unpublished report from The News Analysis Institute, Pittsburgh, PA, received in May 2000, pp. 15–16.

63. Hugh M. Culbertson, "Giving Two Hundred Million Kids a Childhood," in Judy VanSlyke Turk and Linda H. Scanlan, eds., *The Evolution of Public Relations: Case Studies from Countries in Transition* (Gainesville, FL: The Institute for Public Relations, 1999), 131–152.

5

Advertising Research

Tom Bowers

Advertising research reduces the risk and uncertainties in the many decisions or choices advertisers must make at almost every step of the advertising process.

- They have to determine the best consumer prospects for their products. **Target market research** helps advertisers to make that determination.
- They need to know what those products "mean" in the lives of their prospects. **Positioning research** gives them that understanding.
- They have to create advertising messages that will convey the meaning persuasively, and they want to know what impact the message had. **Message research** helps them determine which advertising messages stand the best chance of conveying the desired information to the minds of the consumers to lead to the desired consumer action.
- They want to know how many consumer prospects saw the messages in the media used to deliver them. **Audience research** gives them information about the number of people who saw the media vehicles in which the advertising appeared.

Research will not usually identify the best choice in each decision, but if used correctly, it can reduce the risk of a wrong decision by eliminating alternatives that do not have a good chance of success. Take the example of choosing the right advertising message. An advertiser might conceive of five possible messages—different ways of saying the same thing about a product. By using research—pretesting the five messages on small samples of typical consumers—the advertiser might eliminate two of the alternatives that have less chance of success. While research will not eliminate all the risk and identify the single best message, it can increase the chances of success by eliminating alternative messages that have less chance of achieving the intended goal. The advertiser will have to rely on experience and intuition to decide which alternative will more likely be successful.

Target Market Research

One of the first questions advertisers need to answer is this: Who are the best prospective customers for my product, and what are their characteristics? Knowing the characteristics of people who currently use the product will help the advertiser direct advertising to similar consumers more efficiently.

Target market research typically uses large-scale survey research studies to measure product usage levels, media exposure patterns, and demographic data about the consumers. Simmons Market Research Bureau[1] (SMRB) and Mediamark Research, Inc.[2] (MRI) conduct such research and syndicate the results to advertisers and others willing to pay for them. Those companies typically survey more than 20,000 representative households per year. The careful selection of the households enables the companies to project the results to the more than 100 million U.S. households.

To measure product usage, researchers ask respondents to quantify their product use. For example, to measure soft-drink consumption, researchers might ask this question: "In the last seven days, how many soft drinks have you consumed?" They collapse the resulting data into usage categories: heavy users (5 or more), medium users (2–4), light users (1), and nonusers. Researchers also ask respondents similar questions about their use of hundreds of other products.

The researchers seek two other important kinds of information in the survey: media exposure and demographic characteristics. The demographic categories are standard: gender, age, income, ethnic group, occupation, education, geographic region, employment, and number of children. Researchers also ask the respondents to indicate their media exposure patterns, including the magazines they read, the television programs they watch, and the types of radio stations they listen to.

Results are presented in two-dimensional tables. The horizontal axes of the tables show product consumption categories: all users, heavy users, medium users, light users, and nonusers. The vertical axes show demographic categories or media usage categories. Analysis of the results enables advertisers to describe heavy users in important demographic categories or their usage of major media types. For example, a manufacturer of mascara could learn that the heavy users of her product are primarily single women, aged 18–24, who work primarily in technical, sales, and clerical occupations. They are likely to read magazines such as *Entertainment Weekly*, *Shape*, *Sassy*, and *Vogue*.

Positioning Research

Advertisers use positioning research to determine the meaning that products, brands, and services have for consumers—what product benefits are important and how they use the product. Advertisers can't rely on their own conceptions of what products mean to consumers because those meanings differ from consumer to consumer. This research is more likely to be proprietary—conducted by researchers at the company or agency or for their exclusive use—than syndicated.

In conducting this kind of research, it is important to distinguish between product attributes and benefits. An *attribute* is a feature or characteristic of a product. The attribute of a camera, for example, is the fact that it permits light rays to strike photosensitive material that can be used to produce an image of the actual scene. The **benefit** of a camera is the fact that it captures and preserves memories or gives a person the satisfaction of creating an artistic object.

The same type of product can offer different benefits to different kinds of consumers. For example, some people purchase certain brands of cameras because they are easy to use and facilitate the capturing of memories. Other people purchase other brands because they are professional artists or journalists who want to create works of art or capture reality. To take another example, some consumers perceive certain brands of toothpaste as being beneficial because they help to prevent tooth decay. Others choose competing brands because they provide whiter teeth or fresher breath.

Positioning research helps advertisers determine how to create perceptions of the product (position it) that match the needs of a significant number of consumers. For example, if a toothpaste manufacturer's positioning research shows that a significant number of consumers want a toothpaste that gives them very bright teeth and fresh breath, that brand's advertising will focus on those product benefits. In advertising jargon, that is referred to as positioning the product against consumer needs and desires. Advertisers do that to make their advertising more effective against a niche market rather than trying to meet the needs (provide benefits) of many consumers seeking varied benefits.

How Is Positioning Research Done?

Researchers typically use qualitative research methods—projective techniques and focus groups, for example—to ascertain benefits that are important to consumers. They usually rely on small samples and are more interested in general ideas than representative and statistically reliable data.

Because we doubt that consumers can express their true feelings or give accurate answers to direct questions about product usage and benefits, we ask indirect questions in projective techniques. For example, instead of handing someone a 35 mm camera and asking her to explain why she would buy it, we could ask her to examine the camera and try to describe the kind of person who might buy and use that brand or kind of camera. Or, we could hand her a tube of toothpaste and ask her why people might purchase that brand.

Another indirect questioning technique is sentence-completion, in which we ask subjects to fill in the blank at the end of a partial sentence. For example, we might pose this statement: "The person who buys ready-made pasta sauce instead of making it herself is ___." A variation of this technique is to ask subjects to complete a cartoon illustration with dialogue. We could show a man and woman sitting in a chair with the man saying, "I want tomorrow night's dinner to be a success, and I don't know whether to serve imported or domestic wine." The subject's task would be to provide the responding line of dialogue. We would assume that the subjects' responses to these kinds of questions would reveal their personal feelings in an indirect manner.

Role-playing is another indirect technique for trying to learn the deep or hidden meanings that products have for consumers. We might use this kind of instruction: "Suppose a new person moved into your neighborhood and asked for your advice about the best brand and variety of grass seed to plant in your lawn. What would you tell him?"

The kind of research described above can be conducted with small samples of consumers—one at a time—and the responses are reported in the aggregate. However, we do not collect such data for statistical analysis. Instead, we report general themes and verbatim accounts of what subjects said about the product. While the samples are purposively small and unrepresentative of the population, it is still important to try to find subjects who generally resemble the target population for the product.

Focus Groups

Many of the same kind of projective and indirect questions can be asked in focus-group research—talking to small groups (8–10) of subjects instead of individuals. The advantage of focus groups is that consumers talk to and respond to each other and often provide more and deeper insights than they would if interviewed separately. Conducting a focus group requires special skills to lead consumers with nondirective questioning without suggesting desired responses. Effective focus group facilitators must also encourage participation by all members of the group without allowing a few individuals to dominate.

While a successful focus group session can appear to be self-sustaining among members of the group, it requires considerable preparation and constant monitoring and guidance by the researcher. The researcher has to prepare questions and probes for the group, but also has to "go with the flow" of the discussion and allow the group to take the discussion in natural directions. A researcher has to avoid the tendency to conduct a survey of the group—asking each of them to answer the same set of questions. Instead, the researcher must start with a provocative question, encourage a response, and then gently nudge others in the group to respond to what others have said.

Issues with Positioning Research

Positioning research assumes that consumers can accurately express what the product really means to them. Even with indirect questioning and projective techniques, that assumption is not always accurate. Nevertheless, advertising researchers often have no better alternative, especially considering that this research is relatively inexpensive compared to more quantitative research based on large samples. Here, as in many other aspects of advertising research, researchers have to consider the cost-benefit ratio of doing more precise research. Large-scale research may yield more accurate results, but the increase in accuracy is not proportional to the increase in cost.

Using Research to Measure Brand Strength

The Y & R advertising agency has developed a new way that research can measure the brand strength and potential and help advertisers determine appropriate positioning strategies. As one of the largest marketing communications companies in the world, Y & R wanted to learn more about the concept of a brand and what it means to consumers, so it spent $50 million to interview more than 100,000 consumers around the world. By the researchers' definition, a brand is a set of differentiating processes that links a product to its customers. Furthermore, brands develop in a very specific progression of consumer perceptions, and those perceptions are the dimensions of brand meaning: differentiation, relevance, esteem, and knowledge.[3]

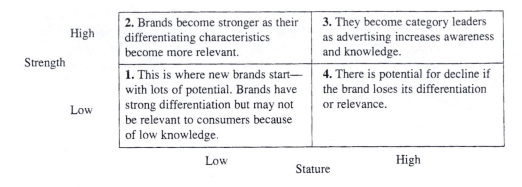

		Low Stature	High Stature
Strength	High	**2.** Brands become stronger as their differentiating characteristics become more relevant.	**3.** They become category leaders as advertising increases awareness and knowledge.
	Low	**1.** This is where new brands start—with lots of potential. Brands have strong differentiation but may not be relevant to consumers because of low knowledge.	**4.** There is potential for decline if the brand loses its differentiation or relevance.

FIGURE 5.1. The Y & R Power Grid of Brand Development.

Differentiation is the distinctiveness of the brand—something that makes it different and unique. This is the first and most important element. It's how the brand is born; it defines the brand and distinguishes it from all others.

Relevance is the second perception in the process—how the brand is personally appropriate or important to consumers. To survive and grow, brands must be relevant to consumers.

Esteem is the extent to which consumers like a brand and hold it in high regard. It is related to their perceptions of the quality and popularity of the brand.

Knowledge is consumer awareness of the brand and what it stands for. It is based on what consumers say they know about the brand and does not necessarily have to be accurate knowledge.

The challenge was to develop a way to quantify those dimensions and use the research results to help make decisions. Y & R researchers developed questions to assess these consumer perceptions, and they use percentile scores—which show the brand's position relative to other brands—to measure a brand on each dimension. More importantly, the scales can be combined into measures of brand strength and brand stature. **Brand strength** is the relationship between (product of) relevance and differentiation and is a strong indicator of the brand's future performance. **Brand stature** is the relationship between (product of) esteem and knowledge.

A brand's strength and stature can be plotted on a *power grid* that shows the brand's potential and suggests appropriate advertising strategy because brands progress through generally predictable stages of consumer perceptions (see Figure 5.1). Starbucks Coffee, for example, began with strong differentiation because it was the first strong brand in the specialty coffee category. Its strength grew and it became the category leader as it became more relevant to consumers. There is always a risk that a brand will lose its differentiation and decline as competitors enter the market.

Message Research

Another important use of advertising research is to determine which advertising messages stand the best chance of conveying the advertiser's desired information to the minds of the consumers in a way that will lead to the desired consumer action. Ultimately, of course, an advertiser is interested in a causal relationship—learning how a specific advertising message in a specific advertising medium affected the sale of the product. Better yet, he or she would like to know if the cost of the advertising can be justified in light of its contribution to sales. In other words, the advertiser wants to know the direct effect of an advertising message on sales and profits. Knowing the answer to that question will enable the advertiser to use advertising more efficiently in future campaigns.

Unfortunately, not even the most careful research can measure such a direct impact, and that is not because of any weakness of research. The problem is due to the fact that advertising (or a specific advertisement) is one of only many forces that affect product sales. Some of the other factors that influence sales are controlled by the advertiser, including the price charged for the product, its availability in stores, information on the package, point-of-purchase displays, and other means the advertiser has to communicate to consumers. It is also impossible to separate the impact of one ad from a repetition of the same ad or from another ad that is similar. Other forces that influence sales are not controlled by the advertiser, including competitors' actions, government regulation, communication from consumer-advocacy groups, the personal influence of other consumers, a consumer's personal knowledge of the company and product, climate, and culture.

Nevertheless, advertisers use research to eliminate messages that seem to hold the least promise. Some of the research is **pretesting**—conducted before the advertising appears—and some is **posttesting**—conducted after the campaign. Because of the difficulty of tracing the impact of one advertisement on a consumer decision to buy the product or take the desired action, advertisers usually measure an indirect relationship between advertising and behavior.

Consider, for example, a magazine advertisement for a personal computer aimed at the consumer market. Consumers must first receive the magazine (the advertising vehicle). Some, but not all, who receive the magazine issue will read or look through it. Only some who read the magazine will see (be exposed to) the computer ad. Only some who are exposed to the ad will read it or a major portion of it. Only some who read the ad will comprehend the ad's message, and only some who comprehend it will recall the ad as part of a process that results in a purchase of the product.

The advertiser would like to know how many consumers reached that final step of recalling the ad and purchasing the product as a result. Because of the difficulty of measuring that direct effect, advertisers sometimes settle for research that is indirect and a step removed from the purchase—measures of *comprehension*—the estimated number or percentage of consumers who learned the ad's message. Comprehension could be measured by asking consumers to recite or explain the salient points of the advertising. Advertisers do such research on the assumption that only those consumers who comprehended the ad could recall the salient points that would lead to a purchase. In other words, comprehension is a necessary condition leading to purchase.

Pretest Message Research

Based on their understanding of the target audience for the product and their knowledge of what consumers want from products and what products and brands mean to consumers, advertising copywriters and art directors can create preliminary or "rough" versions of advertisements and advertising messages. Before advertisers spend the thousands of dollars needed to make finished advertisements, advertising researchers test preliminary versions with small samples of consumers.

One way to do that is to show consumers the ads and ask them to discuss their reactions to the ads. This method is fairly simple, but it is not very realistic because it tends to elicit consumers' opinions about ads instead of the ads' persuasive power. In effect, consumers are placed in the role of experts asked to comment about advertisements. While many may consider themselves to be experts about advertising because of their lifelong exposure to ads, they are more likely to express opinions than to respond to the advertising messages. While consumers' opinions of advertisements may have some value to advertisers, those attitudes are not nearly as useful as even rudimentary assessments of their ability to increase awareness of the brand, convey information, or stimulate the desired purchase response.

Advertisers try to create realistic conditions of exposure to the advertisements being tested and use natural measures of their impact. The methods used and the degree of realism achieved depend on the amount of time and money the advertiser is willing and able to devote to the research.

Magazine ads to be tested can be made to look realistic and attached to actual magazines to simulate real ads. Subjects are directed to look at the magazine with an explanation that the researcher is interested in their readership and opinions about the articles. While "testing" for that readership, researchers can measure recall of the test ads. This kind of message research is not very practical for pretesting television commercials because one cannot produce realistic television ads without spending thousands of dollars.

Split-Run and Inquiry Tests.   Presses that print copies of newspapers and magazines are capable of producing alternative versions of the same ad in copies of the publication as they come off the press. This is called **split-run** capability, and it allows researchers to test print ads under realistic exposure conditions.

For example, we could prepare two versions of a magazine ad, which we would label A and B. These versions should be identical except for one ad element, such as the headline, illustration, or layout. If the ads are dissimilar in more than one element, it will be impossible to tell which element caused the difference in response.

For this kind of research, the ads must seek a direct response from readers. That response can be a request for more information about the product or an actual purchase. Consumers could respond by mailing in a portion of the ad (coupon) or calling a toll-free telephone number. Each of the two versions of the ad would have a different address (e.g., post office box) or telephone number.

As the magazines come off the press, every other copy has version A, and the other half has version B. Because of the relatively random way the copies are distributed to readers, researchers can assume that the "sample" that gets version A will be identical in all important variables (e.g., income) to the sample that gets version B. That means any difference in the number of inquiries to the ad can be attributed to the difference in the ad instead of differences in the samples. This method is realistic because consumers read the magazine (or don't read it) under normal conditions in their homes and respond (or don't respond) without any external stimulation from a researcher.

Two different direct mail brochures could be tested in the same way. In fact, direct-response marketers constantly test different strategies or tactics—type of envelope, color of ink or paper, and the use of short, separate notes or letters in the package. As a direct-response medium, the World Wide Web also lends itself to research about actual ads under realistic conditions.

Researchers could also compare responses to two different television commercials—but with less confidence because of the inability to say with any confidence that the samples of viewers who saw each version were similar in demographic characteristics. Because the two commercials could not be telecast at exactly the same time of the day, there is also a possibility that some viewers would see both. (There are limited opportunities to test television commercials under realistic conditions with cable-television systems that can broadcast different messages to subscribers at the same time.)

Technically, of course, split-run or **inquiry research** is not really pretesting because the research is done after the ads appear. The results, however, can help advertisers create future ads that should be more effective. By accumulating and integrating results from many such tests, advertisers can build a field of knowledge about what seems to work or not work in ads.

Posttest Message Research

Advertisers also conduct message research after the campaign has started (or even after it has ended) to measure how many people read or saw the ads and how much they learned from the ads. The results of such research can guide the creators of the advertising when they prepare subsequent campaigns. Posttest message research relies on measures of recognition and recall.

Recognition research asks subjects if they can remember seeing (can recognize) advertisements at some time interval after they supposedly had an opportunity to see them while watching television or reading. With magazines, for example, researchers determine if subjects read a particular issue—based on the readers' self-report of such readership. If subjects say they read the issue, researchers go through the magazine page by page with the subjects, asking a series of questions about whether they remember reading the headline, reading enough of the ad to determine the name of the advertiser, or reading most of the body copy. This is as much of a measure of the subjects' memory as a measure of what they actually read. However, because it is difficult to measure exactly what subjects read, researchers are forced to rely on consumers' self-report of the memory of readership. Because it would be impractical and too expensive for a single advertiser to pay for readership research on just its advertisements, the research is usually conducted by firms like Starch[4] or Readex[5] for several advertisers at the same time.

Recall testing is different in the sense that it asks subjects if they can remember reading or seeing ads instead of whether they can recognize ads they supposedly read earlier. For example, in a recall measure of ad readership in a magazine, researchers would show subjects the cover of the magazine issue and ask them to recall specific ads they remembered seeing in that issue—without any hints or cues. Because most subjects probably could not recall a single ad under such circumstances, print ad readership is usually measured by recognition.

It is not really practical to measure recognition of television advertisements because researchers would have to play a recording of a television program and ask subjects if they recalled seeing individual ads on that program. Therefore, viewership and memory of television ads is measured by recall. Operating in specific cities, researchers telephone a sample of households to find people who said they watched a particular television program the previous night—the program on which the test commercial was shown. After using screening questions to verify that the subjects did indeed watch the program, researchers ask subjects to name brands for which they saw advertising. That is *unaided recall*, meaning subjects are not given any cues to stimulate their memory. Researchers then ask *aided recall* questions, in which they ask subjects if they remember advertisements for a particular product category or brand.

Audience Research

Advertisers place their messages in advertising vehicles because they want the messages to be seen by certain consumers. Consequently, they need to know how many and what kind of people are likely to be in the audience of various advertising vehicles. That is why audience research is so important. Although advertisers make decisions about expectations of exposure to their advertisements at some future time, they must make those decisions on the basis of data about audiences at time in the past. And, even though they want to know how many people saw their advertisements, they must often compromise and settle for estimates of the number of people who saw the advertising vehicle (e.g., television program or newspaper) in which the ad appeared. It is not practical to try to measure the people who saw the ad. Research about advertising audiences, therefore, is about the audiences of advertising vehicles and not the ads themselves. Furthermore, while it is possible to measure audiences of some types of advertising media (radio stations, television programs, magazines, newspapers, and websites), other types cannot be measured. An advertiser will know how many pieces of direct mail advertising she mailed but cannot tell how many were received and read.

Print Audience Research

One measure of magazine and newspaper readership is circulation, or number of copies sold. Such measures can be quite precise because they are based on physical units that can be counted as they come off the press and are distributed. Publishers can subtract the number of unsold copies to ascertain the number of copies that were sold through subscriptions or single-copy sales. Independent auditing organizations, like the Audit Bureau of Circulations,[6] Business Publications Audit of Circulation (BPA International),[7] and Verified Audit of Circulation[8] verify circulation data of newspapers and magazines and assure advertisers of their accuracy of the circulation data.

However, circulation data show only the number of copies of the newspaper or magazine that were sold, and that is not the same as the number of people who saw a particular issue. More than one person reads each issue, and advertisers are more interested in the number of people who read a publication than the number of copies that were sold. An earlier section of this chapter described how Simmons Market Research Bureau and Mediamark Research, Inc., interview carefully selected national samples of households and consumers about their product consumption. Those same surveys also ask consumers to report their exposure to specific magazines and television programs, local newspapers, and types of radio stations. Data from the samples are projected to audience estimates for the national population, and it is important to recognize that they are only estimates. Those data are used by advertisers to select advertising vehicles because they show which advertising vehicles are likely to be read, seen, and heard by the advertisers' target audience.

Broadcast Audience Research

Researchers also rely on samples to estimate the number of people who watch television programs or listen to radio stations. Nielsen Media Research[9] measures audiences for network and cable television programs and satellite services by placing electronic meters in a carefully selected sample of more than 5,000 households. Those meters measure the program viewing (duration of tuning to particular channels) on every television set in each of the sample households. A major issue about Nielsen's measurement of television audiences is whether anyone is in the room while the television set is turned on. Viewers in each household use a Nielsen People Meter to signal that they are in the room watching the set. Those people meters allow Nielsen to estimate demographics of the viewing audience—provided that viewers in the sample are conscientious about using the people meter.

The meter technology is too expensive to measure audiences of most local television stations, so Nielsen asks viewers in sample households to record their viewing in paper diaries. That diary information is supplemented by meter information (not people meters) in the largest television markets where more money is spent on local television advertising.

Audiences of national and network radio stations are measured by RADAR (Radio's All Dimension Audience Research), a division of Statistical Research, Inc.[10] RADAR conducts 12,000 telephone interviews per year to ask listeners to list the networks and national stations they listen to. Arbitron Radio uses diaries to compile audience estimates for local radio stations.[11] Nielsen/NetRatings measures Internet site visits and audiences by collecting real-time data from a panel of 57,000 home users and 8,000 at-work users.[12]

Test-Market Research

The most realistic way to use research to measure advertising's effects is to conduct actual advertising campaigns in **test-market** cities and compare the sales results in the two cities. This technique is not used very often because it takes a long time and is very expensive. You would have to select two cities that are very similar in important demographic characteristics such as income, race, and age. The two cities ought to be similar in cultural and climatic conditions as well. Ideally, they should be geographically close together but not so close that media vehicles from one city can be seen in the other.

You would have to use advertising strategies that are identical in all respects but one—the variable that you are testing. For example, suppose you wanted to measure the effect of television commercials. You might use the same newspaper ad in both cities. In one city, you would supplement the newspaper ad with television commercials on local television stations. You would run the campaign for two or three months, and then you would compare sales of the product in the two cities. Much of the difference in sales could be attributed to the use of television in the one market. Not many advertisers are willing to take the time to set up such a test, wait two or three months for results, and spend the money required to conduct such research.

Practical versus Theoretical Research

A useful distinction between types of advertising research is practical versus theoretical. *Practical* research is like the research described in the preceding paragraphs. Its objective is to help advertisers reduce risk when making real advertising decisions. It is sometimes **proprietary**, which means it is conducted for the sole use of one advertiser and the results are not revealed to others. Much practical research, however, is **syndicated**, which means it measures phenomena for many different companies and is available (in printed or electronic format) to any organization that pays for it. The research that Nielsen Media Research conducts about television audiences is an example of syndicated research.

Some practical research appears in scholarly journals, such as a study that tested different advertising strategies to increase responses to the 2000 Census.[13] That study is an excellent example of practical research that sought to understand the effect of advertising on socially desirable consumer behavior. It is also a very good model of a research report that explains the background problem, methodology, and results of a research study with important societal implications.

In April 1998, the U.S. Census Bureau researched paid advertising messages that were designed to encourage citizens to return their census forms. The Census Bureau had traditionally relied on free public service advertising to encourage responses, but a low response rate in 1990 forced it to consider paid messages it could control in 2000. This study reports the results of a test campaign in Sacramento, CA, and Columbia, SC.

Before the test campaign started, the Census Bureau's advertising agency used focus group research to develop an appropriate message strategy and media strategy. The agency produced advertising messages for television, radio, newspapers, out-of-home media (billboards, transit advertisements, and bus-shelter ads), and a public information campaign in local schools. The advertising campaign in the test cities ran from March through June 1998.

The Census Bureau conducted a telephone survey at the end of the campaign to measure how the advertising messages increased awareness and knowledge of the census and encouraged citizens to return completed forms. It used a random-digit dialing technique to generate telephone numbers for the survey in the two test sites. That technique increased the likelihood that new or unlisted telephone numbers were included. Surveyors asked respondents about their media use, level of civic participation, recall of Census Bureau advertising, and demographic information.

The researchers were aware of three limitations of their research, limitations that are present in many advertising research studies: (1) Respondents could have heard about the census from sources other than paid advertising messages—including news coverage and activities in the local community; (2) the study would have been improved if the researchers had measured response in a control city that did not receive any of the messages; (3) the test cities were not representative of the U.S. population, and the results could not be generalized to the larger population. As is the case with much advertising research, however, budget restrictions prevented the researchers from conducting a more rigorous study.

To measure exposure to the paid messages, researchers asked respondents if they recalled seeing or hearing advertising in each of several media sources. They created an advertising exposure index for each respondent by adding the number of sources that were recalled, and that index became a dependent variable in the study. The researchers recognized that this index did not measure frequency of exposure and that it treated all sources equally. That was another example of how advertising researchers must sometimes make compromises for practical reasons.

The researchers learned that 80 percent of the people surveyed had heard about the census through advertising from at least one of the media sources. They used regression analysis to assess the impact of demographic and other factors on the dependent variable of advertising exposure. That analysis showed that civic participation, newspaper readership, education, and radio listening had statistically significant effects on exposure to advertising messages about the census. So did ethnicity—the effect was significant for black respondents but no other nonwhite group.

The researchers were also interested in the impact of the paid messages on knowledge about the census, and they created a knowledge index for each respondent based on the number of correct responses to a series of questions about how government agencies used census information. Using regression analysis again, they learned that higher levels of income and education were positively associated with census knowledge. They also discovered that advertising exposure had a positive effect on knowledge, even when they controlled for education, income, and ethnicity. (An appendix to the article includes the questions used to measure media consumption, civic participation, advertising exposure, and census knowledge.)

Having measured the effect of the advertising messages on awareness and behavior, the researchers were most interested, of course, in the effect on behavior—whether respondents mailed back their census form. That dependent variable was operationalized by matching returned forms with names of people in the sample. In other words, the researchers did not have to rely on a self-report measure by respondents.

For that dependent variable, the results were somewhat confounding. Some of the variables (notably income and education) that had been positively associated with awareness and knowledge of the census were not significantly related to completing and returning the census form. On the other hand, level of civic participation, the expectation of receiving a census form, and ethnicity significantly predicted the likelihood of returning the form. Most importantly, exposure to the paid advertising messages had a weak but negative relationship with returning the form.

Did the results of this limited test in 1998 suggest that the Census Bureau should not use paid advertising in 2000? Apparently not, because we know it did use paid advertising. This study did not reveal the nature of the paid messages, so it is possible that the research results suggested that the agency try other message strategies. The Census Bureau also knew the test cities were not representative and that the results could not be generalized to the rest of the country. This may also have been an example of a case where advertising decision makers proceeded in the face of research results.

. The researchers did find that the paid advertising messages appeared to increase knowledge about the census. Respondents with higher exposure levels had higher knowledge scores. This led the researchers to conclude that paid advertising may have had an indirect effect on behavior by creating a higher level of expectation among some groups that they would receive a form in the mail. That level of expectation did seem to have a positive effect on behavior, and the researchers recommended that paid advertising messages in 2000 try to make citizens anticipate the forms in the mail.

Theoretical research, on the other hand, tries to discover and test general principles of advertising that might be applied to many situations. One example of theoretical research attempted to study the effect of different background patterns and colors on viewers' attitudes toward full-motion video commercials on web pages.[14] The study did not have an immediate practical application but could guide future advertising strategies.

Even theoretical research faces limitations. These researchers had to have access to computers capable of running audio and video software to show the commercials on the website. That restricted them to a college campus, and their subjects were students at a Midwestern university.

The researchers prepared three web pages that differed only in their complexity—number of items, color of page elements, and movement or animation of some elements. The topic of all three sites was the same—a state lottery. The website resembled the actual site for the lottery, and the researchers assumed the students would have a natural interest in the lottery. The simplest stimulus condition had a black background, and the background of the moderate (middle) condition was light blue. The complex site had the same light blue background but had blinking phrases and an animated car moving across the screen. To verify that the pages did indeed vary in complexity, the researchers pretested the pages with a sample of students. Those students' ratings confirmed that the pages differed in complexity.

Subjects went to a campus computer lab for the experiment, where they were randomly assigned to one of the three web-page stimuli. They were told to view the assigned site and watch the lottery commercial that was part of the site. When the commercial ended, subjects completed an online survey and emailed it to the researchers.

The dependent variables in the study were attitude-toward-the-commercial (A_{ad}), attitude-toward-the-lottery (A_b), purchase intention (PI), attitude-toward-the-website (A_{ws}), and attention-to-the-commercial (ATT_{ad}). The researchers hypothesized that complex backgrounds on the site would have negative influences on (A_{ad}), (PI), and (A_{ws}). They also hypothesized that the complex background would reduce (ATT_{ad}) more than the simple background. Finally, they hypothesized that the (A_{ws}) would have a positive impact on (A_{ad}), (A_b), and (PI).

The researchers used analysis of variance (ANOVA) and multivariate analysis of variance (MANOVA) to help them understand the results. The data supported the hypothesis that background complexity of the website would reduce A_{ad}, A_b, PI, and A_{ws}. On the other hand, differences in background complexity did not affect attitudes toward the ad (A_{ad}). The researchers suggested that this may have been an artifact of the experiment—that subjects did not want to admit (or could not admit) that they did not pay attention to the ad even though they had been told to do so. The third hypothesis was supported: Subjects' attitudes toward the website had a direct effect on A_{ad}, A_b, and PI.

Summary

Advertisers use research to help them make decisions throughout the process of creating advertising. Research does not usually give them definitive answers or directions, but it does reduce the risks and uncertainties associated with such decisions.

Target market research uses surveys of large numbers of consumers to ascertain product usage levels, media exposure patterns and demographic data about product users. Simmons Market Research Bureau and Mediamark Research, Inc. are two major suppliers of such research.

At the next stage of the advertising process, advertisers rely on positioning research to determine what product benefits are important and how consumers use the product. Such research is more likely to be qualitative (projective techniques and focus groups, for example) than quantitative. An example of such research is that done by Y & R for its clients.

Advertisers use pretest and posttest message research (recall and recognition) to help them craft effective advertisements. It is difficult for such research to show a direct connection between the advertising and sales or knowledge results because so many factors affect such outcomes. Nevertheless, advertisers sometimes use split-run or inquiry tests to establish such connections.

Advertisers want to know how many people saw their advertisements. While audience research cannot show that with certainty, it can estimate how many people were potentially in the audience for the advertising.

By using test cities to compare advertising strategies and measuring sales in those cities, advertisers can identify effective advertising. However, such research is costly and takes a long time, so it is not widely used.

Most advertising research is practical because it is designed to help advertisers reduce risk when making real advertising decisions. One example is the research that was designed to help the U.S. Census Bureau identify ways to increase voluntary response to the Census. Other research is considered theoretical because it tries to identify general principles that might be applied to a number of situations. An example is a study that studied the effect of different background patterns on viewers' attitudes toward web pages.

Endnotes

1. *http://www.smrb.com*
2. *http://www.mediamark.com*
3. *http://www.yr.com/bav/what_is.html*
4. *http://www.roper.com/starch/*
5. *http://www.readexresearch.com*
6. *http://www.accessabc.com*
7. *http://www.bpai.com*
8. *http://www.verifiedaudit.com*

9. *http://www.nielsenmedia.com* For a more detailed explanation of how Nielsen conducts its research, see *http://www/nielsenmedia.com/whatratingsmean/*

10. *http://www.sriresearch.com*

11. *http://www.arbitron.com*

12. *http://www.nielsen-netratings.com*

13. Nancy Bates and Sara Buckley, "Exposure to Paid Advertising and Returning a Census Form." *Journal of Advertising Research*, January–April 2000, 65–73.

14. Julie S. Stevenson, Gordon C. Bruner II, and Anand Kumar. "Web Page Background and Viewer Attitudes." *Journal of Advertising Research*, January–April 2000, 29–34.

6

The Logic of Social and Behavioral Science

Douglas M. McLeod

Phillip J. Tichenor

Scientific inquiry, as a mode of knowledge production, blends abstract theorizing with concrete empirical observation. Scientific approaches ground the gathering of evidence in higher-order theoretical reasoning. Knowledge is pursued in an atmosphere of rigor in logic and measurement that, when thoroughly articulated, allows others to determine whether they, using the same combination of reasoning and procedure, would come to similar conclusions.

"Theory" implies abstraction, which means a drawing back from experience and observation so as to conceptualize a problem in general terms. "Social conflict," "social capital," "social status," and "self-esteem" are abstract concepts that may have particular operational definitions for given research purposes. An "attitude" is an abstraction in the sense that it refers to a predisposition that is not observed directly but is inferred from a series of observations about a person's behavioral responses.

How are abstractions and empiricism jointly employed in the production of scientific knowledge? The answer is that there is no uniform way of blending the two, nor is there a single form of abstract reasoning or empirical methodology that scientists must employ. There is, however, agreement that both abstractions and empirical methods must be used with a high degree of control. "Control" is basic to science, starting with the control arising from rigor in statements of problems, concepts, and conceptual schemes and hypotheses. Science means controlled observation and/or experimental methods that may be replicated by others. It is controlled use of language in presenting statements of theory and procedure that can be understood uniformly by others. Terms that are called the "jargon" of a discipline are necessary consequences of the rigorous use of language for scientific purposes.[1] Such a pattern of control in all phases of intellectual and procedural activity sets science apart from "common-sense" knowledge gained from everyday experience.

In the course of conducting scientific investigations, researchers must make many decisions in the interest of enhancing the growth of knowledge. Many of these most basic decisions are related to the following processes:

1. Defining research problems
2. Constructing explanations
3. Making observations and testing hypotheses
4. Developing research programs

Defining Research Problems

Identification of a problem for social and behavioral research is itself a process of abstraction. From the complexity of events of concern in a topical area of interest, an investigator selects and formulates a problem in terms that give it some generalizability and make it amenable to systematic study.

The identification of a research problem may seem at first glance to involve few if any abstractions. Problem selection is very much influenced by the investigator's ideological orientation; abstraction can remove some of this bias. A researcher might start with a question of how to develop an effective advertising campaign to stimulate demand for Brand X. The research question might be: Which of a given set of test commercials best raises the consumer's desire to purchase the product? Or, what type of advertising appeal works most effectively to raise the consumer's interest in Brand X? Thus far, these questions do not yield to much abstraction and pursuing them will not add much to general knowledge either, if the investigator seeks only to analyze the sales volume of Brand X. Testing various combinations of content characteristics to find the one that works best is one way to get results; such an approach is often called "cut and try" experimentation.[2] Knowledge generated using this procedure, however, is not the ultimate knowledge that a scientist seeks, because it is not systematic and it does not by itself uncover general principles. To state a problem that will produce systematic, generalizable knowledge requires abstraction, stepping back from the immediate case at hand to identify underlying concepts and the principles that link them together.

Suppose the aforementioned advertising campaign is restated: What is the relationship between level of exposure to television advertising and compulsive consumer behavior? Now the question is both more abstract and more likely to contribute to general knowledge. "Advertising" and "consumer behavior" are now treated as abstract concepts dealing with one aspect of the role of the media in U.S. society. There may be both applied and theoretical ingredients in a project, and one may lead to the other. But the problem must be stated in general terms if it is to be subjected to scientific inquiry.

The importance of abstraction in defining research problems is apparent even in situations that may seem to require immediate, concrete answers, such as social policy areas. As Greer[3] points out, such problems are among the foremost in stimulating social research. Part of the value of abstraction in these areas comes from the fact that policy problems reflect value concerns in society. An example is the study of violence in media content and the consequences for members of audiences exposed to that content. A study of youth gang behavior in Los Angeles, conducted merely in the interest of controlling gang violence, is not likely to add much to knowledge, except in an experiential way. However, the research takes on greater importance when the problem is related to behavioral norms in certain environments and the role of conduct codes in the process of adolescent socialization.

While some research problems have their roots in value and policy concerns, abstraction not only contributes to generalizability, but also serves to put the investigator in a more detached position. Some examples may be seen in other areas of research on communication. There are many value and policy reasons why a better understanding of communication relationships between persons may be desirable, and there are many ways of studying those relationships. Research on **co-orientation**[4] (the extent to which communicators and their audiences perceive a situation in similar ways) puts self-other perceptions into a framework that is both abstract and, presumably, generalizable to a wider range of situations.

Constructing Explanations

The ultimate purpose of abstraction in scientific investigation is to develop and test explanations. While many scientific investigations begin with the modest goal of systematically describing the "idiographic"[5] characteristics of a given phenomenon, most research progresses to "nomothetic"[6] concerns for explaining how things work.

We encounter many things in everyday life that may seem like explanations, but are not true scientific explanations. Typologies that categorize observations, while contributing to knowledge, do not provide explanations. Similarly, identifying common features or shared characteristics of phenomena does not constitute an explanation. Such might be the case when a doctor recognizes the symptoms of a disease; identifying the disease in and of itself doesn't explain the symptoms unless the doctor articulates the causal processes that produced the symptoms. Observing that two events co-occur or that two variables covary together may be offered as an explanation, but without a rigorous delineation of the processes that connect them, a true explanation has not been constructed. Simply noting that the decline in U.S. political participation corresponded to the growth of television does not qualify as an explanation. Finally, the ability to make accurate predictions does not necessarily imply that an explanation is driving the prediction. A public opinion poll might be able to make a very accurate prediction of the outcome of an election, yet provide no insight as to why people are voting the way they are. An explanation involves establishing the nature of the relationships between relevant concepts, which may illuminate why objects share characteristics, why factors covary, or why accurate predictions can be made.[7]

Creating explanations for a given phenomenon involves attempts to answer a number of related questions: What are the antecedent factors and processes? What are the consequent factors and processes? What contingent conditions are involved, and are there any potentially confounding factors to be considered? The network of propositions that are used to construct an explanation for a phenomenon and these related processes is called a "theory." In other words, a theory is essentially an explanation.

All scientific explanations are considered tentative, subject to continued testing through the process of empirical observation. These explanations are continually refined, expanded, and even replaced by more effective explanations. The value of a given theory may be evaluated using a number of standards. First, is the explanation logically consistent? Does it make predictions that are not blatantly obvious? Is it abstract enough to explain a range of phenomena? Is the theory capable of being tested, and does it possess a relatively high ratio of testable statements to assumptions? Are there potential observations that could disconfirm it, such that the conditions under which the theory would be considered untenable are readily apparent? Finally, is the theory understandable to other social scientists and do they find it useful?[8]

The construction of scientific theories, and the resultant generation of knowledge, are part of an ongoing process that alternates between abstract reasoning and concrete observation. Abstract reasoning involves constructing a generalized explanation. Concrete observation involves testing these explanations using data collected from the material world. At the abstract level, concepts are the building blocks that are used to form a theoretical explanation. Concepts may take many forms in theory construction. First, there are units of analysis, the objects that are the focus of the explanation. One of the most common units of analysis in mass communication research is the individual. Numerous studies are interested in explaining the antecedents and consequences of individual differences in media use behaviors.[9] Alternatively, research may adopt other units of analysis, such as communities,[10] nation states,[11] or as in many content analysis studies, content units such as the television news story,[12] television program,[13] or television character.[14]

Variable concepts describe ways in which units of analysis differ. Social and behavioral science requires the identification and measurement of variation in units of analysis. The question "Why do television stations broadcast entertainment containing violent content?" implies an assumption that the content might under some conditions be different. Or if the question is about the consequences of violent content for viewers, variation across content and viewer reactions are implied. When a characteristic has different values for different cases of individuals, it is referred to as a *variable*. Amount of viewing of violent content will not be the same for all members of a given audience; it varies from one person to another. "Amount of viewing," then, is variable, as are level of education, degree of alienation of individuals, and degree of urbanization of communities, to mention a few.

Creating explanations is a process of identifying potential relationships between variables at the abstract level of reasoning. At this level, variable concepts are linked by relational concepts. The explanation is then tested at the concrete level by examining the extent of covariation between variable concepts at the level of measured indicators. Testing hypotheses about variable relationships by making concrete observations is a way of testing the validity of an abstract theoretical explanation.

Moving from the abstract theoretical level to the concrete level and back again engages the researcher in two interrelated and recursive processes of concept explication:[15] meaning analysis and empirical analysis. Meaning analysis takes abstract variables used in explanations to the level of concrete indicators by beginning with a conceptual definition that denotes the meanings of concepts in abstract terms. Based on the conceptual definitions, operational definitions detailing how these variables are to be measured are derived. Once these indicators are identified, formal observations can be made. Once the data from these observations are compiled, the researcher engages in empirical analysis of the results to test the validity of both the underlying abstract explanation and the conceptual and operational definitions. Both the theoretical explanation and concept definitions are then refined for future investigations.[16]

In essence then, the production of scientific knowledge is an ongoing cycle: creating an explanation, identifying the concepts in that explanation, performing meaning analysis to derive concrete indicators of those concepts, making empirical observations to test hypotheses about the relationship between those concepts, engaging in empirical analysis of the measured concepts to refine the definitions and measurement of those concepts, and ultimately refining the theoretical explanation that links those concepts together. The cycle then begins again in a new investigation. Theoretical explanations are constructed at the abstract level; hypotheses are tested at the concrete, empirical level. Meaning analysis and empirical analysis link the abstract concepts to concrete indicators.[17]

Constructing hypotheses for testing involves the creation of a logical rationale that is derived from a combination of the following sources: past experience, previous research, existing theoretical frameworks, and logical reasoning. The past experiences and informal observations of the researcher often provide inspiration and intuitive clues about relevant concepts and their interrelationships. Results of prior research can be extrapolated to substantiate the proposed hypotheses. In addition to research results, the existing literature may also provide abstract theoretical explanations that can be adopted or adapted to reinforce the explanatory rationale used to derive testable hypotheses. Finally, the researcher must introduce some degree of unique logical reasoning to cement the linkages between abstract variables and concrete indicators, between the variables of the theoretical explanation, and between the concrete indicators involved in hypothesis testing. Together these factors comprise a theoretical rationale that links concepts together, like mortar to bricks in the wall of scientific knowledge.

Making Observations and Testing Hypotheses

The ultimate dependence on observation and experience holds for all communication research. Two investigators who differ widely in their choice of abstractions will, if following the scientific norm, accept specific observations in the same light. Regardless of their models concerning the consequences of televised violence, they would ordinarily be expected to agree on the fact that in a given experiment, say, 53 percent of the subjects displayed aggressive behavior as operationalized by the investigator. There may be differing interpretations of the meaning of those behaviors, but the observed empirical facts themselves are, in the norms of science, the same for all. Findings must stand the test of interobserver agreement and reproducibility, meaning that observers using the same procedures should get the same result.

Observation alone, however, is not a sufficient criterion for a scientific procedure. The observations must be relevant to a theory, meaning in the specific case they must bear on one or more hypotheses. A **hypothesis** is a statement of relations, based on the best that can be derived from more general assumptions and prior evidence. While hypotheses take different forms, they are generally of the "If A, then B" form. They may be qualified in various ways, depending on the conditional relations between A and B. Is A hypothetically sufficient for B to occur? Or, is it necessary without being sufficient? Or, as still another alternative, is A a contributory condition, *increasing* the *likelihood* of B?

Hypotheses are central to the scientific process. The act of stating a hypothesis forces one to have the basic problem statement in hand and clearly defined.[18] Second, stating a hypothesis requires thinking out the contingent conditions under which the hypothesis should hold and the linkages between this and other hypotheses. Third, the process of establishing a hypothesis forces the investigator to demonstrate how the hypothesis may be deduced from a more general body of theory and higher-order statements. To illustrate this, where does television viewing fit in the total pattern of leisure-time behavior available to a media audience? Is it reasonable to hypothesize about television viewing in general, or does it depend on what kind of viewing one is studying? Does higher education lead to an increase in certain kinds of television viewing and to a decrease in another kind of viewing? By considering such questions in stating and clarifying hypotheses, the investigator increases the likelihood of generating more *specific* knowledge and the likelihood of developing generalizations as well.

The statement of hypotheses is the key to operationalizing the test of a theory. Suppose the above question of television viewing is expressed in a hypothesis, such as: "The higher the level of education of viewers in a metropolitan area, the higher the viewing of documentary programs." Then if, in a sample of viewers in Cleveland, the investigator finds a high positive correlation between number of years of formal schooling and frequency of viewing such programs as "CBS Reports," the conclusion would be that the evidence *supports* the hypothesis.

Furthermore, stating a hypothesis provides the specific points of reference for evidence, or data. *Testability* is a basic criterion of a theory. If a theory is to contribute to the growth of scientific knowledge, it must be expressed in a form such that it may be tested. This allows for the evaluation of theories, which prevents theoretical "chaos." Lakatos[19] labels this view "methodological falsificationism." From this perspective, theories are never proved or disproved; they are retained and abandoned on the basis of "survival of the fittest." Lakatos advocates a "sophisticated" version of falsificationism by which a theory is supported if it both explains empirical observations better than its rivals and yields new facts.

When can a hypothesis be said to be "fully verified"? The answer in a sense is "never," since all empirical knowledge is tentative. There is always the possibility that a hypothesis, however strongly it may be held among scientists at a given time, may be rejected or modified at some time in the future. Hypotheses themselves are generalizations, and future research may turn up situations in which the generalization does not hold. Nevertheless, there is a point at which it is necessary to take stock of the evidence and theories about an issue so important that it may have engaged dozens or hundreds of investigators and an enormous commitment of funds and other resources over a period of years or decades. What can be said today, for example, about the impact that political content of mass media has on voter behavior? What *does* one conclude about the forces affecting whether certain kinds of content gets into newspapers, television programs, and magazines in the first place? The evidence at any given stage must be evaluated, and how should that be done?

The commonly adopted (and conservative) procedure is to evaluate hypotheses according to degree of support, which ordinarily means a joint consideration of amount of testing and the outcome of that testing. Practically, it means testing variations of a hypothesis. In the case of violent media content and individual behavior, there is now a great deal of evidence supporting the general hypothesis that the more aggressive the content viewed, the more likely the subjected individual is to behave aggressively later on.[20] This general hypothesis has received support in settings involving movies, cartoons, adult programming, and news and entertainment formats. At the same time, the media-aggression hypothesis has been sharply qualified and delimited. It has become a series of interrelated hypotheses, couched in an increasingly complex series of conditional statements. This is a normal progression in the development of knowledge and in building theory. An initial hypothesis may be neither rejected, nor supported in all tests and instances. Additional and accumulative research often leads, as it has in this case, to a specification of the conditions under which the hypothesis holds and does not hold.

As a result, accumulated research and evidence rarely provide a definitive answer to whether one or the other of competing theories is more correct. There are contrasting views on the effect chain ownership on the quality of newspapers. Some scholars argue that chain ownership provides more organizational resources, which improves organizational performance and content quality. Other theorists say that chain ownership prompts the newspaper to become more concerned with the well-being of the corporation than that of the community, producing a decline in performance and content quality.[21] Which theory is more correct? Research has yielded evidence showing both positive and negative consequences of chain ownership.[22] The results seem to vary depending on the conditions of the study. The answer to the question "Which theory is correct?" is not simple. The conditions and consequences need to be specified through exhaustive investigation. As a result, the state of knowledge will be much more complete. Specification of complexity is a common outcome of the pursuit of knowledge.

Developing Research Programs

Grounding scientific investigation in past research is one way to link studies to a broader body of scientific knowledge. Isolated studies contribute disproportionately less to the growth of knowledge. Similarly, researchers should strive to develop a research program that links their various investigations into a larger whole. The linkages that bind studies together into a research program may be shared concepts and/or theoretical propositions. There are several incentives, both theoretical and practical, for a researcher to develop an integrated research program.

Most importantly, programmatic research contributes greatly to growth of scientific knowledge. A progressive research program yields more comprehensive, sophisticated, and robust explanations than isolated studies. Initial investigations may lead naturally to new, more provocative research questions. Follow-up studies may provide solutions to initial problems and new ways of looking at old phenomena. Knowledge advances more quickly as a result of serial investigations by producing refinements in theory and method and in conceptual and operational definitions.

Systematic research programs provide practical advantages to the career development of researchers. They provide continuity and visibility to a scholar's body of work. Studies that can be amalgamated into a larger whole add to the impact of the research on the field of study. Finally, programmatic research development is often an important criterion in a scholar's promotion and tenure decisions.

Issues in Social and Behavioral Science

In conducting social and behavioral research, the investigator must go beyond the general standards of scientific inquiry in terms of logical rigor, objective observation, and controlled measurement. The investigator must first define a problem in a way that makes it amenable to study. In conceptualizing that problem, the investigator must address a number of issues including:

1. Epistemology
2. Induction versus deduction
3. Causation versus prediction
4. Micro versus macro models

These issues and questions force a choice about the perspective or frame of reference used in approaching a research problem. The choices that are made may have ramifications for the scope of the problem to be addressed, the specific hypotheses to be tested, and the selection of evidence to be gathered. The researcher must address these issues in the planning phases of research; the issues may be reconsidered at some stage, such as when one project is complete and the researcher moves on to a new stage of inquiry.

Epistemology

Epistemology refers to the origin of knowledge and the routes used to establish it. Social science is generally seen as adhering to the norms of **logical positivism**, sometimes referred to as the *classical empiricist* point of view. The positivistic view is that all knowledge derives from experience or, more specifically, from observational experience. Historically, the move toward positivism was a reaction to what its adherents objected to as purely speculative reasoning.[23] While there are many consequences of a positivist outlook, one of the most frequently stated (and most hotly debated) is that theoretical concepts are defined entirely in terms of things that can be observed or determined empirically.[24] In the most extreme version of positivism, a concept may be broken down into its observational terms, with no surplus meaning. However, this extreme view is not strictly followed in social science; research involves a mixture of assertions, some of which can be tested empirically and some of which are treated as assumptions.

Positivism has been a continuing issue in social and behavioral research as illustrated by the difference between a Freudian approach and a more positivist learning-theory approach to understanding the relationship between the viewing of violent television content and aggressive behavior. Freudian psychoanalytic theory may state that gratification from viewing an aggressive television drama would be based on nonobservable characteristics of the personality. The explanation would be rooted in Freudian theories of the personality. The pleasure derived from viewing violent media content might be seen as the expression of desires repressed by internal psychological mechanisms.

By contrast, a positivist approach, such as might be taken from a learning-theory perspective, would produce a hypothesis that is more clearly limited to observables and research operations. The hypothesis might take a form such as, "The more intense the aggressive stimulus, the greater the likelihood that the subsequent response will be aggressive." Both stimulus intensity and response aggressiveness would be defined in terms of observable characteristics. The hypothesized impact of violent television programming on viewer behavior is then treated largely as an empirically testable stimulus-response process.

There are other approaches to the question of television and aggressive behavior that might strike a compromise between these extremes, but it is correct to say that social science research by and large swings toward the positivistic end of the continuum. Similarly, much mass communication research has been strongly influenced by the positivist tradition. The rationale for positivism rests on the view that observation is an indispensable requirement of scientific investigation.

One objection to the extreme version of positivism is that complete reduction of concepts to measurable indicators implies an unrealistic notion of what scientific theories are or can become. Some critics have questioned the validity of using what they term "hard science"—that is, physical science—approaches to the study of society and human behavior. The Frankfurt School has objected to positivism on three counts: the inappropriateness of mechanistic approaches to the study of humanity, the inherently conservative nature of focusing only on that which currently exists, and the tendency of social science to reinforce "technocratic domination."[25]

A frequently stated perspective portrays an integrated theory as a network of concepts and propositions that are linked in only a few places to observational data.[26] In this portrayal, a body of knowledge or theory is depicted as a system of postulates that hovers or floats above a plane of empirical data.[27] The basic theoretical terms are "primitive" expressions that are implicitly defined by the postulates in which they occur. A lower layer of defined concepts may be identified, and they, in turn, are linked to operational concepts that refer to items that may be observed.

According to this "layer cake" perspective, the primitive terms in the postulate can be given only a partial interpretation, meaning that they and the defined concepts are not reducible to operations or observables alone. It has sometimes been argued that such a view of theory is simply testimony to the current state of development of the social and behavioral sciences. It must be remembered that this idea of a floating and partially uninterpreted postulate system, only partially linked to observables, has been stated largely for the physical, rather than social and behavioral, sciences.[28] The implication is that the linkage between a postulate system and the plane of observation is fundamentally the same, regardless of the substantive field involved.

Induction versus Deduction

The nature of the logic, or reasoning, is an important concern in the construction and testing of theory. Two types of logic are commonly used: **induction** and **deduction**.

Traditionally, a great deal of emphasis in the research literature of the social and behavioral sciences was placed on deductive reasoning, in which a hypothesis or conclusion is implied in the premises. One proceeds, then, from the general to the particular. From a set of assumptions, sometimes called axioms or *higher-order postulates*, one deduces the above hypothesis that the more aggressive the media content to which persons are exposed, the more likely these individuals are to engage in subsequent aggressive behavior. Social and behavioral research, placing a premium on deductive reasoning as *the* highest mode of scientific logic, has tended to endorse the philosophical and procedural perspective often termed *hypothetico-deductive* empiricism, in which specific empirical hypotheses were deduced from a set of higher-order statements taken as assumptions."[29]

Such reasoning might be contrasted with inductive reasoning, in which one proceeds inferentially from particulars to more general statements. Induction is used continuously, both in problem definition and in the interpretation of the results. An investigator might observe a case in which tension in one individual leads to avoidance of certain communications and, as a result, infer a general relationship between tension and avoidance. That would be a rather extreme case of inductive reasoning, but conceivable if the tension-avoidance relationship is then considered as a hypothesis for further testing. Also, generalization from measured results is an inductive process, such as when behavior among a sample of individuals is generalized to a larger population.

There are several reasons why a rigid adherence to the hypothetico-deductive approach alone, as *the* mode of scientific reasoning, is not entirely satisfactory. One is that the basic statements (axioms, postulates, or assumptions) are not necessarily arrived at themselves by a previous chain of deductive reasoning, but may have involved a considerable degree of inductive logic as well. There are the "creative leaps" of reasoning upon which science depends so heavily."[30] Also, the process of generalizing from a given set of evidence to a larger set of events or circumstances is largely an inductive process, and generalizing is a vital phase of scientific activity. It therefore seems more reasonable to conclude that both induction and deduction are used, either simultaneously or alternatively, in scientific activity. One might deduce that, given a set of assumptions about the joint consequences of age, social experience, and imitative behavior at particular developmental stages, aggressive activity is more likely to occur following one kind of media content than another. However, consideration of this reasoning might lead to the realization, arrived at inductively, that such content may have other consequences as well. The investigator may have observations indicating that violent content of a certain type leads some viewers to turn off the program and telephone their objections to the station. Generalizing from these observations (an inductive process), the investigator may reconsider some of the original assumptions about age and social experience and then make another try at the deductive scheme.

Rejecting a rigid deductive approach to the process does not mean denying the importance of either deductive logic or of hypotheses. Both are basic to research. It is more reasonable, however, to recognize that a deductive chain of reasoning is often a *reconstructed* logic, imposed on a set of statements that themselves were arrived at by both induction and deduction. An ultimate test of a chain of reasoning may be whether it is consistent from a deductive perspective, not whether it was reached that way in all its particulars.

Causation versus Prediction

Causation is an idea that has led to so much debate among scientists and philosophers that many investigators avoid using the term altogether. Some point out that science is both causal and predictive. The difference between the two is important. We may be able to use X to predict Y, even though little is known about the causal relationship between them. On the other hand, as Harre[31] observes, the causal mechanism of Darwinian evolutionary theory is well articulated, but it yields little ability to predict the emergence of new life forms.

In its most narrow sense, prediction means accounting for the future status of something, but, more particularly, stating under what conditions that situation may be expected to occur. A projected estimate of the number of television sets in U.S. households in 2010 is a prediction. Or one might base a prediction upon the convergence of two or more variables. The number of television sets in a nation might be predicted from the level of income, level of education, and availability of programming at a given time in a particular nation, based upon evidence already gathered from a sample of nations.

Important as prediction is, it would be difficult to argue that prediction alone is the goal of scientific research without concern for explanation of causes. In fact, some observers (e.g., Hage[32]) see prediction as constituting only a small part of the concern of social science, apart from economics. These observers would see the fundamental goal to be explanation, which implies analysis of causes. Some notion of causation permeates most research activity as well as conscious activity in general, as MacIver[33] has pointed out. This is not to imply that "causation" means the same thing to a scientist as it does to a non-scientist. The intrusion of a common-sense notion about a single cause-and-effect link for any phenomenon may encourage many investigators to abandon the idea of causes. Bronowski[34] is one observer who went so far as to insist that causation is an overemphasized aspect of scientific activity.

Nevertheless, in most research some idea of causation is fundamental. When we ask about the effects of violent media content, why soap operas are viewed, how people decide to adopt an innovation, or whether newspapers set public agendas, we are asking causal questions. Following Hume's[35] three criteria establishing causality, the researcher would look for: whether cause and effect covary, whether the cause precedes the effect, and whether the cause and effect do not appear independent of one another. Cook and Campbell make the additional stipulation that all potentially confounding third variables are controlled.[36]

What we need not accept—and ordinarily should not accept—is the idea of single causes and single effects. The answer to the question "Why?" in social and behavioral science is much more complex than the idea of single causation would suggest. Some of the more commonly used versions of causal thinking tend to emphasize single causes even when a more thorough analysis indicates greater complexity. MacIver pointed out some of the dangers of such oversimplification in causal thinking by his illustrations of *precipitants and incentives* as causal mechanisms.[37]

Consider the notion of precipitant as it might apply in a particular setting to the question of television and aggressive behavior. When John W. Hinckley, Jr., attempted to assassinate President Reagan, media coverage pointed out that the shooting was prompted by Hinckley's infatuation with actress Jodie Foster. Hinckley's preoccupation began after he saw her in the urban drama *Taxi Driver*. In this movie, the main character (Robert DeNiro) plots the assassination of a politician, while he becomes involved with Foster's character. Seeing this movie, then, was one of many potential precipitants to Hinckley's actions and thus was part of a causal pattern, even though a full answer to the question of why requires a far more extensive analysis.

A very familiar causal interpretation in the social and behavioral sciences leans on incentives or motives. Incentives might in turn be seen as related to perceptions of need, to modes of tension reduction, or to pleasure seeking of one type or another. The "uses and gratifications" approach to studying media behavior (see, for example, Blumler and Katz[38]) is in this tradition. Certain types of media behavior are explained as serving certain functions, foremost among which may be fulfillment of certain desires and specific wishes. Classic studies of soap opera listening[39] and newspaper reading[40] lean on causal explanations of this type. Similarly, studies of gatekeeper behavior[41] are based at least partly on interpretations of motivational causes.

Like the precipitant explanation, the incentive or motivation approach to causation may leave some questions unanswered. Explaining soap opera viewing by means of incentives may deal with only one or a cluster of factors, leaving aside the questions, among others, of social reinforcement, family and community setting, available content, communicative skills, and the symbolic characteristics of the soap operas themselves. Again, this is not to imply that any one investigator is not justified in concentrating on incentives or motivation in the study of such phenomena. What the illustration indicates, instead, is that a motivational explanation is inherently a partial explanation of causal forces, just as a selection of any one of the other factors suggested here also would be a partial explanation. The obligation of the scientist is to recognize that fact when it occurs.

The complexity of the causal process and the importance of considering multiple causation are illustrated by the Zamora murder case. When 15-year-old Ronald Zamora was charged with murder, his defense attorney argued that Zamora was not guilty by reason of insanity because of his "prolonged, intense, involuntary, subliminal television intoxication."[42] Did the television exposure "cause" the murder? The jury rejected this contention. The event would seem to be the result of a long history and complex set of conditions; the media violence was part of the causal pattern, but only a part. It is entirely defensible to study the role of television or other media in precipitating acts of violence, but the burden is on the investigator to point out that unless other factors are considered, causation is being studied only in a very limited sense.

In view of the multiple aspects of causation, a more basic approach considers the *necessary and sufficient conditions* for an event. A necessary condition is one without which the event in question will not occur. A sufficient condition is one whose presence always implies that the event will occur. While the difference between these two types of conditions may seem very clear in a logical sense, specifying them for a particular research problem is one of the most important and difficult tasks the investigator faces. One reason is that conditions are often mutually dependent, meaning that a particular condition may be one of a number of conditions that are jointly sufficient for an event to occur. There may be another set of conditions that, as a set, is also sufficient, meaning then that neither set of factors is, as a whole, necessary. There may be many different sets of conditions, each of which might be sufficient to cause someone to commit a murder. In each set or combination of conditions, there are factors that may be necessary in the sense that without each one the other would not suffice. When we speak of violent television content as a precipitant to murder, we mean that the content must be considered jointly with other conditions without which the violent content would not have led to the same result.

In many areas of the social and behavioral sciences, causes are dealt with through functional analysis. Functionalism was introduced in social science by sociologists such as Comte,[43] Spencer,[44] Pareto,[45] and Durkheim[46] and by anthropologists Radcliffe-Brown[47] and Malinowski.[48] These scholars shared a concern for those structures and processes that serve the "function" of system maintenance. Although originally applied at the system level, functional reasoning can be used at various levels of analysis.

Stinchcombe[49] regards a functional explanation as one in which the consequences of some behavior are essential ingredients of the causes of that behavior. If the function of soap opera viewing is to reduce tension, the viewing may be continued for that reason. The researcher must be careful in the use of such causal reasoning: assuming that the cause of a given phenomenon is the same as its effect is tautological. What Stinchcombe is stressing, however, is not a tautology, but reciprocal causation in a dynamic process.

Stinchcombe pointed out that functional explanations may be especially appropriate when the outcomes of action are quite uniform and the behavior causing those consequences is highly varied. This situation, in which different processes or acts produce the same result, is often referred to as equifinality by some systems theorists. A variety of leisure-time behaviors, such as television viewing and comic-book reading, may fulfill an escapist function. Similarly, a wide variety of conventions for reporting news in a community (and not reporting certain kinds), may have identical consequences for maintaining a low level of tension there.

Merton made several important observations about functions.[50] First, functions may or may not be acknowledged or recognized directly by participants in a process. In addition to raising this distinction between manifest and latent functions, Merton pointed out that elements in the system could also be dysfunctional. He argued that something may be both functional and dysfunctional to different elements or to different levels of the system.

Tichenor, Donohue, and Olien[51] observe that in certain situations, media coverage of an issue or event may lead to growth in knowledge for some individuals. Even though this may be functional to these individuals, the resultant increase in the "knowledge gap," based on differential rates of knowledge acquisition, may contribute to social inequality. Thus, what is functional at one level may be dysfunctional at another, which for some observers casts some doubt upon the utility of functional explanations of causality.

However, functional explanations have been widely used in communication research, at both individual and system levels. Berelson's[52] "What Missing the Newspaper Means" was a functionalist explanation for audience use of a mass medium. The "uses and gratifications" research mentioned earlier is equally functionalist.[53] By and large, the literature on impact of mass media on social systems is functionalist.[54]

Micro and Macro Models and Reductionism

Another choice an investigator faces is between microscopic and macroscopic conceptual approaches. At the **microscopic** level, the emphasis is primarily on the individual as a unit of analysis. At the **macroscopic** level, a holistic approach is taken, and the unit of analysis tends to be a collective or larger social unit, such as an organization, a community, or a social system. A distinction must be made here between the unit of observation and the unit of analysis. Gathering data among individual persons does not necessarily mean that the individual is the *unit of analysis*. One might do a study of differences in communication patterns across ten different communities according to a holistic approach, with a hypothesis about community characteristics as they affect television habits. Data for this study may come from samples of individuals from the general population and from persons in leadership roles in the communities. From these data, community characteristics might be determined, such as the overall level of education (which involves averaging) and the type of conversational pattern in the village (which may not involve averaging). The main analytic unit may be the community, even though individuals were measured.

There is no correct answer to the question "Which is better?" The individualistic approach can account for phenomena that a macroconceptual approach may not encompass. Similarly, a macroconceptual approach may provide insights and interpretations that are not possible with a microconceptual scheme. The choice between these approaches should be made in full knowledge that neither necessarily accounts for all the behavior or phenomena of concern. Suppose an investigator is studying performance of reporters in the coverage of local political events. A certain amount of the variance in that performance might be explained by structural characteristics of the communities and by organizational characteristics of the various newspapers for which the reporters write.[55] Reporters working for newspapers in large, diverse urban centers might be hypothesized to cover political affairs in ways quite different from reporter practices on newspapers in small rural communities. Or political coverage might be different in communities with single newspapers under independent ownership than in communities where there is direct competition. At the same time, there may be additional variance in reporter performance than can best be explained by a study of individual characteristics, such as reporter background, adherence to professional values, and personality characteristics. In some cases, it may be possible to determine empirically which approach provides a better explanation. Ordinarily, however, the chosen perspective leads initially to research operations that emphasize one approach or the other throughout the design.

The difference between the two approaches may be illustrated by two contrasting approaches to the study of effects of violence in the media. In many ways, the popular questions raised about effects of media violence have been in a micro framework. The general question, whether violent media content produces more violence in society, has been conceptualized frequently as: "Does violence in media content produce more violent behavior in the individuals exposed to that content?" Conceptually, individual effects from exposure to aggressive content have been viewed as psychological processes, such as imitation, disinhibition, and acquisition.[56] In a number of studies, the results have supported the hypothesis that the more aggressive the content, the more aggressive the consequent behavior of individuals exposed to that content. This is developed further by Donohew and Palmgreen in the Chapter 7.

A quite different, and more macroconceptual, approach to the question of violent content in media has been taken by Gerbner and Gross.[57] Instead of starting with the question of the impact on individuals, Gerbner and Gross ask what the long-term consequences of televised drama are in U.S. society. Their approach is both macroconceptual and functionalist, based on a fundamental assumption about maintenance of cultural values and norms through symbolic content. Television, as a medium different from all its predecessors in scope and kind, is conceived of as a "cultural arm" of U.S. society, presenting symbolic rituals of oughts and naughts in the social order and a reminder of who wins and who loses in the game of life. Dramatization of these rules requires direct, unambiguous portrayals of transgression of rules and the costs of so doing. In this setting, say Gerbner and Gross, the occasional effects of televised violence on individual aggression are less important than are the long-run societal effects, which are to create and reinforce social control measures for containing and repressing crime and violence.

Tichenor, Nnaemeka, Olien, and Donohue[58] suggest that structural characteristics mediate television effects. Television content predominantly reflects the urban environment. Thus, people in rural areas are less likely to perceive the content as being relevant to their environment. Evidence has been found that the effects of violent content are greater when it is perceived as being realistic.[59] According to this reasoning, violent media content may have a greater impact on individuals in urban areas.

In the cases described briefly here, the micro and macro approaches include data gathered on individual respondents. The difference is in the conception and statements of the research problem. The micro approach depends largely on assumptions about individual behavior and motivations; the macro approach depends on assumptions about social and cultural processes, particularly about societal patterns of organized social control. Hypotheses from both approaches may (and do) find support in different bodies of data. There is no more logical inconsistency between these models than there is between micro and macro approaches in other scientific fields. The bottom line is that it is advantageous to the production of scientific knowledge to approach a research problem from different levels of analysis and to even consider "cross-level" explanations to provide a broader understanding of system dynamics.[60]

There is a long-standing and deeply seated division of thinking over the related questions of **holism** and **reductionism**. Investigators favoring a macroconceptual approach generally take the holistic view that elements of the larger social system, such as organizations, communities, and institutions, have existences that cannot be reduced to behaviors of the actual individuals within them. The whole, with "emergent properties" not reducible to individuals, is literally seen as greater than the sum of its parts.

A reductionist view, often termed "methodological individualism," would hold that collective social units are nothing more than aggregations of individuals and may be so treated for methodological purposes. There is often a strong link between methodological individualism and the logical positivist view, which regards statements about social systems as nonscientific to the extent that they are not empirical.

The merit of the reductionist pattern is debated widely in the philosophy of science literature.[61] Hyland and Bridgstock conclude that the debate continues to be a crucial one, pointing out that it is reductionist to state that institutions are reducible to actual individuals, but not reductionist to hold that statements about institutions can be restated in terms of typical individuals.[62] The key term here is *typical*, meaning "ideal" types rather than statistical averages and "average" individuals. The ideal type, Weber[63] said, is an abstract characterization, and a typical individual in this sense could be a characterization of a role. Such a type is constructed and described by the researcher on the basis of a theoretical model and may not be found in reality. Merton[64] offered one of the best known ideal types in communications research in his characterization of "local" influentials and "cosmopolitan" influentials. Tuchman's characterization of news reporter behavior[65] may be seen as an "ideal type" since it embodies a global characterization of one particular role without analyzing variations of the performance of that role in different structures.

Cumulative but Tentative Knowledge

Ultimately, the goal of the social scientist is to produce cumulative, albeit tentative knowledge. The final test, the assessment of the state of knowledge, is conducted in the arena of debate among peers of the scientific community. Social and behavioral science research depends upon confrontation of theories with evidence, and confrontations of the interpretations of that evidence by skeptical outsiders. In any specialized field or subfield, there is an array of procedural and methodological rules for measurement and for increasing the precision of that measurement. Yet, interpretation of evidence ultimately meets the critical appraisal of others. A theory and its supporting evidence must stand the test of debate. The outcome of this debate is rarely conclusive to all, but it increases the likelihood that the theory and the associated evidence will add to the body of knowledge.

Scientific debate and criticism go beyond maintaining intellectual honesty, although they may serve that purpose as well. Debate forces rigor on the presentation and defense of hypotheses, data, and their interpretation. Knowing in advance that a paper will be subjected to peer review and criticism forces the investigator to anticipate weaknesses. The process may well stimulate alternative conceptualizations, strategies, and interpretations that enrich the final product of the research in question.

Criticism and debate have deep roots in the traditions of science and academic inquiry generally. They serve as continual reminders that science is an enterprise of uncertainty whose current knowledge is, therefore, tentative. When investigators regard a question as "settled," that generally means they are willing to accept a given body of evidence, for the time being, as supporting a particular generalization or set of generalizations. They may even regard a particular generalization as a "law," although few social and behavioral scientists today seem inclined to use that expression.

There are some generalizations that approach the status of laws. There may be widespread acceptance in social and behavioral research of the hypothesis that "the higher the level of education, the higher the use of print forms of mass media." The evidence for this hypothesis may be extensive enough to justify it as an assumption in design of other studies. Yet nearly any student of the subject can specify conditions under which this hypothesis might not be supported. The two variables do not occur in isolation, but operate in a social setting and are jointly affected by other conditions. There is also the possibility that new conditions might appear in the future under which the hypothesis would generally not be supported. So when scholars do accept the relationship between education and print media as an assumption, they are implicitly making still other assumptions about the related conditions.

A similar result occurred several decades ago with Lund's "law of primacy," to the effect that the first side in a debate has the persuasive edge. After systematic studies on the question, the Yale research group[66] concluded that under certain conditions a primacy effect would occur. But under other conditions, a recency effect was more likely.

It is generally agreed upon that knowledge may accumulate, but it never loses its tentative nature. However, the relationship between knowledge accumulation and scientific growth and change has been debated in the philosophy of science literature. Kuhn[67] maintains that scientific change is marked by radical "paradigm" shifts from one era of "Normal Science" to another. Knowledge is seen as accumulating within one period of Normal Science, but Kuhn rejects the notion that science proceeds by accretion beween scientific paradigm eras. Toulmin[68] disputes Kuhn's portrayal of the "catastrophic" nature of scientific change, arguing instead for a more "evolutionary" conception. The accumulation of knowledge is said to lead to variation in theory.

In sum, there is no final or ultimate knowledge from science, only the best knowledge and the best interpretation that can be provided at a given time. Knowledge, like other products of human endeavor, always faces the possibility of obsolescence.

Endnotes

1. While "jargon" is necessary for communicating precise meanings, it is crucial that key terms are clearly defined so that not just experts but other interested parties can understand the discussion.

2. James Conant, *Science and Common Sense* (New Haven, CT: Yale University Press, 1951).

3. Scott Greer, *The Logic of Social Inquiry* (Chicago: Aldine Publishing Co., 1969).

4. Steven H. Chaffee and Jack M. McLeod, "Sensitization in Panel Design: A Coorientation Experiment," *Journalism Quarterly* 45 (Winter 1968): 661-669.

5. An orientation designed to render detailed descriptions of the unique characteristics of a given phenomenon.

6. An orientation designed to render generalizable principles or laws that apply across various phenomena.

7. Jack M. McLeod et al., *Concept Explication and Theory Construction: Part I. Meaning Analysis and Part II. Empirical Analysis* (Madison, WI: Mass Communication Research Center, 2000).

8. *Ibid.*

9. For examples, see Alan M. Rubin, "Audience Activity and Media Use," *Communication Monographs* 60 (March 1993): 98–105; Seth Finn, "Origins of Media Exposure," *Communication Research* 24 (October 1997): 507–529; Richard C. Vincent and Michael D. Basil, "College Students' News Gratifications, Media Use, and Current Events Knowledge," *Journal of Broadcasting and Electronic Media* 41 (Summer 1997): 380–392; Douglas A. Ferguson and Elizabeth M. Perse, "The World Wide Web

as a Functional Alternative to Television," *Journal of Broadcasting and Electronic Media* 44 (Spring 2000): 155–174.

10. For example, see George A. Donohue, Clarice N. Olien, and Phillip J. Tichenor, "Reporting Conflict by Pluralism, Newspaper Type and Ownership," *Journalism Quarterly* 62 (Autumn 1985): 489–499, 507.

11. For examples, see the articles on the European Parliamentary elections compiled in Jay G. Blumler ed., *Communicating to Voters: Television in the First European Parliamentary Elections* (London: Sage, 1983).

12. For example, see Travis L. Dixon and Daniel Linz, "Overrepresentation and Underrepresentation of African Americans and Latinos as Lawbreakers on Television News," *Journal of Communication* 50(Spring 2000): 131–154.

13. For example, see James W. Potter and Stacy Smith, "The Context of Graphic Portrayals of Television Violence," *Journal of Broadcasting and Electronic Media* 44 (Spring 2000): 301–323.

14. For example, see Gregory Fouts and Kimberley Burggraf, "Television Situation Comedies: Female Weight, Male Negative Comments, and Audience Reactions," *Sex Roles* 42 (May 2000): 925–932.

15. For an in-depth discussion of the concept explication process, see Steven H. Chaffee, *Communication Concepts 1: Explication* (Newbury Park, CA: Sage, 1991).

16. McLeod et al., *op. cit.*

17. *Ibid.*

18. Fred N. Kerlinger, *Foundations of Behavioral Research* (New York: Holt, Rinehart and Winston, 1973).

19. Imre Lakatos, "Falsificationism and the Methodology of Scientific Research Programmes," in Imre Lakatos and Alan Musgrave, eds., *Criticism and the Growth of Knowledge* (Cambridge: Cambridge University Press, 1970).

20. George Comstock, *Television Portrayals and Aggressive Behavior* (Santa Monica, CA: Rand Corporation, 1976).

21. John Soloski, "Economics and Management: The Real Influence of Newspaper Groups," *Newspaper Research Journal* (October 1979), 19–28.

22. Clarice N. Olien, Phillip J. Tichenor, and George A. Donohue, "Relation Between Corporate Ownership and Editor Attitudes About Business," *Journalism Quarterly* 65 (Summer 1988): 257–264.

23. Herbert Feigl, "Some Major Issues and Developments in the Philosophy of Science of Logical Empiricism," in Herbert Feigl and Michael Scriven, eds., *The Foundations of Science and the Concepts of Psychology and Psychoanalysis.* Vol. 1 of Minnesota Studies in the Philosophy of Science (Minneapolis: University of Minnesota Press, 1956), 3–37.

24. Paul K. Feyerabend, "On the Interpretation of Scientific Theories," in Richard E. Grandy, ed. *Theories and Observations in Science* (Englewood Cliffs, NJ: Prentice-Hall, 1973), 147–153.

25. Tom Bottomore, *The Frankfurt School* (London: Tavistock, 1984).

26. Feigl, *op. cit.*

27. Herbert Feigl, "The Orthodox View of Theories: Remarks in Defense as Well as Critique," in Michael Radner and Stephen Winokur, eds., *Analysis of Theories and Methods of Physics and Psychology.* Vol. 4 of Minnesota Studies in the Philosophy of Science (Minneapolis: University of Minnesota Press, 1970), 7–16.

28. *Ibid.*

29. Bruce H. Westley, "Scientific Method and Communication Research," in Ralph O. Nafziger and David Manning White, eds., *Introduction to Mass Communications Research* (Baton Rouge: Louisiana State University Press, 1958), 238–276.

30. Grover Maxwell, "Induction and Empiricism: A Bayesian-Frequentist Alternative," in Grover Maxwell and Robert M. Anderson, Jr., eds., *Induction, Probability, and Confirmation.* Vol. 6 of Minnesota Studies in the Philosophy of Science (Minneapolis: University of Minnesota Press, 1975), 106–165.

31. Rom Harre, *The Philosophies of Science* (Oxford: Oxford University Press, 1972).

32. Jerald Hage, *Techniques and Problems of Theory Construction in Sociology* (New York: John Wiley & Sons, 1972).

33. R. M. MacIver, *Social Causation* (New York: Harper & Row, 1942); R. M. MacIver, *Community: A Sociological Study* (London: Cass Press, 1970).

34. Jacob Bronowski, *The Common Sense of Science* (New York: Random House, 1962).

35. Thomas D. Cook and Donald T. Campbell, *Quasi-Experimentation: Design and Analysis Issues for Field Studies* (Boston: Houghton Mifflin, 1979).

36. *Ibid.*

37. MacIver, *Community: A Sociological Study.*

38. Jay G. Blumler and Elihu Katz, eds., *The Uses of Mass Communication: Current Perspectives on Gratifications Research.* Volume 3, Sage Annual Reviews of Communication Research (Beverly Hills, CA: Sage Publications, Inc., 1973).

39. Herta Herzog, "What Do We Really Know About Day-time Serial Listeners?" in Bernard Berelson and Morris Janowitz, eds., *Reader in Public Opinion and Communication* (New York: The Free Press, 1953), 352–365.

40. Bernard Berelson, "What Missing the Newspaper Means," in Wilbur Schramm, ed., *The Process and Effects of Mass Communication* (Urbana: University of Illinois Press, 1955), 36–47.

41. David Manning White, "The 'Gatekeeper,' A Case Study in the Selection of News," *Journalism Quarterly* 27 (Fall 1950): 383–390; Ithiel de Sola Pool and Irwin Shulman, "Newsmen's Fantasies, Audiences, and Newswriting," *Public Opinion Quarterly* 23 (Summer 1959): 145–158 .

42. "TV on Trial," *Newsweek* (Sept. 12, 1977), 104.

43. Auguste Comte, *The Passivist Philosophy* (London: Bell, 1896), Vol. II.

44. Herbert Spencer, *The Principles of Sociology* (New York: Appleton, 1896).

45. Vilfredo Pareto, *The Treatise on General Sociology* (New York: Dover, 1963).

46. Emile Durkheim, *The Rules of Sociological Method* (New York: Free Press, 1982).

47. A. R. Radcliffe-Brown, "The Functional Unity of Social Systems: Is MI Incompatible with This Hypothesis? *American Anthropologist* 37 (1935): 394–402.

48. Bronislaw Malinowski, *Magic, Science and Religion* (Boston: Beacon Press, 1948).

49. Arthur L. Stinchcombe, *Constructing Social Theories* (New York: Harcourt Brace Jovanovich, 1968).

50. Robert K. Merton, *Social Theory and Social Structure, 3rd ed.* (New York: Free Press, 1968).

51. Phillip J. Tichenor, George A. Donohue, and Clarice N. Olien, "Mass Media Flow and Differential Growth in Knowledge," *Public Opinion Quarterly* 34 (Summer 1970): 159–170.

52. Berelson, *op. cit.*

53. Charles R. Wright, "Functional Analysis and Mass Communication," *Public Opinion Quarterly* 24 (Winter 1960): 605–620; Blumler and Katz, *op. cit.*

54. For example: Harold D. Lasswell, "The Structure and Function of Communication in Society," in Wilbur Schramm, ed., *Mass Communications* (Urbana: University of Illinois Press, 1949), 102–115.

55. George A. Donohue, Phillip J. Tichenor, and Clarice N. Olien, "Mass Media Functions, Knowledge and Social Control," *Journalism Quarterly* 60 (Winter 1973): 652–659.

56. Comstock, *Television Portrayals and Aggressive Behavior.*

57. George Gerbner and Larry Gross, "Living with Television: The Violence Profile," *Journal of Communication* 26 (Spring 1976): 173–199.

58. Phillip J. Tichenor, Anthony I. Nnaemeka, Clarice N. Olien, and George A. Donohue, "Community Pluralism and Perceptions of Television Content," *Journalism Quarterly* 54 (Summer 1977): 254–261.

59. Albert Bandura, "Social Learning Through Imitation," in Marshall Jones, ed., *Nebraska Symposium on Motivation* (Lincoln: University of Nebraska Press, 1962), 211–274.

60. Jack M. McLeod, Zhongdang Pan, and Dianne Rucinski, "Levels of Analysis in Public Opinion Research," in Theodore Glasser and Charles Salmon, eds., *Public Opinion and the Communication of Consent* (New York: Guilford, 1994), 55–85.

61. May Brodbeck, "Methodological Individualism: Definition and Reduction," in May Brodbeck, ed., *Readings in the Philosophy of the Social Sciences* (New York: Macmillan, 1968), Chapter 16.

62. Michael Hyland and Martin Bridgstock, "Reductionism: Comments on Some Recent Work," *Philosophy of the Social Sciences*, 4: (1964), 197–200.

63. Max Weber, *The Methodology of the Social Sciences* (New York: Free Press, 1949).

64. Robert K. Merton, "Patterns of Influence: Local and Cosmopolitan Influentials," in Robert K. Merton, *Social Theory and Social Structure* (New York: Free Press, 1957).

65. Gaye Tuchman, *Making News* (New York: Free Press, 1978).

66. Carl I. Hovland, *The Order of Presentation in Persuasion* (New Haven, CT: Yale University Press, 1957).

67. Thomas Kuhn, *The Structure of Scientific Revolutions* (Chicago: University of Chicago Press, 1962).

68. Stephen Toulmin, "Does the Distinction Between Normal and Revolutionary Science Hold Water?" in Imre Lakatos and Alan Musgrave, eds., *Criticism and the Growth of Knowledge* (Cambridge: University of Oxford, 1970), 39–47.

7

Constructing Theory

Lewis Donohew

Philip Palmgreen

A principal goal of this chapter will be to offer simple ground rules for constructing theories of communication and to illustrate them from research in the field. As in many of the other chapters in this volume, the subject matter will be approached from a behavioral—or objectivist[1]—perspective. This approach, considerably evolved from logical positivist ancestors, seeks to identify general principles and "causes" of behaviors as one of its basic perspectives and is the only one with an established method for verifying truth claims.[2]

Although there are several distinct perspectives on communication theory, all based on different philosophies and methods, the behavioral/objectionist perspective is the most widely used both in this field and in other social science disciplines and thus perhaps is the closest to a unifying approach meeting requirements of a mature discipline, as defined, for example, by Kuhn,[3] Laudan,[4] and others.

We have proposed[5] that a theory is a tentative explanation invented to assist in understanding some small or large part of the "reality" around us. Ideally, its concepts are measurable and its propositions testable and therefore subject to refutation. A theory comes into prominence when it is noticed and pursued by the scientific community, and it passes into history when better explanations are found.

According to Kerlinger,[6] a theory is "a set of interrelated constructs (concepts), definitions, and propositions that present a systematic view of phenomena by specifying relations among variables, with the purpose of explaining and predicting the phenomena."

This definition highlights the two major purposes of a theory: explanation and prediction. It also indicates that such goals are achieved through developing concepts, the building blocks of theory, and linking them in certain systematic ways. The concepts by themselves possess no explanatory or predictive powers. It is their interrelationship in the form of theoretical propositions that performs these functions.

In communication research, messages often are at the center of our concerns. The authors, for example, have studied what attracts attention to messages and holds it long enough for them to be understood. We have sought to learn what causes messages to have an effect, such as to inform or persuade. This has led us to study what kinds of people, in terms of their psychological or sociological needs, are most likely to attend to what kinds of messages.[7] Our program began with development of an activation theory of information exposure, then later drew upon the propositions of that theory to design messages in prevention campaigns, taking individual differences into account. These studies have involved both media messages[8] and classroom instruction.[9]

The step from basic research on the communication process to employment of theory in achieving some applied goal often is a short one. Although there has been emphasis in recent years on communication as a "practical" discipline,[10] there is considerable argument over the relative values of basic and applied research. Popularization of this dichotomy, in which basic research contributes to theoretical development, but applied research merely helps solve problems of the moment, is attributed to Vannevar Bush, director of the U.S. Office of Scientific Research and Development at the end of World War II.[11] The value of such a dichotomy has been challenged in recent years, both in communication[12] and in the physical sciences.[13] Kreps and associates, for example, argue that:[14]

> There is nothing intrinsically non-pragmatic about basic research. In fact, many scholars contend that the best applied communication research is conceived and conducted with theory firmly in mind. (p.73)

They offer a typology of research ranging from that which is low both on application and theory, which they suggest is not of much worth, to that which is high on both. Donald Stokes offers a similar typology in his argument for the sciences in general, labeling the intersection that is high on both theory and application as "Pasteur's quadrant,"[15] describing the type of research conducted by Louis Pasteur that led to a germ theory of disease. This type of research is both basic, in that it examines fundamental relationships, and *applied*, in that it also seeks to solve specific problems.

In their highest form—cloaked in lawlike statements, propositions, and predictions—formal expositions of theory can be imposing. Yet when there is a grasp of the metatheoretical objectives for their construction, the ground rules referred to above, they become much easier to grasp.

Why should concern over theory be addressed in a book devoted to research methodology? Although theory and methodology are often taught separately, they are, in fact, inseparable. Theory poses the questions that methodology tries to answer.

Constructing Theories and Testing Propositions

Essentially, theoretical reasoning is either *deductive* or *inductive*. The deductive approach proceeds from the general to the specific. There is perceived to be some general law operating to produce a set of outcomes or, as is more realistic in research in communication, there is some basic assumption about a causal relationship. The investigator then proceeds to deductively reason that, given this, if some specific action is taken, then it would logically follow that some other specific action would occur. These deduced propositions are then converted into operational form and tested against the likelihood they could have oc-curred by chance. The inductive approach proceeds from the specific to the general. Here, the researcher seeks to determine if a set of interrelationships occurs with a frequency that makes it very likely that some general law is operating.

The most rigorous model to evolve from the epistemology described above is a de-ductive falsification model sometimes called a *deductive* **nomological** *model.* Under this system of reasoning, the scientific process begins when existing preconceptions (which may already be formalized into theories) are threatened by new observations, suggesting revision of old perspectives or development of new ones entirely.

Under this schema the presence of an already existing perspective is *assumed.*[16] An alternative theory is proposed to account for the disturbing phenomena, propositions are *deduced* from the logical consequences of the theory (in the form of "if this, then this" statements), and **operational** hypotheses are formed and tested. If the hypotheses are not supported, the alternative theory is rejected and a new explanation is formulated. Although there is no established number of times this must occur before the theory is accepted, clearly, consistent support of hypotheses is likely to build confidence in the alternative theory. On the other hand, a single negative instance of failure to support is considered by some to be enough to reject a universal hypothesis. This position has been softened in in-terpretation by a number of philosophers of science to apply to reproducible effects that refute basic propositions. One common-sense explanation of this is that theories that have survived falsification tests long enough to win some acceptance should not then suddenly be abandoned without solid contradictory evidence yielded from valid research methods.

Drawing upon a notational system offered by Hempel,[17] the *deductive-nomological* model is of the form:

$$C_1$$
$$C_2$$
$$C_3$$ Characteristics or "facts" of a particular situation
.
.
$$C_n$$

$$L_1$$
$$L_2$$ Fundamental theoretic assumptions, expressed
$$L_3$$ in lawlike form, followed by propositions logically   EXPLANANS
      derived from these and expressed as other laws
.
$$L_n$$

_____

E   Prediction or predictions based on above
    propositions, converted to operational form   EXPLANANDUM
    as hypotheses and tested.

It should be made clear that the strict interpretation that a proposition must be re-jected as soon as it encounters a single falsifying instance would render this model inappropriate for the study of human communication. It is highly unlikely that invariant laws of a universal nature ever will be found in this area of study. Critics of "covering law" approaches, or of "conventional science," often cite this interpretation as grounds for rejection without giving evidence that they are aware of other interpretations or modifications.

Under the deductive model, either the theory invented under an inductive approach or a theory invented purely from imagination can be subjected to rigorous tests for falsifiability. In either instance, the *theory* is expressed as $L_1, L_2, \ldots L_n$, and E represents the set of specific predictions generated from these general lawlike statements comprising the theory.

Although in studies of communication, inductive research is far more common than deductive research, the most widely employed deductive approach involves a version of the deductive-nomological model. In this approach, propositions (and the general theoretic assumptions from which they are derived) are rejected or allowed to stand on the basis of the level of probability that they could have occurred by chance. The researchers appear to implicitly assume a probabilistic universe in which it is not necessary for all statements to be supported all the time, but rather one in which most propositions—if they are "true"—will be supported most of the time. In other words, some room is left for variation or error, and those seeking apodictic, or *certain*, knowledge—as described below—are likely to be disappointed. This more flexible model appears to be far more appropriate to the type of universe studied by communication researchers.

In general, theories formed through the above procedures describe laws of interaction, which we often describe as *causal* laws. According to Hunt:[18] "Pragmatically speaking, we may refer to causal explanations as those explanations that employ nonspurious, theoretically supported, sequential laws in their explanans." He lists four criteria for acceptance of such laws:

1. *Temporal sequentiality.* The "causal" force must precede that which is "caused." This must, of course, be modified in cases where causality might plausibly work in both directions; that is, where there might be mutually causal processes.
2. *Associative variation.* Changes in that which is "caused" must be associated with changes in the "causal" force. Association alone is not strong enough evidence to support a case for causal change.
3. *Nonspurious association.* Care must be taken to assure in the examination process that there are not underlying and hidden causes. This implies testing to eliminate alternative sources. There is no known procedure under any of the systems of theoretic logic which permits absolute assurance that this has been achieved.
4. *Theoretical support.* Purely empirical statements, such as one that holds that the seasonal temperatures in one part of the world are associated with the seasonal pregnancy rate in another, may be consistently verified but offer no explanatory content. In fact, of course, such associations are completely spurious. Pregnancy rates tend to rise in the winter (we won't attempt here to explain the cause) and may be found to be positively or negatively associated with temperatures in the other location, depending on whether that location is in the same or a different hemisphere (when it's summer in Australia, it's winter in England and the United States, for example). Theoretic statements are intended to explain that because of

some broadly operating principle, if this occurs, then this will follow. Such statements must also:

a. Have empirical content making them susceptible to measurement.
b. Possess nomic necessity; that is, relationships must be potentially causal.
c. Be capable of integration into a system of compatible lawlike statements able to explain some phenomenon.
d. Be intersubjectively certifiable, that is, in a form in which other investigators can ascertain the truth content themselves. Statements derived from the laws and theories must be amenable to confrontation with real-world data.

Examples of Deductive Theories

One illustration of a deductive theory is an activation model of information exposure which has guided the program of research referred to earlier.[19] The basic assumption of this theory—which would be represented as L1 in the deductive-nomological model presented earlier—is that individuals have an optimum level of activation or arousal at which they feel most comfortable. A second assumption, L_2, is that they enter information exposure situations with the expectation of achieving or maintaining this optimal state.

These are general lawlike statements that describe propositions we assume to be true if deduced propositions are more or less consistently supported. In this instance two principal propositions were deduced. They are, L_3, that individuals will experience a positive affect when the optimal state is achieved and, L_4, that they will experience a negative affect when (a) arousal drops below the optimal level or (b) when arousal exceeds the optimal level.

This leads to predictions, E, that individuals will continue to expose themselves to an information source or will turn away from it according to their level of positive or negative affect.

Empirically, we also know certain characteristics or facts of the situation that serve to define, limit, or otherwise specify conditions under which the theory is expected to apply, as noted under the C statements below. Employing Hempel's notational system as before, a formal statement of the theory could be made as follows:

Characteristics or "Facts" of the Situation:

C_1 Individuals vary in their levels of need for stimulation as a function of inherited drives and on learned needs based on rewarded and nonrewarded experiences. High sensation seekers have higher needs for stimulation than low sensation seekers.

C_2 In messages, stimulation is provided by formal features, including (a) action, (b) novelty, (c) color, (d) stimulus intensity, (e) complexity, and others, and by the verbal content, including dramatic qualities and emotional intensity.

Laws:

L_1 Individuals seek to achieve or maintain a level of activation at which they feel most comfortable.

L_2 Attention to a message is a function of (a) individual level of need for stimulation or cognition (or both) and (b) level of stimulation provided by a stimulus source (such as a message).

Deduced propositions:

L_3 Individuals will attend to messages that fulfill their needs for activation.
L_4 Individuals will turn away from messages that fail to generate enough arousal to meet their needs for activation to seek more exciting stimuli.
L_5 Individuals will turn away from messages that generate too much arousal to seek less exciting stimuli.

Explanandum:

E: Operational hypotheses, based on the propositions expressed in L_3, L_4, and L_5 above may concern exposure to information, attitude or behavior changes, or other variables.

In an analysis of the model in a news situation, it has been noted that

when an individual's arousal level is exceeded—for example, when a news story contains a message that is too threatening or otherwise exciting—he or she will become uncomfortable and face internal pressures (see Figure 7.1). Similarly, when the desired level is not reached—the message is too boring—the person also will be likely to turn away. It is only when the message satisfies a desired level of arousal that individuals are likely to stay with it. (pp. 206-207)[20]

Another example of a deductive theory is Zillmann and Bryant's theory of affect-dependent stimulus arrangement.[21] They offer the following as conditions (C_1 etc.):

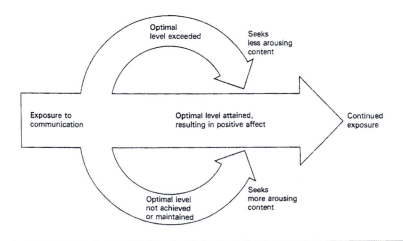

FIGURE 7.1. An Activation Theory of Information Exposure. Reprinted with permission from Lewis Donohew, Howard Sypher, and E. Tory Higgins, eds., *Communication, Social Cognition, and Affect* (Hillsdale, NJ: Erlbaum, 1988), p. 207.

Extreme understimulation (boredom) and extreme overstimulation (stress) constitute aversive states. So does any threat to the welfare of individuals, in both a most direct and broader sense. The experience of gratification, on the other hand, is conservatively defined by the absence of aversive stimulation. It is characterized by the temporary nonexistence of acute, action-instigating needs. Stimulation is nonextreme. (p. 158)

Their fundamental covering law, the basic premise (L_1) from which other propositions are deduced, is that

individuals are motivated to terminate noxious, aversive stimulation of any kind and to reduce the intensity of such stimulation at any time. It is further proposed that individuals are motivated to perpetuate and increase the intensity of gratifying, pleasurable experiential states. (p. 158)

From this premise, they derive a number of propositions, in the form of additional lawlike statements ($L_2 \ldots , L_n$) such as:

Based on this hedonistic premise, it is proposed that individuals are inclined to arrange—to the extent that they are capable—internal and external stimulus conditions so as to minimize aversion and maximize gratification. Both minimization and maximization are in terms of time and intensity. (p. 158)

These propositions eventually lead to predictions about behaviors in general and exposure to mass media entertainment in particular.

Inductive Theories

In practice, theories often are not expressed in such a formal way. They most often evolve from observations arrived at *inductively*, then are restated and tested in the more rigorous deductive manner.

This is represented in another approach evolving from positivism—Carnap's[22] logical empiricism—that also accepts that universal statements can never be verified and relies on confirmation from the accumulation of empirical tests that, when taken as a whole, point to a general explanation. Results of these tests do not have to be conclusive, but they must form the only grounds for determining if propositions are true or false. This can be illustrated by an inductive model widely used in communication research. Drawing upon Hempel's notation system we employed earlier, let us examine this approach as indicated in an *inductive-statistical* model:

C_1
C_2
C_3 Characteristics of "facts" of a particular situation
.
.
.

C_n

SL_1
SL_2 Empirically connected observations, some
             in the form of statistical laws with an   EXPLANANS
SL_3 acceptable level of probability
SLn

E   A general theory that explains the observations   EXPLANANDUM
         reported in SL_1 through SL_n under conditions C

In the deductive-nomological model described earlier, the theory was expressed in the form of lawlike propositions ($L_1, \ldots, L_n$) that predicted outcomes (E). In the inductive model here, however, we are at an earlier stage in the process. Ls represent statistical observations, and we do not get around to formally inventing a theory until the very end, when we arrive at E.

This approach employs both logic and probability. It does not claim to make universal truth statements, but rather, on the basis of empirically connected observations, seeks to form an explanatory theory that is very likely to be true. It should be noted that there is no claim that is universally true and, as noted above when we examined the nature of falsification and deduction, it is only weakly falsifiable. Nonetheless, it serves the function of systematically approaching a set of phenomena, testing their interrelationships, and forming an explanation that then can be tested by more rigorous means.

The inductive model involves examination of sets of interrelated phenomena that occur with a frequency that make it very likely that some general law is true—and even calls for invention of that law—but we have no assurance that the invented law is in fact true. However many times the phenomena described in the lawlike statements (SL_1, SL_2, . . . , SL_n) may occur, they do not permit a strong test of the falsification of the laws. What we have proposed as a theory under E may be a plausible explanation, but it is no more than informed speculation until it is drawn upon to deduce propositions and then formulate hypotheses that are tested to determine if the law itself works.

An example of an inductive model in which confirmation of individual tests taken as a whole point to a general explanation is the theory of evolution. Since Darwin, scientists have been accumulating individual pieces of evidence to the point today when the evidence is so overwhelming that evolution is no longer considered a theory, but fact.

A Hindsight Theory of Television Violence Effects

This inductive-deductive process can be illustrated with an example from a study of the effects of televised violence. Building an adequate theory requires a dash of intuition and at least a modicum of foresight. Although a vast amount of theorizing and research has been devoted to televised violence, let us assume that we are starting from scratch. Where should we begin? What steps should we follow in constructing and testing a theory of the effects of televised violence?

A reasonable description of what takes place is represented by the following outline.

1. Observe.
2. Develop concepts.

3. Relate concepts to form theoretical propositions.
4. Develop operational definitions of concepts.
5. State research hypotheses in operational terms.
6. Design a research study to test these hypotheses.
7. Evaluate the theory in terms of the outcome.

Let us examine each step in detail.

Observe. Most theory building begins with rather crude observations of events or other phenomena that seem to be related. At first, the scientist does not know exactly what to look for. Observation at this point tends to be rather unstructured and informal. But let us assume that we notice that all the children we know who spend most of their free waking hours immersed in video violence seem to pattern their nonviewing behavior after a "hit man" in "The Sopranos." On the other hand, each child of our acquaintance who avoids such fare in favor of "Sesame Street" appears to be a candidate for canonization. On the basis of this admittedly limited and possibly biased sample, we might surmise that the differences in observed behavior are due to the differences in exposure to television violence. At this point we have moved very quickly through the next two steps of the theory construction process.

Develop concepts; relate concepts to form theoretical propositions. The observational stage is very unstructured, although not totally without its governing principles. Our perception of events is influenced by concepts acquired previously. Thus we are likely to perceive the nonviewing behavior of the violence viewers in our previous example as "aggression," and the aspect of their viewing behavior that may contribute to this aggression as "exposure to television violence." It is with such concepts that we build theories. Concepts that have been defined as unambiguously as possible and put to use in theories are known as *constructs*. Taken individually, however, such concepts or constructs can aid only in *description*; they cannot *explain*. We must relate concepts to each other in a systematic fashion before the explanatory apparatus that we call "theory" emerges.

In our example, we have proposed that "exposure to television violence" leads to or is a proximate cause of "aggression." This relationship between two abstract concepts is called a *theoretical proposition* or *theoretic hypothesis*. Actually, this proposition, together with the definitions of the concepts involved and certain underlying axioms whose truth is assumed (such as, "Television content can influence the behavior of those exposed to such content"), constitute a theory in its simplest form. However, at this stage the "theory" has little explanatory value. It does not tell us *how* or *why* exposure to televised violence might lead to aggression. Obviously, our theory requires some elaboration.

One common way in which theories are elaborated to increase their explanatory power is through the addition of "intervening" concepts. To illustrate in an abstract sense, we might insert concept Y between concepts X and Z to help explain why X and Z should be related. Then, instead of the theoretical proposition (X → Z), we have (X → Y → Z). With regard to exposure to television violence (X), we might ask what mechanism or mechanisms (Y) could account for subsequent aggressive acts (Z) apparently related to that exposure. A possible mechanism, of course, is learning, especially observational learning of aggressive acts depicted on television. This may range from a young child's learning how to administer a karate chop to an adult's learning an intricate scheme for robbing a bank. We might expect such learning to be particularly prevalent among young children, since they spend so much time watching television and have relatively little personal experience with violence. Although we need not expect that all aggressive behaviors acquired while viewing television actually will be performed, it is plausible to assume that the larger the repertoire of learned aggressive acts, the greater the probability that some such acts will be performed in appropriate situations. The many accounts of murders, robberies, hijackings, and assaults whose details have closely matched events depicted in television drama provide some support for such a rationale.

Hence, observational learning of aggressive acts seen on television is one plausible explanation for the connection between exposure to televised violence and aggression. But could such exposure instigate or trigger *nonimitative* aggression, that is, aggressive acts that do not closely parallel the behavior seen on television? Could, for example, viewing a brutal murder on television cause someone to rush out of the house and commit armed robbery? Perhaps viewing any kind of aggression lowers our inhibitions against aggression in general, thus making it more likely we will behave aggressively. Or perhaps viewing televised aggression is physiologically arousing. Some theories treat arousal as a drive state serving to activate behavior. If the cues in the postviewing environment seem to call for aggression, any arousal state generated by viewing television violence might serve as the motivational impetus for such aggression. Thus both "disinhibition"[23] and "arousal" emerge as plausible concepts that might intervene between viewing of televised violence and subsequent aggression.

But do these experiences square with what is already known? Before testing our own version of this prediction, we must review the literature. We will not find all the answers here, but it would be foolish and wasteful to proceed to our own test of a three-element theory without knowing what the research of others has told us about each element and the relations among them. There is a large literature on incidental learning, for example, and indeed the propositions stated in our example are based on that literature.

Part of the reason for the literature review is to decide which of the many intervening constructs we might posit are promising. We might have chosen another among many intervening constructs that might have found support in the literature. Indeed, other researchers might well have reached the same point and decided to insert some other intervening construct and put the resulting hypotheses to test. We cannot include them in our own theory because any theory must meet the test of consistency. That is, any theory must be capable of yielding one and only one prediction linking any single set of independent and dependent variables.

This underscores a critical fact about the way science progresses. One experimenter casts his lot with an incidental learning explanation as to why the viewing of television violence may lead to aggressive behavior. Another investigator may cast her lot with a "disinhibition" explanation; for example, that persistent viewing of television violence impairs inhibitions to aggressive behavior that a society has included in its customary socialization processes. Hence, Television viewing → Disinhibition → Aggression. Another investigator, believing that the evidence really tells us that viewing of aggressive acts on television actually leads to reduction in tendencies toward aggressive behavior, erects between independent and dependent variables the intervening construct "catharsis." For that theory, Viewing → Catharsis → Reduced tendency to aggress. The whole point is that science is, in essence, an adversary proceeding, in which each theorist does her or his best to find support for a particular view and points to flaws in the work of others—yet the theorist clings to a position only until the evidence plainly shows that another explanation is superior.

The only test of a theory is to see whether reality is indeed consistent with what the theory says. We must somehow derive predictions from our theory concerning the way in which certain real-world phenomena are related and then make systematic observations to see if these predictions are supported. This process is referred to as *hypothesis testing*. But to make such observations requires first that we take the next step.

Develop operational definitions of concepts. Operational definitions are the crucial links between theory and reality that make theory testing possible. An operational definition specifies the "operations" or procedures necessary to measure or manipulate a concept. Kerlinger[24] sees two kinds of operational definitions: (1) *measured* and (2) *experimental*.

A measured operational definition describes how an abstract concept is quantified, for example, "intelligence" as measured by the Stanford-Binet IQ test, or "mass media exposure" to information on a certain topic as measured by counting the number of media messages on that topic that a respondent can recall having encountered. In our television violence example, "aggression" may be measured by observing and counting the number of times children perform aggressive acts against toys in a playroom setting. We might index "arousal" by measuring heart rate, skin conductance, or blood pressure change. (A lie detector uses two or more of these same measures to infer arousal as a consequence of lying.) In doing so we have defined abstract and thus unobservable concepts in terms of concrete observations that we can quantify. Quantification is important because it lends precision to our predictions and permits mathematical and statistical operations to be applied to the data. A good portion of this book is devoted to such mathematical and statistical operations, but the raw material for such procedures is the product of measured operational definitions.

An experimental operational definition specifies not how to measure a concept but how to *manipulate* it in an experiment. For example, we might manipulate "exposure to television violence" by randomly assigning subjects to two groups, exposing one to a 10-minute television sequence portraying a predetermined number of violent acts and exposing the other (control) group to a benign nature film.

But how can we be sure that an operational definition truly represents the abstract concept it is designed to represent? How do we know that an IQ test is a reasonable indicator of "intelligence," or that the number of times a child subject in an experiment strikes a bobo doll is a measure of "aggression"? When we ask the question "Are we measuring (manipulating) what we think we are measuring (manipulating)?" we are concerned with the *validity* of our operational definition. Stamm treats this topic in greater detail in Chapter 8. We should emphasize here, however, that without valid operational definitions of concepts, it is impossible to test the relations among those concepts specified by a theory. And the task of constructing valid operational definitions is a difficult one. As Blalock has observed:[25]

> We shall take the commonly accepted position that science contains two distinct languages or ways of defining concepts, which will be referred to simply as the theoretical and operational languages. There appears to be no purely logical way of bridging the gap between these languages. Concepts in one language are associated with those in the other merely by convention or agreement among scientists.

Closely tied to the validity question is the topic of reliability. Not only do we want, for example, our measures of "aggression" to reasonably tap what we ordinarily mean by that concept in the abstract, we also want those measures to do so consistently and reliably.

Operational definitions, then, are the primary tools of all scientific research because, as Kerlinger says, "they enable researchers to measure variables and because they are bridges between the theory-hypothesis-construct level and the level of observation."[26] They are also critical to the process of *replication*. Any finding that is obtained in a particular laboratory must be subjected to further scrutiny. Others must repeat the experiment to test the validity of the results. Replication tests whether such a finding can be obtained repeatedly. The importance of operational definitions, then, is that they provide a precise answer as to what we did to obtain our result—both how we measured our attributes and how we manipulated our experimental conditions—so that others may test them. Without operational definitions, replication would be impossible.

State research hypotheses in operational terms; design a research study to test these hypotheses; evaluate the theory in terms of the outcome. Now that we have discussed the nature of the links between theory and observable reality, we are in a position to describe the predictions or *research hypotheses* that such links make possible. *We do not test a theory or its propositions directly.* We test it indirectly through the predictions we make about reality that follow from the theory. For example, we might test the theoretical proposition "the greater the exposure to televised violence, the greater the physiological level of arousal" indirectly through the research hypothesis: "Subjects exposed to a 10-minute violent sequence of 'NYPD Blue' will manifest greater mean physiological arousal as indexed by skin conductance measures than subjects exposed to a nonviolent nature film."

The *theoretic* hypothesis is stated in terms of abstract concepts and is thus untestable in any direct sense, while the *research* hypothesis is stated in terms of operational definitions (one "experimental" and the other "measured," as in the example above) and is therefore testable.

We must now face the troublesome fact that there is still a third level at which hypotheses are stated. Our first statement of expectations, the theoretic hypothesis, was stated in terms of the theory. The second instrument, the research hypothesis, was the same hypothesis stated in terms of the operations to be performed and the relations to be tested by the research. The third-level statement may be termed the *statistical hypothesis* and refers to the technical form in which the hypothesis is stated for purposes of a statistical test. Contrasted with each of these forms is the *null hypothesis*, which (ordinarily) states that there is *no* relationship among the variables under study. When there is a statistically significant relationship, we reject the null hypothesis; that is, we find positive evidence for our prediction. If we must accept the null hypothesis, this means failing to find positive evidence for the predicted relationship. (The null hypothesis is explained more fully by Weaver in Chapter 9.) Being in a position to reject the null hypothesis means we have indirect support for the theory that generated the hypothesis, provided, of course, that our operational definitions are valid.

Note that we did not use the word *proof* in our discussion. One cannot "prove" a theory. We can only accumulate evidence "in support of" a particular theory. If most of the research hypotheses generated by the theory are supported in most cases, then we usually *accept* the theory as a reasonable representation and explanation of how certain phenomena are interrelated. This acceptance is always tentative, because a new theory with better empirical support may come along at any time, as we have said.

The reader may have noticed that we have not discussed step six in the theory-research process, *design a research study to test the hypotheses*. Given that a substantial portion of this book is devoted to research design, we do not deal with that topic in detail here. As the material in these chapters should make clear, it is a gross oversimplification to reduce such a complex undertaking to one "step."

Research design, however, though vitally important, is but one aspect of the overall theory-data-theory process, or "scientific method." This process cannot be reduced to choices between experiment and survey or between chi square and correlation. These are important decisions, certainly, but they are only links in a long chain of decisions that constitute the entire process. It is this decision chain that makes the research process inherently creative. To begin with, any number of concepts might be chosen, and these concepts might be related to one another by theoretical propositions in any number of ways. There are many ways each concept may be operationalized, literally hundreds of research designs from which to choose, and dozens of analysis techniques to pick from depending on the research design selected.

But for all its complexity, the process is characterized by a single underlying structure (see Figure 7.2). Basically, the process involves a continuous shuttling back and forth between two planes, the abstract plane of theory and the earthly plane of the empirical world. We begin with relatively informal observations of some phenomenon in the real world. To explain and predict phenomena, we engage in conceptualization, an inductive step by which we develop concepts and link them in a theoretical structure. To test the propositions of this structure, we must again descend to the real (empirical) world, over the bridge created by our operational definitions. It is important to recognize the essentially arbitrary nature of these definitions. Our operational definitions enable us to make new observations, and, based on the relationships among them, we make inferences concerning the "truth" or "falsity" of our original propositions. If certain propositions did not receive empirical support, then we need to alter the theory, correct our methodological procedures, or both, and put the theory to test once again. This process of reconceptualization prompted by research findings was termed many years ago as "retroduction" by Selltiz, Wrightsman, and Cook:[27]

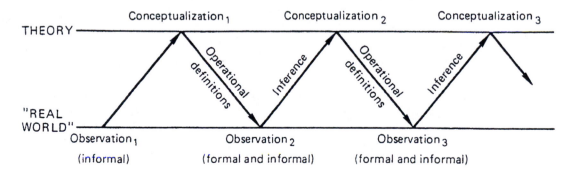

FIGURE 7.2. Relation of Theory and Empirical Observation.

Retroduction is no bastard of science, but its progenitor. We fit data into patterns retroductively: We elaborate the patterns deductively and test them inductively, but the propositions that endure are usually retroduced, not deduced or induced. The scientist shuttles back and forth between data and theory. How else could it be?

Ideally, this process should continue until an elegant and powerful theory emerges, one that is highly explanatory and that repeatedly withstands rigorous testing and replication. Unfortunately, this level of explanation is rarely attained.

Theory before Data or Data before Theory?

There is some disagreement among students of scientific method over which should come first, data or theory. In the seven-stage description of the inductive-deductive process given here, we put observation first, followed by tentative formulations of constructs and propositions. Such observations may, of course, arise unaided by research. But it is more likely that they arise from observations of data, our own and those of others. We scan data for signs of regularity and of anomaly.

A three-stage perspective offered many years ago by Westley[28] continues to be useful today. For Westley, whose ideas are summarized in Table 7.1, the first stage is one of relatively crude observation and highly intuitive interpretation. At this stage observation and interpretation are more or less inseparable, just as in perception observation is guided by expectation.

It is at stage II (inductive empiricism) that we begin to refine our observations (through measurement), treat them systematically (through statistical reduction), and refine constructs and develop operational definitions. This is more or less the correlational stage where we seek as much order as the data provide us, working entirely inductively. Thus, what we carry to stage III is a combination of observation and interpretation.

Searching for Ideas

Now that we have described the steps in theory construction and discussed assumptions, how does one come up with ideas for communication theories? We noted earlier that there is a shortage of theory in the field, yet this does not indicate a lack of research over a wide range of topics. In the preface to an early edition of *Theories of Mass Communication*, DeFleur and Ball-Rokeach have observed that[29]

> various sources have yielded an amazingly diverse set of trends, specialized interests, subareas, and directions. In fact, the heterogeneity of the field has sometimes proved to be an embarrassment of riches. No one can be sure at any given time, or can be sure at the present time, precisely what constitutes the study of mass communication.

This is particularly true today. Not only has the field of mass communication forged even more ties with an ever-expanding set of related areas, but new communication technology has blurred old distinctions like mass versus interpersonal communication. As Reardon and Rogers have put it, "The distinctive aspects of the new technologies force basic changes in communication models and in research methodologies. . . . In particular, the new interactive media mean that the past dichotomy of interpersonal and mass media channels as a means of subdividing the discipline will be deemphasized."[30] If we fail to recognize this, they surmise that "we may be missing a world of research possibilities."[31]

Over a quarter of a century ago, Cole and Bowers[32] asked the twenty-four most productive scholars in the field and the deans of the twenty-five most research-productive schools: "What are the important areas in which we should involve ourselves and in which theory should be developed?" The researchers gave thirty different answers, and the deans gave twenty-five, with no area receiving more than three mentions. Unquestionably, there would be much greater diversity today.

Within the body of literature represented by the numerous journals dealing with communication, annual reviews describing perspectives and new thinking in communication research, a number of special publications, and work in related fields, there is considerable raw material for developing new concepts and reconceptualizing old ones. It also is possible to get some notion about what is likely to be supported in this new perspective, and why, through review of data reported in the tables accompanying these articles and chapters.

In communication we often have borrowed the theories of others as we have sought to understand, explain, and predict behaviors associated with communication. But there are no patents on disciplinary boundaries to theories, and there is nothing to prevent us from going further and inventing new concepts or reorganizing old ones in new ways that allow us to explain in greater detail or in greater depth the phenomena that interest students of mass communication.

Endnotes

1. Robert Bostrom and Lewis Donohew, "The Case for Empricism: Clarifying Fundamental Issues in Communication Theory," *Communication Monographs*, 59 (1992): 109-129.

2. *Ibid.* When developed by the Vienna Circle of scientists in the 1920s, this doctrine generally referred to a strict form of empiricism that recognized as valid only those truth claims based on direct observation and quantification, an approach that has been modified in the social and behavioral sciences to include self-report and other sources of data not directly observed. This epistemology, in turn, springs from Ludwig Wittgenstein's verification theory of meaning. The latter holds that statements or propositions are meaningful only if they can be empirically verified. In other words, if no empirical method for verification exists, inferences are meaningless.

3. Thomas Kuhn, *The Structure of Scientific Revolutions, 2nd ed.* (Chicago: University of Chicago Press, 1970). The fact that after more than half a century as a formally constituted discipline communication still has no agreed-upon metatheoretical perspectives by which its theories are built may derive in part from the historical legacy of the discipline, which involves an unusual degree of eclecticism or, as has been further suggested, from its methodological fixation. Whatever the causes, if a mature discipline requires a research tradition embracing an agreed-upon set of specific theories and philosophical and methodological guidelines for its acceptance, then communication, although in its fifties, continues to struggle through a difficult infancy. Presently, among those most often employed in the field are critical, interpretive, and objectivist perspectives. (See, for example, C.R. Berger, "Communication Theories and Other Curios," *Communication Monographs*, 58 (1991): 101–113.

4. Larry Laudan, "Views of progress: Separating the Pilgrims from the Rakes," *Philosophy of the Social Sciences*, 10 (1977): 273–286. Kuhn, Laudan, and others define a mature discipline as one that has a research tradition embracing an agreed-upon set of specific theories and philosophical and methodological guidelines.

5. See Guido Stempel III and Bruce H. Westley, *Research Methods in Mass Communication, 1st and 2nd eds.* (New York: Prentice-Hall, 1981, 1989).

6. Fred N. Kerlinger, *Foundations of Behavioral Research* (New York: Holt, Rinehart & Winston, 1986), p. 9.

7. A considerable portion of the work cited here grows out of the authors' own long-running program of research in mass communication and health communication, funded for the past seventeen years by agencies of the National Institutes of Health, particularly the National Institute on Drug Abuse (NIDA), the National Institute on Alcohol Abuse and Alcoholism (NIDA), and the National Institute on Mental Health (NIMH). The authors wish to express gratitude to these agencies for their support, which has contributed both to advances in the study of prevention of adverse health behaviors and to advances in the study of human attention and persuasion in the communication process. For a summary of this work, see Lewis Donohew, Elizabeth Pugzles Lorch, and Philip Palmgreen, "Applications of a Theoretic Model of Information Exposure to Health Interventions," *Human Communication Research*, 24 (1998): 454–468, and for an illustration of its application to a contemporary communication campaign, see Philip Palmgreen, Lewis Donohew, Elizabeth Pugzles Lorch, Rick H. Hoyle, and Michael Stephenson, "Television Campaigns and Adolescent Marijuana Use: Tests of Sensation Seeking Targeting," *American Journal of Public Health*, 91 (2001): 292–296.

8. Donohew and Palmgreen, *op. cit.*, 1998.

9. Lewis Donohew, Rick Zimmerman, Pamela Cupp, Scott Novak, Susan Colon, and Ritta Abell (2000). "Sensation Seeking, Impulsive Decision-Making, and Risky Sex: Implications for Risk-Taking and Design of Interventions," *Personality and Individual Differences*, 28 (2000): 1079–1091.

10. Robert Craig, "Communication as a Practical Discipline," in Brenda Dervin, Lawrence Grossberg, Barbara O'Keefe, and Ellen Wartella, eds., *Rethinking Communication, Volume II, Paradigm Issues* (Newbury Park, CA: Sage,1989), 97–122.

11. Vannevar Bush, *Science—The Endless Frontier* (Washington: National Science Foundation, 1990).

12. Gary L. Kreps, Lawrence R. Frey, and Dan O'Hair, "Applied Communication Research: Scholarship That Can Make a Difference," *Journal of Applied Communication Research*, 19 (1991): 71–87.

13. Donald Stokes, *Pasteur's Quadrant: Basic Science and Technological Innovation* (Washington: Brookings Institution Press, 1999).

14. Kreps et al., *op. cit.*

15. Donald E. Stokes, *op. cit.*

16. See, for example, Karl Popper, *The Logic of Scientific Discovery* (New York: Harper & Row, 1986), and Popper's *Objective Knowledge* (Oxford: Clarendon, 1972).

17. Carl Hempel, *Aspects of Scientific Explanation* (New York: The Free Press, 1965).

18. Shelby Hunt, *Marketing Theory: Conceptual Foundations of Research in Marketing* (Columbus: Grid, 1976).

19. Lewis Donohew, Philip Palmgreen, and Jack Duncan, "An Activation Model of Information Exposure," *Communication Monographs*, 47 (1980): 295–303. This has been slightly revised and updated to eliminate a requirement for awareness of the arousal level in Lewis Donohew, Elizabeth Pugzles Lorch, and Philip Palmgreen, Applications of a Theoretic Model, *op. cit.*, 1998.

20. Lewis Donohew, Seth Finn, and William Christ (1988), "The Nature of News Revisited: The Roles of Affect, Schemas, and Cognition," in Lewis Donohew, Howard Sypher, and E. Tory Higgins, eds., *Communication, Social Cognition, and Affect* (Hillsdale, NJ: Erlbaum), 195–218.

21. Dolf Zillmann and Jennings Bryant (1985), "Affect, Mood, and Emotion as Determinants of Selective Exposure," in Zillmann and Bryant, eds., *Selective Exposure to Communication* (Hillsdale, NJ: Erlbaum, 157–190.

22. Rudolf Carnap, "Testability and Meaning," in Herbert Feigl and May Brodbeck, eds., *Readings in the Philosophy of Science* (New York: Appleton-Century-Crofts, 1953), 47–52.

23. For a review of this literature, which retains its quality despite having been made a number of years ago, see L. Rowell Huesmann (1982), "Television violence and aggressive behavior," in David Pearl, Lorraine Bouthilet, and Joyce Lazar, eds., *Television and Behavior: Ten Years of Scientific Progress and Implications for the Eighties, Vol. II* (Rockville, MD: National Institute of Mental Health, 1982).

24. Kerlinger, *op. cit.*, 29.

25. Hubert M. Blalock, Jr., *Causal Inferences in Nonexperimental Research* (New York: W.W. Norton & Co., 1964), 6.

26. Kerlinger, *op. cit.*, 29.

27. Claire Sellitz, Lawrence S. Wrightsman, and Stuart W. Cook, *Research Methods in Social Relations* (New York: Holt, Rinehart, & Winston, 1976), 35.

28. Bruce H. Westley, "Scientific Method and Communication Research," in Ralph O. Nafziger and David M. White, eds., *Introduction to Mass Communications Research, 2nd ed.* (Baton Rouge: Louisiana State University Press, 1963), 260.

29. Melvin L. DeFleur and Sandra Ball-Rokeach, *Theories of Mass Communication, 3rd ed.* (New York: David McKay Co., 1975), ix.

30. Kathleen Reardon and Everett M. Rogers, "Interpersonal vs. Mass Media Communication," *Human Communication Research*, 15 (1989): 297.

31. *Ibid.*, 300.

32. Richard R. Cole and Thomas A. Bowers, "An exploration of factors related to Journalism faculty productivity," *Journalism Quarterly*, 52 (1975): 638–644. See also Cole and Bowers, "Research Article Productivity of U.S. Journalism Faculties," *Journalism Quarterly*, 50 (1973): 246–254.

TABLE 7.1 Schematic Representation of Three Levels of Empirical Investigation*

Level (Stage)	Purpose	Formal System	"Mapping" Devices	Theoretical System	"Mapping" Devices	Reality System	Approached "End Product"
I Orientation, Problem setting	Orientation: problem setting, "hypothesis hunching" Intuitive (no certainty) knowledge of loosely defined segment of reality	"Common sense" Inductive logic	"Common sense"	Fragmentary, intuitive constructs Plausible hypotheses and explanations "Interpretations"	Verbal definitions Subjective relations between observations and constructs	Sweeping, inclusive, holistic, interpretative observations (wholly uncontrolled)	Description; insight, "wisdom" Orientation
II Inductive empiricism	Orientation: problem setting, hypothesis formulating Conceptual clarity Low-certainty knowledge of a more or less defined segment of reality	Inductive logic	Concepts loosely related to formal properties	Hypothetical constructs of increasing refinement Emerging hypothesis	Measurement of attributes Operational definitions? Normative (probability) statistics	Observations defined by operations (statistical control)	"Observed dependencies" leading to testable hypotheses
III Hypothetico-deductive empiricism	Dependable (high-certainty) knowledge of a strictly defined segment of reality	Deductive logic	Formal derivation	Assumptions, postulates, and derived hypotheses	Measurement of attributes Operational definitions? Normative and nonnormative statistics	Observations strictly defined by operations Controlled observation (statistical and/or laboratory controls)	Verified generalizations, statable as laws, and inferring causal connections

*This may also be treated as stages in the development of a science or as stages in the advancement of a particular investigation.

8

Measurement Decisions

Keith R. Stamm

In your view, are the numbers researchers use what most sharply separates science from your professional and everyday life? If you subscribe to this view of measurement and statistics, chances are you may be a little intimidated by the whole subject, which is not very conducive to understanding. Let's try to put you more at ease by beginning with some familiar uses of measurement outside of science, to show what they have in common with "scientific" uses.

With my own students I often bring up weight control as a practical problem for the everyday application of measurement. For health and other reasons, most of us would like to keep our weight within a certain range. The solution to this problem often is "don't eat too much!" But how do we know when we're eating too much? This is where measurement comes in, measurement of something called "calories." It's proved very helpful to me, and I'm sure to many others, to be able to count calories in the following fashion: 5 calories/gram of carbohydrates and 9 calories/gram of protein and fat. Foods high in protein and/or fat are going to add calories a lot faster than carbohydrates. The application of this measurement scale can provide a good guideline when you go shopping. Don't put anything in your shopping cart that gets more than 30 percent of its calories from fat.

Introductory journalism textbooks provide other examples of the practical application of measurement to everyday problems. After all, measurement is basically a set of rules for assigning numbers to observations, which allows us to introduce order to what we observe. Under this definition, the rules that editors employ in counting headlines would qualify as measurement. One such instrument, described by Westley,[1] is used to:

- Count all small letters 1 except l, i, f, t, which count 1/2, and m and w, which count 1 1/2.
- Count all capital letters 1 1/2 except I, which counts 1/2, and M and W, which count 2.
- Count all punctuation marks 1/2 except the dash, question mark, dollar sign, and percent sign, which count 1.
- Count all numbers 1.
- Count all spaces 1.

The basic question to be asked about this measuring instrument, or any other, is how well it serves its purpose. Editors use it to estimate the space a given headline will require—a tool to fit headlines to a designated space—and it usually provides sufficiently precise estimates. Some lack of precision can be tolerated because the headline does not have to fit the space exactly. But of course, if it exceeds the allotted space, the headline will come back from the page editor for revision.

Within the scientific community, the precision (or "power") of a measuring instrument must also be appropriate to its purpose. Many "scientific" instruments are less precise than the headline count, either because the additional precision is not needed or because present techniques do not allow it. The scientist, like the editor, must be aware of this. Greater precision is not an end in itself. (Actually, in today's automated newsrooms, headlines are no longer counted in this way. Instead they are counted by a computer, which signals the editor working at a visual display terminal whether a line is too long or too short. This change has meant the difference between crude estimating and exact measurement.)

If the old headline count were to be used for scientific purposes, how would we describe its measurement properties? The scientist would note, for example, that characters assigned a value of 1 always occupy more space than those that count 1/2, but they do not necessarily occupy twice as much space, although the numbers might imply that they did. Scientists refer to this type of instrument as an *ordinal scale*. The power of an ordinal scale is limited in that the intervals between values are not equal. Thus, for example, a headline that counts 30 will always be longer than one that counts 20, and both longer than one counting 10. But we cannot be sure that the difference in length between the 30-count and 20-count headlines will always be the same as the difference between the 20-count and 10-count headlines. Later we will consider how the inequality of intervals limits the statistical tests that may be performed upon numbers derived from ordinal scales.

Ordinal scales reflect the magnitude or amount of a quality that is being observed. It is thus an instance of what we call quantitative measurement as compared to qualitative. An example of qualitative measurement would be the circulation manager who wants to separate those who take the Sunday edition from those who don't. He uses a simple measurement scheme (called a nominal scale) employing two numerals. The numerals simply indicate whether a quality is present. In this example each household that has the quality of taking the Sunday edition can be assigned the numeral 1, and each household that does not can be assigned the numeral 2 or any other numeral; it doesn't really matter). We call this kind of measurement "nominal" because it names a quality and merely distinguishes its presence from its absence. We want to record, for example, whether each person in a survey is a newspaper subscriber (quality present) or not (quality absent). This simple measurement scheme has facilitated, for example, a series of studies in which newspaper subscribers could be contrasted with nonsubscribers on a variety of other qualities, revealing the many other ways in which these two groups differ.[2]

We can find other cases where the professional requires very powerful measurement tools. For example, a magazine editor may want to assess amount of "interest" in a list of proposed topics. If he or she wants to obtain interest scores that would allow exact comparisons between topics, a type of measurement scale called *equal interval* should be developed. To explain what this means, let's assume that a measurement technique called the *thermometer scale* has been applied. Using this technique, we obtain ratings on the scale from 1 to 100 for all topics. Next, suppose that three topics have received the following interest ratings: Topic 1 = 20, Topic 2 = 40, Topic 3 = 60. When the measurement scale for interest is equal interval, the difference between Topics 1 and 2 is assumed to be the same as the difference between Topics 2 and 3. We could not make this assumption if the scale were ordinal.

An equal-interval scale of interest ratings may suffice for the magazine editor, but the film writer uses even more precise measures of scene length that correspond to the time each scene occupies. Measurements of length can be used because of the exact correspondence between length of a scene (in feet) and the time it will occupy on the screen. Since film is projected at the rate of 24 frames a second, each foot of film occupies 1.6 seconds on the screen. In fact, it is safe to say a 20-foot scene will take twice as much time as a 10-foot scene, an assumption we could not make with equal-interval scales. The reason is that both length in inches and time in minutes have meaningful zero points. That makes both what we call **ratio scales**, the most powerful kind of measurement scale. A ratio scale requires equal intervals and a zero point.

There are common scales of measurement that have equal intervals but no meaningful zero. The thermometer scale described above is an equal-interval but ratio scale. We may say that one film scene is twice as long as another—in either feet or minutes. We cannot say that an interest rating of 40 is twice as high as a rating of 20.

To recapitulate, nominal scales are qualitative rather than quantitative—the numbers are arbitrarily chosen to indicate the presence or absence of a quality. Ordinal scales are quantitative, but the numbers provide only a ranking of the observations being measured. Interval scales provide a ranking but in addition the intervals between the values are equal. Ratio scales have these same properties and a meaningful zero.

In any situation where measurement is employed, professionally or scientifically, questions about the adequacy of the measurement scheme are bound to arise. These questions center on the **power, validity, reliability,** and **efficiency** of the measure, and include questions such as the following:

- Does the measure describe your observations with sufficient precision to satisfy your research objectives? *(power)*
- Will the instrument give us the same result time after time? In different situations, no matter who is using it? *(reliability)*
- How can we be sure it is measuring what it is supposed to be measuring? *(validity)*
- Is the measure easily and readily applied in data collection? *(efficiency)*

We turn now to a consideration of these questions within the various stages of the research process.

There are several different points at which important decisions about the design of a measure need to be made. Although we do not actually begin working with numbers until we reach the analysis stage, measurement must be part of the researcher's thinking from the moment a project is initiated. Here we consider the role of measurement at four stages: (1) conceptualization, (2) operationalization, (3) analysis, and (4) discussion of results. At each of these stages, the four basic measurement questions listed above are raised.

Conceptualization

Let us say the researcher is interested in the concept "television use." Is the concept concerned with exposure to television or with attention to television? These are two different behaviors, requiring different observations and having different theoretical import. A television viewer can be exposed without paying any particular attention to the content. The relationship of, say, political knowledge gain, may be very different for exposure as compared to the relationship with attention.[3] It is therefore very important to have clearly in mind what you intend to measure. It is also important to consider which is most appropriate, a qualitative or quantitative measure. Is the measure intended to distinguish those who attend to a particular program from those who don't (qualitative)? Or is it meant to distinguish those who attend much of the time from those who attend only a little (quantitative)?

From the moment of conceptualization, measurement principles are involved, in this case the power of the number system appropriate to the concept. Whatever the hypothesis to be tested, whatever the relationship to be discovered, we must ask how much measurement power will be required to do the job, whether adequate measures can be obtained, and what time and resources will be needed to develop and pretest appropriate instruments. For example, if you want to find out whether television makes as much difference in political knowledge as newspapers, you might elect to develop quantitative measures of attention to news and public affairs content of television and newspapers.

There is insufficient space here to discuss all the relationships between concepts and measures. For example, Cronbach and Meehl did seminal work more than thirty years ago that identified "construct validity" and distinguished it from other validity problems. They argue that ultimately the validity of any measure rests upon the adequacy with which the concept is defined, including the hypothesized relations among observables.[4] Such hypotheses must be sufficiently explicit to permit unequivocal interpretation of validating evidence.

A good example of the connection between conceptualization and measurement is provided by analyses of the concept of accuracy in interpersonal communication.[5] Since accuracy had not been adequately conceptualized, a number of measurement procedures were being employed that did not pertain to the same concept. In fact, it was often unclear exactly what was being measured, and it was therefore difficult to interpret the meaning of the accuracy scores obtained.[6] The confounding of accuracy scores had to be untangled through sharper definition of the underlying attributes.

Another example of the interrelationship of conceptualization and measurement can be found in recent work on "community ties" and newspaper readership. Conceptual analysis of community ties showed that there were no less than twelve kinds of ties (that is, twelve concepts) that needed to be distinguished.[7] Previous work, however, paid little or no heed to these distinctions, resulting in a variety of confused and ill-defined measures. One could not say with any confidence which concept of "community tie" any of these measures pertained to. Most measures seemed to pertain to more than one concept (that is, they were confounded measures). As a result, findings relating community ties to criterion variables such as newspaper readership varied widely. The fact that different concepts were (unwittingly) being measured probably had a lot to do with the inconsistent findings.

A theoretical contradiction also arose that could not be resolved. Some authors theorized that community ties led to newspaper readership, while others theorized that readership resulted in community ties. The contradiction could be resolved only if one distinguished the kinds of ties that preceded newspaper use from those likely to result from it. Of course, little or nothing could be made of such a theoretical distinction unless one could develop valid measures for particular kinds of community ties. Confounded measures would only perpetuate the difficulty, and it goes without saying that measures are likely to remain confounded until concepts are untangled.

Conceptualization also tells you something about the stability of the condition being observed, which has important implications for the reliability of the measure. For example, most psychologists regard attitude as a very stable characteristic of a person. Attitudes are considered very resistant to change and applicable to behavior in a variety of situations. Given this conceptualization, we should expect a very high degree of consistency in an attitude measure over time and across situations.

For example, observation of an individual's attitude toward a political candidate would be expected to remain consistent over time and across situations. If not, the reliability of the measure may be suspect, unless some reason for change can be identified and documented with evidence.

At the other extreme is a "mood scale," which is conceived as measuring highly volatile emotions. The research utility of such a scale may depend on its sensitivity to moment-to-moment changes in emotion. The appropriate degree of stability lies in the concept itself, and that must be reflected in the research and statistical designs that use it.

The across-time stability of measures (called "test-retest reliability") is of particular relevance when longitudinal studies are done to search for delayed or cumulative effects of media exposure. For example, some researchers hypothesize that effects of exposure to televised violence may show up months or even years subsequent to a history of exposure. However, it is also well known that measures of media exposure and of aggressive behavior (the hypothesized effect) tend to be unreliable. This situation might call for collecting data at three points in time rather than two, and employing statistical techniques in which unreliability is controlled for as a "third variable" in the analysis. For example, Heise has developed a path analysis model by which *error variance* due to unreliability and *true variance* may be separated where three data points are available.[8] Once the reliability coefficients between each pair of the three tests have been calculated, a measure of reliability may be obtained using partial correlation (see Chapter 9). Where there has been change between tests due to "true" change in the variable, this correction will result in a higher coefficient that is a more accurate reflection of the actual stability of the method.

The greatest contributions to the efficiency of a measure are also made at the conceptualization stage. A clean, focused definition of the attribute to be measured pays dividends in at least two ways. First, it prevents confounding the instrument with observations that have little or nothing to do with the concept. Second, clarity of definition leads more readily to standardization of measurement procedures. When there is little doubt about what you want to measure, you can specify all the relevant observations ahead of time and determine what values should be assigned to each type of observation.

Operationalization

The operationalization stage is pivotal for the development of an adequate and appropriate measurement scheme. We look back to the conceptualization to ensure that the empirical operations are faithful to the concept(s)—so-called *concept validity*. And we look ahead to the observations required to provide confidence in the reliability of the measure. We even ask how the obtained measure will satisfy the demands of the statistical model to be used in analysis. Operationalization must be considered a pivotal stage. The measure must be subjected to serious tests here, lest it be found wanting at a later stage when it might be too late to introduce needed improvements.

Both validity and reliability should be established at the operationalization stage. Reliability points to sources of measurement error, error due to lack of stability or consistency in the measuring instrument. To return to the headline example, a headline count that is a reliable measure would assure that two editors counting the same headline would come up with identical (or very similar) values. Or, if the same editor counted the same headline another time, the values should be the same or similar. To the extent that these measurements differ, reliability is lacking. As with validity, it is generally best to pretest so that a preliminary assessment of reliability can be guided by results. These results may lead to changes in either the instrument or the measurement context of the study. The purpose is to increase prospects of obtaining acceptable reliability when the study goes into the field.

To be a little more specific about the difference between validity and reliability, take the example of a caliper. A caliper should measure distance and nothing else. Its validity, thus, is obvious. A caliper should get the same answer every time (within stated tolerances), no matter in whose hands, no matter in what circumstances. That is reliability. In human measurement, validity must be established and so must reliability. The fact that we usually use correlation in both instances requires us to be quite self-conscious about what such correlations mean.

Reliability

In establishing a measure's reliability we are really asking two questions. The first relates to equivalence. For example, will two versions of the same measure consistently yield the same answer when applied to the same subjects? The second is stability. Will the measure yield the same answer at different times? An all-too-common shortcoming in reliability arises from placing too much faith in limited observation. The classic case is to place all one's faith in a single observation as the sole basis for a measure. For example, a typical approach to measuring newspaper exposure is to ask: "How many issues of the newspaper did you read in the past week?" Although this is a relevant observation to make, it is subject to some sources of error. "Last week" may have been an atypical week, in which case the observation is not entirely valid. If issues read fluctuates markedly from week to week, the observation is not very reliable. This makes it very risky to place all our confidence in this one observation.

It is often better to make several observations of the same behavior and then use the average of these observations as your measure. For example, in a recent study the measure of "newspaper reading" was based on three observations: (1) Do you usually read the front page news? (2) Do you sometimes read opinion columns on the editorial page? (3) Do you sometimes read letters to the editor?[9] Why would we have more confidence in this measure? Consider that if we made only the single observation above ("How many issues.....?), a person who frequently skimmed the front page headlines could obtain just as high a score as someone who frequently read the front page, editorial section, and letters to the editor. The measure would end up equating individuals whose newspaper reading is actually very different. The use of multiple observations is important to establishing the reliability of a measure. In general, the reliability of a measure increases with the number of observations included in the measure providing, of course, that the observations all pertain to the same concept. In fact, the use of multiple observation measures—called *indexes*—is quite essential to providing evidence of reliability. Both of these points can be illustrated with a simple example. Suppose that we are doing a study to find out if media attention makes a difference in understanding of an environmental problem (e.g., salmon recovery). One of our measurement goals is to create a reliable index of understanding that we could use in a sample survey. And so we have devised a set of six questions to tap understanding and try them out in a small scale survey—called a *feasibility test*. An important purpose of the test is to verify the reliability of the index before investing in an expensive and time-consuming sample survey. Results from the feasibility test are shown in Figure 8-1 below.

The figure shows the value of the reliability coefficient—called an *alpha coefficient*—that we obtain for various numbers of observations. The reliability coefficient increases as we increase the number of observations on which the measure is based. With only two or three items, reliability does not reach an acceptable level. Alphas of .80 or higher are considered optimal. Notice that in this case six observations were required to obtain optimal reliability. Sometimes more than six items would be required, but seldom fewer than four or five. Notice also that the amount of gain in reliability diminishes with each additional item and reaches a point of diminishing returns around five items. In the interest of efficiency, between four and six observations is often optimal.

This feasibility test is very encouraging, inspiring our confidence that the six items will yield a reliable index when applied in large-scale survey. Of course, such tests don't always turn out so rosy, which is why it's so important to do them. Figure 8-2 shows results from a test of an index to measure opinions toward an environmental problem. The

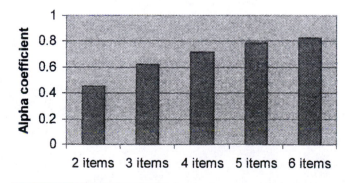

FIGURE 8.1. Relationship Between Reliability and Number of Items.

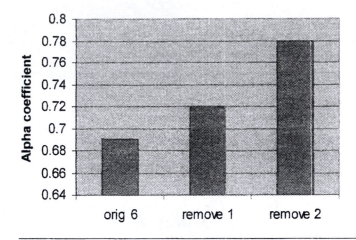

FIGURE 8.2.   Effect of Removing Unreliable Items.

original six items yielded a reliability coefficient of only .69, a bit lower than we'd like to see. What's wrong? Are six items insufficient in this case, or do we have some "bad items?" One or more of the items might be invalid—measuring something other than what we intended, or may be highly unreliable. How do we know?

When an index is not performing as needed, we often examine the correlations between all of the items, based on the principle that observations of the same concept should be positively correlated. Given the relatively low reliability obtained in this case, we might expect weak or even negative correlations between some of the items. The *correlation matrix* (Table 8.1) shows that in fact two of the items have weak correlations with the other four. Referring back to the figure above, you can see the effect of removing these items from the index. Removing both items improves reliability to .78—not quite optimal. At this point we should probably construct four additional items to add to the four reliable items and conduct the feasibility test on another sample.

TABLE 8.1   *Correlation Matrix for Six-Item Index*

	Item 1	Item 2	Item 3	Item 4	Item 5
Item 1	1.0				
Item 2	.31	1.0			
Item 3	.06	.04	1.0		
Item 4	.07	.09	.61	1.0	
Item 5	.13	.17	.45	.46	1.0
Item 6	.16	.05	.38	.39	.51

In recent years, factor analysis has become commonly used for assessing the unidimensionality of a set of items such as those in Table 8.1. In this case the correlations suggest that the set of items is measuring two different variables. If that is the case, a factor analysis may help to identify the specific items associated with each of these two variables. Factor analysis accomplishes this by first correlating every item with every other item and then sorting the items into "factors," each with values indicating what items share variance with other items.[10] Table 8.2 confirms that indeed our preliminary six-item index is measuring two different variables. This might lead us to try to identify the variable being measured by items 1 and 2, then produce additional items to observe that variable in a second index. The application of factor analysis, while widespread, is not advised for those who are not well trained in its use.

Of course, the validity and reliability of instruments may already exist at the time the researcher turns from concept to operations. It only requires a careful search to discover that a measure appropriate to a concept in which the investigator is interested has been used fruitfully many times and its measurement properties are well established. In the computer age, however, there is no reason not to check one's own experience with a measure, since a computer routine often will provide everything that is needed. (For example, SPSS, the Statistical Package for the Social Sciences, contains easy-to-use software that permits tests of reliability and creation of correlation matrixes for item analysis.)

The preceding discussion has assumed that we are talking about multi-item measures. But in both survey and experimental research we often depend upon single-item measures. For identifying information for later analysis, we may use single questions to obtain age, occupation of head of household, political affiliation, and the like. Surveys may use single items to measure attitudes or expected behaviors (Do you favor Proposition 13?) (If the election were held today . . . ?). In validating such items, we are really talking about validating an entire instrument, and Shoemaker and McCombs have much to say on that question in Chapter 13. We can say that the method used is essentially test-retest. In surveys it is customary to check on the work of interviewers by calling a respondent and checking out answers to selected questions—a test-retest procedure.

TABLE 8.2 *Two-Factor Solution for a Six-Item Set*

	Factors 1	2
Item 1	0.0	.80
Item 2	0.0	.80
Item 3	.81	0.0
Item 4	.81	0.0
Item 5	.76	.18
Item 6	.71	.12

Validity

The notion of validity raises two sorts of questions about measures. The first is whether the instrument actually taps the attribute it purports to measure. We will refer to this as *empirical* validity. The second question is much more difficult: It asks whether the instrument taps only the attribute in which you are interested. This question has been called *construct* validity.

To take the empirical validity question first, we may begin by identifying the types of evidence that bear upon whether a measure actually measures what it is intended to measure. Three types of evidence must be considered: *face* validity, *concurrent* validity, and *predictive* validity.

We will begin with face validity. Generally, any measure of a communication variable is begun on evidence of face validity. All this means is that the content of the measure (e.g., its items) appears to represent the attribute being measured. Of course, the validity of a measure cannot rest on face validity alone.

To go beyond face validity requires us to relate the instrument to other measures of the same attribute. An instrument that correlates with scores on another measure of the attribute provides some evidence of concurrent validity. Indexing, as described in connection with reliability, is also one way of producing concurrent validation. Several items, all designed to measure the same attribute, are correlated with one another over a sample of respondents. Such evidence for validity is normally obtained in a pretest. Until some evidence of concurrent validity is found, it is risky to use an instrument for extensive data gathering. There are many other ways of obtaining concurrent validation. Where other instruments have been developed for measuring the attribute, such an instrument may be used together with an untested instrument in a pretest. If they correlate, this is further evidence of concurrent validity. Osgood and others used this method in validating the semantic differential. For example, they showed high correlations between the location of concepts on the evaluative factor of the semantic differential and scores on standard attitude scales. Another approach, called "multiple operationism," has been gaining favor in the research literature recently. The basic argument behind this approach is that concurrent validation can be strengthened by comparing scores obtained through different types of observational procedures. For example, the validity of a paper-and-pencil test as a measure of the popularity of an exhibit might be checked out against a measure of floor erosion in front of the exhibit.

Despite frequent exhortations to multiple operations by Webb and others and Campbell and Fiske,[11] among others, the actual use of multiple operations has not gained much popularity in communication research. This is probably not due to lack of a convincing argument or to ignorance on the part of researchers. Paisley and others[12] have shown that some concepts are adequately measured with a single operation, while others, such as "intelligence" and "ethnocentrism," require triangulation using multiple measures. There is no reason such communication concepts as "empathy," "agenda," "readership," "readability," or "use" and "gratification" could not also be validated by this method.

Campbell and Fiske[13] long ago described a method of concurrent validation, which they called the "multitrait-multimethod matrix." Actually, this method is designed to demonstrate construct validity as well as concurrent validity. Concurrent validation is demonstrated with this method by the "convergence" of measures of the same attribute obtained through different methods. Construct validity is demonstrated through discrimination; that is, measures of different attributes obtained with similar methods should not be highly correlated. If they are highly correlated, one suspects that something other than the trait in question is being measured by the instrument. Paisley and others have elaborated the Campbell and Fiske idea with their "convergent-discriminant matrix" and shown that other "double variation" strategies are also available, including cross-lagged correlation, "Q analysis," and profile analysis.[14] These techniques are too specialized to receive full treatment here.

Turning now to *predictive* validity, the question is whether a measure relates to other measures as expected. Once again, it is at the conceptualization stage that one identifies variables that should be predicted by the measure in question. For example, it would be expected that a measure of the individual "news agenda" should be related to variables describing patterns of media use. Osgood and others demonstrated the predictive validity of the semantic differential by showing that ratings of Stevenson and Eisenhower could be used to predict how people would actually vote in the 1952 elections.[15] For another example, let's return to our index of environmental understanding. We might argue that if it is a valid measure of understanding, it should be positively correlated with education and, further, it should be more strongly correlated with education than a measure of opinions on the same issue. When this test of predictive validity was conducted, a significant, positive correlation ($r = .18$, $p < .01$) was found between understanding and education, and a positive but nonsignificant correlation ($r = .07$) between opinion and education.

There are some things to keep in mind when testing predictive validity. First, when a measure is tested against an extensive list of criterion variables, it is likely that some significant relationships will appear by chance. After all, when we accept the usual p less than 0.05 criterion (see Chapter 9), we may expect one prediction in twenty to be significant by chance. Second, if the expected relationships are not found, we are left with the question: Is the measure invalid, or is the theory that led to those predictions invalid? Lack of predictive validity calls for reassessment of the concept and perhaps the theory from which it is drawn.

Demonstrating *construct* validity is a complex process, and one is not expected to get more than a start on it in a single investigation. It can only occur in a theoretical framework in which the construct can be defined in terms of propositions about relationships to observable variables. As Cronbach and Meehl have stated, "The investigation of a (measure's) construct validity is not essentially different from the general scientific procedures for developing and confirming theories."[16] Many types of evidence may be relevant to the construct validity of measures. But how such evidence is to be interpreted depends largely upon what the theoretical framework leads us to look for and what that evidence means in that framework. Here are some kinds of evidence that might be obtained in demonstrating construct validity:

1. *Group differences.* Does the theory lead one to expect that two groups should differ on the measure? If so, both populations should be sampled and compared on the measure.
2. *Internal structure of the instrument.* Evidence of the unidimensionality of the measure, as discussed in connection with factor analysis of indexes, supports construct validity.

3. *Change over instances.* If the theory suggests experimental manipulations that should produce changes in the measure, we may demonstrate that these changes actually occur.
4. *Logical consequences.* If the theory specifies a certain outcome, measures of that outcome may be related to some logical consequence. For example, when Flesch was first measuring "readability," he reasoned that a consequence of readability should be reading comprehension, which allowed him to correlate his scores with an existing comprehension measure.[17]

Construct validity is established through a continuing program of research involving the development of theory, the creation of hypotheses, and testing of these hypotheses by experiments and other means. The aim of construct validation is the development of a measure that reflects only the attribute in which we are theoretically interested. There are very few measures currently employed in communication research whose construct validity is firmly established.

Analysis

By the time we get to the analysis stage, all the critical decisions have been made. The plan has been drawn and it only remains to carry it out. But sometimes the analysis stage turns up problems due to shortcomings at earlier stages. A case in point may be found in the literature of schizophrenia. Controversy arose over findings that parental communication behaviors were linked with the onset of schizophrenic symptoms in the children.[18] It centered on a measurement problem. The index used to measure parental communication deviance was confounded: Scores on the index were heavily dependent upon the sheer number of words spoken. Thus, the question had to be posed whether lack of validity (of the index) had produced an artificial correlation.

An effort was made at this point to reinterpret the findings by statistically removing the source of confounding by means of analysis of covariance, which is discussed in Chapter 9. It turned out, however, that the sources of measurement error were so complex that a statistical correction was inappropriate. The only way to clear up the controversy was to go back and design a more valid index and collect new data. Attention to conceptual clarity and use of pretesting in the operationalization stage should help avoid serious difficulties of this kind. It is likely, however, that the instrument will not perform exactly as it did under pretest conditions. The preliminary checks that were employed in pretesting must now be repeated to verify that the instrument has performed according to expectations. Also, evidence bearing on predictive validity may be available for the first time at this stage.

We begin by rechecking the internal consistency of the instrument, whether a scale or an index. This procedure includes checking the frequency distributions of individual items. It is important to check the frequency distribution of measures and of the individual items that comprise them. A measure that is badly skewed will present problems since many inferential statistics used in analysis require normally distributed variables (see Chapter 9). To illustrate let's return to our six-item index of environmental understanding.

A check of the distributions shows that all the individual items making up the index are somewhat skewed (Figure 8.3). If we'd used a single-item measure, or even one comprised to two or three items, we'd be in trouble. But because the skewness of the items runs in opposite directions, combining them produces a measure that is normally distributed (Figure 8.4).

In this case, as a result of previous decisions and careful pretesting, we have succeeded in producing a measure of understanding that is normally distributed. But what might have happened if we had decided to rely on four items and had not pretested carefully? To illustrate, let's randomly pick any four items from the previous index and examine the distribution. The distribution of these four items is not normally distributed; it has a fairly strong negative skew (Figure 8.5, skewness = −.18). For some statistical applications, such as analysis of variance, this would be very undesirable. Now we are in the position of needing to do something about the skewness. (In addition, a check on reliability shows that the reliability falls short of optimum—alpha = .72.)

Now we are forced to attempt a mathematical transformation of the variable to achieve a more normal distribution. Usually a transformation can be found that will improve normality. (See the variable transformation menu of your statistical package.) However, the cost of improving normality is that the original metric of the index is lost. It has been transformed into units that are not nearly as straightforward in their interpretation— such as squares, square roots, logarithms, or standard deviation units. In the case of our four-item understanding index, the skewness was reduced from −.18 to −.07 by transforming into standard deviation units.

At the analysis stage, if we have developed our measure carefully, we ordinarily expect to reap the benefits of a valid and reliable measure. This should be apparent in the relationships we are able to obtain with other variables, assuming these variables have been adequately measured. There are two principles here that are worth remembering. The first is the statisticians' oft-repeated aphorism—"if you don't have variance, you can't get covariance." In other words, a measure that doesn't vary can't covary in relationship with some other measure. For example, what if everyone in our sample received a score of 5 on our measure of understanding? There would be no way, statistically, that we could show,

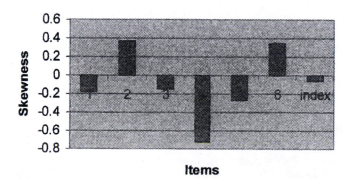

FIGURE 8.3. Skewness of Index Compared to Single Items.

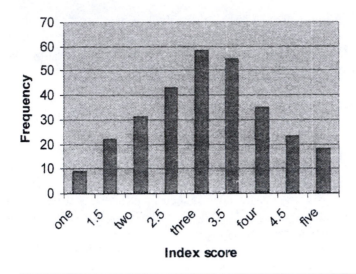

FIGURE 8.4.   Frequency Distribution of Index.

for example, that media use makes a difference in understanding. Regardless of the amount of media exposure, the understanding score would be 5.

The second principle is less obvious: A more reliably measured variable will produce a more accurate estimate of the strength of relationship with other variables. This would mean, for example, that the more reliable measure should produce stronger correlation coefficients, if our hypothesis is sound. Returning to our example, this can be demonstrated in several ways. First, if we simply correlate media use with the single (less reliable) items making up the understanding index, we see that all these correlations are lower than the correlation with the index measure (Figure 8-6). We also notice that the correlations with single item measures give wildly different estimates of the strength of relationship between media use and understanding.

Second, we can create a series of indexes based on increasing numbers of items. As we saw previously (Figure 8-1), increasing the number of items increases the reliability of the index. Therefore, we would expect that the correlation of understanding with media use would become stronger as we add items to the index. This relationship is shown very clearly in Figure 8-7 and is just one more way of demonstrating the payoff from a more reliable measuring instrument. The careful investment in conceptualization and construction of index measures is well worth it.

A question that invariably comes up at the analysis stage is whether the measures obtained can be treated as satisfying interval-level measurement. Unfortunately, readily applied procedures for meeting the requirements of intervality are lacking. The established method of creating interval scales, Thurstone's method of paired comparisons, is laborious and requires an enormous investment in development.[19] Its primary use in communication research has been as an outside criterion for checking the intervality claims of other measures, such as the semantic differential and Likert scales. This use of Thurstone scales is rather limited because so few of them are available.

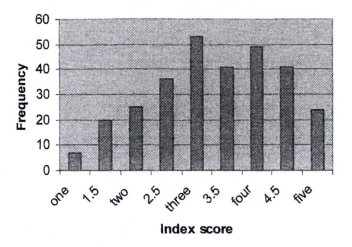

FIGURE 8.5.   Frequency Distribution for Four-Item Index.

In a recent review of the intervality question, Hewes observed that few of the measurement scales currently in use have been adequately tested for intervality, even though they are treated as interval scales. This in itself presents a serious problem for two reasons. First, not very much is known about the effects of violations of intervality, specifically, the use of interval-level statistical models in the analysis of ordinal data. According to Hewes, this widespread practice runs the serious risk that both type I and type II errors may be increased.[20] (A type I error is accepting a hypothesis when in fact it is false. A type II error is rejecting a hypothesis when in fact it is true.) Until further information is available on this question, the cautious researcher is justified in selecting less demanding statistical tools. Second, there is usually no practical way to test the intervality of a measure after the fact. There are few established measures that can be used as standards for checking one's own instrument. Hewes has worked out a path analysis procedure by which a necessary condition for intervality may be tested, but there is not much payoff from conducting such a test unless there is strong reason to believe the measure will pass the test.

Reporting Findings

When it comes to reporting findings, the researcher should give attention to explaining the reasoning behind the measurement model and to describing evidence that pertains (positively or negatively) to the validity and reliability of the measurement. The report should describe the conceptual basis for the measurement model and give a detailed description of the development of the measure, the kinds of observational procedures selected, the results of pretests and what modifications were made in light of pretest results, what kinds of validating evidence were incorporated into the study design, what rules were adopted for scoring, and the like. A complete report requires a listing of the contents of any new instrument.

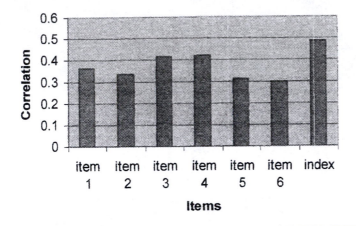

FIGURE 8.6. Correlation of Media Use with Single Items Compared to Index.

The discussion of results should include an evaluation of the adequacy of the measure. Evidence bearing upon validity and reliability should be fully reviewed, since interpretation of findings hinges on this evidence. The choice of a statistical model for analyzing results should also be linked to the measurement procedures. It is not a matter of defending the "correctness" of the approach used, but of the instrument used within the research context.

Despite careful pretesting, it may happen that the obtained validity and reliability turn out to be inadequate. When the evidence for reliability is flawed, there is no point in reporting the study. The same is true where the evidence for validity is flawed. No reportable results can flow from flawed instruments. But if the study requires accepting the

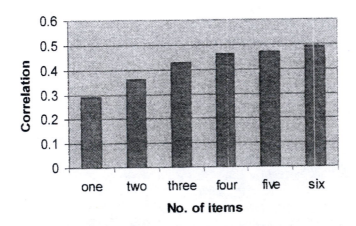

FIGURE 8.7. Relationship between Index Reliability and Strength of Correlation.

null hypothesis, there may be grounds for reporting the study.[21] The failure to predict may have sprung from weak measures or it may have sprung from a weak or inadequate theory. Presenting the study may permit the researcher to explore what needs to be done to revise the theory and may also invite others interested in the work to do so themselves. For further suggestions on reporting research results, see Chapter 21.

Summary

The most important decisions respecting measurement of communication variables are made during the first two stages of a study. The conceptualization of the variable clarifies the choice of measurement model and indicates the types of evidence that will be most relevant to validation of the instrument. Pretesting is important to efficiency. It provides needed information for guiding development of a useful instrument and prevents overinvesting resources in an unproductive measurement approach. Evidence supporting the validity and reliability of a measure is an integral part of any research project and vital to the interpretation of findings.

Endnotes

1. Bruce H. Westley, *News Editing, 3rd ed.* (Boston: Houghton Mifflin Company, 1980), 137.

2. Jeremy Lipschultz, "The Nonreader Problem: A Closer Look at Avoiding the Newspaper," *Newspaper Research Journal* 8 (Summer 1987): 53–59.

3. Steven Chaffee and Joan Schleuder, "Measurement and Effects of Attention to Media News," *Human Communication Research* 13 (1986): 76–107.

4. Lee J. Cronbach and Paul E. Meehl, "Construct Validity in Psychological Tests," *Psychological Bulletin* 52 (1955): 281–302.

5. Norman L. Gage and Lee J. Cronbach, "Conceptual and Methodological Problems in Interpersonal Perception," *Psychological Bulletin* 62 (1965): 411-422; Steven H. Chaffee, "Pseudo-Data in Communication Research," 1971, unpublished paper; Keith R. Stamm and W. Barnett Pearce, "Communication Behavior and Coorientational Relations," *Journal of Communication* 21 (1972): 208–220; Beth Hefner, "Communicatory Accuracy: Four Experiments," *Journalism Monographs* No. 30 (August 1973).

6. Daniel Wackman, "A Proposal for a New Measure of Coorientational Accuracy or Empathy," 1969, unpublished paper.

7. Keith R. Stamm, *Newspaper Use and Community Ties: Toward a Dynamic Theory* (Norwood, NJ: Ablex Publishing Corp., 1985), 23.

8. Donald Heise, "Separating Reliability and Stability in Test-Retest Correlation," *American Sociological Review* 34 (1969): 93–101. Students are advised to study this reference closely before attempting to use Heise's method.

9. Michael McDevitt and Steven Chaffee, "Closing Gaps in Political Communication and Knowledge: Effects of a School Intervention," *Communication Research* 27 (2000): 259–292.

10. See James Stevens, *Applied Multivariate Statistics for the Social Sciences* (Hillsdale, NJ: Lawrence Erlbaum, 1992), 374–402.

11. Eugene Webb and others, *Unobtrusive Measures: Non-Reactive Research in the Social Sciences* (Chicago: Rand McNally & Co., 1966); Donald T. Campbell and D. W. Fiske, "Convergent and Discriminant Validation by the Multitrait-Multimethod Matrix," *Psychological Bulletin* 56 (1959): 81–105.

12. Matilda B. Paisley, W. A. Collins, and William J. Paisley, "The Convergent-Discriminant Matrix: Multitrait-Multimethod Logic Extended to Other Social Research Decisions," 1970, unpublished paper, Institute for Communications Research, Stanford University, Stanford, CA.

13. Campbell and Fiske, *op. cit.*

14. *Ibid.*

15. Charles Osgood, G.J. Suci, and Percy Tannenbaum, *The Measurement of Meaning* (Urbana: University of Illinois Press, 1957).

16. Cronbach and Meehl, *op. cit.*

17. Rudolph Flesch, "The Marks of a Readable Style," Ph.D. dissertation (Columbia University, NY, 1944).

18. A. Woodward and M. J. Goldstein, "Communication Deviance in the Families of Schizophrenics: A Comment on the Misuse of Analysis of Covariance," *Science* 197 (1977): 2096–2097.

19. L.L. Thurstone, *Scales for the Measurement of Social Attitudes* (Chicago: University of Chicago Press, 1931).

20. Dean Hewes, "'Levels of Measurement' Problem in Communication Research: A Review, Critique, and Partial Solution," *Communication Research* 5 (January 1978): 87–127.

21. Successful prediction contributes positive evidence for validity. But the only safe course is to have independent evidence for validity before risking the null hypothesis, because this provides the best basis for judging whether the failure should be attributed to the measure or the hypothesis.

9

Basic Statistical Tools

David H. Weaver

Many students interested in journalism and mass communication express a dislike or fear, or both, of anything quantitative. One typical comment from such a student is: "I never was any good at math; that's why I decided to go into journalism."

This comment reflects a misunderstanding about the nature and uses of statistics in mass communication research. Statistics and mathematics are not the same, and one need not necessarily be adept at mathematics to use statistics effectively in mass communication research.

In most cases in mass communication research, we use statistics to reduce complicated sets of findings or data to simpler terms. We usually are trying to answer one of two sets of questions: (1) How strong is the relationship between variables, or (2) is this difference real, or is it due to chance?

We might find, for example, that modernization of format by newspapers is related to increase in circulation. A correlation coefficient, which we know can range from -1.0 to $+1.0$, enables us with one number to summarize the relationship we have found between modernization of format and circulation. Or we might find that readership of editorials in our survey is on the average 5 points higher for men than for women. A t-test will enable us to find out whether that is merely a difference that happened by chance in this sample or a real difference we might expect to find with all readers of that paper.

Although it used to be argued that one needs to be somewhat familiar with mathematics to calculate various statistics, this is less true as calculators and computers become more available and as programmed statistical packages (such as SPSS, the Statistical Package for the Social Sciences)[1] become easier to use and more available for personal computers. There are preprogrammed calculators and computer packages to produce just about any commonly used statistic from raw data.

Knowledge of the mathematical principles and procedures underlying statistics is valuable in interpreting statistical results and for checking computer programs. But it is not essential for one to be highly proficient in mathematics to understand and use statistics.

Descriptive Statistics

A primary use of **descriptive statistics** in quantitative mass communications research is to summarize large and complicated sets of data. Why are such summaries needed?

Consider a survey of 500 persons or an analysis of 500 court documents. If only ten questions are asked of each person or each document, such a study produces at least 5,000 pieces of information. The hundreds of answers to each question, in their raw form, are very difficult, if not impossible, to interpret without the help of some summary measures, or statistics. This becomes more and more the case as the size and the complexity of a set of data increase.

There are basically two ways to summarize or describe a set of data: (1) according to how the individual pieces of information *cluster* together (measures of central tendency), and (2) according to how individual cases *spread apart* (measures of dispersion).

Measures of Central Tendency

The three most common measures of clustering, or central tendency, are the **mean** (average), the **median** (midpoint), and the **mode** (most frequent value or values).

Mean.   This is the most common measure of central tendency. It is a simply the sum of the individual values for each variable divided by the number of cases. It should be used with interval data. By interval, we mean that the scale of measurement contains equal intervals. Height measured in inches, for example, is an interval measurement because all inches are the same size. Thus, if we interview twenty persons and assign them scores based on how often they use newspapers, radio, and television for news, we find the mean, usually represented as a capital X with a bar across the top, by adding the scores and dividing by the number of cases (20 in this example). In other words,

$$\overline{X} = \frac{sum\ of\ scores}{number\ of\ scores} \quad \text{or} \quad \overline{X} = \frac{\Sigma x}{N}$$

Once the mean is calculated, it tells you the *balance point*, or the average, of the set of values you are interested in summarizing. There are not necessarily an equal number of scores above and below the mean, as is true of the median, but the mean is sensitive to the value of each score and the distance of each score from every other score. With a normal distribution, there will tend to be the same number of scores both above and below the mean (see Figure 9.1). When there are a very few high or very low scores, however, the mean will be pulled toward those extreme scores and will not be as accurate an indicator of the central clustering, or midpoint, of these scores as it would be if there were no extreme scores (see Figure 9.2).

Distributions of scores with a few very high scores or values are said to be *positively* skewed, whereas distributions with a few very low values are said to be *negatively* skewed. In positively skewed distributions, the mean is likely to be misleadingly high (see Figure 9.2). In negatively skewed distributions, the mean is likely to be misleadingly low (see Figure 9.3).

Frequency of Scores	6						x					
	5					x	x	x				
	4				x	x	x	x	x			
	3			x	x	x	x	x	x	x		
	2		x	x	x	x	x	x	x	x	x	
	1	x	x	x	x	x	x	x	x	x	x	x
		1	2	3	4	5	6	7	8	9	10	11

Mean = 6.0   Scores

FIGURE 9.1.   A Normal Distribution.

In short, the mean is an extremely sensitive measure of clustering and is also a very accurate measure of central tendency when the set of measures is fairly equally distributed above and below the midpoint, as in Figure 9.1. In addition, the mean is the most important statistically of all the measures of central tendency, as will become more apparent in the discussions of the t-test and analysis of variance.

Median.   The median is the midpoint of a set of ordered numbers. To find the median, arrange the numbers from the smallest to the largest. Thus, if we had the numbers 1, 5, 8, 7, and 3, we would arrange them 1, 3, 5, 7, and 8. The median would be the middle number, 5. If we add a number, say 10, to the series, then we would have 1, 3, 5, 7, 8, and 10. We use a slightly different procedure to estimate the median of an even number of scores. We would now take the two middle numbers, 5 and 7, and take the midpoint between those two numbers, or 6, as our median. Like the mean, the median can be used with interval data. It can also be used with ordinal data. Instead of measuring height in inches, we could line people up according to height and rank them from tallest to shortest; those ranks would be ordinal measures.

Because the median depends only on the number of measures in a distribution and not their value, it is quite useful as a measure of central tendency for distributions that are positively or negatively skewed, but it is not as useful as the mean in more complicated statistical tests where one is interested in the odds of certain differences occurring by chance.

Modes											
4		x	x		x						
3		x	x		x						
2		x	x	x	x	x	x	x			
1	x	x	x	x	x	x	x	x	x	x	x
	1	2	3	4	5	6	7	8	9	10	11

Mean = 5.04

FIGURE 9.2.   Positively Skewed Distribution.

					Modes					
4					x			x	x	
3					x			x	x	
2		x	x	x	x	x	x	x	x	x	
1	x	x	x	x	x	x	x	x	x	x	x
	1	2	3	4	5	6	7	8	9	10	11

Mean = 6.54

FIGURE 9.3.   Negatively Skewed Distribution.

Mode.   The mode is simply the most frequent score, or scores, in a distribution and may be calculated for variables measured at any level. In the case of a "normal" distribution, as illustrated in Figure 9.1, there will be only one mode and it will equal the mean and the median. In some distributions that are not normally arranged, however, there may be several measures that tie for the most frequent score, and thus several modes (see Figures 9.2 and 9.3). In distributions where all scores are equal, there will be no mode.

Why use the mode? What does it tell you that the mean and median do not? In a normal distribution, the mode offers no additional information to that conveyed by the mean and the median. In a skewed distribution, however, where the mean, median, and mode may all take on different values, the mode tells you not only the most frequent value(s) but also how far from the midpoint (median) and balance point (mean) the most frequent value or values occur.

It is useful to compare the values of the mean, median, and mode for any distribution of scores or values of any kind. If these three statistics are fairly equal, the chances are that the distribution is fairly normal or at least not skewed in some manner. If the mean is larger than the median and the mode, this usually indicates a positively skewed distribution (see Figure 9.2). If the mean is smaller than either the median or the mode, this usually indicates a negatively skewed distribution.

Measures of Dispersion

The three most common measures of scatter, or dispersion, are the *range*, the **variance**, and the **standard deviation**. *Percentiles* are also considered measures of scatter by some researchers.

Range.   This is the simplest measure of dispersion. It is calculated by subtracting the lowest score (minimum) from the highest score (maximum) in a distribution of values. It is not at all sensitive to the distribution of scores falling between the minimum and maximum and so provides very limited information about how a set of scores is dispersed.

Variance.   Sometimes referred to as s^2, variance is a measure of the dispersion of values around the mean. Unlike the range, the variance is sensitive to every score in a distribution of scores and thus provides more information about the dispersion of a set of scores than does the range.

The variance is the average of the squared deviations from the mean. To calculate the variance, the mean must first be determined. Once this is done, each score is subtracted from the mean, and the difference is squared to eliminate any negative values and to give additional weight to extreme cases. These squared differences are then added together and divided by the number of scores in the distribution to get the average squared deviation:

$$s^2 = \frac{\Sigma (x - \overline{X})^2}{N}$$

where Σ means "the sum of," x equals each individual score, $\overline{X}$ equals the mean of the set of scores, and N equals the number of scores in the distribution (see Figure 9.4).

Thus the variance provides a measure of scatter that is sensitive to all the values in a distribution. The larger the variance, the more spread out the scores in a distribution. In addition, variance is important in many other statistical tests and procedures. In mass communication research, one of the main goals is to "explain" or "predict" variance in dependent

Scores (x)	Frequency	$(x - \overline{X})$	$(x - \overline{X})^2$	$(x - \overline{X})^2 \times Frequency$
6	1	−4	16	16
7	2	−3	9	18
8	4	−2	4	16
10	6	0	0	0
12	4	2	4	16
13	2	3	9	18
14	1	4	16	16
	20			$\Sigma(x - \overline{x})^2 = 100$

$$\overline{X} \text{ (mean)} = \frac{\Sigma x}{N} = \frac{200}{20} = 10$$

$$s^2 \text{ (variance)} = \frac{\Sigma(x - \overline{X})^2}{N} = \frac{100}{20} = 5$$

$$s \text{ (standard deviation)} = \sqrt{\frac{(x - \overline{X})^2}{N}} = \sqrt{\frac{100}{20}} = \sqrt{5} = 2.24$$

In a distribution of scores where more than one score has the same value, one must remember to multiply each score by its frequency when adding the scores and to divide by the total frequency of scores rather than the number of different scores. So, in calculating the mean, one multiplies each score by its frequency and gets a total of 200, which is divided by the total frequency of scores (20) to yield a mean of 10.

Each score is then subtracted from the mean of 10, and the difference is squared: $(x - \overline{X})^2$. Then the squared differences are multiplied by the frequency of each score and added to produce the sum of the squared differences about the mean: $\Sigma(x - \overline{X})^2$. This sum (100 in this case) is divided by the total frequency of scores (20) to yield a variance of 5.

The standard deviation is calculated simply by taking the square root of the variance of 5, yielding a value of 2.24 (rounded to two decimal places).

FIGURE 9.4. Calculation of the Variance and the Standard Deviation.

variables by locating independent variables that can account for why some cases deviate more or less from the mean. (A "dependent" variable is one for which the value depends on an "independent" variable. For example, if we hypothesize that the amount of time a person spends reading magazines depends on the person's level of reading ability, then reading ability is the independent variable and time spent reading magazines the dependent variable.)

Standard Deviation.   This is the most commonly used measure of dispersion because it is expressed in the *same* measurement units as the scores it summarizes. The standard deviation is simply the square root of the variance and is often expressed as *s*. The values of the standard deviation are smaller and easier to work with than those of the variance, and standard deviation values have more intuitive meaning because they are expressed in the same units as the original scores. That is, if the variance of the annual income of a sample of workers is 250,000, then we are really talking about 250,000 squared dollars. A standard deviation of 500, though, refers to 500 dollars.

The standard deviation is calculated in exactly the same manner as the variance, except that one additional step is required—taking the square root of the final figure:

$$s = \sqrt{\frac{(x - \overline{X})^2}{N}}$$

where Σ means "the sum of," x equals each individual score, $\overline{X}$ equals the mean of the set of scores, N equals the number of scores in the distribution, and $\sqrt{}$ means "the square root of" (see Figure 9.4).

In addition to being sensitive to every score, or value, in a distribution and being expressed in the same measurement units as the original scores, the standard deviation is very important in estimating the **probability** of how frequently certain scores can be expected to occur in random sampling. In other words, the standard deviation is very important in calculating sampling error and confidence intervals. This will be discussed in more detail in the next section on inferential statistics, where measures of association and differences are included.

Percentiles.   Perhaps the most common measure of dispersion, percentiles are useful for describing how an individual score is related to other scores in a distribution. For example, if you know that an individual score is at the 80th percentile, you know that nearly four-fifths of the scores fall below this score and one-fifth of the scores fall above it.

To compute percentiles, rank the scores from lowest to highest. Take the rank of the score you want the percentile for, divide it by the total number of items, and multiply by 100. For example, we have these scores: 6, 6, 8, 9, 10, 12, 14, 15, 18, and 19. We want to know the percentile value of 15. Ranking the scores, we find that 15 ranks eighth. There are ten scores, so our computation is $\frac{8}{10} \times 100$ or 80.

Summary of Descriptive Statistics

Descriptive statistics are summaries of distributions of measures or scores. These summaries are often needed in mass communication research because of the large and complex nature of different quantitative studies, be they surveys, content analyses, or experiments.

Measures of central tendency (the mean, median, mode, and others) are used to summarize how the individual scores or values cluster together, whereas measures of dispersion (the range, variance, standard deviation, and percentiles) are used to summarize how the individual measures scatter, or spread apart.

When using measures of central tendency, one should not automatically rely on only the mean, or average, but should check the value of the median to see how close it is to that of the mean. If the median differs substantially from the mean, that is probably a sign that the distribution is skewed. A further check of the skewness statistic, if available, should confirm whether the distribution is skewed. If so, the median should probably be used as a measure of central tendency rather than the mean, unless the median differs appreciably from the mode.

If the median does differ substantially from the mode, and there is only one clear mode, it may be that the mode is the truest measure of clustering in a highly skewed distribution.

If the mean, median, and mode are all fairly equal, however, it is best to use the mean because of its usefulness in statistical tests of differences, such as the t-test and the analysis of variance.

When using measures of dispersion, one should not rely only on the range, because it is not sensitive to the scores between the lowest and highest points of the distribution. Percentages are useful for comparing one score or a category of scores with the other scores in a distribution, but percentages cannot provide a single measure of how spread out a set of scores is from the mean, as can the variance or the standard deviation.

In general, the standard deviation is more useful as a single measure of dispersion than is the variance, because the standard deviation is expressed in the same units of measurement as the original scores and can be directly related to the probability of certain scores occurring in random samples, as will be discussed in the next section. The variance, on the other hand, is more useful in statistical tests of relationships and differences among two or more variables.

Inferential Statistics

Inferential statistics differs from descriptive statistics because it is used not only to summarize characteristics of sets of data and relationships between various sets of data, but also to make estimates of how likely it is that such characteristics or relationships exist in the universe (or population) of all possible cases that make up the sets of data, whether these cases be people, cities, newspaper articles, or whatever.

Mass communication researchers usually study only a **sample** of the universe of all possible cases, whether they are persons in a survey, documents or articles in a content analysis study, or cities in a field experimental study. Descriptive statistics, such as the median, mean, and standard deviation, are usually used to describe characteristics of these samples. If these samples are drawn on a **random** basis, such that each case in the universe has an approximately equal chance of falling into the sample, then sampling error may be calculated to make estimates of how those descriptive statistical summaries apply to a universe of all possible cases.

Because most mass communication researchers are interested in generalizing beyond their particular samples, and because they are usually more interested in *relationships* between measures (or variables), rather than simply describing each set of measures individually, measures of associations and differences are needed to summarize the strength of such relationships and to provide an estimate of how likely it is that such relationships exist in the universes from which the samples were drawn.

Thus, inferential statistics differs from descriptive statistics in two fundamental ways: (1) It is usually concerned with the strength of relationships (associations or differences) among two or more sets of measured variables, and (2) it has accompanying tests of statistical significance that indicate how likely it is that a particular relationship would occur by chance, given a certain sized sample.

Before discussing various measures of association and difference, it is necessary to distinguish between statistics and parameters and to briefly review some of the underlying principles of random sampling. A more detailed account of various forms of sampling appears in Chapter 13.

Statistics and Parameters

Simply put, statistics refer to various characteristics of a *sample*, such as the mean, median, and mode, and parameters refer to various characteristics of a *universe*. Statistical inference is the process of estimating parameters from statistics. For example, if we interview a random sample of 400 college students and find that they read an average of four issues of the college newspaper a week, we are dealing with a statistic, a mean of four issues read a week. If we know that a random sample of 400 cases has a certain error due to sampling, and we take this into account in estimating the average number of issues read each week by all 33,000 students, we are estimating a **parameter**—the average number of issues read each week by the universe (all students enrolled on a certain campus).

It is important to remember that parameters are *fixed* values and are generally *unknown* because we can rarely interview all persons in a certain universe or examine all issues of a certain newspaper. Statistics, on the other hand, tend to vary somewhat from one sample to another and, of course, are known quantities.

Random Sampling

If statistics (characteristics of samples) vary from one sample to another, how is it possible to estimate parameters (characteristics of universes) from one sample? The answer, in its simplest form, is that random samples of the same universe, if drawn over and over again, are distributed in a *normal* fashion, and this normal pattern of distribution allows us to calculate the probability of a universe parameter falling within a certain range of values. By random sample we are referring to a sample where each member of a certain universe has an *equal chance* of being included. An example of this is the familiar technique of putting names in a hat and drawing a certain number of names without looking at them.

In other words, if repeated random samples are drawn from a certain universe of persons, newspaper issues, court documents, or whatever, the means of each sample will be distributed in the shape of a normal curve, with the overall mean for all samples coming very close to the actual universe mean (see Figure 9.5).

We also know from two mathematical theorems, the law of large numbers and the central limits theorem, that the larger size of the samples, the more likely it is that the overall mean for repeated random samples (the mean of the sampling distribution) will be identical to the actual universe mean and the spread of sample means about the overall mean will be less. This is true *even though the universe itself may not be normally distributed.*[2]

Figure 9.5 illustrates a nonnormal universe distribution and an accompanying normal sampling distribution, with equal means. Remember that the universe distribution is made up of many individual cases (persons, newspaper issues, court documents), and the sampling distribution is made up of the means from many repeated random samples. Why is it so important that the sampling distribution take the shape of a normal curve?

Because statistics from repeated random samples are arrayed in a normal distribution about universe statistics, it is possible to estimate the amount and the probability of error contained in a single sample. This is so because the normal curve has certain known properties. For example, we know that about 68 percent of the cases in a normal curve fall within plus or minus one standard deviation from the mean. We also know that slightly more than 95 percent of the cases fall within plus or minus two standard deviations from the mean (see Figure 9.6).

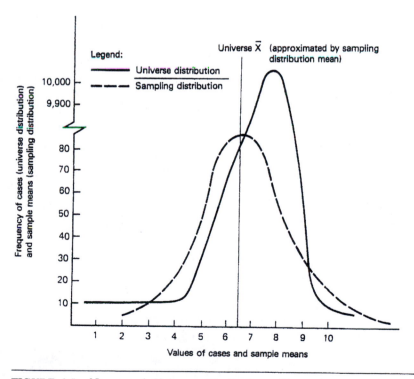

FIGURE 9.5. Nonnormal Universe Distribution with an Accompanying Normal Sampling Distribution.

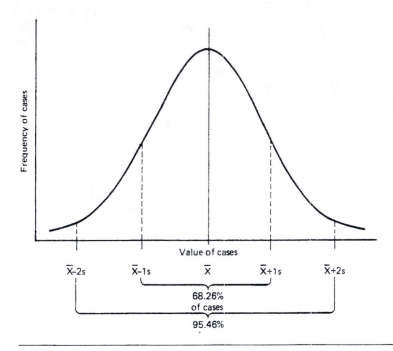

FIGURE 9.6.   Areas under the Normal Curve.

This means that if random samples were drawn from the same universe over and over again an infinite number of times, about 95 percent of these samples would have means of falling within plus or minus 1.96 standard deviations of the overall mean. Therefore, we can be 95 percent certain that when we draw a random sample it will be one of those samples falling within plus or minus 1.96 standard deviations from the overall mean. Likewise, we can be 99 percent certain that when we draw a random sample it will fall within plus or minus 2.58 standard deviations from the overall mean of the sampling distribution.

It should be remembered that the samples must be of a fairly large size for their means to be distributed in a normal manner. That is, the samples should include at least 50 and preferably 100 cases.[3] Samples with fewer than 50 cases cannot be assumed to be normally distributed; therefore, calculating sampling error for such samples is not recommended.

Calculating Sampling Error

Knowing that 95 percent of fairly large random samples fall within plus or minus 1.96 standard deviations from the sampling distribution mean is very useful, but it is not enough information to be able to calculate the amount of the sampling error. An additional piece of information is required: the value of the standard deviation of the sampling distribution for any given sample. This value varies with the size of the random sample and the spread of the scores or values. As mentioned earlier, the spread of repeated sample means about the overall mean for the sampling distribution decreases as the sample size increases. Thus, the standard deviation of a sample distribution decreases as the sample size increases (and increases as the sample size becomes smaller). This means that the amount of sampling error decreases as the sample becomes larger, as one would suspect.

The value of the standard deviation of a sampling distribution is also known as the *standard error*. Although the standard error cannot be computed exactly because one cannot draw an infinite number of random samples of the same size from a given universe, it can be estimated by dividing the standard deviation of a single sample by the square root of the number of cases in the sample.[4] In other words,

$$\text{Standard error} = \frac{\text{standard deviation}}{\sqrt{n}}$$

or

$$s_m = \frac{s}{\sqrt{n}}$$

However, the computation of the standard error as discussed thus far assumes an *interval* level of measurement, a continuous scale. Often in mass communication research, the variables we are interested in are measured at the *ordinal* or *nominal* levels. In other words, we are often dealing with proportions (percentages) when calculating sampling error rather than means and standard deviations.

How is it possible, then, to estimate the value of the standard error for a certain size random sample? By treating proportions as special cases of means, much of the previous discussion of the standard error still applies. It can be shown from the general formula for the standard deviation that the formula for the standard error of a given random sample is

$$s_m = \sqrt{\frac{pq}{n}}$$

where s_m equals the standard error for a given size sample, p equals the proportion of the sample falling into a certain category (say 30 percent), q equals $100 - p$ (70 percent in this example), and n equals the size of the sample.[5]

Once the value of the standard error is calculated, by using either the standard deviation or the proportions formula, one is ready to calculate the sampling error. This is usually done either at the 95 percent level of confidence or the 99 percent level of confidence. Because we know that 95 percent of large random samples will fall within plus or minus 1.96 standard deviations of the overall sampling distribution mean, we multiply the standard error by 1.96 to calculate the sampling error at the 95 percent level of confidence:

$$\text{Sampling error} = 1.96 \, s_m$$

or

$$\text{Sampling error} = 1.96 \sqrt{\frac{pq}{n}} \quad \text{(using the proportions formula)}$$

At the 99 percent level of confidence, the same formula holds, but 2.58 is substituted for 1.96, because we know that 99 percent of large random samples will fall within plus or minus 2.58 standard deviations of the sampling distribution mean (our estimate of the universe mean).

It should be emphasized that repeated large random samples fall *both above and below* the sampling distribution mean, so a plus or minus sign (±) should be inserted before any estimate of sampling error. That is, if the sampling error for a sample of 300 cases is calculated at 5.6 percentage points using the 95 percent level of confidence, this means that we are 95 percent confident that the true universe value lies somewhere between the sample value (say, 30 percent) *plus or minus* 5.6 percentage points. In other words, in this example we are 95 percent certain that the true universe value falls between 24.4 and 35.6 percent (30 ± 5.6 percentage points). This interval (24.4 to 35.6 percent) is known as a *confidence interval*, in this case, a 95 percent confidence interval.

One way of simplifying the calculation of sampling error for an entire study, using the proportions formula, is to assume that p equals 0.5 (or 50 percent) for each variable, and therefore q equals 0.5, making pq equal to 0.25 (0.5×0.5). This is the largest value the standard deviation can assume, using the proportions formula, and therefore is a conservative estimate. If 0.25 is substituted for pq, the formula for sampling error (using the proportions formula for the standard error) becomes

$$\text{Sampling error} = \pm 1.96 \sqrt{\frac{0.25}{n}} \text{ (for the 95\% level of confidence)}$$

In this formula, all that is needed is the sample size (n) to complete the calculation of sampling error.

Through random sampling and the calculation of sampling error and confidence intervals, it is thus possible to estimate parameters from statistics—to generalize from one sample to the universe from which the sample was drawn.

Relationships

As noted earlier, mass communication researchers typically are interested in going beyond the generalizing of certain descriptive statistics of sample variables (e.g., the mean, median, or percentages) to various universes. Researchers are also very much interested in looking at the strength of *relationships* between various sample variables (e.g., level of education and mass media use) and in being able to estimate how likely it is that such relationships exist in the universes from which the samples were drawn.

An examination of relationships in a sample is important for at least three major reasons: (1) for testing research hypotheses, such as "The more education a person has, the more time he or she will spend reading newspapers"; (2) for answering research questions, such as "Do persons who spend much time reading newspapers tend to be more interested in politics than those who spend little time reading newspapers?" and (3) for suggesting new research hypotheses and/or questions (see Chapter 6 for a more detailed discussion of hypothesis testing).

There are two basic ways of looking at relationships among mass communication variables. One can look for *associations* or for *differences*. That is, one can ask if one variable increases (or decreases) as another increases, or one can ask if there are significant differences in one variable that may be due to differences in other variables. Usually survey data are analyzed for associations and experimental data for differences.

Once one has decided to look for associations and/or differences in sample data, two additional questions must be answered: (1) How strong are the associations and/or differences? and (2) How likely it is that these associations and/or differences exist in the universe from which the sample was drawn? The second question applies *only* to sample data. If one collects data from every member of the universe (e.g., U.S. senators in 1965), only the first question is of interest.

There are many different statistical measures designed to indicate the strength of association between two variables. The choice of which one(s) to use depends largely on the *level of measurement* of the variables being related (see Chapter 8 for a detailed discussion of different levels of measurement).

Before discussing specific measures of association, it is necessary to briefly review the nature of correlation and cross-tabulation.

Correlation

When we speak of a **correlation** (positive or negative) between two variables, we are talking about things that are measured on the *ordinal level* or higher; that is, they range from low to high or from few to many. Such variables might include frequency of newspaper readership (measured in number of issues read each week or the amount of each issue read), level of political interest (ranging from low to high), or amount of time spent watching television each week.

A *positive correlation* between political interest and frequency of newspaper readership means that high levels of political interest tend to be associated with high levels of newspaper readership, and low levels of political interest are linked with low levels of newspaper readership. A *negative correlation* between political interest and frequency of newspaper readership would indicate that high levels of political interest are associated with low levels of newspaper readership, and vice versa.

Most correlational measures range from −1 to +1, with −1 indicating a perfect *negative* correlation (all low values of one variable are associated with all high values of another variable), 0 indicating *no* correlation (there is no pattern of association between low and high values of the two variables), and +1 indicating a perfect *positive* correlation (all high values of one variable are associated with all high values of another variable, and all low values of one variable are linked with all low values of the other).

In mass communication research it is very unlikely, given the crudeness of our measures and the lack of any hard and fast linear "laws," that you will find perfect correlations (either positive or negative). Most correlations will range from −0.65 (a moderately strong negative correlation) to +0.65 (a moderately strong positive correlation).

Significance Levels

In addition to indicating the *strength* of a relationship (from −1, a very strong negative correlation, to +1, a very strong positive correlation), most correlational statistics also include a *significance level* (also called a *p level* or probability level), which indicates how likely it is that the relationship could have happened by chance. This significance level may range from almost 0, which indicates that there is almost no likelihood that the relationship could have occurred by chance), to 1, which indicates that it is certain that the relationship could have occurred by chance.

Significance level varies not only with the strength of the relationship (high correlations have lower significance levels, indicating that they are less likely to occur by chance), but also with the size of the sample. In large samples, even weak relationships may be statistically significant, while in small samples only stronger correlations will be significant. Therefore, the choice of a significance level depends upon the size of the sample, among other factors.[6]

There are no hard rules regarding the choice of a significance level in mass communication research, but .05 is generally accepted for samples of 500 or less, and .01 is generally more appropriate for larger samples.

A significance level of .05 indicates that the relationship has a probability of occurring by chance 5 percent of the time, or 5 times in 100 samples, meaning that it would occur in the larger population in 95 of 100 equal-sized samples. Likewise a significance level of .01 indicates that the relationship would occur by chance only 1 time in 100 samples or that it would be present in the larger population or universe in 99 of 100 equal-sized samples.

It should be stressed that statistical significance levels only indicate the likelihood that an observed relationship actually exists in the universe from which the sample was drawn. They do not tell how strong the relationship is. Thus, a statistically significant relationship may not be substantively important. You should consider *both* the strength of the relationship and the statistical significance level before concluding that the relationship is meaningful. There is a guide to strength of a correlation near the end of the section on Pearson's *r* later on in this chapter.

Cross-Tabulation

There are two major methods of obtaining measures of association and their accompanying significance levels: (1) from **cross-tabulation** or contingency tables, and (2) from scatterplots or scatter diagrams. In mass communication research, where most variables take on only a limited number of values (2 to 7), cross-tabulation tables are more common than are scatter diagrams, because scatter diagrams are more appropriate for continuous variables that have many values measured on an interval or ratio scale (e.g., income or temperature).

A cross-tabulation table is simply a joint frequency distribution of cases according to two or more variables (see Table 9.1). The two variables being related in Table 9.1 are taken from an opinion survey of students enrolled on the Bloomington campus of Indiana University. Each person in the survey who indicated his or her class standing *and* who indicated how often he or she usually watched the evening network and/or local news on television was sorted into one of nine categories on the basis of the answers to both questions.

In Table 9.1, only the row percentages are included because of the nature of the two variables being compared. Class standing is considered to be an independent variable (a predictor of watching television news), and frequency of watching evening television news is considered to be a dependent variable (the behavior being predicted or studied).

TABLE 9.1 *College Class Standing and Frequency of Watching Television News*

Class Standing	1–2 Times a Week	3–4 Times a Week	5 or More Times a Week	Total
Freshmen and sophomores	30 37.5%	34 42.5%	16 20.0%	80 100%
Juniors and seniors	25 26.0%	43 44.8%	28 29.2%	96 100%
Graduate students	9 20.5%	7 15.9%	28 63.6%	44 100%
Total	64	84	72	220

Chi square = 27.76, 4 df, p = .0000

Cramer's V = .25

Contingency coefficient = .33

Kendall's tau$_b$ = .24, p = .0000

Gamma = .37

Usually, the percentages in a cross-tabulation table are calculated on the totals for each category of the independent or predictor variable (class standing in this example).

Correlation and Causation

It is important to remember that correlations and cross-tabulations, especially with data gathered at one point in time, do *not* necessarily indicate a causal relationship. Just because a person's educational level is strongly correlated with his or her time spent reading newspapers does not mean that increased levels of education cause increased use of newspapers. It may be that a third factor, such as income or kind of job, can account for the high correlation between level of education and reading a newspaper. It may also be true that increased newspaper reading may lead to a higher level of education, although this seems unlikely in this example.

The point is that the designation of independent and dependent variables is often somewhat arbitrary, depending upon the researcher's interests, and should not be automatically interpreted to mean that the independent variable really *causes* the dependent variable in a real-world setting without additional evidence of time ordering and control for other possible causes.

To prove causality, not only must we be able to establish that the correlation between our variables is nonspurious (that it holds even when we control for as many other factors as possible), but also that the cause preceded the effect in time and that there is a plausible rationale for why one variable should be a cause of another. Even if all these conditions are met, a causal relationship cannot be proven by one study. If the evidence from numerous studies all supports a causal relationship, we can have more faith that such a relationship exists.[7]

Returning to Table 9.1, it's obvious that class standing is considered the independent variable and frequency of watching television news the dependent variable, because the percentages are calculated on the totals for the class-standing categories. Whenever trying to decide which percentages to use, remember to base them on the totals for the *independent* variable categories—the variable that your research question or hypothesis implies is predicting the other variable.

Looking at the percentages in Table 9.1, it's clear that there is a positive correlation between class standing and the watching of television news. As class standing increases (from freshman to graduate student), greater proportions of students fall into the highest category of television news viewing (5 or more times a week). Conversely, lower levels of class standing are associated with lower levels of television news viewing; that is, greater proportions of underclassmen fall into the lowest category of television news viewing (1–2 times a week).

Even if we know that the sampling error at the 95 percent level of confidence for a random sample of this size (220) is about ±6.7 percentage points and therefore differences in individual percentages should be roughly 13 percent or greater to ensure that they really exist in the overall population of Bloomington students, we still do not know how strong the *overall relationship* between class standing and watching television news is, nor do we know how likely it is that this relationship exists in the universe from which the sample was drawn.

At this point, we need to turn specific statistical measures of association to determine both the strength of the relationship and the likelihood that it exists in the universe of all Bloomington students.

Measures of Association

Chi Square.   This measure makes no assumption about the level of measurement. The variables need not be ranked from high to low or from few to many. They may simply contain discrete categories (e.g., sex, religion, political party) that are not ranked in any way. **Chi square** may be applied to tables with variables measured at a higher level (ordinal, interval, or ratio), but chi square is calculated as if the variables are measured at the nominal level.[8]

Chi square is primarily a test of statistical significance, rather than a measure of the strength of an association, because its value can range from very small to very large depending upon the size of the table (the number of rows and columns) and the size of the sample.

In Table 9.1, for example, the value of chi square is 27.76, which by itself says nothing about the strength of the relationship between class standing and watching television news. However, when we also know that there are 4 degrees of freedom (4 df) for this particular table (number of rows minus 1 times number of columns minus 1), then we can check a table of chi-square probabilities to see what the chances are of getting a chi square of 27.76 in a table with 4 degrees of freedom.[9] It turns out that the chances are equal to .0000 (carried out to only four decimal places), or less than 1 in 10,000 (a significance level of 0.01 indicates 1 chance in 100; a level of 0.001 indicates 1 chance in 1,000; a level of 0.0001 indicates 1 chance in 10,000.

Obviously, the odds are very good that the relationship in Table 9.1 is *not* due to chance and therefore *does* exist in the population from which the sample was drawn.

The logic behind the chi square measure is rather simple: the *actual* values in each cell of a table are compared to the *expected* values. The expected value for each cell is calculated by multiplying the column total for that cell by the row total for that cell and dividing the product by the total number of cases in the table. Once each cell's expected value has been calculated, it is subtracted from the actual (or observed) value and the difference is squared and divided by the expected value for the cell. The final figures for all cells in the tables are summed to get the value of chi square.

In other words,

$$X^2 = \sum \frac{(f_o - f_e)^2}{f_e}$$

where X^2 equals chi square, f_o equals the observed (or actual) frequency in each cell of the table, f_e equals the expected value for each cell, and $\sum$ indicates that the values for all cells are summed to equal the overall value of chi square.

The expected frequency for each cell, f_e, is calculated with this formula:

$$f_e = \frac{(cr)}{n}$$

where c equals the column total (or marginal) for a particular cell, r equals the row total for that cell, and n equals the total number of cases in the table.

As can be seen from the formula for chi square, the larger the discrepancies between the actual and expected values for each cell, the greater the value of chi square and the less the probability that the relationship indicated in the table is due to chance.

It should be noted that chi square assumes randomly sampled data, so is not appropriate for data gathered from an entire universe.[10] Also, the chi-square test requires that the expected frequencies in each cell not be too small. In general, for a 2-by-2 contingency table (two rows and two columns), the total number of cases should be greater than forty, and all *expected* cell frequencies should be five or more. In a larger table (more than two rows and two columns), chi square may be used if fewer than 20 percent of the cells have an *expected* frequency of less than five and if no cell has an *expected* frequency of less than 1.[11]

If the expected cell frequencies are less than five, the researcher may combine categories of the table to increase the expected frequency of the cells (if possible), or employ the Fisher exact probability test for a 2-by-2 table.[12] In all 2-by-2 tables, the formula for chi square should be corrected for continuity.[13]

As mentioned earlier, chi square is not a measure of the strength of a relationship because its value fluctuates greatly according to the size of the table and the differences between the actual and expected values in each cell. However, when chi square is adjusted for these factors, it can serve as an indicator of the strength of association between two variables.

Phi. This statistic, which is based on chi square, is appropriate for 2-by-2 contingency tables. It corrects for the fact that the value of chi square is directly proportional to the total number of cases by adjusting for the number of cases in the table. The formula for phi is

$$\phi = \sqrt{\frac{X^2}{n}}$$

where ϕ equals phi, X^2 equals chi square, and n equals the total number of cases in the table. Phi takes on the value of 0 when no relationship exists and $+1$ when the variables are perfectly related, that is, when one value of the first variable is associated with just one value of the second variable and the other value of the first variable is associated with the other value of the second variable (see Table 9.2). It should be remembered that phi, like chi square, is most appropriate for *nominal-level* variables, so a value of $+1$ does not indicate positive or negative correlation; it simply indicates a perfect association of some kind. It is necessary with all nominal-level measures of association to examine the contingency table to see what kind of relationship is (or is not) present. With ordinal-level (ranked) variables and those measured at interval or ratio levels, it is possible to look only at the measure of association to tell if the association is positive, negative, or nonexistent, assuming that the variables are scored consistently such that higher numbers indicate higher values.

It is recommended that chi square be obtained whenever using any nominal measure of association with random sample data.

Cramer's V.   Like phi, Cramer's V is based on chi square and assumes a nominal (categorical) level of measurement. Unlike phi, Cramer's V is appropriate for tables with *more* than two rows and two columns. It ranges from 0 to $+1$, as does phi, with 0 indicating no relationship and $+1$ indicating a perfect relationship.

Like phi and other nominal measures of association, Cramer's V may be applied to tables with variables measured at a higher level, but a positive value of V does not necessarily indicate a positive correlation. In Table 9.1, where two ordinal variables are being related, V equals 0.25, indicating some sort of association, and the chi-square significance level (.0000) suggests that this relationship holds in the universe of all Bloomington students, or that it is not due to chance. A look at the table suggests that the association is positive: as class standing increases, so does the frequency of watching television news (see Table 9.1).

TABLE 9.2   *Chain Ownership of Newspapers and Modern Design (Hypothetical Data)*

Design	Chain %	Not Chain %
Traditional	0	100
Modern	100	0
Phi = +1		
Chi-square significance = 0.0000 (assuming random sample data)		

Note that if the relationship were the opposite—that is, if all chain papers were traditional and all nonchain papers modern—phi would still be +1. This underscores the necessity of looking at the actual contingency table when using nominal-level measures such as phi, Cramer's V, and the contingency coefficient.

The formula for computing Cramer's V is

$$V = \sqrt{\frac{\phi^2}{\min(r-1), (c-1)}}$$

where V equals Cramer's V, ϕ^2 equals phi squared, and min $(r-1)$, $(c-1)$ indicates that ϕ^2 is divided by either the number of rows minus 1 or the number of columns minus 1, depending on which is smaller. One advantage of Cramer's V is that it varies between 0 and 1, even when the number of rows and columns in a table is not equal.

Contingency Coefficient.   This is another nominal measure of association based on chi square, but it is not as useful as phi and V, even though it can be used with a table of any size. Like phi and V, the contingency coefficient has a minimum value of 0 (when no association between two variables is present), but its maximum value varies with the size of the table. In a 2-by-2 table, for example, the maximum value is .71. The contingency coefficient cannot attain an upper limit of 1 unless the number of categories for the two variables is infinite.[14]

Because its maximum value varies with the size of the table, it cannot be directly compared to other measures of association, which vary in range from 0 to +1 or from −1 to +1. Also, the contingency coefficient cannot be used to compare tables of differing sizes.

In Table 9.1, for example, the contingency coefficient of .33 is not directly comparable to Cramer's V, Kendall's tau$_b$, or gamma, because all these measures have an upper limit of +1.

The formula for calculating the contingency coefficient is

$$C = \sqrt{\frac{X^2}{X^2 + n}}$$

where C equals the contingency coefficient, X^2 equals the value of chi square for the table, and n equals the total number of cases in the table.

Although chi square itself is not a measure of strength of association and should be used only with random sample data, the other measures based on the chi square (phi, Cramer's V, and the contingency coefficient) may be used as estimates of the strength of an association between two variables, even if the data are based on the entire universe. If the data are based on all cases in the universe, however, the chi-square significance level is meaningless and should not be computed.

Other nominal-level measures of association are discussed by Blalock, Hays and Winkler, and Siegel.[15]

We turn now to a discussion of measures of association appropriate for variables measures at the ordinal (ranked) level.

Kendall's Tau$_b$ and Tau$_c$.   Kendall's tau and two other measures of association between ordinal-level variables (gamma and Somers' D) employ a similar calculating procedure. They all consider every possible *pair* of cases in a table to see if the relative ordering on the first variable is the same (concordant) as the relative ordering on the second variable or if the ordering is reversed (discordant).

In Table 9.1, for example, a junior who watches television news three times a week is "higher" on both variables (class standing and television news) than a freshman who watches television news two times a week. This is a *concordant* pair because the first person is higher on both variables than the second person. But a freshman who watches television news five times a week compared with a graduate student who watches three times a week is a *discordant* pair because the first person is lower on one variable (class standing) than the second person, but higher on the other variable (television news watching). If two persons in Table 9.1 are in the same position on one or two of the variables, the pair is *tied*.

Kendall's tau$_b$, which is appropriate for square tables (the same number of rows and columns), ranges from -1 (a perfect negative correlation) to $+1$ (a perfect positive correlation), with a value of 0 indicating no association between the two variables. Tau$_c$ is appropriate for *rectangular* tables (those with a different number of rows and columns) and also ranges from -1 to $+1$.

The first step in calculating either tau$_b$ or tau$_c$ is to compute the number of concordant pairs (P), the number of discordant pairs (Q), the number of ties on the row variable (T_1), and the number of ties on the column variable (T_2).[16]

Once these quantities are determined, the formula for Kendall's tau$_b$ is

$$\text{Tau}_b = \frac{P - Q}{\sqrt{[1/2(n^2 - T_1^2)1/2(n^2 - T_2^2)]}}$$

where n equals the total number of cases in the table.

It can be seen that if P (number of pairs ordered in the same direction on both variables) is larger than Q (number of discordant pairs), the final statistic will be positive, indicating a positive correlation between the variables. Conversely, tau$_b$ will be negative if Q is larger than P and will equal 0 if Q equals P.

The formula for tau$_c$, which is used in a rectangular table, is

$$\text{Tau}_c = \frac{2m(P - Q)}{n^2(m - 1)}$$

where m equals the number of rows or columns, whichever is smaller, and n equals the total number of cases in the table.

One advantage of Kendall's tau over other ordinal measures of association such as gamma is that both tau$_b$ and tau$_c$ take ties into account and are generally more conservative measures of association than the other ordinal measures. In Table 9.1, for example, Kendall's tau$_b$ equals 0.24, but gamma equals 0.37.

Another advantage of Kendall's tau is that a significance test may be calculated, assuming random sample data. Finally, Kendall's tau can also be used in partial correlation, where one is measuring the strength of association between two variables while statistically controlling for a third variable.[17]

Gamma. This ordinal-level measure of association makes no adjustments for either ties or table size. Therefore, it tends to be higher in value than Kendall's tau, and it can assume a value of $+1$ (perfect correlation) even if all cases do not fall along the major diagonal of a table. Like Kendall's tau, gamma ranges from -1 to $+1$.

Gamma is simply the number of concordant pairs (P) minus the number of discordant pairs (Q) divided by the total number of concordant and discordant pairs ($P + Q$). This means it is easier to calculate than either Kendall's tau_b or tau_c, but gamma tends to inflate the strength of an association between two variables because it does not take ties into account.

The formula for calculating gamma, once the number of concordant and discordant pairs has been calculated, is

$$\text{Gamma} = \frac{P - Q}{P + Q}$$

Because it does not take into account the number of tied pairs, gamma should not be used with tables where most of the cases fall into one column category or one row category. The cases should be fairly evenly spread among the column and row categories.

Spearman's Rho. This is a very commonly used measure of association between two sets of rankings. It, too, varies from -1 (a perfect negative correlation) to $+1$ (a perfect positive correlation), but it is generally *not* used with cross-tabulation tables where each variable has several categories.

Instead, Spearman's rho is usually used to measure the strength of association between two sets of rankings (see Table 9.3). When used in this manner, rho is an estimate of the value of Pearson's correlation coefficient (discussed in the next section).

TABLE 9.3 *Issues Emphasized by the Charlotte (NC) Observer and CBS Television News during the 1972 U.S. Presidential Campaign*

Issue	Charlotte Observer	CBS News
Vietnam war	1[a]	2
Economy and inflation	3	3
Human rights and welfare	2	4
Government scandal	4	1
Environment and ecology	6	6
International relations	7	7
Crime and violence	5	5
Busing	8	8
	Spearman's rho = 0.83	

[a]The *Charlotte Observer* ranking of issues was established by tabulating the column inches, excluding headlines. The CBS News ranking of issues was determined by adding up seconds devoted to each "issue" story. In both cases, a 1 indicates the issue given most coverage.

In Table 9.3, Spearman's rho, also designated ρ_s, equals .83, indicating that the two sets of rankings are strongly, but not perfectly, correlated. A quick look at the rankings themselves bears out this strong correlation. Five of the eight rankings are identical, and the largest difference between ranks is three (on the issue of government scandal). Clearly, these two rankings are highly similar, and the high value of Spearman's rho reflects this similarity.

Spearman's rho, like Kendall's tau, requires the use of rankings rather than the absolute value of the variables. Hence the first step in computing rho is to rank order the values of the variables from lowest to highest.

In the case of tied ranks, the ranks are averaged, and the same value is assigned to each of the tied values of the variable. For example, if three values of the variable are tied for second place, each value is assigned the rank of 3 (the average of ranks 2, 3, and 4), and the next value is assigned to the rank of 5 because ranks 2, 3, and 4 have already been used.

Once the ranks have been assigned to each value of the two variables for each case (person, issue, or whatever), one rank is subtracted from the other, the difference is squared, and the acquired differences for each rank are added together. Then the following formula is used to adjust this sum of squared differences so that its value will be $+1$ whenever the rankings are in perfect agreement, -1 when they are perfectly opposite, and 0 when they are not related in any way:

$$\rho_s = 1 - \frac{6\Sigma d^2}{N(N^2 - 1)}$$

where ρ_s equals Spearman's rho, Σ means the "sum of," d^2 equals the squared difference between the ranks for each case, and N equals the number of cases or ranks (8 in the case of Table 9.3).

So this formula simply says that one multiplies the sum of the squared differences between the ranks by 6, divides this number by the number of ranks times the number of squared ranks minus 1, and subtracts this number from 1.

How does one decide whether to use Spearman's rho or Kendall's tau to measure the strength of association between two rankings? If one knows that the distances between ranks are unequal (in terms of the absolute values of the variables) and if there are a few cases with extremely low or high ranks, Kendall's tau is a more appropriate measure of association than Spearman's rho. On the other hand, if the data are distributed fairly equally among a fairly large number of ranks (eight or more), Spearman's rho is a better estimate of the degree of correlation between the rankings.

Before moving on to a discussion of the Pearsonian correlation coefficient, we want to make a few brief comments about *nonparametric statistics*. In general, the measures of association considered thus far (chi square, phi, Cramer's *V*, contingency coefficient, Kendall's tau, gamma, and Spearman's rho) are nonparametric statistics because they are appropriate for categorical data (nominal and ordinal), they do not assume that the scores being related were drawn from a population distributed in a certain way (such as a normally distributed population), and they are generally easier to calculate than more complicated parametric statistics such as the Pearsonian correlation coefficient.[18]

Another advantage of nonparametric statistics is that they are useful with small samples. For generalizations from a sample to a universe, however, nonparametric statistics require random sampling just as parametric statistics do. So the use of nonparametric statistics does not mean that one can draw convenience or quota samples and still generalize to a given universe. Random sampling is necessary for generalizing to a universe, regardless of whether nonparametric or parametric statistics are being used. The disadvantages relate to the relatively low power of nonparametric statistics, a concept that is discussed by Stamm in Chapter 8 on measurement.

Pearsonian Correlation Coefficient.   This well-known measure of association between two variables, also known as Pearson's r, assumes that the variables being related are measured at the interval or ratio levels (that we know the distance between different values, as well as the fact that one value is larger or smaller than another), and that the relationship between two or more variables is *linear*; that is, as one variable increases, the other either increases or decreases in a constant manner.

Pearson's r also assumes that the variables being related have many values (that they are more nearly continuous than discrete) and that the joint distribution of two variables is a bivariate normal distribution.[19] When this is the case, it can be shown that r calculated from random sample data is the best estimator of the actual correlation in the universe from which the samples were drawn.[20]

Although Pearson's r assumes at least interval-level data, it is often used by mass communication and other researchers with ordinal level variables. In fact, some social science methodologists have argued that r and other interval-level statistics (such as factor analysis) should be used with ordinal-level data so as not to miss relationships that less powerful nonparametric statistics would not detect.[21]

We have mentioned that there are two major methods of obtaining measures of association, from contingency (cross-tabulation) tables and from scatter diagrams or scatterplots. Although cross-tabulation tables are more common in mass communication research because the variables under study usually have a limited number of values, there are some interval-level continuous variables in mass communication research that require scatter diagrams and Pearson's r as a measure of association (e.g., percentages of literate adults in a country and daily newspaper circulation per 1,000 adult population).

Instead of creating a separate table cell for the intersection of each value of the other variable, one plots the joint values on a two-dimensional plane, with the horizontal axis defined by one variable and the vertical axis defined by the other.

One way to summarize a scatterplot is to draw a straight or curved line through the middle of the points so as to summarize the pattern of points (see Figure 9.7). In the case of a rather clear and consistent linear pattern, a straight line may be used to summarize the relationship between the two variables. This line is placed so as to minimize the vertical distances of all the points from the line, a procedure known as least-squares **regression**.

Pearson's r is a measure of the degree to which a linear regression line (a straight line) fits the data displayed in a scatter diagram. If all the points fall on the line, r equals either $+1$ or -1, depending on the direction of the line. As the squared vertical distance from each point to the line becomes greater, the value of r comes closer to zero. An r of 0

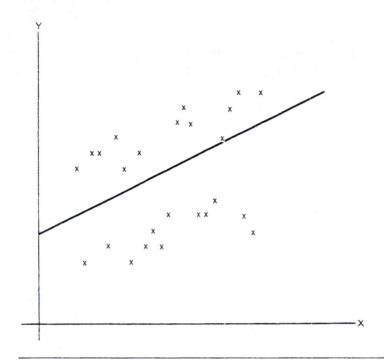

FIGURE 9.7.   Scatterplot and Regression Line.

indicates that there is no *linear* relationship between the variables, but it does not mean that there is no relationship. There may be a well-defined curvilinear relationship.

The calculation of the Pearsonian correlation coefficient is more complex than that required for most of the other measures of association discussed thus far, but the principle behind r is rather simple. Pearson's r is the ratio between the maximum amount of variability that two measures could have in common and the amount that they actually have in common. In other words, r is the ratio of the covariation (the amount of variation two measures have in common) to the square root of the product of the variation in both variables.[22]

Thus r^2 (which is also known as the coefficient of determination) can be interpreted as the percentage of variability in one variable explained by the other variable.[23] Both r and r^2 have a maximum value of $+1$, but the interpretation of r and r^2 is considerably different.

Pearson's r is a measure of the strength of the linear relationship between two variables. An r of 0 denotes no linear relationship, whereas an r of -1 denotes a perfect negative linear relationship (as one variable increases, the other steadily declines), and an r of $+1$ denotes a perfect positive linear relationship (as one variable increases, the other increases at a constant rate). It should be noted that an r of .80 does not signify a relationship that is twice as strong as an r of .40, because r is not a ratio measurement scale.[24]

The interpretation of r depends on several factors, including the purpose of the research. With very large samples (say 1,000 or larger), even small rs of .20 or less may be highly significant statistically. This does not mean that such correlations are journalistically or socially significant. The researcher must consider whether the purpose of the study is to locate variables that are related to each other, or whether the purpose is to predict from one variable to another. In the case of prediction, very strong correlations are required.

Guilford and Williams have suggested the following as a rough guide to interpreting the strength of a correlation coefficient:

Less than .20	slight correlation; almost negligible relationship
.20–.40	low correlation; definite but small relationship
.40–.70	moderate correlation; substantial relationship
.70–.90	high correlation; marked relationship
More than .90	very high correlation; very dependable relationship[25]

Whereas r is interpreted as an indicator of the strength of a linear relationship between two variables, r^2 is interpreted as the proportion of variation in one variable explained by the variation in another. Thus an r^2 of .80 indicates that two variables have twice the variation in common as two variables with an r^2 of 0.40.

Pearson's r may be calculated by the following formula:

$$r = \frac{\Sigma(X - \overline{X})(Y - \overline{Y})}{\sqrt{[\Sigma(\overline{X} - X)^2][\Sigma(\overline{Y} - Y)^2]}}$$

where r stands for the Pearsonian correlation coefficient, X equals each value of the first variable, $\overline{X}$ equals the mean of the first variable, Y equals each value of the second variable, $\overline{Y}$ equals the mean of the second variable, and Σ means "the sum of."

Measures of Difference

The various statistics we have considered thus far (chi square, phi, Cramer's V, contingency coefficient, Kendall's tau, gamma, Spearman's rho, and Pearson's r) are useful for indicating the strength of association between variables or the probability that the association occurred by chance, or both.

But not all research questions and hypotheses are couched in terms of associations. Many are stated in terms of *differences* between individuals and/or groups. This is especially true in experimental research, where comparisons are made between groups that have and have not been exposed to certain experimental treatments (such as certain media messages or television programs).

In such a setting, instead of asking, "Do persons who spend much time reading newspapers tend to be more interested in politics than those who spend little time reading newspapers?" we might ask, "Is there a significant difference in political interest between those persons who spend much time reading newspapers and those persons who spend little time reading newspapers?"

Or, instead of hypothesizing that "The more education a person has, the more time he or she will spend reading newspapers," we might hypothesize, "There is a significant difference in time spent reading newspapers between those persons with low levels of education and those persons with high levels of education."

To address these restated research problems, measures of difference are more appropriate than measures of association. We now turn to some specific examples of these measures of difference.

Difference of Proportions Test.   This is one of the simplest measures of difference, both in terms of calculation and underlying assumptions. This test assumes only nominal-level data and random sampling. As was true in calculating sampling error, a difference between two proportions can be treated as a special case of a difference between two means (see the section entitled "Calculating Sampling Error").

When comparing two proportions from the *same* random sample, we can simply subtract one from the other and ask if the difference exceeds plus or minus the sampling error. In other words, if we have calculated the sampling error to be plus or minus 5 percentage points at the 95 percent level of confidence, we can simply ask if the two proportions differ by 10 points or more. If they do, we can be 95 percent sure that the difference between the proportions really exists in the universe from which the sample was drawn.

Remember that the formula for the sampling error at the 95 percent level of confidence (or the .05 level of significance, depending on how you want to view it) is

$$\text{Sampling error} = \pm 1.96 \sqrt{\frac{pq}{n}}$$

where 1.96 equals the number of standard deviations within which 95 percent of large random samples will fall, p equals the proportion (or percentage) of cases in one category, q equals $1 - p$ (or $100\% - p$), and n equals the number of cases in the sample.

Another way of estimating the probability that the difference between two proportions in the same sample is real is to employ the formula

$$Z = \frac{p_1 - p_2}{\sqrt{\frac{pq}{n}}}$$

where Z equals the number of standard deviations from the mean in a normal curve, p_1 equals the first proportion, p_2 equals the second proportion, p equals either p_1 or p_2, depending upon which is closer to 50 percent, q equals $1 - p$ (or $100\% - p$), and n equals the number of cases in the sample.[26]

For example, if we draw a random sample of 125 newspaper issues from the files of the local newspaper for the past five years and we find that 60 percent of these issues contain editorials critical of local government and 65 percent contain editorials critical of national government, can we conclude that this is likely to be a real difference in all issues of this newspaper for the past five years?

Applying the formula,

$$Z = \frac{.60 - .65}{\sqrt{\frac{(.60)(.40)}{125}}} = \frac{-.05}{.0438} = -1.14$$

Checking this Z-score in a table of areas under the normal curve, which can be found in most statistics books, we find that the odds of this difference occurring by chance are about .13, or 13 times in 100. If we have set our significance level at .05, we must conclude that this difference could have occurred by chance and therefore probably does not occur in the universe of the past five years' issues of the local newspaper.[27]

It is also possible to test the significance of the difference between two proportions taken from two independent random samples, but this procedure is more complicated and less often used in mass communication research. (For the computing procedure, the reader is referred to Blalock, pages 176-178; see note 3.)

The chi square test can also be thought of as a difference of proportions test because it compares expected values of nominal variables with their actual values. (See the section on chi square for a discussion of the computing procedure.)

T-Test. This commonly used difference of means test is appropriate for two-group problems, that is, for situations where one is comparing the mean(s) of one group with the mean(s) of another group. For three or more groups of cases (persons, newspaper issues, etc .), analysis of variance should be used.

The **t-test** assumes interval-level data, random sampling, and a normally distributed population. It produces a t statistic with accompanying significance test, which enables the researcher to estimate the probability that a difference observed between sample means is a real difference in the universe from which the sample was drawn. If one is using data from an entire universe or from a nonrandom sample, the t-test should not be used.

Although the most common use of the t-test is to test the significance of the difference between two sample group means to estimate if such a difference exists in the universe, another use often made of the t-test is to measure the *change* in average scores of the *same* persons after being exposed to an experimental treatment of some kind.

For example, if a group of persons is exposed to a film on techniques of advertising, and their scores on an attitude measure about advertising are averaged before and after the film, the t-test may be used to determine the statistical significance (if any) of the difference between the before and after mean scores. This is sometimes called a *correlated* t-test. Again, the t-test does not indicate how *meaningful* the difference is; it simply indicates how likely the difference is to occur by chance, and therefore how likely it is that the difference would exist in the universe from which the sample of persons was drawn.

The t-test, sometimes called Student's t, is based upon a distribution similar, but not identical to, the normal distribution. This distribution is more appropriate for smaller samples (less than 30 or so) than is the normal distribution.[28] For larger samples, the difference between the t distribution and the normal distribution is trivial.

As mentioned earlier, the t distribution is more appropriate for smaller samples than is the normal distribution, but this does *not* mean that the t-test may be used only with small samples. Blalock argues that it is always preferable to use the t distribution whenever the universe standard deviation is unknown and whenever a normal universe (population) can be assumed.[29]

In addition, there is no advantage to using analysis of variance over the t-test when only two groups are being compared, because it can be shown that exactly the same conclusions will be reached in the two-sample case regardless of whether analysis of variance or t-test is used.[30]

Analysis of Variance.   This test of the difference between sample means should be used when *three or more* means are being compared simultaneously. For example, subjects in an experiment may be randomly assigned to three different groups, one exposed to a very violent television program, one exposed to a moderately violent television program, and one exposed to a neutral (nonviolent) program. After viewing the television program, each group may be asked to complete a test measuring willingness to use violence to solve problems in society.

In such an experiment, the researcher would be interested in the relationship between degree of violence in television programs and willingness to use violence in solving problems. To test this relationship, the researcher would ask if the mean problem-solving scores vary significantly among the three experimental groups. **Analysis of variance** would provide a single *F* test, with accompanying significance level, to tell the researcher how likely these sample means are to differ in the universe from which the samples were drawn.

Once having obtained an overall significant test for all three mean scores, the researcher could then use a t-test of difference to check on the statistical significance between *each pair* of means.

The preceding example is known as a *one-way* (or single factor) analysis of variance because only one independent variable is involved—violence in television programs. It is possible, however, to examine the effects of two or more independent variables simultaneously on the mean scores of a dependent variable by using *n*-way (two-way, three-way, etc.) analysis of variance.

The assumptions required for analysis of variance are basically the same as those for the t-test, but the computation of the *F* test is very different. Analysis of variance assumes interval-level measurement of the dependent variable, independent random samples (or independent random groups within a single sample), a normally distributed population or universe, and equal universe variances.[31] The independent variables (or factors) are usually categorical variables measured on the ordinal level (such as three levels of violence in a television program).

The *F* test underlying the analysis of variance is based on a comparison of the variation of scores *within* each category of each independent variable (factor) with the variation *between* the means of each category. Thus, the *more* variation *between* the means of each category of each independent variable and the *less* variation of the scores *within* each category (about each category mean), the larger the value of *F* and the more certain we are that the differences between categories really exist—and the more certain we are that the independent variable has a real effect on the dependent variable.

In other words, the value of the *F* test may be expressed by the formula

$$F = \frac{SS\ between/(k - 1)}{SS\ within/(N - k)}$$

where "SS between" stands for the sum of squared differences between the means of each category for each independent variable (factor) and the overall (grand) mean for the entire sample, k stands for the number of categories of each factor, "SS within" equals the sum of the squared differences between each score and its category mean, and N equals the total number of cases in the sample.

Another way of expressing the formula for the F test is

$$F = \frac{MS\ between}{MS\ within}$$

where "MS between" equals mean score between, which is the same as "SS between" divided by the number of groups minus 1, and "MS within" stands for mean score within, which is the same as "SS within" divided by the total number of cases in the sample minus the number of groups (or categories) of each independent variable.

Analysis of Covariance. This is a modified version of analysis of variance that enables one to statistically extract variance from the dependent variable that is accounted for by one or more measured control variables *before* assessing the effects of the various experimental factors on the dependent variable.

For example, in assessing the effects of televised violence on the tendency for children to act aggressively, a researcher would be interested in having groups of children as nearly alike as possible exposed to different levels of violence. As pointed out in Chapter 15, *control* is a primary goal of experimental research because without adequate controls one cannot be sure if the observed effects are due to the independent variable(s) or to other influences.

One way of ensuring that the children in each group are as alike as possible is to assign them randomly to each group, hoping that this procedure will tend to cancel out individual differences that might affect the level of aggressiveness in their behavior. Another way to control for individual differences is to match the children on as many characteristics as possible (sex, age, school grade, etc.). Still another way to control for individual differences is to measure things you think might not be equal in the two groups and might affect the dependent variable, then use analysis of covariance to statistically control for these variables (covariates).

For example, in the case of children exposed to televised violence, the researcher might want to obtain a measure of each child's tendency to act aggressively before the experiment (perhaps by unobtrusive observation) and then use analysis of covariance to control statistically for the pre-experiment aggressive score. This procedure would first eliminate the variance in the dependent variable accounted for by the children's pre-experiment tendency to act aggressively, and then perform a normal one-way analysis of variance to determine the effects of the televised violence on the children's tendency to act aggressively.

In applying analysis of covariance, it is necessary to assume that the covariates (the variables being controlled for) do not interact with the factors (the independent variables).

It should be noted that covariates must range from "low" values to "high" values, and they should be measured at the interval level. Therefore, measures of variables one wishes to control for in analysis of variance should ideally be as precise and continuous as possible.

Other Measures of Difference.   The reader should not conclude that the statistics discussed thus far (differences of proportions test, t-test, analysis of variance, and covariance) are the only tests of difference available to the mass communication researcher. Although these tests are commonly used, several others are useful, especially for variables measured at the ordinal level. These include the median test, the Mann-Whitney U test, the Kolmogorov-Smirnov test, the sign test, the Wilcoxon matched-pairs signed-ranks test, the Friedman two-way analysis of variance, and the Kruskal-Wallis one-way analysis of variance. The assumptions and computational procedures of these tests are discussed in Siegel.[32]

Summary and Conclusions

This chapter has attempted to provide an overview of descriptive and inferential statistics useful to mass communication researchers. The treatment of most of these statistics has been brief and, in some cases, oversimplified. The reader is urged to consult some of the standard statistics books, such as Siegel, Blalock, McNemar, Williams, and Hays and Winkler for more details about the assumptions, calculation, and interpretation of these statistics.

Because the chapter was designed to focus on basic statistical tools, no description has been provided for more powerful multivariate techniques such as multiple regression (for assessing the effects of several independent variables on a dependent variable, controlling for the relationships between the independent variables), factor analysis (for locating patterns of relationships in the intercorrelations of a large number of variables), multidimensional scaling or cluster analysis (for locating dimensions, or patterns, of relationships in the associations of a large number of cases), canonical correlation (for simultaneously correlating one group of variables with another group), and discriminant analysis (for simultaneously relating a dependent variable with only two or three nominal values to many independent variables—in other words, for finding independent variables that statistically distinguish between two or more groups of cases).

For additional information on these more sophisticated techniques, the reader is urged to consult more advanced statistics books such as Tabachnick and Fidell, Cooley and Lohnes, Van de Geer, Harman, Stephenson, Anderson, Kerlinger and Pedhazur, Duncan, Heise, Morrison and Bock.[33]

Using Statistics to Describe Data

In trying to decide which descriptive statistics to use to summarize a distribution of data, there are two major considerations: (1) the level of measurement of the data (nominal, ordinal, interval, or ratio) and (2) the kind of summary desired (one emphasizing the clustering of the cases or one emphasizing the amount of scatter of the cases.)

Table 9.4 shows the relationship of these two major considerations to the individual descriptive statistics discussed in the first part of this chapter. Although the measures of central tendency seem to be used more often than the measures of dispersion in mass communication research, it's recommended that both kinds of measures be used wherever possible.

TABLE 9.4   *Commonly Used Descriptive Statistics in Mass Communication Research*[a]

Level of Measurement of Data	Kind of Statistic	
	Central Tendency (Clustering)	Dispersion (Scatter)
Nominal (unranked categories)	Mode (most frequent value)	Range[b] (highest − lowest) Percentile[b]
Ordinal (ranked categories)	Median (midpoint)	
Interval (known distance between ranks)	Mean (average)	Variance (Σ of squared deviations about mean/N) Standard deviation (square root of variance)
Ratio (interval with a true zero)	All of above	All of above

[a]Each statistic is listed under the lowest acceptable level of measurement, but it should be remembered that all statistics are appropriate for all higher levels of measurement. It should also be noted that many interval-level measures are commonly used with ordinal-level data.

[b]It can be argued that the range and the percentile are more appropriate for ordinal-level data because they both imply a ranking of values from "low" to "high." In practice, however, they may be used with nominal-level data.

Simply reporting modes, medians, and means without ranges and standard deviations does not give the reader enough information to compare these measures of central tendency from one distribution of data to another. And reporting only ranges, percentages, and standard deviations does not tell the reader much about the clustering of cases within distributions.

As pointed out earlier, when using measures of central tendency with interval data (or perhaps ordinal, if one suspects that the differences between ranks are not too great), one should not automatically rely only on the mean. In a skewed distribution of values, the median or mode may be more representative of the central clustering of cases than the mean. If the mean, median, and mode are fairly equal, there are statistical advantages in using the mean. When in doubt, report more than one measure.

When using measures of dispersion, one may be limited by nominal measurement to the range and percentiles (or percentages), but if the data are at least ordinal scale and there is no reason to suspect great differences in the distances between the rankings, it is recommended that the standard deviation be reported as well.

In general, when reporting the mode or the median, it is recommended that the range and/or percentages also be reported. When reporting the mean, it is recommended that the standard deviation also be reported.

Using Statistics to Analyze Relationships

The choice of an appropriate statistic to analyze a relationship between variables is more complicated than choosing a descriptive statistic. There are more inferential statistics, the assumptions underlying the use of many of these statistics are more complex, and the nature of one's research questions and hypotheses must be considered.

Two major considerations in the choice of inferential statistics, however, should be dealt with before the others: (1) the level of measurement of the variables and (2) the kind of relationship specified by one's research question or hypothesis: either an *association* between two variables or a *difference* between two or more groups. Table 9.5 groups the individual measures of association and difference discussed in this chapter in terms of these two major considerations.

When considering Table 9.5, one should remember that other considerations enter into the selection of specific statistical tests. These include whether random sampling was employed, whether the samples are independent or related, whether the universes from which the samples were drawn can be assumed to be normally distributed (as in the case of parametric statistics such as Pearson's *r* and analysis of variance), the size of the contingency tables, and whether distinctions are made between independent and dependent variables. Many of these points are touched on in the descriptions of individual statistics, and these should be read before selecting a particular statistical test.

Table 9.5 assumes that both variables being related are measured at the same level (nominal, ordinal, interval, or ratio). In practice, this is often not the case. One may be relating a nominal independent variable (such as religion or selection of a specific newspaper)

TABLE 9.5   *Commonly Used Inferential Statistics in Mass Communication Research*

Level of Measurement of Variables	Kind of Relationship	
	Association	Difference
Nominal (unranked categories)	Chi square Phi Cramer's *V* Contingency coefficient	Difference of proportions test
Ordinal (ranked categories)	Kendall's tau Kendall's tau_b Kendall's tau_c Gamma Spearman's rho	Median test Mann-Whitney U test Kolmogorov-Smirnov test Sign Test Wilcoxon matched-pairs signed-ranks test Kruskal-Wallis one-way analysis of variance Friedman two-way analysis of variance
Interval (known distance between ranks)	Pearsonian correlation coefficient	T-test Analysis of variance Analysis of covariance
Ratio (interval with a true zero point)	All of above	All of above

to an ordinal dependent variable (such as amount of political participation). There are specific statistical tests to handle such situations, such as Somers' *d*, but they are not discussed here because of the limited scope of this chapter.[34]

If both variables are not measured at the same level, it is recommended that a statistical test be chosen according to the *lower* level of measurement. Thus, if one is looking for a measure of association between a nominal and an ordinal variable, it is recommended that one of the nominal measures of association be used, such as phi or Cramer's *V*. This rule applies whenever a nominal and an ordinal variable are being related, but the reader may choose to ignore it when an ordinal and an interval variable are being related because of the advantages of using more powerful parametric tests such as Pearson's *r* and the t-test. When using analysis of variance or covariance, only the dependent variable can be measured at the interval level. The independent variables (factors) are typically measured at the ordinal or nominal level.

If in doubt, the researcher should apply more than one test of association or difference to the data. If the conclusions of the two tests are different, one should use the results from the more appropriate test (the one suited best to the lower level of measurement of the variables).

In looking for statistically significant relationships, the researcher should remember that at the .05 level of significance, 5 instances of every 100 (or 1 of 20) statistically significant relationships at the .05 level may not actually exist in the universe from which the sample was drawn. At the .01 level, 1 of every 100 relationships may not exist in the universe from which the sample was drawn.

Finally, just because a relationship is statistically significant does not mean it is substantively important. A positive correlation of .20 indicates a weak relationship, regardless of the significance (or p) level. (See the section on the Pearsonian correlation coefficient for guidelines for interpreting the strength of correlations.)

This chapter provides a foundation of commonly used statistics for describing mass communication variables and for relating them to one another. In using these statistics, the researcher should keep in mind the need to let the research questions and hypotheses dictate the kind of measurement employed and the specific statistics used. The use of statistics in mass communication research should not become mindless or an end in itself. Statistics should be used only to clarify the understanding of complex sets of findings and relationships, not to embellish and legitimize research reports.

Endnotes

1. See *SPSS Base 10 User's Guide Package* (Chicago, IL: SPSS Inc., 2001), and Jeremy J. Foster, *Data Analysis Using SPSS for Windows Versions 8–10* (Thousand Oaks, CA: Sage Publications, 2001).

2. See David S. Moore and George P. McCabe, *Introduction to the Practice of Statistics* (New York: W. H. Freeman, 1989), 349–351 and 416–419, for a discussion of the law of large numbers and the central limits theorem.

3. See Hubert M. Blalock, *Social Statistics* (New York: McGraw-Hill Book Company, 1960), 142, for a discussion of sample size and the assumption of normality.

4. See William L. Hays and Robert L. Winkler, *Statistics: Probability, Inference, and Decision* (New York: Holt, Rinehart & Wiston, 1971), 284.

5. Blalock, *op. cit.*, 149–153.

6. For a discussion of other factors influencing the choice of a significance level, see Sanford Labovitz, "Criteria for Selecting a Significance Level: A Note on the Sacredness of .05," *American Sociologist* 3(August 1968): 220–222.

7. For a more complete discussion of the necessary and sufficient conditions for inferring causal relationships, see Claire Selltiz, Marie Jahoda, Morton Deutsch, and Stuart W. Cook, *Research Methods in Social Relations*, rev. ed. (New York: Holt, Rinehart & Winston, 1959), 80–88; and W. Lawrence Neuman, *Social Research Methods, 4th ed.* (Boston: Allyn & Bacon, 2000), 52–55.

8. Marija J. Norusis, *SPSS^x Introductory Statistics Guide* (New York: McGraw-Hill Book Company, 1983), 54. See also Marija J. Norusis, *SPSS 10.0 Guide to Data Analysis* (Chicago, IL: SPSS Inc., 2001).

9. As with other tables of probabilities, chi-square tables can be found in the back of most statistics books. See, for example, Frederick Williams, *Reasoning With Statistics: Simplified Examples in Communications Research* (New York: Holt, Rinehart & Winston, 1968), 174–175; Sidney Siegel, *Nonparametric Statistics for the Behavioral Sciences* (New York: McGraw-Hill Book Company, 1956), 249; Blalock, *op. cit.*, 452; and Moore and McCabe, *op. cit.*, A-20.

10. Although this seems to be the most widely held view, there are some scholars who argue otherwise. See, for example, Robert J. Winch and Donald T. Campbell, "Proof? No. Evidence? Yes. The Significance of Tests of Significance," *American Sociologist* 4(1969): 140–143.

11. See Siegel, *op. cit.*, 110, for a more detailed discussion.

12. *Ibid.*, 94–110.

13. *Ibid.*, 110.

14. Hays and Winkler, *op. cit.* 804.

15. See Blalock, *op. cit.*, 212–241; Hays and Winkler, *op. cit.*, 801–813; and Siegel, *op. cit.*, 95–111 and 196–202.

16. For more detailed discussions of these computing procedures, see Siegel, *op. cit.*, 213–223; Blalock, *op. cit.*, 319–324; and Hays and Winkler, *op. cit.*, 845–849.

17. For the formula for computing a partial Kendall's tau, see Siegel, *op. cit.*, 223–229.

18. *Ibid.*, vii, for a more extended discussion of the difference between parametric and nonparametric statistics.

19. *Ibid.*, 195–196.

20. See Hays and Winkler, *op. cit.*, 601, for a discussion of why this is true.

21. See, for example, Sanford Labovitz, "Statistical Usage in Sociology: Sacred Cows and Ritual," *Sociological Methods and Research* 1(August 1972):13–37.

22. For a more detailed discussion of Pearson's r, see Blalock, *op. cit.*, 287.

23. For a more detailed discussion of r^2, see Blalock, *op. cit.*. 298; and Dick A. Leabo, *Basic Statistics* (Homewood, IL: Richard D. Irwin, 1972), 436–437.

24. Williams, *op. cit.*, 134.

25. Williams and J. P. Guilford, *Fundamental Statistics in Psychology and Education* (New York: McGraw-Hill Book Company, 1956), 145.

26. Blalock, *op. cit.*, 149–152.

27. *Ibid.*, 152. (See p. 441 for a table of areas under the normal curve.)

28. *Op. cit.*, 145; and Williams, *op. cit.*, 81.

29. Blalock, *op. cit.*, 149.

30. For a discussion of why this is so, see Blalock, *op. cit.*, 253.

31. *Ibid.*, 242.

32. Siegel, *op. cit.*, chapters 5–8.

33. Barbara G. Tabachnick and Linda S. Fidell, *Using Multivariate Statistics, 2nd ed.* (New York: HarperCollins, 1989); William W. Cooley and Paul R. Lohnes, *Multivariate Data Analysis* (New York: John Wiley & Sons, Inc., 1971); John P. Van de Geer, *Introduction to Multivariate Analysis for the Social Sciences* (San Francisco: W. H. Freeman, 1971); Harry H. Harman, *Modern Factor Analysis* (Chicago: University of Chicago Press, 1967); W. Stephenson, *The Study of Behavior* (Chicago: University of Chicago Press, 1953); T. W. Anderson, *Introduction to Multivariate Statistical Analysis* (New York: John Wiley & Sons, Inc., 1958); Fred N. Kerlinger and Elazar J. Pedhazur, *Multiple Regression in Behavioral*

Research (New York: Holt, Rinehart & Winston, 1973); Otis Dudley Duncan, *Introduction to Structural Equation Models* (New York: Academic Press, Inc., 1975); David R. Heise, *Causal Analysis* (New York: John Wiley & Sons, Inc., 1975); Donald G. Morrison, "On the Interpretation of Discriminant Analysis," *Journal of Marketing Research* 6(1969): 156–163; R. D. Bock, *Multivariate Statistical Methods in Behavioral Research* (New York: McGraw-Hill Book Company, 1975); Paul E. Green and Frank J. Carmone, *Multidimensional Scaling* (Boston: Allyn & Bacon, Inc., 1970); Herbert B. Asher, *Causal Modeling* (Newbury Park, CA: Sage Publications, 1976); and William R. Klecka, *Discriminant Analysis* (Newbury Park, CA: Sage Publications, 1980).

34. For a more thorough and detailed guide for choosing specific statistical tests, see Frank M. Andrews and others, *A Guide for Selecting Statistical Techniques for Analyzing Social Service Data* (Ann Arbor: Institute for Social Research, University of Michigan, 1974).

10

Data Analysis and SPSS Programs for Basic Statistics

Daniel Riffe

Quantitative research often begins with a process of reduction, both in terms of reducing a complex phenomenon through precise measurement and in terms of characterizing vast amounts of data with "reduced" summary measures.

For example, in content analyses (see Chapter 11), communication message variables are reduced to numeric values reflecting precisely measured differences between one unit of analysis and another (e.g., an official source in a news story is given a code value of 1 while a citizen source is a 2). Similarly, survey respondents report how often they read newspapers by responding to a questionnaire item (e.g., daily readers might indicate a value of 7 on the questionnaire, while nonreaders indicate a 0). Attitudes or psychological states among experimental subjects might be indicated by checkmarks on a five-point scale (e.g., on a statement like "I am generally happy," strong disagreement is indicated with a 1 while strong agreement is 5 and 3 is the scale midpoint reflecting neither agreement nor disagreement).

Once that process of measurement yields the "raw" questionnaires or coding sheets, is the process of reduction complete? Raw questionnaires or coding sheets *can* be examined and conclusions drawn. The researcher can report that "most" news stories contain official sources. He or she may even count the number of stories and provide an exact number. Our newspaper readership survey could yield piles of questionnaires, hand-sorted from the 0 pile (nonreaders) through the 7 pile (daily readers). Noting that some analyses could be as simple as recording data on 3- by 5-inch cards and sorting them, Danielson observed: "Nothing is wrong with such an approach. On the contrary, it is to be preferred over other more complicated methods if it produces the desired results and satisfactory levels of statistical significance."[1]

Ultimately, though, the sheer number of questionnaires or sheets may become so large as to be unmanageable and subject to handling error. Some content analyses involve thousands of content units and a survey may involve a sample of thousands of respondents. At that point, the reduction possible through computer data processing is essential. After the hundreds of news stories or completed questionnaires are processed, the researcher is able to examine summary statistics that reduce the hundreds of content units or survey respondents to percentages (20% of stories have official sources in them, while 15% use environmental experts; 80% of survey respondents read the newspaper from three to five days per week), or to averages or ranges of numbers (the mean score on the five-point happiness measure is 3.7). These and other summary statistics describe the entire array of cases in a reduced form, thanks to computer processing.

Of course, few communication researchers are satisfied with mere description or counting. Another advantage of data analysis packages is that they provide tools permitting researchers to test relationships among two or more variables. For example, consider how the summary statistics noted above may be related to or influenced by other variables. How often were the percentages of stories that cited official or environmental expert sources based on reporter enterprise (or digging), and how often did the sources "stage" news conferences? Did male and female subjects differ on the five-point happiness measure? Is newspaper readership related to education level or to the number of out-of-home social or community activities one pursues? (To remain with the "pile-sorting" approach, we *could* answer some of these questions by sorting into smaller and smaller subset piles: sorting all the male subject responses into five piles corresponding to happiness levels and then all the female subject responses into five other piles and examining the resulting ten.)

The number of variables and the number of relationships that may be examined are limited only by the researcher's insight into theory and previous research, the foresight to have collected the appropriate data, and the *capacity to manage multiple operations* at once, a capacity enhanced by computer data analysis.

One of the most common forms of **data processing** involves **SPSS**, introduced in 1970 as *Statistical Package for the Social Sciences*.[2] During the early and late 1970s communication researchers could choose among SPSS, the Biomedical Computer Programs (BMD),[3] and SAS packages.[4] Each offered applications that met the needs of most researchers and each developed loyal followings. But as the evolution of microcomputers led academic researchers from punch-card processing in universitywide mainframe computers, to "dumb" remote terminal interaction with mainframes, and finally to lab or office personal computers, the ease of use of SPSS and its developers' willingness to stay in step with that evolution, have helped SPSS enjoy and maintain popularity. SPSS has itself evolved through various releases and revisions, including its most current personal computer version, SPSS for Windows. Other statistical packages for personal computers include JMP, Minitab, StatView, Statistica, SYSTAT, STATISTIX and EcStatic.[5]

Senior researchers may recall using boxes of keypunched paper data cards, topped with SPSS "data definition" and "procedure" cards, and university-specific "job control" cards that identified the appropriate account to be charged for use of the mainframe central processing unit. They turned over decks of cards to a data-entry clerk who fed them into the computer. Depending on the time of the semester and the volume of work, they might wait hours before a printout was generated, often with an error message. The process of analysis and scientific inquiry was put on hold while the researcher punched corrections into a new card and resubmitted the deck.

These tales yield looks of bored disbelief and disinterest among today's students, many of whom know SPSS as a readily available and easily accessible program in Mac and PC labs on campus. This description of early computer card processing is not offered, however, to bemoan the passing of an era, but to introduce a data processing "model" that helps understand how statistical analysis programs work and how to conduct effective data analysis. The model assumes there are at least four steps in data analysis: preplanning, including design and measurement decisions; data definition, entry, and cleaning; data modification or transformation; and analysis procedures.

Why Preplanning? An Example

The first step in computer data analysis occurs long before the computer is booted. It is, quite simply, thinking. In the classic *Foundations of Behavioral Research*, Kerlinger wrote, "The electronic computer is utterly stupid: It will do exactly what a programmer tells it to do."[6] That observation remains true no matter how advanced the SPSS version or how fast the microprocessor. The researcher, after all, defines what constitutes data and which data are entered for analysis, determines what kinds of operations will be applied to those data, and draws conclusions. SPSS will not correct the researcher on any of these steps, nor does the fastest microchip have the capability to correct faulty thinking or bad decision making; told to "run," the computer will do just that.

Consider a researcher measuring newspaper readership by collecting data from 200 households. How should the data be entered for analysis—for each household as a whole, or for each individual reader (or nonreader)? SPSS cannot intuit whether 200 cases represent 200 households or 200 readers—it must have the distinction made for it.

How will readership be measured? If the household is our focus, do we assign a value of 1 for households that have *any* newspaper readers, and a 0 for households that have no readers? Or do we count the number of readers and nonreaders in the household and compute a percentage for each household?

Or, if the focus is on the individual respondent selected at a household, do we enter a score ranging from 0 (nonreader) to 7 (daily reader) for each person?

What kind of statistical or mathematical operations can be applied with our sample of 200 households or individual respondents? Should an average be calculated? SPSS will happily add up all the scores and divide by 200, whether the numbers to be averaged are *appropriate* to such an operation (e.g., our 0–7 readership score) or inappropriate for it (a score of 1 for households that have any newspaper readers and 0 for those with no readers). Similarly, SPSS does not "know" whether the 200 households were selected via a probability or a convenience sample, whether they represent all households, and whether probability-based concepts such as confidence interval, margin of error and level of significance are appropriate. It will provide such measures, whether they are appropriate or not. Finally, SPSS will not sound a warning bell if the researcher draws incorrect conclusions.

Thinking about Analysis

The term "data processing" generates an image of a machine performing repetitive tasks, almost as if on "automatic pilot." But it should be clear by now that, regardless of that mechanical image, data analysis can be effective only when careful, even creative, thought has gone into the development and design of the research. Most social science research is conducted to test specific hypotheses or answer specific research questions. Good research design enables the researcher to conduct those tests or provide those answers, by ensuring that the right variables are measured, at the right place and time, and in a form that makes analysis possible.[7]

Decisions about variables, then, come from previous research efforts, theory, and experience. The relationship of those decisions to planning the data analysis is, in turn, a prescriptive one: Having chosen the right variables to achieve the goals of the design, one can plan the analysis in advance, even constructing dummy tables that illustrate the form of the analysis and that await only the insertion of the final processed numbers. Public opinion surveyors, in fact, often use their questionnaire or interview schedule as a template to develop the SPSS program, even before the survey is complete; the questions on the questionnaire, after all, were developed to measure the "right" variables for the study.

Unit of Analysis.   What kinds of issues are involved in this planning process? Recall our question of whether data from the readership study would reflect whole households or individuals within households. That question—what is the *unit of analysis?*—has obvious implications for our data analysis. If a single case is a household, then averages, percentages, and other statistics are per-household statistics. If an individual respondent is a case, then statistics describe the average or typical individual, not household.

Content analysts face similar decisions. For example, at least two approaches are possible when examining the gender, ethnicity, and role of characters in television programming. If the unit of analysis is the episode, then one might count how many characters are male, how many are female, how many are of color, and how many are speaking *per episode*. A case or line of SPSS data would represent an episode. Statistics would indicate the average number of females, Asians, and so on, per episode of that program. Or the unit of analysis might be an individual character, so a case or line of data would represent a character, and variables would indicate that character's gender, ethnicity, speaking role, and so on, and the name of the dramatic program. Statistics now would indicate the percentage of *all characters in the television character "population"* who are speaking, of color, female, and so on. The impact of difference in approach is illustrated by a study of television advertising: examining individual characters, researchers found minorities present in the television population of characters in proportions close to actual Census figures (about 15%); examining individual ads, they found minority characters distributed so that a third of the ads had at least one minority character, a distribution the authors called evidence of "a form of tokenism."

Level of Measurement.   Other design decisions that affect data processing and analysis involve the level of measurement used, a decision important because of statistical requirements or assumptions, and the level of precision in the measurement. Some statistical procedures require that variables be measured at the interval or ratio level (see Chapter 8). Recall that an *interval* measure is one where the steps or levels of the measure are of equal sizes and have an order to them (greater than and less than), like degrees on a thermometer, but where the zero is arbitrarily placed. A Fahrenheit thermometer is a good example of an interval scale because its zero is arbitrary (it does not reflect "absence" of heat). A *ratio* measure has the same property of equal and ordered intervals, and its 0 is meaningful, like our 0-to-7 measure of newspaper reading in a week. In that case, 0 indicates absence of reading, not an arbitrary midpoint like the thermometer. Other measures may be **nominal** (simple differences in categories like male/female gender differences, religious denominations, ethnic backgrounds, or ABC/CBS/NBC networks) and **ordinal** (the categories have an order to them but the intervals represented by the categories are not precisely equal; an example is a "never"/"sometimes"/"always" response option to a question about newspaper readership).

These examples are simplistic, but in the practice—and planning—of research, level of measurement is crucial because it affects the kind of arithmetic that can be performed with the data. Good researchers, knowing what kind of statistical procedures are to be employed—and are available—will collect data measured at the "appropriate" level. But it is worth emphasizing once again: Computers cannot divine whether numbers that have been input represent interval, ratio, or lower levels. They will compute a mean out of nominal values (1 = crime stories, 2 = sports stories, 3 = weather, 4 = economic stories, and so on, from a content analysis topic scheme) the same as they will for ratio data from our 0–7 readership scale, yielding an average readership score or an "average topic" with equal zeal, regardless of the latter's pointlessness.

Precision of Measurement.   Precision is an attribute of measurement, sometimes but not always associated with decisions about level of measurement. Precision, in essence, is how *fine* the differentiations are on a variable. A relatively imprecise measure of height would consist of two ordinal categories: short and tall. Such a measure might be of value to a basketball coach, but few others would find it useful. A more precise measure might use a ruler, with scores rounded to a half inch.

More seriously, we can ask a respondent how likely he or she is to buy a particular television, and accept ordinal responses of "not at all likely," "somewhat likely," or "very likely." The three levels obtained might be acceptably precise for some applications, but not for others. For a more precise measure, we might ask the respondent to indicate on a 1–10 scale how likely he or she is to purchase, with 1 being "not at all likely" and 10 representing "definitely will purchase." The ten levels of likelihood certainly have the potential to yield finer discriminations among potential purchasers. But while the greater number of values on the scale may represent a gain in precision, we might ask questions about the *reliability* (the stability or constancy of measures taken at different times with the same instrument), and, therefore, *validity* (whether we are indeed measuring purchase intent) of the 1–10 scale. Simply because respondents *can* be enticed to use the finer discriminations afforded by the 1–10 scale does not mean differences between values are any more valid than between "not at all likely" and "somewhat likely" or that they would reliably give the same responses if measured again. In short, increasing the number of levels on a measure is not an end in itself, regardless of the increased precision.

The precision obtainable when data are collected is sometimes "blunted" when data are reported. For example, in many cases we can record age in real, whole years (18, 21,

53, 22, 72, etc.), and not in ordinal "age brackets" we often encounter (18–21, 22–25, 26–35, etc.). Whenever real numbers can be obtained, researchers should opt for them. Less precise ordinal categories can be created later by "collapsing" numbers into categories.

Similarly, content analysts sometimes use very precise coding instructions that differentiate fine discriminations within larger categories. Deutschmann,[8] for example, developed a coding system for classifying subject matter in dailies with nearly 100 categories. Those categories were later reported as a set of eleven nominal categories because reliability of the larger set was not satisfactory. Riffe examined thousands of international news stories, precisely coding each for the country being covered, but ultimately reported the data in a First World (Western industrialized nations), Second World (communist states), and Third World category system.[9]

Number of Variables.   A related pre-analysis planning decision is how much data to collect per case. Note that the question here is not how many cases, news stories or surveys, subjects, or respondents, but *how many variables*. Do we want to know only the topic of a story coded in a content analysis, or should we also record the length, the headline, the presence of a graphic, the cutline, the sources quoted? If we record the content of the headline, should we also measure and count how many decks it crosses? Does the jump page headline count, too?

Recall that good research design requires and ensures that the "right" data—and only the right data—are collected to answer the research question or test the hypotheses. Danielson warns that "Only data that will contribute to the final product should be collected and stored. The 'carrying along' of unneeded or extra data is a trap that has snared many an unwary researcher."[10] Indeed, trying to measure headlines and numbers of decks and sizing photos and charts can be a nightmare, particularly if working with microforms, and questionnaires can quickly balloon from manageable 15-minute interviews to low-completion 40-minute monsters piggy-backing three or four separate studies!

But what if the researcher anticipates future additional uses for the data, particularly if collecting it initially already involves major investment of time or resources? There may be instances when data not related to the immediate research goal but for which a future use is anticipated are available for minimal additional effort. A content analyst once examined a decade of network television news topics, in order to examine *annual* change in topics.[11] But because he also recorded the month and date, he was later able to group stories *by quarter*, and examine the relationship of economic news to economic indicators released quarterly (consumer price index, unemployment rates, housing starts, etc.).[12]

The key here is whether there is an *anticipated* use for data—an anticipation guided by theory and previous research. Such guidance can help the researcher make the most productive use of resources and time while avoiding the trap envisioned by Danielson.

Where Do the Data Come From?   These measurement issues (unitizing, and the measurement and precision of the appropriate number of variables) that impact data processing—and that should be addressed early in the planning stage—are sometimes simplified, sometimes complicated by *how the data are generated* or collected. Research data are elicited or generated by a variety of techniques, many of them what would traditionally be viewed as "pencil-and-paper" tools. Interview schedules and questionnaires are used in generating and recording telephone, mail, and face-to-face survey data. Coding protocols and coding sheets are used to record data in *content analyses*. Treatment and control group subjects often complete post-exposure measurement instruments that yield *experimental* data for analysis. Researchers once transferred data in these forms to long sheets that were then used by keypunchers. Many, if not most, researchers now avoid this intermediate step and go directly to the keyboard by carefully planning and designing instruments, questionnaires, and code sheets so that data are easily and reliably input from them to the computer.

These examples emphasize instruments and sheets for recording data that are *then* input to create SPSS data files. Some research technologies eliminate several of these steps entirely. Computer-assisted telephone survey interviewing, for example, uses callers at monitors that display survey questions that are read to respondents. Responses are entered at the keyboard and dumped to a central server as data files. Similar direct data collection and file creation is possible in some "dynamic" content analysis applications, such as Viewdac, where coders can simultaneously code up to thirty-two variables, permitting examination of overlapping action and character roles that are difficult in traditional content analysis.[13]

While these direct processes reduce the danger of error associated with transferring from a paper questionnaire or coding sheet to a keyboard, they do require intensive planning and preparation of the system.

Entering SPSS: Defining the Data "Then and Now"

Whatever the data source, the precision, or the level of the measurement, the next step in analysis of a well-conceived, well-designed study is *defining the data* in language SPSS or another program can use. The fine points of the data definition process may vary slightly depending on which version of a statistical package one uses, but the defining process has always been a part of data processing, dating from the early computer punch-card days.

Consider data processing in those days: Cards about the size of a business envelope were preprinted with 80 columns of numbers (Figure 10.1). In each vertical column, ten numbers ranged from 0 at the top to 9 at the bottom. By punching holes in columns, the researcher could make this data card convey a tremendous amount of information, but it was up to the researcher to define the "rules"—that is, to specify the field (number of columns) for that information. For example, age, for most people, could be reported in a two-column field; weight for most adults would require a field of three columns.

For each survey respondent in a readership survey, we might collect five variables: gender, age, years of education, frequency of daily newspaper readership, and number of social or community activities per week. We would need five fields of varying width. In column 1, we would punch gender data (1 for female and 2 for male). Similarly, columns 2 and 3 would be the field for age in years, columns 4 and 5 would be for total years of education, column 6 would contain weekly frequency of daily newspaper readership (0–7), and column 7 would be for number of days per week (0–7) the respondent attends out-of-home activities.

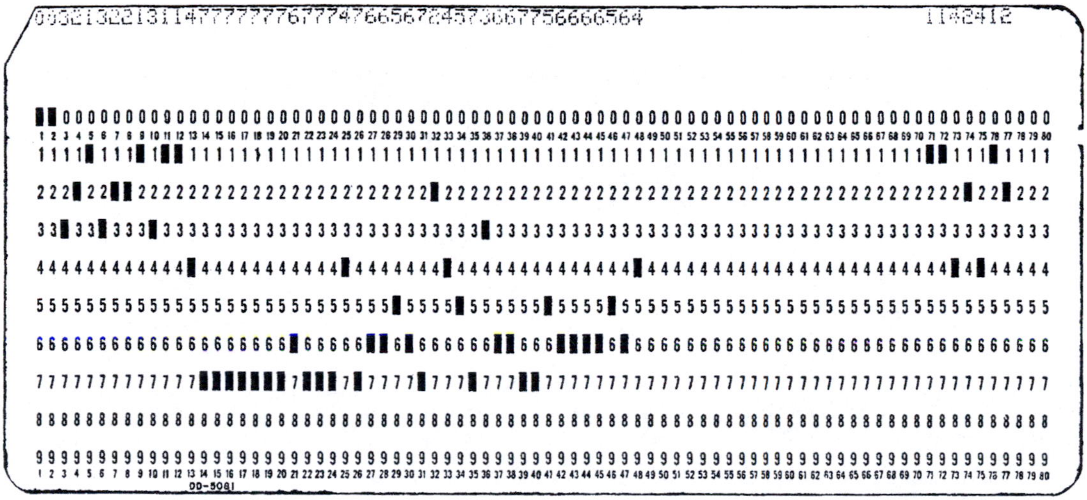

FIGURE 10.1. Computer Card.

For a 30-year-old female college graduate who is a three-times-a-week newspaper reader and who attends two out-of-home activities (church and an aerobics class on Thursday), the data line would read:

1301632

Note that the numbers (1 for female, 30 for age, 16 for years of education, 3 for daily readership, and 2 out-of-home activities) could as easily describe the weight (130 pounds), age (16 years), and vertical leap (32 inches) of a basketball player, *if* we had defined only *three* fields instead of five.

Indeed, when the card was read into the computer, the machine recognized it as a single continuous row of data: 1301632. However, the process of "data definition" ensured that all variables (gender, age, etc.) would be named, along with specification of how many and which columns were needed for each field, and any labels the researcher might want (e.g., output would indicate "Female" if the entry in the gender field was a 1).

In some current microcomputer applications, the process represented by the cards is recreated, though the instructions and the data might be entered as text in SPSS or another text "editor" (MS-DOS, Word text, etc.) for subsequent importing by SPSS. The seven numbers for our sample respondent would be one of many sets entered in a text or data file analogous to a stack of cards. Within the file, typically above the data lines for each of our respondents, are the data definition instructions. The data lines might in turn be followed by a procedure card (telling SPSS what to do with the data), in this case, "CROSSTABS."

```
DATA LIST FILE=READERSHIP /
    GENDER 1 AGE 2–3 EDUCAT 4–5 READER 6 ACTIVITY 7
VARIABLE LABELS EDUCAT 'YEARS OF EDUCATION'
    READER 'NEWSPAPER READERSHIP'
    ACTIVITY 'OUT OF HOME ACTIVITIES'
VALUE LABELS GENDER 1 'FEMALE' 2 'MALE'
    READER 0 'NONREADER' 7 'DAILY'/
BEGIN DATA
1301632
2261245
etc....
END DATA
CROSSTABS
```

In effect, SPSS reads the variables and labels and uses them as a "dictionary" to assign meaning for each number in the data fields.

In another variation of the process, some SPSS/PC+ users employed separate data definition "driver" and data files to accomplish the same goals. A driver is a text file (e.g., A:SURVEYDRIVER) that contains all the data definition information about the variables and their location and labels *and* includes a "path" (e.g., GET FILE=SURVEYDATA) to a second file that contains the lines of data. A researcher would specify particular procedures within the driver file, editing it using an MS-DOS editor, an SPSS/PC+ editor, or even a word processor (provided special word processing codes were stripped out). To execute the run, the researcher would enter the SPSS package itself, then tell it to INCLUDE: 'A:SURVEYDRIVER'. The GET FILE command would bring the data file and the driver together, creating an active file that combines the two.

Why divide the two parts of the process? Though the capacity of personal computers has increased exponentially in the last two decades, one reason for this approach was space. Data sets may be as large as tens of thousands of cases. Researchers could, in theory, write the data definition, labels, procedures, and so on, as part of the same massive file. However, some text editors had limited capacity (perhaps 300 or so lines). They were fine for getting in and out of a relatively small driver file, but had difficulty opening, editing, and saving very large files. Some researchers remain loyal to the dual file system out of habit. They are familiar with that system and prefer its output (printouts) to that generated by the newest SPSS version, SPSS for Windows.

As it did word processing, office tasking, and many other applications, Windows revolutionized SPSS. In SPSS for Windows, the data entry process was streamlined tremendously because the process of defining which columns constitute the "field" for each variable is simplified. SPSS for Windows uses a spreadsheet approach. The analyst opens the program and goes directly to a grid of thousands of cells. Using the tab and arrow keys for maneuvering, data are entered directly into this matrix of rows and columns, with each variable represented by a column, and each row representing a case. The cell size can be adapted to accommodate longer variables. A user can highlight the column heading and input a variable name. The full name of any variable might not be apparent on the grid square, but when the mouse pointer is moved to the variable name, a highlighted label is presented. In the early versions, variable labels and value labels were defined using a variable definition pull-down menu and subsequent dialog boxes. In the most recent versions, the user clicks a tab that toggles the screen between a Variable View (the data as inserted into the cells) and a Data View (see Figures 10.2 and 10.3). The variable view lists each variable, its label and value labels, and other information. Changes in data definition can be made on the variable view screen.

Data Definition, Entry, and Cleaning

Regardless of which version one uses, careful data definition is essential in SPSS or any package. A computer can be made to read a value of 1 as indicating how many cars one owns, the rank of one's favorite football team, the age of a child, or one's gender. But unless the researcher defines exactly which of these is *the* appropriate meaning of 1, SPSS treats them all the same.

SPSS data definition, then, comprises the following four steps: providing "shorthand" names for the study's variables for SPSS system use and researcher convenience; providing longer labels for the variables that might be useful in examining or explaining output; providing labels to go with selected numeric values of the variables; and identifying for SPSS any numeric values it should ignore or treat as missing values.

Data Menus and Variable Views

How one actually goes about completing the four steps in data definition depends on which version of SPSS for Windows is available. A series of pull-down menus with dialog boxes might be used; one example is the Analyze menu (Figure 10.4). More recently, Version 10.1

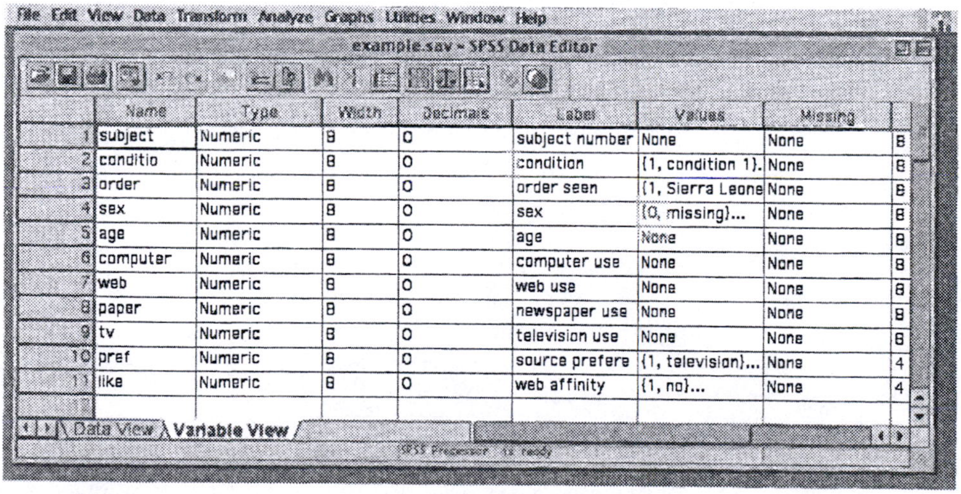

FIGURE 10.2. Windows Variable View Example.

	subject	conditio	order	sex	age	computer	wot	paper
1	11001	1	1	1	19	14	140	14
2	21002	2	1	2	20	20	17	8
3	21003	2	1	1	19	45	30	7
4	21004	2	1	1	22	14	14	14
5	11005	1	1	1	19	30	15	5
6	22006	2	2	1	20	20	20	14
7	22007	2	2	1	18	20	10	0
8	12008	1	2	2	19	48	14	14
9	11009	1	1	1	18	14	6	0
10	12010	1	2	1	20	40	30	3
11	22011	2	2	2	21	14	14	5
12	12012	1	2	1	18	50	50	5
13	11013	1	1	2	19	25	25	10
14	21014	2	1	2	19	20	10	5
15	12015	1	2	1	18	14	14	7
16	21016	2	1	1	18	20	20	6
17	21017	2	1	2	18	4	28	2
18	22018	2	2	1	18	15	8	2
19	12019	1	2	1	18	25	20	5
20	22020	2	2	1	18	28	14	14
21								

FIGURE 10.3. Windows Data Editor Example. Figures 10.2, 10.3, 10.4, and 10.5 are from *A Simple Guide to SPSS for Windows Versions 8.0, 9.0, and 10.0 Revised Edition, 1st edition*, by L. A. Kirkpatrick and B. C. Feeney © 2001. Reprinted with permission of Brooks/Cole, an imprint of the Wadsworth Group, a division of Thomson Learning. Fax 800 730-2215.

introduced the "Variable View" approach. That switches to a listing of variables from top to bottom and offers cells across the row that enable the researcher to insert labels, values, missing values, and so on—the same tasks performed on the pull-down menu and dialog box.

After SPSS is booted, the user indicates at the opening menu that he or she is going to enter new data (as opposed to modifying or using an existing data file). Once in the resulting data window, the first task is to define the variables by replacing the column headings with shorthand labels to specify which variables are in which columns. These variable names will from this point forward be recognized by SPSS as "shortcuts" to the data in particular columns or cells.

Variable names are arbitrary (in fact, SPSS for Windows will identify columns sequentially as var001, var002, etc., if the user does not supply names), but they must meet certain SPSS conventions. They must begin with a letter, may not contain a space, and must be shorter than nine characters (the program will not allow the user to continue if these conventions are violated). Researchers struggling with these conventions come up with odd

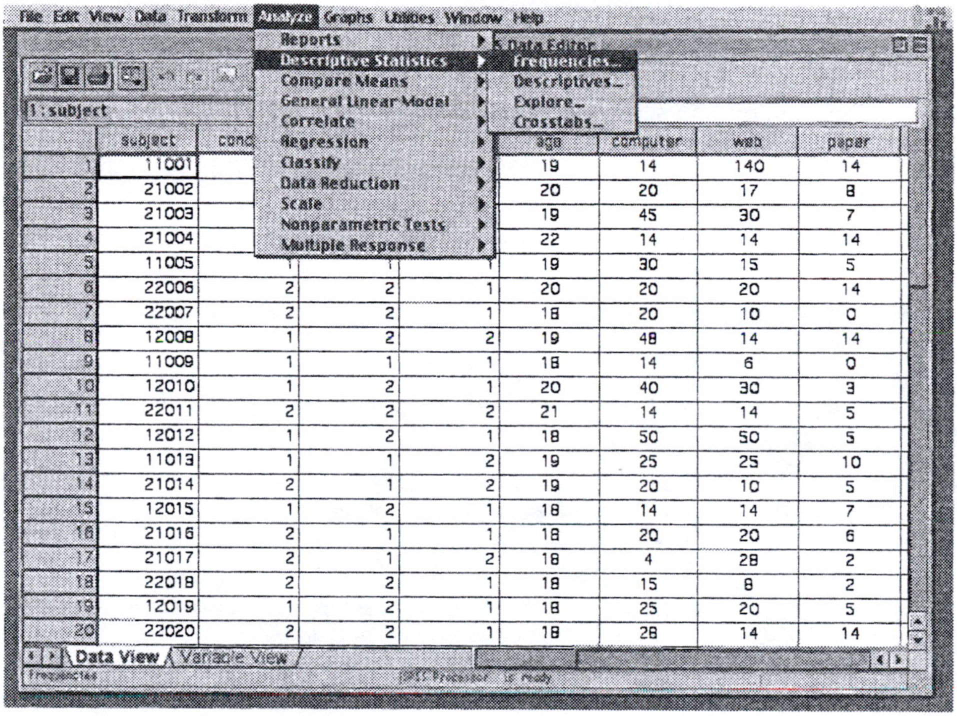

FIGURE 10.4.　Sample Analyze Menu.

names, like NEWSOURC to represent "News Sources Quoted Within the Story," to stay within the 8-character convention. Make careful notes about what these shorthand terms mean for future use, or take advantage of the Labels option on the Define Variable box or in Variable View in order to create some "longhand" labels that provide more information.

Doing so, one can furnish longer variable names that will be used in output. This command makes sure that, while SPSS uses NEWSOURC in system processing and commands may be issued in fairly concise terms, "News Sources Quoted Within the Story" is displayed in computer output.

The same dialog box or Variable View process permits the user to indicate labels used for the individual numeric *values* of individual variables. These value labels are names or categories represented by the numbers in the data set, a process that is deceptively simple, given the disastrous impact of *mislabeling* at this point. Consider this example: If "1" was used to indicate that a respondent's gender was female in the survey data, SPSS should be instructed to display "female" whenever the gender variable is used and the value of "1" is present. Conversely, if "2" was the questionnaire option indicating the male gender, the value label must reflect that. Having those values mislabeled would be a major problem. To assign labels, enter the numeric value ("1"), type in the corresponding label ("female"), and click the Add button. In Variable View, value labels are entered under the Values column.

When extensive sets of categories are used, as in a content analyses, or when survey response options for a particular question are numerous, the process of assigning labels can be lengthy. It is critically important, however, to invest care and necessary time to this process. Shorthand labels might be quicker today but difficult to decipher later.

Obviously, though, it would be pointless to provide value labels for some ratio-level variables (assuming that the variable label itself is clear). A value for a ratio variable such as WEIGHT, for example, would not require a label: "165" suffices as well as a labeled "165 POUNDS" (imagine inputting 165 POUNDS, 166 POUNDS, 167 POUNDS, etc.). On the other hand, it might be useful to provide labels for our ratio-level newspaper readership variable: a score of 0 could be labeled "nonreader" and a score of 7 could be labeled "daily reader."

Both Variable View and the Define Variables dialog box permit dealing with one additional step that is required in many communication studies: specification of *missing values* and instructions for SPSS on how to deal with them. "Missing values" are exactly that. For a variety of reasons, data sets sometimes have missing data for certain cases: a respondent is uncomfortable answering a question, for example, or information is literally unavailable for a few cases (too much such unavailable data, on the other hand, raises questions about how well the study was planned). In these instances, the user must tell SPSS what the "code" is for missing data and how to deal with it. If a variable has a range of values of from 1 (strongly disagree) to 5 (strongly agree), 9 might be preassigned as the missing value (e.g., the interviewer would be instructed to circle or indicate 9 as "no response"). Clearly, SPSS has to be instructed *not* to treat 9 in the first instance as a real number to be used in computing an average agreement score; such an average is meaningful only if based on scores within the prescribed 1–5 range.

Specifying missing values is, in some ways, part of *cleaning the data*, an essential part if one is to perform meaningful analysis. But data cleaning also involves a far simpler process: eyeballing and checking the data. Coding or scoring error can occur (a 99 is inadvertently entered in a cell to indicate missing data on a variable where the agreed-upon code is 9). Keyboarding error can occur (a 9 is entered from the number pad when the 6 just below it should have been entered). Transferring error can occur (glancing between coding sheet and computer screen without hitting "enter" or "tab" means column 26 data on the coding sheet might find its way into the variable 25 cell). Some of these errors would not be visible to the eye; to find them, a second researcher should read from the original data sheets. For other kinds of errors, one can trust one's own eyes. Columns of data can be scanned for out-of-range values: if the values used to indicate gender are "1" and "2," a "3" should catch the eye. Some researchers, in fact, will use nonconsecutive values on some variables ("1" is female and "3" is male), believing this keyboard "distance" reduces the possibility of keyboard error by making such slip-ups more visible.

Some researchers will print out the data, making it easier to find out-of-range values. One of the easiest ways to clean the data, though, is to run a *frequency analysis*. Using the Analyze or Summarize menu (depending on the version), select Frequencies (see Table 10.2). This is a procedure that looks at each variable and counts the number of cases for each of the values used in the variable (e.g., how many males coded "2" and how many females coded "1" are there in the gender variable?). Examine the output to see if there are cases outside the specified range (see Table 10.2). Those will have to be corrected or, in some cases, transformed.

TABLE 10.1 *An SPSS Frequencies Table, Including Missing Value Data." Over the past few years, do you think things where you live have gotten better, stayed about the same, or gotten worse?"*

		Frequency	Percent	Valid Percent	Cumulative Percent
Valid	1 Gotten Better	132	28.6	29.5	29.5
	2 Stayed the Same	231	50.0	51.7	81.2
	3 Gotten Worse	84	18.2	18.8	100.0
	Total	447	96.8	100.0	
Missing	4 Don't Know or Not Sure	15	3.2		
Total		462	100.0		

Data Modification or Transformation

Regardless how much planning and pretesting went into a study, researchers sometimes find themselves with data in a form that is not useful for their purposes. Asked to record survey respondents' time in minutes spent viewing television, some interviewers might record larger increments of time ("$1\frac{1}{2}$ hours"). An interval-level measure (like minutes of viewing) envisioned as providing a high degree of precision might need to be "reduced" to simpler, ordinal categories (light, medium, and heavy television viewers) for analysis purposes.

Or, researchers may find new research questions or purposes—or even patterns within the data—that invite or require changing the data. Through **factor analysis** of a set of ten questionnaire items, for example, a researcher may discover that there are two underlying "clusters" of items: scores on, say, six items cluster together because they are strongly correlated, while the four items in the other cluster are highly correlated with one another but not with the first cluster. The researcher might consider whether there is a way

TABLE 10.2 *An SPSS Frequencies Table, Including Two "Out of Range" Cases (values of "5") That Have to Be Recoded or Corrected." Over the past few years, do you think things where you live have gotten better, stayed about the same, or gotten worse?"*

		Frequency	Percent	Valid Percent	Cumulative Percent
Valid	1 Gotten Better	132	28.6	29.5	29.5
	2 Stayed the Same	229	49.6	51.2	80.8
	3 Gotten Worse	84	18.2	18.8	99.6
	5	2	.4	.4	100.0
	Total	447	96.8	100.0	
Missing	4 Don't Know or Not Sure	15	3.2		
Total		462	100.0		

to sum, first, the six-item cluster and then the four-item cluster to reflect the patterns in the data more accurately.

Whether problem solving or creatively examining new directions, researchers can take advantage of procedures that allow *modification* of existing data or *transformation* of those data into "new" forms. Consider these examples:

A survey might ask each respondent his or her ethnicity, yielding tiny percentages of subjects who are Asian Americans, Hispanics, or Native Americans. Those percentages might be crucial to certain analyses, but other research questions might be better answered with ethnicity categorized simply as "nonwhite" (e.g., 15%) and "white" (85%). Within the ethnicity variable, the frequencies for the small-percentage groups need to be summed.

Or a survey might reveal television viewing time varying from 0 minutes per day to as high as 500 or 600 minutes. Such an extraordinary range is informative, but for analysis purposes, the researcher might prefer to group viewers along a simple, three-category ordinal dimension: light viewers, medium viewers, and heavy viewers. The researcher would need to divide the respondents into those categories so that one-third of the respondents would fall in each category. This division of viewership is exactly the same approach used by scholars examining the process of cultivation.[14]

A survey might ask respondents to indicate on a five-point scale how likely (1 = not at all, and 5 = very likely) they think *most people* are to be affected by negative campaign advertising and, then, "How about *you*? How likely are you to be affected by negative campaign advertising?" The size of the "gap" or difference computed between "most people" and "you" might be revealing to a researcher interested in the "third-person effect," the idea that people tend to estimate that communication messages will generally have greater effects on others than themselves.[15] For each survey subject, the score for "most people" would be subtracted from the "How about you?" score.

Similarly, respondents might be asked to provide 1–10 enjoyment ratings for six different types of television programming (reality-based cop shows, soap operas, news, etc.). Differences in the sample's enjoyment among the programming *types* might be interesting (i.e., Do respondents as a whole enjoy news more than reality-based cop shows?), but so might differentiation among *respondents* in terms of their enjoyment ratings across programming types (i.e., Do some respondents enjoy television programming more than other respondents, regardless of programming type?). One approach for answering the latter question would be to compute an average rating: Add all six ratings for each subject and divide by 6.

A researcher might gather content analysis data on the focus of news stories, determining with fine precision how much news space is devoted to ten or fifteen topics spanning local, state, national, and international dimensions. For purposes of measuring the paper's commitment of resources to its local community, however, a simple distinction between local and nonlocal focus might suffice. The fifteen-topic system could be collapsed into two larger "local" and "nonlocal" categories.

Finally, consider a situation where a researcher might want to examine more closely a subset of cases. She or he might ask telephone survey respondents their preference for Candidates A and B. Before predicting an election outcome, it might be advisable to select those respondents in the sample who are registered voters *and* who voted in the last election (and are thus more likely to vote the next time). Making a pass through the data, the analyst would instruct SPSS to create a subfile that includes only these likely voters.

Each of these examples represents a situation where data modification or transformation is needed. Frequently used data modification options in SPSS are *recoding, computing*, and *selecting*. The examples above suggest how these options are used.

Recoding is a procedure that takes existing values of a variable and transforms them into new values. It is in many instances the same as "collapsing" categories of a variable. If, for example, we have precise data (from 0 to, say, 21) on the number of years a sample of respondents has attended formal schooling, we might recode those data to yield values traditionally associated with educational level: 1–8 recoded to 1 with a new value label defined as "Elementary School"; 9–12 recoded to 2 with a label of "Some High School or High School Graduate"; and 13–21 recoded to 3 with a label of "Some Education Beyond High School."

Or, using our example of ethnicity in the survey above, we might recode the values for the several nonwhite ethnic groups to "1," with a new value label as "Nonwhite," in contrast to the white respondents identified as "2." In the case of the three levels of television viewing, we would need to carry out a frequency analysis and determine at which levels in minutes 33 percent and then 67 percent of the viewers are identified. Assuming, for example's sake, that 33 percent of the sample views fewer than 35 minutes of television daily, and 67 percent views fewer than 120, we would recode the values for viewing: 0–35 minutes recoded to 1 with a new value label defined as "Light Viewing"; 36–119 minutes recoded to 2 with the new label of "Medium Viewing"; and 120+ minutes viewing recoded to 3 for "Heavy Viewers." Other common recodes might involve using the mean score as a point for "breaking" frequency distributions into above- and below-the-mean groups.

The education and television viewing examples demonstrate two of the possibilities represented by the recoding process. Continuous data (like years of education) can be grouped in categories that are meaningful to readers, and large ranges of data (like minutes of viewing) can be reduced to levels that are intuitively understandable. In addition, in each case the recoding was justifiable on conceptual or theoretical grounds. Quite often, though, researchers use the recoding process for a third reason, one highlighted in the example of the survey ethnicity variable: There are simply too few cases in a category to be meaningful. A content analyst using a ten-topic category system to compare two dailies might find it necessary to combine categories with few cases in them. A caveat, however: Faced with categories with few cases, beginning researchers must be cautious about how they tread. It might be tempting to recode or transform the data in such a way as to maximize support for one's hypothesis or theory. Decisions on how to recode or collapse variable categories, however, must be based in strong reasoning, and the recoding process must be reported fully, of course.

Recoding values of a variable in SPSS requires use of the Transform menu and the Recode option. The researcher can choose between recoding the values into new values of the same variable or into new values of a newly created variable. In the case of the former, for example, one might be cleaning up out-of-range values that need correcting. Or a researcher may decide that the differentiation among nonwhite ethnic groups (e.g., black, Hispanic, etc.) noted above will be of no use in the future. Many researchers, however, routinely opt for recoding old values into a new variable (e.g., values for level of education, labeled EDUCAT, recoded into NUEDUCAT), while maintaining the original entries for the original variable. Once the transformation is completed, NUEDUCAT appears as a new column on the far right side of the data window.

A number of features are available in the Recode dialog box (Figure 10.5). A researcher can specify individual values to be recoded into new values, can recode ranges of values, and can use shortcuts like "lowest" through 35, or 120 through "highest." These shortcuts can save a lot of keystrokes. The dialog box also includes an If button, a path to a second dialog box that permits what are called "conditional transformations." Conditional transformations, quite simply, tell SPSS what criteria or conditions *have to be met* before a particular transformation or modification can take place. Recall the example above where we were trying to identify "light," "medium," and "heavy" television viewers. Respondents who reported viewing "zero" television stretch the definition of "light" viewers. We might want SPSS to recode viewing into our three categories but *if and only if* the original viewing score was greater than 0. Conditional transformation options include greater than, less than, greater than or equal to, and less than or equal to, among others. Moreover, conditional transformations may involve more than one condition (e.g., if viewing is greater than 0 and less than 60) or more than one variable (e.g., if television viewing is greater than 0 and income is greater than $40,000 per year).

Another common data transformation option is Compute. Also located on the Transform menu, the Compute dialog box enables the researcher to compute values for a variable—new or old—using transformations of other variables. SPSS permits the user to type in the computation (using SPSS variable names and keyboard elements such as $+$, $-$, $/$,

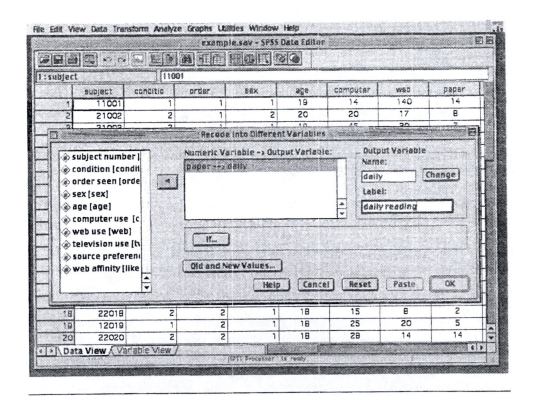

FIGURE 10.5. Windows Recode.

and X) or use preset mathematical functions provided on a keypad in the dialog box. As with the Recode option, conditional transformations, via the If button, are possible in the Compute process.

The Compute process involves naming a "target" variable—the new variable to be created—and then specifying the mathematical functions that are to be used to create it. Returning to our example from above, a new variable labeled TVENJOY, or "TV Enjoyment across Types," might be our target variable. Recall that we elicited scores (on a 10-point enjoyment rating scale) for six types of programs. In SPSS "compute" logic, the expression for TVENJOY would be:

COMPUTE TVENJOY=(TYPE1+TYPE2+TYPE3+TYPE4+TYPE5+TYPE6)/6

Note that the sum of the six program type ratings is divided by 6 to yield an average enjoyment rating across the six types. Obviously, division by 6 is optional. We could use the sum of the ratings for the six types, but computing an average yields an answer that is more easily comparable to the original rating.

While Recode and Compute enable the researcher to change existing data and, in effect, create new variables, another frequently used SPSS command enables the researcher to modify the data set (as opposed to individual variables) by selectively analyzing cases. The Select Cases option, found on the Data menu, gives the researcher a broad range of capabilities and options for how those cases are selected. As with Recode and Compute, the researcher can specify particular conditions that have to be met. Recall the example of registered voters above. Whatever value was used to indicate a respondent's being registered can be used in the Select Cases command. SPSS would then filter or select only the registered voters for subsequent analysis. A researcher interested in gender differences might, in addition, specify two conditions that have to be met—gender and registration status—and command SPSS to select only female registered voters. Two caveats: First, just as the Select Cases command specifies which cases to include, so too it implicitly specifies which cases to *exclude*. The researcher needs to be mindful during the analysis of which cases are excluded: Our example excludes not just males who are unregistered, but all males. Second, the researcher needs to remove the Select Cases filter before returning to the analysis of the full data set.

In addition to selecting cases if particular variable values are present, SPSS can also be instructed to select ranges of cases. If a national survey data set is organized sequentially by, say, state, a researcher could instruct SPSS to select only the cases from a particular state or region by specifying the lowest case number in that state and the highest.

Moreover, SPSS can be instructed to select cases at random. Within the Select Cases option, the researcher can request a random sample of the cases, whether by specifying an exact sample size or by indicating that the sample is to be equivalent to a given percentage of the cases. If the applicability of this option is not readily apparent, consider this: Public and government records are increasingly available in electronic form, particularly in states with open-records laws. A researcher using software like Windows Excel can load records, often from the Web, into a spreadsheet. That spreadsheet, in turn, can be imported into SPSS for Windows. At that point, two applications of SPSS-sampling might occur: First, the researcher might want to reduce a population of hundreds of thousands of records to a more manageable size and could select a representative random sample for closer analysis. Second, a cautious researcher might want to examine a sample of the records to assess their quality and the presence of error.

Good content analysis requires careful examination of between-coder reliability and some researchers believe the reliability test should be conducted on a random sample of the cases in the content analysis data set. The SPSS sampling feature might be useful in identifying such a subset.[16]

Incidentally, Select Cases is quite useful in those instances where, for whatever reason, an out-of-range value for a variable is discovered. If Frequencies output shows one person's date of birth as 2975, a researcher can instruct SPSS—using Find under the Edit menu—to select only that case where the date of birth is entered as 2975, and then change it to 1975.

An Example of Data Transformation

A university committee wanted to determine if students favored a technology fee to pay for increased access to computers involved in coursework. The committee received university permission to study human subjects and recruited a dozen students to phone 250 students randomly selected from the university phone directory. Each respondent's class standing (freshman, sophomore, etc.), age, major, ownership of a personal computer, financial aid status, and estimated family income were recorded, along with opinion statements on current tuition rates and on the proposed fee hike.

After making several checks to verify that interviews had actually been conducted as prescribed, a journalism professor on the committee volunteered to analyze the data and obtained the data sheets provided by the interviewers. The professor examined the sheets to ensure their readability. He entered the data in SPSS for Windows, first opening a blank data editor screen or window—which he promptly saved as filename "Technology Fee." Using the variable definition process, he entered "CLASS" as the name of the variable in the first column. For the successive variables, he named the column headings "AGE," "OWNCOMP," "FINANAID," "INCOME," "TUITION," and "INCREASE." After this shorthand naming of these variables, he provided more detailed variable labels: "Class Standing of Respondent," "Respondent's Age," "Does Respondent Own Computer," "Is Respondent Currently Receiving Financial Aid," "Estimated Family Income," "Is Current Tuition a Good Value," and "Willing to Pay Technology Fee." The next step was to define or label the values used by the interviewers in collecting and recording the data. For "CLASS," interviewers had circled "1" for a freshman respondent, "2" for a sophomore, "3" for a junior and "4" for a senior. The professor used these same values and labels from the questionnaire as SPSS values and value labels. A ratio-level variable, "AGE" required only one label: two respondents had refused to reveal their ages, so the professor instructed SPSS to read the "99" he input as "Refused." For "OWNCOMP" and "FINANAID" values and labels were input for "yes" and "no" and "refused/don't know." For "INCOME" interviewers had read a list of $20,000 increments (less than $20,000 was recorded as "1," $20,000 to $40,000 was recorded as "2," and so forth until $80,000 and above was recorded as a "5") and asked the respondents which level best described their family's combined household income. In defining that variable's values, the researcher needed to supply only the numbers 1–5 and the accompanying labels for the obtained data, a 6 for "don't know" and a 7 for "refused." For "TUITION" and "INCREASE," the two opinion statements ("All things considered, the value the university gives for the tuition I pay is a good one"; "I would be willing to pay a technology fee to improve the quality of my education."), respondents were able to "Strongly Disagree" (recorded as "1"), "Disagree" ("2"), "Neither agree nor disagree" ("3"), "Agree" ("4"), or "Strongly Agree" ("5").

Having invested the effort in defining these variables, the researcher saved the file to ensure the work was not lost. Returning to the pile of data sheets before him, he began inputting the information from each of the respondents. When he reached the twentieth case, he noticed that the last question ("INCREASE") was blank. Tempted to discard the data sheet, he instead went back to the variable definition option and specified that "9" for the variable "INCREASE" was to be treated as a missing value and not used in the computation of averages or percentages for that variable. Ultimately, he found missing data for only one other variable, "CLASS," on one case.

Once all 250 cases were entered and the file saved, the professor went to the Analyze menu in SPSS for Windows. He executed a Frequencies run for all variables except case number and obtained an output screen showing the percentage of respondents who were male and female; freshman, sophomore, junior, and senior; and so on. He noticed that in the frequencies for the "CLASS" variable, one respondent was identified as a "7," a value outside the prescribed set for the variable. He toggled from the output screen back to the data editor, went to the head of the "CLASS" column, instructed SPSS via the Edit command to "Find '7,'" and saw that it was case number 220. He checked the data sheet and saw the actual score should have been a "4," the number just below "7" on the numeric pad on his keyboard. After assuring himself there were no other data entry errors, he remedied the class standing of case 220.

Examining the frequencies for "INCOME," he noticed there were only three respondents who indicated family income below $20,000. Using the Recode function to instruct SPSS to read "1" as "2" in this column, he transformed the income variable so that the three respondents below $20,000 were pooled with the $20,000 to $40,000 respondents.

Deciding that he wanted to begin his analysis of the survey results by looking at descriptive data for only those students currently on financial aid, he used the Select Cases command under the Data menu to instruct SPSS to select only those cases where "Receiving Aid" was coded "1" for "yes."

Simple or Preliminary Analysis Procedures: Frequencies, Descriptive Statistics, Cross-Tabulation, and Comparing Means

As noted above, some data modifications and transformations are associated with cleaning the data, while other modifications are viewed as part of the process of data analysis, per se: the actual exploration and examination of the data in order to find patterns within and relationships among the variables. Indeed, our discussion of cleaning the data has also introduced already one of the most basic analysis procedures, the Frequencies procedure, the tabulation and presentation of the *frequency distribution* on a given variable. More simply put, a frequency distribution tells us how many cases there are for each value of a variable and the percentage of the total represented by that value's cases. Given the many powerful statistical procedures available to researchers and accessible in SPSS, a frequency distribution seems a fairly low-power tool. On the other hand, it is a very important tool. For most researchers, in fact, close scrutiny of a study's frequency distribution is essential and productive.

If we went to the Analyze menu, selected Descriptive Statistics and Frequencies for data from a survey of 420 adults, we might find a simple frequency distribution like this for gender, where "1" represents female and "2" represents male:

Gender	Frequency	Percent
1	234	55.7
2	186	44.3
Total	420	100.0

A variety of other descriptive statistics can be selected in the Frequencies dialog box, though most are not appropriate for a nominal variable like Gender. With interval- and ratio-level measures, however, those statistics—*measures of central tendency* such as means, modes, and medians; *measures of dispersion* such as standard deviation, variances, and ranges—are more appropriate. A separate option on the Analyze menu is Descriptives, which yields means, standard deviations, minimum and maximum values, but not frequencies or percentages.

While the gender example above illustrates how 420 cases can be reduced to summary statistics, it only begins to indicate what an important tool for analysis Frequencies can be. But consider the frequency distribution below, reporting the number of radios per household in a survey conducted in Malaysia, the percentages of the total represented by each value, and the *cumulative percentage:*

Radios	Frequency	Percent	Cumulative Percent
None	2	1.1	1.1
One	75	39.7	40.7
Two	54	28.6	69.3
Three	30	15.9	85.2
Four	20	10.6	95.8
Five	2	1.1	96.8
Six	6	3.2	100.0
Total	189	100.0	

Examining a frequency distribution like this can serve several functions for a researcher. First, it provides answers to substantive questions, like "What percentage of households cannot be reached via radio?" The answer is only 1.1 percent; the cumulative percentage shows that nearly 60 percent of households have two or more radios. Second, this frequency distribution might guide the researcher in transforming or modifying the data. For purposes of analysis, the researcher might want to combine responses of those with four or more radios; little is gained by keeping those 4.3 percent of housholds separate.

Now consider the frequency distributions—and the additional descriptive statistics—for these two questions used in a survey in Appalachia:

"How serious do you think environmental threats are to the health of most people in the area where you live?"

	Frequency	*Percent*	*Cumulative Percent*
Not Serious at All	27	6.3	6.3
Not Very Serious	87	20.2	26.5
Somewhat Serious	173	40.2	66.7
Very Serious	143	33.3	100.0
Total	430	100.0	
Mean: 3.0	Standard Deviation: .888		

"How about you personally? How serious do you think environmental threats are to your health personally?"

	Frequency	*Percent*	*Cumulative Percent*
Not Serious at All	46	10.8	10.8
Not Very Serious	101	23.7	34.5
Somewhat Serious	148	34.7	69.2
Very Serious	131	30.8	100.0
Total	430	100.0	
Mean: 2.85	Standard Deviation: .979		

Each question was scored on a 1–4 scale, with higher values indicating that environmental threats are a more serious health threat.

What can we gather from the frequency distribution on these two questions? First, environmental problems are perceived as a fairly serious health threat: 73.5 percent called them "Somewhat Serious" or "Very Serious" threats to the health of most people. But far fewer respondents see those problems as risks for themselves: Only 65.5 percent saw them as "Somewhat" or "Very Serious" threats to their own health. (Researchers call this "optimistic bias,"[17] a tendency to understimate one's own likelihood of suffering undesirable phenomena.) Yet the "movement" of respondents from the first question to the second is not so much in the "Very Serious" categories (a change of 12 respondents) as it is in the other categories, particularly the "Somewhat Serious" (a change of 25) and "Not Serious at All" (a change of 19) categories.

The point here is not to explicate optimistic bias or even to consider the risk from environmental problems faced by Appalachians. The point, first, is simply to demonstrate how fruitful even simple frequency distributions can be. A second point deals with the analytic "edge" represented in the additional statistics shown, the measure of central tendency (the mean) and variability (standard deviation). This chapter began by noting the reduction that takes place in much research, both in measurement and in the summarizing of data through descriptive statistics. Note that the difference in responses to the two questions—elaborated above in the discussion of percentages and percentage "shifts"—is reflected in the difference between the two means for the two questions. This is an obvious point, of course, but it is a point made to illustrate the value of reducing even simple percentage data to a single statistic or, alternatively, of looking at the same data in different ways.

We noted earlier that few communication researchers are satisfied with mere description or counting—and as fruitful as they may be, frequency distributions and summary statistics by themselves are primarily descriptive. One advantage of data analysis packages is that they provide tools permitting researchers to test relationships among two or more variables. Consider this: We could eyeball the two statements on environmental threats in Appalachia and suggest that respondents who had been very concerned about the risk to others "moved" to a less concerned category when the question asked them about personal risk. But that would be guesswork.

Imagine having the capability of examining the two variables' frequency distributions at the same time, in the same table, with one variable's values representing column headings and the other variable's values serving as row labels. Stated differently, a researcher could take those respondents who see "Very Serious" threats to "most people" and examine their frequency distribution on seriousness of the threat to "you personally." Then the same could be done with those who see "Somewhat Serious" threats to most people. The following may demonstrate this point.

Threat to Most People

	Not Serious At All	Not Very Serious	Somewhat Serious	Very Serious
Threat to You Personally				
Not Serious At All	?	?	?	?
Not Very Serious	?	?	?	?
Somewhat Serious	?	?	?	?
Very Serious	?	?	?	?
TOTAL				

This process—examining two variables' frequency distributions simultaneously—is actually called *cross-tabulation*, a procedure accessed through the Analyze or Summarize menu and the Descriptive choice on that menu. The cross-tabulation of two or more variables yields tables commonly called cross-tabs, or two-way cross-tabs, to distinguish tables with only two variables from those with three or more.

Consider a content analysis of network newscasts exploring how much time in seconds the "Big Three" networks devote to news items. A researcher would direct SPSS to cross-tabulate network and length variables. Thus, a probability sample of dates drawn from a year's newscasts yielded these frequency (or f) data, presented here as they would be used in a manuscript or paper:

Network

Length	ABC f	CBS f	NBC f
1–10 seconds	27	31	71
11–20 seconds	63	58	63
21–60 seconds	38	72	50
> 60 seconds	130	125	129
TOTAL	258	286	311

While the data reveal that a plurality of each network's items are over a minute in length, the similarities among the three are not as apparent as might be desired, simply because each network's total number of sampled items is different. Fortunately, SPSS can easily be directed to provide percentage data to accompany the frequencies, yielding a table that makes clearer the differences among the three networks.

Network

Length	ABC %	CBS %	NBC %
1–10 seconds	11	11	23
11–20 seconds	24	20	20
21–60 seconds	15	25	16
> 60 seconds	50	44	41
TOTAL	100	100	100
(n=)	(258)	(286)	(311)

Note that the table includes an indication of the total column frequencies (n-values) on which the column percentages are based. This is a critical convention when using percentages; a reader needs to know if the table indicates 50 percent of 258 items or 50 percent of four items.

Note also that the percentages are calculated to add to 100 percent within each column. The cross-tabulation procedure in SPSS also has a "cells" option that permits computation of percentages *across rows* and the percentage of the "grand total" of items that are in any single cell in the table. A cell is simply the juncture of a column and a row (e.g., the ABC column and the 1–10 second row cell above has 27 items in it; those 27 items represent 3.2% of the study's total 855 items). In analysis of cross-tabs, the "independent variable" is typically on the top, providing the column headings.

Perhaps more important, a researcher can produce a multilayer cross-tabulation by specifying a third (or more) variable. Using the network news example above, for instance, a researcher might be interested in controlling the focus (domestic versus international) of the news items, reasoning perhaps that international news items might be "disproportionately" represented among the shorter items. While the resulting output can sometimes become unwieldy, the researcher could, when guided by theory or previous research, add even more layers to the three-way cross-tabulation of network, length, and focus (e.g., by adding layers for hard versus soft news; anchor-read versus field correspondent, etc.).

Cross-tabs make it possible to examine a particular kind of relationship, an *association* between variables. Association between variables means simply that one value of the first variable tends to occur when a particular value of the second variable occurs. An observer might notice on several successive days that a particular young man and young lady tend to be in the school library or reading room each day. With no more data than this, and not having spent every day in the reading room, the observer might conclude that there is an association between her presence and his. (Contrast this with a *correlation*: The observer notes that when she leaves, he leaves the reading room; when she arrives, he soon follows; and neither is present without the other.)

"Eyeballing" some of the data examples presented in the tables above, one might be tempted to conclude that a statistically meaningful or significant association *must* be present, simply because of the distributions of frequencies and percentages. To test for statistical significance in cross-tabulations, however, researchers typically use two statistical tests, the chi-square test of association and Cramer's *V*. The value of chi-square for a two-way table indicates the statistical probability or certainty that the observed distribution of frequencies among the cells represents a real association, and not a chance one. Cramer's *V* is one of several additional tests that can indicate the strength of the association.[18] A fuller discussion of these techniques and of statistical probabilities is in Chapter 9.

The two basic analytical techniques presented so far—frequencies and cross-tabulation—have involved for the most part frequencies and percentages, though we did note that other statistics (mean, median, mode, etc.) are available and may be used with the frequencies and descriptive commands *if* the data are at an appropriate level of measurement.

Another basic technique—one that requires data at the interval or ratio level of measurement—involves comparing *means*. This "Means" procedure enables a researcher to designate groupings and subgroups within the data and to compute an arithmetic mean or average (or over a dozen other statistics!) for each of the groups. For example, if we have entrance test score and gender data for all applicants for a graduate program, we could use the Means command to identify gender differences on test scores among applicants. From the Statistics or Analyze menu (depending on the version of SPSS), we would select Compare Means or Means, designate test score as the *dependent variable* and gender as the *independent variable*, and run the analysis. Those group means might be more "meaningful" within the context of which group had the overall high score and the overall low score, so we might select from the Options menu to also see the *minimum* and *maximum* scores. As with cross-tabulation, the researcher can add additional layers of independent variables. For example, after admission decisions are made on the basis of test scores, undergraduate performance, professional experience, recommendations, and so on, an analysis might be done using test score as the dependent variable, gender as the first independent variable, and admission status (yes or no) as the second independent variable. Four separate means would be calculated, one each for admitted and nonadmitted males and admitted and nonadmitted females.

Simple comparison among means, like these, only begin to utilize the usefulness of the Means procedure. Recall our earlier example of the three levels of television viewing, where we conducted a frequency analysis and found that 33 percent of the sample viewed fewer than 35 minutes of television daily and 67 percent viewed fewer than 120 minutes. We recoded 0–35 minutes of viewing to "Light Viewing"; 36–119 minutes to "Medium Viewing"; and 120+ minutes to "Heavy Viewing." As part of the same survey, we asked respondents to tell us, using a 1–10 scale (where 1 = "not likely at all" and 10 = "almost certain"), how likely they were to be a victim of a violent crime during their lifetimes. Using likelihood as the dependent variable and our three levels of viewing as the independent variable, we could compare mean likelihood scores to determine whether heavier viewers are more likely to see themselves as potential victims, the basic premise of cultivation theory.

As was the case with cross-tabulation (and the accompanying chi-square and Cramer's *V* statistics options), there are statistical tests available with the means command for testing the statistical significance of observed differences in means. Those are detailed in Chapter 9.

Summary

This brief introduction to specific analysis techniques like cross-tabulation or comparisons of means, and the statistics that accompany them, cannot overshadow several of the points made earlier in this chapter. Nor should researchers let the many, many possibilities represented by SPSS tempt them into hasty research and data analysis. First and foremost, students must commit to the idea that while careful preplanning is not part of data analysis, it is the essential first step *toward* successful, efficient, and valid analysis. To be blunt: A powerful technique such as comparison of means is useless if the data were not collected at the interval or ratio level. Preplanning includes decisions about measurement level, as well as other aspects of *research design*—that entire collection of decisions about units of analysis, sampling, measurement, and plans for data analysis.

SPSS—whatever the version—is a powerful tool for data reduction, manipulation, and analysis, and the techniques available within SPSS or most other statistical packages will perform virtually any task a researcher chooses, from transforming existing variables to computing new ones, to dividing the data into groups and subgroups. Ultimately, the success of the research enterprise depends less on the sophistication of the data analysis or the impenetrability of the statistical procedure used than it does on the clarity of the research questions or hypotheses and the effectiveness of the research design. A dummy table sketched on a dinner napkin during the planning of the research—showing the anticipated use and analysis for carefully collected data—may be more important than tables and tables of statistics and probabilities that SPSS could generate from "dirty" data.

Endnotes

1. Wayne Danielson, "Data Processing," in Guido H. Stempel and Bruce H. Westley, eds., *Research Methods in Mass Communication, 2nd ed.* (Englewood Cliffs, NJ: Prentice-Hall, 1989), 112.

2. Norman H. Nie, Dale H. Bent, and C. Hadlai Hull, *Statistical Package for the Social Sciences* (New York: McGraw-Hill, 1970).

3. Wilfred J. Dixon, ed., *Biomedical Computer Programs* (Berkeley: University of California Press, 1973).

4. Anthony J. Barr, *SAS User's Guide* (Raleigh, NC: SAS Institute, 1979).

5. Neil J. Salkind, *Statistics for People Who (Think They) Hate Statistics* (Thousand Oaks, CA: Sage, 2000), 275-286.

6. Fred Kerlinger, *Foundations of Behavioral Research, 2nd ed.* (New York: Holt, Rinehart and Winston, 1973), 706.

7. Daniel Riffe, Stephen Lacy, and Frederick G. Fico, *Analyzing Media Messages: Using Quantitative Content Analysis in Research* (Mahwah, NJ: Lawrence Erlbaum, 1998), 42.

8. Paul J. Deutschmann, *News-Page Content of Twelve Metropolitan Dailies* (Cincinnati: Scripps-Howard Research, 1959).

9. Daniel Riffe, "The Stability of 'Bad News' in Third World Coverage: 22 Years of *New York Times* Foreign News," *International Communication Bulletin* 28 (Fall 1993): 6-12.

10. Danielson, *op. cit.*, (1989), 110.

11. Daniel Riffe and Arianne Budianto, "The Shrinking World of Network News," paper presented to the Annual Conference of the Association for Education in Journalism and Mass Communication, Washington, DC, August 2001.

12. This was possible because the researcher had drawn a constructed-week probability sample from each quarter of each year (January to March, April to June. etc.).

13. Riffe, Lacy, and Fico, *op. cit.*, 188.

14. George Gerbner, Larry Gross, Michael Morgan, and Nancy Signorielli, "Growing Up with Television: The Cultivation Perspective," in Jennings Bryant and Dolf Zillmann, eds., *Media Effects: Advances in Theory and Research* (Mahwah, NJ: Lawrence Erlbaum, 1994), 26.

15. W. Phillips Davison, "The Third-Person Effect in Communication," *Public Opinion Quarterly* 47 (Spring 1983), 47: 1-15.

16. Riffe, Lacy, and Fico, *op. cit.*, 124-127.

17. Neil D. Weinstein, "Unrealistic Optimism about Future Life Events," *Journal of Personality and Social Psychology* 39 (May 1980): 806-820.

18. Riffe, Lacy, and Fico, *op. cit.*, 167.

11

Content Analysis

Guido H. Stempel III

Content analysis is a formal system for doing something we all do informally rather frequently—draw conclusions from observations of content. We express opinions about the adequacy of various kinds of coverage by newspapers, magazines, radio stations, and television stations. We talk about violence and sex on television and the Internet. Those opinions are based on what we observe as readers or listeners.

Such opinions make interesting conversation, but we have seen in recent years that casual observations have been the basis for serious suggestions for major changes in the media. For example, Congress almost continually is considering legislation about the Internet, but they are doing so in almost a total vacuum of research data about content of the Internet.

We have seen the same thing for years with regard to the issue of violence and television. The only difference has been that data about television violence have been developed, but Congress has not paid much attention to those data. That is at least part of the reason that the controversy about television violence has continued so long. The impressions of those on both sides are colored by their perspectives. The critic watches a television program and sees gratuitous violence. The producer sees nothing in the same program except violence that is integral to the plot.

Such situations make the need for formal content analysis rather evident. Issues like sex and violence on television and the Internet are too important to be resolved on the basis of people's subjective impressions. We need a better way to assess media content. Content analysis offers that. The place of content analysis in communication research is indicated by the following paradigm:

WHO says WHAT to WHOM with WHAT EFFECT

It is evident that communication research has not dealt equally with all four parts of this paradigm, but we did not introduce it here to make that point. Rather, we bring it up to suggest that communication research can reach its full potential only if it can relate content to communicator, audience, and effects. Yet it cannot do that without definitive information about content. That is why content analysis has been used so frequently in mass communication research.[1]

Definition of Content Analysis

Berelson provided a classic definition of content analysis a half century ago:

> Content analysis is a research technique for objective, systematic, and quantitative description of the manifest content of communication.[2]

The key to understanding content analysis and performing it competently lies in understanding the meanings of *objective*, *systematic*, *quantitative*, and *manifest content*.

> *Objective*, to begin with, means the opposite of subjective or impressionistic. Objectivity is achieved by having the categories of analysis defined so precisely that different persons can apply them to the same content and get the same results. If content analysis were subjective instead of objective, each person would have his or her own content analysis. That it is objective means that the results depend upon the procedure and not the analyst.

> *Systematic* means, first, that a set procedure is applied to all the content being analyzed. Second, it means that categories are set up so that all relevant content is analyzed. Finally, it means the analysis is designed to secure data relevant to a research question or hypothesis.

> *Quantitative* means simply the recording of numerical values or frequencies with which the various defined types of content occur.

> *Manifest content* means the apparent content, which means that content must be coded as it appears rather than as the content analyst feels it is intended.

There has been little quarrel with the first two points in Berelson's definition. To be sure, some content analyses have not been objective or systematic, but no one has advocated that they should not be. With regard to content analysis being quantitative and dealing with manifest content, however, the story has been somewhat different.

There has been the recurring suggestion that content analyses should be qualitative rather than quantitative. This suggestion has assumed incorrectly that these were mutually exclusive. Those who have advocated qualitative content analysis have criticized published content studies for shallowness and lack of meaning. Such criticism, however, may well be an indictment of the failure of the study to be systematic in the full sense of the word, as just defined.

Those who advocate qualitative rather than quantitative content analysis also seem to overlook what would be lost in meaning if a study were not quantitative. For example, it is not particularly meaningful to say that *Time* and *Newsweek* both referred to the impeachment of President Clinton in 1999. The relative frequency of those references is a rather significant fact. It would also, of course, be useful to know how many references were favorable and how many unfavorable and how many were attributed and how many unattributed. These points are as much a matter of being systematic as of being quantitative.

However, we do not advocate assigning arbitrary numerical values to achieve an index score for content. One could, for example, create an attention score for TV news by giving a "2" to the stories before the first commercial break and a "1" to the rest of the stories. In addition, we could give a "2" to stories more than 30 seconds long and a "1" to the rest of the stories. And we could give a "2" to every story that has supporting video and a "1" to those that don't. Each story then would have a score between 3 and 6. We could average these stories for categories of news or for stations or networks. We would have results and conclusions based on these numbers.

The problem with this is that the scores have no validity. There is ultimately no research evidence to support the assumptions here that stories early in the newscast get twice as much attention as stories that come later. Likewise, there is no evidence that longer stories get twice as much attention as shorter stories or that stories with video get twice as much attention as stories without video. This is not what is called for when we say content analysis is quantitative. Furthermore, it probably compromises objectivity.

The concept of **manifest content** has been criticized by those who balk at dealing with the apparent content when they are certain the intent of the communicator is otherwise and are equally certain they know what it is. This viewpoint has a certain appeal, but the question is whether objectivity can be maintained if manifest content is abandoned. The content analyst, after all, is injecting a subjective interpretation. While he or she may feel this is the correct interpretation, whether others will see the situation in the same terms is another matter. If other coders do not agree, then obviously the criterion of two persons getting the same results when applying the categories to the same content will not be met.

Some researchers have expressed concern that taking content at its face value may distort reality. Reality, however, probably can be dealt with more effectively by interpreting the results accordingly than by giving up on manifest content. If two political candidates talk about balancing the budget, it does not mean that their economic views are the same. It does not mean, as has been amply demonstrated at all levels of government, that either of them would really balance the budget. What it does mean is that each candidate recognizes that speaking in favor of a balanced budget is good politics, and that is how a sensible content analyst would interpret it.

Content Analysis Procedure

The person who undertakes a content analysis study must deal with four methodological problems: selection of the unit of analysis, category construction, sampling of content, and reliability of coding.

Selection of Unit of Analysis

What we are asking here is simply whether we are going to consider words, statements, sentences, paragraphs, or entire articles. The answer must be related to the purpose of the study. If our objective is to find out how much coverage newspapers give to South

America, it would be silly to use the word as the unit of analysis and count each mention of South America or a South American country. We would learn as much or more by counting articles as by counting words, and it obviously would take considerably less work. Conversely, if our concern is whether George Bush or Bill Clinton received more favorable coverage during their presidencies, we probably would want to use words or symbols. Most stories about either president would contain both favorable and unfavorable references, and while we probably could make an overall judgment, we would lose information in doing that. Thus the decision about the unit of analysis depends primarily on what information is required for the purpose of the study.

Category Construction

Category systems already developed by other researchers may prove to be appropriate for your study. If you want to deal with television coverage of a presidential campaign, the symbol-coding system developed by Lasswell may be your answer.[3] That would involve simply identifying the pertinent symbols, which would be the names of the candidates and the parties, plus a set of directional categories such a favorable, unfavorable, and neutral. If you want to deal with the subject matter covered about South America in U.S. newspapers, Deutschmann's categories would be appropriate. His eleven categories, covering the full range of content in media, are war and defense, popular amusements, general human interest, economic activity, education and classic arts, politics and government, crime, accident and disaster, public health and welfare, science and invention, and public moral problems.[4]

In other cases you may be able to find a category system that has been used for a similar study to the one you have in mind. That is true even for some fairly narrow topics. There are real advantages to using a category system that has been used in other studies. First, you will know that it is a workable system. By looking at the results of other studies that have used the system, you will get some notion of the kinds of results that are likely. It will be easier to make comparisons of your results with other results. Yet, granting all this, you may find that you need to develop your own set of categories. The decision to do so should be based on the conclusion that no existing system will enable you to meet the objectives of your study.

As you set out to create a set of categories, you should keep three things in mind:

1. Categories must be pertinent to the objectives of your study.
2. Categories should be functional.
3. The system of categories must be manageable.

These three concepts are interrelated, and when a set of categories falls short on one these, it is likely to fall short on all of them.

The simple test of whether categories are pertinent is whether the information they yield will answer the research questions of the study or permit the testing of the hypotheses of the study. For example, if your objective is to determine the adequacy of coverage of South America by U.S. newspapers, you might want to consider where the stories are in the paper. It might be useful to have as categories "Page 1" and "other pages," because the distinction has some significance in assessing coverage. On the other hand, while you could create as categories "odd-numbered pages" and "even-numbered pages," such categories would not seem pertinent. Knowing the proportion of stories on odd-numbered pages would not really tell you anything meaningful about coverage. In many cases, whether a particular category is pertinent can be determined only by careful consideration of the hypotheses of the study. For example, to consider the subject matter of stories about South America may or may not make sense. If the hypothesis is simply that the U.S. public gets less information about South America than it does about Europe, then it does not seem important to note whether the stories are about politics, economics, or accidents and disasters. If, on the other hand, the hypothesis is that coverage of South America, because of the way in which reporters are assigned, emphasizes disasters over political news, the distinction is vital.

In suggesting that categories are functional, we are assuming that a content study intends to say something about a media process and the decision making within that process. Our interest in how television networks cover a presidential campaign assumes that through our content analysis we can gain insight into the decisions that were made by reporters, camera persons, editors, or anchors. If our categories include material over which these people have no control, we may not be able to achieve the objectives of our study. If, for example, we consider the coverage of crowd reaction to the candidate, we are probably dealing with something that is more related to the campaign itself than to what media personnel do in covering the campaign. If the newscast shows the crowd booing the candidate's statement on healthcare, that probably does not tell us anything about the camera person. On the other hand, if every picture of Candidate A shows him with an ugly expression on his face, while every picture of Candidate B shows her with a smile on her face, we must wonder at either the work of the camera person or the selection of pictures by the editor.

Keeping the system of categories manageable is mostly a matter of limiting the number of categories. Once coders are familiar with the set of categories, they should be able to function without frequent reference back to the list and the definitions. With computerized content analysis, this may not be a problem, but the researcher still has to comprehend the whole set. So does the person who reads the report of the study. Somewhere between ten and twenty categories can be handled by coders, researchers, and readers. As you build a set of categories and add new categories, it is important to keep the objectives of the study in mind. It is easy to become fascinated with all the possible categories and in the process lose sight of what you set out to do.

Sampling of Content

In many respects, sampling in content analysis is not different from sampling in surveys. The major concern, often overlooked, is to make sure that the sample represents the population that it is intended to represent.

The prime consideration is that each unit in the population must have the same chance of being represented in the sample. Unfortunately, in content analysis there has been a tendency to accept a less rigorous criterion—this unit is pretty much like any other unit in the population. It is on this basis that we accept the collection of newspapers in a university library or in a given database as a representative sample. Even casual second thought ought to convince you that the library's goal is not to create a representative sample. Likewise, that probably is not what those who select papers for a database are seeking.

In sampling for content analysis, there is the additional consideration of sampling time as well as media. Thus, if you decided to study network news coverage of a presidential campaign, you must either take the total campaign or sample days from within the defined campaign period. Here again, the guiding principle ought to be to give every day an equal chance of being drawn for the sample.

Beyond these fairly basic points of sampling, there are some special considerations in sampling for content analysis. These considerations tend to mean that stratified samples are necessary in some cases and that purposive samples are extremely useful in some cases.

The first of these considerations has to do with days of the week for daily media. Most newspapers have a fairly consistent pattern so far as number of pages is concerned—much larger in the middle of the week than at the beginning or end of the week. The exact details vary, depending on retail trade patterns in the newspaper's trade area, but in any case the variation in number of pages stems from variation in the volume of advertising. This in turn creates variation in the amount of news content. It also means that the decision-making process is not the same every day. This makes it imperative to represent days of the week equally.[5] For example, if you decide to have twenty-four days in your sample, you should select four Mondays randomly, four Tuesdays randomly, and so on. Sundays, of course, are a whole separate problem, partly because Sunday papers are much larger and partly because many papers do not have Sunday editions. Some content analysts have dealt with this by excluding Sunday editions. This is not always a good idea, but if you include Sunday papers, you should be careful in making comparisons of papers with Sunday editions and papers that do not have Sunday editions.

Days of the week are also a problem if you are studying radio or television news, but for a somewhat different reason. Both radio and television tend to maintain a constant amount of time for the news day after day. The problem variable here is the news itself, because news does not happen equally all days of the week. The worlds of commerce and government operate primarily on five-day, forty-hour weeks. All news does not come from those sources, but a substantial amount does. For broadcasters, the amount of news available between Friday noon and Monday noon is perceptibly less than it is for the rest of the week. That is why if you are studying broadcast news, you need to have each day of the week appear equally often in your sample.

For magazines, the issue is seasons rather than days of the week. Whether you are analyzing weekly magazines or monthly magazines, you get more accurate results if you represent each month equally.[6]

A second consideration is how news media and news gathering are organized. If, for example, you want to study coverage of South America by U.S. newspapers, one approach would be to take a random sample of U.S. newspapers. You probably would want to take 100 of the approximately 1,500 daily papers. In doing that, however, you would be overlooking two things. First, the news of South America that comes to Americans is supplied by a very limited number of sources. There is the Associated Press, the New York Times Service, and the British service Reuters. There are perhaps a dozen U.S. newspapers that maintain correspondents anywhere in South America, and they do some syndication. It would seem then that you might learn more by studying fifteen purposively selected papers than by studying the random sample of 100. Second, papers that depend on wire service coverage have some choices that determine how much South American news they will get. Those choices avoid costs, and what a newspaper can afford is related to its revenue, which in turn is related to its circulation size. It is therefore predictable that the amount of news about South America available in newspapers of less than 50,000 circulation will be much less than that available in newspapers of more than 50,000 circulation. It is about at this circulation figure that newspapers find they can afford the Associated Press national-international wire, rather than the condensed compiled state wire. It is also at this circulation level that newspapers discover they can afford a second wire. Again, it can be argued that a smaller sample chosen with reference to these considerations might yield more information.

A third consideration is availability. For studies of coverage by newspapers, this is not a major problem. For studies of coverage by broadcast media, however, it obviously is a major problem. We are getting more TV newscasts into databases, but it still would be difficult to find what you would need for a national study of local TV newscasts. That is why there have not been many. Most studies of television newscasts have been of the network newscasts because they are readily available. For radio, the situation is worse. There really is no source the researcher can turn to for scripts or tapes of radio newscasts. The only option is to seek them from the stations, and the response to such an effort is likely to be uneven.

A fourth and somewhat different concern is whether you intend to draw inferences about the behavior of news decision makers or inferences about what readers and listeners are exposed to. In the first instance you would be sampling newspapers, and a fair sample would be one that represented all newspapers equally. In the second instance you would want to consider weighting newspapers by circulation. This would require drawing newspapers randomly after you had stratified by circulation category. Otherwise, the very largest papers would be unlikely to turn up at all in a random sample of 100 papers among the 1,500 plus. Conversely, a straight random sample would tell us a great deal about the content of newspapers that reach few readers and very little about the content of newspapers that reach a million readers or more a day.

How researchers have responded to this problem is unfortunately rather obvious. Not only do we assess television news solely on the basis of what the networks do, but we do the same thing about entertainment programming. In studies of print media we address this by using purposive samples. That is probably why Riffe and Freitag found that 68 percent of the content studies in *Journalism Quarterly* used purposive samples.[7]

Reliability of Coding

The fact that content analysis is defined as systematic and objective means that the researcher must be concerned with reliability. By reliability, we mean consistency of classification. If, for example, we have two coders viewing a newscast in a study of presidential campaign coverage, we would expect them to agree on the number of times the Democratic candidate was mentioned and on whether a given mention was favorable or unfavorable. As a practical matter, we know that two coders will not agree completely, but unless we achieve some level of agreement, we obviously cannot claim our study is systematic or objective.

Disagreement between coders is usually the result of one of three things: (1) inadequate definition of categories, (2) failure of coders to achieve a common frame of reference, and (3) oversights. It is not uncommon in the early stages of a study for there to be more disagreement than agreement among coders.

The researcher's primary concern needs to be with what he or she can do to increase reliability. The first step is to work out precise definitions of categories. The second is to go over those definitions and the coding process with coders before they begin. Trial runs should be conducted, and the responses of coders should be compared item by item. This will contribute a great deal to the development of a common frame of reference among coders. As much practice coding as resources and the situation permit should be done. It probably takes a group of coders a full week to reach a really common frame of reference.

Once coding has begun, you should make spot checks to be sure that the reliability level is not deteriorating. Briefings should be conducted to deal with problems the coders feel the definitions and instructions do not cover completely.

If you are doing all the coding for the study yourself, the reliability problem remains every bit as real, although perhaps not so complex. If possible, you should have a second person work with you initially and also have that person do some spot checking with you. By working with another person, you will have to clarify some definitions and procedures, and you will have to develop an objective approach.

For any content study, a reliability estimate ought to be calculated and reported. However, Riffe and Freitag found that only 56 percent of the studies in *Journalism Quarterly* reported a reliability figure.[8] A minimum standard for reporting reliability would be to have three passages coded by all coders. A person doing a content study by himself or herself should, near the end of the work, recode some of the earlier material and compare. Also, if you have a second person helping you in the fashion suggested earlier, you could use that person in making your reliability check. After the coding is completed, you should compare item by item.

We believe that the appropriate thing to report here is simply the percentage agreement between coders. However, some content analysts argue that the complexity of the category system and the level of agreement that would be obtained by chance should be taken into account.[9] Still others use correlation approaches.[10] These more complex approaches have their merits. In most measurement situations, reliabilities are given in terms of correlations, and correlating coding distributions permits us to report values that are comparable to other measures. However, percentage of agreement is the most direct measure, and it is an accepted way of reporting reliability.

Training Coders.   For studies using several coders, some things should be said about the selection and training of coders. The first suggestion is to try to find experienced coders, but while that may be obvious, it usually is not practical. The people you recruit to code will, in all probability, never have done any coding before. It probably is desirable to have people with somewhat similar academic backgrounds. We have found that a person's academic background does provide a perspective that is very evident in the early stages of coding.

We once used as coders a group of college teachers in three different fields, journalism, political science, and sociology. These are similar fields, and one might even suggest that college professors are similar, but it was some time before we could get a unified approach. In the early stages, the journalists performed pretty much alike, but distinctly differently from the political scientists, who in turn performed differently from the sociologists.

The major challenge in training coders is to develop the common frame of reference that is vital to the success of your study. It does not come quickly. No matter how carefully you define categories and instruct coders, there will be situations that coders perceive as not being covered. These situations need to be identified, discussed, and agreed upon. Bear in mind that the coder does not need to accept the rationale for handling a situation; he or she merely needs to know what the rule is. It is possible that you will have a coder who simply cannot develop the same frame of reference as the rest of the group. If that happens, you need to drop that coder from the coding group. When this happens, it is usually because of major differences in background between one coder and the rest of the group. It is not a reflection on that person, but merely an indication of a different perspective.

Training should continue throughout a study. The work of coders needs to be checked as the coding progresses. Opportunities should be provided for coders to discuss problems. The major value of such discussions is simply that it promotes the common frame of reference.

Computerized Content Analysis

Computers are being used in two ways in current content analyses. The first way, one that has been used for more than thirty years, is for coding. The other, a more recent development, is the use of computerized indexes to identify stories. Both have their advantages and disadvantages.

The strength of the computer is its ability to do fairly simply tasks extremely fast. Practically, what this means is that the computer is valuable in a study that involves recognition of words or syllables. An early, but good example, of efficient use of **computerized content analyis** is the study by Wilhoit and Sherrill on the visibility of U.S. senators in wire-service copy.[11] The computer's task in this study was basically to recognize 100 words (the names of the senators). Currently, we see examples of assessment of coverage that has been done by having a computer search for certain names. It was this technique, for example, that produced the report that the president's dog was getting more coverage in U.S. media than the secretary of agriculture. On a more serious level, we were able to document the total coverage of Canada by major U.S. newspapers over a period of twenty-one months primarily through the use of databases.[12] Presumably, we will see more use of computer searches to show who and what have been covered.

It is also possible to program a computer to analyze texts. Not much use has been made of this option thus far. In part, this may be because to make use of this potential of the computer, you have to input the text. However, more and more text material is becoming available in databases, which makes it likely that we will see this application of computers to content analysis. There has always been the option of keyboarding the material into the computer, but that has seldom been done because it is so time consuming.

Another way to get text material is to get it from media that are using computerized production processes and therefore could easily create a disk containing text material for a given print issue or broadcast program. For the researcher to get sufficient material for a study requires consideration cooperation. It is not easy, but it is possible. A key factor is that the media have a substantial interest in your project. For example, suppose the National Association of Broadcasters or the National Newspaper Association has a concern with proposed Congressional legislation and your study provides pertinent information. The NAB or NNA would endorse your project, and member stations or newspapers would be more than willing to cooperate by providing you disks.[13] Thus computerized content analysis offers opportunities for more extensive studies and more detailed analysis within those studies. However, a word of caution is in order. Databases have their problems and limitations. Indexing is not unform from one data base to another and sometimes not within a single database. It is therefore highly desirable to go to the specific medium and do some checking of what is in the medium and how that compares to what is in the database. Kathleen Hansen discusses these concerns in Chapter 12 in detail.

Summary

A successful content analysis study is the result of a series of good decisions. The process must start with a clear statement of objectives and hypotheses. The necessary decisions cannot be made intelligently unless you know what it is that you're trying to find out. Once you have determined that, you are ready to move to the basic decisions about unit of analysis, category construction, and sampling. Next comes the selection and training of coders. While all these matters can be and should be decided with careful deliberation well in advance of the start of the study, the need for little decisions will arise continuously throughout a study. These must be dealt with in a way consistent with the basic decisions, but not with total rigidity. Adjustments usually are needed simply because not every problem can be anticipated.

We have tried to indicate in this chapter some of the considerations that enter into these various decisions. It is important for you to remember that there will be more than one good choice in some instances. Researchers may differ as to which of several good choices is clearly the best. Your goal ought to be to make those decisions to the best of your ability, keeping the objectives of the study clearly in mind at all times. If you can achieve that, you undoubtedly will produce a good study.

Endnotes

1. See Daniel Riffe and Alan Freitag, "A Content Analysis of Content Analyses: Twenty-Five Years of Journalism Quarterly," *Journalism Quarterly* 74 (Winter 1997): 873–82 . They report that nearly one-fourth of the articles in *Journalism Quarterly* from 1971 to 1996 were content analyses.

2. Bernard Berelson, *Content Analysis in Communication Research* (New York: The Free Press, 1952), 18.

3. Harold Lasswell, Nathan Leites, and associates, *The Language of Politics* (Cambridge, MA: M.I.T. Press, 1965).

4. Paul J. Deutschmann, *News-Page Content of Twelve Metropolitan Dailies* (Cincinnati: Scripps Howard Research, 1959), 92–95. For another example of use of these categories, see Guido H. Stempel III, "Gatekeeping the Mix of Topics and the Selection of News," *Journalism Quarterly* 62 (Winter): 791–796, 815.

5. See Guido H. Stempel III, "Sample Size for Classifying Subject Matter in Dailies," *Journalism Quarterly* 29 (Summer 1952): 333–334 and Daniel Riffe, Stephen Lacy, and Charles W. Aust, "The Effectiveness of Random, Consecutive Day and Constructed Week Samples in Newspaper Content Analysis," *Journalism Quarterly* 70 (Spring 1992): 133–39.

6. Daniel Riffe, Stephen Lacy, and Michael W. Drager, "Sample Size in Content Analysis of Weekly News Magazines," *Journalism Quarterly* 73 (Autumn 1996): 635–644; Stephen Lacy, Daniel Riffe, and Quint Randle, "Sample Size in Multi-Year Content Analysis of Monthly Consumer Magazines," *Journalism Quarterly* 75 (Summer 1998): 408–417.

7. Riffe and Freitag, *op. cit.*

8. Riffe and Freitag, *op. cit.*

9. W. A. Scott, "Reliability of Content Analysis: The Case of Nominal Scale Coding," *Public Opinion Quarterly* 19 (1955): 321–325.

10. Lasswell et al., *op. cit.*, Chapter 5.

11. G. Cleveland Wilhoit and Kenneth S. Sherrill, "Wire Service Visibility of U.S. Senators," *Journalism Quarterly* 45 (Spring 1968): 42–48.

12. Don Flournoy, Debra Mason, Robert Nanney, and Guido H. Stempel III, "Media Images of Canada," *Ohio Journalism Monograph Series No. 3*, August 1992.

13. See, for example, James A. Anderson, *Broadcast Stations and Newspapers: The Problem of Information Control: A Content Analysis of Local News Presentation* (Washington, DC: National Association of Broadcasters, 1971).

12

Using Databases for Content Analysis

Kathleen A. Hansen

Content analysis has been widely recognized as a research tool since the 1940s. In 1952, Berelson defined content analysis as a "research technique for the objective, systematic and quantitative description of the manifest content of communication."[1] Budd, Thorp, and Donohew expanded this definition by describing content analysis as "a systematic technique for analyzing message content and message handling."[2] Holsti identified three primary purposes for content analysis: to describe the characteristics of communication, to make inferences about the antecedents of communication, and to make inferences about the effects of communication.[3] A major advantage of content analysis is its ability to cope with large volumes of data.

Communication researchers use content analysis to examine any number of questions about news content. For instance, researchers might ask how a particular topic, issue, or event has been covered by different news organizations, such as how different organizations covered a major environmental disaster or a political scandal. Researchers might examine how a specific newspaper or set of newspapers cover news generally, such as the ratio of wire service copy to staff generated copy, male versus female bylines, national and international news versus local news, or types and affiliations of sources in stories. Content analysts might ask how specific types of news content are handled, such as how AP stories are handled by different news organizations or how syndicated materials are distributed. Researchers might ask how different media (television, print newspapers, web publications) cover stories differently. Researchers may be examining these questions using a number of theoretical frameworks such as the sociology of news production, the industrial organization economic model of the news industry, the political economy perspective on news production and dissemination, and many others. The salient factor in these types of analyses is that a large amount of content must be examined in order to make valid and reliable observations and to draw proper inferences.

The year 1985 was a watershed in the wide adoption of electronic database systems in news organizations for the storage and retrieval of the full text of newspaper and magazine articles, broadcast program scripts, and wire service content.[4] Most of these databases were created first for in-house management, storage, and retrieval of the vast quantities of text generated by news organizations' own personnel every day. However, news organizations quickly discovered that their back files were a valuable asset that could be marketed for commercial gain as well. There are now many thousands of full text publication databases that can be searched through a large number of database vendors. In addition, many news organizations make their archives of back issues available through their websites, allowing web surfers to search the back files for free but charging a per-article fee for the retrieval of the full text.

Major Methods for Gaining Access to Databases

There are three main methods for gaining access to electronic **databases** of news content. For the content analyst, the most useful databases are those that provide access to the full text of the articles that appeared in the publication. A number of major proprietary database vendors provide extensive files of full text news sources. News producers have contracts with these vendors and regularly upload their news files to the vendors' computers. The vendors then charge a subscription for access to the files, and most also charge a per-article retrieval fee for each full text article downloaded, printed, or viewed. In the last few years, most of the proprietary database vendors have introduced a web-based version of their service that allows subscribers to search and retrieve articles via the web.

Dialog (*www.dialog.com*) provides access to more than 100 U.S. newspapers and 500 databases covering business, patents, trademarks, science, and government publications. Dow Jones Interactive (*www.djnr.com*) provides 80 million+ articles from 6,000 publications plus market research, analyst reports, and historical market data. Lexis-Nexis (*www.lexis-nexis.com*) provides 1.4 billion+ news stories from more than 22,000 sources arranged into 10,000 databases. They add more than 4.6 million documents each week. The newspaper databases in Lexis-Nexis Universe, alone, include the full text of 840 newspapers worldwide. Burrelle's Information Services (*www.burrelles.com*) includes broadcast transcripts from more than 160 network and cable stations dating back to 1989. NewsLibrary (*www.newslibrary.com*) allows access to more than 80 U.S. newspapers (many of them Knight-Ridder papers). Database services available through many academic and public libraries (which pay institutional subscriptions so patrons may search for free) provide access to full texts of magazines and newspapers through files such as the "National Newspapers" database on Proquest or the "General Reference Center" database on Infotrac.

Another major method for gaining access to electronic databases of news content is through the websites of the publications themselves. In addition to uploading their archives to the major proprietary database vendors and receiving a royalty fee for doing so, many publishers have added an archive search feature as a part of their own website. On the website, searching the archive is free, but retrieving individual articles incurs a fee (usually $3.50 to $5.00). It is important to make a crucial distinction here—one that will arise again later in the chapter. The electronic archive on the website is the full text back file of the articles that appeared in the printed version of the publication. Most websites do not archive their web content for more than two weeks. This poses an extremely difficult problem for content analysts wishing to study website content, because the best news websites contain much material that never appeared in the printed publication. However, that content is not archived and superceded web pages cannot be searched or retrieved.

The third major method for gaining access to the full text of news publications is through the use of the CD-ROM-based publications issued by many news publications or services such as NewsBank that provide abstracts of news publications on CD. In addition to microfilming the printed edition of the newspaper, for instance, many publishers also issue a **CD-ROM** of the printed publication. These CDs can be found in libraries and can be searched using many of the fields and techniques provided by the proprietary vendors of databases online. The disadvantage of the CD databases is that there is a time-lag in their publication, leaving many content analysts with a need for timely information to use the online vendors instead.

The wide availability of these electronic databases of the full text of news content has greatly enhanced content analysts' access to the volume of data needed to conduct a variety of studies that examine newsmaking. Rather than going through the cumbersome process of using print indexes to identify the issues in which the desired articles appeared, and then referring to the microfilm of the back files to retrieve the articles, content analysts can search for and retrieve hundreds of articles on their desired topics in a matter of minutes, download the files to a computer hard drive and proceed with their content analysis tasks.

But there are a number of reasons why content analysts need to be cautious in using databases for the search and retrieval of their data. Scholars of the content analysis process tell us that the selection of the sample is second only in importance to the formulation of the research question or hypothesis. Solid content analysis requires rigor in drawing the sample, and sample selection poses one of the most difficult aspects of using databases for the search and retrieval of data. All databases are not created equal, nor do they all provide the same access to information. Therefore, sample selection becomes highly problematic.

A significant problem in the selection of the sample arises before the content analyst even begins the process of choosing which news publications or broadcasts to analyze. Willey has documented a major hurdle facing content analysts working in academic settings who rely on their college or university libraries for access to electronic databases of content.[5] Willey moved from a privately funded foundation to academia, where she wanted to continue her research focus on the journalism's relationship to democracy. Her work relied on access to newspaper content for analysis. At the foundation, Willey had access to the Lexis-Nexis Universe database, with its thousands of full-text publications and its highly sophisticated search capabilities. However, upon arriving at her university post, Willey learned that the academic version of Lexis-Nexis, called "Lexis-Nexis Academic Universe," is a stripped-down version of the corporate account database service, with much more limited search capabilities and many fewer publications in the database.

In fact, Lexis-Nexis Academic Universe was never intended for the kind of research that faculty content analysts might do. It was designed primarily for undergraduates. Indeed, the corporate version of the database provides full-text access to 840 newspapers. The academic version, in its "General News" file, is restricted to the top 50 circulation U.S. newspapers as listed in *Editor and Publisher Yearbook*. The "U.S. News" file in the academic version of the database includes many more regional publications, but no where near the 840 titles in the corporate version. Because of licensing restrictions and agreements with the source publishers, anyone connected with academia is actually prohibited from purchasing the corporate version of Lexis-Nexis. Some journalism schools have access to yet a *third* version of Lexis-Nexis, limited to restricted use via password for research purposes only. And law school faculty and students have a *fourth* version of Lexis-Nexis, with access to many more legal publications than are available on any of the other academic versions of the service.

Before the content analyst begins any work that relies on the availability of electronic databases of content, this fundamental problem must be addressed. What do I have access to? What do I *not* have access to? Who controls that access? Will I be able to conduct the appropriate types of searches, with the necessary level of specificity, to generate the information I need? Am I going to have to design my study and draw my sample based on someone else's decisions about the access I have to the content I need? Will anyone else be able to reproduce my results if they study the same publications but use a different vendor for access to the content? Once this fundamental hurdle is addressed, a different set of problems arise for the content analyst.

Three Major Problems with Using Databases for Content Analysis

Electronic databases pose three major types of problems for the content analyst. The first problem has to do with the precision of the search and its effects on the subsequent retrieval of articles. The second problem has to do with the comprehensiveness of the databases themselves. The third problem has to do with the quality control that is exercised over the creation and maintenance of the databases. All three of these problems affect the size, reliability, and validity of the sample of articles that become part of the content analysis. Let's take each one of these problems in turn.

Inconsistent and Imprecise Results

Electronic search strategies, even when designed and used by database search professionals, produce inconsistent and imprecise results. This problem is especially harmful for content analysis projects that are designed to examine how a particular issue or topic has been covered across many news organizations. Electronic databases allow for a variety of search strategies. The researcher can search for the appearance of a term that might appear anywhere in the full text of the article, the appearance of a term in the descriptor field (key words assigned to the article by the database producer), the appearance of a term in the abstract of the article, and by many other fields of data (byline, dateline, author name, date of publication, etc.).

In an extensive and well-designed research study by a group of professors at Rutgers School of Communication, Information, and Library Studies, professional database searchers were recruited to search using Dialog.[6] These professional searchers were given the same search questions, but they interpreted the search topic in different ways and structured their searches such that they retrieved different items. The average overlap in search terms for a given search was only 27 percent. The average overlap in items retrieved from the search was only 17 percent! And many of the items retrieved by any one of the searches were totally irrelevant to the actual topic of the search.

What this means is that content analysts face a formidable problem right from the very start of their project. What search terms, used in what combination, will reliably locate all the relevant items from the full text database? The content analysts are unlikely to be expert database searchers themselves, and even if they recruit an expert to help with the search, there is no uniform way to structure a search in a news database for completely accurate results. If your goal as a content analyst is to examine how a particular topic was covered in the news, you may be missing important chunks of the coverage because your electronic search strategy does not adequately capture all of the stories that actually appeared.

Neuzil did another type of study in which he compared how print indexes and electronic databases for the *Chicago Tribune*, *St. Paul Pioneer Press* and *San Francisco Chronicle* compare on topic searches about the environment and about gambling.[7] He discovered that topic searches using print indexes and electronic databases for the same newspaper over the same time period resulted in very different numbers of stories. Also, a database search of the full text of each newspaper resulted in different numbers of stories than a search in the descriptor field. Both types of electronic searches retrieved more items than were included in the print indexes. But the print indexes included some stories that did not show up in either of the electronic searches (full text or descriptor). Furthermore, the full text searches retrieved a very large number of irrelevant items. So comparing your electronic search results against the print index for a news publication is not a sufficient method for guaranteeing that your electronic search strategy was sufficient. The only way to ensure that the results of the search are both reliable and valid is to compare the results of a computer database search against a sample of the actual published newspaper.

Lack of Correspondence between Online News Files and Print Versions

The second major problem with using electronic news databases for content analysis is that the online news files do not correspond to the print versions of the publication in any case. No matter how good your search strategy is, what you find is in no way an accurate guide to what actually appeared in the paper. Before we can examine this problem in detail, however, we need to review one important fact: The only somewhat complete version of any electronic database is the in-house, internal database that is kept by each news organization for use by its own reporters and editors. That version is not available to anyone outside the organization, and it includes material that is not included in any electronic version available to database searchers.

Electronic databases that don't correspond to the print version of the publication are the source of many problems for the content analyst. Kaufman, Reese Dykers, and Caldwell conducted an experiment in 1991 in which they compared the results from electronic news database searches with a hand-search of actual newspaper issues.[8] They did an electronic search in Vu/Text files (an early news database service) and Lexis-Nexis files and a hand search of actual issues of seven major U.S. newspapers. They uncovered a number of extremely important discrepancies between what appears in the electronic files and what appears in print.

Newspapers have different policies for which edition of the print version gets sent to the commercial database provider. Some papers have national, East Coast, Midwest, and West Coast editions, and only one of those becomes the commercial database edition. Other papers have editions throughout the day, and stories get added and dropped for each edition, but only one edition is sent to the commercial vendor. Sometimes the news librarians in charge of sending content to the database vendor send the longest version of a story that appeared in multiple editions; sometimes they send the version that was in the final edition of the newspaper. Content analysts have to be very careful about which edition is electronically stored in the database they happen to be using.

A related problem has to do with the retrieval of the print version of an article that is indexed by the database. The Expanded Academic Index on CD-ROM indexes both the national edition and the late city edition of the *New York Times*. However, the microfilm copy of the *New York Times* held by every library is the late city edition. That means that an article may appear in the database even though it appeared in print only in the national edition, the hard copy of which is discarded by libraries once the microfilm arrives. So despite what the database says, the article retrieved by the electronic search appears not to exist in the microfilm of the newspaper. Indeed, some readers may have seen the article if they read the national edition of the newspaper, but it is incorrect for the content analyst to assert that the article was available to all readers of the *New York Times*.

Another major problem identified by Kaufman, Reese Dykers, and Caldwell was that newspapers have different policies for what content gets uploaded to the commercial provider. Some papers only send their staff-produced and freelance material, in part because the contracts with wire services may limit how much of the wire service content can become part of a paper's electronic database. Some papers include in the database version only those wire service stories they deem to have "significant news value," however they define that. Other papers include in their database only some of the syndicated columns that ran in the print paper, based on internal policy that may or may not be discernible to the database searcher. The uploading policy of each paper is one of the most likely contributors to the discrepancies between what is in the electronic database and what actually appeared in the paper.

For example, on the Dialog service, the *Atlanta Journal* and the *Atlanta Constitution* description states that syndicated columns are excluded and that staff-generated news, features, business, sports, and editorials are included. Does "staff-generated news" mean that wire service stories that appear in the print editions of the Atlanta newspapers are not included in the electronic database? Similarly, the Dialog database description for Columbia, South Carolina's *The State*, the largest newspaper in the state, says that national and international news stories are not included in the database unless there is some direct impact on South Carolina. Who makes that determination and why? The Dialog description for the *Detroit Free Press* says that "some syndicated columns are excluded." Which ones? These decisions pose serious problems for the content analyst who may be studying the ratio of staff-generated to wire service content in the newspaper, or the treatment of national and international news stories in regional newspapers, or the diversity of syndicated opinion columns in newspapers under various ownership conditions (all questions asked by content analysts over the years).

A third problem identified by Kaufman, Reese Dykers, and Caldwell is that no paper sends any agate material such as box scores, funeral notices, stock market listings, calendars, classified advertising, weather lists, games and puzzles, or similar material to the database vendor. Similarly, the current technology for electronic news databases from the major vendors does not allow for anything except a text notice that the story was accompanied by a photo, graph, chart, series logo, or other visual material. So significant portions of the paper are not represented in any way in the electronic database. The best the content analyst finds in the database is a notice that says "this story was accompanied by graphs and charts" or some such indication that the database is incomplete. While much of this material is not particularly important for content analysts, the placement, play, and appearance of a story is usually taken into account in studies, but cannot be using the electronic version.

The final problem identified by Kaufman, Reese Dykers, and Caldwell is that corrections that appeared in the newspaper are handled differently by individual papers and by different database vendors. Some papers send a corrections feed directly to the vendor with software code that is supposed to append the correction to the previous story in the database. Other papers send corrections as separate items in the database and attach a notice on the original story that says a correction was later published. Some other papers have taken the controversial step of actually correcting the original electronic version of the story, with a note saying the story incorporates a correction and directing the searcher to the microfilm of the print copy to see what the original mistake was. Content analysts studying corrections policies at newspapers (another common topic for content analysis) have to understand how the electronic version of the paper handles corrections.

The Kaufman, Reese Dykers, and Caldwell study concluded that content analysts have to be clear about which edition of the paper they're looking at in the electronic files, they must persist in using a variety of search strategies to try to locate all the relevant stories in a database, and they should always try to compare electronic searches with hand searches of the actual print versions of the newspaper.

Another major twist was added to the dilemma of incomplete databases when the United States Supreme Court ruled on June 25, 2001, that freelance writers have a right to separate compensation for electronic copies of their works. The opinion in *New York Times Co., Inc. et al. v. Tasini et al.* meant that hundreds of thousands of articles stored in the database files of major newspapers, magazines, and specialty publications were subject to contract renegotiation or removal. As might be expected, the major database publishers decided to start removing the articles rather than compensate the authors. Within days of the decision, notices began appearing on Dialog newspaper files, for example, notifying users that records had been removed. The New York Times Company announced it was removing 115,000 records from Lexis-Nexis and other sources and shutting down access to all *New York Times* book reviews on its own website.[9] Articles from the *New York Times Magazine*, Arts & Leisure section, and pieces from the Op-Ed Pages, among others, were subject to removal from electronic databases.

The implications of this series of decisions for content analysts are grave. As database publishers further compromise the completeness and integrity of their electronic files, users have even less confidence that their search results and samples are reliable and valid. The online files correspond even less accurately to the actual printed publication or the microfilm version of the newspaper or magazine. Pending the outcome of an Authors Guild class action lawsuit seeking to bar the publishers from removing the articles, content analysts must be even more wary of relying on electronic database searches as the sole method of constructing a sample.

Impact of Database Creation Process on Quality and Accuracy

The third problem with using electronic news databases for content analysis is one that is rarely discussed, but one that news librarians talk about a lot among themselves. These are the dirty little secrets of database creation that worry those who care about quality of information and accuracy of searches. Many of these quality control problems have been documented by Bruce William Oakley, with a follow-up by Jackie Chamberlain.[10] For the content analyst, the database creation work that goes on behind the scenes at news organizations has an indirect, but critical, effect on the quality of a content analysis project.

Despite the appearance of automation, the creation and maintenance of an electronic database of news content is an extremely labor-intensive activity. Stories created and edited in the newsroom are sent through the pagination system to the printing presses, but they are also routed to the news library, where individual entries must be "enhanced" before being archived in the database. News librarians use a variety of "enhancing" techniques when they prepare content for the electronic database. If search terms are added by news enhancers, they may or may not be consistently added every day and with careful attention to consistency. With cutbacks and retrenchments, many news libraries do their subject heading enhancing on a "staff available" basis, meaning that a database search that relies on the subject heading field will not retrieve every relevant article in the file because headings weren't attached in the first place.

A related issue involves the way changes are handled by database enhancers. Sections change headings (something once called the business section is now called marketplace, for instance). Reporters change their bylines and how they want their names to appear in the paper. If the news enhancers do not go back and make cross-references and links between the old and new versions of the way something is entered in the database, there will be no way for a search in the section or byline field across time to be consistent. Also, enhancers are supposed to check to be sure that fields haven't been transposed (byline and dateline get entered in the wrong field, sometimes). But they don't always catch those errors.

In addition, database vendors' quality control standards have been going down, and as news librarians are pressed into service doing more and more work, they have less time to follow up on vendors who aren't keeping up standards. For instance, one newspaper was sending corrections to the electronic database vendor for more than a year before realizing that the vendor wasn't attaching the corrections to the stories *or* including the corrections as separate items. The corrections were simply not there at all. Another newspaper diligently sent corrections to their database vendor on a regular basis. When the quality control person at the vendor quit, the new person assigned to the job by the vendor thought that the corrections fed from the newspaper meant that the original article was supposed to be deleted from the database and was operating on that basis until a news librarian talked to the vendor and realized what had been happening.

Another issue in quality control has to do with making sure that everything transmitted by the news organization to the vendor is actually received by them and jibes with what was sent. Strange things can happen. Stories can disappear, duplicate themselves, get mixed up with previous files. If the news organization transmits 353 stories, ideally the vendor should verify that it actually received 353 stories, and the 353 the news organization sent, not 350 plus 3 left over in the system from some other day. But these kinds of follow-up practices are not consistently applied by the papers and are not reliably followed by the vendors.

Another quality control problem has to do with trying to capture stories that are heavy with graphics and design elements. For example, one newspaper published an extensive series that incorporated many graphic design elements in each segment. The reporter and editor did a lot of editing and made corrections after each series segment was sent to the Macintosh computers for design. But the electronic database system in that newsroom could not handle any changes from the Mac. So the version of the series stories that appeared in the electronic database could only be tagged with a note saying "This version differs significantly from what actually appeared in print. Please check the microfilm for the final published version."

In fact, Oakley found problems at every step of the process of database creation. He examined the commercial electronic archives and the print editions of four newspapers on arbitrarily chosen dates and not one archived version flawlessly matched the newsprint. Errors ranged from incorrect punctuation to incorrect headlines and bylines, absence of corrections in the database even though they had appeared in print, and lost parentheses around explanatory information embedded in quotations in the database version of a story, opening the publication to serious charges of misattribution of words never spoken by a quoted source. For the content analyst studying corrections policies, publication performance on accuracy measures, or such fundamental issues as whether a publication committed a libelous error, these types of database archive problems are devastating.

The World Wide Web and the Content Analyst

A growing problem for the content analyst concerns the total lack of an archiving system for online publications, many of which roughly correspond to the print publication but include many other things such as hot links, discussion forums, audio and video clips, and more. Many websites are updated almost continuously. There is no "final" edition of an online publication. The Internet provides access to thousands of publications, but most websites do not archive more than two or three weeks of pages before the materials disappear forever.[11] This poses a serious problem, especially for historians who wish to study the development of a website over time.

In addition, the licensing rights for most syndicated material that appears in print publications (wire-service content, stock prices, etc.) explicitly state that the publisher has the right to electronically archive only that content that was actually published in the newsprint version of the paper. Online publishers have to negotiate separate contracts with each information provider for their online products. Very significant changes in these licensing stipulations will have to be made before online publishers can regularly archive the entire content of their sites.

Aside from the fact that most content on the Web disappears after a few weeks, McMillan identified additional problems with applying content analysis to the World Wide Web.[12] Once again, questions about sampling raise serious challenges for the content analyst. McMillan's analysis of nineteen published studies that applied content analysis techniques to the World Wide Web determined that few of the studies she cited provided any discussion of how to address sampling difficulties. One common way of defining a sampling frame was to use an online list of sites in a given category. Another popular technique was to use search engine(s) to identify sites that met criteria related to the study. Some studies used off-line sources to identify websites and one study of three newspaper websites didn't discuss the sampling frame at all.

McMillan concluded that the stable research technique of content analysis can be applied in the dynamic environment of the Web, but that there are potential problems for researchers. In particular, she identified questions about whether the use of different search engines results in empirically different findings, what sample size is adequate, how sample techniques from traditional media (e.g., selection of "representative" newspaper or broadcast content) can be applied to the Web, and whether sample methods for the Web have been held to lower standards than have been accepted for traditional media.

The Autumn 2000 issue of *Journalism and Mass Communication Quarterly* focused on the Internet, with a summary article by Stempel and Stewart that outlined the opportunities and challenges the Internet poses for communication researchers.[13] The authors concluded that "The Internet thus appears to be a mixed blessing for researchers. It can make research easier, and it can make our data better, but it won't happen automatically."[14] As the discussion in this chapter has shown, the same can be said for the use of any electronic databases for content analysis. The watchword is "database content analyst beware."

Endnotes

1. Bernard Berelson, *Content Analysis in Communication Research* (New York: Free Press, 1952), 18.

2. Richard W. Budd, Robert K. Thorp, and Lewis Donohew, *Content Analysis of Communications* (New York: The Macmillan Company, 1967), 2.

3. Ole R. Holsti, *Content Analysis for the Social Sciences and Humanities* (Reading, MA: Addison-Wesley, 1969).

4. Marcia Ruth, "Electronic Library Systems Reach Watershed Year," *Presstime* (July 1985): 10–11.

5. Susan Willey, "The Pitfalls of Cyberspace and Electronic Database Research," *Journalism & Mass Communication Educator* 21 (Summer 2000): 78–85.

6. Tefko Saracevic, Paul B. Kantor, and Alice Yanosko Chamis, "A Study of Information Seeking and Retrieving, I: Background and Methodology," *Journal of the American Society for Information Science* 39 (May 1988): 161–176; Tefko Saracevic and Paul B. Kantor, "A Study of Information Seeking and Retrieving, II: Users, Questions, and Effectiveness," *Journal of the American Society for Information Science* 39 (May 1988): 177–196; Tefko Saracevic and Paul B. Kantor, "A Study of Information Seeking and Retrieving, III: Searchers, Searches, and Overlap," *Journal of the American Society for Information Science* 39 (May 1988): 197–216.

7. Mark Neuzil, "Gambling with Databases: A Comparison of Electronic Searches and Printed Indexes," *Newspaper Research Journal* 15 (Winter 1994): 44–54.

8. Philip A. Kaufman, Carol Reese Dykers, and Carole Caldwell, "Why Going Online for Content Analysis Can Reduce Research Reliability," *Journalism Quarterly* 70 (Winter 1993): 824–832.

9. Barbara Quint, "Stop the Trash Trucks: A *Tasini* Case Damage-Control Proposal," available at *http://www.infotoday.com/newsbreaks*.

10. Bruce William Oakley, "How Accurate Are Your Archives?" *Columbia Journalism Review* (March/April 1998): 13; Bruce William Oakley, "Accuracy in Electronic Archives: An Investigation" (April 1997), available at *http://www.ibiblio.org/journalism/oaktre.html*; Jackie Chamberlain, "Survey of Selected Full-Text Online Newspaper Database Quality Control Policies and Procedures" (April 1998), available at *http://www.ibiblio.org/journalism/dbqcsur3.html*.

11. Shannon E. Martin and Kathleen A. Hansen, *Newspapers of Record in a Digital Age: From Hot Type to Hot Link* (Westport, CT: Praeger, 1998).

12. Sally J. McMillan, "The Microscope and the Moving Target: The Challenge of Applying Content Analysis to the World Wide Web," *Journalism and Mass Communication Quarterly* 77 (Spring 2000): 80–98.

13. Guido H. Stempel III and Robert K. Stewart, "The Internet Provides Both Opportunities and Challenges for Mass Communication Researchers," *Journalism and Mass Communication Quarterly* 77 (Autumn 2000): 541–548.

14. *Ibid.*, 546.

13

Survey Research

Pamela J. Shoemaker

Maxwell E. McCombs

Media professionals spend a lot of time dealing with the products of survey research. Journalists write public opinion poll stories to tell Americans who's going to win the next election or to report what we think about the latest issue. Advertisers assure us that "9 out of every 10 dentists surveyed" support their products. And media management's marketing strategies are based on what surveys say the audience wants. Surveys have even invaded the Internet.

A *survey* is a study that collects information by asking people questions. The information collected—the data—is generally numerical and suitable for statistical analysis. Although the United States Constitution specified that a survey of Americans be conducted every ten years in order to ensure proper representation in the House of Representatives,[1] this census of all U.S. households is not what we commonly think of as a survey. The vast majority of survey research projects are *sample surveys* in which data are collected from a subset of individuals in the population. Inferences about the larger population are made from the information gathered from those people in the sample. U.S. public opinion polls commonly include survey interviews with 1,000 to 1,200 people, even though the adult population of the United States exceeds that by millions.

Surveys have proven to be an effective way to assess people's voting intentions, to explain their votes, to predict use of products, and to assess changes in opinions. In fact, the effectiveness of the telephone survey has resulted in the public being bombarded with polls. Unfortunately, many polls are thinly disguised attempts to sell products and services, thus making survey research more difficult for the legitimate pollster.

Surveys of Americans' actual or intended votes have been conducted for 200 years, with one of the earliest polls on record being conducted after the election for Massachusetts governor in 1787.[2] Supporters of the incumbent Governor James Bowdoin conducted a poll to explain why John Hancock won the race. The Bowdoin poll showed that Hancock's support came primarily from "labourers, servants, and so on," whereas Bowdoin's base was among "merchants and traders."

Three days later a Hancock supporter revealed his own poll, a recategorization of the vote that he called the "authentic breakdown," which showed that Bowdoin's support was actually among "speculators in publick securities," whereas Hancock's vote came primarily from "merchants, tradesmen, and other worthy members of society" and from "friends to the revolution." The Hancock poll also revealed that the one wizard voting in the election supported the losing candidate![3]

Although such canvassing of voters became fairly common in the 1800s, surveys of people's opinions on issues of the day were rare. One of the first U.S. opinion polls was conducted in the 1880s by the Iowa Labor Statistics Bureau. As part of its survey on labor and economic conditions, the bureau asked farmers' attitudes on the liquor issue and immigration.[4]

The advent of modern random sampling techniques in the early 1900s made surveys more practical, since a smaller number of interviews meant savings in time and expense,[5] but surveys using random samples also proved to be more accurate. In the 1936 U.S. presidential election, pollsters George Gallup, Elmo Roper, and Archibald Crossley used the expertise of statisticians, psychologists, and market researchers to correctly predict Franklin D. Roosevelt's victory over Alf Landon, whereas the less methodologically sound *Literary Digest* magazine poll of 10 million people picked Landon by a wide margin.[6]

Gallup and other pollsters enjoyed popularity until they predicted incorrectly that Thomas Dewey would beat Harry Truman in 1948. Confidence in polling collapsed until in the 1960s, when secret polls captured the imagination of politicians.[7] John Kennedy used polls in his 1960 election campaign, thus dignifying them for use by others, and Jimmy Carter was the first U.S. president to have access to continuous opinion polls.[8]

Much of the interviewing in opinion polls now is being done by telephone, rather than in face-to-face interviews, because of the rising costs and lower response rates face-to-face interviewing has yielded in recent years.[9] About 98 percent of U.S. households are reachable by telephone.[10] Internet polling is also becoming increasingly popular.

Survey Designs and Applications

One of the first decisions to be made in planning a survey involves the *design*—who will be interviewed, over what period, and how many times? There are three basic survey designs: the **cross-sectional** survey, the **panel study**, and the **trend study**.

The decision about whom to interview is largely a theoretical one driven by the hypotheses that are to be tested, but it is not a trivial decision. For example, in an election survey, we could interview adults, or only adult citizens, or only registered voters, or only people who actually intend to vote. The population we select for study will affect the data we collect and the conclusions we draw.

The period of time during which interviews are conducted—generally called being "in the field"—is also crucial. Some polls are in the field for less than one day, meaning that interviews have been conducted only with those individuals who are home at the instant that the interviewer calls. Such a sample of respondents may underrepresent busy individuals. Other polls are conducted over several months, making the results vulnerable to events occurring while the study is in the field. For example, a poll asking about people's attitudes toward AIDS could yield two very different data sets if a cure for AIDS is revealed in the middle of the field period. The optimal field period is long enough to make several attempts to complete an interview in each sampled household, but short enough to minimize threats to validity due to intervening events.

In a *cross-sectional* survey, the respondents are interviewed only once, and the data collected provide a snapshot of the population at the time the field work (the interviewing) is done. Cross-sectional surveys are common, because they are far more economical than longitudinal studies. Cross-sectional surveys can describe the characteristics of the sample (e.g., respondents' attitudes or behaviors) at a given point in time, but such one-shot studies cannot address questions about change (e.g., is a change in a person's attitude followed by a change in his or her behavior?). To study changes among the elements in a sample (and, by inference, in the population from which the sample is drawn) requires that data be collected at more than one point in time—a *longitudinal* study. The panel study and the trend study both involve longitudinal data collection.

The *panel study* involves interviews with the same individuals at more than one point in time. The panel design permits the comparison of a person's responses at each time point, thereby allowing us to assess the extent and direction of any changes that may have occurred *within that individual*. For example, we might compare changes in an individual's media use with changes in support for a political candidate.

The *trend study* is also used to study change, but change in the population as a whole rather than changes in individuals. In a trend study, a new sample of individuals is drawn from the population at each point in time—the trend study is composed of several cross-sectional studies that are compared over time. This permits the researcher to evaluate change in the population over time (e.g., changes in support for two presidential candidates); however, because such changes (e.g., in vote intention) are attributes of individuals, the trend design limits our ability to explain change. Because different individuals are interviewed at each point in time, we do not know why the observed changes have occurred, and we cannot easily separate changes in individuals over time from possible differences between the samples drawn at each time point.

The panel is a superior design for explaining change, but data from a panel study may be flawed by *panel mortality*—the loss of individuals from the panel between each interviewing wave. Individuals leave panels for many reasons: They decline to participate; they move during the study or change telephone numbers and are now unreachable; they go on vacation or business trips or become ill; or they may even die during the study. Panel mortality is generally not the result of a random process, and therefore the individuals who leave a panel generally have characteristics in common. Their failure to participate in the entire study may make the panel unrepresentative of the population, thereby limiting the inferences we can make about the population.

Attempts to limit panel mortality can make the panel study more expensive than the trend design, but the panel remains the more valid way of assessing changes in individuals. The trend design is useful in the *secondary analysis* of preexisting data sets. Many survey organizations (such as the University of Michigan Institute for Social Research and the National Opinion Research Center) archive survey data and make data sets available to others. Secondary analysis is "the extraction of knowledge on topics other than those which were the focus of the original surveys."[11] When the same questions are asked in successive surveys, the secondary analyst can perform a trend analysis of several data sets. For example, McCombs used the well-known Michigan national election surveys to trace increasing political participation by blacks through their use of newspapers and television for political information during the 1952–1964 civil rights era.[12]

A fourth design is not recommended—the *pseudopanel*. If a researcher asks her respondents to report their past and current attitudes or behaviors, she may decide to treat her data as if they represent different time points. Such a design is vulnerable to many problems, however, not the least of which is the human being's ability or willingness to remember and report what he or she thought or did in the past. The pseudopanel design is subject to many potential errors and should be avoided.

Using Survey Data to Establish Causal Relationships

Establishing a causal relationship requires: (1) showing covariation between the presumed cause and the presumed effect; (2) establishing appropriate time order, that is, that the cause precedes the effect and not the reverse; (3) ruling out alternative explanations for the observed relationship; and (4) controlling error variance, that is, keeping errors to a minimum and explaining as much of the independent variable as possible.

The cross-sectional design—representing the bulk of all survey projects—can address only three of the four criteria necessary for establishing a causal relationship: covariation, alternative explanations, and error. Covariation can be shown between two or more variables through the use of statistics that test the strength of the relationship between two variables (e.g., Pearson's correlation coefficient). But, as the saying goes, "correlation is not causation"—showing that changes in one variable (e.g., exposure to a daily newspaper) are associated with changes in another (e.g., levels of political interest) is only one step, but a necessary one, toward proving causality.

Survey researchers have become adept at *multivariate statistical techniques* that help rule out alternative explanations for a relationship by statistically controlling for the effects of other variables on the observed relationship. The use of statistical controls, however, is only as good as the researcher's ability to identify and measure possible alternative explanations. It is far easier to rule out alternative explanations in a randomized experiment, where the experimenter randomly assigns subjects to treatment groups, thereby controlling for a vast array of unidentified and unmeasured variables. In a survey, respondents select themselves into high or low political interest groups, thus making differences in these groups related to many causes.

Time order can be established in survey research through the use of longitudinal designs, with the panel's ability to study changes within individuals making it far superior to the trend or cross-sectional design in establishing causality. In a panel study, we can look at whether, for example, individuals first change their level of newspaper reading and then their level of political interest, or vice versa. If we observe that newspaper reading and political interest change simultaneously, then we have evidence of a third variable affecting both reading and interest or a methodological problem with the time intervals between our panel waves. The waves of interviewing need to be frequent enough to "catch" changes in variables that may occur rapidly one after the other.

Controlling error variance is a major challenge in all research, and, to the extent that our studies are flawed, our data will not permit the establishment of valid causal relationships. Later in this chapter, we will discuss the types of errors that must be considered in survey research.

Types of Surveys

Survey interviews are either *self-administered* or conducted by an *interviewer*. Self-administered questionnaires are either distributed in group settings or by mail (or, occasionally, through home delivery), whereas interviewer-conducted surveys can be done by telephone or face to face.

Self-Administered Questionnaires

This popular survey method involves giving a potential respondent a questionnaire, usually by mail. The respondent is asked to complete the questionnaire and return it to the study director. The major advantage of the self-administered questionnaire is a savings of time and expense when compared to telephone and face-to-face surveys. Self-administered questionnaires also avoid biases due to interviewers, ensure standardized presentation of questions, give respondents more privacy (important for sensitive questions), and may increase the validity of responses that require the respondent to check information or to think about his or her answer. Their major weakness is that response rates are generally lower than in telephone or face-to-face studies, thus increasing threats to validity due to the lack of representativeness for the sample.

Mail Surveys. Intensive follow-ups in **mail surveys** are often necessary to increase the response rate above 50 percent, thus increasing study time and expense. A variety of techniques has been used to increase the percentage of returns in a mail survey.[13] Follow-up contacts by mail have been shown to increase return by 20 percent for one follow-up and about 12 and 10 percent for second and third follow-ups, respectively. Supplementing telephone follow-ups with mail follow-ups can increase the return by another 15 to 30 percent. The role of monetary inducements has not been clearly established.

Some questionnaires seem to get better returns than others. Questionnaires that are particularly salient to the respondent can yield a 30 to 40 percent higher response than non-salient questionnaires. Those dealing with sensitive topics may get lower response rates. The length of the questionnaire was not related to response rate in one experiment, where length varied from one to twenty-two pages. A regular stamped return envelope yields higher responses than a business reply envelope. In addition, the best response rates have been associated with questionnaires printed in booklet format and with an attractive cover page. Among other factors influencing response rate is the type of population being surveyed. Response rate is positively related to the education level of the respondents; non-readers are automatically excluded from responding. Altruistic appeals and an institutional sponsor can also be helpful in increasing responses.

Internet Surveys.   An increasing number of self-administered questionnaires are being delivered via email or through web pages on the Internet. The decision of whether to include the questionnaire as part of an email message is related to the amount of bandwidth it takes—how long it is. Very long questionnaires may irritate potential respondents as a breach of "netiquette."[14] It is probably more reasonable to send an email message as a "cover letter," with an accompanying link to a web page where the questionnaire can be accessed. Other Internet questionnaires begin with a link from another web page, such as a browser that is used by many people. Either way, **Internet surveys** are easily ignored or deleted by a single keystroke, thus contributing to response rates that are dramatically lower than other methods.

An advantage, however, is that the length of Internet questionnaires does not seem to affect response rates, as is the case with mail surveys.[15] If respondents begin the questionnaire, they are likely to finish it. Another advantage is the quick turnaround. Most Internet surveys can be completed in 48 to 72 hours,[16] the time period shortened dramatically by automatic entry of the data into a file readable by statistical software. In addition, there is some evidence that respondents may give more complete answers to open-ended questions.[17]

Although the cost of Internet surveys may potentially be less than mail (or interviewer-conducted surveys), an experiment comparing mail and Internet modes of questionnaire delivery demonstrated that there were substantial costs associated with managing the email sample, including answering technical questions about the electronic questionnaire. Costs of the Internet and mail versions may be close if similar quality and response rates are desired.[18]

Interviewer-Conducted Surveys

The **telephone survey** is quickly supplanting the **face-to-face survey** in the United States, primarily due to the lower costs of the telephone interview and to falling response rates of face-to-face studies in urban areas. Refusal rates often exceed 40 percent of potential respondents.[19] The probability of social class biases due to the availability of telephones has greatly diminished. For studies on subpopulations such as the poor, the elderly, or young adults (who are often transient), the face-to-face interview may provide more reliable data than the telephone survey. Comparisons of data collected by the two methods show few statistically significant differences, although there is some evidence to suggest that respondents find telephone interviews to be less rewarding and more tiresome than face-to-face interviews, even though the telephone interview is generally faster paced.[20]

The telephone survey requires much less administration than the face-to-face survey. For example, a face-to-face study requiring 200 interviewers, each completing 7 or 8 interviews, could be accomplished by 30 to 40 telephone interviewers, each doing 40 to 50 interviews. Supervisory staff is similarly reduced.

If telephone interviews are completed from a central phone facility, the telephone survey can result in higher quality data, because supervisors can monitor interviewers and give immediate feedback to correct interviewer errors. Face-to-face interviewers work under far less supervision.

Telephone surveys have the additional advantage of being far more economical than face-to-face surveys, often averaging half the expense. Telephone surveys also take less time to complete than do an equivalent number of face-to-face interviews.

Comparing Self-Administered to Interviewer-Conducted Surveys

Interviews with a sample of respondents can be conducted through the mail, face-to-face, or over the telephone. Each of these modes of interviewing has its advantages and disadvantages. Which should you use?

Although there is no fixed number of criteria to be weighed, five are suggested here: cost, response rate, kinds of questions, numbers of questions, and social desirability bias. While the mail questionnaire ranks well on cost, it receives relatively low marks on the other four criteria. The face-to-face interview has the advantage in terms of the kinds and number of questions that can be included. For response rate and social desirability bias, there is little difference between face-to-face and telephone interviews. But telephone interviews have a distinct advantage in cost. Increasingly in recent years, the telephone interview has been the mode of choice for most research projects.

Survey Data Collection

Survey questionnaires traditionally have been printed on paper, and the responses have been recorded in pencil or pen directly on the questionnaire. The data were entered in a computer file and proofread before analysis.

Today most large survey research organizations use **CATI (computer-assisted telephone interviewing)** systems for data collection in telephone surveys. In CATI the survey questionnaire is programmed into a computer file. Interviewers sit at computer terminals and directly input the respondents' answers to all questions. In most systems, both numerical (closed-ended) and text (open-ended) responses can be easily handled. Numerical data go directly into a data file, where they can be available for analysis almost immediately after the interview is completed. Text responses require additional coding before statistical analysis can be performed.

The key advantage of CATI systems is the quality of the data collected. In most systems, out-of-range responses will not be accepted by the system (e.g., if the interviewer hits "6" for a scale that ranges only from 1 to 5, the CATI software may ask him or her to "try again," resulting in very clean data). CATI also easily handles complicated questionnaires that require the interviewer to skip around the instrument depending on the respondent's answers to previous questions. Such skips and branches are programmed into the CATI instrument by the study managers and do not rely on the interviewers' judgment and memory. CATI instruments can easily handle questionnaires far too complicated for any human interviewer to correctly follow. Skips and branches occur automatically based on the respondent's previous answers, thereby eliminating many interviewer errors. Previous answers can be inserted into subsequent questions in order to personalize the questions to the respondent.

Some survey directors also feel that CATI increases the speed with which a telephone survey can be completed, but such time savings are debatable for the inexperienced CATI user and for small projects. The major drawbacks to CATI are the complexity of the systems and the time required to master them. The more flexible the system (and hence the more options the study director has), the more complicated the system is to learn and to use. Six months to a year is the usual shakedown period for the more complicated CATI systems. Survey personnel must in general be more highly trained for CATI projects than for pen-and-paper surveys.

Any time savings to be realized with a CATI system fall at the end of the study period. Once the data are collected, they can be made available for statistical analysis almost immediately, since the data entry and proofreading steps are eliminated. More time is required in CATI projects at the beginning of the study, however, since it is far more difficult to program and debug a questionnaire into CATI language than it is to type and photocopy a pen-and-paper instrument.

Computerized data entry is also occasionally used for face-to-face and self-administered surveys. *CAPI (computer-assisted personal interviewing)* software packages are now available for use on laptop computers that can be taken to the respondent's location. *CADE (computer-assisted data entry)* software enables fast and accurate entry of data from mail surveys. Some software packages also have a self-administered feature that permits respondents to sit at terminals and enter their own responses.

Survey Sampling

Sampling is the process of selecting *elements* (in survey research, usually telephone numbers, households, or individuals) from a population (the aggregate of elements about which the researcher wants to make inferences). For example, a nationwide telephone opinion poll might use a sample composed of 1,200 household telephone numbers within the United States. Assuming that interviews are conducted only with adults, the researcher could use the data gathered from people in the sample to make inferences about the opinions of U.S. adults living in households that have working telephones.

Samples can be classified as either probability or nonprobability samples. In **probability samples**, the elements are selected by a random process involving chance; therefore each element has a known chance of being selected into the sample. In *nonprobability* samples, the elements are selected by other means (such as the researcher's convenience or ideas about the types of clients that should be included in the study), and there is no way of estimating each element's chance of selection. Knowing the odds of an element being selected allows us to estimate how representative the sample is of the population. Much error in our data is due to sampling. **Sampling error** can be estimated for probability samples but not for nonprobability samples. Although it is theoretically possible for a nonprobability sample to be representative, we have no way of evaluating its worth.

Types of Probability Samples.   The easiest to understand, but the one used least often for surveys, is the *simple random sample*, in which each element of the population has an equal chance of being selected into the sample on each sampling round. Simple random sampling requires a list of all elements in the population, and this is one of the method's major drawbacks: Some populations are impossible to list, and some are so large that listing all elements would be impractical. For example, a directory of all 40,000 students at a university could be considered a list of the university's student population. Each student in the directory could be sequentially numbered from 1 to 40,000. Numbers (and the students attached to the numbers) would then be selected at random, such as by computer, by using a table of random numbers, or even by selecting from among 40,000 numbered balls. On the first round, every student's chance of being selected is 1/40,000. After the first student has been selected for the sample (without replacement, meaning that the student is ineligible for selection again), each remaining student's chance of being selected is 1/39,999. Although the probability of selection changes between the selection rounds, each student has an equal chance of being selected within each round.

A less cumbersome sampling method, but one that also requires a list of elements, is the *systematic sample*. A sampling fraction is computed by dividing the number of elements in the desired sample by the number of elements in the population. If we want to sample 1,000 students from the university population of 40,000, then our sampling fraction would be 1/40; the sample will include one-fortieth of the population. Using the directory of students, we select a random number between 1 and 40 as the starting point, and then select every fortieth student from that random start. Systematic sampling is an efficient method that can result in a representative sample, unless there is some periodicity in the list, such that the sampling fraction corresponds to a cycle inherent in the list. For example, the interval for a systematic sample of newspaper "days" should never be seven, for such an interval will yield a sample made up entirely of the same day of the week.

Some samples make use of **stratification**, a process that requires the researcher to identify one or more variables on which the sample elements can be categorized, generally at the time of sampling. Independent sampling procedures are then carried out within each stratum. For example, we might want to compare people from the Midwest with those from the South, West Coast, and East Coast. We would stratify our sample by geographic region and draw separate samples from each region.

If those separate samples yield different sample-to-population proportions (e.g., a Midwesterner's chances of being selected into the sample are 1 in 1,000, whereas a Southerner's chances are 1 in 750), then we have *unequal probabilities of selection*. Generalizations made about the country as a whole will be biased by the fact that Southerners are more likely to be selected than Midwesterners. To make the total sample representative of the nation as a whole, the researcher must *weight* the sample to bring all strata back into proportion to the population.

Stratified samples with unequal probabilities of selection are common in studies where the researcher is stratifying on a variable that is not evenly distributed through the population, such as ethnicity. If 70 percent of the population is Anglo, 20 percent Hispanic, and 10 percent black, then a sample of 1,000 individuals would yield only 200 Hispanics and 100 blacks – samples that are generally considered too small to be representative of those populations (see "sampling error" later in this section). If Hispanics and blacks are *oversampled* in order to have sufficient numbers for separate analysis, then the total data set will require weighting before it is analyzed to yield a picture of the overall population.

Most telephone surveys use *cluster sampling*, which takes advantage of the fact that telephone numbers are assigned in groups. Telephone numbers are assigned first in groups of area codes (the first three digits of the long-distance ten-digit number), and second in groups of exchanges or prefixes (the first three digits of the seven-digit local number). *Random digit dialing (RDD)* is a process of sample generation that uses known lists of area codes and exchanges and combines these with randomly generated suffixes (the last four digits of the seven-digit local telephone number). RDD samples are not dependent on telephone directories, which do not include unlisted telephone numbers and which become out-of-date and inaccurate over time. A nationwide RDD sample also would be a multi-stage sample. The first stage might include sampling from among the population of area codes. In the second stage the researcher might sample from among all prefixes in the area codes selected in stage one. In stage three randomly generated four-digit suffixes would be added to the prefixes and area codes to complete a list of ten-digit numbers.

The problem with such an RDD sample is that it generally yields only about 25 percent working residential telephone numbers; the remaining numbers are not assigned or not residential. Waksberg[21] suggested an RDD cluster design that generally yields 50 to 60 percent working residential numbers. The researcher first randomly samples from among the population of area code prefix combinations, as described above, then adds a randomly generated four-digit suffix to each area code prefix combination. This number is dialed. Once the number is determined to be a working household number, then the last two digits of the ten-digit number are removed and the eight-digit number remaining is designated as a *primary sampling unit (PSU)*. One hundred two-digit numbers are then generated in a random order for the PSU in order to create 100 potential ten-digit telephone numbers. Interviewers are then instructed to complete a predetermined number of interviews in that cluster.

Respondent Selection.   For most telephone and in-person surveys, the sample element (e.g., the telephone number or address) represents a household. We still have the task of selecting the individual to interview within that household. It is not adequate to interview whomever answers the telephone or door, since such individuals turn out to have characteristics in common. For example, women are more likely to answer the telephone than men. The researcher must decide whether his or her population includes all residents of the household (including children), only adults (i.e., at least 18 years old), only heads of households, or some other subset of household residents.

One commonly used method requires that all adults within the household be listed by the interviewer. The selection method is then based on the number of men, the number of women, and the last digits of the telephone number. This results in a probability sample of individuals within households.

Another common method is to select the individual who has most recently had a birthday. This results in a nonprobability sample of respondents, since the probability of a given individual being selected depends on the memory of the individual who answers the telephone and on the distribution of birthdays throughout the year and throughout the population. However, it is easier and quicker to carry out than the household-listing method.

Sampling Error.   Table 13.1 includes estimates of sampling error at the 95 percent confidence level—usually called *margin of error*—for simple random samples of 50 to 2,400 elements. The estimates are computed by multiplying the standard error of a *proportion* by 1.96 (the appropriate value for the 95 percent confidence level.)[22]

TABLE 13.1 *Margin of Error (at the 95 Percent Confidence Interval) for Proportions Ranging from 10/90 to 50/50 and for Simple Random Sample Sizes Ranging from 50 to 2,400*

Sample Sizes	50/50	40/60	Proportions 30/70	20/80	10/90
50	13.86	13.58	12.70	11.09	8.32
100	9.80	9.60	8.98	7.84	5.88
200	6.93	6.79	6.35	5.54	4.16
300	5.66	5.54	5.19	4.53	3.39
400	4.90	4.80	4.49	3.92	2.94
600	4.00	3.92	3.67	3.20	2.40
800	3.46	3.39	3.18	2.77	2.08
1000	3.10	3.04	2.84	2.48	1.86
1200	2.83	2.77	2.59	2.26	1.70
1400	2.62	2.57	2.40	2.10	1.57
1600	2.45	2.40	2.25	1.96	1.47
1800	2.31	2.26	2.12	1.85	1.39
2000	2.19	2.15	2.01	1.75	1.31
2200	2.09	2.05	1.91	1.67	1.25
2400	2.00	1.96	1.83	1.60	1.20

The margin of error sets boundaries around an obtained percentage that will contain the true population value in 95 out of 100 samples of the size shown. For example, for random samples with Ns of 400 and an obtained percentage of 50, the true population value of the percentage will be found somewhere between 45.10 and 54.90 in 95 out of 100 samples. The margin of error decreases as sample sizes increase and as percentages move away from 50/50.

Margin of error for a proportion at the 95 percent confidence level =
+/− 1.96 * (square root of $p(1 - p)/n$)

where n = the number of elements in the sample and p = one of the percentages in the observed proportion.

If, for example, 60 percent of the 1,000 people interviewed favor candidate A and 40 percent favor candidate B, then the margin of error for this observed 60/40 proportion is +/− 3.04 percent. We are 95 percent confident that candidate A's true support in the population is between 56.96 percent and 63.04 percent.

A similar margin of error for a *mean* can be computed by multiplying the *standard error of the mean* by 1.96.

Margin of error at the 95 percent confidence level for an observed mean =
+/− 1.96 * (square root of Var/n)

where Var = the observed variance, the sum of squared deviations from the sample mean and n = the number of elements in the sample.

Table 13.1 shows that the margin of error decreases as the sample size increases and as the observed proportion moves away from 50/50. Not only are data from 1,000 individuals more likely to correctly represent the population than are data from 100, but also it is easier to correctly detect the majority position when the proportion is 10/90 than when it is closer to 50/50.

How big should a sample be? The researcher should select the sample size with the smallest margin of error he or she can afford (within time and monetary constraints). Although it seems counterintuitive, error due to sampling depends almost entirely on the absolute size of the sample, not on the proportion of the sample size to the population size, *when the sample elements constitute less than 10 percent of the population.*[23] Therefore, a sample of 1,200 people can as precisely represent a country of 220,000,000 as it can a city of 100,000.

The formulas given above are appropriate for simple random samples or systematic samples with no stratification. If the sampling plan calls for a stratified sample, then sampling error will be lower "for the variables that are more homogeneous within strata than in the population as a whole."[24] Higher sampling errors are associated with samples involving clustering and unequal rates of selection. It is also important to remember that margin of error estimates only errors due to sampling. A discussion of other types of survey errors is at the end of this chapter.

Nonprobability Sampling on the Internet. Although the Law of Large Numbers requires a randomly selected large sample to reduce bias,[25] the problem with most Internet surveys is that there is no sampling frame of the population being studied. This is especially true in general population surveys, where not only does an unknown percentage of the population have access to the Internet (and the characteristics of these people is generally unknown), but also there is no list of email addresses for those who do have access. It is impossible to select a random sample in such a situation, thus raising questions about validity. For small populations made up solely of individuals who have Internet access with known email addresses, a random sample may be possible. It is important to know that people are not responding more than once, and asking them for their email addresses can help filter out duplicates. However, even where sampling frames may be acquired and duplicates screened out, there is no way to control for the multiplicity of email addresses, some even with false information.[26] In addition, not all email addresses are valid or current.

There have been two basic strategies to general population sampling on the Internet. The first involves selecting a traditional random sample for a telephone survey, and then making calls that screen for Internet users. This method is expensive and fails to make use of the speed of electronic interviewing, requiring telephones, interviewers, data entry, and so on. The second strategy involves sampling directly online through either/or advertising or direct selection.[27] Many such polls result in very small response rates and invalid data sets, but the use of multiple methods of sampling can allow polls to approximate representativeness. Some pollsters have posted announcements about their surveys on newsgroups, placed banners on browsers like Yahoo!, used their own email lists, and advertised in print publications. This approach does not result in a random sample, but by exposing the study to many sources of the online population, it increases the odds of an unbiased sample.[28]

If the goal is to represent a general population, however, we must remember that the online population is not itself representative of the general population. It generally is better educated, with higher income, and younger.[29] A 1998 study conducted by the National Telecommunications & Information Administration of the U.S. Department of Commerce showed that 26 percent of United States households had Internet access and 33 percent of those living in the U.S. had access to the Internet either at home or work.[30]

Nonetheless, Internet polling can yield good data. In the 1998 midterm elections, the Harris Black/Excite poll correctly predicted 21 of the 22 races in the 16 states they studied. Large samples from each state were said to be the key.[31] But for pollsters educated with the traditional routine of random sampling, it is difficult to accept what amounts to a convenience sample as representative. Harris Black International is studying the extent to which carefully weighted Internet polls can be as representative as random polls.[32]

Instrument Design

The term *instrument design* refers to writing and formatting the survey questionnaire. Questionnaires should be easy to read and should have an easy-to-follow format. Pen-and-paper questionnaires should put plenty of space around each question; they should also make clear whether the correct answer is to be circled or checked in a box or circle. Skips and branches need to be clearly marked with text instructions and/or arrows. CATI instruments are usually formatted to have one question per screen, but the programmer should take care to type the text so that ends of lines and punctuation make the questions easy to read. Tabs can be used to make the screen visually attractive and easy to follow. Although CATI skips and branches must be programmed accurately, they are "transparent" to the interviewer and require no special graphic presentation.

The questions in the instrument represent *operational definitions* for the variables under study. It is desirable for the researcher to specify his or her *hypotheses* prior to data collection and to provide explicit *theoretical definitions* for all concepts in the hypotheses. Then the operational definitions relate directly to the theoretical definitions. The researcher should have a clear idea of how every question will be used; respondents should not be abused by asking them questions that may not be used because the researcher did not carefully think through his or her project. It is a good idea to make up dummy tables prior to questionnaire construction that specify the analyses necessary to test the hypotheses of interest. Here are some keys to designing a good questionnaire:

1. Make sure your language is appropriate for the respondent and pick words that have the same meaning for everyone. For example, unless you're interviewing college professors, don't ask, "Do you favor or oppose the tenure system?"
2. Avoid long questions.
3. Limit questions to a single idea. Don't ask, "Do you favor or oppose televised presidential debates and equal coverage for all candidates?" Ask, "Do you favor or oppose televised presidential debates? Do you favor or oppose equal coverage for all candidates?"
4. Don't assume that your respondent has factual information or that he or she can report another's opinions. For example, parents may or may not be able to list

the television shows their children watch, but they are unlikely to accurately report their children's opinions.

5. Establish your frame of reference. For example, when asking about behaviors like television viewing, be sure to set a time frame such as *hours per day*.

6. Be considerate of your respondent's ego. For example, "Do you *happen* to know the mayor's name?" is better than "Do you know the mayor's name?" Also, phrase questions so that they are not objectionable. Don't ask, "Did you graduate from high school?" Instead ask, "What is the highest grade of school that you completed?"

7. Avoid biased or leading questions. Don't ask, "Do you let your children watch violent television shows?" Instead ask, "What shows do your children watch on television? Any other shows?"

8. Decide whether the question should be open- ("What do you think about George W. Bush's performance as president?") or closed-ended ("Some people say that, overall, George W. Bush has been a good president. Do you strongly agree, agree, remain neutral, disagree, or strongly disagree that George W. Bush has been a good president?"). They don't necessarily yield the same results. Be certain that closed-ended response categories are mutually exclusive and exhaustive.

9. Consider whether general or specific questions are needed. For example, is it enough to ask, "How well did you like the television show?" or should you also ask, "Have you recommended the show to anyone?"

10. Decide whether the question should be stated personally or impersonally. Impersonal: "Is the amount of television that your children watch too much, not enough, or just about right?" Personal: "Would you like your children to watch more television, less television, or is the amount that they're watching now okay?"

11. Avoid ambiguous wording. For example, do not ask, "Do you usually vote?" Instead ask, "Did you vote in the last presidential election?"

12. When asking for sensitive information, use introductory statements and transition phrases to ensure that the respondent understands why you need the information. Respondents will answer even the most sensitive questions if they understand the reason for the questions and believe the request to be legitimate.

13. Begin the interview with questions that will be interesting and easy for the respondent to answer.

Before using the questionnaire to collect data, it must be *pretested*. Test interviews are conducted with members of the population being studied; for general population surveys, around fifty pretest interviews are usually adequate. Be sure that respondents who participate in the pretest are not included or interviewed again as part of the actual study. When pretesting, interviewers look for errors in the instrument (e.g., spelling, punctuation, grammar, incorrect skips or branching) and for questions that may be misunderstood by the respondents or to which respondents may take offense. Pretest interviewing is more difficult than the actual data collection interviewing, because interviewers have to think critically about the instrument at the same time they are reading questions and recording answers. Pretest interviewers should always make notes about each pretest interview for review by the study directors.

Hiring and Training Interviewers and Supervisors

Interviewing—whether on the telephone or face to face—is a tough job. The interviewer has to get important factual information from a stranger who probably doesn't want to be bothered and, at the same time, accurately record that information. If the interviewer is working on a CATI or CAPI system, then he or she has the additional challenge of mastering hardware and software that may not always work properly. Being able to distinguish a hardware problem from a software problem from interviewer error is a treasured talent in an interviewer. Unfortunately, such individuals don't remain interviewers very long; they are promoted to supervisors at record speed.

What else makes a good interviewer? A pleasant telephone voice is essential for phone surveys, but not sufficient. The best interviewers seem to be highly empathetic and confident about their ability to carry out the interview. Good interviewers listen to respondents' words and tone of voice and circumvent the respondent's suspicions and uncertainties. Good interviewers convey the legitimacy and importance of the survey project by projecting a professional demeanor. And above all, good interviewers quickly learn procedures and carry them out. If CATI or CAPI systems are used, then typing proficiency is necessary and a familiarity with computers will speed training.

In many parts of the country, it is advisable to conduct interviews in languages other than English. Hiring bilingual interviewers presents some special problems. You must be certain that the individual really is proficient in both languages; being able to speak Spanish when you're face to face with someone may not equal speaking Spanish fluently on the telephone. In addition, you must consider what level of proficiency is necessary (colloquial or formal speech and/or the ability to grammatically write the language), how accurately the individual can translate between the languages, and how similar the person's accent is to that used by the population being studied.

It is advisable to provide bilingual telephone interviewer applicants with a one-page bilingual questionnaire and arrange for a bilingual tester to telephone them at a later date for a test interview. The tester should evaluate the applicant's ability to switch easily from one language to the other, translate accurately, write in both languages coherently, answer questions from the interviewer that are not on the script, and speak in an acceptable manner *before* training the individual in survey procedures.

Some organizations pay interviewers an hourly rate for training and some pay a flat fee or nothing. Paying the same hourly rate for training as for actual interviewing conveys to the interviewer that his or her time is valued and that the training is important. This may translate into more learning and better efficiency.

Most training programs include the following: administrative procedures, such as filling out time cards and other record-keeping; using CATI or CAPI technology or recording answers on pen-and-paper instruments; tone of voice, pacing, and reading questions; probing and clarifying answers; how to elicit respondent cooperation; answering respondent questions and comments; dealing with hostile respondents and converting refusals; setting up callback appointments (a scheduled time for completing the interview with the respondent) and making callbacks; how to use the sample; and lots of practice interviews.

The best supervisors are promoted from among the interviewers; they already know the system and can anticipate interviewers' problems. Supervisors need additional training on sample control and maintenance, personnel supervision, hardware and software use, monitoring interviewers, and verifying interviews.

Additional training for interviewers and supervisors is generally needed before beginning a new study. Interviewers should be given a chance to make several practice interviews in order to familiarize themselves with the questionnaire, and supervisors need to practice sample control. Both interviewers and supervisors must be briefed about the study's purpose and goals. Frequently, *question-by-question objectives* are provided in writing by the study director for each item in the questionnaire. Several hours of training may be necessary to explain each question's objectives to interviewers and supervisors.

Conducting the Interview

The interviewer has at least seven basic tasks to perform in the interview. His or her first job is to *elicit the cooperation* of the person who answers the phone or doorbell. Professional dress can be important for face-to-face interviews, and a professional tone of voice is critical for telephone interviewers. The interviewer may have to answer the respondent's questions or comments before proceeding with the interview. Respondents often want to know who is sponsoring the study, why someone else in the household can't be interviewed instead, what the information collected will be used for, and how long the interview will take. The project director should provide the interviewer with answers to the most common questions and comments; giving the interviewer some stock phrases to rely on can help her or him persuade the respondent to cooperate.

Second, interviewers must *read the questions exactly as written* in exactly the order given. Even slight deviations can cause the respondent to provide a completely different answer. Standardization in interviewer performance is important. Some words in the questions may be underlined or written in capital letters; these should be emphasized by the interviewer. Occasionally a respondent will provide an answer before the full question text has been read; if there is *any* doubt that the respondent would answer differently after hearing the rest of the question, the full question text should be reread.

Third, the interviewer must *record* the respondent's answers exactly. This usually means writing down (or typing on the CATI/CAPI keyboard) the appropriate number for a response, but it may also include recoding verbatim open-ended responses. If the respondent talks quickly or at length, the interviewer may need to interject a phrase such as "I'm writing this down (typing what you've said), please wait a moment." It is very important that interviewers write down exactly what the respondent has said; many times the exact words used by the respondent are crucial to interpreting the respondent's meaning.

Fourth, the interviewer must *clarify* questions when the respondent is uncertain what a question is asking for. The question-by-question objectives provided by the study director should include definitions of key words and phrases when allowed—sometimes the study director wants the respondent to provide his or her own interpretation: "Whatever _____ means to you." The question-by-question objectives should also tell the interviewers what they are allowed to say about the goals of each question.

Fifth, interviewers should be prepared to *probe* for more complete answers or when they think that the respondent has given an inappropriate answer. Sometimes probes are scripted on the instrument, with explicit instructions for their use. For example, in an open-ended question like, "Why do you watch television?" interviewers would probably be instructed to probe "Any other reason?" after each response. Most probes, however, cannot be scripted, because they must be used to improve a particular respondent's performance. For example, if the interviewer asks, "How many days per week do you read a daily newspaper?" and the respondent says, "Oh, three or four," then the interviewer should probe for a specific answer: "Would you say it is closer to three or to four?" The key to probing is that the probe used is neutral; that is, it does not lead the respondent toward a particular answer. Often the best probe is silence. Other good probes include repeating the question, "anything else?", "in what ways?", or "how is that?"

Sixth, interviewers should provide neutral *feedback* occasionally to let respondents know that they are performing adequately. Feedback is not used to congratulate respondents on the type of response they are giving (i.e., a certain attitude), but rather to reward them for responding at all. Short feedback is used most often: "Thank you," "Uh huh," and "That's helpful." Longer phrases should be mixed in every few items: "Thank you, that is helpful to our research," "That is useful information," or "I appreciate your cooperation." Feedback should not include any phrases that indicate approval of the type of response; interviewers should avoid such terms as *okay*, *right*, and *good*.

Finally, the interviewer may have to set up a *callback* appointment if the respondent is unable to begin or complete the interview at the current time. The interviewer should try to make the appointment for a specific date and time. If that is not possible, then he or she should try to set up a general time, such as "tomorrow afternoon."

If the survey questionnaire has been prepared in more than one language, the interviewer must also evaluate which language the respondent wishes to speak. Often this can be deduced from the way the telephone or door is answered, but sometimes the interviewer may need to ask. Once the choice of language is made, however, the interviewer must also be sensitive to the needs of the respondent, switching back and forth between languages as is necessary to communicate effectively.

In addition, for Internet surveys, it may be necessary to have someone answer telephone calls about the study, often of a technical nature.

Quality Control

Collecting data of the highest quality should be the primary goal of the survey researcher. There are several ways in which the quality of the data can be maintained. First, the project director must provide sufficient *training* for both interviewers and supervisors. Training is important not only for basic survey procedures, but training specific to each new study is also crucial.

Second, the interviewers should be monitored for at least one hour's worth of interviewing on each study. For telephone surveys, this generally means having a supervisor listen to interviews over an extension telephone that allows the supervisor to hear the interviewer, but not the reverse. The supervisor should follow the interview with a copy of the questionnaire being used. For CATI studies, a "slave" terminal can be tied into the interviewer's terminal: This allows the supervisor to hear what the interviewer says, what the respondent says, *and* see exactly what the interviewer records when she records it. After an interview is monitored, the supervisor should meet with the interviewer to give feedback on the performance. Frequently, an evaluation sheet is used, with a copy being put in the interviewer's personnel file.

Third, a small percentage of interviews conducted in a study (such as 5 or 10 percent) should be verified. To verify an interview, a supervisor calls a randomly selected respondent to confirm that the interview actually was conducted. Verification is more important in face-to-face surveys and in those telephone surveys that are not conducted in centralized phone facilities because falsification of data is easier when supervisors are not present when the interviews are conducted.

Fourth, the researcher should use sample control methods that result in the highest possible percentage of completed interviews and the lowest possible percentage of refusals. There are many formulas for response rates, completion rates, and refusal rates, and the selection of one is more a matter of choice than science. Frey[33] gives a simple formula for each:

- The ***response rate*** reflects the percentage of potential eligible respondents who cooperated in providing information. It may be calculated as the number of completed interviews divided by the number of eligible respondents. "Eligible respondents" include those who completed interviews, who partially completed interviews, who refused, who could not speak the language, who were ill or otherwise indisposed, or who were away for the duration of the study. "Ineligible respondents" might include those who do not meet the respondent profile (e.g., not 18 years of age or older), but "ineligible elements" in the sample could also include (in a general population household survey) businesses, nonworking numbers, and numbers that are *always* busy or that ring but are never answered.
- The *completion rate* reflects the proportion of cooperating respondents as a percentage of all sample elements contacted, eligible or not. It is calculated by dividing the number of completed interviews by the total number of sample elements (e.g., telephone numbers or households) used.
- The *refusal rate* is the opposite of the response rate. It reflects the percentage of eligible respondents who refuse to be interviewed. It is calculated by dividing the number of refusals by the number of eligible respondents.

Evaluating Survey Research

Measurements derived from survey research are subject to two main sources of errors— *sampling error* and *nonsampling error*.[34] Sampling error, as we discussed earlier, can be empirically estimated for data collected from a probability sample. Nonsampling errors are equally important, but they are extremely difficult to estimate empirically with any degree of confidence.

Nonsampling errors are of two types. *Random errors* reduce the reliability of measurements, but they generally cancel each other out over numerous measurements (e.g., one person overestimates the number of hours per day that he watches television and another underestimates her viewing). *Nonrandom error* or ***bias*** is more troublesome, because these errors are systematic and do not cancel out over repeated measurements. One type of nonrandom error is *nonresponse bias*, which results from differences between those who complete interviews and those who refuse to cooperate and between those who answer a given question and those who refuse. Refusals are not random; these individuals tend to have qualities in common that are consequently underrepresented in the pool of completed interviews,

Response bias is another type of nonrandom error—the systematic distortion of answers by respondents. Response biases frequently occur when respondents are asked to report socially unacceptable behaviors or attitudes. For example, if respondents are asked to report whether they use illegal drugs, some drug users may refuse, but others may lie. Such distortions are systematic, in that few nonusers would say they use drugs, but some users will say that they do not. Therefore, whatever level of drug use is estimated by the survey probably represents the minimum level in the population, and the true value is probably much higher.

Other types of nonrandom errors include those made by interviewers, by coders, by data transcribers, and so on. For example, an interviewer's tone of voice or choice of feedback may suggest disapproval of answers, thereby causing the respondent to modify his or her responses. Coders may misunderstand their instructions, thereby categorizing open-ended responses incorrectly. Checks and double-checks of procedures can help minimize such errors.

Reliability and Validity of Survey Research

With cost factors and decreasing response rates making the telephone survey increasingly more popular than the face-to-face survey, we need to consider the reliability and validity of the two methods. *Reliability* refers to the accuracy of the data obtained, whereas *validity* refers to whether we are measuring what we think we're measuring. Miller[35] reports that the telephone survey results in data very similar to that obtained in a face-to-face study, although there may be more respondent-selection errors in the telephone surveys, and response rates outside of urban areas continue to be higher for face-to-face surveys. The telephone survey is probably as good as the face-to-face survey for general populations, but for subpopulations that have lower telephone coverage, the validity of the telephone survey is in question.

As we indicated earlier, establishing causal relationships may be difficult through survey research, making the *internal validity* of survey research lower than that of randomized experiments, although the use of statistical controls helps rule out alternative explanations for observed relationships in survey data. The *external validity* of the survey is superior to that of the randomized experiment, since survey data are collected in the natural environment (that is, in the household) rather than in the laboratory.

Ethical Issues

The vast majority of surveys represent intrusions into people's private lives:[36] a stranger knocking at the door or calling on the telephone in order to serve his or her research organization's purpose. Telephone survey samplers have even devised random-digit dialing methods to ensure that individuals with unlisted numbers—who clearly do not want phone calls from strangers—are included in the study. Therefore, researchers have an obligation to restrict their surveys to important issues and to keep the number of questions to a minimum. Internet-based surveys may be more intrusive if they are sent by email than if by some other method; "spamming" of unwanted email messages is undesirable. On the other hand, because it is so easy to delete or ignore, an Internet survey is far less intrusive than a telephone call or household visit.

The researcher also has an obligation to be truthful to the respondent. Interviewers should identify themselves and their organization before requesting any information from a respondent. In addition, interviewers should never underestimate the amount of time the interview will take. Although respondents sometimes ask for information that could bias their subsequent answers, such as who is sponsoring the study or whether they got knowledge questions right or wrong, this information can be given to the respondent at the end of the interview without fear of increasing response errors. Respondents should also be told enough about the study to judge whether they want to participate. This includes the kinds of information they will be asked to provide and the uses to which it will be put.

Interviewers should never badger respondents into answering questions that they don't want to answer. Probing "don't knows" once is standard practice, but respondents should be permitted to refuse to answer or to give a neutral response without undue pressure or negative feedback from the interviewer.

Survey researchers also have a responsibility to keep respondents' answers anonymous—to never identify particular data with an individual respondent. It is common practice for study directors to assign code numbers to sample units, whether they be telephone numbers, household addresses, or email addresses. The routine procedure is to destroy the link between the code number and the data once all data are collected and cleaned. However, the fact that email messages may be intercepted by others makes them more vulnerable to breaches of confidentiality.[37]

Summary

Survey research is by far the most common methodology used in mass communication research. The ability to simultaneously canvas many variables and to project the parameters of these variables to entire populations has made survey research popular and valuable for three major research tasks: describing the uses and effects of contemporary mass communication, testing specific hypotheses about relationships involved in these uses and effects, and developing comprehensive theoretical explanations for mass communications.

In short, survey research covers the gamut from applied to basic theoretical research. Its findings appear on the front pages of our newspapers and in the pages of scholarly treatises.

Endnotes

1. Floyd J. Fowler, Jr., *Survey Research Methods*, Applied Social Research Methods Series, Volume 1 (Beverly Hills, CA: Sage Publications, 1984), 9.

2. Richard Jensen, "Democracy by the Numbers," *Public Opinion* (February/March 1980), 53.

3. *Ibid.*, 53.

4. *Ibid.*, 54.

5. L. John Martin, "The Genealogy of Public Opinion Polling," in L. John Martin, ed., *Polling and the Democratic Consensus*, The Annals of the American Academy of Political and Social Science (Beverly Hills, CA: Sage Publications, March 1984), 19; Jensen, *op. cit.*, 58.

6. Martin, *op. cit.*; Jensen, *op. cit.*, 58.

7. *Ibid.*, 59.

8. Charles Roll, "Private Opinion Polls," in Gerald Benjamin, ed., *The Communications Revolution in Politics*, Proceedings of the American Academy of Political Science (*American Academy of Political Science* 34 (4), 1982).

9. James H. Frey, *Survey Research by Telephone* (Beverly Hills, CA: Sage Publications, 1983), 9.

10. *Ibid.*, 13.

11. Herbert H. Hyman, *Secondary Analysis of Sample Surveys* (New York: John Wiley & Sons, 1972), 1.

12. Maxwell McCombs, "Negro Use of Television and Newspapers for Political Information, 1952–1964," *Journal of Broadcasting* 12 (1968): 261–266.

13. Delbert C. Miller, *Handbook of Research Design and Social Measurement* (New York: Longman, 1983), 110–114.

14. Diane F. Witmer, Robert W. Coleman, and Sandra Lee Katzman, "From Paper-and-Pencil to Screen-and-Keyboard," in *Doing Internet Research*, ed. Steve Jones (Thousand Oaks, CA: Sage Publications), 157.

15. *Ibid.*, 156.

16. Cheryl Harris, "Developing Online Market Research Methods and Tools," *Marketing and Research Today* (November 1997): 269.

17. David R. Schaefer and Don A. Dillman, "Development of a Standard E-mail Methodology: Results of an Experiment," *Public Opinion Quarterly* 62 (1998): 390.

18. Mick P. Couper, Johnny Blair, and Timothy Triplett, "A Comparison of Mail and E-mail for a Survey of Employees in U.S. Statistical Agencies," *Journal of Official Statistics* 15 (1999): 53.

19. Gordon S. Black and George Terhanian, "Using the Internet for Election Forecasting," *The Polling Report* (October 26, 1998).

20. Miller, *op. cit.*, 121–125.

21. Joseph Waksberg, "Sampling Methods for Random Digit Dialing," *Journal of the American Statistical Association* 73 (1978): 40–46.

22. Fowler, *op. cit.*, 36–37.

23. *Ibid.*, 40–41.

24. *Ibid.*, 39.

25. Alan J. Rosenblatt, "On-Line Polling: Methodological Limitations and Implications for Electronic Democracy," *Harvard International Journal of Press/Politics*, 4/2 (1999): 32.

26. *Ibid.*, 33.

27. *Ibid.*, 33–34.

28. *Ibid.*, 34.

29. *Ibid.*, 38.

30. "Falling Through the Net II: New Data on the Digital Divide," U.S. Department of Commerce National Telecommunications & Information Administration, July 1998.

31. James Ledbetter, "You Surfed It Here First," *The Industry Standard* (November 6, 1998).

32. Black and Terhanian, *op. cit.*

33. Frey, *op. cit.*, 38–40.

34. James Alan Fox and Paul E. Tracy, *Randomized Response: A Method for Sensitive Surveys* (Beverly Hills, CA: Sage Publications, 1986), 8–10.

35. Miller, *op. cit.*, 125–126.

36. Fox and Tracy, *op. cit.*, 10–12.

37. Couper, Blair, and Triplett, *op. cit.*, 49.

14

Secondary Analysis

Lee B. Becker

Secondary analysis is the reuse of social science data after they have been put aside by the researcher who gathered them. The reuse of the data can be by the original researcher or someone uninvolved in any way in the initial research project. The research questions examined in the secondary analysis can be related to the original research endeavor or quite distinct from it.

In a very real sense, then, secondary analysis is the use of available records, the records of other social scientists.[1] Because social scientists, particularly within the last forty years, have been diligent in the preservation of some important records, **data archives** now exist that make the possibilities for secondary analysis quite astounding. The Roper Public Opinion Research Center at the University of Connecticut, for example, contains records of sample surveys dating back through the 1930s. Thousands of polls from the United States and from approximately seventy other countries are housed there.

Advantages of Secondary Analysis

Secondary analysis has a bad connotation for some researchers, particularly those unfamiliar with some of its potential. Students who do not have the resources for primary data gathering are sometimes encouraged to reuse existing data to complete course or degree requirements in the allotted time. It would be better to gather new data, these students are advised, but they may have to get by with secondary analysis.

To be sure, there is great value in gathering new data. Students learn most about the problems of design and measurement when they direct a project from beginning to end. And there are some very real problems with secondary analysis.

The secondary analyst is quite removed from the initial data-gathering procedures and consequently can be unaware of flaws and data limitations. Details of sample design and field operations, for example, are not always known. Peculiarities of data storage, in-

Aswin Punathambekar assisted in the preparation of this chapter.

cluding information on weighting or recoding of initial responses, may not be available. And because many of the archived data sets have been created by reputable organizations, some researchers may not be critical enough in their reuse. There is a tendency to think of archived data as "cleansed," as if aging makes them finer than they were when "put down."

The most serious limitation of secondary analysis, however, results from the fact that the primary researcher was unaware of the interest of the secondary analyst. While efforts are made by some organizations to anticipate future uses and plan for them, it is impossible to anticipate future research questions completely. The result is that archived data may not provide for an adequate test of the research questions of the secondary analyst. In such cases, the researcher has to weigh the advantages of secondary analysis and the advantages and disadvantages of new data-gathering operations.

The practical benefits of secondary analysis are rather obvious. Using data already gathered is cheaper and quicker than undertaking a second study. Many communication researchers lack the financial resources to field studies of the scope of many of those presently archived. Survey research is expensive because it is relatively labor intensive, involving banks of interviewers and teams of supervisors. The employment of coders for content analysis and supervisory personnel for laboratory work also is expensive. Payment of interview respondents or experimental subjects, when necessary, adds to costs.

Data archives, in addition to providing relatively inexpensive records for the researchers, also allow social scientists to save what good will exists in society for those situations in which it is necessary to gather new data. Most people have been contacted at least once by someone claiming to be a pollster, and many have participated in school or some other setting in some form of experiment.[2] While there is evidence that many people are supportive of such research, others are not, and there is, to be sure, a real danger of "pollution" of the social environment by researchers.[3]

Perhaps the greatest benefit of secondary analysis, however, results from its potential contribution to theory and substantive knowledge of the social processes. Sociologist Herbert Hyman, in his comprehensive text on secondary analysis, argued that existing data archives provide extensive opportunities for such contributions.[4] These data, for example, allow for an examination of important aspects of the past. The pollster can be thought of as a "contemporary historian," and the pollster's data are a rich source of information on opinion during important periods of our past.[5] These data also provide an opportunity to study social change in ways that are impossible in present-day primary analysis. Researchers would be forced to rely on retrospective reports by current respondents were it not for existing archives.

Secondary analysis of comparable data sets gathered in different countries or sections within a country also allows for comparative tests and consequent broadening of inferences. Because few researchers have the capability to field comparative studies, cross-cultural inferences are not often made from primary analysis. Similarly, secondary analysis allows researchers to replicate findings and in so doing enlarge on the original interpretation. Findings from one community or state, for example, can be tested with data gathered by a national organization. Or the findings can simply be replicated in another, somewhat different, setting.

Finally, Hyman argues, secondary analysis provides researchers with the impetus to elevate and enlarge their theories. Partly because secondary analysts seldom find perfect measures of needed concepts, they are forced to treat the measures as indicators of some general concept. In the process, they may change the level of abstraction, seeing the old concept as only a small component of some more abstract, and perhaps more important, social phenomenon.

Existing Archives

Archives of experimental data are of less value to communication researchers than archives of survey data. Secondary analysts cannot add manipulated independent variables to experimental data sets and seldom have the opportunity to examine the effects of the manipulations on dependent variables other than those intended by the primary researcher. As a result, no major archive of experimental data from communication research exists.

The largest general archive of public opinion data in the world is located at the Roper Public Opinion Research Center at the University of Connecticut. Founded in 1947 by public opinion research pioneer Elmo Roper, the Center holdings include polls conducted by ABC News, CBS News, Fox News, The Gallup Organization, the *Los Angeles Times*, the National Opinion Research Center, NBC News, *The New York Times*, Princeton Survey Research Associates, *USA Today*, *The Washington Post*, and others. The Center's U.S. holdings reflect a strong interest in social and political information drawn from national samples. Market and audience research is given less attention. The Roper Center's collections from outside the United States give special emphasis to survey findings on political preferences, policy judgments, and social and cultural values.

It is possible to search the catalog of the holdings of the Roper Center from its website (*www.ropercenter.uconn.edu*). For a fee, users of the site also can obtain univariate frequency distributions for answers to the approximately 350,000 questions stored in the Center's U.S. public opinion poll holdings going back to 1935. Those who pay a membership fee to the Roper Center (and many universities around the country are members) can obtain raw data files from the Center for secondary analysis.

The Roper question database also can be accessed through the Lexis-Nexis news and retrieval archive, to which many university libraries subscribe. Lexis-Nexis is composed of several electronic "libraries," each consisting of searchable files. The libraries include the following categories: General News, Legal, Public Records, International, Medical, and Financial. The Roper Center database can be accessed from the CMPGN (Campaign Library), under the RPOLL listing. The data archived in the Roper Center database can be searched by time, period, and by organization. The search results include the question asked of the people, the population sampled, the number of respondents, the interview method, the organization that conducted the survey, the date of release of the results, and the frequencies for each response category to the question. In some cases, the results include bivariate frequencies, such as by age, gender, and race.

Included in the holdings of the Roper Center are the General Social Surveys, conducted by the National Opinion Research Center at the University of Chicago on a nearly annual basis since 1972. Between that year and 1998 more than 35,000 respondents have answered more than 2,500 different questions, including a number of questions dealing with the media. Since 1982, the GSS has had a cross-national component, and since 1985, the GSS has included a module of the International Social Survey Program, organized by Australia, Great Britain, Germany, and the United States.[6]

The Inter-University Consortium for Political and Social Research (ICPSR), located in the Institute for Social Research at the University of Michigan, provides access to the world's largest archive of computerized social science data. ICPSR is a membership-based organization serving colleges and universities in the U.S. and abroad. Faculty, staff, and students at member institutions can obtain data files in such areas as political science, sociology, demography, economics, history, education, criminal justice, public health, and law. Included are the data files from the National Election Studies, which have been conducted since 1948 and contain various measures of media use.

The Howard W. Odum Institute for Research in Social Science at the University of North Carolina at Chapel Hill maintains an archive of social science data dealing with national and international economic, electoral, public opinion, and health and demographic issues. Its Louis Harris Data Center is the exclusive national repository for Louis Harris public opinion data. The Odum Institute's website contains its Public Opinion Poll Question Database allowing users to search for specific poll questions in the Institute's archives by key words, date, study number, study title, or state. The system displays the full question text, frequency distribution, and study details. It also is possible to download many of the data files from the archives directly from the website of the Institute (*www.irss.unc.edu*).

Another website of considerable value to those interested in locating data for secondary analysis is maintained by the University of California, San Diego. The site has a listing of more than 850 other Internet sites containing social science data, data catalogs, data libraries, and more. The address for the site is *www.ssdc.ucsd.edu/ssdc*.

Also of considerable interest is the website of the Pew Research Center for the People & the Press (*www.people-press.org*). The Pew Center investigates public attitudes toward the news media, creates a news interest index to measure how closely the public follows major news stories, and tracks the public's use of the Internet and traditional news media outlets. The Pew Center website contains a data archive, from which data can be downloaded directly. Survey data are generally released six months after reports are issued and posted on the web as soon thereafter as possible.

Summaries of recently published poll data, many of which are or will be archived, appear in "The Polls" section of *Public Opinion Quarterly*, *Gallup Opinion Monthly*, and *Public Perspective*, published by the Roper Center.

Types of Secondary Analysis

Research projects relying on secondary analysis are of two general types. Many such projects follow the traditional model of research. A question is developed and shaped, perhaps with the assistance of some established theoretical perspective, into a hypothesis. The hypothesis is then subjected to an empirical test with data having been collected by some other researchers. Were it not for the latter fact, that the data were not gathered by the persons performing the test, it would be impossible to distinguish this type of research project from any other.

Many secondary analysis projects, however, are of a different sort. They begin when the researcher becomes aware of data already collected and is stimulated by some rather narrow, often descriptive, finding of the original researcher. A hypothesis is formulated, sometimes to explain that descriptive finding. Existing theory may be used to buttress the hypothesis, which is tested with the existing data set. In other words, existing data have given rise to the hypothesis and provided its empirical test.

For the most part, researchers do not report which of these descriptions best fits their research using secondary analysis. The reason is rather simple. The second situation, where an interesting data set stimulated the secondary analysis, seems more opportunistic, less programmatic, and less rigorous. That need not be the case. And it is probably true that more secondary analysis results from the fact that the data are available than from the formulation of research questions derived wholly independently of such data sets.

Because the process of conducting secondary analysis differs to some extent under these two types, they are discussed separately here. No value judgment regarding their worth is being made.

Hypothesis-Then-Data Type of Secondary Analysis

The beginning stages in this type of secondary analysis are indistinguishable from those in primary analysis. The researcher develops a research problem, defines the concepts included in the problem statement, and formulates a **hypothesis**. At this point, however, the paths of the primary and secondary analyst diverge.

The primary analyst, having stated the hypothesis, attempts to enumerate the various ways of measuring each of the concepts included in the hypothesis. From this list of possible measures, the researcher then selects the measure or measures that best reflect the concept of concern. The feasibility of actually using the measure is then explored. The choice of a measure results from a weighing of its appropriateness and the likelihood that it can be taken.

The secondary analyst, on the other hand, does not have the luxury of selecting the best measure from a list of possible measures. Rather, he or she is constrained to select the best measure from those available, in other words, from those used by other researchers.

This process is illustrated fairly well by recounting some of the decisions made by Stroman and Becker in their secondary analysis examining racial differences in media use habits.[7] The general research problem arose from ambiguities in the previous literature regarding the exact nature of differences in the ways blacks and whites in this country use the mass media. Some research suggested they were the result of socioeconomic differences in the two population subgroups; other evidence indicated the differences were more deeply ingrained in the two subcultures.

In their search for existing data that would allow for a closer examination of these two positions, Stroman and Becker had two goals. First, they wanted to obtain as much diversity as possible in the types of media use measures included on the original questionnaire. Second, they wanted to obtain as large a sample of black respondents as possible to allow for a robust test of each position. They eventually settled on the 1974 University of Michigan election study, made available to them through the Inter-University Consortium for Political Research. The study included a wide range of questions on media that were asked of a relatively large number of black respondents.

The decision to use the 1974 Election Study, however, reshaped the original research question. Many of the questions included on the interview schedule had to do with the election or public affairs in general, so the analysis dealt with that subject matter. Because the schedule included questions on the gratifications audience members reported seeking from the political content of the media, the research question was expanded to examine differences in this aspect of media behavior.

The authors concluded that some real racial differences existed in key aspects of media behavior, and the differences were not entirely attributable to differences in social class. In some important respects, however, the two racial groups were quite similar. This is particularly true where gratifications sought from the political content of television were concerned. The conclusions, quite clearly, were influenced by the measures available for analysis. Those decisions on measurement had been made by the primary, not the secondary, analyst.

A second and much more prominent example of the use of secondary analysis to test a hypothesis formulated before the data to test it were located is the research by Robert Putnam reported in his book, *Bowling Alone*.[8] Putnam acknowledges in the book that his original thesis that civic engagement and social participation in the United States had declined in the last decades of the twentieth century, in part because of the advent of television, rested on relatively weak data until he was able to identify two additional archived data sets.[9] The first of these was the Roper Social and Political Trends archive, housed at the Roper Center but in need of additional cleaning before it could be used. The second was a commercial data set consisting of results of DDB Needham Life Style surveys conducted each year since 1975.[10] The addition of these two rather robust data files added considerable weight to Putnam's arguments about the decline of what he calls social capital and the various contributors to that change in U.S. society.

Data-Then-Hypothesis Type of Secondary Analysis

The secondary analysis project stemming from an existing data set has quite a distinct history from those for which the hypotheses are generated in the more traditional manner. The research endeavor begins when the secondary analyst stumbles on or is somehow made aware of an existing data set. The availability of the data set, rather than some prior research problem, is responsible for the secondary analysis.

The problems encountered by the researcher in this second situation are quite distinct from those encountered in the more traditional approach. The problems are ones of operationalization, to be sure, but they have a different direction. Rather than asking whether existing measures adequately tap a concept of interest to the researcher, the secondary analyst working from the data is more likely to be consumed initially with identifying the concept measured by existing questions: The analyst is asking, What is it that is measured here?

Once the researcher has answered that question, or at least made some attempt at it, he or she can start to ask whether that concept is related to others measured in the data set. If the answer seems to be affirmative, the researcher has stumbled onto a hypothesis. If the hypothesis is of substantive interest, the secondary analysis may be warranted.

The secondary analysis by Becker, Beam, and Russial of the New England Daily Newspaper Survey data was of this second type.[11] It began when the authors became aware of the data set, which included evaluative essays of New England's daily newspapers written by trained critics, as well as large amounts of other data. It ended with empirical tests of a substantive hypothesis relating to correlates of press performance.

Through content analysis of the evaluative essays, the authors were able to derive performance scores for the approximately 100 newspapers included in the original study. Newspaper performance became the dependent variable in the analysis. The authors also sifted through the data reported for each newspaper to identify independent variables—factors that might be expected to be functionally related to performance. Measures were first grouped into two general headings: those measuring characteristics of the community served by the press and those measuring characteristics of the news organization itself. After having made this distinction, the authors attempted to group and combine measures that seemed to tap similar concepts. Included in the community group were measures of market growth and newspaper competition. Examples of organizational measures were size of news staff and type of ownership.

The analysis showed that community factors measured were less important in understanding newspaper performance than organizational characteristics. As was true in the Stroman and Becker analysis, the conclusions were somewhat tentative because other measures not included by the primary analyst might have altered the empirical picture.

The process of naming variables, and defining them conceptually, is probably the most challenging activity in the type of secondary analysis that stems from existing data. Until that is done, however, it is not possible to formulate meaningful hypotheses. So it is the crucial step that transforms what could be a "fishing expedition" using available data into substantive theoretical research.

In naming and defining the measured variables, the secondary analyst also takes important steps toward elevating and enlarging existing theories. As Hyman has argued, when researchers use measures created by others, they often break out of their own conceptual narrowness and push toward higher levels of abstraction. The researcher is forced to think "broadly and abstractly in order to find overarching concepts or categories within which these varied specific entities can be contained."[12] The result may well be better theory.

Designs in Secondary Analysis

For the most part, researchers are restricted in the secondary analysis to the designs of the primary analyst. This often means a cross-sectional design, though experiments, particularly involving variants in question wording, are now quite common components of surveys.[13] Through use of more than one archived data set, however, researchers often can perform trend and cohort analyses not otherwise possible. In this way, secondary analysis can be used for rather sophisticated and theoretically important studies of change.

Trend and cohort analysis can be conducted by the primary analyst, of course. But the existence of data archives increases the possibilities for such analyses. For that reason, and because secondary analysis can present some rather distinct problems in employing these designs, they merit discussion here.

Trend Analysis

In its simplest form, **trend analysis** merely involves the laying side-by-side of research results that are comparable except for the date of data gathering. In this way, change in some criterion variable can be assessed. Although actually only a surrogate for some more substantive factor, time becomes the independent variable in the analysis.

Gallup data shown in Figure 14.1 are illustrative of the kinds of data that are often used for this type of trend analysis.[14] They consist of responses to a single item repeated on a large number of national Gallup surveys over the six-year span of the presidency of Richard Nixon. The question was designed to measure the electorate's approval of the job performance of the president.[15]

The raw data merely show the high and low points of Nixon's approval rating. That rating was relatively stable during the first year and a half of when Nixon was in office. It

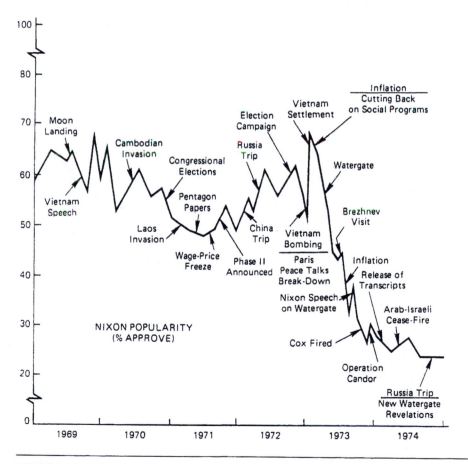

FIGURE 14.1. Trends in Job Approval Rating of Richard Nixon. From *The Gallup Opinion Index*, Report No. 111, September 1974. Copyright © The Gallup Organization, Princeton, NJ. Reprinted by permisson.

dropped in 1971 and built again to a new high in 1973. At that time, it began to fall, almost without serious interruption, until the summer of 1974 when Nixon resigned in shame.

By coupling these raw data with an understanding of historical events, it is possible to get some rough indication of what might have been the cause of Nixon's loss of popularity. All presidents witness shifts in their support. Often the shifts seem quite unrelated to specific presidential activities.[16] The drastic downturn in Nixon support as Watergate unraveled, however, would seem to be tied to that event. Nothing the president said or did during that time seemed to be able to pull him from the Watergate quagmire.[17]

The difficulty with this kind of interpretation, however, is that it is impossible to argue with certainty that something other than the identified historical event produced the change in the criterion variable. While the drastic drop in 1973 and 1974 in Nixon support is easy to tie to such an event (Watergate clearly dominated the domestic and international scene during the period), other changes shown in Figure 14.1 are less easily explained. Did the Laos invasion in early 1971, for example, lead to a decrease in presidential popularity, or was Nixon's support on the wane as a result of other forces that preceded the invasion? Or perhaps it was a combination of factors, including the invasion, that produced the decrease in support.

The situation becomes even more complex when dramatic events occur but public opinion remains relatively stable. Figure 14.2 shows just such a case. Here the job approval rating for President Bill Clinton is shown during the crucial months before and during his impeachment trial. The measure is the same as that shown in Figure 14.1; the data also come from the Gallup Poll.[18] Clinton entered the crucial second half of 1997 with a

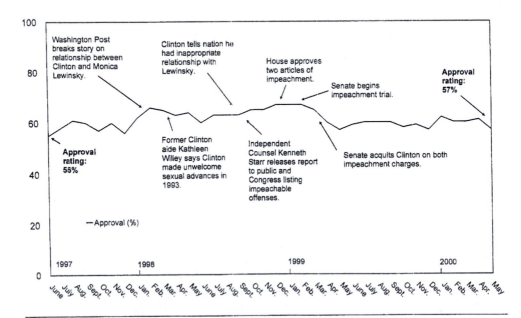

FIGURE 14.2. Trends in Job Approval Rating of Bill Clinton. Where multiple polls were conducted in a single month, the figures shown are averages.

job approval rating of 55 percent. His approval rating three years later was nearly the same, at 57 percent. In the interim, the scandal involving White House intern Monica Lewinsky filled the news. The House voted articles of impeachment. The Senate acquitted Clinton despite evidence that the president, at a minimum, misled almost everyone who tried to learn the true nature of the relationship he had with intern Lewinsky.

On the face of it, it appears that the scandal actually helped improve Clinton's standing in the polls. It is hard to imagine why the lurid details of Clinton's sexual activities and his duplicity would have had this effect. In fact, other data show people largely disapproved of his activities and his character. Clearly a simple examination of the trend data in Figure 14.2, matched to real-world events, as well as the trend data in Figure 14.1, is not sufficient.

At least two distinct solutions to this problem present themselves. The first is to attempt to disaggregate the trend. The second is to find correlates of it over a long period of time. Disaggregation of a trend is illustrated by a secondary analysis reported by Tichenor, Donohue, and Olien.[19] The researchers, using Gallup data, identified a general increase in the belief on the part of the public between 1949 and 1965 that man would reach the moon. The authors believed that this increase was due at least in part to discussion of the topic in the media during the period. If this was the case, those most likely to be in a social environment facilitating this media effect should show a higher level of change in this belief than those in less facilitating environments. Using education as an indication of this type of environment, the researchers were able to disaggregate the trend and show that those with less formal education increased less in this belief than those with more formal education. The result was a better understanding of the overall trend in beliefs about man reaching the moon.

The second strategy, isolation of correlates of the shift in the criterion variable over time, is illustrated by a secondary analysis of data gathered by the National Opinion Research Center in the annual General Social Survey, an omnibus national survey conducted each year since 1972.[20] The authors were able to show that changes in national evaluation of the press followed a pattern opposite that of evaluation of the executive branch of government, at least over the short period for which data were then available. This finding was used to support the authors' inference that popular support of the press is dependent at least in part on support of other institutions in the society with which the press is often in conflict.

In evaluating trends, of course, the possibility exists that the change observed in the criterion variable is not real, but rather an artifact resulting from sampling error, changes in the techniques of data gathering across the studies being analyzed, or changes in question wording. Problems of question wording will be dealt with later in this chapter. Suffice it to say at present that any variation in question wording poses a serious threat to an inference of real change, because, strictly, trend analysis assumes identical measurement across time.

Difficulties with sampling errors can be dealt with in a rather straightforward manner. Slight shifts in survey data are expected when they are derived from a sample of the population. Samples are estimates; as such, they are likely to contain error. By means of a simple difference of proportions test, however, it is possible to determine that shifts greater than 4 percent between any two data collection points in Figures 14.1 or 14.2 would be likely to occur by chance (or as the result of sampling) only one time in twenty.[21] Using a slightly more complicated procedure developed by Glenn, it is possible to evaluate the overall pattern of fluctuation due to sampling error in trends like those shown in the Gallup data in Figure 14.1.[22]

Changes in field or other techniques of data gathering are less easily overcome. The original researcher may have changed sample designs, altered field strategies, or obtained different overall return rates in the various studies the secondary analyst is using in the trend analysis. In the early years of the Gallup Poll, for example, the method of quota sampling used resulted in an underrepresentation of the less educated and lower-status members of the U.S. population. Changes in sample design were initiated around 1950 so that data gathered after that point do not have this bias.[23] But trend analysis of the long series of Gallup polls is marred by this artifact.[24]

A final problem in trend analysis results from the fact that the lags between field dates are not always the ones the secondary analyst desires. Sometimes the spans between the field dates are not equal. In the Tichenor, Donohue, and Olien research, for example, four time points were used.[25] Five years elapsed between the first data point and the second and between the second and the third. Between the third and final survey, however, six years elapsed. While it is doubtful this slight difference had any effect on the conclusions these researchers reached, there are other situations in which this might not be the case. At times large spans such as five years are completely inadequate to measure the type of change the secondary analyst is interested in studying.

Cohort Analysis

Cohort analysis refers to any study in which there are measures of some characteristic of one or more cohorts at two or more points in time.[26] A cohort is a population subgroup whose members have some particular experience or characteristic in common. Most often, cohorts are defined in terms of birth. The 1946–1950 birth cohort, for example, would consist of those individuals born during those five years. The cohort members have birth years in common.

Cohorts can be studied using panel designs, where the same persons are observed at more than one point in time. Or independently drawn samples of the various cohorts can be studied at more than one time point. The panel study allows for an examination of individual change. The independently drawn samples allow only for study of net change. This second type of cohort analysis can be seen as a subtype of trend analysis in which age is used to disaggregate the trend. Some of the problems that plague cohort analysis also affect other efforts at disaggregating trends.

Generally, researchers employ cohort analysis to test inferences about what have been labeled age effects, cohort effects, and period effects. *Age effects* are changes in the criterion variable attributable to the process of aging. For example, some have argued that individuals become more conservative as they get older for a number of psychological and social reasons. *Cohort effects* are those associated with cohort membership. To argue that individuals born during the advent of television are different from those born before or after that period in terms of subsequent use of the media is to argue for cohort effects.[27] *Period effects* are the result of influences within a given time span. For example, a general drop in trust in government among all voters during a given period would be a period effect.[28]

Because few researchers have the opportunity to gather data that allow for comparisons of cohorts across long periods, secondary analysis is commonly employed. These data, as might be expected, can present some problems.

Changes in study design, which restrict all trend analysis, can have particular importance for the cohort analyst. Because it is essential that cohorts remain identical across time, any changes that could produce fluctuation in small segments of the population (and consequently not be overly important in simple trend analysis) might jeopardize cohort analysis. Researchers need to be aware of these problems, which can be overcome to some extent by introduction of appropriate controls. For example, race or educational level of cohort members might be used as a control for differential mortality (or changes in cohort composition) across time.

The particular way the cohort-defining variable is measured and coded in the archived data set is of critical importance to the cohort analyst. If birth cohorts are being studied, age must be measured and coded finely and consistently. The secondary analyst, of course, must be able to reconstruct relevant cohorts at each date of data gathering. If age is coded into ten-year groups in one study and into fifteen-year groups in a second, use of the data will be difficult.

The final restriction (other than measurement problems, which is dealt with in the following section) resulting from use of archived data for cohort analysis has to do with the limited time span of the existing data. A most optimistic estimate is that, at present, a cohort could be studied for about sixty years using existing data sets. A more realistic estimate is that change could be studied in a cohort for about half that time. The result is that it is not possible, at present, to follow cohort members from early adulthood through retirement and termination using archived data. But the archived data are probably richer in this regard than any other data sets available.

Measurement Problems

Difficulties of measurement are so pervasive they permeate the entire discussion of secondary analysis. The research using previously gathered data to test a hypothesis generated independently of the data must assess how well existing measures tap the concepts of concern. Most often the measures are imperfect, and the researcher must decide whether the analysis is worth the time and other resources it will consume, given the difficulties of measurement.

The secondary analyst employing trend and cohort designs must not only deal with these general problems of measurement but also with others that may result from noncomparability across the studies used. The primary analyst simply may have made a slight change in question wording or even response categories, which threatens the inference that the observed trend is a real one. Sometimes the change may be in the use of a filter question, which results in changes in the sample across time. This problem sometimes can be dealt with through use of appropriate controls that make comparison groups comparable, but at a minimum this solution limits the generalizability of the findings. Sometimes, the difference in questions results not from changes in wording but rather from changes in what the words themselves mean. The term "liberal," for example, has taken on different meaning across time, as has the term "conservative." Questions using such words may seem comparable, and yet may artificially produce quite distinct responses across time.

The seriousness of this problem of question wording can be illustrated by a brief recounting of the controversy surrounding research that culminated in publication of *The Changing American Voter*.[29] The work was based on secondary analysis of the Michigan Voting Studies and reached the conclusion that, among other things, the U.S. electorate had become more issue oriented during the 1960s and 1970s when compared with earlier periods. The critical turning point in this trend was the 1964 election. Critics have noted, however, that important question wording changes were introduced into the Michigan studies at precisely that point.[30] The result, these critics argue, is that the movement may not have been real at all. The U.S. electorate may not have changed. The way some important questions were asked did change.

There are few easy solutions to these problems of measurement. Researchers who have opted for secondary analysis, indeed all researchers, must confront such difficulties straightforwardly. If there is a solution, it probably rests in continued discussion of concepts and their operationalizations and replication of findings.

The Future of Secondary Analysis

Communication researchers, as well as their colleagues in other disciplines, were slow to recognize the value of secondary analysis. That situation has changed considerably in the last twenty years. It is now quite common to see articles in the journals of the field of mass communication based on the re-analysis of data gathered by others. The breadth and depth of holdings of the major archives, the ease of access to them, and the simplicity of distribution of data files has contributed greatly to this change.

Researchers themselves can do a great deal to further even more the prospects of secondary analysis by thinking of the secondary use of data they gather when they begin their research projects. The American Sociological Association now includes sharing of data in its list of ethical standards for its members. Sociologists are told they are expected to make their data available after completion of a project and to anticipate data sharing as an "integral part" of the research plan. Those who do not place their data in public archives are expected to "keep data available and retain documentation relating to the research for a reasonable period of time after publication or dissemination of results."[31]

While none of the major associations for communication researchers has taken such a public position on data sharing, it is a basic tenet of science that the process is open and that data are made available for scrutinizing. Secondary analysis, then, is simply a logical extension of the basics of scientific work.

Endnotes

1. Many other kinds of records containing information of value to researchers exist. Governmental agencies, for example, gather and store massive amounts of information. Census data, birth, death, marriage, and similar records, and various health statistics are only a few examples. In general, such records differ from the records of social scientists is that they are less obtrusive. In other words, the person or organization providing the information is unaware that a researcher is observing. There are many

social scientists in government, however, and the distinction is not always very clear. To be sure, Census data are usually thought of as social science archives. See Eugene J. Webb and others, *Unobstrusive Measures: Nonreactive Research in the Social Sciences* (Chicago: Rand McNally & Co., 1966) for a general discussion of the use of available records.

2. A survey of Wisconsin residents 18 years old or older conducted by the Survey Research Lab at the University of Wisconsin in 1995 found that 6 percent of those interviewed had been contacted to participate in another survey within the thirty days prior to being interviewed by the Lab! The Wisconsin survey is archived at the Howard W. Odum Institute for Research in Social Science at the University of North Carolina at Chapel Hill.

3. A 1993 poll, conducted by the Field Institute, found that 68 percent of the Californians 18 years old or older surveyed found information derived from polls or surveys to be "very" or "somewhat" useful to the public at large. The California Poll is archived at the Howard W. Odum Institute for Research in Social Science at the University of North Carolina at Chapel Hill. A Gallup Poll in 1999 found high levels of interest in polls on a variety of topics. For example, 90 percent of the national sample reported they were "very" or "somewhat" interested in polls about "how America feels about the major political issues of the day." The frequencies for the July 22–25 Gallup Poll were taken from the Gallup website, *www.gallup.org* in the section Gallup Poll Topics: A–Z under the heading "Public Opinion Polls." Of course, it is difficult to generalize about feelings about polls from data gathered only from those willing to participate in them. Those who refused to participate in the poll in the first place are likely to hold more negative views of them.

4. Herbert Hyman, *Secondary Analysis of Sample Surveys* (New York: John Wiley & Sons, 1972).

5. Paul F. Lazarsfeld, "The Historian and the Pollster," in Mirra Komarovsky, ed., *Common Frontiers of the Social Sciences* (New York: Free Press, 1957), 242–262.

6. The GSS data are housed in a number of archives. In addition, it is possible to analyze the data from the GSS online at the Survey Documentation and Analysis website of the University of California, Berkeley (*www.csa.berkeley.edu:7502/archive.htm*).

7. The author is relying on research with which he has firsthand knowledge to accurately portray the different decisions made. See Carolyn A. Stroman and Lee B. Becker, "Racial Differences in Gratifications," *Journalism Quarterly* 55 (Winter 1978): 767–771.

8. Robert D. Putnam, *Bowling Alone: The Collapse and Revival of American Community* (New York: Simon & Schuster, 2000).

9. The original work was published as: Robert D. Putnam, "Bowling Alone: America's Declining Social Capital," *Journal of Democracy* 6 (1995): 65–78. It, too, was based on secondary analysis, including of the General Social Survey data and the archives of the National Election Studies.

10. Dhavan V. Shah, who also has conducted secondary analyses of the DDB Needham Life Style Survey data, told Putnam of the availability of these commercial data after Shaw read Putnam's journal article. See Dhavan V. Shah, "Civic Engagement, Interpersonal Trust, and Television Use: An Individual-Level Assessment of Social Capital," *Political Psychology* 19 (No. 3, 1968): 469–496. Putnam provides an interesting account of how his book was developed in an afterward to the volume. See Putnam, *Bowling Alone: The Collapse and Revival of American Community*, 505–513.

11. Lee B. Becker, Randy Beam, and John Russial, "Correlates of Daily Newspaper Performance in New England," *Journalism Quarterly* 55(Spring 1978): 100–108. The data originally appeared in Loren Ghiglione, ed., *Evaluating the Press: The New England Daily Newspaper Survey* (Southbridge, MA: Published by the editor, 1973).

12. Hyman, *op. cit.*, 23, 24.

13. Howard Schuman and Stanley Presser, *Questions and Answers in Attitude Surveys: Experiments on Question Form, Wording, and Context* (New York: Academic Press, 1981).

14. Hyman would label this "semisecondary analysis," since it is reported by the organization that gathered the original data. It clearly fits under the broad definition of secondary analysis used in this chapter.

15. The exact question asked is, Do you approve or disapprove of the job Nixon is doing as president?

16. For a discussion of patterns in presidential popularity, see James S. Stimson, "Public Support for American Presidents: A Cyclical Model," *Public Opinion Quarterly* 40 (Spring 1976): 1–21.

17. David Moore, managing editor of The Gallup Poll, argues that more than half of the drop in Nixon's approval rating from the beginning of 1973 until June of that year can be explained by economic issues. The economy suffered the largest cost of living increase in twenty-two years in March of that year,

following the end of wage and price controls at the beginning of the year. See David Moore, "Economy, as Much as Watergate, Felled Nixon," in Lawrence T. McGill, ed., *Polls and Scandal, from Nixon to Clinton* (New York: Freedom Forum Media Studies Center, 1998), 3–4.

18. The data on job approval ratings for the various presidents is available from the website of the Gallup Organization, *www.gallup.org*.

19. P. J. Tichenor, G. A. Donohue, and C. N. Olien, "Mass Media Flow and Differential Growth in Knowledge," *Public Opinion Quarterly* 34 (Summer 1970): 159–170.

20. Lee B. Becker, Robin E. Cobbey, and Idowu A. Sobowale, "Public Support for the Press," *Journalism Quarterly* 55 (Autumn 1978): 421–430.

21. See Herman J. Loether and Donald G. McTavish, *Inferential Statistics for Sociologists* (Boston: Allyn & Bacon, 1974) for a discussion of the difference of proportions test. Since national surveys, including those conducted by Gallup, are never simple random samples, the difference of proportions test, as well as other common statistical tests based on simple random sampling models, is not strictly applicable. It does provide, however, a rough guide in evaluating trends. See Norval D. Glenn, *Cohort Analysis* (Beverly Hills, CA: Sage Publications University Paper Series on Quantitative Applications in the Social Sciences, Series No. 07-001, 1977), particularly pages 41–45, for a detailed discussion of this problem.

22. Norval D. Glenn, "Problems of Comparability in Trend Studies with Opinion Poll Data," *Public Opinion Quarterly* 34 (Spring 1970): 82–91. For a more detailed discussion of measurement of change, including a discussion of time-series analysis appropriate for evaluating the comparability of trends in two variable, see Chester W. Harris, ed., *Problems in Measuring Change* (Madison: University of Wisconsin Press, 1963).

23. Steven H. Chaffee, "George Gallup, and Ralph Nafziger: Pioneers of Audience Research," *Mass Communication and Society* 3 (Spring and Summer 2000): 317–327.

24. See Glenn, *op. cit.* for a discussion of this problem and a means of correcting for it.

25. Tichenor and others, *op. cit.*

26. Glenn, *op. cit.*

27. Peiser found evidence of this effect in the United States, but not in Germany. See Wolfram Peiser, "Cohort Trends in Media Use in the United States," *Mass Communication and Society* 3 (Spring and Summer 2000): 185–205, and Wolfram Peiser, *Die Fernsehgeneration* (Opladen, Germay: Westdeutscher Verlag, 1996).

28. In actuality, cohort data alone may not be able to differentiate among these effects. In other words, most findings can be explained in more than one way. See Glenn, *op. cit.*, for an elaboration of this argument.

29. Norman H. Nie, Sidney Verba, and John R. Petrocik, *The Changing American Voter* (Cambridge, MA: Harvard University Press, 1976).

30. George F. Bishop, Alfred J. Tuchfarber, and Robert W. Oldendick, "Change in the Structure of American Political Attitudes: The Nagging Question of Question Wording," *American Journal of Political Science* 22 (May 1978): 250–69.

31. Code of Ethics of the American Sociological Association, approved by the ASA membership in June of 1997 (Washington, DC: American Sociological Association), 14.

15

The Controlled Experiment

Maria Elizabeth Grabe

Bruce H. Westley

The controlled experiment is, when carried out rigorously, the most powerful method of seeking answers to research questions about cause and effect available to the social scientist. Indeed, the controlled experiment is our best—and very nearly only—way of investigating causal processes. In this sense experiments are integral to research aimed at understanding and *predicting* media effects. The survey method (see Chapter 13) also has the potential to produce predictive findings, but often results in *descriptive* research that describes or explains rather than predicts behavior or opinions. On the other hand, it is virtually impossible for an experimental study not to aim at some level of prediction. Also important to keep in mind is that experimenters test theoretical ideas on relatively small groups of people. Unlike survey researchers, experimenters are not interested in making statistical estimates about large populations. Yet, as we will explain later on, the results of an experimental study can be generalized based on logical rather than statistical inferences. A final point of comparison between the two methods: Experiments are used far less often in mass communication research than surveys. About 30 to 34 percent of research studies published in major communication journals employ the survey method; only 9 to 13 percent are experiments.[1]

One might wonder how the complicated course of mass communication, which involves variance within every component of the process (channel, message, and audience), could be reduced to the required components of the controlled experiment. The logic of such reductionism is addressed first in this chapter, followed by experimental design matters, and practical information about procedures.

To illustrate the application of the method, let us begin with an example of a published experimental study by Franklin Gilliam and Shanto Iyengar.[2] As we have seen at

The first author would like to thank Annie Lang and Erik Bucy for their thoughtful suggestions on an earlier version of this chapter.

various points in this book, nothing can happen until a question presents itself. In this case, the question was: Do television viewers adopt the journalistic stereotype of criminals as predominantly African American as a filter for observing daily events? To investigate this question, the researchers first conducted a content analysis of local television news and established the presence of what they termed a "crime script" in which minorities are more likely than Caucasians to be depicted in the role of suspect. While important, this documentation of patterns in mass media content alone does not provide evidence of causal effects. The researchers therefore set out to test the impact of the "crime script" on viewer attitudes about crime suspects.

To isolate the phenomenon of interest, subjects were exposed to one of four different levels of the experimental manipulation. In the first condition subjects viewed a television news story in which the alleged perpetrator of a murder was an African American man. The second level of the experimental manipulation featured exactly the same news story except that the alleged perpetrator was a Caucasian man. The third experimental group viewed the same story but without information about the identity of the perpetrator. The fourth group of subjects comprised a control group—they did not view a crime news story. By introducing such distinct conditions, Gilliam and Iyengar were able to exercise an impressive level of control over the experiment. They kept all visual elements of the news stories constant while only varying the race or appearance of the alleged perpetrator in the first three conditions. Race in the news stories was varied by means of a "mug shot" of the perpetrator, which Gilliam and Iyengar digitally manipulated to change skin color. Thus the "African American" and "Caucasian" perpetrators featured in the stories were identical except for skin tone. In this way the researchers had reason to be confident that if there were differences in how subjects responded to the African American and Caucasian perpetrators, these differences would almost surely be the result of the perpetrator's race.

A cross-section of Los Angeles metropolitan area residents was recruited for the study through flyers and announcements in newsletters offering $15 for participation in media research. Upon arrival participants filled out a questionnaire gathering information about their demographic status. They then watched a 15-minute newscast with one version of the crime story inserted toward the middle of the newscast. In an attempt to overcome the artificiality of watching the news in a laboratory, the researchers provided a viewing room that was furnished casually and subjects were free to browse through newspapers and magazines, snack on cookies, and talk with other participants. After viewing the newscast, subjects completed a questionnaire probing their attitudes about crime and news as well as asking free recall questions about the crime story.

The results showed that subjects were generally accurate in recalling whether a perpetrator was present in the crime story. Yet, those in the African American perpetrator condition were significantly more accurate in recalling that a perpetrator was mentioned. Most striking is the finding that over 60 percent of subjects in the condition that did *not* feature a perpetrator reported that they could recall having seen one. In 70 percent of these cases, the nonexisting perpetrator was identified as African American. The researchers concluded that what they identified in their content analysis as the "crime script" creates specific expectations about crime, which motivates viewers to fill in the gaps when they don't have information about the perpetrator. These leaps of judgment involve inferences that mirror what television news has been shown to emphasize in crime reports, namely the portrayal of criminals as predominantly African American.

While certain aspects of this investigation could be criticized, most elements of a carefully controlled experiment are present. By taking measures immediately after the manipulation (the newscast) and by randomly assigning subjects to different treatment conditions (versions of the crime story), it was possible to say with some degree of certainty that the variation in the perpetrator's skin color must have caused the differences in subject responses. But what makes this a "controlled" experiment? In this case control was exercised through random assignment of subjects to different treatments, command over the environment in which the test was carried out, manipulation of the independent variables (skin color and presence of perpetrator), design of the testing instrument (the response questionnaire), and the use of a control group.

We note in passing that this is an **after-only** or posttest-only **design**. That is, no measures were taken before the manipulation as a basis for comparison with the measures taken after the manipulation. Subjects did provide demographic information about themselves before they were exposed to the newscasts but these responses were not used as a pretest of the independent variables. As we shall see, there are problems with after-only designs. In this case, though, the memory questions asked by Gilliam and Iyengar make sense only after the manipulation. Thus, there was no reason to employ a **before-after design**.

The experiment conducted by Gilliam and Iyengar was a *laboratory* experiment. In other words, it was conducted in a controlled environment. But we also make use of other, often somewhat less controlled, experimental designs, including the *field experiment*. The difference can crudely be described as a matter of locus. In the laboratory experiment, the investigation is carried out on the experimenter's own turf; the subjects come to the laboratory. In the field experiment, the experimenter goes to the subjects' turf. In general, the physical controls available in the laboratory are greater than those in the field. For that reason, statistical controls are often substituted for physical controls in the field. This chapter title refers to the *controlled* experiment and assumes that the quality of any experiment must be judged on whether the controls were adequate, not whether they were maintained in the laboratory.

Readers of Chapter 13 might ask how experimental research differs from *panel* studies, which survey the same subjects at two or more times. The difference lies in the manipulation. Panel studies are designed to identify trends. Whatever happens between survey 1 and survey 2 is eligible to be considered a potential "cause" of the differences observed. Consequently, panel studies can deal with causality only speculatively except where special conditions are met. When, in a now classic study, Tannenbaum and Greenberg[3] sought to test the effects of watching the 1960 presidential debates between candidates Kennedy and Nixon, they did not entirely control the manipulation (i.e., the first debate) but they knew the debate would take place. So they obtained attitude measures from a sample of voting age adults beforehand, exacted a pledge to view the first debate, and left with the respondents a questionnaire containing further items to be completed immediately after the debate. Their field experiment used a before-after design without a control group and was not a panel study. In their case, the intervention of a media event was what made the difference. Thus, the manipulation in this study was the debates. Due to the lack of controls, it may not qualify as a fully controlled experiment, but it does meet the criteria for a field experiment.

This introduction to the use of experiments to test mass communication hypotheses reveals some of the options in experimental design. These nuances will be examined throughout this chapter.

The Logic of the Controlled Experiment

When performed correctly, the controlled experiment tests cause-and-effect relationships within a setting that permits maximum control over extraneous variation. The procedure allows the experimenter to observe the effect of one or more variables on another in such a way as to demonstrate that no other variable could have produced the same effect. It is probably the most sophisticated means of testing causal propositions and, represented by the independent variable, particularly suits efforts to conduct research that puts theoretically grounded propositions to direct test. How such propositions are generated from theory and how measures stand for concepts are discussed in Chapter 8.

The simplest way to show the effect of one variable (called the independent variable) on another (called the dependent variable) is to measure an attribute at time 1, then introduce a manipulation, and then measure the same attribute at time 2. As we shall see, it is not always that simple; but for purposes of illustration, let us imagine testing the proposition that the more a persuasive message arouses fear, the less effective it will be persuasively. The manipulation in this case will be the level of fear (low, medium, and high) contained in the message. "Manipulation" may sound chiropractic, but actually it is a crucial feature of the controlled experiment. The dependent variable, persuasion, will be measured by a set of attitudes toward something. In this case, let us imagine it is strength of belief that speed is the principal cause of death on highways.

To control for individual variation we will randomly assign subjects to treatments so that each subject has an equal chance of receiving one of the three message versions (high, medium, or low fear content). Ideally, the experimenter should make the verbal message identical in all treatments to hold it constant and introduce fear in another way, for example, showing graphic visual images. Take note that the visual fear induction is the manipulation, not the verbally persuasive message that is constant in low, medium, and high fear conditions. Subjects will first be tested for agreement with the statement that speed is the principal cause of death on highways, then exposed to one of the persuasive conditions (low, medium, or high level of fear appeal) and then tested again for agreement with the statement that speed is the principal cause of death on highways.

Inferring Cause

How does an experiment permit us to infer a causal connection between independent and dependent variables? In other words, how can we be sure that the independent variable (varying levels of fear in a persuasive message) caused the dependent variable (persuasion) to appear or change? Common sense would suggest that we search for a single cause for each single event and, when we find it, we can say A causes B or high levels of fear make persuasive messages less persuasive. But scientific endeavor does not assume single causes. Indeed, it searches for the *conditions* under which a particular phenomenon may be expected to occur. We say, "may be expected" deliberately; in the social sciences we demonstrate the *probability* that a phenomenon will occur under certain conditions. We search for invariance or uniformity in behavior, but what we find are never certainties. Invariance is demonstrated in probability terms. When a set of conditions consistently (i.e., with a high degree of probability) produces the predicted results, we show that such a relationship, while not absolute, could not have been accounted for by chance. The best predictor variables are the ones that account for more variance in the dependent variable than any other set of predictors.

Instead of seeking *causes*, we search for necessary and sufficient conditions for particular behavior or phenomena to occur. If B can occur only in the presence of A, then A is a necessary condition of B. If B occurs whenever A is present, A is both a necessary and a sufficient condition of B. Causality cannot be demonstrated without (1) concomitant variation and (2) precedence or time order. Concomitant variation means that B varies consistently with A. That is what correlation demonstrates. But in showing concomitant variation, we are only showing that two variables vary together. We need more: Does change in A *precede* a change in B? When A and B vary together, and A precedes B in time (and the reverse is not also true), we have a basis for saying that A is causally related to B. Then, if we can be sure that A and only A produces B, we may say that B is caused by A. In social science it is often difficult to claim that A is the *sole* cause of B but it is important to rule out, as much as possible, any outside influences other than A that might cause the change in B.

This issue is further discussed in the following section. To summarize, there are three conditions necessary to infer causal relationships between variables:

- Cause precedes effect in time.
- Covariation between variables: Change in one correlates with the other.
- There is a high level of probability that nothing but the independent variable explains the change in the dependent variable because other possible causes have been controlled.

Control

At the heart of an experiment's effectiveness for discovering causal relationships is control over the order of events. But in demonstrating *a* causal relationship, we have not shown that the independent variable is *the* cause of the dependent variable. Other variables that share concomitant variation with the dependent variable when they precede it in time may also be shown to be causally related. For example, the pre-existing personal experience of a high-speed car accident might be causally related to the persuasiveness of a message, regardless of the level of fear appeal contained in the message. The goal becomes one of either showing that other explanations are spurious, for example that an extraneous variable's apparent causal relationship to the dependent variable arises out of its correlation with the independent variable, or seeking out the set of conditions that most consistently produces change in the dependent variable. If two independent variables together cause change in the dependent variable, we have a basis for a finding of multiple causality. The goal is then to detect what combination of conditions causes change in the dependent variable.

But just as we may search for multiple causes in the experimental setting, the experiment also permits us to control for extraneous or spurious variables. Control ideally means control over all other possible explanations. A well-designed experiment allows us to show that a set of conditions accounts for a large amount of the variance in the dependent variable and that no other causal agents could have accounted for that variance. In survey research we may be able to show that one variable is more strongly correlated with the dependent variable than are other variables in the survey. We may apply multiple regression, partial correlations, and other sophisticated multivariate techniques to investigate these relationships. But because all these variables occur and are measured together, we have no basis for inferring cause unless, in some way, we can show (or assume) that one preceded the other in time. An experiment must then be devised in a way to ensure that nothing but the independent variable or variables, or an interaction between them, could account for the behavior of the dependent variable, and partial and quasi-experiments may properly be called experiments only when they, too, meet these conditions.

Random Assignment to Experimental Conditions versus Random Sampling.   The controlled experiment conjures images of the aseptic confines of a white-walled laboratory. But whether within a research laboratory or in some real-life setting such as a community center, randomization is often the critical means of control. As discussed in Chapter 9, random samples are required for meeting assumptions of probability statistics. In survey research this means that if we were to conduct a test of a hypothesis using such statistics, we must draw a random sample of respondents.

Although experiments and surveys both rely centrally on the principles of probability theory (with random selection as a key ingredient), the application of random selection differs markedly between these two research methods. As discussed in Chapter 13, when random selection is imposed on a carefully defined universe for a survey, researchers are able to make inferences about what to expect if samples, drawn under identical rules, were endlessly repeated. The condition of random selection is critical to the use of probability-based statistics. Yet, in the laboratory we do not rely on random sampling of subjects from a defined universe. Researchers are not fooling themselves to reason that college sophomores, who often participate in experiments, are somehow a *random selection* from the human race. Instead, they are treated as *instances* of the human race. When sophomores are randomly assigned to treatment groups (e.g., low, medium, high levels of fear) all characteristics not involved in the comparison—characteristics that would affect the outcome—are controlled by random variation. This means that characteristics are allowed to vary within groups but are prevented by means of random assignment from varying between groups and becoming sources of unpredicted and uncontrolled variance in whatever is being predicted for the dependent variable.

This methodological procedure offers more insight into what we meant in the opening paragraphs of this chapter when we said that experiments are effective in testing causal relationships but not effective in making population estimates. If the goal is to estimate parameters in an adult population (as nationwide surveys allow), it would be foolish to sample college sophomores, obviously. But in the laboratory we are not estimating parameters in a defined population. Instead, our goal is to carry out controlled experiments that test for relationships between variables. Experiments produce subject responses to stimuli, and the insights derived from these responses are stable and generalizable under the conditions specified in the experimental design. In other words, what can be statistically inferred and generalized is that under the same experimental conditions the same cause will have the same effect. We cannot make statistically accurate generalizations of the findings to a larger population. Statistical generalization depends on random sampling that is typically not practiced in experimental research. Yet, that does not mean we are completely unable to make generalizations about experimental findings. In fact, by replicating experiments with different groups of subjects over time and finding the same results, experimental researchers are empowered to make nonstatistical generalizations, or logical inferences, about their findings.[4]

Because experimental researchers are usually less concerned about generalizing to large populations than survey researchers, *random sampling* from a population is not important to experimentalists. What is important is *random assignment* of subjects to experimental conditions.[5] In fact, random sampling from a population is often impractical and counterproductive to the goals of an experimental study. Consider a study testing the impact of public service announcements about condom use on subject attitudes about the practice of safe sex. First, unlike survey participants who could respond to a questionnaire via phone, the Internet, or by mail, interpersonal contact between experimental subjects and the experimenter is unavoidable. Experimenters administer subject exposure and responses to stimuli in a relatively controlled physical environment. This makes the possibility of drawing a random sample from a national population impractical. Second, even if a random national sample were practically feasible, the range in subject demography and behavior captured in such a sample might not serve the goal of the inquiry. Including subjects who are in monogamous relationships or perhaps in age groups associated with little sexual activity is clearly not a reliable way to test the effectiveness of a public service announcement in shaping attitudes about safe sex.

A more productive approach is to sacrifice sweeping generalizability empowered by random sampling and purposefully select subjects who are not in committed relationships and who are sexually active. In fact, what would be gained by generalizing the findings in this case to the entire U.S. population? The pressing question is if the public announcement has the potential to impact the spread of a deadly sexually transmitted disease among a specific group of sexually active people. This discussion of the trade-off between wholesale generalizability and sample relevancy further unpacks what we meant in the opening paragraphs of this chapter by arguing that experiments are quite potent in testing causal relationships but not in making large population estimates.

Random Order of Experimental Stimuli.   In addition to randomly assigning subjects to experimental conditions, experimenters also randomly order exposure to stimuli. Practically, this means that the series of media messages used as stimuli is organized into different sequences so that all subjects are not exposed to the stimuli in the same order. The specific goal of random order is to control for unknown consequences in the succession of tests and tasks in the experimental setting, namely primary and recency effects. Miller and Campbell[6] have demonstrated that when there is a time delay in measuring attitudes after exposure to two persuasive messages, the first message is generally more effective (primacy effect). Yet, the second message becomes more effective when there is a time delay between exposure to the two messages and the attitude measure is taken directly after the second message (recency effect). In this case the first message is forgotten while the second is still fresh in memory.

When ordering is arbitrary we can control for order effects by deliberate variation and randomization. For example, if subjects will be exposed to multiple television messages about speed-related accidents on highways, the experimenter could create at least two random orders of the messages. Half the subjects will view one order and the other half the other order, while making sure that who gets what order is determined purely on the basis of random assignment.

Purposive Sampling.   There are additional means of obtaining control over variables that may produce sources of uncontrolled variation. Often demographic differences, even when experimenters do not hypothesize differences, are controlled to avoid their becoming artifacts of the study (i.e., uncontrolled factors that may offer alternative explanations of the outcome). For example, say we are concerned about (but do not wish to vary deliberately) the possibility that gender may be a significant variable in a predicted result. **Purposive sampling** will give us an equal number of men and women from the subject pool. What remains important is that the women and men are *randomly assigned* to experimental groups.

In studies using schoolchildren, researchers often group them by grade so that early, middle, and later grades can be compared. But in combining, let us say, first, second, and third graders into the early treatment group, it would be desirable to purposefully select an even number of students from the three grades to represent the early treatment group.

It should be added that by purposefully controlling demographic variables in this way the ideal distribution is obtained for studying the effect of the variable because it is equally distributed within the subject pool. Which brings us to the next method of control.

Including a Source of Potentially Uncontrolled Variance as a Variable in the Experimental Design.   Another method of controlling the influence of variables is to treat them as explicit factors in the experimental design rather than controlling them. For example, the experimenter has the option to include gender as a factor in the experimental design. This enables observation of how gender might influence the dependent variables as well as interact with other independent variables in the study. This technique of control might make more sense after reading the section on factorial designs. Do take note, though, that adding a factor to a factorial experimental design complicates the design and generally requires collecting data from more subjects.

Validity

The unknown effect of pretreatment influences, the treatment itself, and dependent measures are potential threats to experimental validity. Campbell and Stanley[7] have listed twelve of them. The first six sources of invalidity impede on the soundness of the experiment, referred to as *internal* validity. Researchers have to assess if they have indeed measured what they intended or claimed to have measured. Thus, when a study has internal validity there is sufficient reason to argue that the changes in the dependent variable are due to the influence of the independent variable(s) and not some other extraneous influences. The last six items refer to *external* validity and pertain to whether the results of an otherwise valid experiment could be generalized (through logical inference) to human populations within the scope of the experimental design.

- *History* refers to uncontrolled events occurring between initial and posttreatment measurements. This is a problem particularly in conducting field experiments.
- *Maturation* is what happens to a subject, group, or community as a direct consequence of the passage of time that influences the study outcome without the researcher's knowledge or intention.
- *Testing* subjects before and after exposure to a treatment could have an unintended and undesirable impact on the dependent variable. For example, the effect of a pretest on the scores of the subsequent posttest is a concern in studies where memory is measured, especially when the same questions are used in the pretest and posttest.
- *Instrumentation* pertains to changes in either the technical instruments of measurement or the researcher conducting the experiment. When technically advanced equipment—such as physiology sensors or computer-controlled stimuli presentations—is used, there is the chance that equipment could become faulty over the course of data collection without the researcher's realizing it. This will introduce error variance into measuring the impact of independent variables and threatens validity. It is also quite likely that over time, the experimenter will change. Fatigue and bias, or even a more experienced outlook in conducting the experiment and making observations about subject behavior, could cause unintended variance. These inconsistencies in either equipment or researchers cause concern about experimental validity.
- *Statistical regression* of extreme scores toward the mean is a well-known concept to measurement specialists. In some experimental designs potential subjects are subjected to a pretest to help researchers identify a target subject group with extreme scores (either very good or bad) to participate in the experiment. Yet, chance factors play an important role in test taking that might artificially inflate or deflate a subject's performance. Because of chance the good or bad luck that might have played a role in the first test is not likely to be present in following tests and subjects will perform closer to their average capacity. Yet, the researcher might mistake the regression to the mean as the effect of the experimental treatment.
- *Bias in respondent selection* results when respondents are assigned to treatments or controls on any other basis than random assignment.
- *Experimental mortality*, or the loss of subjects on some basis other than random deletion, is often a problem in panel studies.
- *Interaction between maturation and selection factors* arises when, based on the selection of subject groups, subjects mature at different rates. Observed differences between the groups might then be attributed to this interaction between maturation and selection rather than exposure to the treatment. Comparing a group of freshman college students with high school graduates who are in their first-year of full-time employment clearly presents maturation differences. The changes that occur

in first-year college students might be very different from the transformation that takes place during the first year of full-time employment after high school. These two groups might appear quite comparable and homogeneous in that they both are comprised of, say, 19-year-old subjects who consume more than 7 hours of television per day. Yet, the maturation differences might account for more variance in dependent measures than the treatment.

- *Effects of testing*, both reactive and interactive, are potential threats to experimental validity. Reactive outcomes are effects on the dependent variable attributable to a premanipulation test; interactive effects relate to interactions between selection biases and the dependent variable. In these cases the testing or selection effects are said to "confound" the dependent variable, which means that the experimenter cannot know whether the results are the product of the predicted relationship or some uncontrolled cause.
- *Uncontrolled interaction between selection biases and the dependent variable* creates concern about validity. For example, failure to control gender differences in assigning subjects to treatments where gender is related to the behavior being predicted is likely to result in invalid findings.
- *Ecological validity* is threatened when the experimental arrangements are in some way unrelated to the general behavior being predicted. In some cases the laboratory situation is so complex or artificial that the results bear no similarity to the relationships the experimenter wishes to study.
- *Confounding caused by multiple treatments* can arise, of course, only in particular designs that call for more than one treatment for a subject or group and the effects of the first are not successfully erased.

Experimental Designs

This section will elaborate on key issues of experimental design. Three different types of designs will be discussed: "true" or classical designs, pre-experimental designs, and factorial designs. Before we get going on the discussion of experimental designs, it might be helpful to review five concepts central to most experimental designs:

- *Treatment.* This refers to the experimental stimuli that contain manipulations of the independent variable(s) of the study. The central goal of any experiment is to test the effect of a treatment on the dependent variables of the study.
- *Pretest.* This is a measurement of dependent variables administered before subjects receive a treatment.[8]
- *Posttest.* This is a measurement of dependent variables administered after subjects receive a treatment.
- *Experimental group.* The group of subjects who receive the experimental treatment.
- *Control group.* The group of subjects who do not receive an experimental treatment. Control groups are often subjected to pretests and posttests even though they don't receive the treatment, to act as a point of comparison.

"True" Experimental Designs

A true experiment is marked by certainty that the experimental treatment influenced subjects. In this way the experimenter is able to gather evidence that the experimental treatment, and nothing else, is responsible for change in the dependent variables of the investigation. The three most widely used experimental designs are the pretest-posttest design with control group, the posttest-only design with control group, and the pretest-posttest design with additional control groups to deal with the effects of testing.

In a nutshell, the **pretest-posttest design** *with control group* assigns subjects randomly to at least two groups, administers a pretest, exposes one but not the other group to an experimental manipulation (treatment), and then posttests both groups (see Figure 15.1).

The *posttest-only design with control group* randomly assigns subjects to an experimental group and a control group and tests both groups after the treatment but not before. Only the experimental group is subjected to the experimental manipulation (see Figure 15.2).

The *four-group pretest-posttest design with controls* combines the procedures of the pretest-posttest control group and posttest-only control group designs. Solomon[9] is often credited for creating this experimental design. Subjects are randomly assigned to four groups. Group 1 is tested before and after the manipulation. Group 2 is subjected to a pretest and posttest but receives no treatment. Group 3 is exposed to the experimental manipulation and posttested only. And Group 4 receives the same posttest as the other groups but is not subjected to either a pretest or the experimental manipulation (see Figure 15.3). This is the most elegant of the three most frequently used classical experimental designs because it provides evidence not only that the experimental group gained significantly more than did the control group (the one not manipulated) in whatever direction the theory predicted, but that this gain could not be accounted for by any interaction between pretest experience and the manipulation.

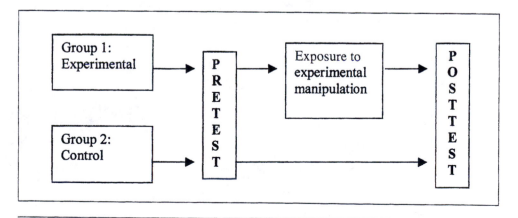

FIGURE 15.1.   Pretest-Posttest Design with Control Group.

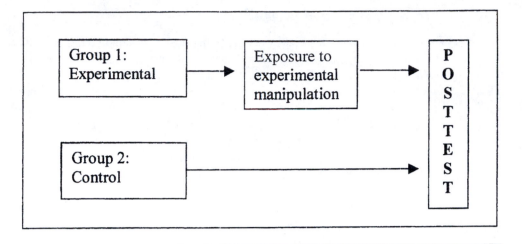

FIGURE 15.2.   Posttest-Only Design with Control Group.

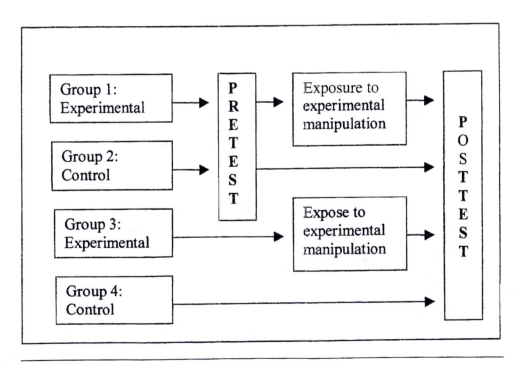

FIGURE 15.3.   Solomon Four-Group Pretest-Posttest Design.

Pre-Experimental Designs

Pre-experimental designs are alternatives to classical experimental designs in situations where laboratory control is not feasible. They differ most prominently from "true" or classical experimental designs in that subjects are not randomly assigned to experimental and/or control groups. It is important to note that pre-experimental designs are not fully reliable for detecting causal relationships. While some experimentalists recommend against their use, they are still employed, most commonly in evaluation research. In other words, rather than refraining from evaluating the effectiveness of, say, a media campaign to make women aware of the importance of mammograms, pre-experimental designs can be employed to form some evaluation of the campaign.

In the *one-shot case study* (Figure 15.4) no pretest is administered and control groups are not used. Random assignment of subjects to groups is irrelevant because there is only one group. Because pretests or control groups are not included in this procedure, the experimenter cannot be sure if the treatment is the cause of what is measured in dependent variables.

The *one-group pretest-posttest* (Figure 15.5) design is a slight improvement on the one-shot case study. As the term suggests, one group is subjected to a pretest and a posttest. Yet, the absence of a control group and random assignment of subjects keep the researcher from having certainty about causal relationships. Without a control group there is no way of knowing if something other than the treatment that might have occurred between the pretest and posttest is responsible for the change in the dependent variables.

The *static-group comparison* (Figure 15.6) design consists of two subject groups and a posttest. It lacks a pretest and subjects are not randomly assigned to the two groups. The first group is exposed to the experimental manipulation, then receives the posttest. The second (control) group receives the posttest without the manipulation. Because there is no random assignment and pretest, the experimenter cannot be certain that posttest differences between two groups are due to the treatment because the group differences could have existed prior to the treatment.

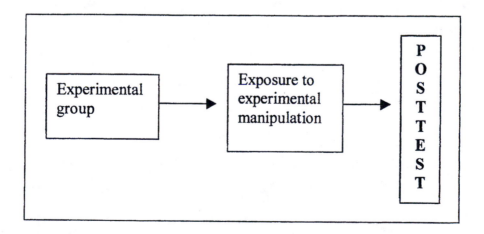

FIGURE 15.4. One-Shot Case Study.

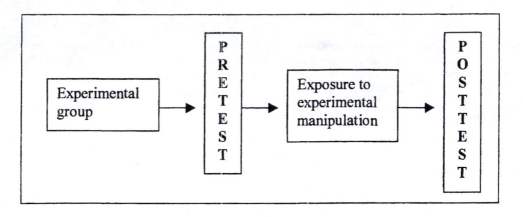

FIGURE 15.5.   One-Group Pretest-Posttest Design.

Factorial Designs

When a researcher is interested in investigating the simultaneous effects of more than one independent variable on dependent variables, a **factorial design** is necessary. Let us use a specific example to explain a number of issues related to factorial designs. Say a researcher is interested in knowing which specific mass communication channels (television, radio, newspaper, or World Wide Web) are most effective in conveying memorable news information to people in two different age groups (Generation Y versus early Baby Boomers). The independent variables, known as factors, are channel and age group; the dependent variable is likely to be some measure of memory.

The design for such a study will be described in a research report as a 4 × 2 (four-by-two) factorial design. The channel factor has four levels (television, radio, newspaper,

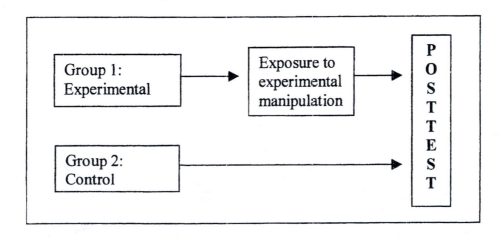

FIGURE 15.6.   Static-Group Comparison Design.

World Wide Web). The age factor has two levels: Generation Y (young people between 15 and 20) and early Baby Boomers (people in their fifties).

The treatment consists of the different combinations of the levels *within* each independent variable. In this case eight different treatment combinations or cells (literally, 4 channel levels x 2 age levels) will be considered during data analysis (see Figure 15.7).

Independent Variables

Characteristics. There are a few dichotomous characteristics associated with independent variables that influence experimental design decisions. Independent variables could either be discrete or continuous.[10] *Discrete* variables change in distinct categorical leaps. For example, in our sample study above, both the age and channel factors are discrete variables. Subjects are either Baby Boomers *or* part of Generation Y, and media channels are distinct: radio, television, newspaper, or the Web. Many demographic variables such as political party affiliation, gender, race, and marital status are discrete in that they contain distinct categorical subunits: Democrat, Republican, Reform Party, politically unaffiliated or male, female, transgendered, and so on. *Continuous* variables, on the other hand, change in steady increments on a continuum from high to low. For example, a television message could range from emotionally arousing to dull, or from emotionally positive to negative. In experimental research continuous independent variables are usually transformed into discrete variables with fixed subcategories. Indeed, the age factor in our sample study was operationalized to contain two categorical levels (Baby Boomer and Generation Y) instead of the natural

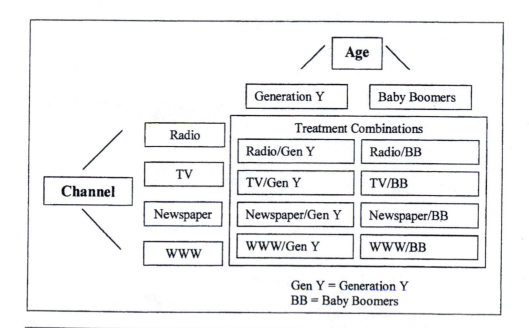

FIGURE 15.7. Factorial Design.

continuous range in age (e.g., 0 to 100). Experimental researchers do this because discrete independent variables are required for factorial designs. Every independent variable must have distinct levels that can be tabulated as shown in Figure 15.7.

Independent variables can be either internal or external to subjects. *Internal* variables originate from subject characteristics. Researchers cannot create these variables; they emerge from observations about subjects. In our hypothetical study of memory for news stories, the age factor is an example of a variable internal to subjects. Not all variables internal to subjects are easily observable. Cognitive and emotional dimensions such as sensation seeking, political sophistication, and fear of crime cannot be assessed based on the physical appearance of subjects. When cognitive or emotional attributes are used as independent variables, researchers must measure potential subjects' ranking on these variables to determine how much or little they have of these characteristics before selecting them to represent a specific level of an independent variable. *External* variables originate from things outside subjects. In mass communication research external variables usually comprise some dimensions of media messages that are manifested in stimuli subjects are exposed to. The media channel variable is an example of a factor external to subjects.

After deciding on the *experimental factors* (e.g., age and media channel), researchers also have to consider adding *control factors* to the design. Clearly, in the above example the two experimental variables, age and channel, are the two factors that drive this investigation. Their influence on memory is at the center of *theoretical* interest in our hypothetical study. On the other hand, control variables are *methodological* tools to improve the accuracy of observations about the experimental variables. Two control variables in particular could be added to most factorial designs as a check on systematic error. These two control variables are message repetition and order. These are also important issues to consider in other experimental and pre-experimental designs discussed earlier in this chapter. The following discussion focuses on how to implement control variables in factorial designs.

The *message repetition* factor refers to how many messages, or examples of the experimental manipulation, subjects ought to be exposed to. In other words, in our memory study, how many news stories should subjects view, read, and listen to in four different channels (radio, TV, newspaper, and WWW)? Related to this issue, should each story be presented in all four media channels or should different news stories be selected for each of the four media channels?

There are no quick answers to these questions. Stanford Professor Byron Reeves[11] points out that media messages rarely, if ever, exemplify only one thing. It is therefore virtually impossible to completely isolate the single feature of interest to a researcher in an experimental stimulus. At first, the implication of this insight appears devastating: the natural variation between media messages introduces severe threats to internal and external validity of experiments. Internal validity is compromised because we are unable to completely isolate the experimental manipulation, and this makes us unsure about which part of the media message is affecting the dependent variable. In the case of our sample study we have reason to question whether an uncontrolled message characteristic such as violent content, rather than media channel, might be responsible for affecting memory for news.

This dilemma offers a clue as to why it is more desirable to use the same story across versions. Put differently, it is preferable to use radio, television, newspaper, and Web versions of the same story—for example, a lawsuit about the patent for the drug Prozac. If we test the same message across media channels, natural variation between messages is less of a problem than when we test different messages across different media channels. Yet, it is not always possible to manipulate the same message to represent different versions of the independent variable. For example, we may not be able to find news reports of the Prozac story, or any other stories, in all four media channels. Even if we are able to find reports of the story in all four media channels, they may differ so substantially that we are not able to do what we set out to achieve: reduce variance across messages.

If we truly want to control natural variation between messages, the solution then seems to create four channel versions of the Prozac story, using exactly the same information and making the stories roughly equal in length. Even this apparent solution poses problems, specifically related to ecological validity. Broadcast writing differs dramatically from print writing. Thus do we take the newspaper story and add visual material to it to create the television story? Or do we take the television or radio story scripts to represent the newspaper story? After all, the four versions of the Prozac story should each be typical of the four different media channels that they represent if we want to be able to generalize our findings to radio, television, newspaper, and the Web.

In other studies, searching for or creating the same story across versions might not be an option. For example, if we want to compare the effects of "real" and fictional television violence on physiological arousal, it would be impossible to manipulate the same message to represent both fiction and nonfiction versions. Instead we might represent "real" violence by selecting material from Fox network shows such as "The World's Scariest Police Chases" and "When Animals Attack" and choose fictional violence from cop shows such as "NYPD Blue" or "Nash Bridges."

This discussion should reveal that often there are not clear-cut answers to design issues. That is precisely why the process of designing an experiment requires creativity combined with logical thinking and an understanding of the method. Our advice is thus to carefully contemplate the options and justify design decisions in the methods section of the research report—and be able to defend your decisions on scientific grounds.

Let us return to the discussion about the threats of natural message variance to experimental validity. We have just elaborated on the threats to internal validity. External validity in such situations is also compromised because variance between messages makes generalizability of findings difficult. Indeed, these threats to internal and external validity hold true if subjects are exposed to only one example of the experimental manipulation. If subjects are exposed to multiple messages, on the other hand, each containing some uncontrolled differences as well as the controlled experimental manipulation, the variance *between* messages is reduced to random error, which is less damaging than systematic error. Using multiple messages benefits experiments in which the same message is used across versions and when different messages are chosen to represent different versions of the independent variable. It cannot be emphasized enough that using multiple messages is key to rigorous experimental investigations of mass media effects. In fact, some experimentalists argue that we should be more concerned about sampling messages than subjects.[12]

The response, then, to the question about how many messages subjects should be exposed to is: as many good examples of the experimental manipulation as the researcher can find and the subjects can reasonably attend to. Typically, fatigue and boredom set in after about one hour of viewing and actively responding to dependent measures.[13]

In a factorial design multiple messages are treated as a control factor, usually referred to as the *message repetition factor*. In the case of our memory study, let us assume that after considering fatigue and availability of suitable messages, we select three different stories to represent each of the four levels of the independent variable, media channel. Thus the four channels will be represented by a total of twelve different stories, which will be collapsed (three per channel) during data analysis. Their impact—in combination with the other independent variables—will be investigated on the dependent variable. The previous experimental design for our hypothetical study only featured experimental factors. Now we will add the first control variable, message repetition, to the design: age (2) x channel (4) x message repetition (3).

The second control factor to consider is order. To assess the impact of primacy and recency effects as discussed earlier in this chapter, multiple experimental messages must be presented in a different sequence to different subjects. If we expose all subjects to the same order of experimental messages we cannot be certain that the independent variables, and not the sequence in which stories were viewed, is affecting the dependent variables. How many different message orders should be created? Again, there is no convenient formula to determine this, but clearly more than one order is necessary if we want to control order effects. Some researchers are comfortable using as many orders as the number of levels in the message repetition factor. Sometimes it is too expensive or practically impossible to meet that standard. How are the message sequences determined? Researchers typically use what is referred to as semi-random procedures to compile message sequences for each order. By semi-random we mean that rules are set to ensure the suitability of each order before standard random assignment procedures are followed. True random assignment often results in orders that resemble each other to a small degree, thereby introducing bias and diminishing the control over order effects. For example, two orders could have the same messages in positions three and four, which might create an uncontrolled primacy or recency effect in the experiment. If random procedures produce sequences that will not be effective in controlling order effects, sequences are purposefully altered to enhance control, making this a semi-random procedure. In the case of our memory study, let us assume we decided to create three (same number as the levels in the message repetition factor) message sequences. By including the order factor in the experimental design we could statistically assess order effects during data analysis. The full design with both control factors will look like this: age (2) x channel (4) x message repetition (3) x order (3). Subjects from both age groups will be randomly assigned to one of three stimuli orders. Figure 15.8 shows how three orders could be created in which the twelve stories are semi-randomly assigned. Note how each order has all twelve stories in unique sequences: (1) subjects will not be exposed to the same channel in two consecutive stories; (2) each order starts and finishes with different stories and different channels, and (3) looking across the order rows it is clear that stories are not duplicated in any position.

With the conceptualization of the independent variables for our memory study now completed, including the experimental and control factors, there is another design issue that deserves attention: who will receive what level(s) of the independent variable. The most typically considered options are between subjects, within subjects, and mixed experimental designs. Although experiments are often thought of as either between or within subject designs, mixed designs are quite common and often the only choice.

Order 1	Order 2	Order 3
WWW story 3	Radio story 1	TV story 2
Newspaper story 1	WWW story 2	Radio story 3
Radio story 2	Newspaper story 3	WWW story 2
TV story 1	WWW story 3	Newspaper story 3
WWW story 2	TV story 2	Radio story 1
TV story 3	Radio story 3	WWW story 1
Newspaper story 2	Newspaper story 1	TV story 3
WWW story 1	TV story 3	Newspaper story 1
Radio story 1	Newspaper story 2	Radio story 2
Newspaper story 3	TV story 1	WWW story 3
TV story 2	Radio story 2	Newspaper story 2
Radio story 3	WWW story 1	TV story 1

FIGURE 15.8. Example of Three Random Stimuli Orders.

Using the *between subjects* design, also called the *independent groups design* (Figure 15-9), subjects are assigned to different versions of the independent variables. In our memory study, Baby Boomers would be divided into four groups and each group would be exposed to only one of the media channels: radio, television, newspaper, or the World Wide Web. The same procedure would be followed for the Generation Y subjects. Thus, each subject would see three news stories in only one channel. Both the age and the channel factors are treated as between subject factors; in other words, they do not overlap or repeat for any subject.

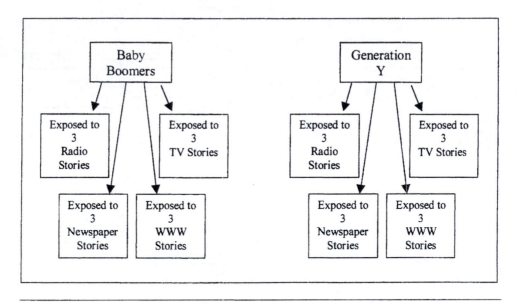

FIGURE 15.9.   Between Subjects Design.

Using **within subjects designs**, also known as *repeated measures designs*, the same group of subjects is exposed to all versions of the independent variable. In other words, the responses of the same group of subjects are measured repeatedly. Whereas the independent groups design compares separate experimental groups, the repeated measures design exposes all subjects to all levels of all independent variables. In this design each subject serves as his or her own control. Put differently, each subject is compared to him- or herself in the various experimental conditions. Yet, some variables simply cannot be tested using a within subjects design. Demographic variables, such as the age factor in our sample study, are good examples of variables that can only be investigated using between subject comparisons. The channel factor, on the other hand, could be subjected to either between or within design analyses. Clearly, in a repeated measures investigation of memory, subjects cannot respond to a test first as a Baby Boomer and then as a Generation Y member. On the other hand, subjects can respond to four different media channels in a repeated measures design. We can thus apply a repeated measure to the channel factor, but not the age factor, in our memory study by exposing subjects in the two different age groups (Baby Boomers and the Generation Y group) to the twelve news stories in all four media: radio, television, newspaper, and the World Wide Web. This combination of repeated and independent group measures is referred to as a *mixed design* (Figure 15.10).[14]

There are three benefits to using the within subjects design. First, this design requires fewer subjects than independent groups designs, which makes it ideal in situations where the subject pool is small or difficult to recruit. Second, using relatively few subjects makes within subjects studies more efficient and cost effective than between subjects designs. Third, within subjects designs are more sensitive than between subjects designs in detecting significant differences caused by the independent on dependent variables. By

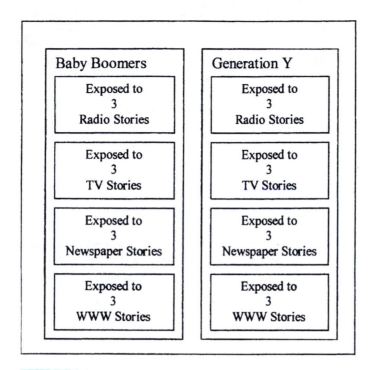

FIGURE 15.10.   A Mixed Design.

sensitive we mean there is less error variation in repeated measures designs. Consider the nature of the repeated measures design: The experimenter measures the impact of all the experimental conditions on *the same group of subjects*. In the independent groups design, researchers measure the impact of experimental conditions on *different groups of subjects*. Logically, there is more variation *between different people* than *within the same subjects*. Thus the repeated measures design has less error variation and is particularly useful in studies where the independent variables might have subtle or hard-to-observe effects on the dependent variables.

Yet, the repeated measures design is not always an appropriate choice. Repeated exposure to messages could produce sensitization effects that are especially problematic when memory measures are administered. Let us consider our hypothetical experiment again. If we had produced three news stories in four media channels instead of using twelve unique stories to present the four different media channel versions, subjects would have been repeatedly exposed to the same information presented in different channels. Being repeatedly exposed to the same experimental stimuli increases rehearsal of the information and is likely to improve memory. Thus a measurement of memory for news may not be attributed to the manipulation of the independent variable but rather to repeated exposure to the experimental stimuli.

With the knowledge of what between, within, and mixed designs entail, let us reconsider the status of each factor in our sample study: age (2) x channel (4) x message repetition (3) x order (3). Age is, and can only be, a between subjects factor because it is a variable internal to subjects. Channel is a within subjects factor in our sample study, but if the same stories were used across channels it is necessary that channel be a between subjects factor. In this way memory sensitization can be avoided. Message repetition is always a within subjects factor because it entails repeated exposure to messages that each exemplify levels of the experimental factors. Order is by definition a between subjects factor. Nothing could be gained by exposing the same subject to different orders of the same stimuli. Because we have both between and within subjects factors in our design, it is mixed. To summarize, statistical comparisons in mixed designs, and in particular the memory study, are simultaneously made:

- *Within subjects.* Each subject's memory scores will be compared within the story repetition (three levels) and channel (radio versus TV versus newspaper versus WWW) factors.
- *Between subjects.* Baby Boomer memory scores will be compared with scores from Generation Y. The three stimuli order groups will be compared to assess primacy and recency effects.

Effects.   The final dimension of independent variables that needs consideration is the effects they produce. Independent variables can either have a *main effect* or an *interaction effect* on the dependent variable. All the previously discussed single treatment nonfactorial designs result in main effects only—changes in the dependent variable caused by a single independent variable or treatment. Testing for main effects in a factorial design means that the impact of each independent variable on the dependent variable is tested separately. Let's consider main effects for the two independent variables (channel and age) on our hypothetical study. Testing for a *main effect for channel* will produce an answer to the question: "Did the four media channels produce significantly different memory scores?" The statistical procedure for this test will compare the memory scores of subjects across channels, collapsing the two levels (Baby Boomers and Generation Y) of the age factor. Figure 15.11 illustrates this idea of statistically collapsing the age factor temporarily to consider the unique effect of channel on memory scores.

Figure 15.12 reveals graphically what a main effect for channel in the example study might look like if illustrated in a bar chart. Recall of news in this hypothetical case is highest for newspaper stories, followed by the World Wide Web, television, and radio. The idea that there are differences between subjects in terms of age is not considered in this analysis. The focus is exclusively on the overall impact of the independent variable channel (radio, TV, newspaper, WWW) on the dependent variable, memory, regardless of subject age.

The next order of business is to see if there is a *main effect for age.* When memory test scores for Baby Boomers are compared to scores for Generation Y, this time collapsing across the channel factor, and a significant difference emerges, one could conclude that there is a main effect for age. Figure 15.13 illustrates graphically the nature of such a comparison: Age groups are compared on memory scores, this time collapsing the levels (radio, TV, newspaper, WWW) of channel.

Figure 15.14 graphically illustrates a main effect for age. In this example finding, overall, Baby Boomers were better at recalling news facts than Generation Y. This analy-

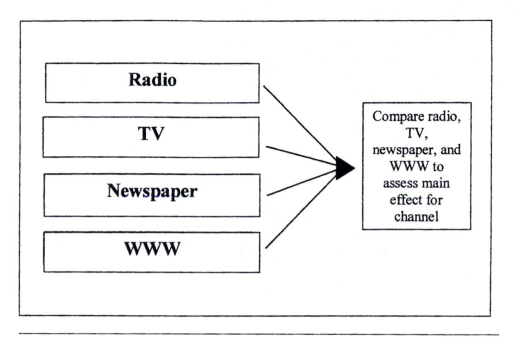

FIGURE 15.11.   Testing for a Main Effect for Channel.

sis assesses the unique impact of age on memory for news by collapsing the levels of the second independent variable, channel.

Unlike a main effect, where the impact of a single independent variable on the dependent variable is investigated, *interaction effects* come about when a combination of independent variables together affects the dependent variable. Thus levels of the independent variables *interact* with each other to produce an effect. For example, the effect of the independent variable age on memory for news could vary by levels of the other independent variable, media channel. In other words, an interaction in this case means that the direction and effect size of age on memory is altered by media channel. The procedure for testing an interaction effect considers all the levels of all independent variables of interest in the factorial design at the same time. In the case of our study on memory, four levels of the channel variable and two levels of the age variable will simultaneously be compared using the dependent variable, memory for news. It is not a procedure that invites a simple or effective graphic illustration. Perhaps it is best to pause for a second and imagine the cobweb of intercomparisons.

Let's assume that in the case of our example study, the experiment produced an interaction effect for age on the memory scores for the World Wide Web. How the illustration of the scores might look when plotted in a line graph is shown in Figure 15.15.

Figure 15.15 shows an interaction effect. In this case the direction of the influence of age on memory for news facts is different for different media. In particular, exposure to news on the WWW produced markedly different results for memory by age group than any of the other three media. The crossing of the line representing the WWW scores with the

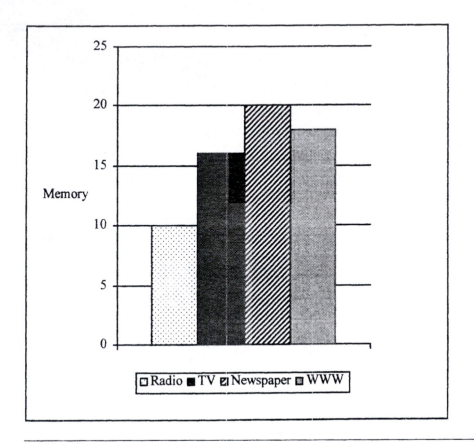

FIGURE 15.12.   Main Effect for Channel.

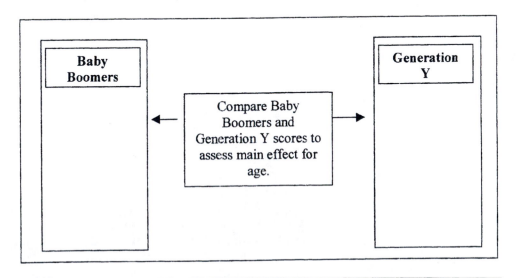

FIGURE 15.13.   Testing for a Main Effect for Age.

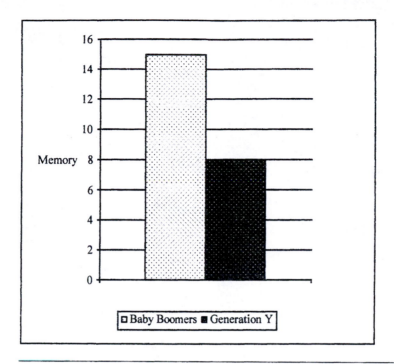

FIGURE 15.14.   Main Effect for Age.

lines for radio, TV, and newspaper indicates the interaction. When subjects watched news presented on the WWW, Generation Y was better in recalling facts (the dependent variable of interest) than Baby Boomers. At the same time, Baby Boomers were better at recalling information from the three other channels than Generation Y. This means that Baby Boomers had better memory for information that appeared on radio, TV, and in newspapers, whereas Generation Y had the highest memory scores for information that appeared on the Web. As a result, we can conclude that in this experimental setting the Web improved memory for news among Generation Y subjects.

It is possible to plot a statistically significant interaction and see lines converging, but not crossing. Figure 15.16 represents this phenomenon. The lines representing the levels of the channel factor do not cross, yet the lines are clearly approaching each other and extending them will eventually produce a crossing. It is also possible to plot the means of an interaction that is not statistically significant and observe crossed lines. Only the results of statistical tests (e.g. analysis of variance) can determine whether the interaction is *statistically significant*. The point here is to understand that plotting the means of the dependent and independent variables might not visually indicate the interaction or might suggest a statistically significant interaction where there is none. Yet, graphs do help researchers to see the *direction* of the significant interaction findings and are considered an essential part of the research report, as Chapter 17 points out.

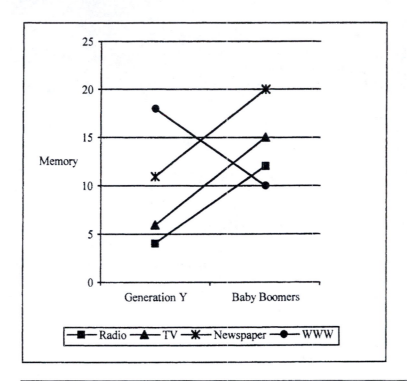

FIGURE 15.15.   Interaction Effect.

So far we have discussed main and interaction effects in terms of the two experimental factors, age and channel. There would be reason for concern if we found significant interaction effects for either of the two control variables, order and story repetition. If order has a significant interaction effect on either of the experimental variables, we have to assume that the order in which subjects viewed the stories is at least partially responsible for affecting memory for news. Significant interaction effects associated with the story repetition factor would suggest that the effects attributed to the independent variables differed for individual stories. Thus, while we would hope to see main and interaction effects associated with the experimental variables, there is some reason for concern when control variables produce significant interaction effects.

It is also important to consider the implication of significant main and interaction effects associated with experimental variables in one data set. Two main effects like those we have illustrated in the case of our sample study means that each independent variable, age and media channel, affects memory for news when collapsing across the other variable. The interaction finding means that the two independent variables change each other's impact on the dependent variable, memory for news. This interaction effect is quite different from the main effects that were illustrated for each independent variable separately. Also keep in mind that an interaction is not dependent on main effects or vice versa. In other words, a given data set might produce no main effects and a significant interaction; or no interaction but one or more significant main effects.

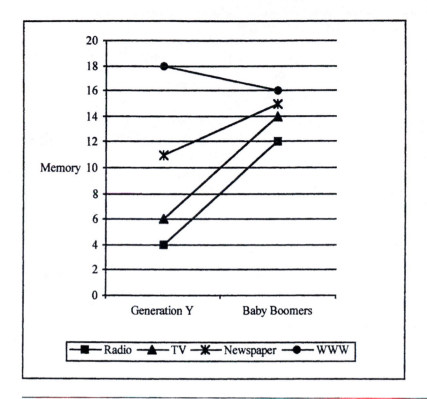

FIGURE 15.16. Interaction Effect Showing Converging, Not Crossed, Lines.

The influence of independent variables on a dependent variable revealed by a significant main effect versus an interaction effect has vastly different implications and should therefore be interpreted accordingly. When an interaction effect is *absent*, the main effect of each independent variable can be generalized across the levels of the other independent variable. Yet, when an interaction effect is *present*, main effects should be interpreted with caution. Let us turn to the hypothetical findings in our sample study. Say a significant interaction effect was found for age and channel on memory for news; Generation Y is best at remembering facts when exposed to WWW versions of news stores, whereas Baby Boomers have the worst memory for news when they get it from the Web. There is also a significant main effect for age; overall Baby Boomers have better memory for news than Generation Y. Thus the answer to a question about which age group performed the best in the news memory test is that it depends on which medium the two age groups were exposed to.

Practical Matters

The process of conducting experimental research cannot be condensed into a set of instructions to be followed in a linear fashion like a recipe for baking lemon meringue pies.

Yet, there are procedures common to every experiment and there is a logical flow to the steps taken to conduct experimental research. The following outline, presented in a suggested chronological order, offers guidelines for planning experimental research.

- *Formulate theoretically grounded research questions or hypotheses.* See Chapter 7 for a discussion of theory building.
- *Consider experimental design issues.* As discussed, the major options are between pre-experimental, true experimental, and factorial designs and a choice of between subjects, within subjects, or mixed designs.
- *Assess the potential for threats to internal and external validity.* Review discussion earlier in this chapter.
- *Operationalize independent variables and prepare stimulus manipulations.* Depending on the medium under study and the nature of the manipulation, experimenters have three basic options for creating stimuli: (1) with permission, existing professionally produced or published messages can be used; (2) existing media messages can be altered to contain the experimental manipulation; or (3) experimental stimuli can be created from scratch. The last option is clearly the most challenging and time consuming and probably poses the most serious threats to the ecological validity of experimental stimuli. Yet, creating your own stimuli gives you the most control over the experimental manipulation. Television news directors, newspaper editors, and webmasters are sometimes agreeable to providing material for academic studies. In some cases media producers are thrilled to have their messages experimentally tested on an audience. A valuable source of television news material (video material and scripted abstracts) is the Vanderbilt University Television News Archive (*www.tvnews.vanderbilt.edu/eveningnews.html*). The Archive began taping evening news broadcasts of the three major networks (ABC, CBS, and NBC) on August 5, 1968.
- *Operationalize dependent measures.* Although Likert or **semantic differential** items, traditional to survey research, are often used as evaluative measures in experiments, there are a number of other, less traditional measures available to experimenters. Consider for example the SAM (Self-Assessment Manikin) created by psychologist Peter Lang.[15] This pictorial scale is designed to measure three dimensions of emotion: valence, arousal, and dominance. A number of studies have validated the scale as a reliable measure of emotional responses to media fare.[16]

Thought-listing is a handy and perhaps underemployed dependent measure in mass communication studies.[17] Subjects are asked to report all their thoughts during or after performing a task. These open-ended comments help researchers gain insight into mental processes at work during the creation of meaning. Content analysis is then used to uncover patterns in subject responses. It is a time-consuming and labor-intensive measure but provides rich qualitative data that could provide insight into cognitive responses to media messages.[18]

Physiological measures are widely used in psychology experiments. A small contingent of mass communication scholars is employing this method of data collection. Heart rate and skin conductance are the two most common responses recorded during exposure to experimental stimuli. Heart rate is generally used as a measure of attention while skin conductance reflects the physiological arousal of subjects.[19] In the United States, there are currently at least seven physiology laboratories supervised by mass communication scholars. In addition, many psychology departments have physiology laboratories and are sometimes open to collaboration with mass communication scholars.

- *Specify the procedures for the experiment.* Part of maintaining control in an experiment involves effectively managing the data collection environment. If data are collected in multiple sessions, measures must be taken to ensure that all participants are subjected to exactly the same experimental procedures. The development of a detailed and often scripted protocol or series of explicit instructions is necessary. The protocol should include an extraordinary amount of detail, from very practical things like "Turn the lights on before subjects arrive" to exact scripted instructions for explaining different measures to subjects. Scripting instructions promotes consistency and is especially important when more than one experimenter contributes to data collection.

- *Obtain human subject's approval.* To protect the rights of people from whom data are collected, review committees ethically evaluate studies that involve the participation of human subjects. For experimental research, it is therefore necessary to submit information as stipulated by your research institution's human subjects review board or committee. A summary of the goals of the study and detailed descriptions of experimental procedures, as well as independent and dependent measures, are usually required. It is not uncommon for review committees to ask for clarification or revisions of experimental procedures. Most important, data should not be collected until official approval from your institution's human subjects committee has been secured.

- *Pretesting stimuli.* The experimental stimuli and dependent measures should be tested before data collection officially begins. By doing so a number of potential problems, such as unclear questionnaire items, not allowing enough time to respond to dependent measure items, and technological problems can be detected and resolved. A pretest can also be used to validate the experimental manipulation. For example, if experimental stimuli are designed to trigger emotional arousal in subjects, the pretest can give some indication of how effective the stimuli are.

- *Determine subject recruitment procedures.* Much of what we have learned about mass communication effects through experimental research is based on responses from undergraduate students. While some experimentalists are concerned about this convenience, others have defended the practice.[20] There are, of course, many alternatives to using undergraduate students in experiments. For example, researchers sometimes make donations to community organizations in return for members of the organization agreeing to participate in the study. Many universities have established adult subject pools, typically associated with research units within Psychology or Education departments. Moreover, paying a member of a target group (e.g., someone who is HIV positive) to help recruit subjects for a study on the effectiveness of an AIDS awareness information campaign is a creative alternative to using undergraduates enrolled in introductory mass communication classes.

- *Collect and analyze the data and write a research paper based on the findings.*

Examples of Experimental Research

Mastering the experimental method requires a combination of conceptual understanding and practice. Reading experimental studies and textbook chapters on this topic combined with a program of collaboration with experienced experimentalists would provide the groundwork for independent research. The published experimental studies cited in this chapter are all examples of rigorously conducted research. In addition, the following list of studies is recommended for further reference to advance an understanding of experimental research.

Joanne Cantor and Cynthia Hoffner, "Children's Fear Reactions to a Televised Film as a Function of Perceived Immediacy of Depicted Threat," *Journal of Broadcasting and Electronic Media* 34 (1990): 4, 421–442.

Joseph N. Cappella and Kathleen Hall Jamieson, "Broadcast Adwatch Effects: A Field Experiment," *Communication Research* 21 (1994): 3, 342–365.

Wolfgang Donsbach, Hans-Bernd Brosius, and Axel Mattenklott, "How Unique Is the Perspective of Television? A Field Experiment on the Perception of a Campaign Event by Participants and Television Viewers," *Political Communication* 10 (1993): 1, 37–53.

Dan G. Drew and Thomas Grimes , "Audio-Visual Redundancy and TV News Recall," *Communication Research* 14 (1987): 4, 452–461.

Doris A. Graber, "Seeing Is Remembering: How Visuals Contribute to Learning from Television News," *Journal of Communication* 40 (1990): 2, 134–155.

Albert C. Gunther and Esther Thorson, "Perceived Persuasive Effects of Product Commercials and Public Service Announcements: Third-Person Effects in New Domains," *Communication Research* 19 (1992): 5, 574–596.

Annie Lang, Shuhua Zhou, Nancy Schwartz, Paul D. Bolls, and Robert F. Potter, "The Effects of Edits on Arousal, Attention, and Memory for Television Messages: When an Edit Is an Edit Can an Edit Be Too Much?," *Journal of Broadcasting and Electronic Media* 44 (2000): 1, 94–109.

John E. Newhagen and Byron Reeves, "The Evening's Bad News: Effects of Compelling Negative Television News Images on Memory," *Journal of Communication* 42 (1992): 2, 25–41.

Karla Schweitzer, Dolf Zillmann, James B. Weaver, and Elizabeth S. Luttrell, "Perception of Threatening Events in the Emotional Aftermath of a Televised College Football Game," *Journal of Broadcasting and Electronic Media* 36 (1992): 1, 75–82.

Shyam S. Sundar, Sunetra Narayan, Rafael Obregon, and Charu Uppal, "Does Web Advertising Work? Memory for Print vs. Online Media," *Journalism and Mass Communication Quarterly* 75 (1998): 4, 822–835.

Endnotes

1. See Michel Dupagne, James W. Potter, and Roger Cooper, "A Content Analysis of Women's Published Mass Communication Research 1965–1989," *Journalism Quarterly* 70 (1993): 4, 815–823; Rasha Kamhawi and David Weaver, "Mass Communication Research Trends from 1980 to 1999," unpublished manuscript (2001).

2. Franklin D. Gilliam and Shanto Iyengar, "Prime Suspects: The Influence of Local Television News on the Viewing Public," *American Journal of Political Science* 44 (2000): 3, 560–573.

3. Reported in Sidney Kraus, ed., *The Great Debates* (Bloomington: Indiana University Press, 1962).

4. See Annie Lang, "The Logic of Using Inferential Statistics with Experimental Data from Nonprobability Samples: Inspired by Cooper, Dupagne, Potter, and Sparks," *Journal of Broadcasting and Electronic Media* 40 (1996): 422–430.

5. For more information on this debate, see Leonard Berkowitz and Edward Donnerstein, "External Validity Is More Than Skin Deep: Some Answers to Criticisms of Laboratory Experiments," *American Psychologist* 37 (1982): 3, 245–257; Joseph E. McGrath and David Brinberg, "External Validity and the Research Process: A Comment on the Calder/Lynch Dialogue," *Journal of Consumer Research* 10 (1983): 1, 115–124; John G. Lynch, "The Role of External Validity in Theoretical Research," *Journal of Consumer Research* 10 (1983): 1, 109–111; Douglas G. Mook, "The Myth of External Validity," in Leonard W. Poon and David C. Rubin eds., *Everyday Cognition in Adulthood and Late Life* (New York: Cambridge University Press, 1989), 25–43; Douglas G Mook, "In Defense of External Invalidity," *American Psychologist* 38 (1983): 4, 379–387.

6. Norman Miller and Donald T. Campbell, "Recency and Primacy in Persuasion as a Function of the Timing of Speeches and Measurements," *Journal of Abnormal and Social Psychology* 59 (1959): 1–9.

7. Donald T. Campbell and Julian C. Stanley, *Experimental and Quasi-Experimental Designs for Research* (Chicago: Rand McNally & Co., 1962).

8. Pretest also refers to the validation check of the experimental stimuli *before* the study is conducted. The data collected are used only to assess if experimental procedures and stimuli are practically working the way they were intended to.

9. Richard L. Solomon, "An Extension of Control Group Design," *Psychological Bulletin* 46 (1949): 137–150.

10. For more discussion of this issue, see Mary John Smith, *Contemporary Communication Research Methods* (Belmont, CA: Wadsworth, 1988), 198–199.

11. Byron Reeves and Seth Geiger, "Designing Experiments That Assess Psychological Responses to Media Messages," in Annie Lang, ed., *Measuring Psychological Responses to Media Messages* (Hillsdale, NJ: Lawrence Erlbaum, 1994), 165–180.

12. Ibid.

13. For a more detailed discussion of these issues, consult Byron Reeves and Seth Geiger, *op. cit.*

14. See also fractional designs: B. J. Winer, Donald R. Brown, and Kenneth M. Michels, *Statistical Principles in Experimental Design* (New York: McGraw-Hill, 1991).

15. Margaret M. Bradley and Peter J. Lang, "Measuring Emotion: The Self-Assessment Manikin and the Semantic Differential," *Journal of Behavior Therapy and Experimental Psychiatry* 25 (1994): 1, 49–59.

16. See Annie Lang, Kuljinder Dhillon, and Qingwen Dong, "The Effects of Emotional Arousal and Valence on Television Viewers' Cognitive Capacity and Memory," *Journal of Broadcasting and Electronic Media* 39 (1995): 3, 313–327; Jon D. Morris, "Observations: SAM: The Self-Assessment Manikin: An Efficient Cross-Cultural Measurement of Emotional Response," *Journal of Advertising Research* 35 (1995): 6, 63–68.

17. See, for example, Erik P. Bucy and John E. Newhagen, "The Emotional Appropriateness Heuristic: Processing Televised Presidential Reactions to the News," *Journal of Communication* 49 (1999): 4, 59–79.

18. For more detail, see Michael Shapiro, "Think-Aloud and Thought-List Procedures in Investigating Mental Processes," in Annie Lang, ed., *Measuring Psychological Responses to Media Messages* (Hillsdale, NJ: Lawrence Erlbaum, 1994), 1–14.

19. See, for example, Annie Lang, Shuhua Zhou, Nancy Schwartz, Paul D. Bolls, and Robert F. Potter, "The Effects of Edits on Arousal, Attention, and Memory for Television Messages," *Journal of Broadcasting and Electronic Media* 44 (2000): 1, 94–109; Daniel Linz, Edward Donnerstein, and Steven M. Adams, "Physiological Desensitization and Judgments about Female Victims of Violence," *Human*

Communication Research 15 (1989): 4, 509–522; Matthew Lombard, Robert D. Reich, Maria Elizabeth Grabe, Cheryl Campanella Bracken, and Theresa Bolmarcich Ditton, "Presence and Television: The Role of Screen Size," *Human Communication Research* 26 (2000): 1, 75–98; Glenn G. Sparks, Marianne Pellechia, and Chris Irvine, "The Repressive Coping Style and Fright Reactions to Mass Media," *Communication Research* 26 (1999): 2, 176–192; Dolf Zillmann, Jennings Bryant, and Rodney A. Carveth, "The Effect of Erotica Featuring Sadomasochism and Bestiality on Motivated Intermale Aggression," *Personality and Social Psychology Bulletin* 7 (1981): 1, 153–159.

20. See, for example, Michael E. Gordon, L. Allen Slade, Neal Schmitt, "Student Guinea Pigs: Porcine Predictors and Particularistic Phenomena," *Academy of Management Review* 12 (1987): 1, 160–163; Robert Plutchik, *Foundations of Experimental Research* (New York: Harper and Row, 1983); L. Allen Slade; Michael E. Gordon, "On the Virtues of Laboratory Babies and Student Bath Water: A Reply to Dobbins, Lane, and Steiner," *Journal of Organizational Behavior* 9 (1988): 4, 373–378; Alvin Y. Wang and Florian G. Jentsch, "Point-of-Time Effects across the Semester: Is There a Sampling Bias?," *Journal of Psychology* 132 (1998): 2, 211–219.

16

Ethical Issues in Conducting Mass Communication Research

Bradley S. Greenberg

Matthew S. Eastin

Gina M. Garramone

With its emphasis on objectivity and empirical facts, mass communication research might seem limited in its ethical implications. Yet the study of mass communication involves people as researchers, respondents, and interested observers—people whose interactions are not always morally neutral. The purpose of this chapter is to sensitize the reader to ethical issues evolving from these interactions and to provide resources for the reader's personal resolution of such issues.[1]

The chapter is organized into four main sections. The first examines the nature, significance, and origin of ethical dilemmas confronting mass communication researchers. The second section focuses on the ethical issues arising from human subjects research—specifically, informed consent and privacy—and the third introduces various strategies for resolving these issues. The final section discusses researchers' responsibilities to the society that supports and is influenced by their efforts.

This is now the third version of this chapter. Each version has added another co-author and additional dilemmas. This revision is no exception. It pays special attention to a source of ethical dilemmas that did not exist (or was not being used) at the time of the earlier versions. Today's fastest growing database for "mass" communication researchers is online data gathering. Access to the Internet, its users, and their messages exacerbate the ethical issues originally posed in this chapter. At the same time, online data gathering poses some altogether new issues for discussion. A fundamental difficulty with doing research online is, at this time, a complete lack of professional and scientific guidelines. Therefore, we do some abstraction from guidelines in place before online research became fashionable in order to help readers make sound judgments about their research behaviors.

Ethical consideration of research issues vis-à-vis the Internet has not received consideration commensurate with the research being conducted. While such groups as the American Psychological Association are considering guidelines, no currently accredited guidelines exist for conducting online research. Each area of ethical concern in research discussed in this chapter applies to online research. Each—confidentiality, deception, debriefing, and privacy—will be examined to the extent that online research poses ethical questions. Further, recommendations will be offered as to methods researchers may use to safeguard the integrity of their online research. Albeit a brief addition to this chapter, it likely will become a major component of concern to researchers whose primary medium of study is online communication.

Ethical Dilemmas

To better understand the nature of the ethical dilemmas confronting mass communication researchers, consider the following hypothetical research situations and the types of ethical questions these situations may elicit.

1. A researcher interested in the effects of news proximity on editorial treatment randomly assigned his editing students to read one of two versions of newswire material and to prepare a front page from the material. One version included a story reporting a toxic chemical spill in a nearby community; the other version reported a spill as occurring in a community in another state. To increase the realism of the manipulation, the students were intentionally misled to believe that the newswire material had been taken from the school's UP1 hookup only moments earlier.

Did the students give their informed consent to participate in the study? Were they debriefed following participation regarding the fabricated nature of the spill story? Even if debriefed, is such deception ethical? What does lying to subjects do to the professional image of mass communication scientists? How will it affect the subjects the next time they find themselves in a research situation?

2. For her senior thesis, a public relations student decided to conduct a participant observation study of the PR function within a local nonprofit organization. She obtained a summer internship with the organization and collected her data by covertly observing the behavior of the organization members.

By observing the organization covertly, did the student violate the privacy of its members? May social scientists go digging wherever they wish and in whatever fashion? Since the members were unaware of the study, how could they consent to participate? Is their consent necessary if the risks to them are minimal?

3. Prompted by news stories describing the impact of AIDS on the entertainment and fashion industries, a researcher conducted a mail survey of all creatives (i.e., writers, artists, etc.) employed by the twenty largest U.S. advertising agencies.

The questionnaire, which was to be returned anonymously, included items regarding the respondent's health, sexual preferences, and sexual practices. The aggregate findings of the survey were reported in an academic journal and later picked up by the advertising trade press. The ensuing publicity caused many respondents to experience suspicion and alienation from their colleagues.

Are questions inquiring about another's sexual behavior an invasion of privacy? Although the respondents' individual identities were indeed anonymous, the researcher identified the population of the study. Is it the researcher's responsibility to maintain the confidentiality of both individual and aggregate responses?

4. A team of researchers was asked to evaluate the effectiveness of a government-funded health information bulletin. They found no significant differences between communities receiving the bulletin versus those not receiving it, but discovered that this was likely due to the government's poor distribution of the bulletin. Individuals who were exposed to the bulletin demonstrated both increased health-related knowledge and more healthful behavior as a result of their exposure. Although the researchers provided a full report of their findings to the government, the results were portrayed by the government as demonstrating that the bulletin had "no effects on knowledge or behaviors of the recipients" and were used as justification for canceling the program.

Are the researchers responsible for the misleading interpretation and subsequent effect of their data? Should they make a public statement to correct the misinterpretation? Is there anything they might have done to prevent such a misinterpretation from happening?

5. First graders in a government-sponsored research project were subjects for a television study. Permission to ask the youngsters to participate came from the school principal. The youngsters were asked, "Would you like to watch some television?"

Did the study involve informed consent from the first graders? Could there be? What child would reject the opportunity to watch television, particularly in the middle of the school day? Should consent have been obtained from the parents as well?

6. In an experiment investigating the effects of pornography on attitudes toward rape, subjects were randomly assigned to one of two conditions. In the first condition, they viewed six hours of pornographic films; in the second condition, they viewed six hours of nonerotic films. Several weeks after the exposure treatment, the subjects were surveyed as to their attitudes toward rape.

If the experimental treatment *did* affect the subjects' attitudes toward rape—for example, make them more callous regarding violence toward women—then didn't the manipulation itself have a harmful effect on society? Was any attempt made to restore the subjects' pre-experimental attitudes? If so, how do we know that the debriefing was successful?

7. The researcher entered fourteen different chat rooms on the Internet, posing as a woman in seven of them, posing as a man in seven, and offering identical messages on the topic under discussion in all instances. The researcher recorded the responses of other participants in the chat room to the messages in order to examine gender bias.

Is the on-line researcher obligated to inform those he is studying that he is studying them? That he is deceiving at least half of them as to his gender? That he is deceiving all of them as to the purpose of his presence? This example could exist in a laboratory situation as well, but the opportunity (and inclination?) for deception is so much easier to implement online that it merits additional consideration in this context.

Hypothetical examples? Yes, but not without real-life counterparts. Enough to make the issue significant? Consider this exchange between Gross[2] and Zillman and Bryant[3] about the incidence and reporting of subject debriefing practices. Gross chastised his colleagues for failing to report subject debriefing in their study[4] concerning pornography and rape:

> I would fault them for not discussing this crucial component of their experimental procedure if for no other reason than because failure to address ethical concerns makes such "glamorous experiments dangerous examples " for novice researchers to learn from.[5]

Zillman and Bryant answered that:

> Debriefing is so obviously a part of experimental procedure that it is mostly indicated as having occurred; at times, it is merely implied. Moreover, our accuser must have known that research procedures have to be approved by some form of human-subjects committee and that careful debriefing is a requirement imposed by such committees.[6]

Perhaps there is a high degree of consensus among researchers regarding the appropriate procedures for conducting ethical research. Or perhaps external control mechanisms—such as institutional review boards or human subjects committees—guarantee that the proper procedures are used. Yet, before dismissing the issue as insignificant, consider the results of a survey investigating the frequency with which specific informed consent and privacy protection procedures are used by mass communication researchers.[7]

Contrary to what one might expect from Zillman and Bryant's argument, subject debriefing practices are not universal among the researchers surveyed: 71 percent of the researchers indicated that they "usually" debrief subjects, 19 percent "sometimes," 8 percent "rarely," and 2 percent "never." And while oral debriefing would seem necessary to assess subject understanding of any explanation provided, only 68 percent of the researchers indicated that they "usually" debrief orally, while 54 percent indicated that they either "usually" or "sometimes" debrief by providing a handout explaining the project.

There was also considerable variation in the information typically provided experimental subjects. Only 31 percent of the researchers indicated that they "usually" tell subjects the experiment's purpose (38 percent "sometimes" do, 20 percent "rarely," 11 percent "never"). While 58 percent "usually" disclose experimental procedures, 23 percent "sometimes" do, 11 percent "rarely," and 8 percent "never." Only 65 percent "usually" tell subjects that they may discontinue participation at any time, 16 percent "sometimes" do, and 13 percent "rarely."

There was greater consistency in the information typically provided survey participants. The most frequently provided information is a confidentiality guarantee (96 percent indicated they "usually" provide this information) and the identity of the research organization (92 percent indicated "usually"). The research topic is "usually" provided by 72 percent of the researchers, "sometimes" by 21 percent. Only 66 percent "usually" tell survey participants that participation is voluntary, 14 percent "sometimes" do, 13 percent "rarely," and 7 percent "never." The length of the survey is "usually" provided by 61 percent, "sometimes" by 30 percent.

A fourth set of items concerned specific steps researchers may take to protect the privacy of their subjects. Most researchers claimed to train interviewers and others with access to participant identification in their ethical responsibilities (84 percent "usually" do; 10 percent "sometimes"). Many remove all names and addresses from questionnaires as soon as possible (71 percent "usually" do; 15 percent "sometimes"). But fewer regularly tell subjects who will have access to the information they provide. Only half "usually" provide subjects such information; one-fourth "sometimes" do.

As a whole, the survey results indicate that while some informed consent and privacy protection procedures are used regularly by the majority of the researchers surveyed, many procedures are used less consistently. Whether any of these specific procedures is essential to obtaining informed consent or privacy protection is, of course, open to debate. But the lack of uniformity in their use suggests that the issue of appropriate procedures for conducting research is not a trivial one.

The fact that mass communication researchers may find themselves facing ethical dilemmas does not make them evil persons. In social science research, most ethical dilemmas arise not because of bad faith on the part of anyone, but because certain conflicts of legitimate interest are inherent in the research context.[8] These conflicts of interest may involve opposing individual rights such as the scientist's right to conduct research versus the subject's right to privacy. Or the conflicts may pit individual rights against benefits for society such as the individual's right to freedom from the risk of harm versus the potential for diminishing some social ill. Some critics suggest that with the proliferation of governmental and institutional requirements designed to protect the rights of human subjects, researchers may find their role as social benefactors threatened with extinction.[9] This perception of a conflict between individuals' rights and potential benefits for society is evident in Zillman and Bryant's response to criticisms of their pornography research:

> The reader should realize that a simplistic moral premise like "nobody may be placed at risk for any purpose" is unworkable. Such a formula protects the human subject far more than the citizen. Under these conditions, social science research cannot protect the citizen. The stronger protection of the subject actually prevents socially significant research that would benefit the citizen, at times through protection.[10]

The remainder of this chapter will explore in greater detail the types of dilemmas evolving from these conflicts.

Ethical Issues in Human Subjects Research

Mass communication research which involves observations of human beings must ensure that the rights of these human beings are not violated. But the fact that one individual's rights may conflict with those of another, and that an individual's rights may conflict with what is beneficial for society, suggests that it may not always be possible for the researcher to simultaneously respect all rights for all involved. Instead, it may be necessary to demonstrate that respect by asking research participants to forgo certain rights. The forgoing of one's rights is generally referred to as giving **informed consent**.[11]

Informed Consent

Four legal standards are involved in informed consent to participate in research: (1) the capacity to make a rational, mature decision; (2) information about what is to occur; (3) comprehension of the possible effects; and (4) freedom from coercion or undue pressure.[12]

While these standards may provide a useful guide to mass communication researchers, they leave many questions unanswered. In Hypothetical Research Situation 5, we faced the problem of obtaining informed consent from first graders. While we may agree that first graders do not have the capacity to make rational, mature decisions, we may disagree about seventh graders. And how much information are we obliged to provide about our study in order to solicit the cooperation of participants? One might give extensive detail regarding research procedures, but is such detail necessary for the participant to make an informed decision? Perhaps more important, how much information must the participant comprehend? The requirement for informing participants carries with it some responsibility for assessing whether that information has been understood. But how can we expect potential participants to comprehend the possible effects of our study when even we cannot anticipate all such possible effects?

Informed consent is compromised if the individual is coerced or pressured into participation. Do incentives constitute pressure? More and more, material rewards are being offered by researchers to obtain participation. It is argued that the participants' time is valuable and they should be compensated in some tangible fashion for their effort. This argument comes from an equity standpoint. Why should I take something from subjects and not give them something in return that is more tangible than the incentive in my motivating message to them? Can't the participation of students be rewarded by additional points toward a grade? Can't the participation of a Girl Scout organization be compensated for by contributing $50 for its next outing? But can there be informed consent where rewards are offered for participation? How will one know if participation is based on the size of the reward?

The issue of coercion also is raised because many data-gathering operations are done with groups of individuals for whom compliance is either explicit or implied. The college classroom is a prime example of a situation in which individuals are expected to provide consent; some classrooms go further and demand student participation. Isn't the student sitting there thinking, "If I don't participate in this study, my instructor will find out and I am going to suffer"? Furthermore, the pressure of peers participating can also yield a high degree of coercion. We probably overestimate the degree of voluntarism created in any intact group assembled in an authority-laden context. It is not only the teacher-student situation that carries this kind of burden. It is similar when soliciting data from employees on the job.

Compounding this is the extent to which consent is obtained from some authority figure almost as a substitute for consent being obtained from a participating individual. For example, if one is doing research with a Girl Scout organization, one solicits consent from the troop leader; and if one is doing research with public schools, one solicits consent from the school administration. Is this an acceptable substitute for individual consent or only a precursor for obtaining consent from individual participants or their guardians?

While such questions regarding informed consent may seem sufficiently troublesome, they pale by comparison to the internal and external validity problems arising from informed consent procedures. It is evident that providing subjects complete information about a research project can have a substantial effect on some phenomena.[13] For example, if participants are informed that they are in a study of verbal conditioning, the phenomenon itself disappears.[14] Consent procedures themselves may confound findings. Stressed subjects who are explicitly informed via consent forms of their freedom to withdraw from an experiment perform significantly better on cognitive tasks than do subjects not so informed.[15]

Informed consent procedures can affect generalizability by reducing the consent rate and biasing one's sample. For example, a request for signatures in face-to-face interviews produced a statistically significant reduction in consent rate.[16] In a study requiring the disclosure of sensitive lifestyle information, a limited waiver of confidentiality decreased volunteering. Furthermore, in three of eight comparisons of volunteers versus nonvolunteers, significant differences in social desirability and sensation seeking were observed.[17] In general, people who volunteer for experiments tend to be more intelligent, more sociable, and have more need for social approval than nonvolunteers.[18] While arguments can be made for informing subjects that they may withdraw from participation in research,[19] the inclusion of withdrawal-without-prejudice clauses can substantially reduce actual participation levels.[20] Consent rate and sample bias are also affected when parental consent is sought for student participation.[21]

Participation in international research offers additional hazards. Host countries may have no similar set of safeguards for human subjects and may not require informed consent or parent approval for minors to be studied. Does this obviate the need for the U.S. research partner to insist on safeguards that parallel those required at the U.S. institution?

In response to the validity threats associated with informed consent procedures, researchers have devised alternatives to informed consent.[22] One approach to circumventing the effect of subject knowledge on the study phenomenon is to deceive the subject about the real nature and purpose of the study. The ethical implications of that approach are discussed below. An alternative approach is to use individuals comparable to the participants to provide surrogate informed consent for the actual participants.[23] While some research indicates that such surrogates provide a generally reliable indication of actual participants' feelings,[24] other studies cast doubt upon such a tactic because the method used to obtain surrogate consent can have major effects on the surrogate's response.[25] Even if the surrogate approach were accurate, it still leaves unanswered the question of what percentage of the surrogates must approve a project before it is initiated.[26] Another alternative is role playing, in which subjects are presented with hypothetical situations and asked what they would do in such situations. However, a substantial amount of evidence suggests that role playing does not provide an adequate substitute for the reactions and behaviors of subjects in situations they have defined as real.[27]

Online Consent.   Survey research is currently the most common method used to conduct online research. Respondents are asked to answer questions primarily by (1) email, where they electronically complete the survey within the email, and by (2) webpage, where the participants are directed to a website to find the questionnaire.[28] Oral consent is not an option, but written and participatory consent are available. Written consent can be initiated by sending or posting a consent form asking participants to electronically respond that they understand the nature of the project and are willing to participate. An advantage of electronic consent is the ability to allow respondents to opt out of the study and thus not receive additional unwanted email. Consent also can be indicated by the respondent's willing and uncoerced completion of the questionnaire. Consent through participation does not confirm that the participant has read or understood the consent form, although we may be no more certain of this in traditional research settings.

Online instruments present a special problem for the researcher in terms of identity verification (e.g., age, gender, income). Because the Internet is an arena in which false identities are seemingly encouraged in some settings,[29] online researchers may be at greater risk of respondents pretending they are someone they are not. It may be no greater a threat than our assumptions as to who has completed a traditional mail questionnaire, but the point is that we do not yet know the likelihood of such pretenses. Thus, while the anonymity of the Internet can be advantageous to data collection, it may belabor the fundamental process of obtaining informed consent and valid responses. This problem has been aggravated by a recent Federal Trade Commission ruling that makes it illegal to collect data from under 13-year-olds without parental permission.[30] The law requires researchers to gain parental compliance prior to collecting any information from those children, something academic researchers have been obligated to do for decades. While the law appears to be aimed at providers of children's websites who rely on cookies to gather information, others may believe they are collecting data from adults in public domains, whereas they may unwittingly be collecting data from children posing as adults, given little if any opportunity to verify their age. (To date, no one has raised the question of adults posing as children!)

Deception

The problems with surrogate consent and role playing have led many researchers to rely upon deception as their primary alternative to informed consent.[31] An analysis of the use of deception in articles published in four leading social psychology journals between 1969 and 1979 found that more than half used some type of deception.[32] Yet the question of using deception in the conduct of experimental research runs smack into the notion of informed consent. These tend to be contradictory. How can you obtain informed consent when deception is used in an experiment? Actually, the question is too imprecise. It ought to be, "Can *fully informed consent* be obtained when deception is used in an experiment?" If you take the position that informed consent exists along a continuum from some information to complete information, then it is still possible to slip in deception at earlier points on that continuum than at the extreme of fully informed consent. Serious doubts have been raised about the use of deception in social research.[33] Some deception critics who are very active social scientists themselves have taken the strong position that all deception in research is wrong. Others maintain that it is a necessary tool for the conduct of some research and unnecessary for others. For example, was the deception in Hypothetical Research Situation 1 necessary to study the news proximity and editorial treatment variables? Typically, the use of deception in mass communication research focuses on whether it is more important to avoid deceiving anyone, or to deceive a small number of subjects temporarily, with the expectation that many persons will benefit from the knowledge gained.

Let us summarize the major arguments of those who oppose the use of deception:

1. Deception takes away the subject's freedom to make a fully informed decision about participating in a given experiment. Given the typical status of experimenters to the subjects, they are likely to obtain consent most of the time. Presumably not disclosing the deception to be involved in the experiment further enhances the experimenter's ability to obtain consent. What would be the consent rate if subjects were informed that they were about to be deceived and if the nature of the deception were disclosed?
2. The use of deception by social scientists institutionalizes deception. Using deception in social research transforms the subject into an object of manipulation, and that is demeaning to the person involved. The dignity of human relationships is being subordinated to the desires of the experimenter.
3. By using deception and contributing to the development of an expectation about deception in subjects, the subject has fewer qualms about deceiving the experimenter.
4. The public's attitude toward social science research will be diminished as the public becomes aware of the use of deception in such research.

The counterarguments, those that advocate the acceptance of deception as an appropriate research tool, also merit identification:

1. Deception has long been used as a research instrument without any apparent negative results.
2. Deception may be the only way to obtain valid information in certain situations.
3. Any potential harm will be offset by the contribution of the research results to the subject, to society, and/or to the scientific discipline.

In addition, deception often is used in situations in which the researcher wishes the subjects to engage in ethically questionable behavior, for example, lying, cheating, and aggression. It is problematic as to how to induce such antisocial responses in the absence of deception.

Gallo and others[34] assessed the effects of deception in a conformity experiment. In the full information condition, subjects were informed that the experiment was about conformity and that they would be tested to see the extent to which they did conform to the judgment of others. In another condition the conformity nature of the experiment was completely masked. The results indicated that subject knowledge about being in a conformity experiment did not decrease their conformity at all. The authors speculated that "This type of response indicates that psychologists are disbelieved even in those rare situations in which they are caught telling the truth."

In an experiment, the subjects themselves have a number of things at stake. They want to believe that their task performance is meaningful. Most are aware that they are only supposed to know as much about the experiment as they have been told and that internally hypothesizing about the study might disqualify them or invalidate their data. Strickler and others[35] suggest that this results in a "pact of ignorance" between the subject and the experimenter. The subjects do not confess that they have some strong guesses about what is going on. At the same time the researcher is not interested in finding out what portion of his or her data may be useless. Strickler[36] found that only 24 percent of all studies using deceit provided data on how much subject suspicion of deception there was. Subjects may frequently not be deceived but behave as if they were. And if the same subject pool is used repeatedly, subjects ought to become more test-wise.

There is also the concurrent problem that participation in deception research by subjects, whether with beforehand or post hoc knowledge about the deception, may result in less favorable attitudes toward the results of such research. Cook and others[37] found that subjects who had participated in five deception experiments had less favorable attitudes toward experimental research than those who had participated in a single deception experiment. However, Schwartz and Gottlieb[38] found that most participants in bystander experiments using deception viewed the research as ethically justified and found their experience both instructive and enjoyable.

Several scholars[39] have suggested guidelines for the use of deception in research. For example, Elms suggests that deception is justifiable in social scientific research:

> when (1) there is no other feasible way to obtain the desired information, (2) the likely benefits substantially outweigh the likely harms, (3) subjects are given the option to withdraw from participation at any time without penalty, (4) any physical or psychological harm to subjects is temporary, and (5) subjects are debriefed as to all substantial deceptions and the research procedures are made available for public review.[40]

Debriefing

Elms's recommendation that subjects be debriefed is also appropriate whenever subjects' perceptions or feelings about themselves or about others may have been altered by participation in a study. As an example of this latter situation, consider the pornography study of Zillman and Bryant.[41] Their subjects were randomly assigned to experimental conditions involving various levels of erotic film exposure. Several weeks after the exposure treatment, the subjects were asked, among other things, what sentence they would recommend for a convicted rapist. The researchers found that the "massive exposure" subjects recommended lighter sentences than other subjects. It appears, then, that participation in the study altered the subjects' feelings toward women as rape victims. If so, the researchers are obliged to attempt to return their subjects to their preparticipation state. This aspect of **debriefing** has been referred to as "desensitizing" the subjects.[42] When we have engaged in deception, debriefing becomes even more imperative and requires "dehoaxing" as well as desensitization. In dehoaxing, we inform the subject of the true nature of our procedures in order to eliminate the deception.[43] Thus, if we have deceived our subjects into believing that a newswire story regarding a toxic chemical spill is real, we reveal our deception to them.

Debriefing is a tool for limiting or eliminating the potential harms of both deceptive and nondeceptive research practices. But if debriefing is to fulfill these ethical obligations to human subjects, it must be effective and it may not be. Consider the study by Walster[44] and others that manipulated the perceived sociability of experimental subjects. Half were told they were very high on sociability and half were told they were very low. All were given a thorough individual debriefing. After the debriefing, those subjects who had been told that they were stronger in sociability continued to rate themselves significantly higher on the sociability index that those who received an unfavorable report. This debriefing obviously did not eliminate the effects of the manipulation. On the other hand, debriefing can be strikingly effective. Malamuth and Check[45] found that subjects exposed to pornographic rape depictions followed by a debriefing designed to dispel a number of rape myths were less accepting of certain rape myths than subjects exposed to mutually consenting intercourse depictions. The variable success of debriefing practices may be due to the fact that we know very little about how to create an effective debriefing. Although there has been an increase in recent years in the percentage of journal articles reporting debriefing,[46] the content and style of debriefing as an experimental procedure remain largely unexamined.

This ignorance leaves many unanswered questions regarding current debriefing practices. Must a debriefing be oral, or will a handout suffice? What if the handout is given to the class instructor to read? That person may be incapable of explaining beyond what it says on the handout or may fail to announce the information at all. How does one debrief young children, who may be incapable of understanding the debriefing message? May a group of subjects be debriefed orally en masse, or should debriefing be conducted on a one-to-one basis? What is the appropriate time to debrief? The most common debriefing time is immediately after participation as a research subject. However, it is not uncommon that debriefing be delayed until all subjects have participated in an experiment. Sometimes this may be weeks or months after a particular subject has participated. Can we trust subjects who are sworn to secrecy to keep that vow? Some evidence available suggests that subjects do remain still, and there is at least as much evidence that suggests they do not.

If the questions regarding the efficacy of specific debriefing practices are not sufficiently perplexing, add to them the proposition that debriefing may do more harm than good. Campbell suggests that there are arguments against debriefing:

> While debriefing has come to be a standard part of deception experiments in the laboratory, it has many ethical disadvantages. It is many times more a comfort to the experimenter for his pain at deceiving than to the respondent who may learn in the process of his own gullibility, conformity, cruelty, or bias. It provides modeling and publicity for deceit and thus serves to debase language for the respondent as well as for the experimenter. It reduces the credibility of the laboratory and undermines the utility of deceit in future experiments.[47]

It is a very interesting proposition to suggest that telling subjects what has been done to them may be more harmful than if they were not told. One can argue the merits of this proposition, but as yet no available evidence confirms or denies it. Consider this argument in the context of two experimental situations. In the first, you have identified and manipulated a group of subjects into believing that they are very popular with their classmates and have the potential for being even more popular. In the second, you have suggested to a group of young men that they have latent homosexual tendencies. Can one take the direction of the manipulation, place a value on it as socially constructive or socially destructive, and then determine where the debriefing will do more or less good?

But the uncertain effectiveness of debriefing practices and the chance that debriefing may do more harm than good should be weighed against the possible ethical advantages of debriefing outlined by Elms:[48]

1. It provides the occasion to diminish anxiety and other unpleasant emotional reactions and to give the subject a sense of the true value of his or her participation as a research subject.
2. It restores a sense of honesty to the researcher, and, by interrupting the role of archmanipulator, it brings him or her back toward the human level of the subjects.
3. It provides an ethical model to researchers, subjects, and others of how a necessary deception can be limited in its consequences and how deception can be used without destroying the integrity of human social contacts or the autonomy and self-esteem of the subjects.
4. It means that a researcher must at some point publicize his or her deceptive research procedures to the individuals most likely to be at risk as a result, namely the subjects, and must therefore be able to justify the deceptions to them or risk some kind of retaliation.

Online Debriefing.   Deception and debriefing in online studies are not as separable as they are in more traditional research venues. The major argument against deception in online studies is not different from "offline" studies—that deception negates the freedom to make an informed decision about participation. In traditional research settings, participants are usually debriefed immediately after their participation in order to repress or negate the effects of the deception. Debriefing online is more challenging.

To debrief online, the researcher can send email to each participant or post a webpage to convey information about the deception and the legitimate purpose of the study. From a researcher's perspective, the problems in debriefing in these ways involve data validity. Normally, instruments are posted for several days and samples are gathered from various discussion groups, chat rooms, and listservs. Often, these sites have rules that disapprove of such an intrusion into their online community. Thus, the researcher has to worry whether the true nature of the study is exposed before completing the data gathering and whether there will be a backlash from the online groups who may be annoyed from receiving unsolicited emails. If the latter, the researcher risks the possibility of online retaliation tactics. These include flame email (an email message in which the writer attacks another participant in very harsh and often personal terms) and screaming (sending an unmanageable amount of email) in an attempt to hack into and disable the server.[49] Furthermore, since these online community members are networked among each other, any early participant in the study could inform others as to the study's content, placing all data gathered in jeopardy.

Privacy

Privacy has been defined as "the freedom of the individual to pick and choose for himself the time and circumstances under which, and most importantly, the extent to which, his attitudes, beliefs, behavior and opinions are to be shared with or withheld from others."[50] The very nature of social science research, with its focus on personal information, threatens privacy.[51]

Privacy issues may be placed into two broad categories of concern: the effects of data collection per se and the possible effects of the disclosure of these data. Some data collection methods themselves may be considered invasions of privacy. Consider the form of data collection known as *participant observation*, illustrated in Hypothetical Research Situation 2. There are classic studies in which investigators have become members of such social groupings as religious cults, political organizations, and campus organizations wherein their primary purpose was to observe the behavior of nonresearch members and to come away from that setting with sufficient information to prepare a report. This form of data collection, seldom questioned before, now merits concern. Certainly, it is a method in which investigators have neither revealed their true purpose for their presence nor informed anyone within those organizations that they are there for a primary purpose different from those of the organizations. This makes for a confounding of both deception and privacy issues. Further, an investigator's information may clearly identify particular individuals being observed. A less blatant example would consist of telephone requests for information from an organization whose mission requires providing that information. These might be telephone calls to the Internal Revenue Service, local crisis centers, or to the local newspaper where the research is to determine the reliability of information being offered over a period of time. This form of nonobtrusive data collection places the investigator in a tenuous position in terms of potentially invading the privacy of the individuals or organizations involved. To resolve this dilemma, the investigator might gain agreement from the group or individuals who are to be studied, indicating that observation is going to occur in some form but without necessarily completely identifying that form.

Data collection also has the potential to embarrass the participant if the questions concern such topics as sexual behavior. More often, however, it is the possible effects of the *disclosure* of sensitive data that are the concern of the respondent, rather than the *collection* of the data. While respondents may be willing to answer questions regarding illegal behaviors, abortions, the use of marijuana, or sexual behavior, they may be justifiably concerned regarding the potential effects of the disclosure of that information. An interesting parallel can be made between the questions of privacy and confidentiality of social science data with the confidentiality journalists accord their sources of information. There is a long-established tradition that journalists will choose to submit themselves to legal repercussions rather than reveal their sources of information. There is no such tradition regarding the data the researcher collects. To the extent the data contain sensitive information, there must be concern with the respondent's right to privacy about those data.

Can the data collection processes guarantee anonymity or confidentiality to the individual? Anonymous data supposedly do not permit identifying the individuals from their responses. Thus, given no link between data and subject, the subject is presumably not at risk. However, truly anonymous data may be more rare than we are willing to admit. If one collects enough demographic indicators, a shrewd individual may piece together individual identifications. On the other hand, if we offer not anonymity but confidentiality, the respondent is asked to trust us, to believe that we will protect information considered sensitive as well as that not considered sensitive. If one is doing panel analyses over time, it is mandatory to have some means to identify respondents. Although we can create special codes for individuals to use over repeated time periods, possibilities occur for tracing the individual. The purpose of these guarantees or offers of anonymity and/or confidentiality is to preserve the trust of the subject. Any belief on the subject's part that the researcher cannot keep the privacy promise may lead to less than complete responses, particularly with sensitive questions.[52]

A few years ago, the senior author oversaw a telephone survey of businesses to determine if the similarity in names of two companies was a source of confusion. Eventually, a civil court ruled that the original questionnaires (still bearing the names of the surveyed business) were to be turned over to the other side in the legal dispute. Confidentiality we had promised was overturned by a court order.

Another difficult point is asking one respondent questions about another person. To what extent is some form of permission necessary from the person being asked about? If I ask someone if his wife beats him, am I not tampering with the other person's privacy?

The researcher's responsibility for the privacy rights of the respondent does not end once the information has been transformed into a data set. Researchers often make their data sets available for secondary analyses. Does this constitute any form of privacy jeopardy? Are we not obligated to explain to research participants that the data they provide us may be used by others for quite different purposes than the purpose we explain to them at the time we obtain informed consent? Furthermore, privacy may be violated by the presentation of *aggregate* survey results in which individual respondents are not identified. While respondent anonymity is usually protected by the large number of persons who contribute to the data set, the disclosure of results from a very well-defined population may have negative effects for that population. Hypothetical Research Situation 3 presented such a problem.

Researchers have developed methods for protecting subject privacy.[53] In addition to offering guarantees of anonymity and/or confidentiality, researchers may present questions in a manner that shields the respondent. In the randomized response approach, interviewers record the answer to a randomly determined question so that they are unable to determine the question that any given respondent is actually answering.[54] For example, in order to estimate the prevalence of illegal pay-cable access, each respondent in a sample of cable subscribers might be presented with two questions: one innocuous ("I own a VCR") and one related to the sensitive topic ("I am illegally accessing a pay-cable channel"). Only innocuous questions where the distribution of responses is already known can be used. The respondent is asked to choose one question at random and answer that question without telling the interviewer which question was answered. Knowing the proportion who will answer Yes to the innocuous item, the percentage who answered Yes to the sensitive item can be estimated. Researchers also may protect their respondents by teaching interviewers that questionnaires identifying respondents should not be left lying about for unauthorized eyes to see. Once the data are ready for processing, a code number may be used for each respondent to keep the identity of the respondents separate from their answers.

Online Privacy.   Considerable online data can be collected without dealing with anonymity or confidentiality issues. However, there often is need to acquire some personal information. Because of the ability to electronically track people online, anonymity cannot be given with certainty. Anonymity is nearly impossible when the instrument is an email item, and the respondent is dependent on faith in the researcher to delete identifying information that may be stored. Worse, a skilled hacker can tap into the email files. Using an "anonymizer" or "e-mailer" (methods used to hide email identity) has been suggested as an option for increasing security.[55]

A website survey provides more viable options. For example, it is not necessary to ask for direct personal identifiers, creating the same level of anonymity given to students who complete questionnaires during class time. If follow-up email for debriefing or resurveying is needed, participants can be directed to a different site to obtain or leave additional information without fear of being connected to their responses. This method also allows online researchers to offer and dispense incentives. Even with this approach, a skilled hacker or cookies could obtain confidential information. Still more advanced methods, such as special encryption techniques, can be used to further protect individual privacy, if affordable and available.[56]

While anonymity suggests confidentiality, the inability to guarantee anonymity requires researchers to more closely attend to confidentiality. Traditionally, response rates have tended to increase on surveys dealing with sensitive topics when participants were informed about confidentiality procedures.[57] Password-protected systems for electronically stored data are recommended. The U.S. Electronic Communication Privacy Act is designed to protect against computer hacking, but it does not protect email that is sent and received at work organizations, including universities. Within the consent form, then, it is important to inform respondents that others may have access to your email. Further, if the data are being stored on a third-party server or an organization's server that others may access, that information also should be shared.

Strategies for Resolution

Mass communication researchers ought to be cognizant of the types of human subjects issues described in the previous section and be prepared to resolve dilemmas they encounter in their own investigations. They are not without guidance, however, because both professional associations and the federal government codify the treatment of human subjects.

Professional Codes

Professional codes of ethics have been adopted by associations of psychologists, sociologists, and public opinion researchers, as well as others. Some of these codes provide considerable direction regarding the treatment of human subjects. Consider that section of the

American Psychological Association's Ethical Principles of Psychologists that concerns research with human subjects:[58]

> The decision to undertake research rests upon a considered judgment by the individual researcher about how best to contribute to psychological science and human welfare. Having made the decision to conduct research, the researcher considers alternative directions in which research energies and resources might be invested. On the basis of this consideration, the researcher carries out the investigation with respect and concern for the dignity and welfare of the people who participate and with cognizance of federal and state regulations and professional standards governing the conduct of research with human participants.

> a. In planning research, researchers consider its ethical acceptability under the Ethics Code. If an ethical issue is unclear, researchers seek to resolve the issue through consultation with institutional review boards, animal care and use committees, peer consultations, or other proper mechanisms.

> b. Researchers design, conduct, and report research in accordance with recognized standards of scientific competence and ethical research.

> c. Researchers conduct research competently and with due concern for the dignity and welfare of the participants. Researchers are responsible for the ethical conduct of research conducted by them or by others under their supervision or control. Researchers and assistants perform only those tasks for which they are trained and prepared.

> d. Prior to conducting research (except research involving only anonymous surveys, naturalistic observations, or similar research), researchers enter into an agreement with participants that clarifies the nature of the research and the responsibilities of each party. Researchers use language that is reasonably understandable to research participants in obtaining their appropriate informed consent. Such informed consent is appropriately documented. Using language that is reasonably understandable to participants, researchers inform participants of the nature of the research; they inform participants that they are free to participate or to decline to participate or to withdraw from the research; they explain the foreseeable consequences of declining or withdrawing; they inform participants of significant factors that may be expected to influence their willingness to participate; and they explain other aspects about which the prospective participants inquire. For persons who are legally incapable of giving informed consent, researchers nevertheless (1) provide an appropriate explanation, (2) obtain the participant's assent, and (3) obtain appropriate permission from a legally authorized person, if such substitute consent is permitted by law.

> e. Researchers do not conduct a study involving deception unless they have determined that the use of deceptive techniques is justified by the study's prospective scientific, educational, or applied value and that equally effective alternative procedures that do not use deception are not feasible. Researchers never deceive research participants about significant aspects that

would affect their willingness to participate, such as physical risks, discomfort, or unpleasant emotional experiences. Any deception must be explained to participants as early as is feasible, preferably at the conclusion of their participation, but no later than at the conclusion of the research.

f. Researchers provide a prompt opportunity for participants to obtain appropriate information about the nature, results, and conclusions of the research, and researchers attempt to correct any misconceptions that participants may have. If scientific or humane values justify delaying or withholding this information, researchers take reasonable measures to reduce the risk of harm.

Although quite explicit in its proscriptions, there are two major problems with such a code. First, it typically lacks any type of meaningful sanctions. The harshest punishment given violators may be to oust them from the association. Given the absence of real sanctions, members may fail to take the code seriously.[59] Even more problematic is the short-lived relevance of any particular code. Reynolds[60] notes that any code of ethics represents the current societal standards regarding current research procedures applied to phenomena of current interest to researchers, and that all three of these are likely to change in unpredictable ways. This chapter's discussion of online research problems exemplifies this dilemma.

That observation also explains why any strictly empirical attempt to resolve ethical issues is of limited usefulness. While we might attempt to determine empirically the answers to many of the questions posed in the previous section—such as, What is the relative effectiveness of one-to-one debriefing versus debriefing en masse?—the questions themselves may change as our research procedures change. It is analogous to efforts to resolve empirically ethical issues in medicine; no sooner are studies completed to establish ethical guidelines regarding one medical procedure than another procedure is developed. Thus, a strictly empirical approach to human subjects issues ensures that ethics will typically be one step behind research methods.

Nevertheless, such codes of ethics can provide researchers with a set of issues to consider when contemplating the ethical status of a particular research project.

Federal Regulations

A second set of prescriptions for resolving human subjects issues is the U.S. Department of Health and Human Services (DHHS) Policy for Protection of Human Research Subjects. The regulations explicitly apply only to research conducted with the DHHS or supported by DHHS funds, and certain broad categories of research are exempt—for example, routine surveys and interviews in which the respondents are not identified and sensitive information is not collected. However, many institutions (e.g., universities) require that *all* research conducted at the institution conform to the federal guidelines and apply standards for human subjects research that go above and beyond those specified in the federal regulations. Therefore, researchers should check with their own institutions to determine the regulations applicable to them. Adherence to the federal regulations is supervised by a system of institutional review boards (IRBs). At many universities, the IRB is a university-level committee that conducts prior reviews of all human subjects research, including that proposed as masters' theses and doctoral dissertations.

While the federal regulations are more binding than professional codes, they may not be any more effective. A study examining the impact of ethical regulations on the research published in social psychological journals from 1979 to 1983 found that the proportion of studies that reported obtaining informed consent or explicitly giving subjects the freedom to withdraw was negligible and that the practice of deception has not been reduced by ethical regulations.[61] Why should communication journals (among others) not require a copy of the author's IRB approval before reviewing an article whose study clearly required such approval? Furthermore, the IRB reviews themselves may be biased. Consider the study of Ceci[62] and others in which university human subjects committees reviewed hypothetical proposals that were identical in their treatment of human subjects but differed in sociopolitical sensitivity. The results showed that socially sensitive proposals were twice as likely to be rejected and that the primary reason for rejection of sensitive proposals was the potential political impact of the proposed findings. Such biased reviews, and the possibility that researchers alter their research priorities on the basis of anticipated IRB approval, indicate that federal regulations have substantial potential to control research agendas.

Ethical Safeguards.   One pressing issue involves the process by which ethical concerns are safeguarded. Currently, IRBs are charged with maintaining the standards for all research involving human subjects. Hamilton[63] claims that most IRB members lack the technical knowledge to properly review an online proposal. He estimates that while half the reviewers had received online proposals, only a few indicated that their IRB had developed guidelines for online research. This is a fundamental oversight for the proper conduct of online research.

Reviewers need to understand how to evaluate the online process of consent, deception, debriefing, and privacy. For example, specific knowledge of how the Internet works is required to address concerns about the identity of online participants, including IP address, email address, and other electronic identifiers. Specific knowledge is needed as to what affects confidentiality when third-party software and storage facilities are used. Debriefing issues for online studies are also more complex. For example, if participants complete half the survey, will they still be debriefed? Is returning the survey a condition of debriefing? If a researcher cannot insure that a debriefing statement will be read or heard, should deception be permitted? Will IRB members have access to data stored on third-party servers if ethical questions about the study are raised? Given the constant technical changes in the online environment, it is reasonable to expect the IRB to develop staff, skills, and guidelines that will accommodate this rich database. In addition, technically competent reviewers must be sought out to review research proposals that depend on online data.

Individual Ethical Analysis

Both professional codes and federal regulations may be used by mass communication researchers in their efforts to resolve human subjects issues. Codes and regulations are imperfect tools at best. Perhaps the most useful decision-making tool to add to the researcher's collection may be a strategy for developing a personal judgment about the moral character of a research activity.

Reynolds[64] offers such a strategy. The strategy is based on three orientations for resolving moral dilemmas—respect for individual rights (defined by society), evaluation of the effects (costs-benefits), and the personal treatment of others. It consists of a set of questions reflecting the three different orientations to moral dilemmas to guide the review of any research project. They are:

Effects on Rights	1. What rights of various parties associated with the research activity—participants, investigators, society at large—may be affected?
Program/Project Effects	2. What are the costs and benefits of the research program and this project?
Participant Effects	3. What are the costs (or risks) and benefits for the participants?
Distribution of Effects	4. What is the expected distribution of the costs and benefits?
Respect for Rights, Welfare	5. How has respect for the rights and welfare of the participants been demonstrated?
Personal Treatment	6. To what extent has the personal treatment of the participants by the investigator(s) approached the ideal?

To demonstrate the application of such a strategy, consider the following study and corresponding ethical analysis.

The Study. Reaching certain audiences with the information they most need can be a difficult task. In a *Journal of Communication* article, Hawkins and others report their evaluation of the Body Awareness Resource Network (BARN).[65] The BARN system of interactive computer programs was designed to provide adolescents with information, behavioral change strategies, and sources of referral in several health areas, including alcohol and other drugs, human sexuality, and smoking prevention and cessation. BARN systems were introduced into one rural and one urban high school in the Madison, Wisconsin, area and into their three associated middle schools. The BARN schools adopted the system as part of their curriculum and made it available to all students at the school. Use of, reactions to, and impact of the BARN system were assessed primarily from two surveys of seventh, ninth, and eleventh graders in 1982 (before BARN was introduced) and in 1984 (after BARN had been in the test schools almost two full years). Students who were seventh graders and ninth graders in 1982 were resurveyed in 1984. Surveys were administered at all five test schools and at five matched control schools. The 350-item questionnaires covered knowledge, attitudes, and behaviors in each of the topic areas.

Effects on Rights. The right of investigators to explore any topic of interest would allow them to choose a health information system designed for adolescents as a phenomenon of study. Considering the societal implications of adolescent health-related behaviors, research on this topic seems consistent with society's right to expect mass communication researchers to investigate important topics. However, the participants had a right to withhold information regarding such personal concerns as alcohol use and sexual behavior. Since the participants were minors, their parents also had some right to control the type of information to which they were exposed, as well as the type of information revealed. And since the health information systems were introduced in the schools and the questionnaires were administered in the schools, these schools had the right to approve the research.

Program/Project Effects. The present study is a contribution to knowledge of both theoretical and applied importance. It is a common finding that traditional information campaigns do the most good where the need is least and widen the very knowledge gaps they intend to close.[66] The present research provides information regarding the ability of an alternative medium of communication—interactive computer programs—to overcome the knowledge gap problem. On the applied side, the costs to society of such health-related behaviors as tobacco, drug, and alcohol use and "unsafe" sex are well-documented. Since adolescence is a critical time for the formation of both positive and negative health behavior patterns, knowledge regarding how to communicate constructive health information to this group could have substantial benefits for society. The major negative effects of the research project were the financial costs (for software development, hardware, research assistants, etc.) and the multiyear time commitment required of the investigators.

Participant Effects. The study involved three categories of participants: BARN access/survey respondents, BARN access/survey nonrespondents, and control group/survey respondents. The survey respondents experienced the cost of completing a rather lengthy questionnaire and some participants completed the questionnaire twice. The questions regarding sexual behavior may have been embarrassing to some participants, and the questions regarding alcohol and drug use had potential legal ramifications. However, responses were made on a machine-score sheet separate from the questionnaire booklet, and the answer sheets were identified only by a code number. But those participants who were reinterviewed could not remain completely anonymous, since their questionnaires needed to be combined for analysis. To protect the privacy of these panel participants, lists containing their names and corresponding code numbers—but no data—were retained between 1982 and 1984 by the schools in locked file drawers. The investigators retained the data with code numbers only. Benefits to the control group were limited; they may have gained self-knowledge as a result of completing the questionnaire or found the questionnaire itself interesting. BARN access participants stood to accrue additional benefits. Besides the sheer enjoyment of using the computer system, they learned important health information in the process.

Distribution of Effects. The study participants were urban and rural high school and middle school students in the Madison, Wisconsin, area. Consequently, the costs of the research experience were not shared by younger or older citizens or by those living in other parts of the United States. Although the various categories of participants received few to moderate direct benefits from their research experience, society as a whole would benefit substantially from knowledge that might be used to improve adolescent health-related behaviors. And while the costs of the research were not shared by all, the distribution of costs does not seem particularly unfair; that is, the disadvantaged were not used to benefit the advantaged.

Respect for Rights, Welfare.   Several activities of the investigators demonstrated respect for the rights and welfare of the participants. Informed consent to introduce the BARN system into the schools was obtained from the school districts. Since the schools adopted BARN as part of their curriculum, no further consent for its introduction was required. However, the investigators did inform parents about the system and invited them to preview BARN before it was placed in the schools. Written consent for student participation in the survey(s) was obtained from both parents and students; either one could revoke their consent at any time. The computer systems were located such as to provide privacy of interaction for the user. Answer sheets were kept separate from questionnaire booklets, and testing sessions were monitored by research staff with no school staff present.

Personal Treatment.   Since the investigators sought to obtain sensitive information and to collect such information from some participants at two points in time, one may assume that they treated the participants in a courteous manner. Furthermore, their treatment was straightforward, as no deception was involved.

  The preceding ethical analysis is not presumed to be a definitive evaluation of the moral appropriateness of the Hawkins and colleagues research. Other critics, even those using the same analysis strategy, could arrive at different conclusions. But a lack of agreement does not mean that the exercise is pointless, since the analysis itself leads to greater understanding of the problems involved, and, in and of itself, it is progress.[67]

Am I My Colleague's Keeper?

Are we responsible for monitoring the professional ethics of others who also go about doing research? If one is asked to carry out the federal regulations on human subjects by serving on an institutional review board, then the prescribed response may be "yes." But we may monitor the professional ethics of our colleagues in other situations as well. A common professional situation in which we have an opportunity to deal with the professional practices of others is when we are in the role of professional peer reviewer (e.g., as a reader of a journal manuscript or a research proposal that seeks funding). The anonymity usually associated with this role makes it easier to espouse any particular ethical stance that appears needed. A second situation that permits a wide degree of authority is in monitoring the behaviors of students, particularly graduate or undergraduate advisees. In these situations, there is little onus in suggesting that some practices they are considering may be questionable. A third situation is that of senior investigator with junior investigator, perhaps even senior professor with junior professor. This is a bit murkier in that the collegial association is closer to parity than any of the prior situations described. We are now talking about offering criticism, perhaps unsolicited criticism, to an individual whose privileges, benefits, and association with us probably extend beyond the professional into the social and/or personal realms. An even more difficult situation is that of senior investigator to senior investigator.

These examples point out varying degrees of interpersonal difficulty in proposing to monitor others who do research. While monitoring as a manuscript reviewer or student adviser may not be particularly problematic, intercollegial checks may be seen to imply mistrust or distrust of the practices of a colleague. The fact that we have more authority in the former than in the latter situations does not render our ethical analysis of a research procedure any more correct. It simply makes it easier to proclaim. But our role should be the same in each situation, and that role is not to force others to abide by our ethical evaluations. Rather, our role is to sensitize others to the ethical issues inherent in various research procedures and to foster thought and debate about those issues.

This position is appropriate even in the teacher-student situation, where one might assume that the teacher's greater experience and knowledge should be transferred to the student for future application. Drawing a parallel to another educational position may strengthen this point. Some educators hold that it is not enough to provide students with *answers*, since the questions they face in the future may be quite different from the ones confronted today. Instead, the educator must train students in *strategies* for answering future questions. A similar position may be held for the analysis of human subjects issues. Since research procedures and societal values are likely to change over time in unpredictable ways, the student is better prepared with a competency in ethical decision making than with a pocketful of fixed answers.

While discussion of human subjects issues may be initiated quite naturally in the teacher-student situation, its initiation in other situations is less formalized. But steps could be taken to formalize ethical discussion in other situations. For example, journal editors might request that a brief ethical analysis be given by authors and reviewers. In the process, both parties would become more attuned to human subjects issues and perhaps learn from each other's analyses.

Even more constructive than such an after-the-fact dialogue would be a preproject discussion. Investigators—from undergraduates to senior faculty members—might be asked to submit a statement of proposed research practices and an ethical analysis of their project within their academic unit. Anonymous reviewers would point out additional ethical considerations, offer alternative viewpoints and perhaps make specific recommendations for altering proposed research procedures to eliminate or minimize questions related to ethical difficulties. Perhaps the proposed deception could be changed in minor ways such that the practice is more acceptable than in its original form. Recommendations of the committee would remain advisory. Final decisions regarding any research project would remain with the investigator.

In addition to increasing awareness of ethical issues, such a review process could serve other functions as well. Would not such collegial oversight result in better research procedures and therefore higher-quality research results? The kinds of suggestions made by colleagues attentive to our research interests and proposals could be useful ones. Research evaluations of our work by journal editors and grant readers may become more favorable over the period of time in which we have been able to receive suggestions for alterations in procedures. And the number of questions raised by university IRBs might be fewer if our submission already included the results of a department review process.

Responsibilities to Society

The ethical responsibilities of the mass communication researcher do not end with human subjects. Since our research may have implications for society at large, we have further responsibilities. As mentioned in the individual ethical analysis, society has the right to expect mass communication researchers to investigate important topics. But society also has an interest in the process and *outcome* of such efforts. By process we mean the conducting and reporting of research, and by outcome we refer to the application of scientific knowledge.

Conducting and Reporting Research

At the minimum, the researcher should be *honest* in the conducting and reporting of research. While this may seem obvious, it is not universally practiced. Recent cases of scientific fraud demonstrate that deviance in science exists and belie the argument that the normative structure of science makes such acts unlikely.[68] Scientific fraud includes such practices as plagiarism, theft of ideas and concepts, and falsification of data.[69] This means that investigators must not present another's words or ideas as their own, or fabricate or alter their data or findings. While some contend that science has an inherent set of controls against false practices—for example, the training of scientists; the constant communication among them, including the sharing of data and materials; and the use of existing data in replication studies[70]—these controls may be less certain than we assume. We know of no graduate program in communication research and theory that formally trains its about-to-be-scientists in the ethics of conducting research. Nor are replications in our field as common as might be expected.[71] In fact, in their study of communication researchers' responses to replication requests, Wimmer and Reid[72] found that only 48 percent indicated that the raw data and other information necessary for replication were readily available.

While sins of commission such as plagiarism and data fabrication seem clear-cut, certain sins of omission are less obvious. Consider the researcher who fails to report nuances of his or her research design that might affect the meaning of the results. Or fails to report the survey response rate, effectively camouflaging the limitations of the findings. An answer to such sins of omission is to insist that we describe our methods accurately and in appropriate detail. But what constitutes appropriate detail? And what of researchers who accurately report their findings, but only those findings that support their hypotheses? Clearly, we ought to present all relevant evidence—pro and con—regarding our hypotheses. This issue, in turn, raises our final ethics question: Are mass communication researchers responsible for the applications of their findings?

Applications of Scientific Knowledge

There is disagreement in the scientific community about the ethical responsibility of behavioral scientists for the use and misuse of their findings. Some hold that knowledge is ethically neutral; others call attention to the application of social scientific knowledge for the improvement of the human condition.[73] There is no question, however, that our findings can and will be used by others and sometimes in a manner contrary to our values.

Consider the First Amendment champion who learns that her media effects data are being used to justify censorship. Or the critic of advertising directed at children who finds that his research on children's processing of television messages is being used by advertisers to increase their appeals to children. Researchers also may find that the knowledge they have generated is misinterpreted, as portrayed in Hypothetical Research Situation 4. Even the failure to use findings in a positive way could be viewed as objectionable.[74] Thus the researcher who demonstrates that youngsters can learn prosocial behavior from television may complain when network programmers ignore her findings.

But mass communication researchers are not totally powerless in the face of such dilemmas. While many scientists feel there is little to be gained *within* science by engaging in public dissemination of information,[75] an attempt to inform the general public about their data, and the appropriate interpretations of those data, can do much to discourage misuse and misinterpretation. And if misapplications or misinterpretations do occur, the investigator may speak publicly to correct these.

Conclusions

This chapter has attempted to increase your awareness of the ethical issues that may arise from certain research practices and prepare you to resolve the ethical dilemmas you confront in the conduct of your own research. We have described several strategies—professional codes, federal regulations, and individual ethical analysis—that may help you to resolve particular issues.

Although these resolution strategies vary in the extent to which they are compulsory—for example, researchers may be required by their universities to abide by the federal regulations—adherence to even compulsory regulations does not release the researcher from personal ethical responsibility. The responsibility for ethical practice in research rests ultimately with the individual investigator. Therefore, researchers should become accustomed to conducting individual ethical analyses of each and every prospective project, as naturally as they assess the appropriateness of their research design or the reliability and validity of their measures.

Endnotes

1. Paul Davidson Reynolds, *Ethics and Social Science Research* (Englewood Cliffs, NJ: Prentice-Hall, 1982).

2. Dolf Zillman and Jennings Bryant, "Pornography and Social Science Research: Higher Moralities," *Journal of Communication* 33 (Autumn 1983): 111–114.

3. Dolf Zillman and Jennings Bryant,"Pornography, Sexual Callousness, and the Trivialization of Rape," *Journal of Communication* 32 (Autumn 1982): 10–21.

4. Larry Gross, "Pornography and Social Science Research: Serious Questions," *Journal of Communication* 33 (Autumn 1983): 107–111.

5. *Ibid.*

6. Zillman and Bryant, "Pornography and Social Science Research: Higher Moralities," 111.

7. The study was funded by the Communication Theory and Methodology Division of the Association for Education in Journalism and Mass Communication and conducted by the third author and

Dr. J. David Kennamer of Virginia Commonwealth University. Mail questionnaires were sent to all members of the CT&M Division. Of the 413 questionnaires sent, 201 were returned for a 49 percent return rate. Respondents were asked to indicate the frequency with which they used specific research procedures, with response categories of "usually," "sometimes," "rarely," and "never." If a particular procedure was not applicable to the respondent (e.g., the item concerned an experimental research procedure and the respondent did not conduct experimental research), the respondent was asked to indicate "not applicable." The "not applicable" responses were treated as missing data.

8. Joan E. Sieber, "Ethics without Models," *Society* 18 (November–December 1980): 48–51.

9. John E. Atwell, "Human Rights in Human Subjects Research," in Allan J. Kimmel, ed., *New Directions for Methodology of Social and Behavioral Science: Ethics of Human Subject Research* (San Francisco: Jossey-Bass, 1981), 81–90.

10. Zillman and Bryant, "Pornography and Social Science Research: Higher Moralities," 113.

11. Reynolds, *op. cit.*

12. G. J. Annas, L. H. Glantz, and B. F. Katz, *Informed Consent to Human Experimentation: The Subject's Dilemma* (Cambridge, MA: Ballinger, 1977).

13. Jerry M. Suls and Ralph L. Rosnow, "The Delicate Balance between Ethics and Artifacts in Behavioral Research," in Kimmel, *op. cit.*, 55–67.

14. Jerome H. Resnick and Thomas Schwartz, "Ethical Standards as an Independent Variable in Psychological Research," *American Psychologist* 28 (1973): 134–139.

15. Charles A. Dill, Eugene R. Gilden, Peter C. Hill, and Larry L. Hanselka, "Federal Human Subjects Regulations: A Methodological Artifact?", *Personality and Social Psychology Bulletin* 8 (September, 1982): 417–425.

16. Eleanor Singer, "Informed Consent: Consequences for Response Rate and Response Quality in Social Surveys," *American Sociological Review* 43 (1978) 144–162.

17. Ashton D. Trite and Epp P. Ogden, "Informed Consent: I. The Institutional Non-Liability Clause as a Liability in Recruiting Research Subjects," *Journal Behavior and of Social Personality* 1 (July, 1986): 391–396.

18. Robert Rosenthal and Ralph L. Rosnow, *The Volunteer Subject* (New York: Wiley, 1975).

19. Lisa H. Newton, "Agreement to Participate in Research: Is That a Promise," *IRB: A Review of Human Subjects Research* 6 (March–April, 1984): 7–9.

20. Ashton D. Trite and Benjamin H. Bailey, "Informed Consent: II. Withdrawal Without Prejudice Clauses May Increase No-Shows," *Journal of General Psychology* 113 (July, 1986): 285–287.

21. Lloyd Lueptow, Samuel A. Mueller, Richard R. Hammes, and Lawrence S. Master, "The Impact of Informed Consent Regulations on Response Rate and Response Bias," *Sociological Methods and Research* 6 (1977): 183–204; Kathleen A. Kearney, Ronald H. Hopkins, Armand L. Mauss, and Ralph A. Weisheit, "Sample Bias Resulting From a Requirement for Written Parental Consent," *Public Opinion Quarterly*, 47 (1983): 96–102.

22. For a discussion of some research methodology alternatives, see D. Mark Mahler, "When to Obtain Informed Consent in Behavioral Research: A Study of Mother-Infant Bonding," *IRB: A Review of Human Subjects Research* 8 (May–June, 1986): 7–11.

23. David W. Wilson and Edward Donnerstein, "Legal and Ethical Aspects of Nonreactive Social Psychological Research: An Excursion into the Public Mind," *American Psychologist* 31 (November 1976): 765–773.

24. Marilyn Aitkenhead and Jackie Dordoy, "What the Subjects Have to Say," *The British Journal of Social Psychology* 24 (November 1985): 293–305.

25. Terry R. Barrett and Thomas J. Muehleman, "Problems of Including Potential Subjects as Ethical Consultants," *Psychology Reports* 49 (October 1981): 575–580.

26. Reynolds, *op. cit.*

27. For example, see A. G. Miller, "Role Playing: An Alternative to Deception?" *American Psychologist* 27 (1973): 623–634; D. S. Holmes and D. H. Bennett, "Experiments to Answer Questions Raised by the Use of Deception in Psychological Research," *Journal of Personality and Social Psychology* 29 (1974): 358–367.

28. Robert LaRose and Hyunyi Cho, "Privacy Issues in Internet Research," *Social Science and Computer Review* 17 (4)(1999): 421–434.

29. A. Fromkin, "The Internet as a Source of Regulation Arbitrage," in Brian Kahn & Charles Nesson, eds., *Borders in Cyberspace* (Cambridge: MIT Press, 1997), 129–163.

30. Federal Trade Commission (1998). "Privacy Online: A Report to Congress" [online] *http://www.ftc.gov/reports/privacy3/toc.htm.*

31. Herbert Kelman defines deception as "any deliberate misrepresentation of the purposes of the research, of the identity or qualifications of the investigator, of the auspices under which the research is conducted, of the experiences to which participants will be subjected, or of the likely uses and consequences of the research" in "Ethical Issues in Different Social Science Methods," Tom L. Beauchamp, Ruth R. Faden, R. Jay Wallace, Jr., and LeRoy Walters, eds., *Ethical Issues in Social Science Research* (Baltimore: Johns Hopkins University Press, 1982), 40–98.

32. Alan E. Gross and India Fleming, "Twenty Years of Deception in Social Psychology," *Personality and Social Psychology Bulletin* 8 (September, 1982): 402–408.

33. See, for example, Diana Baumrind, "Research Using Intentional Deception: Ethical Issues Revisited," *American Psychologist* 40 (February, 1985): 165–174.

34. Philip Gallo, Jr., Shirley Smith, and Sandra Mumford, "Effects of Deceiving Subjects upon Experimental Results," *Journal of Social Psychology* 89 (February 1973): 99–107.

35. Lawrence J. Strickler, Samuel Messick, and Douglas N. Jackson, "Suspicion of Deception: Implications for Conformity Research," *Journal of Personality and Social Psychology* 5 (1967): 379–389.

36. Lawrence J. Strickler, "The True Deceiver," *Psychological Bulletin* 68 (July, 1967): 13–20.

37. Thomas D. Cook and others, "Demand Characteristics and Three Conceptions of the Frequently Deceived Subject," *Journal of Personality and Social Psychology* 14 (March 1970): 185–194.

38. Shalom H. Schwartz and Avi Gottlieb, "Participants' Postexperimental Reactions and the Ethics of Bystander Research," *Journal of Experimental Social Psychology* 17 (July 1981): 396–407.

39. Alan C. Elms, "Keeping Deception Honest: Justifying Conditions for Social Scientific Research Strategems," in Beauchamp et al., *op. cit.*, 232–254; Herbert C. Covey, "Deception in Research: Some Ethical Issues," *Sociological Practice* 4 (1981–1982): 25–54; Herbert C. Kelman, "Human Use of Human Subjects: The Problem of Deception in Social Psychological Experiments," *Psychological Bulletin* 67 (January 1967): 1–11.

40. Elms, *op. cit.*, 234.

41. Zillman and Bryant, "Pornography and Social Science Research: Higher Moralities."

42. Reynolds, *op. cit.*

43. *Ibid.*

44. Elaine Walster and others, "Effectiveness of Debriefing Following Deception Experiments," *Journal of Personality and Social Psychology* 6 (1967): 371–380.

45. Neil M. Malamuth and James V. Check, "Debriefing Effectiveness Following Exposure to Pornographic Rape Depictions," *Journal of Sex Research* 20 (February 1984): 1–13.

46. Daniel Ullman and T. Jackson, "Researchers' Ethical Conscience: Debriefing from 1960 to 1980," *American Psychologist* 37 (August 1982): 972–973.

47. Donald T. Campbell, "Prospective: Artifact and Control," in Robert Rosenthal and R. L. Rosnow, eds., *Artifact in Behavioral Research* (New York: Academic Press, 1969).

48. Elms, *op. cit.*

49. *Ibid.*, 28.

50. Oscar M. Ruebhausen and Orville G. Brim, Jr., "Privacy and Behavioral Research," *Columbia Law Review* 65 (1965): 1189.

51. For a discussion of the conflict between social science research and the problem of invasion of privacy, see David L. Wiesenthal, "Sweating at Night: Some Ethical Paradoxes Confronting Social Psychological Research," *Social Science and Medicine* 15F (March 1981): 33–37.

52. In a survey of public attitudes toward informed consent in social research, Singer found a significant interrelationship between concern over confidentiality of response and willingness to answer sensitive questions on an interview; Eleanor Singer, "Public Reactions to Some Ethical Issues of Social Research: Attitudes and Behavior," *Journal of Consumer Research* 11 (June, 1984): 501–509. However, in an experiment with a confidentiality reminder in a telephone survey, Frey found that assurances of confidentiality did not have much impact on response rates or data quality; James H. Frey, "An Experiment with a Confidentiality Reminder in a Telephone Survey," *Public Opinion Quarterly* 50 (Spring, 1986):

267–269. Frey's finding may be attributed to the fact that many respondents do not believe such confidentiality guarantees. In a national survey examining trends in consumers' attitudes toward the survey research industry, Schleifer found that only 54 percent of the 1984 sample believed that survey research firms maintain the confidentiality of answers, compared to 61 percent who held this belief in 1982; Stephen Schleifer, "Trends in Attitudes Toward and Participation in Survey Research," *Public Opinion Quarterly* 50 (Spring, 1986): 17–26.

53. For descriptions of various procedural, statistical, and legal solutions to privacy problems, see Robert F. Boruch, "Methods for Resolving Privacy Problems in Social Research," in Beauchamp et. al., *op. cit.*, 292–314; Kathleen A. Kearney, Ronald H. Hopkins, Armand L. Mauss, and Ralph A. Weisheit, "Self-Generated Identification Codes for Anonymous Collection of Longitudinal Questionnaire Data," *Public Opinion Quarterly* 48 (Spring, 1984): 370–378; Dane Archer and Lynn Erlich, "Weighing the Evidence: A New Method for Research on Restricted Information," *Qualitative Sociology* 8 (Winter, 1985): 345–358.

54. J.A. Fox and P. E. Tracy, "The Randomized Response Approach," *Evaluation Review* 4 (1980): 601–622; P. E. Tracy and J. A. Fox, "The Validity of Randomized Response for Sensitive Measurements," *American Sociological Review* 46 (1981): 187–200.

55. Yitzchak Bink, Kenneth Mahl, and Sara Kiesler, "Ethical Issues in Conducting Sex Research on the Internet," *The Journal of Sex Research* 36 (1)(1999): 82–90.

56. *Ibid.*, 51.

57. E. Singer, N. Mathiowetz, and M. Cooper, "The Impact of Privacy and Confidentiality Concerns on Survey Participation," *Public Opinion Quarterly* 57 (1993): 465–482.

58. Since these codes are revised from time to time, interested persons should contact an association directly for the current version of its code. Codes relevant were obtained from the American Psychological Association, Inc. (1992). *Ethical Code of Psychologists and Code of Conduct.* [Online] *http://www.apa.org/ethics/code.html.*

59. A survey of sociologists found few familiar with the American Sociological Association's Code of Ethics and few believing that the Code had had any impact on their ethical behaviors; Gary L. Long and Dean Dorn, "An Assessment of the ASA Code of Ethics and Committee on Ethics," *The American Sociologist* 17 (May, 1982): 80–86.

60. Reynolds, *op. cit.*

61. John G. Adair, Terrance W. Dushenko, and R. C. Linsay, "Ethical Regulations and Their Impact on Research Practice," *American Psychologist* 40 (January, 1985): 59–72.

62. Stephen J. Ceci, Douglas Peters, and Jonathan Plotkin, "Human Subjects Review, Personal Values, and the Regulation of Social Science Research," *American Psychologist* 40 (September, 1985): 994–1002.

63. James Hamilton, "The Ethics of Conducting Social-Science Research on the Internet," *The Chronicle of Higher Education* 46 (15)(1999): B6–B7.

64. Only six of the seven questions in Reynold's strategy are treated in this section. Readers interested in a detailed description of the entire strategy are referred to Reynolds, *op. cit.*

65. Robert P. Hawkins, David H. Gustafson, Betty Chewning, Kris Bosworth, and Patricia M. Day, "Reaching Hard-to-Reach Populations: Interactive Computer Programs as Public Information Campaigns for Adolescents," *Journal of Communication* 37 (Spring, 1987): 8–28. Dr. Robert P. Hawkins, personal communication.

66. Philip J. Tichenor, George A. Donohue, and Clarice N. Olien, "Mass Media and Differential Growth in Knowledge," *Public Opinion Quarterly* 34: (Summer, 1970): 158–170.

67. Donelson R. Forsyth, "A Psychological Perspective on Ethical Uncertainties in Research," in Kimmel, *op. cit*, 91–100.

68. Kenneth H. Bechtel, Jr. and Willie Pearson, Jr., "Deviant Scientists and Scientific Deviance," *Deviant Behavior* 6 (1985): 237–252.

69. For a discussion of recent efforts to develop scientific fraud prevention policies, see Nicholas H. Steneck, "Commentary: The University and Research Ethics," *Science, Technology, and Human Values* 9 (Fall, 1954): 6–15.

70. Patricia Woolf, "Fraud in Science: How Much, How Serious?" *The Hastings Center Report*, 11 (October, 1981): 9–14.

71. Leonard N. Reid, Lawrence C. Soley, and Roger D. Wimmer, "Replication in Advertising Research: 1977, 1978, 1979," *Journal of Advertising* 10 (1981): 3–13.

72. Roger D. Wimmer and Leonard N. Reid, "Willingness of Communication Researchers to Respond to Replication Requests," *Journalism Quarterly* 59 (Summer, 1982): 317–319.

73. John Lamberth and Allan J. Kimmel, "Ethical Issues and Responsibilities in Applying Scientific Behavioral Knowledge," in Kimmel, *op. cit.*, 69–79.

74. *Ibid.*

75. Sharon Dunwoody and Michael Ryan, "Scientific Barriers to the Popularization of Science in the Mass Media," *Journal of Communication* 35 (Winter, 1985): 26–42.

17

Presenting Quantitative Data

Claude Cookman

Quantitative research produces data that need to be communicated. Your options range from describing the data verbally to listing them in a table to presenting them pictorially with graphs or charts. Although verbal description may occasionally be adequate, when your data are extensive, complex, or both, the table, graph, and chart options can increase reader comprehension. They can also be more efficient, presenting large amounts of data more clearly and in less space than text can. For the researcher, understanding these visual formats is important conceptual knowledge. Knowing how to produce them is an important professional skill.

Cultural critics like to say we live in a visual era, but visual tools have been used to communicate for many thousands of years. Maps and drawings predate recorded history. Explanatory graphics are generally considered to begin with Leonardo da Vinci, the Renaissance artist and engineer who filled his notebooks with annotated drawings explaining how his inventions would function.[1] René Descartes, the seventeenth-century French mathematician, laid the foundation for graphs. His work on analytical geometry led him to develop a grid of horizontal and vertical lines to plot the position of points.[2] Modern graphs result from the work of William Playfair, a Scottish researcher, who towards the end of eighteenth century invented the line-, bar- and pie-graph formats to present data on European economies.[3]

This chapter explains the theory of tables, graphs, and, to a lesser extent, charts. It discusses ethical issues related to graphs. It offers guidelines for effective visual communication, suggests a procedure for creating graphs, and notes computer applications that make creating graphs relatively easy.

The chapter's guidelines and suggestions are based on two scenarios: If you are submitting your research to a mass communication journal, you must learn and follow its stylistic guidelines for tables, graphs, and charts. If you are preparing them for a course assignment, a conference presentation, or for the popular press, you have more latitude in your stylistic decisions. Neither situation is right or wrong; it is a matter of making your work appropriate to the audience and its expectations.

Definitions and Vocabulary

Some definitions and vocabulary need to be established before proceeding. A table presents actual numbers, organized in rows and columns. A graph represents numbers with physical markers such as columns, lines, wedges, and data points. A chart diagrams relationships, explains theoretical models, schematizes hierarchies or flows, and conveys other concepts that can best be understood visually. In your text, refer to tables as tables. Call graphs, charts, and all other illustrations figures. The distinction is based on printing requirements. Because tables are typeset, they can be incorporated into the body of the article without much additional effort. Until recently, all other illustrations had to be engraved to be readied for the printing press. Computerized publishing can now perform the engraving functions and easily flow type around images. Although the engraving operation continues at some journals, it seems likely that after a transition period it will pass.

Until recently graphs and charts had to be made by graphic artists. Computer software now allows students and researchers to create them. With this facility comes the responsibility to learn how to make ethical and effective ones.

Restraint is the first requirement. Present only the data sets that are necessary to communicate your research. Tables and figures should complement the written account of your research. In your text, refer to every table and figure. You might analyze them, interpret them, perhaps cite one or two key statistics, or point out correlations, but *do not duplicate their data* in the text. Tables and charts should be sequenced and numbered in the order in which you discuss them in the text. To avoid ambiguity, refer to them as Table 1, Table 2, and Figure 1, Figure 2, not "in the table above" or "in the figure below."

The major difference between tables and graphs is the way they present data. Tables list the actual numbers, organized in rows and columns. This organization makes it easy for the reader to scan down a column and across a row to find a datum of interest. Graphs represent the numbers with physical markers such as columns, lines, or wedges. They make it easy to compare quantities. Current practice in mass communication journals privileges the table. There are situations when the table is the only viable format. In addition, when the data are numerous or when the variation among them is very small or extremely large, a graph may not be able to fulfill its function of visualizing a comparison.

In the 1989 edition of this book, Wayne Danielson maintained that tables and graphs must communicate their meaning to people who have not read the accompanying article. "Ideally, in a well-written scientific article, the tables should be able to stand alone," Danielson wrote. "This means that the main ideas of the report should, as a rule, find expression in a set of key tables or figures that can be read by themselves without reference to the text."[4] Guido H. Stempel III and Bruce H. Westley endorsed this position, adding, "Many who 'consult' articles turn to the tables first. They should not have to read columns of theory and method in order to understand exactly what the tables show."[5] Both statements remain excellent advice.

Conventions for Making and Reading Tables

There are conventions, or general agreements among their creators and users of tables, on what their components mean and how they should be arranged. For example, in statistical research the dependent variable goes in a table's columns; the independent variable, in its rows. Just as you learn the syntax and grammar of English, you must learn these conventions to communicate effectively with tables. Even within these guidelines, however, there is still latitude for emphasizing what you consider important about your research results.

The first conventions relate to the anatomy of a table, that is, its various parts and what they represent. Table 17.1 identifies the major parts of a typical table. From top to bottom these components and their conventions are:

1. The title begins at the top. Its first part is the number, and the second part describes the table's contents, in this case *Religious Backgrounds* .... Some writers recommend beginning titles for academic papers and journals with nouns that describe the data—for example, "Percents of ..." or "Frequencies of ... ."[6] Because they lack verbs, such titles are labels. The convention in the popular media is to write a headline with an active verb. For an academic paper, unless your professor specifies an approach, you may choose either option. Stylistic decisions include whether the table number designation goes on a separate line or on the same line as in this example, whether it and the contents are centered or

Title   Spanner headings   Column headings

TABLE 17.1. *Religious Backgrounds of U.S. Journalists Compared with U.S. Adult Population (percentage in each group)*

	Journalists			U.S. Adult Population		
Religion	**1971**[a]	**1982–83**[b]	**1992**	**1974**[c]	**1981**[d]	**1992**[e]
Protestant	61.5	60.5	54.5	60	59	55
Catholic	24.5	26.9	29.9	27	28	26
Jewish	6.4	5.8	5.4	2	2	1
Other or none	7.7	6.8	10.2	11	11	18
Total	100.1[f]	100	99.9[f]	100	100	100

Stub column ↗   Data cells →

Notes ↙

[a]From Johnstone, Slawski, and Bowman, *The News People*, pp. 90, 225. Figures calculated from Table 5.9.

[b]From Weaver and Wilhoit, *The American Journalist*, p. 24.

[c]From George H. Gallup, *The Gallup Poll: Public Opinion*, 1972–1977. Vol. 1 (Wilmington, DE: Scholarly Resources, 1973), p. 393.

[d]From *The Gallup Poll: Public Opinion*, 1982, p. 37.

[e]Gallup Organization national telephone survey of 1,001 U.S. adults, July 31–August 2, 1992. Question: What is your religious preference? Data provided by the Roper Center, University of Connecticut.

[f]Does not total to 100% because of rounding.

aligned at the left, whether to capitalize every word or use a capital and lower case style, and so on. Again, follow the style of the journal, the direction of your professor or, absent these, make your own choices. Many graphic designers prefer left alignment and a capital and lower case style because they promote readability. Whatever you choose, take care to maintain consistency within a single table or figure and, if there are more than one, across all of them.

2. Column headings, which go at the top of each column, are labels that define your data. Just as important, they show how you collected and have organized the data. They should be as brief as possible, while still conveying the necessary content. *Libertarians*, for example, is better than *Libertarian Party Members*. When column headings are considerably wider than the data in their columns, they expand the width of the table. When wide headings cannot be avoided, break them into two lines.

3. Column spanners are headings that are one level up in the organizational hierarchy. They extend across two or more column headings; in Table 17.1, *Journalists and U.S. Adult Population* are spanners. Column spanners have a rule line beneath them that extends the width of the columns that they define.

4. Stubs are the labels for the rows. They go in the extreme left column, which is called the stub column. This column also takes a heading. In Table 17.1, *Religion* is the stub heading and *Protestant* is the stub for the first data set. Typically, stubs are the independent variables.

5. Table spanners are analogous to column spanners in that they show relationships and organize complex arrays of data into more comprehensible displays. They are set off by rule lines above and below. Not every table requires table spanners. If Table 17.1 had a second, comparable set of data for Canadian journalists and Canada's adult population, the two data sets could be combined in a single table by using table spanners.

6. The body is the aggregation of all the data presented. In the example, the numbers from 61.5 at the top left to 100 at the bottom right constitute the body. The intersection of a column and a row, where an individual datum resides, is called a cell. In some cases there may not be a value for every cell. The *Publication Manual of the American Psychological Association*, 4th ed., (APA) an authoritative guide followed by many academic journals, specifies the following:

[If a cell] cannot be filled because data are not applicable, leave the cell blank. If a cell cannot be filled because data were not obtained or are not reported, insert a dash in that cell and explain the use of the dash in the general note to the table.[7]

The APA manual offers these additional guidelines for the contents of a table's body:

To help your reader absorb the data and make comparisons, consider rounding off the values instead of presenting precise ones. Because comparisons are more easily made down columns than across rows, arrange your data so that the comparisons that are most important fall in columns. Where appropriate, include averages or totals for columns and rows.[8]

7. Footnotes to a table are placed at the bottom of the table below a horizontal rule line, not at the bottom of the page. There are three kinds of notes, and they should appear in the following sequence: (a) General notes come first and provide information that pertains to the entire table. They also define abbreviations and give citations for sources. In research journals, general notes begin with the word Note., which is followed by a period and underlined. (b) Specific notes pertain to only parts of a table, for example, a column or a specific datum. Use lower case, superscript letters in the body of the table to refer to the same letter in the note below. Begin sequencing the letters with a lower case *a* at the top left, moving from left to right and top to bottom. One note may apply to several items in the body, in which case the same letter is used for all. However, specific notes are unique to their tables; they do not apply across two or more tables. In the example, *a* through *f* are the specific notes. (c) When your results warrant, use probability notes, which display levels of statistical significance. They should come last in the sequence of notes. Indicate them in the body with a sequence of asterisks, and use asterisks in the notes area. For example, $*p < .05$, $**p < .01$, $***p < .001$, and $****p < .0001$. Assign one asterisk to the largest p-value and continue sequencing them to the greatest number of asterisks for the smallest p-value. The APA manual specifies that the use of asterisks for probability notes should be consistent for all the tables in your article or paper.[9]

8. There are also conventions for rule lines and spacing in tables. Rule lines separate elements from each other; they should be used to add clarity to the organization. In Table 17.1, for example, lines at the top and bottom separate the table from the text. A third line separates the body of the table from its notes. Two additional lines indicate column spanners, which differentiate the two sets of three columns from each other. Because it is difficult and costly to insert vertical rule lines into a typeset table, they are generally avoided. In fact, vertical rule lines are not necessary. Ample white space can clearly separate columns.

An additional note about verbal content applies to both tables and figures: Avoid esoteric terms that require reading the text to understand. Common symbols such as % and $ and standard abbreviations used in statistics such as n=, df, χ^2 or p< can be used without explanation. Other symbols and abbreviations should be defined in a note. Depending on their length, it may save space to write out, instead of abbreviate, terms.

Graphs

Although graphs may be tainted in some researchers' thinking by their association with the "chartoon" approach of *Time* magazine or *USA Today*, they are a serious form of visual communication. Graphs are not mere decoration and should not be tacked on at the last minute without thought. Instead, consider plotting your data as a useful step in your research process. Numbers are abstractions. When there are many numbers or when they are very large, even the most experienced researchers may have trouble holding them in mind or making comparisons. Representing numbers pictorially can reveal relationships that may otherwise be overlooked. Computer software makes it easy to plot a data set in several graph formats, revealing relationships that may expand and enrich the way you think about your findings.

At the publication stage, representing numerical relationships with physical markers creates a gestalt, a visual pattern that lets your readers immediately perceive and compare relationships and retain a pictorial impression of those relationships. To experience this, compare Table 17.1 with Figure 17.1. Both present the same data, but the graph makes the comparisons concrete.

Conventions for Making and Reading Graphs

Conventions have been established that researchers need to follow in creating graphs and readers need to understand in interpreting them. The fundamental convention is that a graph represents numbers with pictorial markers that correspond in size to the quantities

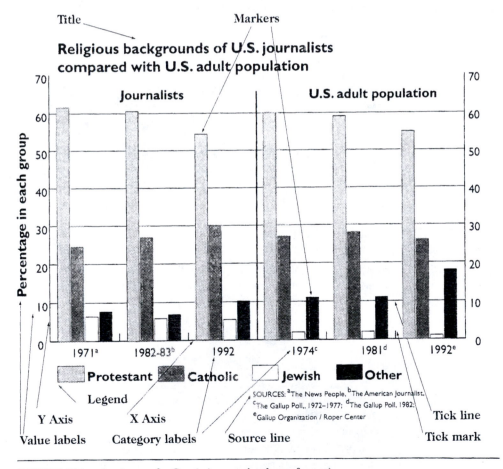

FIGURE 17.1.   Anatomy of a Graph (grouped-column format).

they represent. It is this proportionality of columns, data points, and wedges to their respective values that makes the graph effective in comparing two or more quantities. For graphs to be clear and accurate, their creators and users must agree on several additional conventions. This section discusses them.

The second convention is an agreement on the various parts of a graph. Figure 17.1 provides an anatomy of graphs. A graph communicates its information in two dimensions: A horizontal axis and a vertical axis extend from the lower left corner to form an L-shape. (The pie-chart format, which is based on the circle instead of the Cartesian grid is an exception.) You may also hear this horizontal axis called the X axis, the category axis, or the abscissa. In statistical research, the X axis is typically used to plot the independent variable(s). The vertical axis, which is also called the Y axis, value axis, or the ordinate, represents the quantities or numbers. In statistical research, the Y axis is typically used to plot the dependent variable(s). Both axes should be clearly labeled. Physical markers—columns, bars, lines, wedges, data points—represent the numerical quantities being compared.

Columns, bars, and wedges are differentiated by white, black, and shades of gray, or by hatching patterns. In the popular media they are typically in color. Tick marks extend out from the axes. Tick lines extend across the entire width or height of the graph. Both are intended to make it easier to read the marker values.

The verbal components provide the context necessary for a correct understanding of the data. They include the headline or title, a caption or blurb, and the source line. They also include labels, which define the categories and units of value, and legends, which define the markers. In academic journals, conventions for titling graphs are the same as for tables. For popular media, course assignments, or conference presentations, you may choose to write headlines with active verbs.

Graph Formats

There are several types of graphs, each of which has additional conventions. This section describes four major formats and their variations, notes their purposes and explains what interpretation each format gives to a data set. It also points out when certain formats are inappropriate because of ethical issues or communication limitations. The formats are column/bar with grouped and stacked variations, line with the area variation, pie, and scatter. Additional formats, which are not discussed but which you may want to explore, are radar and doughnut.

Column and Bar Graphs. The column and bar formats are identical, except for their orientations. Column markers are vertical; bar markers are horizontal. For brevity, this chapter will discuss only the column format, with the understanding that the markers may be rotated 90 degrees to produce the bar format.

The purpose of the column graph is to show comparisons among quantities. Because each datum is represented by a separate column and the columns are displayed side by side, this format offers an immediate visual comparison of the quantities. There are two variations of the column format, the grouped- and the stacked-column graphs. They offer alternative ways to organize quantities into subcategories. Figure 17.1, which is a grouped column, is organized into two subgroups; each of those is organized into three subcategories of time. This grouped-column format lets your readers compare the variables in each subcategory and also across the entire graph.

Figure 17.2, the stacked-column format, organizes the same data into six columns, representing the subcategories. It stacks the dependent variables on top of each other, which makes it easier to compare totals across the time frame. At the same time, it makes it more difficult to compare the variables, because except for the bottom range, they start at different points on the value axis.

The column format loses its effectiveness at facilitating comparisons when there are too many items in the data series or when the columns are too thin and too close together. Regarding the number of columns, cognitive psychologists say nine discrete items mark the upper limit of what the human visual apparatus can process as a gestalt. However, if the columns are grouped into patterns—for example, two subgroups, with three subcategories, with four values each as in Figure 17.1—larger number sets can be absorbed. What constitutes too thin and too close together depends on the number of columns and the width available for the graph. While there are no prescribed dimensions that will fit all situations, the column widths and the gaps between them must be large enough so the columns are clearly distinguishable. Figure 17.1 has 24 columns, which is near the maximum.

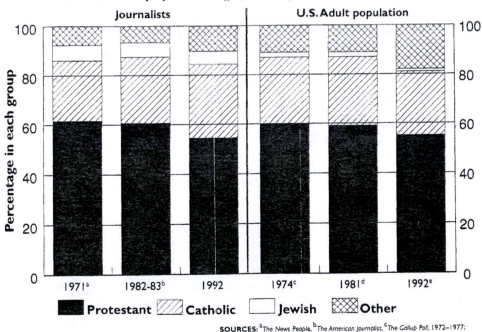

Religious backgrounds of U.S. journalists compared with U.S. adult population (percentage in each group)

SOURCES: [a]The News People, [b]The American Journalist, [c]The Gallup Poll, 1972–1977; [d]The Gallup Poll, 1982; [e]Gallup Organization / Roper Center

FIGURE 17.2. Stacked-Column Graph Format.

Column graphs are also inappropriate when there is a very small difference between the largest and smallest items so that all the columns are about the same height. For example, there would be no visible difference among columns representing 67.8%, 68.1%, and 68.3%. At the other extreme, they are not appropriate when the difference between the largest and smallest items is extreme. In a graph comparing 85.3% and 0.6%, the second column would have no height. In both cases, the data do not justify the space necessary for a graph. If you must display such data, use a table.

A fourth problem results when data are missing for some quantities. Rather than run the columns solid, a gap should be left to alert the reader that information is missing. A footnote should also be added explaining what is missing and why.

Line Graphs. The line graph (Figure 17.3) shows trends by connecting data points with a line. The purposes of the line format are to show changes in the dependent variable across the independent variable and to show interactions between two or more independent variables on a dependent variable. In the popular media, because the category axis often represents time increments, this format is closely associated with showing trends over time. It is frequently called a fever graph, in reference to the graphs that nurses keep on

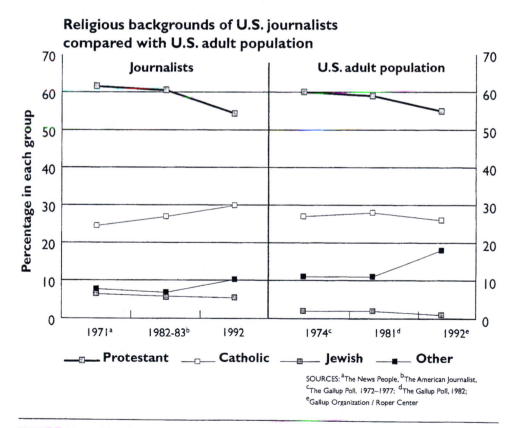

FIGURE 17.3. Line Graph Format.

the temperatures of hospital patients. Typically, two or more data series are plotted on the same grid, which allows readers to compare their respective trends. When the value axis scale is linear, the physical increments are equal and represent equal numerical amounts. In Figure 17.3, for example, all value units on the Y axis are the same height, and each represents 10 percent. Value axis scales can also be logarithmic or log-linear.

If time is the independent variable, the presumption in line graphs is that there will be a value datum for each unit of time. When data are missing for one or more time units, there is a potential to be misleading. A line connecting 1998 to 2000 implies a continuous change, but the missing datum for 1999 may fall above or below the connecting line. One solution is to break the line to alert the reader to the missing information and to explain the gap with a footnote.

The area graph is a variation on the line graph that is analogous to the stacked column graph. Each data series is added to the top of the previous ones, thus showing both the individual data series and their totals. While this format emphasizes totals as trends over time, it makes it difficult to read the component data series because all except the bottom series have shifting base lines. The same issues of appropriateness that apply to the line graph also apply to the area graph format.

Pie Graphs.   The pie graph (Figure 17.4), also called a "100% graph," shows a total quantity broken down into its constituent parts. The purpose of the format is to compare the relative proportions of the parts that constitute the whole. The markers for the parts are wedges of a circle, hence the analogy to a pie with its slices. Because of its purpose, the pie format is not appropriate when the components do not add up to 100 percent of a quantity. The pie format loses its effectiveness when there are too many divisions to process visually. Most graphic designers consider eight to be the maximum number of wedges that

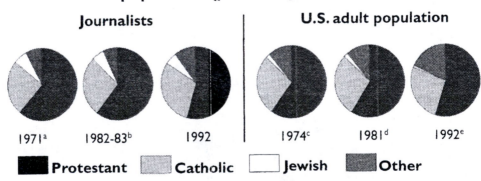

Religious backgrounds of U.S. journalists compared with U.S. adult population (percentage in each group)

Journalists   **U.S. adult population**

1971[a]   1982-83[b]   1992   1974[c]   1981[d]   1992[e]

■ **Protestant**   ▨ **Catholic**   □ **Jewish**   ▦ **Other**

SOURCES: [a]*The News People.* [b]*The American Journalist.* [c]*The Gallup Poll, 1972–1977;* [d]*The Gallup Poll, 1982;* [e]Gallup Organization / Roper Center

FIGURE 17.4.   Pie Graph Format.

can be processed. Similarly, when an individual wedge is smaller than 2 percent, it is difficult for the reader to register.

By convention, the wedges are sequenced from largest to smallest with the largest beginning at the top center of the circle. Most graphing programs will do this sequencing automatically, regardless of how you enter the data. To emphasize one component, its wedge may be pulled out from the rest of the circle.

Scatter Graphs.   Scatter graphs plot data on a grid, representing each intersection of two variables with a dot or point. The grouping of these dots together in clusters may indicate meaningful correlations between two variables. Scatter graphs are most appropriate for interval- or ratio-level data where there are many values, for example, income or age. See Chapter 9 on statistics for an example.

Ethical Issues

Like other communication systems—including writing or photography—graphs can communicate clearly and accurately or they can mislead readers by giving ambiguous or false representations of the data they represent. The more graphs mislead, the more they will lose credibility as a visual communication tool. In some fields, such as advertising and politics, some practitioners deliberately use graphs to distort data in order to promote their product, candidate, or issue. Such unethical usage deserves to be exposed and condemned. More often, however, misleading graphs result from their preparers' not being aware of the ethical issues. Such uninformed usage needs to be recognized and corrected.

As noted, the fundamental premise of a graph is that the columns, wedges, or other markers are in correct physical proportion to the numbers they represent and, thus, to each other. Readers assume that a marker that is physically twice as large as a second marker represents a number that is twice as large as the second number. The graph offers a visual gestalt that the mind can absorb more easily than a set of numbers. When the components of this gestalt are out of proportion, a false impression of the relationship among quantities is given. At best it is misleading. At worst, it is lying. Ethical problems with graphs typically fall into three categories:

Not Beginning with a Zero Baseline.   This problem applies primarily to column, line, and area graphs. Markers should compare totals, not parts. When the horizontal base of a graph is not zero, then the markers compare only parts. The higher above zero the baseline is, the greater the distortion. In the popular media, variations on this ethical violation include not showing the baseline, making it ambiguous through artwork, or not specifying its value.

Figure 17.5a shows a violation of the zero-baseline standard based on an actual advertisement for a pickup truck that was published as a national campaign in the major news magazines. The actual difference between the left and right numbers is 2.9 percent, but the left marker is 13.73 times as high as the right. Because the baseline begins at 95 percent, the markers only compare the top 5 percent of the totals. Figure 17.5b shows the same data plotted with a zero baseline. It is an honest representation of the data, not visual hyperbole.

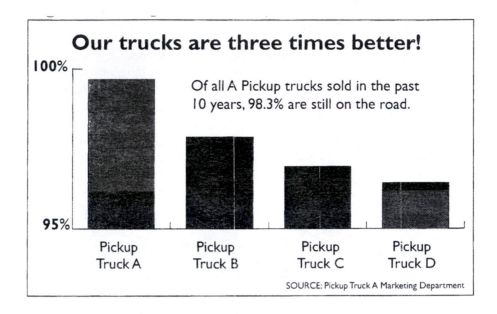

(a)

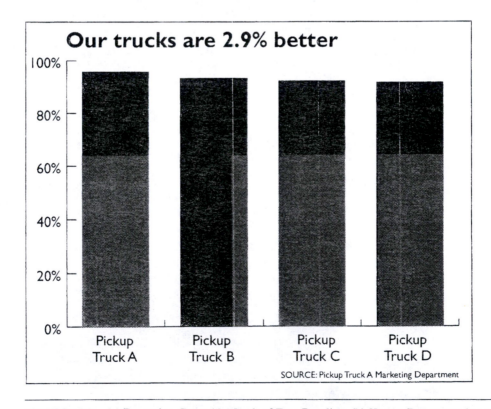

(b)

FIGURE 17.5.   (a) Deception Caused by Lack of Zero Baseline. (b) Honest Representation with Zero Baseline.

Space Used as a Justification for Not Starting a Graph at Zero.   The contention is that the graph would take up less space if the columns did not begin at zero. This argument is false, because the height of a graph has no effect on whether its columns are in proportion to each other. Even so, if there is pressure to shorten the height of markers, you should use a convention that acknowledges that truncation. In column graphs, a zigzag gap is put into the columns near their baseline (Figure 17.6a) In line graphs, a zigzag line interrupts the value axis near the baseline (Figure 17.6b). Readers understand these signs as visual warnings that the markers are not in correct physical proportion. With large numbers in a series some graphing programs plot the baseline above zero. You need to be alert for this and know how to override it by reestablishing a zero baseline. Typically, you change the value axis's starting point to zero in a style panel. Skewing the grid applies primarily to the line and area graph formats. The same data set can generate graphs with dramatically different lines, simply by varying the height or width of the grid. Increasing the grid vertically exaggerates the changes because it makes each value unit taller. Increasing the grid horizontally minimizes changes because it makes each value unit proportionally shorter. Figures 17.7a and 17.7b illustrate these distortions. Both show the same data set. In Figure 17.7a, which skews the grid vertically, the changes seem very dramatic. In Figure 17.7b, which skews the grid horizontally, the changes seem modest. For the most honest representation, grid units should be square. That is, the height of each value unit should equal the width of each category unit (Figure 17.7c).

Enlarging Markers Geometrically instead of Arithmetically.   This problem occurs in column graphs when drawings, instead of rectangles, are used for the markers. Such graphs are rarely used in research journals, but they are prevalent in the popular media. Drawings make comparisons difficult because they vary in both height and width, while columns have the same width. As shown in Figure 17.8a, a researcher may construct one marker twice the height of a second one with the intention of representing twice the numerical value. However, because drawings increase or decrease geometrically, the area of the first drawing is not double, but quadruple, the area of the second. Readers will compare the drawings based on their areas, not their heights, and will mistakenly interpret the difference to be fourfold. When drawings are used in the column graph format, the ethically correct practice is to make them repeating modules as in Figure 17.8b, with each module representing the same quantity. This kind of modular chart is also called a pictorial graph.

An issue analogous to the geometric-versus-arithmetic problem is the trend toward showing columns and bars in three-dimensional perspective, which can also distort accurate physical proportionality. Perspective is rarely used in scholarly journals, but you should be aware of it in the mass media. It is a common option in graphing software, but should be avoided.

To these visual issues can be added two ethical cautions about the verbal components of graphs. First, if the data you are presenting do not result from your own research, you must cite the source(s). This will help readers evaluate the veracity of the data. Second, enough verbal context must be included through a title, subtitle, caption, labels, legends, and so on, to make the meaning of the graph unambiguous. Do not assume that the reader will intuit your intentions. Also, do not assume that the reader has read your

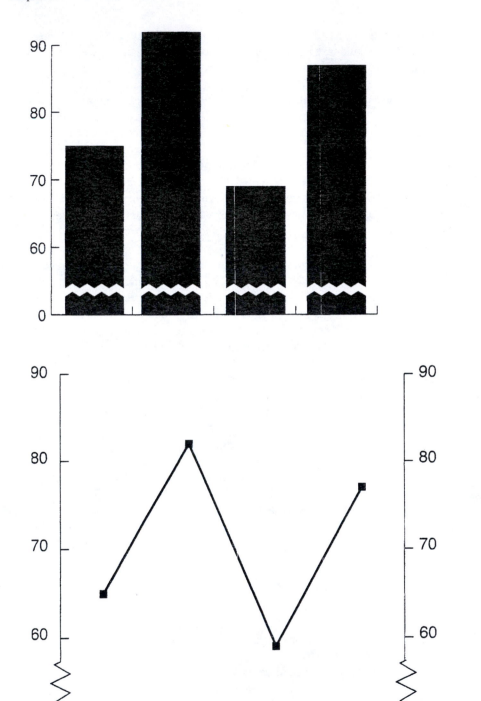

FIGURE 17.6.   (a) Broken Columns. (b) Broken Value Axis.

article and brings that knowledge to your table or graph. As noted in the introduction, tables and graphs should stand on their own.

Charts

There is not space in this chapter for an extended discussion of the many types of charts. The basic stylistic guidelines noted for tables and graphs apply. It is difficult to offer other guidelines, because charts differ greatly depending on the research, theory, or process you are presenting. Several excellent examples of charts are shown throughout this book. See, for example, Chapter 15 on experiments.

Visual Communication Principles

In addition to a conceptual understanding of theory and a commitment to ethical practices, researchers who create tables, graphs and charts need a third area of knowledge and skills: the broad principles and specific guidelines necessary for effective visual communication.

Clarity is the primary principle for achieving effectiveness. All the visual and verbal components should combine to present your data so clearly that they cannot be misunderstood. Keep in mind that in the case of graphs and charts, you are trying to encapsulate your data in a visual gestalt that can be immediately understood and retained. While this principle is easy to articulate, it is not achieved without an understanding of visual literacy. Clarity implies other major principles: The first is unity, which requires that you have a purpose for the table or figure and that you focus all of your editorial and design decisions to support that purpose. Among other factors, unity results from consistency in typography, graphic elements, spacing, alignment, and so on. Another principle is simplicity, which requires that you eliminate everything not necessary to communicate your core idea. A third principle is emphasis; when one part of your data is more important to your argument, you should know how to emphasize it visually. This section discusses these principles and offers guidelines for achieving them.

The graph designer has available the following visual elements to achieve clarity, unity, and emphasis: typography, tonality, rule lines, borders, space, and alignment. As a student preparing tables and graphs to illustrate a course assignment, you have considerable latitude in employing these elements. As a researcher preparing your work for publication, your options are more constrained. As noted, you must learn and follow the guidelines for the journal to which you plan to submit your article. If it has no guidelines or the guidelines do not address your questions, consult the *Publication Manual of the American Psychological Association*, 4th ed., which is comprehensive and authoritative. Even within such guidelines, there is some latitude.

While this section discusses graphs and tables as individual items, if you create several for the same article, be sure to use a uniform style of typography, rule lines, space, and other elements, for all of them. Similarly, make your verbal terminology consistent across all the images. If you label a group "preteens" in one figure, do not call the same group "children" in another.

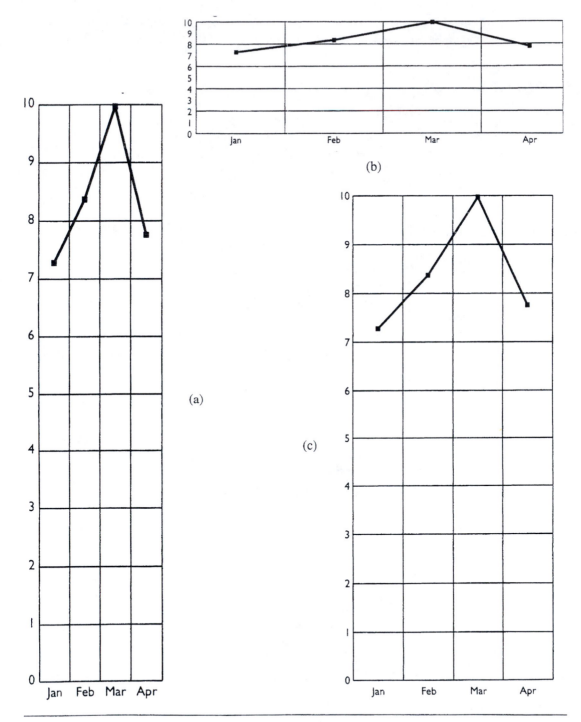

FIGURE 17.7. (a) Grid Skewed Vertically. (b) Grid Skewed Horizontally. (c) Ethically Correct Grid, with Equal Value and Category Units.

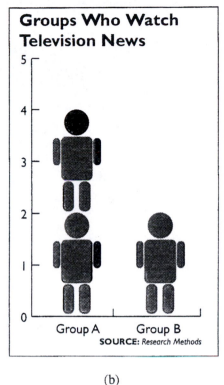

(a)   (b)

FIGURE 17.8.   (a) Misleading Geometric Marker. (b) Modular Markers.

The large number of typefaces that come bundled with most computer operating systems may tempt novice designers to use several in a table or graph. You can do excellent work with only one typeface and should limit yourself to that when preparing work for a journal. In the United States, almost all books, journals, and academic papers use serif typefaces for their primary text. To distinguish your tables and graphs from the text, choose a sans serif typeface. *Serif* refers to the short strokes that run perpendicular to the letters' primary strokes. *Sans serif* means without serifs. [This is serif type. This is sans serif type.] If you are creating tables or graphs for a course assignment or a popular media outlet, you might use a second face. Limiting your tables and graphs to one, or at most two, typefaces will help unify them. Use typefaces that have proven themselves over time. Among serif faces, good choices are Bookman, Caslon, Century Schoolbook, Garamond, Palatino, Times, and Times New Roman. Among sans serif faces, good choices are Avant-Garde, GillSans, Geneva, Helvetica, and Univers. In no case should you use script (calligraphic) or decorative faces.

Typography should function to differentiate the various levels of verbal and numerical information. For example, it should distinguish between a title and a subtitle. The caption or blurb should be distinct from notes. Legends and labels should be identical with each other, but clearly different from the source line. Create these distinctions with the following variables: the two typefaces, all capitals versus capitals and lowercase, a range of point sizes, regular versus bold weights, and regular versus italic, or oblique, angles.

One overriding principle of typographic clarity is that the point size must be large enough to read. This sounds obvious, but in the editorial process as tables and graphs are scaled down to fit the available space, type elements such as labels, footnotes, and source lines can become too small to read. In no case should type be smaller than 8 points in its published version. The APA style manual specifies that there be no more than four points difference in the typographic elements in a table, ranging from 8 to 12 points. For other work, consider a wider range.

Be aware that the point sizes you designate as you are creating your chart may not be the finished sizes that appear in the journal; the printing process may cause them to be enlarged or reduced. Most journals publish tables and figures the full width of the line of type. If a journal uses a two-column format, tables and figures may be either one or two columns wide. When preparing graphs or charts for a journal, it is a good practice to measure the width of its columns or pages and size your work to that width. With this approach, 8-point type in your work should appear as 8 points in the journal.

Because tables are typeset, their width is even more crucial. If the numbers of characters in your table exceed the number of possible characters in a line of type, the editor may have to turn your table sideways, which is undesirable for the readers, or not use it. While it may seem tedious, count the numbers of characters in a line, count the character width of your table and compare them. If your table exceeds the line width, edit it to a workable width.

Just as typography should distinguish verbal elements, tonality and hatching should differentiate the markers that represent the various number sets. Hatching refers to parallel diagonal lines used to fill columns, wedges, or other solid areas. With crosshatching two sets of diagonal lines run in opposite directions, crossing each other. Figure 17.2 shows examples of both. The alternative is using black, white, and shades of gray. There is disagreement over hatching and crosshatching with concerns about reproduction pitted against issues of perceptual psychology. The APA manual recommends hatching based on the experience that "fine stippling and shading can 'drop out,' or disappear, when reproduced."[10] From the perspective of perceptual psychology, many graphic designers dislike hatching, and especially crosshatching, because the resulting patterns with their strong contrasts call attention to themselves, and away from the overall gestalt. Many designers consider hatching to be a kind of visual static and lump it into a larger category of faults called graph junk. This is especially a problem when the markers filled with hatching and crosshatching are small.

How should you resolve this disagreement in your own work? If you are submitting to a journal, learn and follow its style by reading its guidelines but also by studying the graphs it publishes. For your course assignments, print and evaluate your graph(s) to see if the tonality holds up and if it makes the necessary distinctions. On laser-printed pages a tonal difference of 25 percent should distinguish markers clearly. This standard will accommodate five different markers—white, 25%, 50%, 75%, and black—which is probably adequate for most graphs. For four markers, use white, 35%, 65%, and black. Overhead slides for a conference presentation present a different problem. Tonality often gets lost as the original is transferred by a copy machine onto an acetate slide. The safest practice is to make and test some examples. If the tones break down, use hatching.

Rule lines separate elements. Boxes or borders unite the contents inside them while separating those contents from elements outside the box. Most mass communication journals do not box tables and figures. For course assignments, conference presentations, and the popular media you may want to use boxes. They will unify the image and emphasize its contents. Most computer applications offer a variety of widths and dot and dash patterns for rule lines and boxes. Avoid them, because they call undue attention to themselves, detracting from the more important markers. For simplicity, use a solid line, 1 point in width. If your data are complex enough to require a second width to differentiate various levels, use 0.5 point, called a hairline in most programs.

Space can also be an effective tool for organizing data and differentiating various components. It can help clarify the organizational structure of your table or graph. Relatively larger amounts of space separate items. Relatively smaller amounts unify items. The primary guideline for using space is to arrange elements that are related closer together and elements that are not related further apart. Tables 17.2 through 17.4c show how this works in a table. In Table 17.2, proximity among the lines and distance among the tab stops emphasizes the relationships as columns. Table 17.3 emphasizes the relationship as rows. In Table 17.4, the equal horizontal and vertical spacing around all the numbers leaves the relationship ambiguous. As a researcher you must decide what relationship, if any, you want to emphasize. As a communicator, you need to know how to create the table that produces the emphasis you want. While not difficult, it requires that you go beyond the default settings on standard word processing software. You must control the width of the tabular stops and the line spacing to set up these relationships of proxemics.

This general principle of spacing related elements together applies to graphs as well as tables. Whenever possible, for example, labels should go inside or adjacent to markers, instead of in a legend at some remove.

Like spacing, alignment is also a subtle but important factor in design. It has the potential to unify your tables and graphs. Though most readers do not register it consciously, alignment and especially the lack of alignment do affect humans on a subliminal level. In tables, lines of type are typically aligned along their left edges and columns of numbers along their right edges. Numbers with decimals should be aligned on their decimal points. Most word processing programs let you create decimal tab stops, but you must override the default ones.

The human visual perceptual apparatus is strongly attracted to pattern. Too much pattern, especially if it is not related to the core idea of your graph, can compromise your message. Numerous tick lines, dotted and dashed rule lines, and excessive hatchings call attention to themselves and divert it from your data. You might think about them as visual static or "graph junk." While it may be tempting to try out all the possibilities when you

TABLE 17.2 *Proxemics Emphasizing Columns*

Democrat	61	60	54	41
Libertarian	37	26	29	57
Republican	46	35	83	35
Reform	82	73	48	26

TABLE 17.3 *Proxemics Emphasizing Rows*

Democrat	61	60	54	41
Libertarian	37	26	29	57
Republican	46	35	85	35
Reform	82	73	48	26

TABLE 17.4 *Proxemics without Emphasis*

Democrat	61	60	54	41
Libertarian	37	26	29	57
Republican	46	35	85	35
Reform	82	73	48	26

are making your first graphs, it will brand you as a neophyte among graphic designers. Worse, it will obscure what you want to communicate.

Getting Started on the Computer

If you have never created a graph on a computer, you need some guidance to get started. This section discusses several decisions you will need to make and offers a process to take you through the creation of your first graph.

Again, your first decision is whether or not a table or graph is necessary. Graphs take up space, which is a serious issue for journal editors. In a course assignment, cost and space are usually not issues, but, even so, you do not want to inundate your professor with unnecessary graphics that are not germane to your argument. If you can adequately describe what is important about your data in a sentence or two, do not create a graph that takes up a third of a page. On the other hand, if the data you need to establish your argument are extensive or complex or if the comparisons or trends are not readily apparent from the numbers themselves, do not hesitate to create the necessary tables or graphs. As pointed out in the introduction, running your data through the graph formats for your own understanding can be a valuable research tool. Doing this should help you decide which data series you need to display with your paper or article and in which formats.

The second decision is about technical tools: What software should you use to create your graph? The Statistical Package for the Social Sciences (SPSS) and Microsoft Excel may be obvious choices for many researchers. Both can be used for your calculations. Both have functions that let you turn your calculations into graphs without changing software or re-keystroking the data. In addition, Excel comes installed on many computers and is relatively simple to use. Its Chart Wizard walks you step by step through the process of creating the chart by offering and explaining options at each stage.

The major disadvantage of Excel is its lack of precision design controls. The standard graphing software used by graphic designers is Adobe Illustrator, which offers superior control of all the visual aspects of the graph. While Illustrator does not have a spreadsheet function, it does let you import or copy and paste spreadsheet data into its graph environment. Other graphing applications include Cricket Graph, Freehand, and some word processing programs such as Microsoft Word. For charts, a drawing program such as Illustrator is the best option. Some word processing programs include drawing tools, but they are cumbersome and imprecise compared to applications whose primary function is drawing.

Because of space limitations, it is not possible to give instructions for creating all the graph formats on the various computer applications. Instead, this section offers an overview of the steps that are standard in most programs. This, coupled with individual coaching from an instructor or classmate plus the application's online help function, should prepare you to create graphs.

1. First, launch the program, find and select its graph tool, and then choose the graph format that will best display your data. In most graphing programs, you can easily change the format after the initial graph is plotted.

2. Next, enter your data into the cells created by the intersection of the columns and rows. At this point, it looks like a table. In software like SPSS or Excel, you will already have done this in the calculation phase. In Illustrator, you can import the data, copy and paste it, or re-keystroke it into the data panel. If you want your graph to have subcategories, such as the grouped column format (Figure 17.1), you must know where to put category and legend labels. As shown in Figure 17.9, leave the top left cell blank. Type the category labels (independent variables) down the first column at the left. Type the legend labels (dependent variables) in the row across the top. Type the data in the appropriate cells.

3. When you tap the enter key or go on to the next stage, the software transforms your data into a graph. Among other operations, it calculates the size of the markers to be in proportion to their numbers, creates the legend, adds the category and value labels, and draws the axes and tick marks. Working from this basic graph, you may decide to change formats, adjust the graph's height or width, manually override a baseline that begins above zero, customize the markers' tonality, or make other stylistic refinements as discussed above.

4. The category and legend labels that you entered in the data panel will appear as part of the graph. You may want to customize their typography, changing typeface, point size, weight, and so on. You may also want to relocate some of these default elements. For example, putting labels inside the pie wedges rather than leaving them in a legend is a convenience for your readers. You will also need to add the other verbal components, including the title, caption, source line, and so on. Customize the typography of these elements and locate them on your graph. By convention, readers expect the title and subtitle to start at the top left and the source line to be at the bottom right. In mass communication journals, the caption is located beneath the table or graph. If you are preparing graphs for the popular media or a course assignment, you have more freedom in locating these elements. For example, you might place the caption or blurb in any open area within the graph. The primary consideration is that your choices enhance, rather than impede, a clear reading of the graph.

	Protestant	Catholic	Jewish	Other	
"1971"	61.5	24.5	6.4	7.7	
"1982–83"	60.5	26.9	5.8	6.8	
"1992"	54.4	29.9	5.4	10.2	
"1974"	60.0	27.0	2.0	11.0	
"1981"	59.0	28.0	2.0	11.0	
"1992"	55.0	26.0	1.0	18.0	

FIGURE 17.9.   Data panel.

5. The final steps represent a quality control process. Print your table or graph at the size it will actually appear in your paper or in the journal. Study it carefully for accuracy, clarity of communication, and observance of ethical guidelines. Show it to a classmate or colleague and ask for that person's constructive criticism. Based on your own evaluation and that of others, refine the table or graph before you print your paper or submit your article to a journal editor.

In current practice, some mass communication journals want "camera-ready copy"—that is, figures that are ready to put on an engraving camera. In this case, you have the final responsibility for the content, style, and effective communication of your tables and figures. Other journals want graphs and charts submitted as computer files on magnetic disks. In this case, a graphic designer or editor will probably edit your table, graph, or chart to make it conform to the journal's typographic and graphic style and also fit the required size. Still other journals ask for both camera-ready copy and computer files. If you are in doubt, communicate with the journal's editorial office.

Conclusion

Making effective tables, graphs, and charts is not difficult, but it does require thought and planning. The payoff in increased communication of your research makes this effort worthwhile. A sizable number of readers are likely to look at your tables, graphs, and charts first and, based on them, decide whether to read the entire article. Even if they do not read your article, the combinations of numbers, pictures, and words in these visual formats should provide them with an overview of your research.

Endnotes

1. Leonardo da Vinci, *The Notebooks of Leonardo da Vinci* arranged, rendered into English and introduced by Edward MacCurdy (New York: G. Braziller, 1956).

2. René Descartes, *Discourse on the Method of Rightly Conducting the Reason and Seeking Truth in the Sciences*, 1637 (New York: Readex Microprint, 1973).

3. William Playfair, *The Commercial and Political Atlas* (London: Printed for J. Debrett, G. C. and J. Robinson, and J. Sewell, 1786).

4. Wayne A. Danielson, "Data Processing," in Guido H. Stempel, III, and Bruce H. Westley, eds., *Research Methods in Mass Communication* (Englewood Cliffs, NJ: Prentice Hall, 1989), 118.

5. Guido H. Stempel, III, and Bruce H. Westley, "Presentation of Research Results," in *op. cit.*, 391.

6. *Ibid.*, 391.

7. *Publication Manual of the American Psychological Association*, 4th ed. (Washington, DC: American Psychological Association, 1994), 129.

8. *Ibid.*, 121.

9. *Ibid.*, 137.

10. *Ibid.*, 155.

18

Separating Wheat from Chaff in Qualitative Studies

Robert S. Fortner

Clifford G. Christians

Assessing the merit of our research and scholarship is a perennial dilemma. We insist on footnotes in essays so our arguments can be reviewed and our sources checked. We replicate experiments to verify their findings. The problem of proper assessment is inherent in all academic life. However, separating the wheat from the chaff is particularly difficult in the humanities, and even more so as a result of interpretive demands in the wake of post-modernism. Communication research that takes its inspiration from the humanities shares in this larger uneasiness. However, the vitality and continued development of "humanistic models"[1] depend greatly, it seems to us, on the manner in which qualitative communication research engages the ongoing problem of verifying results.

Our concern in this chapter is to suggest means for producing competent humanistic research, with particular reference to the cultural approach, or what is sometimes called qualitative studies. We want to become more precise about valid investigation in this area. Statistically verifiable results are not appropriate in qualitative studies, since they operate with a mentality rooted in the humanities. However, while this fact may mean that qualitative research will lack the elegance of statistical tests, it should not imply a lack of rigor.

Precision and verification are particularly elusive for culturalists because their concern is meaning that has been generated and used by persons who would influence others, by those who have created cultural materials as interpretations of existence (such as music, film, and newspapers), meaning that has been generated and used as explanation by human beings coping with daily existence (and its intrinsic components, such as work, play, family, and peers), meaning that can be identified that helps form a matrix, a web, of meanings, which eventually allows the culturalist to explain the ways human beings have organized community and family life. An orientation to meaning has come under vigorous attack from that scholarship presuming a meaningless existence and negativity as its starting point. It is assailed too by scholars claiming that all meaning is subjective and that it is illegitimate to abstract more general meanings from the particular. We insist on social meaning here as central to the culturalist's understanding of communication theory. We further insist on the legitimacy of constructing such social meaning from the collective meaning-making activities of individuals and institutions in society, and on interpreting these collective acts through careful analytical strategies. Communication could be defined from our perspective as the process by which meanings are created and exchanged.[2]

Internal and External Validity

How can research make meaning such an all-encompassing notion and yet accept some recognizable boundaries within which to pursue this elusive term? Here we confront that question directly, suggesting that cultural studies need their own version of internal and external validity and must meet acceptable standards of logic.

It should be apparent that the cultural approach to communication research remains interested throughout in empirical data. It does not accumulate such data with a highly refined methodology, and it avoids what C. Wright Mills called abstracted empiricism.[3] Yet pursuing evidentiary detail is as fundamental to the humanistic endeavor as it is to all academic life. Reliable data are crucial to responsible conclusions in this mode of scholarship, even though it does not aim to test hypotheses statistically but to gain sensitive understanding.

Instead of laboratory experiments and field surveys as traditionally understood, cultural analyses tend to favor natural, noncontrived settings. The Chicago School of Sociology in the early twentieth century, for example, treated the hobo, the street gang, an ethnic minority, slum dwellers, the professional thief all in their natural habitats. Data were collected in the form of people's own words, gestures, and behavior. Personal documents are the mainstays in discovering how people experience life in concrete situations, as Florian Znaniecki illustrated so dramatically in his afterword to *The Polish Peasant*. We mean, obviously, not just the self-revelations of geniuses or members of an elite class, but the folk wisdom of ordinary people. Thus archival searches for letters, diaries, autobiographical notes, memorabilia, memoirs, verbatim reports, artistic reports, and all manner of private records have special significance as inside revelations. They permit us to study intimate facets of human drama that are not directly observable.[4]

In addition to first-person accounts, open-ended, unstructured interviewing plays a prominent role in discovering how people define their realities. The voluntary character of the interview process is considered paramount, so that the interaction occurs as freely and in as nonstandardized a fashion as interviewing can permit, given the inevitable awkwardness in the relationship of strangers. Moreover, participant observation is recommended for plumbing the depths of a group's experience. The ideal experimenter, in this view, is not an "immaculate perceiver of an objective reality,"[5] but a person so unobtrusively steeped in people or documents that the investigator becomes an intimate, even thinking in the language of those being studied.

Ideally, the data must always be collected unobtrusively; yet the culturalist still seeks to do so systematically. Even though it does not rise from randomized samples or within tightly controlled variables, the aim is solid evidence nonetheless. In fact, the overriding importance of concreteness and the goal of illuminating real-life situations place unusual demands on the researcher. Students of culture select their material not by fixed rules but by Pascal's *esprit de finesse*, not reducing it to isolated variables but consistently viewing it as a whole. The often unstructured nature of the qualitative approach demands that users be very self-conscious, even critically so, of their procedures. Along these lines we offer several suggestions for effective data gathering.

It is widely understood and accepted that field surveys and laboratory experiments must be externally and internally valid; cultural studies need to meet these criteria as well (albeit in a manner peculiar to their own assumptions). External validity forces naturalistic observers to be circumspect in generalizing to other situations; have they, this guideline asks, selected cases and illustrations that are representative of the class, social unit, tribe, or organization to which they properly belong? Cultural studies arise in natural settings and not contrived ones, yet overgeneralizing remains a danger. The more densely textured our specifics, the more we can maintain external validity. Our concern here is particularly apropos in preparing case studies, a favorite qualitative tool since it allows in-depth and holistic probing.[6] In Norman Denzin's felicitous phrasing, the objective is representative rather than anecdotal (i.e., spectacular but idiosyncratic) cases.[7]

Regarding internal validity, our research mode must satisfy the requirement that the observations reflect genuine features of the situation under study and not aberrations or hurried conclusions that merely represent observer opinion. We are not interested in gathering only measurable details such as mortality rates; the culturalist, instead, disentangles the several layers of meaning inherent in any human activity. As Clifford Geertz puts it, "What the ethnographer is in fact faced with is a multiplicity of complex conceptual structures, many of them superimposed upon or knotted into one another, which are at once strange, irregular, and inexplicit, and which he must contrive somehow first to grasp and then to render."[8] We ask, "Is there sympathetic immersion in the material until one establishes, in Blumer's phrase, 'poetic resonance' with it?" Do we know enough to establish the principal aspects of the event being studied and to distinguish these main features from digressions and parentheses? Using the body as an analogue, do we separate the blood and brain from fingernails and skin, all of which are parts of the whole organism but of differing significance? It is usually assumed that such participatory observation can only serve an exploratory function, but we consider this a false assumption. If true interiority has occurred, that is, if data accurately reflect the natural circumstances, those data are valid and reliable even though not based upon randomization, repeated and controlled observation, measurement, and statistical inference. Our concern is for a research style that reduces situations and simultaneously maintains a broad understanding.

Another guideline for unearthing evidence involves the practice of exegesis, our effort at reading situations or documents with grammatical precision. Cultural studies consider failure on this expository level to be especially debilitating since their objective is rich detail. Ability to do accurate exegetical work requires cultivation so that a twitching eyelid is correctly interpreted as either a mischievous wink or incipient conspiracy (or simply a twitch). Simile is distinguished from allegory. Erving Goffman's work excels primarily because it diligently attends to every behavioral nuance. Admittedly, this norm, a developed grammatical sense, can only be placed on a sliding scale from meager to rich, yet culturalists insist on its being an important axis separating competent from incompetent study. Too much cultural work appears with blurred grammatical categories and without the laborious attention to lexical details, which demonstrates that the analyst has distinguished literal and figurative, has established historical antecedents and origins, has discovered words and their social patterns, knows exact meanings of synonyms and parallels, and the like. Often qualitative research proceeds arbitrarily and does haphazard exegesis of either documents or events (or both).

This attention to the character of expressions is not a scholastic exercise. No one knows better than the author of a document (whether a novel, law, judicial opinion, historical essay, letter, telegram, testimony, newspaper article, song, or script) what particular sense he or she attaches to a word. This is initially assumed to be authentic; judging inauthenticity comes later. Culturalists consider it their highest priority to see the world as the actors themselves imagine or interpret it. The culturalist attempts to see the world through others' eyes, using all the possible textual material available from the most obvious (the authored statute, perhaps) to the most obscure (the individual letter to a legislator, for instance). Such evidence is used to provide the most comprehensive view of an issue or era possible. Relevant actors include all persons who elect to become involved, or who are involved even involuntarily, in events or movements under study. The culturalist does not assume a priori that only the views of the major figures in events or controversies are germane. The texts themselves establish the parameters of interpretation, classification (typification), and eventual explanation (valuation).

Cultural studies deliberately center on real-life settings and written personalia, but not to the total exclusion of secondary sources (those not directly expressing a meaning structure) and information abstracted from everyday events. In fact, the culturalist's historical penchant often allows no other choice but to pursue public archives in addition to private ones and encourages submersion in every kind of human record, no matter how far removed from real life.[9] Normally, the public archives yield only secondary material—court testimony, newspaper accounts, business documents, actuarial statements, budget records—and thus are incomplete by themselves. Because these items usually represent a peculiar motivation and posture toward the issues, the selective bias must be ferreted out by careful attention to contexts.

The researcher does not merely cite these secondary documents, but rather weighs, evaluates, and then reconstructs them fairly. That principle obviously holds for all secondary materials; researching them is worthwhile only to the extent that they are painstakingly contextualized. Therefore, in dealing with such secondary material, we must ask several pertinent questions in order to measure this material appropriately: Is the evidence verifiable from other sources or corroborated by similar material in other locations? Can the testimony of the evidence be explained by its own bias? Is the evidence internally consistent or do contradictions occur that cannot be logically resolved? As a detective follows clues and then evaluates the evidence according to established rules, so we insist on our secondary sources' meeting certain basic requirements. Was the author an insider with credentials? To whom were the materials addressed–to a confidant, the public, an official? Was the statement made only out of self-interest? Taking evidence away from its context is a cardinal sin. We must never lose the flavor of the original, even though our task is reconstructing the material into a usable approximation to the truth. Deliberate care in dealing with imperfectly constructed records will help achieve a more complete and accurate rendering of events.[10] Secondary sources can be helpful in the triangulation process described next and in expanding the scope of the inquiry.

Effective use of **triangulation** is another mark of competent humanistic research. Norman Denzin elaborates the concept in detail.[11] The goal is to build up a fully rounded analysis of some phenomenon by combining all lines of attack, each probe only revealing certain dimensions of the symbolic reality. The point is not to advocate eclecticism as such, but to avoid the personal bias and superficiality that stem from one narrow probe. Triangulation takes seriously the way we attach meanings to social reality and the fundamental elements of symbolic interaction embedded in the research process. The assumption is that the different lines of action each reveal different aspects of reality, "much as a kaleidoscope, depending on the angle at which it is held, will reveal different colors and configurations of objects to the viewer."[12]

Triangulation occurs in several forms. It may refer, for example, to method, that is, combining document analysis with unstructured interviewing with unobtrusive observation, and combining this mixture in order to improve perspective. One can also take a social problem, pornography in the media, for instance, and triangulate it by viewing it historically (how does our modern view differ from previous eras and cultures), synchronically (what are the relevant facts on the problem today), and theoretically (what ethical or anthropological system does one use in gaining perspective on it). Theoretical triangulation is an obvious possibility, too, focusing several theoretical outlooks on a single object to see which one explains more.

Beyond these approaches is a kind of multiple triangulation in which all the various facets and insights generated are placed in interaction and cross-fertilization until the structural features of a setting or event are illuminated. Comprehension of actual context only accumulates gradually, so the search is always an ongoing one until we finally reveal the exact contours of the facts unearthed. "The facts never 'speak for themselves.' They must be selected, marshaled, linked together, and given a voice."[13]

Total description is only possible to the anthropologist working on a tribal culture of small numbers; yet depth and complete intelligibility remain the ideals in humanistic research. The process of disentangling from within is complicated by the fact that we are interpreting a world that has been interpreted already. Our aim, then, can only be increasing insight. Thus the emphasis in cultural studies is on discovery rather than applying routinized procedures. We concur with a key notion of John Dewey that research methods are really "intelligence in operation," with intelligence being Dewey's term for directed operations "which eventually transform unsettled doubtful situations into situations that are determinate."[14]

In gathering data from natural field settings, then, cultural studies must pass the tests outlined previously—external and internal validity, exegetical awareness, accurate assessment of secondary sources, and imaginative triangulation. By these indexes one cannot always separate the wheat from the chaff, nor always guarantee valid data, but conscientious attention to them will serve the more modest goal of improved authenticity and meaningfulness in our analysis, interpretations, and explanations. At a minimum, our guidelines indicate that research should be cautious, deliberate, reasoned, and accurate. We oppose sloppiness as much as anyone. We raise these standards as a minimum basis for improving this type of research while keeping imagination and meaning genuinely central. Rather than presenting them as restraints, we view these standards instead as aids for maximizing the adventuresome scholar's productivity.

Presentation of Results

We come now to the problem of presenting our research. At one level this activity is simply an extension of the search for verification that has been the nemesis of research activity all along. During the data-gathering phase the problems have been, as mentioned, separating the idiosyncratic from the representative, as well as recognizing the biases of the sources and of the researcher. When we reach the reporting stage, also, we must take care to identify our position in reference to the material. How have our predilections affected the conduct of the research? What a priori assumptions were confirmed or denied as the research progressed? What nagging doubts do we still have about findings?[15]

On another level our presentation must be in a form that allows the scholarly community to make independent evaluations of the validity of our arguments. We should note, too, that even in the case of the presentation with a purely descriptive intent, we are arguing for the validity of the description. At the other end of the presentation spectrum is the polemic, which is obviously argumentative in character. In other words, any claim we make, if challenged, must be of such nature that it can be made good or justified.[16] Our task in this regard is well stated by Stephen Toulmin:

> A man who puts forward some proposition, with a claim to know that it is true, implies that the grounds which he could produce in support of the proposition are of the highest relevance and cogency; without the assurance of such grounds, he has no right to make any claim to knowledge. The question, when if ever the grounds on which we base our claims to knowledge are really adequate, may therefore be read as meaning, "Can the arguments by which we would back up our assertions ever reach the highest relevant standards?" and the general problem for comparative applied logic will be to decide what, if any particular field of argument, the highest relevant standards will be. Now there are two questions here. There is the question, what standards are the most rigorous, stringent or exacting; and there is the question, what standards we can take as relevant when judging arguments in any particular field.[17]

Toulmin also proposes a system of argumentation that we believe to be well suited for presenting the findings of cultural or qualitative studies. Our goal, obviously, is to move forward from the data we have collected to a claim, or a series of claims, about those data and our interpretations of their meanings. Toulmin's model for such an argument appears as follows:

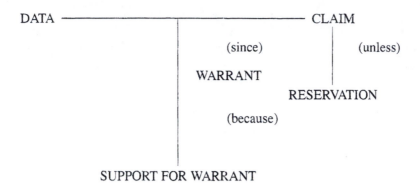

SUPPORT FOR WARRANT

The question "Is that claim warranted?" captures nicely the notion of "warrant" in Toulmin's model. It is another way of asking, "Why do you think so?" We respond, "*since* I know this to be the case," "*because* this is true," or the like. We can stay on a correct path if we think in terms of justifying our claims by stating and demonstrating our assumptions to be true, or mapping out the cognitive process we use in verifying our intuition or revelation about the material we have studied. We can avoid making fundamental logical errors (*post hoc ergo propter hoc, argumentum ad hominem,* and so forth) by continually questioning our own move from data to claim in the process of straining the move through the screens of "since" and "because."

The reservation to our claims is in the form of a qualifier or a condition or exception or rebuttal. Such screens prevent a globalization of findings and force us to recognize the existence of contrary facts, counter currents, or explanations that offer alternatives to our own conclusions.

To give an example of this process at work, in the case of Canadian response to technological innovations in communications prior to World War I, the factual data seemed to indicate, *prima facie,* that Canadians had enthusiastically embraced the telegraph.

But why should such quantitative data necessarily lead to that conclusion? *Since* there would have been little continuing incentive for telegraph expansion into new areas if it were not being accepted and used, *because* the telegraph in Canada operated as part of the private economic sector and was dependent on revenues generated by its operation, any rapid expansion must indicate (*claim*) enthusiastic reception. But there are extenuating circumstances. Therefore, we admit that the claim is true *unless* the extension was due, for instance, to the growth in the west where towns were located at great distances from one another and where the government was involved in telegraph expansion for security purposes, and/or *unless* the usage was principally by government or business interests, which would have had little impact on public enthusiasm. What was, *prima facie*, a simple conclusion is made ever more complex by the use of such a system of argument. (The actual results are even more complex than this simple example indicates.)[18]

Of course, such a system makes the presentation of our findings much more complicated. But it also provides us with the means to validate our conclusions before we publish them and to defend them if they are challenged. The system also allows the community of scholars within which we work to confirm or deny our conclusions independently and to do so within a context that we understand and share. And finally, this form facilitates the use of data, interpretations, and conclusions by other scholars who readily understand our work.[19]

That community may be thought of as an aspect of what Dewey called "communal life," which he said was "moral," or "emotionally, intellectually, consciously sustained."[20] The implications of being part of such a communal enterprise in which one's work is subjected to community interpretation and judgment are profound. In the first place, it reminds us that we do not conduct our research in a vacuum: We are subject to communal "laws" of inquiry, which serve to validate or invalidate our work by adding or refusing imprimature to our personal revelations and conclusions. Our relevant community acts, in other words, as a mutual authority that judges the fruits of our endeavors.[21] Also, to be a part of such an enterprise implies that we have accepted both the historical and mythological constructs of the community to which we belong.

We are fully cognizant of the postmodern objection to authoritative knowledge. Jean-Francois Lyotard's rejection of grand narratives is at odds with Frederic Jameson's cultural logic of late capitalism. And neither takes account of Jean Baudrillard's post-historical simulacra. Poststructuralism develops an independent argument linking language, power, subjectivity, and competing meanings. However, the common core of postmodernism is the doubt that any method or theory has universal and general validity as correct or privileged knowing.

Science is not superior to literature, or statistics to poetry. All methods are distrusted equally. All claims to truth mask particular interests. However, whether postmodern doubt is defensible or not, qualitative researchers can "know something without claiming to know everything." They don't have to write

> ... as disembodied omniscient narrators claiming universal, atemporal general knowledge; they can eschew the questionable metanarrative of scientific objectivity and still have plenty to say as situated speakers, subjectivities engaged in knowing/telling about the world as they perceive it.[22]

In the realm of historical constructs, Hirsch has noted that, "On the simplest level, the members of the community [of inquirers engaged in a communal enterprise] cannot even maintain an increasing body of evidence unless past evidence is stored and is brought to bear, when relevant, on hypotheses presently entertained."[23] Bloomfield has also addressed this aspect of the scholar's work, writing that, "Although nothing is enough, informed enjoyment and a historical dimension to one's experience, a conviction of accuracy, have the power to answer nagging questions and demands and can civilize a man more than destroy him."[24] We might call this phenomenon a historical imperative, for it compels all honest scholars to acknowledge history as it has been explained and interpreted for us by other members of the community of scholars. Because culturalism is necessarily a historical method, scholars using the cultural approach must recognize that history circumscribes, and impinges on, their interpretation and explanation. This is not to say that history is a dictator, for interpretations abound in this field, particularly over events or personalities that have been seen as axial by members of the history community. History is rather an arbiter that applies appropriate limits to imaginative scholarship, counseling caution to those heady from the brew of their own imaginings.

Because the conduct of cultural studies borrows so heavily from historical methods, we need to be especially aware of the pitfalls that haunt historical research. Fischer has isolated a series of fallacies that infect historical study, dividing them into fallacies of inquiry, of explanation, and of argument.[25] Although all are of interest, we shall confine ourselves at this point to the fallacies of argument. Limitations of space prevent us, too, from reproducing Fischer's explanations, and his book is recommended as a necessary complement to this brief summary. Fischer acknowledges the need to "conform to a logic of argumentation" if the historian's arguments "are to cohere as truth."[26] But Fischer does not deal with formal fallacies of argument (a wise decision that we have decided to emulate), discussing, rather, informal fallacies of a semantic or substantive nature. The semantic fallacies include those of ambiguity, amphiboly (meaning muddled by slovenly syntax), figures (abuse of figurative language), accent (distortion by emphasis), equivocation, quibbling, and black-or-white (misconstruction of vague terms).[27] The remedy, Fischer says, for all semantic fallacies is "formal definition faithfully applied" (of which he provides multiple examples).[28] The second set of informal fallacies is substantive. "They all operate by shifting attention from a reasoned argument to other things which are irrelevant and often irrational."[29] He includes sixteen of the more common ones.[30] In addition to such fallacies are the problems associated with polysemia, or the fact—as post-modernist philosophers have pointed out—that any text may have multiple meanings depending on who is doing the interpreting. This is of course, the reason for careful triangulation and the presentation of our scholarship in a self-reflective way. Meaning must not be forced on a text, and alternative explanations may often have to be presented as a kind of "minority opinion" in the final analysis.

We have not been able to discuss in detail here all the problems with argument that we inevitably face in making interpretations. Nevertheless, this all too brief discussion is intended to demonstrate the need for humanists to present research in a mode that responds to the standards of logic in both inquiry and argument. The positive result of such presentation will be a substantial difference in the acceptance of humanistic findings by the community of scholars, the tribunal of last resort. Acceptance of a more formal system for arguing positions will also lead to greater understanding of qualitative work as well as to the framework for more meaningful discussion of one another's work.

Summary

We have reviewed in broad strokes some of the dynamics that characterize a qualitative, humanistic approach to communication research. In our summary we have emphasized the central role of imagination and meaning and have suggested several minimum standards by which evidence is pursued and the results presented. We are concerned that many future academicians gather under the humanistic umbrella for practical reasons, rather than out of a philosophical sensitivity to humanistic aims. Thus we begin staking out in this essay a framework whereby cheap forms of culturalism can be exorcized.

Outside our arena, many who have questioned the use of cultural methods have done so not from malicious designs, but owing to a genuine desire to understand what we who practice it are doing and what our contributions to communication research are likely to be. Many of our colleagues, unfortunately, have misinterpreted the intent of these queries. As a final statement, therefore, on a philosophical plane, let us caution both our questioners and our defenders. We believe, with Hirsch, that total freedom of inquiry is necessary, particularly in communication research, owing to our very inability to predict the future value of any particular form of inquiry.[31] That being so, let us acknowledge that the choice of method is not the result of a conscious selection of an inherently superior tool, but of the selection of instruments most appropriate to our purposes. "Method is primordial judgment become cohesive, deliberate, and qualified within a specific perspective."[32]

Each of us, whatever our perspective, has something to offer the others. In the words of I. A. Richards, "the Total Meaning we are engaged with is, almost always, a blend, a combination of several contributory meanings or different types."[33] Qualitatively oriented offerings may not all be immediately important to everyone else, but they do deserve our attention and constructive criticism. Therefore, we should be able to resolve our differences through the application of that which we study, communication. Finally, we should each take to heart an explanation and admonition from Michael Polanyi:

> Man lives in the meanings he is able to discern. He extends himself into that which he finds coherent and is at home there. These meanings can be of many kinds and sorts. Men believe in the reality of these meanings whenever they perceive them—unless some intellectual myth in which they also come to believe denies reality to some of them.[34]

Endnotes

1. The classic work for academic scholarship generally is Ernst Cassirer, *The Logic of the Humanities*, trans. C.S. Howe (New Haven, CT: Yale University Press, 1960). Paul M. Hirsch in introducing humanistic models of communication research properly suggests that such studies "constitute a neglected resource in which theories and insights for systematic testing are easily located." See Hirsch and James W. Carey, "Communication and Culture: Humanistic Models in Research," *Communication Research*, Special Issue (July 1978): 236. Michael Real brings together the various critical, cultural, and institutional strains in a review essay, "Demythologizing Media: Recent Writings in Critical and Institutional Theory," *Critical Studies in Mass Communication* 3 (1986): 459-486. For an application of humanistic perspectives to research and writing, see Stephen Lynn, *Texts and Contexts: Writing About Literature with Critical Theory*, 2nd ed. (New York: Longman, 1998). Norman Denzin integrates the humanities and social sciences in his *Interpretive Ethnography: Ethnographic Practices for the 21st Century* (Thousand Oaks, CA: Sage, 1997).

2. Thus Clifford Geertz writes: "I take the analysis of culture to be not an experimental science in search of law but an interpretive one in search of meaning . . . meaning, that elusive, ill-defined pseudo entity we were once content to leave philosophers and literary critics fumble with, has now come back into the heart of our discipline." From *The Interpretation of Cultures* (New York: Basic Books, 1973), p. 529;

for elaboration, see Fred Inglis, "Portrait of a Method," in his *Clifford Geertz: Culture, Custom and Ethics* (Cambridge, UK: Polity Press, 2000), ch. 5, 107–132. For an overview in terms of communication studies, see James W. Carey, *Communication as Culture: Essays on Media and Society* (Boston: Allen and Unwin, 1989) and Norman K. Denzin, *Symbolic Interaction and Cultural Studies* (London: Blackwell, 1992). Defining communications as meaning-making, John J. Pauly outlines the implications for the research process in "A Beginner's Guide to Doing Qualitative Research in Mass Communication," *Journalism Monographs* 125 (February, 1991): 1–29.

 3. C. Wright Mills, *The Sociological Imagination* (New York: Oxford University Press, 1967).

 4. Robert Bierstedt, ed., *On Humanistic Sociology: Selected Papers* (of Florian Znaniecki) (Chicago: University of Chicago Press, 1969). Cf. also Norman Denzin, *Interpretive Biography* (Newbury Park, CA: Sage, 1989).

 5. Neil Friedman, *The Social Nature of Psychological Research* (New York: Basic Books, 1967), 179.

 6. For a summary of the issues and procedures and an extensive bibliography, see Robert E. Stake, "Case Studies," in N.K. Denzin and Y.S. Lincoln, eds., *Handbook of Qualitative Research*, 2nd ed. (Thousand Oaks, CA: Sage, 2000), 435–464. Cf. Robert E. Stake, *The Art of Case Study Research* (Thousand Oaks, CA: Sage, 1995), and Charles Ragin and Howard Becker, eds., *What Is a Case: Exploring the Foundations of Social Inquiry* (Cambridge, UK: Cambridge University Press, 1992).

 7. Norman K. Denzin, *The Research Act: A Theoretical Introduction to Sociological Methods*, 3rd ed. (Englewood Cliffs, NJ: Prentice Hall, 1989), chapters 3, 6.

 8. Geertz, *op. cit.*, 10; also see his "Anti Anti-Relativism," *American Anthropologist* 86 (1984): 263–278.

 9. Jacques Barzun and Henry F. Graff, *The Modern Researcher*, 5th ed. (Orlando, FL: Harcourt College Publishers, 1992).

 10. Umberto Eco warns against simplistic causal connections when dealing with original and secondary sources, particularly in a mass-mediated culture: "The media have multiplied, but some of them act as media of media, or in other words, media squared. And at this point, who is sending the message? . . . Power is elusive, and there is no longer any telling where the plan comes from. Because there is, of course, a plan, but it is no longer intentional, and therefore it cannot be criticized with the traditional criticism." From *Travels in Hyper Reality*, trans. W. Weaver (New York: Harcourt Brace Jovanovich, 1983), 149. See N. Bouchard and Veronica Pravadelli, eds., *Umberto Eco's Alternative: The Politics of Culture and the Ambiguities of Interpretation* (New York: Peter Lang, 1998).

 11. Denzin, *op. cit.*, 234–247. For an examination of triangulation and the multi-method character of qualitative research, see Uwe Flick, *An Introduction to the Qualitative Research: Theory, Method and Applications* (London: Sage, 1998).

 12. *Ibid.*, 235.

 13. Barzun and Graff, *op. cit.*, xii.

 14. John Dewey, *The Quest for Certainty* (New York: Minton Balch, 1929), especially chapters 8 and 9.

 15. See the last chapter of Alvin W. Goudner's *The Coming Crisis in Western Sociology* (New York: Equinox Books, 1971) for a classic statement of the prejudices with which he wrote the book.

 16. Stephen E. Toulmin, *The Uses of Argument* (Cambridge, UK: Cambridge University Press, 1964), 97.

 17. *Ibid.*, 218.

 18. Robert S. Fortner, "Messiahs and Monopolists: A Cultural History of Canadian Communications Systems 1846-1914," unpublished Ph.D. dissertation, University of Illinois, 1978. For an excellent discussion of the various philosophical perspectives that influence our understanding of technological history, see Carl Mitcham, *Thinking Through Technology: The Path Between Engineering and Philosophy* (Chicago: University of Chicago Press, 1994).

 19. See Chapter 3 of Toulmin's *Uses of Argument* for a more complete explanation of the system.

 20. John Dewey, *The Public and Its Problems* (New York: Henry Holt and Co., 1927), 151.

 21. Michael Polanyi and Harry Prosch, *Meaning* (Chicago: University of Chicago Press, 1977), 194.

 22. For this quotation and elaboration of these paragraphs, see Laurel Richardson, "Writing: A Method of Inquiry," Denzin and Lincoln, *op. cit.*, 928. For an overview of the issues, see chapters 20 and

34 in this volume: William G. Tierney, "Undaunted Courage: Life History and the Postmodern Challenge," 537–554; and John K. Smith and Deborah K. Diemer, "The Problem of Criteria in the Age of Relativism," 877–896. A standard book-length treatment of the thinkers and issues is Steven Best and Douglas Kellner, *The Postmodern Turn* (New York: Guilford Press, 1997).

23. E.D. Hirsch, Jr., "Value and Knowledge in the Humanities," in Morton W. Bloomfield, ed., *In Search of Literary Theory* (Ithaca, NY: Cornell University Press, 1972), 65.

24. Morton W. Bloomfield, "The Two Cognitive Dimensions of the Humanities," in Bloomfield, *op. cit.*, 79.

25. David Hackett Fischer, *Historians' Fallacies: Toward a Logic of Historical Thought* (New York: Harper & Row, 1970).

26. *Ibid.*, 263.

27. *Ibid.*, 265–277.

28. *Ibid.*, 277–280.

29. *Ibid.*, 282.

30. *Ibid.*, 283–306.

31. *Ibid.*, 68.

32. Justus Buchler, *The Concept of Method* (Lanham, MD: University Press of America, 1985), 67.

33. I.A. Richards, *Practical Criticism: A Study of Literary Judgment* (New York: Harcourt Brace Jovanovich, 1929), 174.

34. In Polani and Prosh, *op. cit.*, 86.

19

The Practice of Historical Research

David Paul Nord[1]

*History is basically a contested discourse, an embattled terrain wherein
people(s), classes and groups autobiographically construct interpretations of
the past literally to please themselves. . . . In the end history is theory and
theory is ideological and ideology just is material interests.*

—Keith Jenkins[2]

*Thus it is that the "poetics" of history becomes the "politics" of history.
Postmodernism, even more than Marxism, makes of history—the writing of
history as much as the "praxis" of history—an instrument in the struggle for
power. . . . The modernist accuses the postmodernist of bringing mankind to
the abyss of nihilism. The postmodernist proudly, happily accepts that
charge.*

—Gertrude Himmelfarb[3]

The Toils of History

In the 1990s history stood at the vortex of the culture wars in the United States. How to
mark the 500th anniversary of the arrival of Columbus in the New World, how to com-
memorate the fiftieth anniversary of the bombing of Hiroshima, how to set national standards for teaching history in elementary and secondary schools, how to mount museum ex-
hibits and television documentaries for popular audiences, how to preserve/rewrite U.S.
history for an increasingly multicultural America—all of these issues and more were
seized by pundits and politicians as occasions to attack a historical profession in thrall to
interest-group politics, to feminist and racialist doctrines of victimology and political correctness. In popular books, magazines, and newspaper columns, critics denounced academic history as arcane, doctrinaire, jargon-ridden, and un-American. They vilified historians as smug tenured radicals and reckless nihilists who despised their country. If literary

theory bore the brunt of popular cultural criticism in the 1980s, it was history's turn in the 1990s. In a word, history was news.[4]

Debate over the practice of historical research swirled within the history profession as well. In 1998 a group of academic historians, fed up with their colleagues in the American Historical Association and the Organization of American Historians, founded a new professional association, immodestly named the Historical Society. Eugene Genovese, the society's founder and first president, declared that "contemporary academic history is being systematically gutted of the breadth, the drama, and, most dangerously, the tragedy that have accounted for its abiding hold over the public imagination. What remains is a series of vignettes of everyday life that bear an eerie resemblance to the contemporary sensibilities of identity politics. The demand that historians privilege race, class, and gender is occurring in an atmosphere that uncomfortably resembles the McCarthyism of the 1950s."[5]

In many ways the wrangling over history, both inside and outside the profession, sounds familiar. Historians have always fought over politics, for history has always resonated with current political concerns. But in the closing decades of the twentieth century a new villain appeared: postmodernism. Especially within the profession, the critique of historical practice targeted methodology and epistemology as well as politics. Those who moved into the new Historical Society criticized history's infatuation with new strains of philosophy and literary criticism that see reality as a social/cultural/political construction. They lamented "historians' apparent flight from the ideals of objectivity and the honest use of evidence."[6] The postmodern notion that human reality exists as a kind of text or discourse, that everything is interpretation, struck critics as a philosophy of "anything goes." "If objectivity is a myth, how can our understanding of the past be anything but an artifact of our political beliefs?" asked one of the founders of the Historical Society. "Indeed, if all interpretation is political anyway, then why not give free rein to one's own political views? Why not use whatever power one happens to have to 'privilege' one's own brand of history?"[7]

Historians and philosophers have long pondered the question, Is history a form of science or a genre of literature? The arrival of postmodernism rendered that question considerably more fundamental and urgent, for at the radical extreme, postmodernism seemed to say that history is indeed fiction—but, then, so is science. No wonder the critics worried.

But their worry was exaggerated. Though many historians have been preachy ideologues, few have actually embraced radical postmodernism in either theory or practice. The postmodern challenge has influenced history in important ways, but the fundamental nature of historical research has changed little. At the beginning of the twentieth-first century, academic historians still inhabit the libraries and archives, sifting through the residue of the past, just as they have always done. They gather evidence, test ideas, make comparisons, fashion generalizations, build arguments, tell stories. The purpose of this chapter is to explore what has changed in historical practice in recent years and what has not. Along with most other academic disciplines, history has been chastened by postmodernism's critique of empiricism and objectivity. The convergence of philosophical stance and method across disciplines has been especially important for history because history has traditionally worked on the hazy boundary between the humanities and social sciences. In general, however, change and convergence have simply made history more diverse in subject matter without altering its essential empirical nature. While change has had its vices as well as its virtues, for the most part it has been good, especially for the kind of history that interests the readers of this book: the history of journalism and mass communication. At the dawn of the new century, communication history seems to be moving to center stage of mainstream historical practice.

The Postmodern Challenge

Postmodernism insists on the multiplicity and elusiveness of meaning in human affairs, so it is apt that the meaning of the term itself is multiple and elusive. Sometimes postmodernism refers to an artistic style of ironic self-reference; sometimes it is said to be the condition of contemporary life, also ironic and self-referential; in the academic realm postmodernism serves as an umbrella term for several strains in philosophy and literary criticism that have emerged in the twentieth century. For the practice of history, the elements of postmodern philosophy that are most important are these: (1) the rejection of the Enlightenment ideal of realism and objectivity; and (2) the related claim that all human experience is mediated through language, and thus the only reality we can know—and the only reality people in the past could know—is socially constructed. This has been called the "linguistic turn" or the "hermeneutical turn." The key idea is that humans live their lives in a world of words and interpretations that draw meaning from other words and interpretations, not from direct, unmediated experience. In human affairs we cannot break out of this circle of interpretation (sometimes called the "hermeneutical circle")—nor need we seek to break out, for our entire social reality lies within it. "We have to think of man as a self-interpreting animal," Charles Taylor wrote in a classic essay thirty years ago. "He is necessarily so, for there is no such thing as the structure of meanings for him independent of his interpretation of them; for one is woven into the other." Striking the keynote of the "linguistic turn," Taylor stressed the artificiality of the distinction between social reality and the language that describes that reality: "The language is constitutive of the reality, is essential to its being the kind of reality it is. To separate the two and distinguish them as we quite rightly distinguish the heavens from our theories about them is to forever miss the point."[8]

The historian Keith Jenkins describes historical practice in similar terms: "History (historiography) is an inter-textual, linguistic construct; . . . the past comes to us always already as stories and . . . we cannot get out of these stories (narratives) to check if they correspond to the real world/past, because these 'always already' narratives constitute 'reality.'" This is history's rendition of the "linguistic turn," framed in the favored jargon of postmodernism.[9]

Has the postmodern challenge transformed history, either for good or ill? The answer seems to be "no" and "yes." In fundamental ways, the practice of history carries on pretty much as it always has. But the "linguistic turn" has had an impact on both the subject matter of history and on how historians do their work. It has also affected history's relationship with other disciplines in the humanities and social sciences.

If postmodernism implies a disjuncture between the actual past and writing about the past, then historians have long been postmodernists and likely always will be. Though they usually spurn the label, they tend to be relativists, at least in the pragmatic sense that the historian Carl Becker was a relativist in the 1930s. In a famous essay published in 1932,

Becker drew a sharp distinction between history as the actual past and history as our reconstruction of the past. The latter was relative, always changing. Even so-called "facts" were relative. "To set forth historical facts is not comparable to dumping a barrow of bricks," Becker wrote. "A brick retains its form and pressure wherever placed; but the form and substance of historical facts, having a negotiable existence only in literary discourse, vary with the words employed to convey them." Like other pragmatists of his generation, such as John Dewey, Becker worried not at all that relativism and presentism pushed history in the direction of epistemological skepticism. On the contrary. The thought seemed to inspire him with a sense of democratic efficacy. "It should be a relief to us to renounce omniscience," he wrote, "to recognize that every generation, our own included, will, must inevitably, understand the past and anticipate the future in the light of its own restricted experience, must inevitably play on the dead whatever tricks it finds necessary for its own peace of mind."[10] Certainly, not all historians since Becker have embraced relativism so ardently and cheerfully, but nearly all have admitted the indeterminancy, the elusiveness, and the multi-perspectival nature of historical "truths." Whatever the past actually was, it was incomprehensibly complex and is now utterly gone, a foreign country where we can never go.[11]

On the other hand, if postmodernism, therefore, implies a rejection of any possibility of empirical research in history, then historians have never been postmodernists and likely never will be. Conservative combatants in the U.S. culture wars of the 1990s criticized academic historians for their cynical methods and nihilistic philosophies, yet the actual work of history today is still based upon traditional methods, most notably painstaking research into documents and other forms of what historians call primary sources. The historian Lawrence Levine is correct to declare that "the primary criticism of contemporary historiography has little to do with what kind of history we practice and almost everything to do with the subjects of that history."[12] U.S. historians now write about previously ignored people (women, African Americans, Indians, gays and lesbians) and previously neglected subjects (sex, race, childhood, domesticity, popular culture), but they do it in the usual way. History has not so much been postmodernized as democratized.[13]

And what is the usual way of doing history? Though its subject is ostensibly the past, history resembles other forms of research in the sciences and social sciences because the actual research work occurs entirely in the present. The materials that historians study are the records of the past (documents, letters, newspapers, artifacts, memories), but they exist as objects in the present. Written history may be forever disconnected from the past as it actually was, but it is a form of empirical inquiry nonetheless. Murray Murphey made this point rather well in the early 1970s. He argued that historical facts are like subatomic particles: They are theoretical constructs postulated to explain present data. In this sense, historians act like scientists. They study the available evidence and form "theories" to explain it. The "theories" are not only the interpretations and narratives, but the facts themselves. For example, the facts of George Washington's life are really theoretical constructs that historians offer to explain the existence of present data, such as documents, letters, memoirs, and Mount Vernon. As Murphey put it, "George Washington enjoys at present the epistemological status of an electron: Each is an entity postulated for the purpose of giving coherence to our present experience, and each is unobservable by us." In a rough parallel to science, historical "theories" that George Washington lived, acted, and thought in a certain way can be evaluated in the usual fashion—on whether they are plausible, parsimonious, heuristically useful, and so on. Thus, our knowledge of the past is based on empirical evidence, though it must remain forever tentative in the way all theories are tentative.[14]

Though he took history to be fundamentally similar to social science, Murphey believed that for practical reasons historical research could never be truly scientific because history could never solve crucial problems of sampling bias in historical records, informant bias in unknown direction and degree, and problems of measurement of past social change. Thus, he concluded that "present methods for confirming general hypotheses regarding past populations cannot meet the standards which now prevail in the social sciences."[15] But Murphey was writing thirty years ago, near the end of a heroic age of confidence in social science. Today many social scientists would admit that their disciplines cannot solve those problems either, that all the human sciences are plagued by a radical indeterminacy. Across the disciplines, postmodernism has rendered knowledge less sure today than it was a generation ago.[16] But empirical research—argumentation with evidence—continues in the social sciences and in history, too.

In the most fundamental ways, then, the postmodern challenge did not revolutionize the discipline of history. Strident proclamations of the "death of reason" and the "murder of history" proved idle. Historians still churn out articles and books that build arguments with empirical evidence, just as if the Enlightenment were alive and well. Yet postmodernism has changed history in other important ways that touch both subject matter and method, and those changes are especially relevant to the practice of communication history and the relationship of history to communication research. These changes include: (1) the movement of history to center stage in the social sciences and literary criticism, a movement sometimes called the historicizing of social science and the humanities; (2) the transformation of social history into cultural history, in the wake of the "linguistic turn" in historical research; (3) a revival of interest in narrative in history, not so much as a form of historical explanation but as a form of historical data; and (4) the rise of a new pragmatic realism in history that depends less on universal truth standards and more on standards held by professional communities of scholarship. This is the historicizing of history itself. I will explore each of these changes in turn.

1. Forty years ago historicism was a term of reproach in social science. The mainstream social sciences—economics, sociology, political science—had been founded in the nineteenth century as historical disciplines, but they had abandoned history in the early twentieth century in their drive to achieve the status of science. As science, their goal was theory unbound by time and space; their method was the objective measurement of human behavior.[17] By the 1970s, however, the postmodern strain in philosophy and sociology of knowledge suggested that decontextualized, ahistorical behavioral research was impossible, for people's behavior, indeed their entire reality, their "meaning world," is constituted in language, in self-interpretation. Thus, behavior alone tells us nothing. To know what people *did* we must know what they *meant*; and meaning is necessarily situated in the contexts of time and place. It is historical. For social science, then, postmodernism prompted a return to history and a turn from behavioralism to interpretation.[18] In the words of the anthropologist Clifford Geertz, "Many social scientists have turned away from a laws-and-instances ideal of explanation toward a cases-and-interpretations one, looking less for the sort of thing that connects planets and pendulums and more for the sort that connects chrysanthemums and swords."[19] One of the leaders of the revival of historical sociology, Theda Skocpol, put it this way: "Against the abstractions and timelessness of grand theory—and especially in opposition to Durkheimian-style modernization theory, as reworked by Parsonian structure-functionalists—historically minded sociologists have reintroduced the variety, conflict, and processes of concrete histories into macroscopic accounts of social change."[20]

A "new historicism" also appeared in literary studies about the same time and for similar reasons. Like social science, mid-century literary scholarship, under the rubric the "New Criticism," had banished old-fashioned literary history and biography in favor of formal textual analysis. The "objectivity of the text," as literary critic Jane Tompkins called it, was the New Criticism's pretension to the scientism that reigned in the natural and behavioral sciences. The new historicism of the 1970s and 1980s attacked the text-based formalism of both the New Criticism and the more recently favored methodology of deconstruction. "New historicists" of various stripes sought to make sense of literary texts by setting those texts into social, economic, religious, and political context. Some scholars explored the contexts of production: the realms of authors, editors, publishers, typographers, and booksellers.[21] Others stressed the contexts of reception: readers' response to literature.[22] Whether the emphasis was on production or reception, the argument was the same and ran parallel to the argument made by the historical social scientists: A literary text is socially constructed by authors, publishers, and readers. Its meaning lies not in the text itself but in the social contexts in which it was written, published, and read. To make sense of the nineteenth-century sentimental novel, for example, Jane Tompkins wrote that she had "to reconstruct the very sense of reality from which the novel sprang—its theology, its definition of power, its thematics, its language, its psychology, its conception of everyday life."[23]

The turn to history in social science and literary criticism coincided with the postmodern assault on history itself. Ironically, while historians worried that postmodernism had rendered history impossible to do, other disciplines were embracing history to save themselves from their own postmodern nightmares.[24] In the end, though, the postmodern challenge seemed to knock no discipline into the Nietschean abyss of nihilism; it just bumped them down a step or two on the methodological stairway to epistemological heaven.

2. The transformation of social history into cultural history was another legacy of the linguistic turn of postmodernism. In some ways, research practice within history in the last half of the twentieth century followed the trajectory of the social sciences, though trailing a bit behind: a rising tide of behavioralism, quantification, and scientism in the 1960s and 1970s, followed by a turn to language, interpretation, and culture in the 1980s and 1990s. In the face of the postmodern challenge, historians did not abandon their fundamental commitment to empirical research, but they did change how they did it.

Economic history led the way into behavioral social science in the 1960s with an open-armed embrace of economic theory, mathematical modeling, and quantitative methods. Historians of politics quickly followed, borrowing models of voter behavior and methods of voting analysis from political science. Urban and labor historians also shifted from their traditional focus on events and institutional biographies to the study of broad socioeconomic processes.[25] Perhaps most interesting, the move to social science in the 1960s gave birth to entirely new subfields of study that came to be called the "new social history," including the history of the family, kinship, ethnicity, race, women's work, gender roles, and sexual relations. To put it simply, these were histories of ordinary people and everyday life.[26] Some new social historians borrowed theory from social science; more borrowed quantitative methods. In a sense, they had to. The processes they sought to study were collective, and the actors whose behaviors constituted those processes were ordinary people who left behind little or no written record. So, historians turned to whatever individual-level social data they could find: marriage and baptismal registers, military musters, tax books, wills and estate inventories, census schedules, voting records, and so on.[27]

The flood of social history in the 1960s and 1970s reflected a symbiotic blending of faith in empirical social science with then-current political enthusiasm for civil rights, feminism, and cultural radicalism. This was to be not just social history but history "from the bottom up."[28] To this end, the thrust of the "new social history" was to reject literary evidence in favor of evidence of the behavior of ordinary people. To the new social historian, actions spoke louder than words. Indeed, for understanding the past lives of most common people, words spoke not at all. And even for understanding literate elites, the written record was considered not just biased but largely epiphenominal, a misleading gloss on "real" history—the study of human behavior.

But what if the meaning of human behavior lies in the words used to describe it, not in the behavior itself? What if human action has social significance only if that significance is signaled in language? What if reality itself is constructed in human consciousness and human discourse? Those are the troubling questions that loomed in the path of the behavioral social history juggernaut in the 1970s. And those are the questions to which cultural history was offered up as the answer. Like social history, cultural history is interested in the lives of common people. But cultural history is concerned not with what those people did but what meanings they attached to what they did, not collective behavior but *mentalité*, the collective consciousness of a people. In other words, behavioral social history in the 1960s and 1970s brought new people into the spotlight of history; new heads were counted. In the 1980s and 1990s, historians tried to get inside those heads. Above all, cultural history takes language seriously. Of course, people use language to lie, as the behavioralist warns us. But they also use language for everything else, too, because the meaning of behavior inheres in the words that name and describe it.[29]

As social history evolved into cultural history, anthropology replaced sociology as history's favorite social science discipline. Following the lead of Clifford Geertz, historians switched from statistical sampling and inference to "thick description" of cultural practices set into the detailed contexts of time and place.[30] This was "history in the ethnographic grain," in the words of Robert Darnton, who helped to introduce Geertz to the practitioners of history. Unlike either the traditional historian's study of elites or the new social historian's study of populations and processes, "the ethnographic historian studies the way ordinary people made sense of the world."[31] The cultural historian not only paid close attention to language as a symbolic system but also treated behavior—such as riots and festivals, rituals and fashions, even cockfights and cat massacres—as a kind of discourse. In short, texts were read as culture and culture as text. This is a semiotic concept of culture, and Geertz was the guru of it. "Man is an animal suspended in webs of significance he himself has spun," said Geertz. "I take culture to be those webs, and the analysis of it to be therefore not an experimental science in search of law but an interpretive one in search of meaning."[32]

A good illustration of the movement from social history to cultural history is the transformation of the history of the family. In 1970 three books, now classics in the field, appeared on the history of the New England family in colonial times.[33] Steeped in social and psychological theory and brimming with quantitative behavioral data, they represented the new social history in full flower. Today family history is quite different. For example, recent studies of early American family life include a book on men's roles in child rearing and another on gender relations in marriage. But these are not social surveys; they are thick descriptions of a handful of individual experiences. (The marriage book is about a single marriage.) They draw not on demographic data but on the rich particularities of diaries and letters, not on external behavioral trends but on internal self-interpretations. These authors believe that the meanings of fundamental social descriptors such as childhood, manhood, and marriage were culturally constructed and historically specific.[34] To understand past reality means to understand the language, the discourse, that made it real. This is the message of the new cultural history.

3. The turn to language and culture also returned narrative to the center of historical research and writing, but in new forms and for new purposes. The traditional mode of explanation in history, narrative, came under heavy fire in the mid-twentieth century from both social science history and postmodern philosophy of history. Hit from two directions, traditional narrative was staggered. But it did not collapse altogether. And, perhaps more importantly, narrative reappeared in history in a new postmodern, ethnographic guise. Social and cultural history seemed to proclaim: Narrative is dead; long live narrative!

For centuries historians have explained the past by telling stories. On the surface, a narrative seems merely a kind of description. It is description especially suited to history, which is often interested in the unique and the particular. Analyses and behavioral generalizations may be of little help in understanding individual thought and action. Lawrence Stone put the matter rather well: "To use Machiavelli's terms, neither *virtu* nor *fortuna* can be dealt with except by a narrative, or even an anecdote, since the first is an individual attribute and the second a happy or unhappy accident."[35]

But a narrative is more than a description; it is a logical organization of material into a chronological sequence for the purpose of explanation. The historian's task is to explain change over time, and this is accomplished by connecting, via narrative, a beginning with an end. The explanatory power of a narrative lies in the causal connection between each step and the following step in the sequence. Behavioral generalizations and probabilities may be helpful along the way in making the connections plausible and persuasive. But, in the end, the explanation inheres in the story, not in the generalizations. Put another way, a narrative may be the only appropriate response to the question that historians often ask: How did it happen that . . . ? Thus, a narrative *is* an explanation, but not only that. Historians have long believed that a narrative may also offer understanding that is not explanation at all; it is simply the understanding that comes through experience, through what J.H. Hexter called "confrontation with the riches of the event itself, a sense of vicarious participation."[36]

The social science history of the 1960s scorned this kind of traditional narrative, arguing that such storytelling was at best epiphenomenal. The proper subjects of history were broad underlying structures and processes, and these would be revealed through the testing of theory and the analysis of data, not through stories about particular events and individuals.[37] But this was a rejection of the utility of narrative, not a direct epistemological assault upon it.

The epistemological assault would come from philosophers of history influenced by the linguistic turn. The key figure was Hayden White, who has argued since the 1960s that historical narrative is a mode of discourse constructed, not discovered, by the historian. **Narrative history** consists of specific linguistic, grammatical, and rhetorical features that belong to the discourse, not to the reality of the past. Historians draw upon actual events and strings of events, but they emplot those events into stories that are fully their own. And they do this in precisely the same way that writers create fictional narratives. "Recent theories of discourse," White argues, "dissolve the distinction between realistic and fictional discourses." Thus, "history is no less a form of fiction than the novel is a form of historical representation."[38] Even an older generation of philosophers of history, reluctant to move as far as White down the road to relativism, were persuaded that historical narrative was fundamentally indistinguishable from fiction. Louis Mink wrote that "the significance of the past is determinate only by virtue of our own disciplined imagination. Insofar as the significance of past occurrences is understandable only as they are locatable in the ensemble of interrelationships that can be grasped only in the construction of narrative form, it is we who make the past determinate in that respect."[39] In short, the stories are ours, not theirs.

The kind of historical narrative that fell most easily before the critiques of social science and postmodernism was "grand narrative" or "master narrative." These are the great synthesizing stories—progress, decline, modernization, class revolution—that have made coherent the histories of entire peoples. The grand narrative, once assumed to be God's own untold story, now seems the obvious product of human artifice, of ideology, politics, and chauvinism.[40]

But the collapse of faith in grand narrative did not drive historical narrative itself from the field. Some historians, focusing on specific people and events, continued to tell their stories just as they always had. No change at all. Others, emboldened by the postmodern effacement of difference between history and fiction, happily embraced fictional technique as simply another way to do history. Serious historians such as Simon Schama and popular biographers such as Edmund Morris spun stories that mixed traditional historical research with imagined scenes and invented dialogue, giving new potency to Carl Becker's definition of history as "an engaging blend of fact and fancy."[41] Meanwhile, social historians also returned to narrative, but neither as grand narrative nor as openly fictional narrative. Even in its most empirical, scientific guise, social history operated from the premise that history could be viewed from multiple perspectives. History "from the bottom up" did not look like history from the top down. Writing the history of groups, social historians hoped to fashion "alternative narratives" that would make sense to those groups. Different groups, different stories. They resisted calls for broad synthesis and unifying narrative, without necessarily rejecting narrative altogether.[42] They were pleased to let a hundred stories bloom.

The new cultural history affirmed the narrative form for another reason, not so much as a mode of historical explanation but as a species of historical data. Historians tell stories, but so did the people they study. Philosophy after the linguistic turn taught that humans construct their reality in discourse, and often that discourse is narrative. People live their lives inside the stories they tell. The ethnographic turn in cultural history applied this idea to the study of people in the past. Following the example of Clifford Geertz and other cultural anthropologists, historians sought neither to discover nor to construct master narrative/explanations, but rather to recover the stories that people told themselves about themselves.[43] Cultural historians of all sorts took increasing interest in past narrative, and a new subfield of history emerged based almost entirely on the study of stories people told themselves—the history of public memory.[44] After the linguistic turn, in other words, some historians were more brash in telling stories, some were more circumspect in telling stories, but nearly all were more open to listening to them.

In its new passion for narrative as an object of study, history ran parallel to other disciplines in the social sciences and humanities. After the linguistic turn, scholars in psychology and sociology followed the lead of folklore and anthropology into the study of talk, of conversation, of narrative—the stories ordinary people tell. Even political scientists turned their attention to narrative, to "tales of the state."[45] Like historians, the proponents of the new methodology of "narrative analysis" argued that stories exist in language not in nature. "Language is understood," writes Catherine Kohler Riessman, "as deeply constitutive of reality, not simply a technical device for establishing meaning. Informants' stories do not mirror a world 'out there.' They are constructed, creatively authored, rhetorical, replete with assumptions, and interpretive." And they are stories.[46]

4. Finally, postmodernism, which undermined all foundations, challenged historians to think seriously about the foundations of their own discipline. If standards of truth and objectivity are not universal, then what are they? Are they purely personal, idiosyncratic, self-serving, and political, as conservative critics charge? After the linguistic turn, historians seemed more comfortable in admitting the contingent, even relative nature of historical research, while insisting that standards can exist, do exist. They are not individually but socially constructed standards. Like everything else, historical research itself has been historicized, rooted into the contexts of time and place. The practice of history—reasoned argument based on empirical evidence—is a cultural practice, not a sure reflection of reality, a mirror of human nature. It is our invention, historians seem increasingly willing to say. And that is good enough.

This was not an easy position to take at the end of the twentieth century. The cheery relativism of Carl Becker in 1932—"every generation . . . must inevitably play on the dead whatever tricks it finds necessary for its own peace of mind"—sounds far less benign today after successive waves of Nazi historical pageantry, Stalinist "realism," CIA disinformation, and Holocaust denials. If anything goes, anything surely will go, it seems. If no objective standards of judgment exist in either epistemology or morality, of what value is history? This is the fear expressed by the founders of the new Historical Society—and others as well.[47]

But many historians have argued that standards need not be arbitrary just because they are understood to be cultural conventions. They need not be universal truths to work well enough within the communities of reason and morality that we have created.[48] In the United States at least, there is a kind of pragmatic, democratic tone to this communitarian constructionist philosophy, a tone captured nicely by the neopragmatist philosopher Richard Rorty. For Rorty, the Enlightenment search for objectivity, for external epistemological foundations, has been an attempt to evade contingency, to escape history. It has been a hope for the indubitable, the ineluctable. But, he writes, it is a forlorn hope, one unworthy of our humanity:

> If we give up this hope, we shall lose what Nietzsche called "metaphysical comfort," but we may gain a renewed sense of community. Our identification with our community—our society, our political tradition, our intellectual heritage—is heightened when we see this community as *ours* rather than *nature's*, *shaped* rather than *found*, one among many which men have made. In the end, the pragmatists tells us, what matters is our loyalty to other human beings clinging together against the dark, not our hope of getting things right.[49]

In this provisional and pragmatic sense, then, historical practice—history itself—is understood to exist within what Stanley Fish has called an "interpretive community." Assumptions, beliefs, codes, canons, and conventions of reason and method are not individual but communal, embraced by and embracing historian and reader alike. Radical relativism and solipsism are actually impossible, in Fish's view, for none of the interpretive strategies available to an individual are uniquely his or her own. Whether in a scholarly discipline or the society at large, objective understanding rests upon intersubjective agreement within a community of inquirers.[50] In a spirited defense of what he calls "moderate historicism," Thomas Haskell argues that history can function well enough on the basis of communal rather universal standards of judgment:

> There is fear in some quarters that by assigning convention and history such a large role in moral thinking, we open the door to all the worst excesses of the neo-Nietzscheans. In my view, that fear is misplaced. By mapping more precisely the pale beyond which morality is irredeemably historical, we do concede some territory to the criterionless wilderness and bring a regrettable measure of satisfaction to the radical wing of historicism. But we also demarcate a domain—spacious, even if not as expansive as we might like—within which rights and other claims to objective moral knowledge can enjoy something like "universal" sway. That historically defensible sense of objectivity, that *provisional* immunity to incursions of time, place, and circumstance, is all we can realistically hope for. More important, it is also all we need.[51]

The philosopher of science Thomas Kuhn perhaps said it best: "Like solidarity, objectivity extends only over the world of the tribe, but what it extends over is no less firm and real for that."[52]

Everyone a Cultural Historian?

In 1983 a little book appeared called *Which Road to the Past? Two Views of History*, a point-counterpoint debate by Robert William Fogel and G.R. Elton. Fogel, an economic historian, argued the case for "scientific" history, or "cliometrics," which he defined as historical practice based on explicit models of human behavior, formal testing of theory, and systematic gathering of evidence, usually quantitative. For Fogel, a key distinction was this: "'Scientific' historians tend to focus on collectivities of people and recurring events, while traditional historians tend to focus on particular individuals and particular events."[53] G.R. Elton, a historian of early modern Britain, accepted Fogel's distinction but argued that particular individuals and particular events are precisely what historians need to understand. The study of collectivities and recurring patterns overlooks the quirky, ill-fitting pieces of the puzzle that may prove most important. "An understanding of the past as a pattern of forces can help to clarify one's understanding of circumstances and influences," Elton wrote, "but it offers at most a start on the task of understanding the past as event and experience."[54]

Fogel and Elton's distinction between the pattern and the event is an expression of the distinction between the *nomothetic* (generalizing) and the *idiographic* (particularizing), a distinction that marks the traditional divide between the social sciences and the humanities.[55] At the height of their identification with natural science, the social sciences imagined their theories to be law-like statements about human behavior, akin to physical laws in the natural sciences. Meanwhile, at the height of their identification with great art and great literature, the humanities imagined that their subject was the individual human being in all his (rarely her) singularity, spontaneity, and free-willed autonomy. "Not the scientific exploration of things," wrote Nathan Pusey, "not the scientific examination of the behavior of groups of people, but the living, vivid acquaintance with the adventures of the human spirit"—this was the traditional province of the humanities.[56]

Today, twenty years after Fogel and Elton published their colloquy, such a debate between an ascendant social science history and a defensive humanistic history seems utterly passé. The historicizing of social science, literary studies, and history itself, together with the rise of cultural studies across the disciplines, has dissolved the distinction between social science history and traditional history and has blurred the differences between the social sciences and the humanities. Grand theory in social science and textual formalism in literary criticism have both been washed over by a flood of history. What the social scientist once saw as general structures and law-like patterns of human behavior now seem the product of particular times and places, of contingency and context. And what the humanist once saw as the unexampled genius of individual thought now appears much more closely wedded to the culture from which it sprang. This is genuine convergence in the social sciences and humanities. Both social theory and individual agency are seen as drenched in culture and history. After the linguistic turn, it seems, everyone is a cultural historian.

What attracts scholars to the idea of culture and to history is the notion of *contingency*. Historians, historical sociologists, and the practitioners of the new historicism in literary studies all share a sense that human reality is and was constructed by human beings in particular contexts of culture. The past could have been otherwise; this is the essence of historicism. But, despite the claims of the radical postmodernists, historicism also accepts what might be called the *fixity* of the past. The past could have been otherwise—but it was not. The probabilities of social science may apply at the time something happens, but not after. Once something has happened, no matter how unlikely, it is permanently part of the past and of the future of that past. And sometimes the most improbable occurrence is the most important—if it occurred. This was G.R. Elton's point. Another traditionalist, J.H. Hexter, put it nicely as well: "An historian who will not count the French Revolution because it was unpredictable does not earn the golden opinion of his colleagues."[57] In short, the pastness of the past makes a difference.

Thus, both social structure and individual choice, both probability and accident, both the general and the particular, can all carry weight in causal explanations in history.[58] After the linguistic turn, the generalizations may be less general and the particulars less particular—the distance between social science history and humanistic history has closed—but generalization and particular still play their roles in history writing. And the distinction between them still marks tendencies in the work of historians. Some historians still seek to explore social change across broad sweeps of time and geography; others tell stories of specific events and individual people. Indeed, every historian is likely to move back and forth (or perhaps up and down is the better image) between the particular and the general, between narrative and analysis, between thick description and broad contextualization.

Furthermore, the tendency to lean toward either the particular or the general still defines the relationship between history and the social science disciplines. The pioneers of convergence in social history and historical sociology remarked on the difference years ago. "The historian," wrote Philip Abrams, "uses a rhetoric of close presentation (seeking to persuade in terms of a dense texture of detail) while the sociologist uses a rhetoric of perspective (seeking to persuade in terms of elegant patterning of connections seen from a distance)." Theda Skocpol added, "These differences will remain, ensuring that social historians will continue to have more to say about lived experiences, while historical sociologists will have more to say about structural transformations."[59]

The sociologist William G. Roy tells the story of a literal meeting ground of social historians and historical sociologists: Charles Tilly's house in Ann Arbor, Michigan. Tilly, both sociologist and historian himself, held weekly seminars for graduate students, faculty, and visiting scholars from both disciplines. These were wonderfully productive meetings of minds and disciplines. "But it wasn't always easy," Roy recalls:

> Graduate students, especially when rubbing shoulders with "alien" scholars, are typically caricatures of their disciplines. And so we acted out our assigned stereotypes. When historians would present their work, we sociologists would inevitably respond, "That's nice, but what does it mean?" When sociologists would present, the historians would ask, "That's nice, but what happened?"[60]

Though the edgy differences between the disciplines have softened considerably in recent years, such conversations still go on when scholars meet. For there is no one right way to do history. What makes history history is not a single method or proper level of analysis. It is simply the pastness of the past.

History of Journalism and History of Communication

The historicizing of social science and literary studies and the rise of cultural history have been a blessing for the history of journalism and for an incipient history of communication. Though most historical writing in journalism history remains quite traditional in form, the subject matter of the field was expanded considerably by the growth of social history in the last several decades. And in related subfields—notably the history of books, literacy, and reading—the new cultural history has had an impact as well. Perhaps most important, the history of journalism and media has begun to seep into other fields of history. With words thrust back to the center of historical inquiry, the linguistic turn has encouraged historians and literary critics to take more seriously the media that carried and shaped those words.

The old sacred scripture of American journalism history, like holy writ in many fields, was hagiography. The saints were Benjamin Franklin, James Gordon Bennett, Joseph Pulitzer, and other Great Men who built Great Institutions.[61] This literature was biographical and institutional, and it had running through it—sometimes vividly, often subtly—a master narrative: the progress of journalism in freedom and professionalism. The historical institutions of interest were those that seemed to carry the seeds of the present. For traditional journalism history, as for the classic Whig historiography of nineteenth-century England, the present was the glorious apotheosis of the past.[62]

This is just the kind of history that came under fire in the 1960s in the movement to social history from the bottom up; and that movement has had a substantial influence on journalism and media history. The social science aspects of social history had only a modest impact, with some use of quantification (sampling and systematic content analysis) and some borrowing of social theory (modernization, professionalization, technological determinism).[63] The greater impact was the expansion of subject matter. In journalism and media history, as in U.S. social history in general, women, African Americans, Hispanics, and Indians now crowd the historical stage, alongside the traditional great white men. One of the standard textbooks in the field, *The Press and America*, reflects this striking diversification. Early editions in the 1950s and early 1960s cast only the usual actors: Franklin, Bennett, Pulitzer, et al. The 801-page 1962 edition carried a single ten-line paragraph on the Black press. By comparison, the eighth edition in 1996 is a rainbow of color. Just as the literary canon now includes Phyllis Wheatley and Charles Chesnut, so the canon of journalism history, codified in the leading textbooks, now embraces Mary Katherine Goddard, David Walker, Elias Boudinot, Ida B. Wells-Barnett, and Robert S. Abbott.[64]

Though new people have appeared and new voices have spoken, the master narratives of journalism history have not been overthrown as fully as they have in other fields of U.S. history (or even in nonhistorical communication research). In journalism and media history, the standard frames of economic, technological, and democratic progress still shape the stories historians tell, especially in the monographic literature.[65] But just as in social history more generally, the raucous arrival of new people and new voices has begun to generate alternative narratives. Commercialization, for example, is now portrayed more often as decline than progress.[66] Embedded within the old grand narrative was a liberal secularism; an alternative narrative now places religion at the center of U.S. journalism history.[67] Perhaps most important, social history "from the bottom up" has thrust dissent, conflict, and even violence into the mainstream of U.S. journalism history.[68]

What has not yet happened in journalism history, however, is a major move to the new cultural history. More than twenty-five years ago, James W. Carey, a leading advocate of cultural studies in mass communication research, urged journalism historians to adopt the cultural approach, to take the linguistic turn. His counsel was precisely that of Charles Taylor, Clifford Geertz, and Robert Darnton. He saw journalism as a vital source of the language that people in the past used to construct their social reality:

> When we study the history of journalism we are principally studying a way in which men in the past have grasped reality. We are searching out the intersection of journalistic style and vocabulary, created systems of meaning, and standards of reality shared by writer and audience. We are trying to root out a portion of the history of consciousness.[69]

To do what Carey proposed would seem to require a focus not just on writers, publishers, and content, but also on the *readers* of journalism and on the cultural contexts in which those readers read. In nonhistorical communication research, a Carey-style cultural studies has blossomed luxuriantly. Once the exclusive province of survey and experiment, media audiences today are routinely studied in the ethnographic vein. How do people read? How do they construct meaning? How do they use the language and symbols of media to construct their lives, their social reality?[70] The Geertzian turn from behavior to interpretation has had a dramatic impact in the cultural studies wing of communication research. But the historical version of this cultural approach has lagged, at least in journalism history.

Outside the field of journalism history, however, a cultural history of communication has begun to emerge. Following the linguistic turn, historians in a variety of fields have been drawn to the historical contexts of language, which include the media of communication—especially books, but also magazines, newspapers, and other popular media. Indeed, the broad story of social history's transformation into cultural history is vividly illustrated in the story of how the social history of *literacy* evolved into the cultural history of *reading*. Thirty years ago, the history of literacy stood in the vanguard of the new social history. The methods for measuring historical literacy rates rested on sampling and quantification of behavioral evidence (such as signing vs. marking wills and estate inventories) and the testing of social theory (such as modernization and social mobility).[71] But, gradually, scholars of literacy began to ask more interpretive questions: What did reading mean to readers? What role did it play in their lives? How did people use reading to construct identity and community? The cultural turn in literacy studies merged with the historicist turn in literary criticism to produce a cultural history of books, readers, and reading.[72] Today, rather than correlating signature rates on a random sample of wills with quantitative indices of social class, historians of reading are much more likely to draw on letters and diaries to explore, say, how one young woman used reading to fashion her identity in late-nineteenth-century America.[73]

The history of reading has concentrated on the reading of books because that is the kind of reading that readers tended to leave a record of. In diaries, letters, and other sources, people talked about how reading played into their lives, perhaps especially religious reading and the reading of fiction.[74] But just as newspapers are more ephemeral than books, so the cultural history of reading journalism is more elusive than the history of reading books. Readers have left behind very little evidence of their reading experience with newspapers and magazines. But there is some evidence, and a few historians have begun to reconstruct how people in the past used journalism in their daily lives. Some of the most interesting work has been the study of newspaper reading in the contexts of popular politics and community life. David Waldstreicher, for example, has described the interaction between political reading and popular street demonstrations and celebrations during and after the American Revolution. Thomas Leonard has explored the physical settings in which people read newspapers in the early American republic, suggesting how news reading shaped and was shaped by family and community life. Ronald and Mary Zboray have shown how newspapers helped to build political communities among women readers in antebellum Boston. I have written about how people used newspapers to survive a community crisis in the late eighteenth century and how political interest groups in the early-twentieth-century taught readers how to read their daily newspapers in a particular ideological way.[75]

For journalism history, the most important outcome of the new cultural history of reading has been the integration of journalism into the broader history of culture, the history of "the consciousness of the past" (Carey's term). One of the best examples of this emergent communication history is Richard D. Brown's *Knowledge Is Power*, which reconstructs, as fully as the evidence allows, the entire communication milieu—word of mouth, handwriting, books, newspapers, etc.—of two men and their families in seventeenth- and eighteenth-century Massachusetts and Virginia. In going after the mental worlds of Samuel Sewell and William Byrd II, rather than going after journalism specifically, Brown finds that journalism simply pops up from time to time in context. Never before in journalism history has the first newspaper published in America, *Publick Occurrences*, played so minor a role; but never before have we better understood what that newspaper meant to one reader and to the community in which he lived.[76] Other imaginative efforts to treat newspaper reading as merely one element of a broad and complex culture of print in early nineteenth-century United States include David M. Henkin's *City Reading: Written Words and Public Spaces in Antebellum New York* and Isabelle Lehuu's *Carnival on the Page: Popular Print Media in Antebellum America*.[77]

Dangers lurk in the cultural history of journalism, however. Whether coming from the communication research angle of James Carey or the literary studies angle of reader-response criticism and new historicism, the new cultural history of readers and reading supposes that people used words to construct their own social realities. People live, as Clifford Geertz put it, in webs of significance that they themselves have spun. But just how free were individual readers to imagine and invent themselves and their mental worlds? Clearly, some of the webs in which readers were suspended were spun by others, and in the case of journalism those others may have been some of the most powerful business corporations and political institutions of their time. The Geertzian ethnographic approach to cultural studies seems weak on the structures of economic and political power, whether the subject is the lives of U.S. slaves, U.S. workers, U.S. women, or the readers of U.S. novels and newspapers. Thick description—reading the texts of culture over the shoulders of ordinary people—takes us deep into the drama of everyday life, so deep that we can lose sight of the theater, the structures, in which the drama was played.[78]

But this is not a critique in principle of all historical research in reader response; it is merely a plea to historians to set their reception studies more fully into context, including the contexts of production—of business and technology, government and politics, professional conventions and practices. This should not be difficult, for this is traditional fare in journalism history, and much excellent work has been done in recent years in each of these areas on the production side.[79] The key point is a simple one: If the reader-in-context is the quarry of cultural studies, then the context is as important as the reader.

A fascinating example of reader-oriented, yet nicely contextualized cultural history of journalism is Robert Darnton's "An Early Information Society: News and the Media in Eighteenth-Century Paris." In this thick description, Darnton seeks to reconstruct all the ways that news was shaped, shared, and pondered at a particular place and time. There were newspapers in Paris during the Old Regime—official gazettes with official court news—but Darnton is after the real news and the media that carried it: novels, broadsides, ballads, handwritten newsletters, notes on scraps of paper, public gardens, benches, rumors, poems, songs, salons, twenty-nine cafés, and even a tree, the tree of Cracow, where local people, diplomats, and spies hung out to hear what Parisians were saying. Luckily for Darnton, Paris was a kind of police state where municipal authorities gathered and preserved the evidence they would need to prosecute libelers and seditionists and that Darnton would need 250 years later to prosecute his cultural history of the news. In Paris, Darnton writes:

> The communication process took place by several modes in many settings. It always involved discussion and sociability, so it was not simply a matter of messages transmitted down a line of diffusion to passive recipients but rather a process of assimilating and reworking information in groups—that is, the creation of collective consciousness or public opinion.[80]

For Darnton the "information age" in Paris, 1750, was this: ordinary people reading, writing, listening, speaking, and singing the news, but in the contexts of social hierarchy, commercial printing, government regulation, and police dragnets.

In following the trails of news, Darnton moves easily between the event and the context, between the particular and the general. His story is a narrative of news in a particular place and time, a story of accident and contingency. But Darnton sees patterns as well as peculiarities, and he is bold to suggest that his history of Paris in 1750 may shed light on the eventual collapse of the Old Regime and on the role that the "communication system" played in that collapse. More boldly still, he suggests that in every age communication systems shaped events. This notion, he says, is "something that might be called the history of communication."[81]

James Carey's 1974 call for a cultural history of U.S. journalism was prescient but premature. "The cultural turn has not quite happened yet," Michael Schudson wrote in 1997 in a Carey *festschrift*.[82] True enough, but perhaps not true for long. The cultural history of readers and reading, born in other disciplines and often nurtured abroad, has migrated to U.S. journalism history. The linguistic turn in history and the new historicism in literary studies have inspired in scholars from a variety of fields a renewed fascination with language and, consequently, with the media that shaped and conveyed it. Journalism may yet get the kind of history it deserves.

Endnotes

1. Author's Note: My coauthor on this chapter for the first edition of this book was Harold L. Nelson, mentor and friend.
2. Keith Jenkins, *Re-Thinking History* (New York: Routledge, 1991), 19.

3. Gertrude Himmelfarb, *On Looking Into the Abyss: Untimely Thoughts on Culture and Society* (New York: Alfred A. Knopf, 1994), 153, 155.

4. Gary B. Nash, Charlotte Crabtree, and Ross E. Dunn, *History on Trial: Culture Wars and the Teaching of the Past* (New York: Alfred A. Knopf, 1997), chap. 1; Lawrence W. Levine, *The Opening of the American Mind: Canons, Culture, and History* (Boston: Beacon Press, 1996), chap. 1. See also Edward T. Linenthal and Tom Engelhardt, eds., *History Wars: The Enola Gay and Other Battles for the American Past* (New York: Metropolitan Books, 1996).

5. Eugene D. Genovese, "A New Departure," in Elizabeth Fox-Genovese and Elisabeth Lasch-Quinn, eds., *Reconstructing History: The Emergence of a New Historical Society* (New York: Routledge, 1999), 6–7. The first issue of the new society's journal, the *Journal of the Historical Society*, appeared in Spring 2000. Author's disclosure: In the 1990s, I was associate editor and acting editor of the *Journal of American History*, the journal of the Organization of American Historians.

6. Elizabeth Fox-Genovese and Elisabeth Lasch-Quinn, "The Imperative: The Historical Society as a Critique and a New Ideal," in Fox-Genovese and Lasch-Quinn, *Reconstructive History*, 3. For a lively attack on postmodernism from the right, see Keith Windschuttle, *The Killing of History: How Literary Critics and Social Theorists Are Murdering Our Past* (New York: Free Press, 1997). For an attack from the left, see Bryan Palmer, *Descent Into Discourse: The Reification of Language and the Writing of Social History* (Philadelphia: Temple University Press, 1990). Views on all sides of the debate are collected in Keith Jenkins, ed., *The Postmodern History Reader* (New York: Routledge, 1997).

7. Marc Trachtenberg, "The Past Under Siege," in Fox-Genovese and Lasch-Quinn, *Reconstructive History*, 9.

8. Charles Taylor, "Interpretation and the Sciences of Man," *Review of Metaphysics* 25 (September 1971): 18, 26, 34, also in Charles Taylor, *Philosophy and the Human Sciences* (Cambridge: Cambridge University Press, 1985), chap. 1; Richard Rorty, *Philosophy and the Mirror of Nature* (Princeton, NJ: Princeton University Press, 1979), chap. 7. Seminal anthologies on the linguistic turn in philosophy, literary criticism, and social science include Richard Rorty, ed., *The Linguistic Turn: Recent Essays in Philosophical Method* (Chicago: University of Chicago Press, 1967); Richard Macksey and Eugenio Donato, eds., *The Languages of Criticism and the Sciences of Man* (Baltimore: Johns Hopkins University Press, 1970); and Quentin Skinner, ed., *The Return of Grand Theory in the Human Sciences* (Cambridge: Cambridge University Press, 1985). Power and oppression play a larger role for French prophets of postmodernism than for North Americans such as Taylor and Rorty. See Michel Foucault, *The Order of Things: An Archaeology of the Human Sciences* (New York: Vintage Books, 1994); and Jacques Derrida, *Of Grammatology* (Baltimore: Johns Hopkins University Press, 1976).

9. Jenkins, *Re-Thinking*, 7, 11; Robert F. Berkhofer, Jr., *Beyond the Great Story: History as Text and Discourse* (Cambridge, MA: Belknap Press of Harvard University Press, 1995), 10–11; George G. Iggers, *Historiography in the Twentieth Century: From Scientific Objectivity to the Postmodern Challenge* (Hanover, NH: Wesleyan University Press, 1997), chap. 10. See also Richard J. Evans, *In Defense of History* (New York: W.W. Norton, 1999); Norman J. Wilson, *History in Crisis? New Directions in Historiography* (Upper Saddle River, NJ: Prentice-Hall, 1998); and Frank Ankersmit and Hans Kellner, eds., *A New Philosophy of History* (Chicago: University of Chicago Press, 1995).

10. Carl Becker, "Everyman His Own Historian," *American Historical Review* 37 (January 1932): 233, 235, also in *Everyman His Own Historian: Essays on History and Politics* (Chicago: Quadrangle Books, 1966); Richard Rorty, "Pragmatism, Relativism, and Irrationalism," in *Consequences of Pragmatism* (Minneapolis: University of Minnesota Press, 1982). See also Peter Novick, *That Noble Dream: The "Objectivity Question" and the American Historical Profession* (New York: Cambridge University Press, 1988), chap. 4.

11. David Lowenthal, *The Past Is a Foreign Country* (New York: Cambridge University Press, 1985). Lowenthal takes his title from L.P. Hartley's *The Go-Between*.

12. Lawrence W. Levine, *The Unpredictable Past: Explorations in American Cultural History* (New York: Oxford University Press, 1993), 8–9; Nash, Crabtree, and Dunn, *History on Trial*, 23–24.

13. Joyce Appleby, Lynn Hunt, and Margaret Jacob, *Telling the Truth about History* (New York: W.W. Norton, 1994), 10–11.

14. Murray Murphey, *Our Knowledge of the Historical Past* (Indianapolis: Bobbs-Merrill, 1973), 15–16; Appleby, Hunt, and Jacob, *Telling the Truth*, 255–56.

15. Murphey, *ibid.*, 155–56, 201. Murphey revisited these issues in 1994 but didn't change his mind in any substantive way. See Murray Murphey, *Philosophical Foundations of Historical Knowledge* (Albany: State University of New York Press, 1994).

16. James Bohman, *New Philosophy of Social Science: Problems of Indeterminancy* (Cambridge, MA: MIT Press, 1991), vii–viii; Richard J. Bernstein, *The Restructuring of Social and Political Theory* (Philadelphia: University of Pennsylvania Press, 1976), 228–31; Appleby, Hunt, and Jacob, *Telling the Truth*, chap. 5. Some philosophers and sociologists argue that natural science is just as indeterminate and hermeneutical as the human sciences, but that is not a debate I feel the need to explore in this chapter. See Noretta Koertge, ed., *A House Built on Sand: Exposing Postmodernist Myths about Science* (New York: Oxford University Press, 1998); Ian Hacking, *The Social Construction of What?* (Cambridge, MA: Harvard University Press, 1999); and Steve Fuller, *Thomas Kuhn: A Philosophical History for Our Times* (Chicago: University of Chicago Press, 2000).

17. Dorothy Ross, *The Origins of American Social Science* (Cambridge: Cambridge University Press, 1991); Robert C. Bannister, *Sociology and Scientism: The American Quest for Objectivity, 1880–1940* (Chapel Hill: University of North Carolina Press, 1987); Mark C. Smith, *Social Science in the Crucible: The American Debate Over Objectivity and Purpose, 1918–1941* (Durham, NC: Duke University Press, 1994).

18. Taylor, "Interpretation and the Sciences of Man," 56–57; Bernstein, *Restructuring*, 61–62; Richard J. Bernstein, "Philosophy, History, and Critique," in *The New Constellation: The Ethical-Political Horizons of Modernity/Postmodernity* (Cambridge, MA: MIT Press, 1992). Classic works that had an enormous impact on the historicizing of U.S. social science include C. Wright Mills, *The Sociological Imagination* (New York: Oxford University Press, 1959); Thomas Kuhn, *The Structure of Scientific Revolutions* (Chicago: University of Chicago Press, 1962); and Peter L. Berger and Thomas Luckmann, *The Social Construction of Reality: A Treatise in the Sociology of Knowledge* (Garden City, NY: Doubleday & Co., 1966).

19. Clifford Geertz, "Blurred Genres: The Refiguration of Social Thought," *American Scholar* 49 (Spring, 1980): 165–79, also in Geertz, *Local Knowledge* (New York: Basic Books, 1983); Clifford Geertz, "Thick Description: Toward an Interpretive Theory of Culture," in *The Interpretation of Cultures* (New York: Basic Books, 1973), 29–30.

20. Theda Skocpol, "Social History and Historical Sociology," *Social Science History* 11 (Spring 1987): 17–30. See also Terrence J. McDonald, ed., *The Historic Turn in the Human Sciences* (Ann Arbor: University of Michigan Press, 1996); and Eric H. Monkkonen, ed., *Engaging the Past: The Uses of History Across the Social Sciences* (Durham, NC: Duke University Press, 1994).

21. Jeffrey N. Cox and Larry J. Reynolds, eds., *New Historical Literary Study: Essays on Reproducing Texts, Representing History* (Princeton, NJ: Princeton University Press, 1993), 6, 8. See also Catherine Gallagher and Stephen Greenblatt, *Practicing New Historicism* (Chicago: University of Chicago Press, 2000); H. Aram Veeser, ed., *The New Historicism Reader* (New York: Routledge, 1994); and John Brannigan, *New Historicism and Cultural Materialism* (New York: St. Martin's Press, 1998).

22. Jane P. Tompkins, "Introduction to Reader-Response Criticism," in Jane P. Tompkins, ed., *Reader-Response Criticism: From Formalism to Post-Structuralism* (Baltimore: Johns Hopkins University Press, 1980); Stanley Fish, *Is There a Text in This Class? The Authority of Interpretive Communities* (Cambridge, MA: Harvard University Press, 1980); Norman N. Holland, *The Critical I* (New York: Columbia University Press, 1992).

23. Jane Tompkins, *Sensational Designs: The Cultural Work of American Fiction, 1790–1860* (New York: Oxford University Press, 1985), 39.

24. Berkhofer, *Beyond the Great Story*, ix; Novick, *That Noble Dream*, 537.

25. Douglass C. North, "The New Economic History After Twenty Years," *American Behavioral Scientist* 21 (November/December 1977): 187–206; Allan G. Bogue, *Clio and the Bitch Goddess: Quantification in American Political History* (Beverly Hills, CA: Sage Publications, 1983); Michael Frisch, "American Urban History as an Example of Recent Historiography," *History and Theory* 18 (1979): 350–77; Michael Ebner, "Urban History: Retrospect and Prospect," *Journal of American History* 68 (June 1981): 69–84; Michael H. Frisch and Daniel J. Walkowitz, eds., *Working-Class America: Essays on Labor, Community and American Society* (Urbana: University of Illinois Press, 1983).

26. Alice Kessler-Harris, "Social History," in Eric Forner, ed., *The New American History*, rev. ed. (Philadelphia: Temple University Press, 1997), 231–32. See also Oliver Zunz, ed., *Reliving the Past: The*

Worlds of Social History (Chapel Hill: University of North Carolina Press, 1985); and Theodore K. Rabb and Robert I. Rotberg, eds., *The New History: The 1980s and Beyond* (Princeton, NJ: Princeton University Press, 1982).

27. Allan G. Bogue, "Systematic Revisionism and a Generation of Ferment in American History," *Journal of Contemporary History* 21 (April 1986): 135–162; J. Morgan Kousser, "Quantitative Social-Scientific History," in Michael Kammen, ed., *The Past Before Us* (Ithaca, NY: Cornell University Press, 1980); Robert P. Swierenga, ed., *Quantification in American History* (New York: Atheneum, 1970).

28. Kessler-Harris, "Social History," 233. An early example is Jesse Lemisch, "The American Revolution Seen From the Bottom Up," in *Towards a New Past: Dissenting Essays in American History*, ed. Barton J. Bernstein (New York: Pantheon Books, 1968).

29. Kessler-Harris, "Social History," 238–39; Lynn Hunt, "Introduction: History, Culture, and Text," in *The New Cultural History*, ed. Lynn Hunt (Berkeley: University of California Press, 1989), 5–7; Dorothy Ross, "The New and Newer Histories: Social Theory and Historiography in an American Key," in *Imagined Histories: American Historians Interpret the Past*, ed. Anthony Molho and Gordon S. Wood (Princeton, NJ: Princeton University Press, 1998), 97–98.

30. Hunt, *New Cultural History*, 11; Clifford Geertz, "Thick Description," 6–7. See also Ronald G. Walters, "Signs of the Times: Clifford Geertz and Historians," *Social Research* 47 (Autumn 1980): 537–556; and Eve Rosenhaft, "History, Anthropology, and the Study of Everyday Life," *Comparative Studies in Society and History* 29 (January 1987): 99–105.

31. Robert Darnton, *The Great Cat Massacre, and Other Episodes in French Cultural History* (New York: Basic Books, 1984), 3; Darnton, "History and Anthropology," in *The Kiss of Lamourette: Reflections in Cultural History* (New York: W. W. Norton, 1990), 335–336.

32. Geertz, "Thick Description," 5; Geertz, "Deep Play: Notes on the Balinese Cockfight," in *Interpretation of Cultures*, 448–49; Hunt, *New Cultural History*, 16. See also Iggers, *Historiography*, chap. 9.

33. John Demos, *A Little Commonwealth: Family Life in Plymouth Colony* (New York: Oxford University Press, 1970); Kenneth A. Lockridge, *A New England Town: The First Hundred Years, Dedham, Massachusetts, 1636–1736* (New York: W.W. Norton, 1970); Philip J. Greven, *Four Generations: Population, Land, and Family in Colonial Andover, Massachusetts* (Ithaca, NY: Cornell University Press, 1970).

34. Helena M. Wall, "Notes on Life Since *A Little Commonwealth*: Family and Gender History Since 1970," *William and Mary Quarterly*, 3rd series, 62 (October 2000): 809–825; Lisa Wilson, *Ye Heart of a Man: The Domestic Life of Men in Colonial New England* (New Haven, CT: Yale University Press, 1999); Anya Jabour, *Marriage in the Early Republic: Elizabeth and William Wirt and the Companionate Ideal* (Baltimore: Johns Hopkins University Press, 1998).

35. Lawrence Stone, "The Revival of Narrative: Reflections on a New Old History," in *The Past and the Present Revisited* (London: Routledge & Kegan Paul, 1987), 82.

36. Thomas L. Haskell, "History, Explanatory Schemes, and Other Wonders of Common Sense," in *Objectivity Is Not Neutrality: Explanatory Schemes in History* (Baltimore: Johns Hopkins University Press, 1998), 21; Arthur C. Danto, *Analytical Philosophy of History* (Cambridge: Cambridge University Press, 1965), 141, 233, 246; J.H. Hexter, *Doing History* (Bloomington: Indiana University Press, 1971), 29–31, 42–43; Louis O. Mink, "The Autonomy of Historical Understanding," in *Historical Understanding*, ed. Brian Fay and Richard T. Vann (Ithaca, NY: Cornell University Press, 1987).

37. Stone, "The Revival of Narrative," 76–79. See also J. Morgan Kousser, "The Revivalism of Narrative: A Response to Recent Criticisms of Quantitative History," *Social Science History* 8 (Spring 1984): 133–49.

38. Hayden White, *The Content of the Form: Narrative Discourse and Historical Representation* (Baltimore: Johns Hopkins University Press, 1987), x, 27, 57; Hayden White, *Tropics of Discourse: Essays in Cultural Criticism* (Baltimore: Johns Hopkins University Press, 1978), 83, 122. See also Novick, *That Noble Dream*, 599–601.

39. Louis O. Mink, "Narrative Form as a Cognitive Instrument," in Fay and Vann. ed, *Historical Understanding*, 202.

40. Dorothy Ross, "Grand Narrative in American Historical Writing: From Romance to Uncertainty," *American Historical Review* 100 (June 1995): 651–77; Allan Megill, "Recounting the Past: 'Description,' Explanation, and Narrative in Historiography," *American Historical Review* 94 (June 1989): 627–653.

41. David Samuels, "The Call of Stories: Abandoning Their Charts and Tables, Many Influential Historians Are Returning to Narrative," *Lingua Franca* (May/June 1995): 35–43; Becker, "Everyman His Own Historian," 229. See also Simon Schama, *Dead Certainties: Unwarranted Speculations* (New York: Alfred A. Knopf, 1991); and Edmund Morris, *Dutch: A Memoir of Ronald Reagan* (New York: Random House, 1999).

42. Jeffrey Cox and Shelton Stromquist, "Introduction: Master Narratives and Social History," in *Contesting the Master Narrative: Essays in Social History* (Iowa City: University of Iowa Press, 1998), 8; Eric Monkkonen, "The Dangers of Synthesis," *American Historical Review* 91 (December 1986): 1146–1157. See also Thomas Bender, "Wholes and Parts: The Need for Synthesis in American History, *Journal of American History* 73 (June 1986): 122.

43. Geertz, "Deep Play," 448; Darnton, *Cat Massacre*, 63–64; Henry Glassie, "The Practice and Purpose of History," *Journal of American History* 81 (December 1994): 961–968.

44. David Thelen, ed., *Memory and American History* (Bloomington: Indiana University Press, 1990); John E. Bodnar, *Remaking America: Public Memory, Commemoration, and Patriotism in the Twentieth Century* (Princeton, NJ: Princeton University Press, 1992); Edward T. Linenthal, *Sacred Ground: Americans and Their Battlefields* (Urbana: University of Illinois Press, 1991).

45. Jerome Bruner, "The Narrative Construction of Reality," *Critical Inquiry* 18 (Autumn 1991): 1–21; Cristopher Nash, ed., *Narrative in Culture: The Uses of Storytelling in the Sciences, Philosophy, and Literature* (New York: Routledge, 1990); Arthur Asa Berger, *Narratives in Popular Cultura, Media, and Everyday Life* (Thousand Oaks, CA: Sage Publications, 1997); Sanford F. Schram and Philip T. Neisser, eds., *Tales of the State: Narrative in Contemporary U.S. Politics and Public Policy* (Lanham, MD: Rowman & Littlefield, 1997).

46. Catherine Kohler Riessman, *Narrative Analysis* (Newbury Park, CA: Sage Publications, 1993), 4–5. See also George Psatha, *Conversation Analysis: The Study of Talk-in-Interaction* (Thousand Oaks, CA: Sage Publications, 1995).

47. The Holocaust as a problem in historiography is explored in "Representing the Holocaust," a special issue of *History and Theory* 33 (1994); and Saul Friedlander, ed., *Probing the Limits of Representation: Nazism and the "Final Solution"* (Cambridge, MA: Harvard University Press, 1992). On outright Holocaust denial, see Michael Shermer and Alex Grobman, *Denying History: Who Says the Holocaust Never Happened and Why Do They Say It?* (Berkeley: University of California Press, 2000).

48. Iggers, *Historiography*, 10–12; Appleby, Hunt, and Jacob, *Telling the Truth*, chap. 7.

49. Rorty, "Pragmatism, Relativism, and Irrationalism," 166; Rorty, *Mirror of Nature*, 9. See also Novick, *That Noble Dream*, chap. 15.

50. Fish, *Is There a Text*, 320–321; Allan Megill, "Introduction: Four Senses of Objectivity," in *Rethinking Objectivity*, ed. by Allan Megill (Durham, NC: Duke University Press, 1994), 7. See also David A. Hollinger, *In the American Province: Studies in the History and Historiography of Ideas* (Bloomington: Indiana University Press, 1985), chap. 7.

51. Thomas L. Haskell, "The Curious Persistence of Rights Talk in the Age of Interpretation," in *Objectivity Is Not Neutrality*, 139.

52. Thomas Kuhn, quoted in *ibid.*, 142. "The tribe" could be interpreted very narrowly and has been so interpreted by some radical postmodernists. Kuhn, Fish, and Haskell have a broader understanding: the community of reason and liberal humanism.

53. Robert William Fogel, "'Scientific' History and Traditional History," in *Which Road To the Past? Two Views of History* (New Haven: Yale University Press, 1983), 24–25, 31–32, 42.

54. G.R. Elton, "Two Kinds of History," in *ibid.*, 78.

55. Fogel, " 'Scientific' History and Traditional History," 20, 29.

56. Nathan M. Pusey, "The Centrality of Humanistic Study," in Julian Harris, ed., *The Humanities: An Appraisal* (Madison: University of Wisconsin Press, 1962), 80–81.

57. Hexter, *Doing History*, 111.

58. Haskell, "History, Explanatory Schemes and Other Wonders," 14–16.

59. Philip Abrams, *Historical Sociology* (Ithaca, NY: Cornell University Press, 1983), 194; Olivier Zunz, "Toward a Dialogue With Historical Sociology," *Social Science History* 11 (Spring 1987): 39; Skocpol, "Social History," 27–28.

60. William G. Roy, "Time, Place, and People in History and Sociology," *Social Science History* 11 (Spring 1987): 53–62.

61. Willard G. Bleyer, *Main Currents in the History of American Journalism* (Boston: Houghton Mifflin, 1927); Frank Luther Mott, *American Journalism*, 3rd ed. (New York: Macmillan, 1962); Edwin Emery, *The Press and America: An Interpretative History of Journalism*, 2nd ed. (Englewood Cliffs, NJ: Prentice-Hall, 1962).

62. Associating American journalism history with "Whig history" is James Carey's apt idea. See James W. Carey, "The Problem of Journalism History," *Journalism History* 1 (Spring 1974): 3–5, 27. See also Joseph McKerns, "The Limits of Progressive Journalism History," *Journalism History* 4 (Autumn 1977): 88–92; and Wm. David Sloan, *Perspectives on Mass Communication History* (Hillsdale, NJ: Lawrence Erlbaum, 1991), chap. 1.

63. Jean Folkerts and Stephen Lacy, "Journalism History Writing, 1975–1983," *Journalism Quarterly* 62 (Autumn 1985): 585–588; Donald Lewis Shaw and Sylvia L. Zack, "Rethinking Journalism History: How Some Recent Studies Support One Approach," *Journalism History* 14 (Winter 1987): 111–117.

64. Emery, *Press and America*, 682; Michael Emery and Edwin Emery, *The Press and America: An Interpretative History of the Mass Media*, 8th ed. (Boston: Allyn and Bacon, 1996); Jean Folkerts, "American Journalism History: A Bibliographic Essay," *American Studies International* 29 (October 1991): 4–27; Margaret Blanchard, "The Ossification of Journalism History: A Challenge for the Twenty-first Century," *Journalism History* 25 (Autumn 1999): 107–112. The two specialized journals in the field, *Journalism History* and *American Journalism*, also reflect this new diversity, as do other textbooks. See, for example, Jean Folkerts and Dwight L. Teeter, Jr., *Voices of a Nation: A History of Mass Media in the United States*, 2nd ed. (New York: Macmillan, 1994); and Wm. David Sloan and James D. Startt, eds., *The Media in America: A History*, 3rd ed. (Northport, AL: Vision Press, 1996).

65. Michael Schudson, "Toward a Troubleshooting Manual for Journalism History," *Journalism and Mass Communication Quarterly* 74 (Autumn 1997): 463–476; John Nerone, "Theory and History," *Communication Theory* 3 (May 1993): 148–157.

66. Schudson, "Toward a Troubleshooting Manual," 466–467. See, for example, Gerald J. Baldasty, *The Commercialization of News in the Nineteenth Century* (Madison: University of Wisconsin Press, 1992); Robert W. McChesney, *Telecommunications, Mass Media, and Democracy: The Battle for the Control of U.S. Broadcasting, 1928–1935* (New York: Oxford University Press, 1993).

67. Marvin Olasky, *Central Ideas in the Development of American Journalism: A Narrative History* (Hillsdale, NJ: Lawrence Erlbaum, 1991); Wm. David Sloan, ed., *Media and Religion in American History* (Northport, AL: Vision Press, 2000); David Paul Nord, "Teleology and News: The Religious Roots of American Journalism, 1630–1730," *Journal of American History* 77 (June 1990): 9–38.

68. William S. Solomon and Robert W. McChesney, eds., *Ruthless Criticism: New Perspectives in U.S. Communication History* (Minneapolis: University of Minnesota Press, 1993); Hanno Hardt and Bonnie Brennen, eds., *Newsworkers: Toward a History of the Rank and File* (Minneapolis: University of Minnesota Press, 1995); John Nerone, *Violence Against the Press: Policing the Public Sphere in U.S. History* (New York: Oxford University Press, 1994); Susan Herbst, *Politics at the Margin: Historical Studies of Public Expression Outside the Mainstream* (New York: Cambridge University Press, 1994); Jane Rhodes, *Mary Ann Shadd Cary: The Black Press and Protest in the Nineteenth Century* (Bloomington: Indiana University Press, 1998); Martha M. Solomon, ed., *A Voice of Their Own: The Woman Suffrage Press, 1840–1910* (Tuscaloosa: University of Alabama Press, 1991).

69. Carey, "Problem of Journalism History," 5; Michael Schudson, "Introduction/The Problem of Journalism History, 1996," in *James Carey: A Critical Reader*, ed. Eve Stryker Munson and Catherine A. Warren (Minneapolis: University of Minnesota Press, 1997). Carey's "Problem of Journalism History" is reprinted in this volume, along with other essays and critical commentaries. See also James W. Carey, *Communication as Culture: Essays on Media and Society* (Boston: Unwin Hyman, 1989). Carey has been more the pragmatist than the critical theory advocate, i.e., he seems more inclined toward the optimism of Dewey and Rorty than the pessimism of Foucault and Derrida.

70. David Morley, "Active Audience Theory: Pendulums and Pitfalls," *Journal of Communication* 43 (Autumn 1993): 13–19, also in Mark R. Levy and Michael Gurevitch, eds., *Defining Media Studies: Reflections on the Future of the Field* (New York: Oxford University Press, 1994); Tamar Liebes, "On the Convergence of Theories of Mass Communication and Literature Regarding the Role of the 'Reader,'" in *Progress in Communication Sciences*, vol. 9, ed. Brenda Dervin and Melvin J. Voigt (Norwood, NJ: Ablex, 1989). See also Ien Ang, *Living Room Wars: Rethinking Media Audiences for a Postmodern World* (New York: Routledge, 1996); David Morley, *Television, Audiences & Cultural Studies* (New York: Routledge,

1992); Ellen Seiter, *et al.*, eds., *Remote Control: Television, Audiences, and Cultural Power* (New York: Routledge, 1989).

71. Kenneth A. Lockridge, *Literacy in Colonial New England: An Enquiry into the Social Context of Literacy in the Early Modern West* (New York: W.W. Norton, 1974); Harvey J. Graff, *The Literacy Myth: Literacy and Social Structure in the Nineteenth-Century City* (New York: Academic Press, 1979).

72. Carl Kaestle, et al., *Literacy in the United States: Readers and Reading since 1880* (New Haven: Yale University Press, 1991), chaps. 1–2; David D. Hall, "Readers and Reading in America: Historical and Critical Perspectives," in *Cultures of Print: Essays in the History of the Book* (Amherst: University of Massachusetts Press, 1996). For American examples, see William J. Gilmore, *Reading Becomes a Necessity of Life: Material and Cultural Life in Rural New England* (Knoxville: University of Tennessee Press, 1989); Cathy N. Davidson, ed., *Reading in America: Literature and Social History* (Baltimore: Johns Hopkins University Press, 1989); James L. Machor, ed., *Readers in History: Nineteenth-Century American Literature and the Contexts of Response* (Baltimore: Johns Hopkins University Press, 1993); Michele Moylan and Lane Stiles, ed., *Reading Books: Essays on the Material Text and Literature in America* (Amherst: University of Massachusetts Press, 1996).

73. Helen Lefkowitz Horowitz, "'Nous Autres': Reading, Passion, and the Creation of M. Carey Thomas," *Journal of American History* 79 (June 1992): 68–95; Barbara Sicherman, "Reading and Ambition: M. Carey Thomas and Female Heroism," *American Quarterly* 45 (March 1993): 73–103.

74. David D. Hall, *Worlds of Wonder, Days of Judgment: Popular Religious Belief in Early New England* (New York: Knopf, 1989), chap. 1; David Paul Nord, "Religious Reading and Readers in Antebellum America," *Journal of the Early Republic* 15 (Summer 1995): 241–272; Mary Kelley, "Reading Women/Women Reading: The Making of Learned Women in Antebellum America," *Journal of American History* 83 (September 1996): 401–424; Kate Flint, *The Woman Reader, 1837–1914* (New York: Oxford University Press, 1993).

75. David Waldstreicher, *In the Midst of Perpetual Fetes: The Making of American Nationalism, 1776–1820* (Chapel Hill: University of North Carolina Press, 1997); Thomas C. Leonard, "How Americans Learned to Read the News," in *News for All: America's Coming of Age with the Press* (New York: Oxford University Press, 1995); Ronald J. Zboray and Mary Saracino Zboray, "Political News and Female Readership in Antebellum Boston and Its Region," *Journalism History* 22 (Spring 1996): 2–14; David Paul Nord, "Readership as Citizenship in Late-Eighteenth-Century Philadelphia," in J. Worth Estes and Billy G. Smith, eds., *A Melancholy Scene of Devastation: The Public Response to the 1793 Philadelphia Yellow Fever Epidemic* (Canton, MA: Science History Publications, 1997); David Paul Nord, "Reading the Newspaper: Strategies and Politics of Reader Response, Chicago, 1912–1917," *Journal of Communication* 45 (Summer 1995): 66–93.

76. Richard D. Brown, *Knowledge Is Power: The Diffusion of Information in Early America, 1700–1865* (New York: Oxford University Press, 1989), chaps. 1–2. See also Richard D. Brown, *The Strength of a People: The Idea of an Informed Citizenry in America, 1650–1870* (Chapel Hill: University of North Carolina Press, 1996).

77. David M. Henkin, *City Reading: Written Words and Public Spaces in Antebellum New York* (New York: Columbia University Press, 1998); Isabelle Lehuu, *Carnival on the Page: Popular Print Media in Antebellum America* (Chapel Hill: University of North Carolina Press, 2000).

78. I develop this line of critique more fully in David Paul Nord, "Intellectual History, Social History, Cultural History, and Our History," *Journalism Quarterly* 67 (Winter 1990): 645–648; and David Paul Nord, "A Plea for Journalism History," *Journalism History* 15 (Spring 1988): 8–15. Scholars of contemporary media, working in the "critical studies" tradition, seem much more attentive than historians to institutionalized media power. See, for example, Robert W. McChesney, *Rich Media, Poor Democracy: Communication Politics in Dubious Times* (Urbana: University of Illinois Press, 1999); Dan Schiller, *Digital Capitalism: Networking the Global Market System* (Cambridge, MA: MIT Press, 1999).

79. See, for example, Gerald J. Baldasty, *E.W. Scripps and the Business of Newspapers* (Urbana: University of Illinois Press, 1999); Richard R. John, *Spreading the News: The American Postal System from Franklin to Morse* (Cambridge, MA: Harvard University Press, 1995); Menahem Blondheim, *News Over the Wires: The Telegraph and the Flow of Public Information in America, 1844–1897* (Cambridge, MA: Harvard University Press, 1994); Janet E. Steele, *The Sun Shines for All: Journalism and Ideology in the Life of Charles A. Dana* (Syracuse: Syracuse University Press, 1993); James L. Baughman, *The Re-*

public of Mass Culture: Journalism, Filmmaking, and Broadcasting in America since 1941, 2nd ed. (Baltimore: Johns Hopkins University Press, 1997); Jeffery A. Smith, *War and Press Freedom: The Problem of Prerogative Power* (New York: Oxford University Press, 1999); Charles A. Johanningsmeier, *Fiction and the American Literary Marketplace: The Role of Newspaper Syndicates in America, 1860–1900* (New York: Cambridge University Press, 1997); Michael Schudson, *The Good Citizen: A History of American Civic Life* (Cambridge, MA: Harvard University Press, 1998); David Z. Mindich, *Just the Facts: How "Objectivity" Came to Define American Journalism* (New York: New York University Press, 1998); David Nasaw, *The Chief: The Life of William Randolph Hearst* (Boston: Houghton Mifflin, 2000).

80. Robert Darnton, "An Early Information Society: News and the Media in Eighteenth-Century Paris," *American Historical Review* 105 (February 2000): 26. See also Robert Darnton, "First Steps Toward a History of Reading," in *Kiss of Lamourette*.

81. Darnton, "Early Information Society," 1–2, 35.

82. Schudson, "Introduction/The Problem of Journalism History," 82.

20

Legal Research in Mass Communication

Erik Ugland

Everette E. Dennis

Donald M. Gillmor

To the student learning the traditions and tools of communication research, **legal research** in mass communication may seem at first to present a conceptual puzzle. Law, like history, is an area of *substance knowledge*, but legal scholarship is also linked to specific *legal research methodologies*. Confusion increases when you realize that studies of legal issues and problems in mass communication (or in other fields, for that matter) also lend themselves to a variety of other methodological approaches. The methods of history, philosophy, sociology, and other disciplines have been applied to the law for many years.

It is important, therefore, to distinguish substantive legal topics that might interest researchers in various fields using differing scholarly methods from the woods of legal scholarship that have a direction and purpose of their own. At the same time, it is imperative that substantive legal issues and problems of interest to mass communication researchers be put in the context of the law generally.

When it comes to substantive legal topics, historians might want to know something of the evolution of libel law in the English courts; philosophers might want information about the reasoning process of judges in making particular legal interpretations; sociologists might be interested in the influence of the law on social class; and political scientists might explore the relationship between election returns and judicial decisions. In carrying out these studies, the scholarly investigator will use whatever research methodology is appropriate to the problem. These might include the historical method, linguistic analysis, participant observation, survey research, content analysis, experimental design, and other approaches. Researchers will conduct their work in accordance with the standards and norms of their scholarly disciplines. The result of this research might be a better understanding of law and legal institutions, but this is not legal research per se.

Legal research methodology for the student of mass communication falls into a number of general areas. First, there is traditional legal research, which involves an exhaustive examination of legal materials in a law library setting; second, there is empirical and behavioral legal research, which employs the methods of social science while recognizing the unique circumstances and problems of law. Both approaches will be examined.

Another consideration for the student of mass communication law is *context*. Most mass communication researchers are not fully grounded in all areas of law, nor are they generally concerned with them. Yet, from time to time it is necessary to understand the communication of the law problem that has no origins in earlier legal areas unrelated to communication law.

For example, one of the authors of this chapter, in a study of the Pentagon Papers, found it necessary to explore rather than obscure reaches of the ancient law of trover and conversion in order to understand the concept of information as property in the public sector.[1]

Areas of law of greatest interest to mass communication researchers have been (1) *torts*, especially libel, privacy, and, since *New York Times* in 1964, constitutional privilege; (2) *criminal law*, affecting sedition, criminal libel, contempt, and journalist's privilege; (3) *personal property*, including copyright, trademark, and commercial speech; (4) *constitutional law*, freedom of speech and press guarantees of liberty under due process of law; (5) *legal procedure*, the enforcement of substantive rights, including free press, and fair trial; and (6) *administrative law*, the regulation of broadcast and other areas of telecommunication and advertising communication. Important as these topics are, they are not the whole of federal and state law.

Frederick S. Siebert, a notable communications scholar, put the point well:

> Research in the field of legal problems of communication, like research in other areas of social sciences, cannot be sharply segregated either as to subject matter or as to methods. Almost every research project in the broad areas of communication involves economic, political or social as well as legal problems, and in many cases it is impossible to separate the strictly legal from other aspects. To add to the complications involved in any attempt to segregate the legal aspects is the modem tendency of legal research to branch out into the social sciences and to utilize the findings of those areas in the solution of juridical questions.[2]

The Status of Communication Law Research

Although legal research is one the oldest areas of communication research, legal studies in schools and departments of journalism had been modest in number until the early 1970s. Central to a sustained interest over the years has been the need for current information on law as it applied to the press. At a time when there was less public interest in issues of press law, journalism education provided colleagues with careful, though sometimes narrowly focused, updates on current cases and their effects.

Doctoral dissertations and master's theses in journalism and mass communication add to the literature, as do occasional articles in the major communication journals. From time to time historical treatises and textbooks on mass communication law appear. A few communication researchers publish in the law reviews. Fortunately for the field, scholars in other fields (law, political science, and history, for example) have provided a substantial yield of communication law studies and theorizing on freedom of expression.[3] Notable exceptions to the overall paucity of legal literature in earlier journalism education are the works of Siebert (legal history)"[4] and J. Edward Gerald (constitutional law and the press),[5] both of whom held journalism appointments.

Articles on legal research methodology in mass communication have been included in books on communication research since the 1970s, and, increasingly, a unit on legal and jurisprudential methods is taught in graduate courses in communication and media studies.[6] Several doctoral programs in mass communication have strong communication law components with some offering joint Ph.D.–J.D. programs with law schools. The Law Division of the Association in Journalism and Mass Communication, which dates from the early 1970s, encourages legal scholarship through an active papers competition and also has its own substantial journal, *Communication Law and Policy*, launched in 1996. The International Communications Association similarly has a law and policy division. Serious students of the field also draw on regular meetings and publications of the Practising Law Institute program on communication law, which is aimed at attorneys concerned with media law.

What Is Legal Research?

For those conversant with the scientific method, a first encounter with traditional legal research may be disappointing. Sometimes law review articles will unabashedly advocate a position based in normative assumptions. Other legal research will seem tediously encyclopedic and pedantic.

Legal research, however, serves several explicit functions, including

> clarifying the law through analysis of procedure, precedent and doctrine; reforming old laws and creating new ones; providing a better understanding of how law operates in society; and furnishing materials for legal education.[7]

These are somewhat distinctive and differing purposes. Many, if not most, legal researchers would like their research to have an impact on the law itself. It is considered a mark of considerable prestige for a piece of legal scholarship to be cited in a court decision as secondary authority for a new interpretation of the law. Of course, not all legal scholarship finds its way into judicial opinions, but as an ultimate goal, the role of the legal scholar is different than that of a researcher who is satisfied simply to observe, analyze, explain, and sometimes predict. The observation-analysis role is more common to the social scientist engaged in empirical and behavioral legal research.

Legal research of the traditional, documentary mode is largely adversarial. The legal researcher sets down a provocative proposition and marshals evidence to support its plausibility, and that evidence may come from opinions for the court, dissenting opinions, legislative histories, constitutional interpretation, and legal commentaries.

The Tools of Legal Research

Cases, statutes, and constitutions are the primary stuff of the law. If you cannot retrieve and read them, you are forever doomed to secondary sources; someone else will have to read and interpret them for you.

Many campuses will not have law school libraries, but there are alternatives. Metropolitan counties often have substantial law libraries in their courthouses or government centers. State capitols usually house law libraries. In addition, general libraries, political science departments, and private law firms may be able to assist you. If there are no law libraries in your area, you might find what you need by searching the growing constellation of law-related sites on the World Wide Web.

With continued computerization and the exponential growth of new media, legal research has been greatly simplified. Web-based systems have made it possible to conduct some legal research from the home or office, vast databases have been recorded onto searchable CD-ROMs, and other technologies have made finding cases, statutes, and articles a process that can take minutes instead of hours.

Despite the benefits of computer-assisted legal research, the traditional resources remain indispensable. Most legal research tasks cannot be completed without spending time in the library, and anyone not acquainted with those resources will inevitably encounter problems.

There are many ways to begin the legal research process, one of which is to learn the language—the legal vocabulary—of the problem you are studying. Any of a number of law dictionaries can serve this purpose (*Black's, Ballentine's*). For those studying libel, for example, *Black's* provides a detailed definition and a series of related terms. A deluxe version will also point you to cases and statutes applying your word.

From there, you might want to know in more detail how courts have construed the concept of libel, or perhaps a more specific term like "malice." One way to do that is with *Words and Phrases*. This set of volumes contains common legal words and phrases followed by abstracts of judicial decisions using them. Pocket parts or supplements inside the back cover of each volume keep this and other legal publications up to date. Do not overlook them.

Legal encyclopedias can provide a still wider sweep of information on your topic. The most commonly used are *Corpus Juris Secundum* (C.J.S.) and *American Jurisprudence 2d* (Am. Jur. 2d). C.J.S. and *American Jurisprudence 2d* are alphabetically arranged sets of volumes containing detailed entries on hundreds of topics and subtopics. Both encyclopedias provide definitions and interpretations, as well as citations to relevant state and federal court decisions, statutes, and regulations. Both are also very detailed. "Libel and slander" takes up nearly 300 pages in C.J.S. and nearly *500* pages in *American Jurisprudence 2d*.

For information on a more specific legal issue, particularly an unsettled one on which lower courts have divided, *American Law Reports* (A.L.R.) is an excellent place to turn. A.L.R. volumes contain detailed annotations with essays, notes, and citations to the most significant court decisions on your topic. The two most current A.L.R. series are A.L.R. 5th, which covers state topics, and A.L.R. Fed., which covers federal topics. State and federal topics are mixed together in A.L.R.lst, A.L.R.2C1 and A.L.R.3d. Locate topics by using either the single-volume *Quick Index*, which accompanies each series, or the multivolume *A.L.R. Index*, which covers all of the main A.L.R. series. Locate specific annotations using the *A.L.R. Digests*.

Newer A.L.R. series do not replace earlier ones; however, annotations in the older series are more likely to be out of date. Use the pocket parts in each volume for updates on your annotation,[8] and *always* check the Annotation History Table, located in the *A.L.R. Index* volumes to find out if your annotation has been supplemented or superseded.

Once you have found case citations using a dictionary, *Words and Phrases,* an encyclopedia, A.L.R., or some other source, you need to know how to locate them. All reported state cases can be found in West Publishing's National Reporter System. West has seven different regional "reporters," each covering a different part of the country. *West Southern Reporter* (So. or So. 2d), for example, contains state court cases from Alabama, Florida, Louisiana, and Mississippi. The other states are grouped within either *Atlantic* (A. or A.2d), *North Western* (N.W. or N.W.2d), *North Eastern* (N.E. or N.E.2d), *Pacific* (P. or P.2d), *South Eastern* (S.E. or S.E.2d), or *South Western* (S.W. or S.W.2d). Additional reporters exist for New York (*New York Supplement*) and California (*California Reporter*). Each of these nine reporters contains the full text of reported cases from the state courts in its region.[9]

State court decisions are cited as: *LeDoux v. Northwest Publishing, Inc., 521* N.W.2d 59 (Minn. Ct. App. 1994). LeDoux is the name of the appellant (the person who appealed the lower court decision), Northwest Publishing is the respondent, 521 is the volume number, N.W.2d is the reporter the case is in, 59 is the page number the case begins on, and Minn. Ct. App. indicates that this is a decision of the Minnesota Court of Appeals.

Federal cases are found in the *Federal Supplement* (F. Supp.), which contains the full text of federal district court decisions, and the *Federal Reporter* (F., F.2d or F.3d), which contains the decisions of the federal appellate courts (circuit courts).

Federal district court decisions are cited as: *Ayei v. CBS,* 848 F.Supp. 362 (E.D.N.Y. 1994). Many states have more than one federal district court. E.D.N.Y. indicates that this is a decision of the U.S. District Court for the Eastern District of New York. Federal appellate court decisions are cited as: *Hunt v. NBC,* 872 F.2d 289 (9th Cir. 1989). You can see that this is a decision of the U.S. Court of Appeals for the Ninth Circuit.

United States Supreme Court decisions are found in three parallel reporters, one official, published by the Court itself (U.S.), another published by West (S.Ct.), and a third, this one annotated, published by the Lawyers Cooperative Publishing Co. (L.Ed.2d). S.Ct. is an abbreviation for Supreme Court and L.Ed. is an abbreviation for Lawyers Edition. A complete citation for Supreme Court decisions refers to all three reporters and is cited as: *New York Times v. United States,* 403 U.S. 713, 91 S.Ct. 2140, 29 L.Ed.2d 822 (1971).

Supreme Court opinions take a long time to appear in the U.S. reporter, so the S.Ct. reporter is used most often for recent cases. Court decisions are initially sent out to law schools as paperback "advance sheets." These look the same as decisions in the bound reporter volumes and they can be cited the same way. When each new bound volume arrives, the advance sheets are discarded.

Another source for recent court opinions is *United States Law Week* (U.S.L.W.). U.S.L.W. provides the full text of U.S. Supreme Court opinions shortly after they are rendered, as well as the latest agency rulings, news notes, statutory developments, and summaries of significant lower-court decisions. It also traces the status of appeals before the U.S. Supreme Court and indicates which have been granted or denied review (certiorari).

The best source for staying on top of the latest court cases affecting the mass media is the Bureau of National Affairs *Media Law Reporter* (Med. L. Rptr.). On an almost weekly basis it reports all cases having a bearing on journalism and communication law, often providing the full text of those decisions. It also provides news notes on media law issues, occasional bibliographies, special reports, and court schedules and dockets.

Perhaps the easiest way to access the most recent court opinions is through computer-based systems. Westlaw is the most comprehensive computer database for the legal profession, followed by Lexis, which is part of the Lexis-Nexis Network. Westlaw and Lexis are both extraordinary services that dramatically simplify many legal research tasks. Their databases allow you to search and access full texts of law review articles, court cases, bills and statutes, agency regulations, and virtually every other source of law imaginable. Unfortunately, both are expensive subscription services that few individuals can afford.

For those who have Westlaw or Lexis access, most court decisions are accessible within days of being handed down. For those who do not have access, the Internet can be the answer. U.S. Supreme Court decisions are available on many sites, but are best accessed through Findlaw (*www.findlaw.com*) or Cornell University (*www.law.cornell.edu*). Findlaw has full texts available from 1893. The Cornell site has decisions from 1990 and more than 600 historic cases from before 1990. Both sites also provide links to the decisions of the federal circuit courts and to state courts, although for many of those courts, only their more recent decisions are accessible on line.

Once you have located one or more cases on your topic, you can quickly find others using digests. Digests provide summaries of court decisions, organized around topics and key numbers. Key numbers are numbers assigned to identify and distinguish different legal topics and points of law. U.S. Supreme Court decisions can be found in the *U.S. Supreme Court Digest*, federal district and circuit court decisions are in the *Federal Practice Digest 4th*, and state court decisions can be found using either regional digests, such as the *Northwest Digest 2d* (covering the same states as the *Northwest Reporter* 2d), or digests for individual states (e.g., *Alaska Digest*). For a more comprehensive range of cases, use the *General Digest*, which covers all of the most recently reported cases from both state and federal courts. For earlier (pre-1996) cases, use the *Decennial Digests* (there are ten of them, each covering a different ten-year period from 1897 through 1996).

Digests are arranged alphabetically by topic, and each set of digests contains an index to help you quickly locate relevant cases. You can also locate cases using key numbers. Once you know the key number for a particular topic, you can quickly find cases in other digests.

Once you have found a case, you need to trace its life history using a citator to make sure it is still "good law." The most commonly used is *Shepard's Citations*, which can tell you whether your case has been modified, reversed, affirmed, superseded, criticized, distinguished, explained, limited, overruled or questioned by other courts. Shepard's can also tell what attorneys general and law review authors have said about your case. There are *Shepard's Citations* for every state, each region of West's National Reporter System, for lower federal courts and the U.S. Supreme Court. Using citators is a necessary step in the legal research process. Bypassing it can be disastrous.

In addition to being able to find and track court cases, legal researchers must know how to locate statutes and regulations. Federal statutes are found in the United States Code (U.S.C.), which is the official, government-produced reporter of federal law. There are two unofficial sources, however, that are often more useful to researchers—*United States Code Annotated* (U.S.C.A.) and *United States Code Service* (U.S.C.S.). Both U.S.C.A. and U.S.C.S. contain the full text of the federal code but add annotations that cite court cases and secondary sources applying and interpreting the law.

Federal statutes are organized by topic into numbered "titles," and each title contains many different laws, which are presented as different "sections" and "subsections" of those titles. The citation 15 U.S.C. §26 (1976) is a reference to federal antitrust law, is located in title *15*, section 26 of the U.S. Code, and was adopted in 1976. In the absence of a specific citation, you can locate laws using the multivolume indices that accompany the U.S.C., U.S.C.A., and U.S.C.S.

To trace the legislative history of a statute, use the *U.S. Code Congressional and Administrative News* (U.S.C.C.A.N.), which publishes the text of each law as it appeared at the time of passage, committee reports, and a variety of other documents and data. You can also consult the *Congressional Record*, which is published daily and contains edited transcripts of floor debates and votes.

The entire U.S. Code is now available on the World Wide Web in searchable form through a number of websites. The most useful and comprehensive is the Government Printing Office's site (*www.access.gpo.gov*). That site also contains the *Congressional Record*, Congressional reports, transcripts of hearings, copies of public laws, and a wealth of other information. Similar information can be found on the Cornell and Findlaw sites noted earlier, as well as the Library of Congress site (*www.loc.gov*), which also contains a link to the Thomas system (*www.thomas.loc.gov*). Thomas provides the most current information on developments in Congress. With Thomas and the GPO sites alone, researchers have comprehensive access to the past and present work of Congress.

To access state law on the Internet, go to the Cornell site or the Findlaw site and find links to every states' statutes and courts. Updates, court interpretations and secondary source treatments of both state and federal statutes can be found in *Shepard's State Citations* and *Shepard's United States Citations*, respectively.

Administrative agency rules and determinations are another important source of law. Rules and regulations of federal agencies are presented in the *Code of Federal Regulations*, supplemented daily by the *Federal Register*. The latter includes official notices of rulemaking and other proceedings conducted by agencies such as the Federal Communications Commission (FCC).

Both the Federal Register and the Code of Federal Regulations are available on the GPO website. The Findlaw and Cornell sites, among others, provide links to sites containing state administrative regulations. Check *Shepard's Code of Federal Regulation Citations* for updates on agency rules.

FCC and other agency regulations affecting communications industries are also found in *Pike & Fischer's Communication Regulation* (C.R.). This is an excellent resource that provides comprehensive access to all of the statutes, treaties, cases, and agency rules that affect communications. C.R. is really the third installment of *Pike & Fischer's Radio Regulation* (R.R. regulation and R.R.2d). The new name reflects the current breadth of its coverage, which has moved far beyond just radio.

C.R., like R.R. and R.R.2d, comes in three sections—current service, digests, and cases. The current service volumes include a complete index and the texts of all statutes, treaties, and agency rules affecting communications. Digest volumes contain summaries of all cases found in C.R. and R.R.2d (back to 1990). And the cases volumes present the full text of all court decisions, FCC rulings, and other materials.

The latest activities of federal agencies can also be monitored by going directly to their websites. The FCC (*www.fcc.gov*) and FTC (*www.ftc.gov*) websites provide detailed information on their latest hearings, rules, and projects. You can also consult the *Trade Regulation Reporter*, or industry periodicals like *Broadcasting, Broadcasting & Cable*, and *Advertising Age* for timely reports on FCC and FTC actions.

Once you have located all of your primary sources—cases, statutes, administrative rules, etc.—you might want to examine some secondary sources to learn more about your topic and to consider what others have written about it. These sources can occasionally be good as starting points to legal research, but you should avoid the temptation to rely on them too early and too often. The best legal research tends to be built around primary sources.

Law reviews are one of the most widely used secondary sources.[10] They can be found in most law libraries, and specific articles can be located using *Legaltrac* (a searchable database available in many law libraries), the *Index to Legal Periodicals*, the *Legal Resource Index*, or the *Current Law Index*. Most law reviews are also available in full-text form on Westlaw and Lexis. A few law reviews offer full text on the World Wide Web, while most others offer only abstracts or tables of contents. To see how articles have been treated by courts and other authors, use *Shepard's Law Review Citations*.

Treatises, hornbooks, and *nutshells* are other useful secondary sources. A hornbook is a single-volume summary of a field of law. A nutshell is an even more concise summary. A treatise is similar to a hornbook but is more likely to reflect the opinions of the author whose comments are interspersed with the presentation of the "black-letter" law.

Restatements are books that attempt to identify the enduring principles governing a particular area of law and to present them in almost code form. Of particular interest to communication scholars are the *Restatement of Torts 2d* and the *Restatement of Contracts 2d*.

In addition to these secondary sources, it should be noted that the Internet now provides thousands of websites and other online resources for legal research. Government agencies, academic departments, media organizations, foundations, industry associations, and law firms provide volumes of information on their websites that can be useful research material. But you must exercise extreme caution when using any of these sources, which can be imprecise, slanted, incomplete, out of date, or just plain wrong.

Before you begin tackling your research project, be sure to take advantage of the growing list of books devoted to legal research on the Internet,[11] as well as the abundance of traditional legal research tutorials.[12]

Finally, when conducting legal research, you must know how to cite items properly. While styles for different publications vary, most legal work and research follows the guidelines presented in *A Uniform System of Citation*, typically referred to as the "blue book." When in doubt, use this citation standard.

Types of Legal Research in Mass Communication

We have indicated that several explicit functions are performed by legal research generally. These also apply to legal research in mass communication. *Some research clarifies the law and offers explanation through an analysis of procedure, precedent, and doctrine.* Pember, in his important book *Privacy and the Press*, used historical analysis and a synthesis of leading cases affecting the press to clarify the law of privacy.[13] In such works as the American Law Institute's *Restatement of the Law of Torts, 2d*, an effort is made to codify and otherwise make sense out of court decisions in libel law.[14]

Some legal law research tries to reform old laws and suggest changes in the law. Law professors Jerome Barron and Benno Schmidt, Jr., have pushed and pulled the concept of "access to the press." Barron, in a landmark law review article and in his book *Freedom of the Press for Whom?*,[15] calls for "realistic reinterpretation of the First Amendment so as to accommodate the public to have access to the major media in order to express one's opinions where they will matter." Barron lost a decisive battle for his proposed changes in the law before the U.S. Supreme Court in the case of *Miami Herald Publishing Co. v. Tornillo* (1974).[16] Recent studies of libel law also reflect on possible changes in this troublesome area of law.[17]

Research may be conducted to provide a better understanding of how law operates on society. Levy's *Freedom of Speech and Press in Early American History: Legacy of Suppression* deals with the social and political effects of constitutional interpretations of the crime of seditious libel in the formative years of the U.S. republic. The endurance of the crime of sedition in the U.S. experience is the chilling theme of this revisionist history, although Levy modifies his thesis in *Emergence of a Free Press.*[18]

Preston's *The Great American Blow-Up*[19] is a legal analysis of the social effects of false and deceptive advertising (puffery) and of the inability of the courts and regulatory agencies to deal with it. Most of the empirical behavioral studies discussed later in this chapter also fall under the general heading of "social effects."

Research may analyze the political and social processes that shape our communication laws. Here the focus is not on the effect of the law on society; rather, it is on the effect of society upon the law. Krasnow, Longley, and Terry's *The Politics of Broadcast Regulation*[20] is a perceptive analysis of how formal legal institutions, such as the FCC, Congress, and the courts interact in social and political terms with citizen groups and the communication industry lobby to create and enforce broadcasting law.

Research may furnish materials for legal and journalistic education in mass communication. Here we think of two kinds of textbooks that provide the basis for mass communication law courses. These include the hornbooks that synthesize and present in easily understood categories the law of mass communication. Examples are the works of Dwight Teeter and Don Le Duc, Kent Middleton and Bill Chamberlin, as well as Donald Pember.[21] Another kind of text is the casebook that presents a series of analytical comments and questions integrated with edited selections of leading cases. The best known casebooks are by Gilimor and Barron; Carter, Franklin, and Wright; and—for the electronic media—Carter, Franklin, Anderson, and Wright.[22]

Beyond the general materials of mass communication law there are programmed instruction materials in libel law, treatises on advertising, and broadcast and cable law and regulation. Communication law research also focuses on news media coverage of courts and the law. A major work on news coverage of the U.S. Supreme Court is Grey's *The Supreme Court and the News Media*. Drechsel does the same for trial courts.[23]

Empirical and Behavioral Legal Research in Mass Communication

Sir Henry Finch observed in his *Discourses on Law* in 1627 that "the sparkes of all the Sciences of the World are raked up in the ashes of the Law."[24] If Sir Henry intended to convey the idea that law, like other realms of human thought and action, is amenable to a variety of mental disciplines, he was prophetic. That is where we are today.

Methodologies applicable to the study of legal questions have been called traditional, **empirical**, and **behavioral**. Yet the most insistent advocates of each recognize the inevitable overlap. The traditional legal material retrieval system we have described depends for its logic upon words and numbers; thus the relative ease of its computability. Methodologies diverge, however, when their adherents are pressed to define what they mean by "theory." For the traditionalist, theory may be no more than a preference for a particular ordering of values, a model of action that can be applied generally and with feeling to a set of everyday occurrences. Oliver Wendell Holmes' "clear and present danger" test, Thomas Emerson's "speech/action" dichotomy, and the Rehnquist court's doctrine of judicial restraint are such models, lending themselves to the logical process of analogy, discrimination, and power deduction.

Behavioral theory is presented as something grander. It assigns to itself the of prediction, but perhaps not its invention. Holmes, in his 1897 address to the Massachusetts Bar, "The Path of the Law," has already staked a claim to prediction:

> The object of our study, then, is prediction, the prediction of the incidence of the public force through the instrumentally of the courts. . . . The prophecies of what the courts will do in fact, and nothing more pretentious, are what I mean by the law.[25]

Legal sociologist Aubert believes it important to understand the characteristics of traditional legal research that set it apart from scientific thinking. They are:

1. Scientific approaches tend to emphasize, often to the exclusion of everything else, that aspect of a phenomenon which is general. Judicial opinions, and also legal theory, tend . . . to stress the unique aspects of the case.
2. The web of relationships which legal thought throws over the facts of life is not a causal or functional one. Legal thinking, legislation, and judicial decision making are (only) peripherally touched by schemes of thought in terms of means and ends.
3. Legal thinking is characterized by absence of probabilism, both with respect to law and with respect to facts. Events have taken place or they have not taken place. A law is either valid or invalid.
4. Legal thinking is heavily oriented to the past. . . .
5. Law is a comparison process. . . . The legal consequences expected to follow a certain action. . . .
6. Legal thinking is dichotomous. Rights or duties are either present or absent.[26]

The goal of legal scholarship in mass communication is not always knowledge for the sake of knowledge; it is often an applied knowledge in keeping with the lawyer's adversarial purpose. Political behavioralist S. Sidney Ulmer writes:

> In choosing among hypotheses concerning historical fact, the lawyer seeks victory, not truth. The adversary process repels evidence as do delays in litigation. In making

decisions the judge recognizes (1) that the case must be decided one way or another, whether or not the evidence is sufficient for a scientific conclusion; (2) that judicial fact-finders are not bound by rules of consistency; and (3) that facts may be bent by the judicial process to serve an ulterior purpose.[27]

It is perhaps unfortunate that much legal scholarship methodologically parallels the opinions of judges. The mass communication researcher, less wedded to the judiciary than the legal scholar, has an opportunity to make more scientific applications and to develop a more disinterested scholarship. Unfortunately, however, the communication scholar gets caught up in another kind of adversarial system and often becomes an advocate for the press and the communication theory; he or she looks for the effects of law on the absolute command of the First Amendment that "Congress shall make no law, abridging freedom of speech or of the press. . . ."

But it is overstatement to say, as Schubert does in the introduction to his landmark book, *Judicial Behavior*, that "the traditional approach is interested in neither the descriptive politics of judicial action (i.e., the facts) nor the development of a systematic theory of judicial decision making (through the use of scientific theory and methods).[28] The aversion is not that strong, and such methodology may simply not be appropriate to some kinds of research. Often the legal scholar works with the singular instance, that is, the individual case. A new court decision is regarded as a landmark and the law changes. That singular instance can be related historically to earlier cases and to external influences that may have brought it about. But does this lead to theoretical formulation?

"Theory" in mass communication studies generally implies a set of related and highly abstract statements from which propositions testable by scientific measurement can be drawn and upon which explanations and predictions about human behavior can be based. Theoretical models in legal research are different since they must accommodate changes in the law created by case adjudication and statute. This difficult task is compounded by the fact that "theory" in law, according to *Black's Law Dictionary*, is explicitly defined as " facts on which the right of action is claimed to exist." When a judge asks the question, "On what theory?" he wants to know the basis of liability or grounds of defense. From Mill to Mieklejohn to Emerson, First Amendment claims have issued from theoretical frameworks that validate the asking of these questions. To lack a persuasive theory of freedom of expression is to lack any explanation for individual cases.

Drawing too rigid a line between traditional and empirical methodologies, however, can be misleading. Traditional legal methodologies, it is true, are qualitative, their outcomes sometimes inexplicable, even unique, but not always. Scientific methodologies are quantitative, their outcomes lawful and noncontradictory, but not always.

Basic steps in the empirical test of generalizations might be (1) reviewing the relevant literature, (2) deciding upon testable hypotheses, (3) setting up a research design, (4) collecting and analyzing data, (5) testing the hypotheses with the data collected, and (6) offering conclusions and explanations for one's findings.

The traditional researcher, though in a less formal and systematic way, follows the same procedure. But again there are differences. If the trial is substituted for, say, the experimental research design, the difference becomes dramatic. The trial can never be repeated or replicated. It can only happen once. The legal hypothesis can be retested in an appeal, and often is, but the appeal process is finite. In principle, the retesting and reformulation of hypotheses in science may continue endlessly. The legal scholar, however, unlike the trial lawyer, can enjoy some of the experimentalist's theoretical opportunities.

The application of social science methods to the study of mass communication law and other legal problems is of relatively recent origin, and there is a paucity of literature. The new approach is an outgrowth of scholarly trends in jurisprudence and political science away from natural law toward positivism (legal realism, political jurisprudence, and judicial behavioralism). Legal realists, including Holmes, Roscoe Pound, Liewellyn, Frank, and Olivecrona,[29] reacted to traditional legal philosophy and the self-contained structure of legal research. They saw the judiciary as an integral element of contemporary social life, amenable to systematic observation and analysis.

Motivated by the legal realists, a number of political scientists and legal scholars observed that traditional legal research, relying on the exhaustive reading of cases and statutes, focused only on an intrinsic aspect of the law: The law is what the courts and the legislatures say it is, nothing less, nothing more. But thoughtful observers knew that extrinsic factors like politics and elections also influences the court and the law, although these influences were seldom acknowledged in the decisions of courts or in the opinions of individual judges or justices. This concern led to a school of political jurisprudence that included the study of judicial lobbying, the political functions of judges, and constitutional politics.[30]

Political jurisprudence concerns itself largely with the impact of politics on judicial institutions. Judicial behavioralism looks more closely at the behavior of individual judges, blocs of judges (liberal versus conservative, for example), and the courts generally. Using theoretical models created by social psychologists to study individual and group behavior, a number of political scientists began to analyze judicial behavior in order to explain and predict what courts were doing and would do.[31]

Again it is important not to overlook the overlap in methodologies. Courts, of course, have not been oblivious to social science techniques. Indeed, legal empiricism may have begun with the *Brandeis Brief* in 1908,[32] a legal argument based on sociopsychological data. And scientific data collection was advocated by Loevinger, a former Federal Communications Commissioner, jurist, and law professor, in a system he called "jurimetrics." All other jurisprudence, said Loevinger, is

> based upon speculation, supposition, and superstition; it is concerned with meaningless questions; and, after more than two thousand years, jurisprudence has not yet offered a useful answer to any question or a workable technique for attacking any problem.[33]

Judicial behavioralism is designed to take the scholar beyond any one court decision or line of cases into an examination of patterned behavior. It might also look at judges in attitudinal terms or explore ethnic and religious variables in their decisions. Ulmer points out some of the virtues of the behavioral approach in legal research:

> It is both pertinent and instructive to study the interpersonal relationships and behavior patterns of the members of a collegial court. By doing so, we recognize what legal analysis ignores, namely, that the law, the courts and the judges are something

more than mere abstractions. The nature of the endowments, outlooks and attitudes which judges bring to the discharge of their duties may be revealed in the identification of individual behavior patterns. The discrepancies among these patterns, in turn, reflect the differences among the actors.[34]

Examples of Nontraditional Methods in Communication Law Studies

Judicial behaviorism moves away from the factual web of particular cases and their idiosyncratic nuances and moves toward generalization. Space will permit only a few examples of empirical and behavioral studies from mass communication.

Thomas A. Schwartz, a journalism professor at Ohio State University, did pioneering work in a master's thesis, "A Study of the Relationship Between the Ideological Tendencies of the United States Supreme Court Justices and Their Young Behavior in Selected Cases Affecting the Press, 1946–74." Schwartz tested three hypotheses:

1. Basic attitudes of Supreme Court justices contribute to their voting behavior.
2. Basic attitudes of Supreme Court justices toward civil liberties contribute to their voting behavior in civil liberties cases.
3. Basic attitudes of Supreme Court justices toward press issues contribute to their voting behavior in press cases.[35]

Schwartz used judicial behaviorism in this mass communication law study. The Supreme Court case was his unit of analysis. He drew his data from all nonunanimous cases decided on their merits by the Supreme Court between October 1946 and February 1974 and two subsamples of civil liberties and economic cases. Units of measurement included Supreme Court justices, "courts" formed by the justices, ideological outcomes of cases, press favorableness of outcomes, and votes of individual justices. Schwartz was able to use a data package collected by the American Political Science Association and to computerize his work.

Patterning his study on the work of Schubert, Schwartz replicated tests of justices' attitudes using factor analysis. His conclusions: (1) Supreme Court justices tend to form blocs; (2) in all instances in civil liberties cases these blocs can be identified as liberalism, conservatism, moderation, neutralism, and independence; (3) in cases affecting freedom of the press, these blocs normally can be identified as favorableness, unfavorableness, and neutralism.[36] More important perhaps were the implications of his work for the study of mass communication law:

1. The establishment of the existence of distinct voting blocs in First Amendment cases can facilitate study of Supreme Court justices' attitudes toward a system of free expression.
2. Since the justices vote in blocs in First Amendment cases, mass communication law researchers can have more confidence in describing the attributes of blocs and in explaining First Amendment freedoms.

3. Explication of Supreme Court bloc arrangements in such areas as economic and civil liberties adjudication is well developed. Comparisons between those arrangements and First Amendment block arrangements could be worthwhile.[37]

In another instance, Cecilie Gaziano, as a graduate student at the University of Minnesota, became interested in the relationship between Supreme Court decisions and public opinion about freedom of expression for deviant political groups. Relying on a sociopsychological model of judicial behavior—the higher the tension and the greater the uncertainty, the more likely the group will seek a dominant outside referent such as public opinion—Gaziano stated the hypothesis: Decisions of the Supreme Court on freedom of expression for deviant political groups are related to public opinion on this issue. Data fitting her research design were available in Court decisions and poll results over her stipulated thirty-four-year period, and she found support for her hypothesis.[38]

Although the data do not account for judicial *behavior*, they do provide for an empirical test of at least a significant statistical relationship. If empirical studies do not permit us to predict judicial behavior, they begin to explain it, and they help to reveal the nature of the rules of law. As has been noted, these rules are expressed in constitutions, statutes, ordinances, regulations, judicial opinions, and scholarly writings. And these are systematically preserved and catalogued. The traditional study of law is more than hunch and hope, and it lends itself to rational analysis in a number of modes.

Other mass communication law studies include Robbins' examination of the uses of social science data in deciding First Amendment decisions,[39] Anderson's empirical investigation of social responsibility theory,[40] Holim's look at a conflict between two professions (lawyers and journalists),[41] Stempel's scale analysis of Burger Court press decisions,[42] and the important Iowa libel study.[43]

These studies and others that could be cited were careful to take into consideration linkages between and among court cases, as well as that long march of the law sometimes called the "dead hand of precedent" or *stare decisis*. The point is this: One does not "sample" cases in the sense of drawing a random sample. Conventional sampling procedure could be disastrous in legal studies if employed without real knowledge of all the cases in a particular area of law.

No doubt, the authors suggested in an earlier book chapter,[44] there are many paths one might follow in searching for a research model. The creative researcher will find one best suited to his or her own needs. However, some considerations are immediately evident. For legal scholarship to become part of the totality of communication research it must:

1. Consider the systematic, step-by-step procedures of the scientific method from the problem formulation to hypothesis development, methodological strategy, data collection and analysis, and discussion of findings.
2. Frame hypotheses that move away from normative, adversarial positions and are instead based on a preponderance of evidence growing out of a complete review of the relevant literature.
3. Present the often-important dissenting views of judges in their full historical context so that they can be understood as part of the fabric of judicial behavior and

not simply as exercises in legal reasoning (it is here that the distinction must be made between holdings and dicta).

4. Make efforts to temper normative assumptions when analyzing the admittedly normative behavior of jurists. That is, while recognizing the value-laden quality of court decisions, the communication researcher should nonetheless seek systematic and value-free modes for dissenting and discussing them and their implications.[45]

Publication Outlets for Research in Mass Communication Law

Scholars seeking publication in this field have a variety of outlets from which to choose. These include the periodicals of journalism and mass communication and numerous law reviews and journals. As noted earlier, *Communication Law and Policy* is devoted solely to research in mass communication law, but other journals use articles on mass communication law.

Two factors may determine where the scholar will publish: (1) form and style of the research paper and (2) the audience one desires to reach. Most journalism and mass communication publications do not want traditional law review articles with their length, heavy documentation, and adversarial tone. They simply would not *fit*. By the same token, brief analytical papers without detailed backgrounding and exhaustive precedential referencing will not make it in the law reviews.

The scholar's purpose in doing legal research may be varied, but inevitably one hopes that one's work will be read. By whom is the question. If one wants to become part of the standard legal literature, be indexed in the *Index to Legal Periodicals*, be accessible on Westlaw and Lexis, and included in *Shepard's Citations* periodical references, the legal periodicals are one's outlet. However, legal periodicals are parochial in their nonlibrary circulations and not likely to be well read by persons in mass communication law, unless your article is discovered as part of the specific search. If one wishes to be read by the journalism community, the mass communications periodicals are the primary outlet. To find research journals in mass communication, and to learn more about their publication procedures and requirements, consult the *Iowa Guide: Scholarly Journals in Mass Communication and Related Fields*, published by the University of Iowa's School of Journalism and Mass Communication. For legal publications, see *Current Publications in Law and Related Fields* and also the *Index to Legal Periodicals*.

Communication Journals

Publications such as *Journalism and Mass Communication Quarterly*, *Journal of Broadcasting and Electronic Media*, and the *Journal of Communication* are interested in short, scholarly studies on legal topics. Behavior studies can find an audience in *Communication Research* or *Public Opinion Quarterly*. Short articles with broad implications for media and society can be directed to *Mass Media and Society*, and updates, essays, and analyses can be submitted to *Media Law Notes*. Legal historical work on a wide range of communication topics is sought by *Journalism History*, *American Journalism*, and the *American Journal of Legal History*. Critical, cultural, and other qualitative studies are seen in such publications as *The Journal of Communication Inquiry*, *Critical Studies in Mass Communications*, *Media Culture & Society*, and *Communications*. Lengthy legal articles sometimes growing out of dissertations are occasionally published in *Journalism and Mass Communication Monographs*. An article on teaching mass communication law might find a home in the pages of *Journalism and Mass Communication Educator*. Articles of current interest written in traditional magazine style might (after a query to the editors) be sent to such publications as *American Journalism Review*, *Columbia Journalism Review*, *Nieman Reports*, *The Quill*, *Editor & Publisher*, *Broadcasting & Cable*, *Brill's Content*, and others.

Legal Periodicals

There is a significantly greater number of legal periodicals than there are communication publications. Legal periodicals are published mainly by law schools, but also by professional associations, groups of legal specialists, and commercial legal publishers. *Index to Legal Periodicals* is the *Reader's Guide* of the law field. Included in it are most American legal periodicals, both scholarly and professional. Articles about the law in more general circulation publications, as has been indicated, are indexed in *Legal Resources Index* and *Current Law Index*, international materials in the *Index to Foreign Legal Periodicals*. One of the best publication outlets for legal research is *Communication Law and Policy*. Its editorial board is composed of mass communication educators and scholars, lawyers, law professionals, and others, and it is designed to bridge the substantive gap between purely legal publications and traditional mass communications journals. It welcomes submissions on all areas of mass communication law and policy and is open to all methods and approaches.

Communication and the Law, a commercially published journal, is another publication to consider. This is a specialized law journal that, like *Communication Law and Policy*, contains articles from mass communication scholars as well as from lawyers and legal scholars.

The major publication outlet for the serious legal scholar who wishes to reach a legally minded audience is the law reviews, published mainly by an elite corps of third-year law students. These are *student* publications only in a technical sense. They feature articles by important legal scholars, judges, political scientists, and others. Nearly every law school has a law review, and most are general publications interested in a brief spectrum of legal topics. As one might expect, some give special attention to proximate federal circuit courts or the special legal problems of a region. But, for the most part, the law reviews are not parochial in content. An article on the Freedom of Information Act, for example, would be of interest to a wide variety of law reviews. Like most publications, law reviews have a pecking order. The Harvard, Yale, Columbia, Michigan, Chicago, and Stanford law reviews are the most prestigious.

Content differs from review to review, but two types of content constitute the prevailing pattern. There are (1) *articles* and (2) *comments* or *notes*. Articles are substantive legal studies, usually well documented in nearly exhaustive, and exhausting, footnotes chronicling the judicial and legislative histories of particular cases, statutes, and legal concepts. Articles often begin with a hypothesis or proposition offered forcefully in an introductory section. This is followed by supporting units set off by subheads, a conclusion, and a discussion of implications. Legal scholars are the main contributors, but other disciplines may be represented as well. A number of communication law scholars publish regularly in the law reviews.

Comments are briefer treatments of legal issues and frequently focus on recent cases, putting them in context and analyzing their meanings. Most comments are written by the law review staff, although outside comments are welcomed. A few law reviews favor review essays on current books and recruit outside specialists for this purpose.

The neophyte legal scholar may be overwhelmed by the number of law reviews in a law library. How is one chosen for publication purposes? The *Index to Legal Periodicals* is a place to start. It will tell you where recent articles on your topic have been published. It will help you decide when to query an editor. By looking under headings such as freedom of expression, freedom of the press, or specific media headings, one can begin to detect the editorial patterns of particular law reviews.

There is some specialization in the law reviews. Some emphasize public law, others administrative law or property law. There are a few law journals that emphasize media and communication law and should be given special attention as possible venues for your research. These include the *Hastings Communications and Entertainment Law Journal* (*Comm/Ent*), published by the University of California's Hastings College of Law; the *Federal Communication Law Journal*, published by the UCLA School of Law; the *Cardozo Arts & Entertainment Law Journal*, published by the Benjamin N. Cardozo School of Law; and the *Loyola Entertainment Law Journal*, published by the Loyola of Los Angeles School of Law.

Another possible publication outlet, but less varied in its approach, is the professional legal journal. Virtually every state and major metropolitan bar association has one. Some are scholarly, others newsy. For topics with a particular state or jurisdictional bias, these are outlets to consider.

Endnotes

1. Everette E. Dennis, "Leaked Information as Property: Vulnerability of the Press to Criminal Prosecution," 20 *St. Louis University Law Journal* 610 (Spring 1976); "Purloined Information as Property: A New First Amendment Challenge," *Journalism Quarterly* 50 (Autumn 1973): 456–462, 474; "Purloined Papers or Information as Property: A Study of Press-Government Relations," unpublished Ph.D. dissertation, University of Minnesota, 1974.

2. Frederick S. Siebert, *Freedom of Press in England, 1476–1776* (Urbana: University of Illinois Press, 1952); Siebert, "Research in Legal Problems of Communication," in Ralph O. Nafziger and Marcus Wilkerson, eds., *Introduction to Journalism Research* (Baton Rouge: Louisiana State University Press, 1949), 46.

3. Zechariah Chafee, Jr., *Free Speech in the United States* (Cambridge, MA: Harvard University Press, 1954); Alexander Meiklejohn, *Free Speech and Its Relation to Self-Government* (New York: Harper & Row, 1948); Leonard W. Levy, *Freedom of Speech and Press in Early American History: Legacy of Suppression* (Cambridge, MA: Harvard University Press, 1960); Leonard W. Levy, *Emergence of a Free Press* (New York: Oxford University Press, 1985); Lee C. Bollinger, *The Tolerant Society: Freedom of Speech and Extremist Speech in America* (New York: Oxford University Press, 1986); Paul L. Murphy, *The Meaning of Freedom of Speech: First Amendments Freedom from Wilson to FDR* (Westport, CN: Greenwood Press, 1972); Ithiel de Sola Pool, *Technologies of Freedom* (Cambridge: Belknap Press, 1983); Thomas I. Emerson, *The System of Freedom of Expression* (New York: Random House, 1970); Frederick Schauer,

Free Speech: A Philosophical Enquiry (New York: Cambridge University Press, 1982); F.S. Haiman, *Speech and Law in a Free Society* (Chicago: University of Chicago Press, 1981). See also Jeremy Cohen, *Congress Shall Make No Law: Oliver Wendell Holmes, The First Amendment and Judicial Decision Making* (Ames: Iowa State University Press, 1988).

4. Siebert, *op. cit.*

5. J. Edward Gerald, *The Press and the Constitution* (Minneapolis: University of Minnesota Press, 1948).

6. Donald M. Gillmor and Everette E. Dennis, "Legal Research and Judicial Communication," in Steven H. Chaffee, ed., *Political Communication*, Sage Annual Reviews of Communication Research (Beverly Hills, CA: Sage Publishing Co., 1975), 283–305; and the present chapter. Also see Jeremy Cohen and Timothy Gleason, *Social Research in Communication and Law* (Newbury Park, CA: Sage Publications, 1990).

7. "How Does the Law Change," *Research News* (Ann Arbor: Office of Research Administration, University of Michigan, February 1971), 4.

8. The first two A.L.R. series are *not* updated with pocket parts. The first series is updated by *A.L.R. Blue Book of Supplement Decisions*. The second series is updated by the *A.L.R. 2nd Later Case Service*, which itself is updated with pocket parts.

9. Case reporters exist for individual states as well. Some of these are offical, government-produced reporters while others are produced by commercial publishers like West Publishing.

10. Law reviews are academic/professional journals edited by law students. They contain articles by lawyers, law professors, and other scholars.

11. Stephen Elias and Susan Levinkind, *Legal Research Online and in the Library* (Berkeley, CA: Nob Press, 1998); Diana Botluk, *The Legal List: Research on the Internet* (St. Paul, MN: West Publishing Co., 1997); Paul Jacobsen, Net Law: *How Lawyers Use the Internet* (Sebastopol, CA: Songline Studios, Inc., 1997); Josh Blackman, *How to Use the Internet for Legal Research* (New York: Find/SVP, 1996).

12. Larry L. Teply, *Legal Research and Citation* (St. Paul, MN: West Group, 1999); J. Myron Jacobstein, Roy M. Mersky, and Donald Dunn, *Fundamentals of Legal Research* (Boston: Little Brown, 1996); Morris L. Cohen and Kent C. Olson, *Legal Research in a Nutshell* (St. Paul, MN: West Publishing C., 1996).

13. Don R. Pember, *Privacy and the Press* (Seattle: University of Washington Press, 1972).

14. *Restatement of the Law of Torts, 2d.*

15. Jerome A. Barron, *Freedom of the Press for Whom?* (Bloomington: Indiana University Press, 1973). See also "Access to the Press—A New First Amendment Right," 80 *Harvard L. Rev.* 1641 (1967).

16. *Miami Herald Publishing Co. v. Tornillo*, 418 U.S. 241 (1974). See also Benno Schmidt, Jr., *Freedom of the Press vs. Public Access* (New York: Praeger Publishers, 1976). Significant proposals for reform on the most contentious area of media law—libel—are made in the following works: Renata Adler, *Reckless Disregard* (New York: Alfred Knopf, 1986); Lois Fore, *A Chilling Effect* (New York: N.W. Norton & Co., 1987); Norman Rosenberg, *Protecting the Best Manian Interpretive History of the Law of Libel* (Chapel Hill: University of North Carolina Press, 1986); Rodney A. Smolla, *Suing the Press* (New York: Oxford University Press, 1986).

17. Everette E. Dennis and Eli Noam, *The Cost of Libel: Economic and Policy Implication* (New York: Columbia University Press, 1989).

18. Levy, *Freedom of Speech* and *Emergence of a Free Press*.

19. Ivan Preston, *The Great American Blow-Up: Puffery in Advertising and Selling*, 4th ed. (Madison: University of Wisconsin Press, 1996).

20. Erwin G. Krasnow, Lawrence D. Longley, and Herbert A. Teny, *The Politics of Broadcast Regulation*, 4th ed. (New York: St. Martin's Press, 1988). See also Barry Cole and Mal Oettinger, *The Reluctant Regulators: the FCC and the Broadcast Audience* (Reading, MA: Addison-Wesley Publishing Co., 1978).

21. Dwight L. Teeter, Jr. and Don R. Le Duc, *Law of Mass Communications: Freedom and Control of Print and Broadcast Media*, 8th ed. (Westbury, NY: Foundation Press, 1995); Kent R. Middleton and Bill F. Chamberlin, *The Law of Public Communication*, 3rd ed. (New York: Longman, 1994); Don R. Pember, *Mass Media Law*, 8th ed. (Madison, WI: Brown & Benchmark, 1993).

22. Donald M. Gillmor, Jerome A. Barron, and Todd F. Simon, *Mass Communication Law: Cases and Comment*, 6th ed. (Belmont, CA: Wadsworth Publishing, 1998); Marc A. Franklin, and David A.

Anderson, *Cases and Materials on Mass Media Law*, 5th ed. (Westbury, NY: Foundation Press, 1995); T. Barton Carter, Marc A. Franklin and Jay B. Wright, *The First Amendment and the Fourth Estate*, 7th ed. (Westbury, NY: Foundation Press, 1997); T. Barton Carter, Marc A. Franklin, and Jay B. Wright, *The First Amendment and the Fifth Estate: Regulations of Electronic Mass Media*, 3rd ed. (Westbury, NY: Foundation Press, 1993).

23. David L. Grey, *The Supreme Court and the News Media* (Evanston, IL: Northwestern University Press, 1968); Robert E. Drechsel, *News Making in the Trial Courts* (New York: Longman, 1983).

24. Quoted by Edgar A. Jones, Jr., in foreword to Layman E. Allen and Mary E. Caldwell, eds., *Communication Sciences and the Law: Reflections from the Jurimetrics Conference* (Indianapolis: Bobbs-Merrill Co., 1965), ix.

25. Oliver Wendell Holmes, Jr., "The Path of Law," in Ephraim London, ed., *The Law as Literature* (New York: Simon & Schuster, 1960), 614, 617.

26. Vilhelm Aubert, "Research in the Sociology of Law," *American Behavioral Scientist* 7 (December 1963): 17.

27. S. Sidney Ulmer, "Scientific Method and Judicial Process," *American Behavioral Scientist* 7 (December 1963): 22.

28. Glendon Schubert, ed., *Judicial Behavior* (Chicago: Rand Mc Nally & Co. 1964), 3.

29. Holmes, "The Path of the Law," 10 *Harvard Law Review* 457 (1897), and Mark DeWolfe Howe, ed., *The Common Law* (Cambridge, MA: Belknap Press of Harvard University Press, 1963); Roscoe Pound, "The Need of Sociological Jurisprudence," 19 *The Green Bag* 607 (October 1907), and *An Introduction to the Philosophy of Law*, rev. ed. (New Haven, CN: Yale University Press, 1954); Karl N. Llewellyn, "Some Realism about Realism," 44 *Harvard Law Review* 1222 (1931) and *The Bramble Bush* (New York: Oceana Publications, 1951); Jerome Frank, *Law and the Modern Mind* (New York: Coward McCann & Geoghegan, 1949) and *Courts on Trial: Myth and Reality of American Justice* (Princeton, NJ: Princeton University Press, 1950); Karl Olivecrona, *Law as Facts*, 2nd ed. (London: Stevens, 1971).

30. See for example, Arthur A. North, *The Supreme Court: Judicial Process and Judicial Politics* (Englewood Cliffs, NJ: Prentice-Hall, 1966), James Eisenstein, Politics and the Legal Process (New York: Harper & Row, 1973); and Samuel Krislov, *The Supreme Court and Political Freedom* (New York: Free Press, 1968).

31. Stuart Nagel, *The Legal Process from a Behavioral Perspective* (Homewood, IL: Dorsey Press, 1969); Glendon Schubert, ed., *Judicial Behavior, The Judicial Mind: Attitudes and Ideologies of Supreme Court Justices, 1946–63* (Evanston, IL: Northwestern University Press, 1965), and *The Judicial Mind Revisited, Psychometric Analysis of Supreme Court Ideology* (New York: Oxford University Press, 1974); S. Sidney Ulmer, ed., *Introductory Readings in Political Behavior* (Chicago: Rand McNally & Company, 1961).

32. See *Muller vs. Oregon*, 208 U.S. 412 (1908), wherein Louis Brandeis, then an attorney, furnished the Court with what for its time was overwhelming social scientific documentation of the deleterious effect of long periods of work on working women.

33. Lee Loevinger, "Jurimetrics: The Next Step Forward," 33 *Minnesota Law Review* 455 (1949).

34. S. Sidney Ulmer, "The Analysis of Behavior Patterns on the United States Supreme Court," *Journal of Politics* 22 (1960): 630.

35. Thomas A. Schwartz, "A Study of the Relationship Between Ideological Tendencies of United States Supreme Court Justices and Their Voting Behavior in Selected Cases Affecting the Press, 1946–1974," unpublished master's thesis, South Dakota State University (1977), 16. For a discussion of models used in the study of judicial process see Schwartz, "A Call for Alternative Approaches to Research in Communication Law," *Media Law Notes* 11 (June 1984): 4.

36. Schwartz, "A Call," 240.

37. *Ibid.*, 241.

38. Cecilie Gaziano, "Relationships Between Public Opinion and Supreme Court Decisions, Was Mr. Dooly Right?" *Communication Research* 5 (April 1978), 131.

39. Jan C. Robbins, "Deciding First Amendment Cases: Part I," and "Deciding First Amendment Cases: Part II, Evidence," *Journalism Quarterly* 49 (Summer and Autumn 1972): 263–270, 569–578; see also Robbins, "Social Science Information and First Amendment Freedoms: An Aid to Supreme Court Decision Making," unpublished Ph.D. dissertation, University of Minnesota, 1970.

40. H.A. Anderson, "An Empirical Investigation of What SR Theory Means," *Journalism Quarterly* 55 (Spring 1978): 33.

41. Kim Holim, "Free Press and Fair Trial: An Attitudinal Study of Lawyers and Journalists in a Conflict Between Two Professions," unpublished Ph.D. dissertation, Southern Illinois University, 1972.

42. Guido H. Stempel III. "A Guttman Scale Analysis of the Burger Court's Press Decisions," *Journalism Quarterly* 59 (Summer 1982): 256–259.

43. Randall P. Bezanson, Gilbert Cranberg, and John Soloski, *Libel Law and the Press: Myth and Reality* (New York: The Free Press, 1987).

44. Gillmor and Dennis, "Legal Research."

45. *Ibid*, 299.

21

Presentation of Research Results

Guido H. Stempel III
Bruce H. Westley

We began this book by talking about the rapid expansion of mass communication research and knowledge. The mass communication researcher is at the frontier of knowledge, and on this frontier, the pen truly is mightier than the sword.

Whatever techniques we develop and however many researchers are at work, knowledge in our field can progress only as rapidly and as effectively as we can communicate our findings. It is the journal article or the convention paper or the book that brings knowledge into our field. Without publication, any piece of knowledge is restricted to a few, and the growth of knowledge is impaired. To fail to publish is to fail to do one's elementary duty. Whether the work is published rests both on the quality of the research and the quality of the presentation.

The mass communication researcher probably brings more training and experience to this task than researchers in most other fields. That edge, however, is at least partially offset by the diversity of audiences he or she must attempt to reach. That diversity is reflected in the wide range of publications that report research findings in mass communication. You may find yourself writing for a research journal like *Journalism and Mass Communication Quarterly*. Such an audience probably is at least as interested in the method as in the finding. You may find yourself writing for a trade publication such as *Presstime*. The reader of that publication probably hopes to find a practical application in your research that will make his or her newspaper better. Or you may find yourself writing for a daily newspaper. That audience will be interested in results and little else about the study.

You will not be writing for all these publications at once, although we have written about the same study for all three of these audiences. You are likely to find at some time or other that you want to reach each of them. This is not an easy assignment, but it is one that has been carried out well by a number of mass communication researchers.

Format for the Research Article

While format will necessarily vary as the research method varies, the standard format for empirical studies is a useful one that can be adapted to most other types of studies. It consists of four parts: statement of the problem, method, results, and conclusion. It may also include a summary at the end or an abstract at the beginning, but seldom both.

The statement of the problem consists largely of a sharply focused **review of literature**. As our field has grown, we have come to the point at which the literature review must be highly selective. A person doing a readership study of advertising forty years ago might have included even studies of news-editorial readership in the review of literature. Today, the researcher should be prepared to limit it to something as narrow as four-color food advertising in newspapers in the top 100 markets. Anything less narrow is likely to introduce studies that offer relatively little to the definition of the current research problem. Unfortunately, computer searches offer the opportunity to compile lengthy literature reviews that are disfunctional.

We need to say a word here about how the literature review is developed, although the process should start long before the writing begins. As a researcher develops concepts, there is a need to place them in a context. Various research databases are probably the place to begin. The big problem is finding the first article—once you have it, your bibliography snowballs. Each article contains citations of other articles, and those articles contain citations of still other articles. While it may seem to you at the outset that you are never going to find anything, you will soon come to the point that focusing of your bibliography is needed.

One word of caution: When you find an article in the literature review of another article, look it up. Don't simply take what is in that literature review. Sometimes, statements in those reviews are incorrect. We know because it has happened in mentions of our own articles in other people's literature reviews. You do not want to assimilate the mistakes of others in your article.

The literature review should provide a justification for the study's hypotheses. The author should put the existing studies together in a logical sequence that leads to those hypotheses and in doing so makes it clear what he or she proposes to accomplish with this study and in what way this study will add to the knowledge in the field. You may also want to draw on statements indicating the importance of the problem.

Method

The method section has two purposes. The first is to give readers an indication of what was done so that they can better understand the results. The second is to provide enough detail about what was done so that the researcher who wants to replicate the study will be able to do so. Many methods sections achieve the former purpose but not the latter one. Many writers do not take the matter of replication seriously and really do not attempt to provide such detail.

An important part of the method section is a clear explanation of the differences between various stimuli or experimental conditions. It is not enough to say that one group of respondents saw black-and-white ads while the other saw color ads. The reader is entitled to know whether color means four-color or one-color plus black-and-white. The reader also is entitled to know whether we are talking about photographs, tint blocks, colored body type, or some other nonpictorial uses of color.

With a survey, the reader is entitled to know the question wording. If there are too many questions, then at the minimum the author should indicate how one can get a copy of the questionnaire.

In short, what we are looking for in a method section is analogous to what we find in a cookbook. Nothing should be left to the imagination; the reader should not have to guess what was done.

Results

In writing the results section, the author must be guided by his or her statement of hypotheses at the end of the statement-of-problem section. The hypotheses should be dealt with in sequential order, with a clear statement for each hypothesis as to whether it was accepted or rejected. Appropriate figures should be cited in the text, and reference should be made to appropriate tables.

While there should be an interweaving of table and text, the author should avoid repeating large portions of the contents of tables in the text. Only a few data from each table should be included in the text.

In reporting differences in the hypothesized direction, the author should be careful to focus on those differences that are statistically significant. Some nonsignificant differences may be of interest, but that is the exception. Unfortunately, it is not uncommon to find results sections that contain more references to differences that are not statistically significant than to those that are.

The author should avoid introducing material that is unrelated to the hypotheses. Again, there may be a some data of interest even though they are unrelated to the hypotheses, but when such data begin to dominate the results section, they disrupt the entire section.

The author should keep in mind that the standard significance level in mass communication research is the 0.05 level. Anything with a higher chance probability than that should be considered potentially a chance difference. However tempting it may be with a given set of data, there can be no compromise on this standard. Reporting probabilities such as 0.10 will not be seen as insightful, but rather as an attempt to inflate the results.

Conclusions

Just as the results should be tied to the hypotheses, so should the conclusions. When the hypotheses are confirmed, that is a rather easy and obvious thing to do. Likewise, when none of the hypotheses is confirmed, it is relatively easy to deal with the conclusions in those terms.

What is more difficult and yet more urgent is to stick to that rule when some of the hypotheses are confirmed and some are not. The search for alternate conclusions has a built-in tendency to stray rather far afield. The danger is that a conclusion will be offered on the basis of limited support from the results and none at all from the literature cited at the outset.

Where the results are not clear-cut, some speculation and some opinion may be in order, but they should be limited. It is easy to find alternate explanations given a set of data that turned out somewhat differently than predicted. The trouble is that the number of possible alternate explanations approaches infinity, and what may have great appeal to you may strike the reader as grasping at straws.

The conclusions section can include a statement about future research. Such statements should be focused on what would seem to be the next logical thing to do in the particular area being studied. At the same time, the proposals should be plausible. If one looks at statements about future research over a period of time, one cannot help but notice how little of it has been done.

If an abstract is to be included, it should be a miniature of the article, not only in content but also in form. It should follow the same pattern, starting with a summary statement of the problem, moving on to the method, the results, and the conclusions.

If a summary is included, it should be somewhat different from an abstract. It should focus more heavily on the results and conclusions and give only passing notice, if any, to the statement of the problem or the method. Those matters should have been addressed adequately at their respective places, and we assume the summary's main function is to serve as a wrapup for someone who has read the article. It is true, of course, that some people scan summaries and do not read the entire article, but the writer's first responsibility is to those readers who arrive at the summary having read what has come before.

Other Types of Studies

All this fits the empirical study well, such as the experiment designed to determine whether the use of color in cigarette ads produces higher brand recognition. But what of the survey designed merely to find out what the readership of cigarette ads in color is or how the readership of black-and-white ads compares? There isn't really a hypothesis, is there?

We think there should be a hypothesis. If there is not, the absence of one most likely reflects the failure of the researcher to do his or her homework, to delve into the pertinent background. Few surveys in this day and age completely break new ground. Part of the meaning of most surveys comes from how the results compare with the results of similar surveys. That is another way of saying that there is, or should be, a hypothesis provided by previous studies being tested by this study.

Take, for example, the frequent surveys of the popularity of the president of the United States. Are these merely descriptive studies of attitudes at a particular moment? Hardly. By now, those studies have been done long enough that the researcher knows what to expect. The news story on the Gallup Poll does not tell you what the hypothesis being tested is. It does, however, talk about how the current results compare with the pattern we have come to expect. A president's popularity is high when he takes office. It drops. It will rise again in moments of genuine national crisis or national triumph. An assessment of current events tells us where we might expect to be in that model, and the poll story will tell us whether we are there.

For most surveys, then, the empirical model will in fact fit pretty well. There may be some unexpected results. In particular, the interrelationships may be hard to predict, but the more you know the easier it is to predict. It may be argued that in any survey there are questions that are not directly related to the hypotheses. We would suggest that this is neither a necessary condition nor a sign of strength.

In studies without numerical data, it may be more difficult to see the connection with the empirical model. Yet, as Nord and Gillmor, Dennis, and Ugland indicate in their discussions of historical and legal research (Chapters 19 and 20), the movement in those fields is toward the empirical model. Mountain climbers may climb mountains just because they are there, but historians no longer study newspapers or their editors or television news and their anchors just because they are there. The historical study is undertaken for a reason. Just as with the empirical study, the purpose of the study follows from the pertinent literature. The person writing the historical research article, therefore, should begin with a statement of purpose similar to that in the empirical study.

What comes next may be somewhat different. The need to elaborate on method is at least somewhat less. To the extent that the historical researcher quantifies, he or she will have the same need to explain sampling and measurement procedures as the experimental researcher. For many historical studies, however, the method may be self-evident and require little explanation.

The historical researcher should then move to an explication of what has been found. This may be organized in accord with the logic of the statement of the problem or it may simply be organized chronologically. In either case, the total evidence the researcher has on the problem should be presented, and the section should be restricted to evidence. Subjective judgment and speculation do not belong here.

The conclusions section will more nearly resemble the conclusions section of the empirical article. Again the conclusions must be tied closely to the statement of the problem and to the evidence. Subjective statements that range far beyond the evidence should be avoided. Logical inference relating the various pieces of evidence is, however, highly appropriate.

The outline presented here for the historical research article also applies to legal studies and descriptive research. There always should be a clear statement of the problem. It must be based on an accurate and precise analysis of the literature on the topic. Evidence bearing on the problem should be presented, and it should be kept apart from the author's opinions about the evidence or the problem. The conclusions section should be tightly linked to the statement of the problem and the evidence, but should go beyond the evidence to interpret meaning.

Thesis and Dissertation Writing

For many readers of this book, the research-writing task that lies immediately ahead is the master's thesis or doctoral dissertation. Much of what we have said about the research article holds for the thesis or dissertation as well, but there are differences. The basic scheme of organization remains the same. The usual chapter headings are Statement of Problem, Review of the Literature, Methodology, Results, and Conclusions.

One major difference is the Review of the Literature, which becomes much more extensive than it can be in an article. The review reaches out farther away from the central topic of the study, and it discusses each piece of literature in more detail. It is not unusual for thirty of forty studies to be mentioned and for the chapter to be twenty to twenty-five pages long. There is a danger that the review will stray too far from the topic and because of this will not lead logically to the research questions or hypotheses.

Another major difference has to do with details about the method. We suggested earlier that it ought to be possible for someone to replicate your study on the basis of your description of the method. In a thesis or dissertation, this is normally carried to the point that the actual questionnaire, stimulus material, and the like are included. Most such material is put in appendices, but it is available. Likewise, more statistical results are included, again, in many cases, in the appendices.

While all this makes the thesis or dissertation longer, it probably does not make it any more difficult to write because the writer does not have to make a lot of decisions about what to include and what to leave out. The rule on a thesis or dissertation is: If in doubt, include it.

Writing Style

Good writing is clear thinking made visible. The format discussed in the preceding section will certainly promote clear thinking. It is up to the researcher to carry it forward in the writing of the manuscript. He or she must begin where any writer begins—with a clear image of the audience.

Clarity of expression is particularly important in scholarly publication because of its special character. Scholarly writing is aimed at an audience of scholars and neophyte scholars. It is submitted in a form to answer the standard questions raised by all scholarship. Is the evidence to be believed? If one entertains doubts, how can evidence be checked? What assurance do we have that all precautions were taken to obtain the best possible evidence? Do the author's conclusions follow logically from the evidence? Given the evidence, could other, even contradictory conclusions, be drawn? If the evidence is sound, what does the study tell us about how our present knowledge must be revised? Almost every feature of scholarly reporting may be traced to the researcher's attempts to answer these questions.

Clarity and precision arise as criteria from the need to impart to other scholars exactly what was done. For the historian, this refers to what sources were consulted, for the legal scholar what cases and briefs were consulted. For the behavioral scientist, it means telling exactly how many subjects were included in the control group, exactly how each concept was measured, how the sample was drawn, how the sample compared with parameters in the population from which it was drawn, and what rules governed the assignment of content to categories. The reader has a right to expect answers to such questions. In other words, the precision demanded by those who might want to repeat an experiment or search a new source for further evidence is the kind of precision required of scholars in reporting their research. The clarity required is of the sort that answers these questions unambigiously.

Organization is critical because so much scholarly writing is meant to be consulted by many, read by few, and examined closely only by the very few who intend to abstract the essence of the study for their own purposes or to verify it by replication. Consultation is aided by several features of a research report, monograph, or journal article. First there is the highly condensed account of the study provided by either an abstract at the top of the report or by a summary and conclusions section at the end. Both should give all the essentials so that the reader may decide whether to look more closely. The next step may be to examine the tables. As is emphasized in Chapter 17, tables must be meaningful by themselves—must "stand alone." The reader may next be interested in how the hypotheses were derived. That points toward the formal statement of hypotheses, which should be found at the end of the problem statement section and just before the methodology section. Another reader might turn from the tables to the "operations" segment of the methodology or procedures section. The best service the writer can provide for the reader is to specify exactly where everything can be found.

Most of the readers of this book will at this point in their lives have had too much experience writing for an audience of one—the instructor who assigned the paper. We have all lived through the frustration of discovering that this instructor evaluates our writing in a different way than the last instructor. That is frequently compounded by the failure of the instructor to articulate very clearly just what it is that is wanted. Frustrating as this is, it is instructional, if we care to let it be. It tells us first of all that communicating is not a sure thing. What we feel we have made extremely clear may be totally misunderstood by our audience. We find that we must concentrate not merely on writing what sounds good to us, but on writing for others. We must think about how to communicate an idea. We must recognize that nobody else in the world has had exactly the same experience that we have had. Nobody else perceives things in exactly the same context that we do.

Scholarly writing need not be dull. This particularly applies to the statement of the problem. The writer has considerable latitude here and should use it. It is not against the rules of scholarship to say something interesting. The writer who fails to do so is likely to leave the reader with the impression that the problem being studied is both uninteresting and unimportant. We might profit by the example of Archimedes. He did not run through the streets of Athens shouting, "An interesting problem that has perplexed alchemists for generations is the measurement of the relative density of metallic substances." He simply yelled "Eureka!" It is worth noting that the principle of Archimedes remains one of the most widely known scientific facts and the name of Archimedes one of the best-known names in the history of science.

The story of Archimedes also reminds us that the most powerful tool the researcher has at his or her disposal is the simple declarative sentence. Compound and complex sentences are used more often than they should be. Sometimes they are necessary, but the greatest need in scholarly writing is for greater use of the simple sentence.

Likewise, the use of common words is important. A reader who cannot understand the words you use cannot understand the idea you are trying to express. The scholarly writer cannot stay within the limits of commonly known words, but excursions outside that realm should be limited.

There is, of course, a language unique to the field of mass communication research. As is the case with most fields, that language is by now a mixture of sheer jargon and terms with a precise special meaning. It is important that you distinguish between the two and choose words accordingly. Rarely is it necessary to call it "media consumption" rather than "reading" or "listening." On the other hand, "cognitive dissonance" may sound like jargon, but it is the most precise and concise way of expressing an idea that is important in our field.

Another matter worth some discussion is redundancy. The format we have described has redundancy built into it. The writer must be careful not to overdo it. If you find that you have written the same sentence for the third time in the same manuscript, you have a redundancy problem. To guard against this, you must constantly refer back and forth between sections. You may think you will remember everything you have written, but you may not.

Slanting the Manuscript

Every magazine writer knows that no two publications have the same editorial requirements, style, or expectations. The writer's ability to succeed will depend a great deal on how well she or he understands the particular publication and can adjust and write accordingly. If it has not occurred to you that you cannot send the same manuscript to *National Geographic* and *Field and Stream*, you perhaps should pause to reflect on that. Scholarly writing is no different. Different publications have different editorial requirements and different styles. They define different topics as being within their scope.

For the scholarly writer, this problem begins with the thesis. There are style requirements. There are specifications as to the size of margins and the weight of paper. In addition, there are the expectations of the members of the thesis committee as to what the thesis should be and how it should be presented. The problem, however, becomes more complex when we consider publications.

The most frequent problem of the writer who is submitting something to a particular journal for the first time is his or her unfamiliarity with the journal. As a journal editor, one of the authors has seen this unfamiliarity in a variety of ways, some amusing and some critical, but all detrimental to the prospects of the manuscipt. There were manuscripts addressed to the previous editor for at least fifteen years after he had retired as editor. There were those addressed to the business office. There were those addressed to a similarly named university and those to the right university but the wrong city. All obviously were sent by people who did not look up the address that appears on the first editorial page of the journal. Those errors are not harmful except that they usually are harbingers of more serious ignorance of the publication.

On the more serious side, there were manuscripts sent with abstracts, which our publication had never used, and with references rather than footnotes, which our publication had not used for many years. There were footnotes not only not in our style but that did not contain the same information, which meant it would be impossible for us to convert them. There were manuscripts with tables in formats that were so different from our normal formats that we could not have used them. All these things indicated that the author was not familiar with our publication. All these matters could have been ascertained rather readily by the author. The failure to do so made his or her efforts look amateurish. Furthermore, not only did these matters concern us as editors, but we also found that our editorial board members became almost as concerned as we did. Many were reluctant to give serious consideration to a manuscipt with such flaws.

Footnotes and references are among the concerns of citation style, which varies widely from journal to journal within and between disciplines. Authors need to be aware of the difference between notes and references. Notes are numbered consecutively throughout the manuscript, and a superscript indicates the point of references. Some journals use footnotes, which means the note itself is at the bottom of the page. Others put all the notes at the end of the article. On the other hand, references are indicated by the name of the author and date in parentheses at the point of reference. The citations then are arranged alphabetically at the end of the article. When you submit an article to a journal, you should be aware of whether the journal uses notes or references.

No two journals in our field seem to use exactly the same style for footnotes or references. Furthermore, journals change style, often unannounced. The author needs to check the most recent issue of the journal to make sure he or she has notes or references in the correct style. A point of confusion is that there are options. Some publications say, for example, that they use University of Chicago style. However, within that style there are some choices—arbitrary choices—that a given journal can make.

Contributors also should be careful to note not only differences in both footnotes and references as they appear at the end of the manuscript, but also where footnote numbers are placed in the text and how references are cited in the text: Are they numbered in order or do they give author's name(s), followed by the year of publication in parentheses? How are page numbers in the citations handled? Attention to these niceties not only relieves editors of great tedium, but also makes submission appear to be more competent and professional.

The matter of topic is more subtle. There are certain topics that might logically appear in a number of journals, but there may be a tendency for a given topic to be almost the exclusive property of one publication. Somehow articles on that topic naturally gravitate toward that journal. If you are writing on such a topic, you might as well take advantage of the natural tendency. Most journals have "Instructions for Contributors," and these may define what the appropriate topics are for that journal. However, in some cases the instructions are too general to be useful. A good guideline is to consider what journals are cited in your footnotes. If you have not found references in *Journalism and Mass Communication Quarterly*, but you have found a handful in *Public Opinion Quarterly*, chances are you should send your manuscript to *Public Opinion Quarterly* and not to *Journalism and Mass Communication Quarterly*. Of course, this problem intensifies if both journals cover the topic equally, but you somehow found only the references in one.

Determining which journal to send a manuscript to is an educated guess, not an exact science. Nobody has ever published a study of this, but we know that in many instances the manuscript is rejected by the journal it was sent to first and accepted by the second, or even the third or fourth.

All this adds up to the simple fact that a little time spent learning something about the journal to which you plan to submit your manuscript is indispensible. The investment of an hour can protect or enhance the research investment that already has run into hundreds of hours. On that basis, it seems foolish not to take the time.

What Editors Look For

In the previous section we have already indicated some of the things editors look for. They can be summed up under the heading of an indication that the manuscript was written specifically for their journal. There are, however, a number of other considerations. Some of them, of course, have to do with the quality of the research itself. Each journal has certain standards with regard to methodology and scope of study. Again, the researcher certainly has a sense about some of this and would be well advised not to send a manuscript that clearly does not meet the journal's requirements. For one thing, it very well could hurt his or her chances with a better manuscript in the future.

At the same time, we should recognize that the topic may have a bearing in ways the author really cannot predict. This can be either a plus or a minus. An editor may decide that he or she has had enough articles on a given topic or may feel that the real substance of the topic has been exhausted. Or the editor may be looking for a manuscript on a particular topic because it is timely in some sense and thus be highly receptive. None of this is true of the "open channels" type of journal, which reviews all relevant manuscripts received and publishes them in order of acceptance, leaving little room for an editor's preferences.

Beyond this, the quality of writing becomes a vital factor. This starts with simple matters such as correct spelling and grammatically correct sentences. This may seem almost trivial to some of you, but the unbelievable fact is that we have on occasion received manuscripts with between a dozen and two dozen errors in grammar and spelling. Those are fortunately rare and not really what we have in mind when we talk about quality of writing. Rather, we are thinking of such things as clarity, conciseness, and aptness of phrasing. The clearer the manuscript, the better its chances of acceptance.

We have suggested earlier that clarity is something you achieve by working at it.

Conciseness tends to reflect two things—the care the writer takes with each sentence and the degree to which the entire article has been organized. Some manuscripts turn out to be twice as long as they need be because the writer does not have goals clearly in mind. If the writer is fortunate, the editor will give him or her the chance to cut it in half.

The writer may, however, pay the price of rejection for failure to keep the manuscript within reasonable length limits. The writer should approach this question from a standpoint of maximum length, not minimum length. We see clear evidence in some instances that the author was striving to achieve a minimum length. That approach is likely to cause problems.

How well a writer turns a phrase is a matter of deeply rooted characteristics. The writer may not be able to effect much of this, but it is a factor that will have something to do with the chance of acceptance of the manuscript. Attention to this may produce some slight improvement, however.

The next thing the editor will look for is the reaction of the author to suggestions for revision and improvement of the manuscript. Relatively few manuscripts will be accepted without comment. It is up to the author to respond intelligently to the suggestions and thereby produce a better manuscript. If, instead, effort is spent in resisting the suggestions, the editor will not be favorably impressed. The author should remember that the suggestions come from established experts in the field. Some suggestions may be wrong and some may be based on misunderstanding, but most are not. The author should approach the suggestions with a positive frame of mind; the goal should be to gain as much as possible from the suggestions, not to debate them.

Editors want to be certain that what is offered to them is original work and that it belongs exclusively to them. As to original work, we are not talking about plagiarism, which is all but nonexistent, and we are not talking about originality in style or presentation.

What we are talking about is that the work is that of the author and not a rewrite of someone else's work or too similar to work already published or in press.

Most journals accept manuscripts with the understanding that they have not been submitted elsewhere and that the author is offering exclusive publication rights. However, there are instances when two or more articles are published out of the same study using mostly the same data. There also are instances in which book chapters or parts of chapters are published as articles. It is essential that authors be completely candid with the journal editor in such situations. There are copyright issues, and the author needs to recognize that once his or her article or book is published, he or she does not usually retain full control over its subsequent use.

Thesis or disseration completion does not constitute publication, but editors want writers to acknowledge the relationship between the article and its origins. Presentations to scholarly gatherings do not constitute publication either, but again such a history should be reported. Authors also need to be aware that scholarly conventions have their ground rules about whether a study in print can be the basis for a convention paper. Published abstracts, such as *Dissertation Abstracts*, and the proceedings of scholarly meetings do not constitute publications and need not be acknowledged.

It is perfectly proper to spin off more than one article from a dissertation. What is not proper is to publish the same data in more than one publication. Where a methodological innovation is itself worthy of publication, there is nothing wrong with publishing it separately. The substantive article may then be reported with a citation to the methodological piece.

Readers as well as editors are entitled to know where the data came from and how else it has been used. The author note or footnotes should spell out such details.

Acknowledging the Work of Others

Scholars are expected to pay their intellectual and pedagogical dues. The former involves giving credit for ideas, theoretical postures, even methodological innovations where they or some part of them originated with another scholar. It is more a matter of reporting than an ethical obligation, but it can be seen as both. Again, owing to the cumulative nature of a reasonably mature science, one traces connections between what is being reported now and what has been posited in the past. Paying pedagogical debts applies particularly to reporting work done under the supervision of others, as in work done for theses and disserations. It is the student's work, to be sure—or it had better be—but surely the student owes something to his or her mentor.

Sometimes work done under close supervision of a faculty member points to joint authorship, especially when the student work is part of a larger program of research directed by a faculty member. This brings us to the etiquette of joint authorship and sponsorship. To take the latter point first: The author should include in any submission to editors information about any assistance received that directly financed all or any part of the investigation being reported. Such assistance may have been provided by an outside funding source such as a foundation or by an agency of the university, college, school, or department where funds are granted to assist research. Normally, this includes funding for specified costs, such as computer time, reseach assistants, even funds to hire interviewers and coders and to provide for publication costs such as "page charges" required by some journals or "prior publication" offered by others.

The etiquette of collaboration is more complex. In some parts of the academic world it is traditional that, for all work carried out under the auspices of a research center or institute, the name of the head of the research teams automatically goes on every article published. This is not usually the case in the behavioral sciences, where the issue usually turns on the question of whether a major professor or the head of a research team does in fact deserve to be listed as an author. There are not hard and fast rules, but editors would like to believe that joint authorship signifies genuine collaboration, that both authors contributed significantly to the work. Supervision does not constitute participation. Some faculty members feel that they should not be listed as a co-author of any work based on a dissertation. The argument is quite compelling: The dissertation is a demonstration of ability to carry out independent scholarship. To share authorship of any article or monograph spun off that dissertation contradicts that principle. The same may be said of a master's thesis, except that often students carve out part of a larger investigation and willingly share authorship with the senior person who heads the team, especially when the latter is actively involved with and responsible for the entire project.

Many of these problems do not arise in the pursuit of scholarship in history, law, and qualitative studies. Collaborations are rare in these fields because of the close intermingling of evidence and inference. In history, for example, the traditional scholar adduces evidence before subjecting it to interpretation, of course, but rarely farms out the gathering of evidence and separates it from the process of drawing conclusions. The same may be said for original scholarship in law and qualitative studies. The latter, in fact, as Chapter 18 points out, are highly individualized.

Team research, on the other hand, is the norm in behavioral research, and hence issues of collaboration and co-authorship are not hard to find. Even the order of names has potential significance. Here, especially, the rules are poorly drawn and exceptions abound. There is a tradition of "senior authorship," which assigns "first" authorship to the most senior and responsible member of the team. But there also is a contrary principle based on the magnitude of the contribution.

One interpretation suggests that the head of the team should be listed first, but another suggests that the person "who did the work" should be listed first. The results may be diametrically opposed. When co-equal colleagues collaborate, they may arrive at first authorship on the basis of who did the most work or whose idea it was. Or they may actually draw straws. Or, if colleagues are involved in a series of studies, they may take turns being listed first. The sensible solution may be to list alphabetically. We may seem to be splitting hairs, but conscientious scholars nevertheless follow the etiquette of co-authorship as they know it.

Research Articles for the Media

Some of you will write or edit articles about research for the media. The format will be different, but much will remain the same. Newspapers expect a summary lead, which means telling about your results before you have described the study. They also expect inverted pyramid structure. It is, however, still necessary to tell the reader how the study was done, by whom it was done, who paid for it, and when it was done. All of this needs to be done in rather limited space. For surveys, you need to tell the reader the sample size. For nonquantitative studies, you need to indicate sources that were used. A lower level of abstraction may be needed. Some writers write journal articles at an abstraction level suitable for the general public, but others do not.

If you are editing stories that report research, the same considerations apply. Too often newspapers run reports of research that is interesting, but inadequately described. And sometimes this indicates poor quality of the research. The editor needs to protect his or her readers from poor research.

Magazines do not usually use summary leads or inverted pyramid structure, but still the format is different from that for a journal article. The first paragraph must entice the reader to read on. Inevitably, results may come before descriptions of how the study was done. Still, the required information remains much the same.

The Company Report

Some of you may find yourselves reporting research either orally or in writing to executives in the company your work for. It is well to remember Archimedes. Your report may be important, but it must be interesting. Details of how the study was done need to be kept to a minimum. Those who are reading or listening to your report always can ask for additional details, but if you bury the results in detail, the effect of your report will be lessened.

Another problem is that you may be dealing with fairly technical material with an audience that varies widely in its specific knowledge. The ten people seated around the conference table do not all know the same thing, and some may know virtually nothing about the topic your research covers. In giving an oral rport, you may be able to sense this and adjust. A written report does not provide the same opportunity, but it will help if you become familiar with the background of your intended audience.

A Concluding Comment

We have stressed in this chapter that good writing does not just happen. Scholarly writing is demanding. It is also rewarding. There is to begin with the satisfaction the writer gets from putting thoughts down on paper and from finding that he or she can tie together the various aspects of the research. There is, in addition, the satisfaction from seeing one's work in print. We might call this pride, in the most positive sense of that word. When you have achieved publication of a piece of research, you are entitled to feel some pride and personal satisfaction. Given the effort required, this seems only appropriate.

There is also the pragmatic point that in the academic world publication is expected and required. Tenure, promotion, and salary are affected. Furthermore, you will be judged by your peers in substantial part by your published research. It is, after all, the most visible part of your work.

In other arenas—the media, the corporation, the public relations firm—the ablity to write about research effectively will always stand you in good stead. Not everybody does this well, and good writing is usually appreciated by those who have read it.

We recognize that writing research will be more rewarding for some people than others. We think, however, that how rewarding it turns out to be for you may depend a good deal on the extent to which you go in the directions suggested in this chapter. Our intent is to save the writer a good deal of wasted motion. Scholarly writing is, in the long run, one of those things that frequently takes less time and effort to do the right way.

Glossary

After-only design   An experimental study design in which the only measurement is after exposure to the stimulus.

Arbitron   The best known of the radio audience ratings; produced by the Arbitron Company.

Analysis of variance   A statistical test of difference between means that essentially does what a t-test does when you have more than two means.

Audience research   Research that determines numbers and demographics of the readers, viewers, or listeners of a given medium.

Behavioral research   Research about how people behave.

Before-after design   An experimental study design in which there are measurements before and after exposure to the stimulus.

Bias   A systematic factor that distorts the results of a study, thus invalidating it.

Brand identity   Focusing on the brand name rather than product characteristics.

Brand stature   The esteem brand has with public and extent of public knowledge of the brand.

Brand strength   Popularity of a particular brand.

CATI (Computer Assisted Telephone Interviewing)   Interviewing with use of a telephone connected to a computer. Answers go directly into a central computer, which greatly reduces tabulation time.

Causation   Deals with determining the cause of a particular phenomenon.

CD-ROM   A compact disk containing printed material, especially newspaper and magazine articles.

Chi square   The most widely used statistical test where the data are in the form of frequencies. It is not, however, the only test and not always the best test.

Circulation   The number of copies of a publication that are distributed; distinction is made between paid and free circulation.

Cohort analysis   Analyzing a given age group at a particular time and then following that up with an analysis of that age group at a later date. Thus, we might analyze newspaper reading by people between the ages of 21 and 30 and then twenty years later analyze newspaper reading by people between the ages of 41 and 50 to see whether the extent of newspaper reading had changed.

Computerized content analysis   Content analysis done by programming a computer to recognize certain words or combination of words.

Control group   A group in an experimental study that is not exposed to any stimulus and presumably does not change, thus providing basis for comparison with the experimental group.

Co-orientation   The extent to which different groups of respondents have the same or similar attitudes or perceptions. It also may mean the extent to which one group believes another group shares their attitudes or perceptions.

Correlation   A measure of degree of association between two variables.

Cross-sectional survey   A survey in which respondents are interviewed once, which provides a snapshot of the population at that point in time.

Cross-tabulation   Comparing two variables to see the extent to which they vary together or perhaps do the opposite.

Data archive   Collections of survey data that are available to researchers.

Database   A collection of computerized material. At first it was used to mean numerical data, but now it is most often use to mean a collection of verbal material. Most important for our field are databases of newspaper and magazine articles.

Data processing   Computerized statistical analysis of data.

Debriefing   Informing participants in an experimental study (after the study is completed) about details of the study (including any deception or misrepresentations).

Deduction   Arriving at a conclusion by going from the general to the particular.

Dependent variable or measured variable   A variable whose values "depend" on the values of the independent or controlled variable.

Descriptive statistics   Statistics used to summarize large sets of data.

Designated market area (DMA)   The market area for television stations broadcasting from a given city. There are 210 DMAs in the United States.

Efficiency   How easily a measure can be applied.

Empirical research   Research bases on verifiable evidence.

Experimental group   Group exposed to stimulus in experimental study.

Face-to-face interview   An interview in which the interviewer and the respondent are face to face; sometimes called a personal interview.

Factor analysis   A data reduction technique used with correlational data whose purpose is to reduce large set of variables to a small number of factors, with each factor being a grouping of like items.

Factorial design   A design used when there is more than one independent variable that the researcher wants to determine the effect of on one or more dependent variables.

Factor score   A numerical value indicating the strength of a particular variable in a factor.

Focus group   A small group selected from the general public that is brought together to discuss a particular topic. These are helpful in producing insights for use in subsequent research. However, focus groups may or may not give an accurate picture of the attitudes of the total population.

Holism   The view that larger institutions such as organizations and communities cannot be reduced to simply the behavior of individuals.

Hypothesis   A predictive statement about the relation between two or more variables.

Independent variable or controlled variable   A variable that is manipulated by the researcher to see what effect it has on the dependent variable.

Induction   Arriving at a conclusion by going from the specific to the general.

Inferential statistics   Statistics used to estimate population from statistics from a sample.

Informed consent   Subjects in an experimental study must consent to participate, with the understanding that they are fully informed of the nature and risks of the study.

Inquiry research   Audience research that calls for a response by mail or telephone.

Interaction   Two or more variables affecting each other.

Intercoder reliability   Extent of agreement between two coders in a content analysis.

Internet survey   A survey in which a questionnaire is delivered to a preselected sample by e-mail or web pages on the Internet.

Interval data   Data expressed in numbers with the interval between consecutive numbers being the same throughout. For example, a thermometer uses an interval scale.

Intervening variable   A variable that is between two related variables and helps explain why those two are related.

Item analysis   Analysis focusing on individual items rather than aggregate data.

Legal research   The study of law that clarifies it and enhances our understanding of law and how the legal system operates.

Logical positivism   The view that all knowledge derives from observational experience.

Macroscopic analysis   Analysis based on a large unit such as an organization, a community, or a society.

Mail survey   A survey in which a questionnaire is mailed to a preselected sample of respondents.

Manifest content   A term used in content analysis to mean the apparent content or what the content actually says, not what we suppose the hidden meaning is.

Mean   The average of a set of numbers.

Measure of association   A statistic used to determine the extent of relationship between two variables.

Median   The midpoint in a set of numbers.

Metro survey area (MSA)   The area served by a radio station. Arbitron reports radio audiences by MSAs.

Microscopic analysis   Analysis that emphasizes the individual.

Mode   The value that occurs most often in a given set of data.

Multivariate statistics   Statistics used in analyses of data in which there is more than one source of variation. Factor analysis and regression are the most widely used multivariate statistics.

Narrative history   History told as a story, with the writer employing real events but creating the story himself or herself.

Nielsen ratings   The best known of the television ratings. They are produced by the A.C. Nielsen Company, using recording devices and viewer diaries.

Nominal data   Data in which there are varied characteristics but no numerical sequence. An example would be color of eyes.

Nomological   Of or related to laws of the mind.

Null hypothesis   An hypothesis that predicts no relations between variable being studied.

Operational   Operational definitions or operational hypotheses are based on how things really are as opposed to what they might be in theory.

Ordinal measure   Measure using data that are not numbers but that have quantitative implications. For example, we frequently express education in terms of these high school graduate, college graduate, and postgraduate. There are no numbers, but the amount of education is indicated by these labels, and they are presented here in quantitative order.

Oversampling   Increasing the sample of a particular audience segment beyond its normal proportion of the population.

Panel study   A survey in which respondents are interviewed two or more times to help determine trends.

Parameter   Values of a universe that are estimated from a sample.

Pearson's r   The most widely used measure of correlation. Most other correlation coefficients are said to be estimates of Pearson's r.

Personal-interview survey   A survey in which respondents are interviewed in person. While such surveys produce the best data, they are seldom used because of their high cost.

Positioning   Emphasizing certain characteristics of a product or political candidate that will make either the candidate or the product more acceptable to the public.

Post-testing   Testing of subjects after exposure to given communication.

Postmodernism   A perspective on history that rejects realism and objectivity and claims all human experience is mediated through language.

Power   Precision of a measure or statistic.

Pretesting   Trying out a questionnaire before the survey begins. Also, trying out an ad.

Pretest-posttest design   An experimental design in which there are measures before and after exposure to the stimulus.

Probability   The chance value of an occurrence.

Probability sample   See *Random sample.*

Proprietary research   Research done by a company or organization for its sole use.

Purposive sample   A sample that is not random but in which items are chosen because of characteristics important in the study.

Random digit dialing   Selecting respondents in a telephone survey by drawing telephone numbers randomly.

Random sample   A sample of a given population drawn in such a way that all members of the population have an equal chance of being included in the sample.

Ratings   Measures of radio or television audiences done by recording devices attached to sets or by dairies kept by listeners or by telephone surveys.

Ratio scale   Numerical data in which the distance between numbers is the same throughout and, in addition, are true ratios—that is 4 is really twice 2, etc. For example, a thermometer is not a ratio scale because 60 degrees is not really twice 30 degrees. Test scores usually are ratio scales—that is, a score of 60 really is twice a score of 30.

Reach   How much of the intended audience a given piece of mass communication reaches.

Recall   Asking respondent to recall a story or an ad. With unaided recall, respondent is asked what he or she can recall from a given publication or broadcast. In aided recall, a respondent is given clues that help him or her remember.

Recognition   Determining whether respondents recognize an ad or other content by showing it to respondent and asking if respondent knows where it appeared or other facts about it.

Reductionism   The view that collective social units are nothing more than aggregations of individuals.

Regression   A multivariate technique for determining the extent of effect of a number of independent variables on the dependent variable.

Relevance   In advertising, how important a brand is to a cosumer. In communication generally, the significance of a particular concept or idea.

Reliability   Consistency in measurement.

Research   When we speak of research, we are talking about an original investigation of a problem that may use any of these various techniques discussed in this book. What is not meant is a synthesis based on secondary sources as one typically does in "research papers" for high school and college classes.

Response rate   The proportion of people in a survey sample who respond.

Retroduction   Shuttling back and forth between data and theory to maximize the explanation of theory by a particular set of data.

Review of literature   A concise, focused presentation of studies related to the study the author is writing about.

Sample   A small portion of the people, the media, or the events under study.

Sampling error   The difference between a given value from a sample and the value in the population.

Secondary analysis   Analysis of survey data by someone other than the original investigator to test hypotheses or research questions other than those of the original study.

Semantic differential   A measurement device in which respondent is asked to rate a concept on a series of 7-point polar scales such as good-bad, fast-slow, etc.

Share   Proportion of all TV sets turned on that are tuned to a specific program.

Significance test   A test to determine whether the degree of association or difference between two variables is a matter of chance or an indication of a real difference in the population.

Split run   Creating two or more versions of the same publication that differ in some aspect (of either content or design). The purpose is to determine the effect on the audience of different versions.

SPSS (Statistical Package for the Social Sciences)   The most widely used computer program for data analysis in the social sciences. It includes an extremely wide range of statistical techniques.

Standard deviation   The most commonly used measure of the dispersion of values around the mean. It is the square root of the variance.

Stratification   A process whereby a sample is put together by drawing separate samples of subgroups of the population to insure adequate representations of those groups in the total sample.

Syndicated research   Research done for many companies and usually made available to interested persons or groups as promotion for those who sponsored the research.

Target market   A market segment seen as most likely to purchase a given product.

Telephone survey   A survey in which respondents are interviewed by telephone.

T-test   The most widely used measure of the difference between two means.

Test market   A community chosen for testing a product or advertising either because certain characteristics make it seem ideal for the product or because it is a typical community.

Trend analysis   Use of data from several surveys to show changes in public opinion over time.

Triangulation   Analyzing a phenomenon by combining several aspects to provide a fully rounded analysis.

Uses and gratifications research   Research that focuses on reasons people use a certain medium and the satisfaction they get from it.

Validity   The extent to which a technique really measures what it says it is measuring.

Variance   A measure of dispersion of values of a set of data around the mean.

Within-subjects design   Design for experiment in which subjects are exposed to all stimuli and thus act as their own controls.

Yesterday readership   The most common standard for measuring newspaper readership, done by asking respondent if he or she read any newspaper or a specific newspaper yesterday.

Name Index

Subject Index